The
ENGLISH
YEAR

*A month–by–month guide to
the nation's customs and festivals,
from May Day to Mischief Night*

STEVE ROUD

PENGUIN BOOKS

PENGUIN BOOKS

Published by the Penguin Group

Penguin Books Ltd, 80 Strand, London WC2R ORL, England

Penguin Group (USA) Inc., 375 Hudson Street, New York, New York 10014, USA

Penguin Group (Canada), 90 Eglinton Avenue East, Suite 700, Toronto, Ontario,
Canada M4P 2Y3 (a division of Pearson Penguin Canada Inc.)

Penguin Ireland, 25 St Stephen's Green, Dublin 2, Ireland
(a division of Penguin Books Ltd)

Penguin Group (Australia), 250 Camberwell Road, Camberwell,
Victoria 3124, Australia (a division of Pearson Australia Group Pty Ltd)

Penguin Books India Pvt Ltd, 11 Community Centre,
Panchsheel Park, New Delhi – 110 017, India

Penguin Group (NZ), 67 Apollo Drive, Rosedale, North Shore 0632,
New Zealand (a division of Pearson New Zealand Ltd)

Penguin Books (South Africa) (Pty) Ltd, 24 Sturdee Avenue,
Rosebank, Johannesburg 2196, South Africa

Penguin Books Ltd, Registered Offices: 80 Strand, London WC2R ORL, England

ISBN: 978-0-141-02106-5

For Jacqueline and Stephanie

Contents

List of Illustrations

Acknowledgements

Thanks to the numerous local studies library staff across the country who have welcomed me to their domains and have answered my somewhat bizarre questions with professionalism and good grace. Thanks particularly to my friends and colleagues at Croydon Local Studies Library, Chris C., Chris B., and Lizzie, for their help and cheerful forbearance; thanks also to what is left of the staff of the LSU section at Croydon for assistance with obscure inter-library loan requests, the library staff at the Folklore Society and the Vaughan Williams Memorial Library, and, most of all, the London Library for simply being a wonderful place for would-be scholars like me.

Thanks also to my fellow Penguin folklore authors Jacqueline Simpson and Jennifer Chandler; to Nigel Wilcockson, late of this parish; the many folklore writers and researchers who have helped with general guidance and specific pieces of information, including Peter Robson, Roy Palmer, Brian Shuel, Derek Schofield, Christine Bloxham, Bob and Jackie Patten; and to Kate Faulkner for preparing the index.

Thanks also to Countryside Books of Newbury, for permission to reprint the extract on Christmas puddings from their *Surrey Within Living Memory*; Persephone Books of London for recipes from their edition of Florence White's *Good Things in England*; and Lillian Barlow for her memories of Whit Walks from the *Have Your Say Magazine* website.

Introduction

The English Year concentrates on 'traditional' customs and festivals that take place within communities and are organized by members of that community, and have been around long enough to have been passed on to successive generations. The focus of the book is mainly historical, and for those customs that still exist, only a brief description of what now takes place is given, followed by a longer discussion of their history and development. In part, this is simply a reflection of my own particular interest in the subject, but it is also because this history has been so poorly served in recent years. Many books and websites describe what goes on nowadays at traditional events, but few give the history of these customs any real attention beyond reiterating standard popular explanations, which, as will be seen, are often spurious. It will also be seen that although we in England often pride ourselves on our love of tradition, numerous customs that were previously popular items in the calendar have simply disappeared, and the ones that have survived are but a small percentage of those of which past eras could boast.

Even with the relatively narrow focus on traditional customs, the events included in this book are too many and various to admit of any one overarching theory of origin, function, purpose, or meaning, except at the most superficial level. In the rare cases where we have solid information about origins, it seems that some customs were simply carried out for fun, others for the preservation of rights. Some function to foster social solidarity and to include members of the community, or to exclude outsiders, and many have religious overtones or origins. Some are parodies or burlesques, others are pious or deadly serious, and some start as one and end up as the other. Many customs had an economic basis, in that participants expected to collect money, food, or drink. Some are genuinely old, while others are surprisingly recent. New events are nowadays regularly created, usually as fun activities designed to raise money for charity, and a sample of these has been included. But it remains to be seen how many will last long enough to become 'traditional' in their own right, handed on from generation to generation. Numerous pieces of conscious official pageantry at national and local level still exist, and a representative sample, such as the Lord Mayor's Show and the Royal Maundy distribution, is also included. Organized sport is not covered, although some of the most common traditional games are described.

It has to be said that any attempt to portray a single 'year', relevant to every English person, is doomed to failure, as the whole notion of time in this context is highly subjective. Historically speaking, the calendrical year is a complete mess. The adoption of the Gregorian calendar in 1752, eminently sensible from an astronomical point of view, introduced widespread uncertainty and confusion with regard to the timing of traditional events and customs, and the fact that the most important religious festivals (Shrovetide, Easter, Whitsun, etc.) float about from year to year plays havoc with any idea of a regular, ordered sequence of events. But an individual person's 'year' is not necessarily made up of official high days and holidays. The lives of many people in the past were dominated by the agricultural cycle, and this varied considerably depending on whether the main farming activity was arable or pastoral, and on local weather conditions. At the national level, the inexorable secularization of society has now stripped most saints' days of their special character, and surviving public customs have tended to drift from holy days towards secular bank holidays. But while the official religion has been seriously weakened, there is now a much wider variety of religions and sects in English society, each of which has its own calendar of special times and events, and for devout followers, this is the 'year' that really matters.

Apart from agriculture and religion, there are other factors that dictate a person's year. Many occupations, for example, have long had a seasonal rhythm of their own, and for those who work in education, the year still begins in the autumn. International days of this, and national days of that, are now spread throughout the year, and most of the bigger charities use the idea of 'a day' to focus attention on their cause and raise money. But nowadays, it is personal hobby and leisure interests that influence the way many people see the year, and the sporting calendar dominates many people's lives.

The historical approach adopted in this book means that, with two exceptions, the customs of newer immigrant communities have not been included. The customs of new communities are already 'English' in the sense of taking place in this country, but if they have been simply imported from elsewhere they need time to become naturalized. Again, once they are passed on to second and third generations, and once they break out of the host community to become more widely known, they will become 'English' in every sense, whatever their origin. The Chinese New Year and the Notting Hill Carnival are included for precisely this reason. They are both public celebrations of the traditions of the communities that initially fostered them, but they now have a resonance on a much wider scale.

The loss of many of the customs of yesteryear has already been indicated. We may bemoan this loss of local colour and national heritage, but in many cases it was not necessarily a bad thing. The treatment of animals in many of our ancestors' games was barbaric, and few would like to see cockfighting or bear-baiting returned to the traditional calendar. Other mass gatherings were indeed excuses for drinking and fighting, just as the moralists of the time claimed, and the struggle over these activities made it clear that just because a pastime is old and customary does not make it acceptable or guarantee its survival. Many customs simply went out of fashion or faded away from lack of interest, but the headline grabbers were those that were forcibly suppressed, often after a bitter local struggle.

When matters of change, suppression, or revival are concerned, the central point to be considered is who owns the custom, and who therefore has the right to take action for or against it. This may seem a fatuous question, with a very simple answer – 'the community', or 'everybody' – but this does not adequately address a surprisingly complex matter. In any community there are different groups and factions, including those who carry out the custom and those to whom it is done. The bonfire boys of Victorian Lewes who wished to continue their riotous behaviour on 5 November shared their community with the shopkeepers, councillors, and clergymen who opposed them, and both sides believed they had the right to dictate the future of the event. On closer inspection, many a community has little real social cohesion, and breaks up into ever smaller groups before our eyes. Many older customs were performed and perpetuated by a small definable group, linked by the particular area in which they lived, by family ties, or by their occupation, and while these people could be fiercely protective of their own traditions, they were often prone to internal dissension, which resulted in acrimonious splits. There are two 'Osses at Padstow and three morris sides at Bampton, for example.

It has been largely the fashion since the 1970s for social historians to view the battle over the control of traditional customs in the nineteenth century in terms of class conflict, and such writers are almost always in sympathy with the workers. In case after case, the records of nineteenth-century public events show that they were firmly in the hands of the lower or working classes of the area, with active opposition coming from the middle- and upper-class residents. Increasingly during the nineteenth century, mass working-class customs were seen as harmful, distasteful, even dangerous, and those in authority began to condemn them and then actively interfere. In many cases, such as the celebrations surrounding May Day, their interference took the form of remodelling – cleaning up and constructing safe, child-based events. In other cases, however, where the customs were unsuitable for such accommodation, they were usually opposed outright and suppressed. National legislation provided assistance, by outlawing games involving cruelty to animals, forbidding the lighting of fires or discharging of guns in the street, and allowing fairs that had existed for centuries to be phased out or moved from town centres. Countless fairs, games of street football, bonfire night celebrations, and raucous mock-mayor ceremonies were banned by local authorities and broken up by the police. A few survived by cleaning up their act, or by chance circumstance, but most simply disappeared from the local scene.

The idea that we all have the right to control other people's leisure pursuits has not gone away, and, indeed, appears to be on the rise again. Some customs, such as Padstow's Darkie Day, and Cliffe's annual burning of the Pope at Lewes, cause widespread concern, but those involved claim the right to do as they please, as they have always done, citing notions of liberty and 'tradition' to justify their arguments. Meanwhile, other customs, such as the cheese-rolling at Cooper's Hill, fall foul of local government health and safety regulations, and, on another level, there were interminable arguments in the twentieth-century morris dance revival about whether women should be 'allowed' to take part. However, the most interesting recent example of control xvii

Introduction

to take part. However, the most interesting recent example of control imposed by outsiders was the successful campaign to ban hunting with dogs – a traditional pastime with a long history, enjoyed by a particular group but condemned and bitterly opposed by others. Although the hunters' contention that it was a town-versus-country issue was simplistic, it contained more than a grain of truth, and there is no doubt that class antagonism played an important role, this time in an interesting case of role reversal.

In the past, it was not just high-profile mass events that came under fire: many small-scale customs also felt the cold disapproving eye of certain sections of society. Up to about the First World War, for example, it was generally accepted that people who performed traditional customs could collect money for themselves. But from about this time such activity was increasingly redefined as begging, and a general resistance began to build in the public mind. This disapproval was even extended to children's customs. An example is provided by Rose Gamble in her autobiography, *Chelsea Child*, concerning her early years in London in the 1920s. In this instance, Rose's older sister Lu had constructed a 'grotto' and had installed it, with Rose beside it, on a doorstep to sing the song she had been taught, 'Please remember the grotto . . .', to gather some pennies to go swimming. Some passers-by gave money, but others clearly disapproved:

Then a man in his shirtsleeves came out of a door next to my step and stood glaring down at me, so I started to sing. 'You with anyone?'; I went on singing. 'And hold that bloody noise,' he shouted. 'Who's with you?' 'My sister, over there.' 'You'd better clear off,' he shouted, turning round to Lu. 'You're begging you are, and you'll get locked up!' 'No we ain't,' cried Lu indignantly, hurrying the pram across the road. 'We got something. We made something for them to look at!'

Seventy years later, the loud protests that greeted the fad of American-style house-visiting (trick or treating) at Hallowe'en, which involved youngsters roaming the streets and knocking on doors, demanding money with threats, showed that children's customs still have the power to raise adult hackles.

However, the history of traditional customs is not simply a tale of opposition and decline and, indeed, the future for most of our surviving public events looks positively rosy. The biggest change in calendar customs in recent years has been that the communities have quite suddenly become proud of their local traditions, and even those who are not directly involved often view their customs as a way of celebrating distinctiveness and community tradition. In sharp contrast to their nineteenth-century counterparts, many local authorities are also taking an active interest, as they recognize the potential of traditional customs for fostering local pride and attracting tourists. Many give grants, include details of customs on their websites and in their tourist publicity, and provide venues and stewards. But this support comes at a price. Councils and other official bodies have agendas of their own, and the desire to reshape and control what they are supporting is often too strong to resist. The Greater London Authority, for example, in their perfectly understandable desire to champion London's cultural diversity and grassroots vitality, have seen the Notting Hill Carnival and the Chinese New Year celebrations as just the sort of thing that should be encouraged and supported. But this always means imposing changes, and the usual questions arise: Wouldn't it be better if the celebrations were moved out of the narrow streets? Why don't we extend this part because the crowd loves it, but that bit is rather boring? What about a prize for the best costume? Even without official 'support', there is often pressure at local level to 'improve' things. These impulses come from within the community and are therefore part of a custom's natural growth or development, and it cannot be said too often that communities have every right to do what they will with their traditions, whatever outsiders like me may think. However, these impulses also bring with them dangers, and the very distinctiveness that the community wishes to champion can be at risk from a creeping homogeneity: the custom may involve more and more participants, to 'make a day of it', or 'a better show'; ways are found to get children involved; people start dressing up in pseudo-historical Merrie England costume; and every custom becomes a pageant, with supplementary morris dancers.

Popularity itself brings problems and changes things. In the 1971 edition of his book *Padstow's Obby Oss*, for example, local writer Donald Rawe commented:

Modern publicity brings vast crowds, which impede the Mayers, tend to discourage dancing, and make it difficult for the singers to follow the leader's words. The night singing is more apt to begin in a general hubbub than the expectant silence of former years during which the church clock could be heard to strike twelve.

And in the 1982 edition, he added the following postscript:

Today . . . we are faced by what may be termed the Publicity Problem. Until 1970 or so, Padstow had never been loth to publicise its Great Day . . . but television and the folk movement changed all that. Within a few years hordes of people were to descend on the little town: many behaved well and were genuinely interested, but others of somewhat dubious character apparently came here to drink themselves insensible, lying across our streets and quaysides, sleeping rough in Stile Field or in public shelters . . . A reaction was sure to follow, and in 1975 television camera crews were told they were not welcome. Since then no one in Padstow has talked to radio or television interviewers or the press.

Again there is a reversal: nowadays the onlookers misbehave, rather than the participants.

Almost without exception, the communities that possess the traditional customs included in this book also have 'historical' stories to explain how and when the custom originated. Some communities have more than one story, but one version usually becomes the dominant, orthodox explanation, and is taught to local children and told to any stranger who asks, appearing in local newspapers, booklets, and websites. These tales are a fascinating study in themselves, as interesting examples of narrative folklore, but they should never be taken at face value as real history. They are in fact legends, which for present purposes can be defined as traditional stories told as true but not supported by evidence. Nor should it be assumed that all legends have a kernel of truth in them. They very rarely do, and the vast majority are simply fictitious tales that have been repeated often enough to take on the veneer of accredited fact. They are believed because they function well as stories, they are neat and plausible, and people like them. They seem to correspond to what we think we know of the past, and we often hear them from respected informants. Like all traditional narratives, they come in all shapes and sizes, and they evolve and adapt, but their basic credibility relies on the dubious authenticity of oral tradition, and on internal corroborative details that support and seem to prove the basic story. However, these very details generally indicate that the story has been fabricated, often quite recently, to explain a custom that already exists.

An example of this is the name of the object that the Haxey Hood players strive to get to their goal – 'the Hood'. The prevailing story relates that the game was founded to commemorate the time when one Lady de Mowbray lost her hood in the wind, and local men tried to catch it for her. Once they had caught it, the Lady called one of the men a 'fool' and another a 'lord', which is said to explain why two characters in the game have these names. Similar *post facto* tales are found elsewhere. At Tichborne, in Hampshire, a story involving crawling has been invented to explain the name of a field, 'The Crawls'; and at Biddenden, in Kent, a story about conjoined twins is given to explain the image that is now printed on a commemorative biscuit, given as part of an annual dole there.

To the practised eye, these legends can be easily spotted and deconstructed in various ways. Because they are of quite recent origin themselves, their historicity is often decidedly shaky. I was recently told by a local resident in Croydon, Surrey, that a 1960s block of flats is called Cromwell House because Cromwell beat the French army on nearby Duppas Hill. This is a facetious example, but stories are usually based on the contemporary popular idea of what life was like in the past, rather than how it really was. Origin legends also regularly include motifs which occur in other stories and which are, in themselves, traditional. The explanation for the Penny Hedge custom at Whitby, for example, includes the motif of a hermit defying and being attacked by angry noble huntsmen. This same story is told of numerous saints and hermits across Europe.

The details woven into these stories necessarily chime well with the modern form of the customs, but this implies that every detail of the current version of a custom was present from the beginning. The one thing we know for sure about traditional customs is that they change over time, often quite dramatically. The neater the story, and the more complete its explanation of current detail, the more dubious it is. Alarm bells also sound when a story claims an origin far more remote than any independent evidence can support. Thus, if a custom that can only be traced back to the nineteenth century has an origin story set in the time of the Crusades, the story itself is insufficient evidence of the custom's earlier existence. Lastly, the details themselves rarely bear close examination. The idea that bedridden and dying Lady Tichborne could crawl around twenty-three acres of land, while holding a burning brand in one hand, is ludicrous. If you do not believe me, try it.

Understandably, those who like and believe the stories themselves do not take well to this type of deconstruction, and many people clearly believe that any legend is better than none. Talk of interchangeable motifs and historical accuracy is no match for romance, and folklorists and historians are regularly portrayed as inveterate wet blankets and wanton killjoys. To this charge we must plead guilty, especially as we cannot often offer any clear explanations to replace the stories we are so keen to debunk. Our only defence is the plea that there is no reason why fact and fiction cannot exist happily side by side, and there is nothing wrong with a legend as long as we take it for what it is. We can still enjoy a John Wayne film (well, some of us can), even though we know that he himself was not a real cowboy, and that the film is not a true historical portrait of cowboy life. We do not have to believe that hobbits really exist to enjoy *Lord of the Rings*, and our children can believe in Father Christmas and are not permanently damaged when they learn the brutal truth.

One problem with accepting legends as truth is that it stops us enquiring further, and we thereby miss the opportunity to investigate how these customs originated. By accepting the historical legend of Lady Mowbray, which makes the Haxey Hood game seem unique, we forget to notice the similarities with other seasonal contests, usually known as 'football', at Ashbourne, Atherstone, and dozens of other places.

But the cold hard stare of the unromantic folklorist is not the real threat to the traditional 'historical' legends. The real danger is from a far more virulent virus – the idea that all customs, indeed all superstitions, nursery rhymes, and anything that smacks of 'folkiness', are direct survivals of ancient pagan fertility rites, and are concerned with the appeasement of gods and spirits. Although the suggestion of an ancient origin for our folklore was the central tenet of the Victorian and Edwardian pioneers of folklore collection, this notion has only become generally known in the last forty years or so, and has taken hold with astonishing rapidity; the majority of the population now carry the virus in some form or other, while some are very badly infected. The problem here is not simply that these theories are unsupported by any evidence, but that their blanket similarity destroys any individuality. All customs will soon end up with the same story.

Legends aside, there is no evidence that our customs have pre-Christian origins. Not one single custom can be proved to have such ancient roots, and there is usually a thousand years and more separating the nominal conversion of the English in the seventh century from the first evidence of a custom's existence; the idea that such customs formed part of a secret underground alternative religion is therefore risible. The whole panoply of vegetation spirits, earth goddesses, and the like has been invented in recent years, with no factual support, to provide a simplistic romantic and mystical backstory suited to the needs of the late twentieth and early twenty-first century. As a rule of thumb, apart from academic treatises, any description of the origin of a specific traditional English custom that uses the words 'pagan', 'fertility', or 'Celt' should be treated with extreme caution, and any description that uses the words 'sacrifice', 'Druid', 'earth goddess', or 'vegetation spirit' as complete nonsense.

A book entitled *The English Year*, which focuses on traditional customs, is bound to be drawn into the current debate on what constitutes *Englishness*. For a variety of reasons, including devolution elsewhere in the United Kingdom, the European Union, immigration, and the increasing influence of the USA, many sections of the population have started to fret about the potential loss of our national character. Leaving aside the ambiguity of the word 'English' in the context of this debate – does it mean found in England, originated in England, or invented by the English? – it has already been noted that the traditional customs listed here are too various to provide any meaningful summary.

On the national level, it is often stated that a 'love of tradition' is one of the strongest characteristics of the English, but this too is questionable, and it could easily be argued that the English have never been particularly good at preserving their traditions. As already indicated, countless customs have ceased to be performed, and not just because the powers-that-be have suppressed them: in numerous cases, the 'ordinary folk' were no longer interested. Other countries have plenty of similar customs and take them far more seriously. Indeed, there is probably very little mileage in calendar custom for the seeker after Englishness.

However, if traditional customs have little clear intrinsic meaning at national level, they certainly have more meaning on the smaller scale. The flourishing condition of the Padstow Hobby Horse, for example, may not tell us anything about being English, but it certainly says something about being Padstonian, and, perhaps, about being Cornish. It is on this more personal level that people's pride is evidenced, and feelings of belonging and continuity are fostered. Such feelings are a complex mixture of pride and nostalgia, and it is often said that Padstonians who are away from home on May Day, will sing the 'Obby 'Oss song to themselves to remind themselves of home.

Nevertheless, there is still something to be said about the attitude of the English to folk customs on a national scale. Historically, many countries have needed their folklore and traditions to help forge a national identity, either for political unification or in defence against a culturally dominant neighbour. But English culture has for so long been the dominant, even predator, culture in the neighbourhood that it has never needed to bolster national pride by drawing on traditional roots, and, because it has never needed it, the notion took hold that England had no valuable traditional culture; hence the almost total absence of academic support for the collection and study of folklore or cultural traditions in England, in stark contrast to the USA and most European countries. There is a School of Scottish Studies, a Welsh Folk Museum, a Department of Irish Folklore, but no official centre for specifically English folklore, and it has largely been left to amateur scholars and bodies like the Folklore Society to collect and document our traditions.

Yet, paradoxically, the result is not all bad. While English folklore has definitely been neglected, ignored, even derided, much of it has, in essence, been left alone. Scotland, Ireland, and Wales may have gained immeasurably from their thriving folk arts, and have each used their folklore to create and support a vibrant national identity, but they have also had to suffer the indignity of the ersatz and fake: the music hall 'stage Irish', the rampant shamrockery, the tourist leprechauns, the Chieftains; the White Heather Club, and pipe-bands perpetually playing *Amazing Grace*. It is symptomatic of this state of affairs that England does not have that arch-symbol of official fakelore, a 'national costume'. Nor have we ever taken much notice of St George's Day, much to the annoyance of patriots of various hues, and I, for one, am proud of that.

How to Use This Book

Anyone who attempts to render the English year in a single straight-forward and logical sequence immediately faces three fundamental problems: what to do with the moveable feasts linked to Easter; how to deal with customs and events that are not really geared to the calendar at all; and, less obviously, how to accommodate the customs that have not been fixed to one particular day since time immemorial, but have actually shifted from year to year, as circumstances dictate. There is no completely satisfactory solution to these questions, and all one can do is to explain the decisions made in each category.

As regards the moveable feasts, I have placed them in the position in which they fall in 2007. Fortunately, in that year Easter happens to fall on 8 April, which is roughly in the middle of its possible span. Headings for dates dependent on Easter are distinguished by an Easter egg motif. To help any reader interested in pinning down the actual festive calendar of any particular year, a table of dates for Easter Sunday for the next decade or so is provided on page 594.

In the absence of any logical or systematic way of ordering the non-calendar items such as bull-baiting and wife-selling, I have simply placed them where they seem to fit best, and readers must rely on the built-in cross-references and index to guide them to specific entries.

Similarly, there is little that can be done about the fact that many custom organizers and participants have proved pragmatic rather than romantic when choosing the day on which they hold their event, but I have placed most entries on the nominally 'correct' day, and such entries are marked by a double rule at the beginning and end. If anyone wishes to visit one of the many surviving public customs, they are cautioned *always* to check the date first. Most customs now have websites.

The Calendar

An Abbreviated History of the Calendar

There is little doubt that most of us take the structure of the calendar completely for granted, which is exactly how it should be. A universally agreed, regular, well-ordered system of time management is all we ask. We may occasionally wonder why there are twelve months of unequal length, or who decided that we needed an extra day every fourth year, but on the whole we are confident that the calendar has been worked out scientifically for us. Christmas will always fall in the middle of winter, and any diary we buy will agree with all the others on sale.

The history of the human race's attempts to understand and regulate time, and of the calendars which have been devised over the centuries, is extremely complex and fraught with false dawns, bitter controversies, and wasted opportunities. It has not been simply the inexorable march of the human intellect, based on an increasingly sophisticated understanding of the universe and the natural world, and backed by better methods of measurement, calculation, and recording. The real long-term struggle has been to wrest control of the calendar from the hands of religious leaders and move it into the secular sphere. In most cases, this has been a question of jettisoning lunar thinking and replacing it with solar.

In the following account, only the major events which have contributed to the development of the modern calendar as we know it in England receive attention, and the four key players in this story are the ancient Egyptians, the Roman Empire, the Catholic Church, and the Protestant Church. The fact that other civilizations, such as the Chinese and the Mayans, had sophisticated calendar traditions is largely ignored. It was the Romans, under Julius Caesar, that gave us the basis of the modern calendar, although they borrowed the idea from the Egyptians.

First it is necessary to understand something of the factual basis of time measurement as we understand it today. The earth's orbit round the sun takes 365.24219 mean solar days (365 days, 5 hours, 48 minutes, and 45 seconds), slightly more than the 365 days in our nominal year; hence we need an extra day every four years to prevent an accumulated disjunction between the physical solar year and our human year. The 'leap year', which includes this extra day, is normally any year whose number is exactly divisible by four, with the occasional exception. One extra day every four years is not quite accurate enough, as it overshoots the target, so the last year of each century is not a leap year unless it is divisible by 400 (1800 and 1900 were not leap years, but 2000 was).

There are four key points in the earth's annual journey round the sun: the two solstices and the two equinoxes. The solstice is the point at which the sun reaches its greatest distance from the equator, north or south, and appears to stand still for a few days (Latin *sol* means 'sun'; *sistere*, 'to stand still'). The summer solstice, which occurs around 21 June, is the longest day in the year, and the winter solstice, around 22 December, is the shortest. The two equinoxes, vernal (around 20 March) and autumnal (around 22 September), are the points at which the sun crosses the equator, when day and night are equal (Latin *equi* means 'equal'; *nox*, 'night').

To modern western eyes, the cycles of the sun are more important in terms of determining seasons, the weather, agricultural practices, and so on, but to early man it was the moon, with its cycles of waxing and waning, that seemed the more obvious candidate for time measurement. All the earliest known calendars are lunar, based on the phases of the moon, which is why we use the word 'month' to describe each of the twelve periods into which the year is divided. But this is where most of our problems start, because it takes long and complicated calculations to correlate the moon with the sun. A lunar month (the time from new moon to new moon) is 29.5306 days, so a twelve-month lunar year is just over 354 days long and thus runs almost 11 days out of step with the solar year. If the lunar year were followed, it would take only sixteen years or so for the seasons to be completely reversed. Whatever the religious investment in lunar phenomena may have been, it must have been obvious from an early date that the moon has little physical effect on nature or human life, but that the sun does. It is the sun's phases that bring the seasons, and determine when crops should be sown and when harvested, or when the weather is good enough to set sail. For centuries, the authorities attempted to keep their traditional lunar calendars while tinkering with them to bring them into line with the sun's movements. Centuries before the birth of Christ, the Babylonians tried to combine lunar and solar by intercalating extra months, the Greeks added ninety days every eight years but not always systematically, and the ancient Jewish calendar added one month every three years and another month every now and then to straighten things up. None of these amendments was sufficient, and all were immensely complex and open to corruption. As early as 4000 BC, the Egyptians were the first to calculate the solar year at 365 days, which gave them 12 months of 30 days each, plus 5 days, and they later calculated that the year was actually 365¼ days long.

The Romans had originally used a ten-month lunar year of approximately 304 days, but around 700 BC they added two more months, bringing the year to 355 days. Priests were in charge of inserting extra months periodically, but they performed this task in such an inconsistent and corrupt way that by Julius Caesar's time the calendar was seriously awry. Caesar learned of the solar calendar from the Egyptians – at a party thrown in his honour by Cleopatra, so legend has it – and in 45 BC he introduced the Julian calendar, based on the 365-day year, with an extra day every four years. Each year had twelve months, with thirty or thirty-one days (except February), and 1 January was confirmed as the beginning of the year.

Although not a perfect system, the introduction of the Julian calendar was by far the biggest step forward in the history of the calendar, and only the leader of the greatest empire on earth could have had the power to impose uniformity on such a grand scale. The month of Quintilius was later renamed 'Julius' in Caesar's honour, and after some small modifications became necessary in the year AD 8 under Emperor Augustus, the month Sextilis was renamed after him.

The calendar as we know it today was now more or less in place – regular, secular, based on the real movements of the sun, with an extra day every four years to take up the slack, and the year divided into twelve roughly equal months. The only real difference between the calendar then and now was the lack of seven-day weeks; instead, the

Romans reckoned days before or after fixed points called 'kalends' (the 1st of each month), 'nones' (the 5th or the 7th), and 'ides' (the 13th or the 15th). The accepted calculation of 365¼ days for the length of the year was still not quite correct, and would cause problems centuries later, but for the time it was a brilliant achievement.

If only it were plain sailing for the calendar from this point, but this is far from the case. Emperor Constantine (d. AD 377) imposed Christianity as the official religion of the Empire, introducing the seven-day week, and Sunday as a regular holy day. Unfortunately, he also put the design of the calendar back into the hands of religious groups still wedded to traditional lunar movements for their major festival, Easter, and they could not even agree on how to calculate that. Constantine summoned Christian leaders from all quarters to their first major council at Nicaea in year 325 with the express purpose of settling differences and creating a credible, unified Church. In most areas they were largely successful, but their failure to agree a basic formula for the calculation of Easter laid the foundations for division and bitter dispute for centuries.

After the collapse of the Roman Empire and the spread of the 'barbarian hordes' across Europe, the Christian Church was the nearest thing to an international controlling body, but there were still major disputes and schisms, and the West entered a long dark period in which scientific enquiry was frowned upon. Apart from the complex calculations needed to fix the date of Easter every year, religious leaders regarded any enquiry into the calendar as at best unorthodox and at worst downright heresy, and this state of affairs lasted well into the early modern period.

By the sixteenth century, the western world was sufficiently stable for new attempts to be made to reform the calendar. The small errors in the Julian system had now become noticeable and annoying, and in 1582 Pope Gregory finally announced changes in the calendar to correct these faults and to prevent them happening again, including the 400-year rule for leap years already described. He introduced what became known as the Gregorian Calendar, and ordained that 5 October be named 15 October to bring the calendar back into line with the physical world. This was a much-needed and sensible move, but with two major problems. The secular calendar may have been put on to a sounder footing, but Easter was still to be calculated on the basis of new moons; moreover, newly Protestant countries such as Britain

labelled the reforms a Popish plot designed to undermine their credibility, and refused to join in. For more than a century following this
change, half of Europe was ten days ahead of the other half.

Over the succeeding years, although other Protestant countries
gradually surrendered to reform, Britain held out until 1752, by which
time it had to correct by eleven days to bring it back in line. The eventual adoption of the Gregorian reforms in Britain was initiated by
Philip Stanhope, fourth Earl of Chesterfield, who introduced a Bill
to correct the 'inconvenient and disgraceful errors of our present calendar', which was finally signed into law by George II on 22 May 1752.
'Chesterfield's Act' decreed that Wednesday, 2 September 1752 was to
be followed immediately by Thursday, 14 September 1752, and also that
the New Year was to start officially on 1 January (for more on the timing of the New Year, see below).

For a long time it has been believed that there were widespread riots
in Britain under the slogan of 'Give us back our eleven days', initiated
by people who were too stupid to understand that the reforms were
simply nominal and did not actually shorten their lives. The existence
of these riots has been seriously questioned by modern scholarship,
but there is no doubt that the reforms were misunderstood and unpopular in some quarters. Many people believed that the customary
days of the calendar, and particularly the major religious festivals, were
inextricably linked to the physical days on which they were held, and
they used such spurious arguments as the alleged blossoming of the
'Holy Thorn' on Christmas Day to show that the reforms were against
God's pattern. Many people stubbornly continued to celebrate 'Old
Christmas Day' right up to the late nineteenth century.

One of the problems for the historian of customs and festivals is that
a double standard was created, which throws a shadow of doubt over
much subsequent evidence. For example, Abbotsbury Garland Day,
which now takes place on 13 May (1 May Old Style), appears to be a
May Day custom which was moved when the calendar was reformed.
But we have no evidence that the Abbotsbury custom even existed in
1752 (the earliest reference is 1867), and it is only by comparison with
other garland customs that we expect it to have any connection with
May Day. It might conceivably have been a custom that took place on
13 May from its inception, whenever that was.

The other major problem is that in the past the official calendar was
only one of several ways in which time was viewed and regulated, and

the further back in time one looks, the harder it is to discern any co-herent pattern. The disjunctions and disagreements between religious and civil calendars have already been indicated, but it is clear that for many in the past it was the physical year of days and seasons, of sun, rain, and frost, which really mattered. However in thrall the farmer may have been to saints' days for visiting fairs, attending markets, and paying rents and wages (for more on saints' days, see below), the fact of the matter is that lambs are born when they are ready, and corn does not ripen on a set day. The agricultural year helped to set the educa-tional year, with the long holiday timed to enable children to help with the all-important harvest, and a new year starting soon afterwards. Parliamentary sessions also start in the autumn, traditionally the time when gentlemen could be spared from their country estates. The legal profession had its own calendar, the fashionable set its seasons, the horse-racing fraternity its high and low points, and many trades their own peculiar annual rhythms.

Which New Year?

The idea that the New Year commences on 1 January is so deeply en-trenched in our psyche that it will be a surprise to many modern read-ers that there should be any doubt about it, or that it ever took place on a different day. In fact, the question of when the New Year starts is enormously complex and in the past caused a great deal of debate and confusion. Echoes of this confusion still resonate whenever an English person wonders why the financial year runs till the end of March, or the tax year begins on 6 April.

In the ancient pre-Julian Roman calendar, there were ten months and the New Year started on 1 March (which is why the names of the months September to December derive from the words 'seven' to 'ten'). It was Julius Caesar, when introducing what became known as the Julian calendar, who changed it to 1 January. This was the ac-cepted 'international standard' when Christianity was being formed, but when the new religion began making headway, many followers thought that a specifically Christian view of the calendar should be adopted, and once the Nativity of Christ had been set at 25 December, many naturally argued that this day should be regarded as the begin-ning of the year. Others, counting nine months back from Christmas Day, argued that the Feast of the Annunciation, the conception of Christ (25 March), should really mark the beginning of the Christian year. The supporters of 25 March won the day, and devout Christians celebrated that day as New Year. A dual system of New Years was thus created, which persisted for centuries, and as so much of civil administration was in the hands of monks and clerics, the religious definition was long adopted as the norm.

Pope Gregory, however, when ordering the introduction of the calendar system named after him in 1582, decreed that from that moment the official New Year would be 1 January. This detail had nothing to do with the reform of the Julian calendar per se, but was an added bonus for those who wished to introduce an international common calendar. As mentioned previously, half the western world followed suit, but those Protestant countries that held aloof from the calendar change also ignored the instruction about the New Year, although Scotland, while rejecting the main reform, adopted 1 January as its New Year in 1600.

England rejected the whole Gregorian reform, including the January New Year, and thus perpetuated a bizarre double standard, consigning the country to a further 200 years of confusion. Despite the fact that 25 March was the official start of the year, 1 January had been *called* New Year's Day by people high and low, from at least the thirteenth century. Henry III, for example, received New Year gifts in January 1249, and in the following 500 years there are numerous examples of letters, diaries, and other documents that name 1 January as 'New Year's Day'. However, and this is the really strange point, the people who wrote these documents did not change the number of the year in January, but in March, in line with official practice. Thus Samuel Pepys, in his famous *Diary*, regularly refers to 1 January as New Year's Day but only changes the year, without comment, on 25 March. Historians have long had to deal with this dating anomaly, and the practice of referring to the first three months of the year in the form of, for example, '1663/4' has been adopted to improve precision.

This state of affairs lasted until 1752, when the reform of the English calendar and the adoption of the Gregorian standard, was finally enacted. The first of January had finally received official recognition as 'New Year's Day', for most purposes. Unfortunately for those who value simplicity, the Exchequer decided not to change, and opted to continue the old New Year formula, although this was compounded by the loss of the eleven days occasioned by the change of calendar. The start of the tax year therefore became 6 April.

Almanacs

Almanacs were a hugely popular form of publication which could be found in nearly every household in the land. They were churned out in their hundreds of thousands every year, and they easily outsold any other form of printed works. They were paper-covered, pocket-sized, and cheap enough for almost anyone to afford. The first examples were produced soon after printing was invented, and from the mid fifteenth century, as their circulation grew in leaps and bounds, they were a major feature of the new printing trade. Exact figures are hard to come by, but it is clear that they were enormous; as historian Keith Thomas comments, 'The figure of 3 to 4 million which is sometimes suggested as the total production of almanacs in the seventeenth century, is a distinct under-estimate; the ten years after November 1663 alone nearly reached that total. Not even the Bible sold at this rate.' Many different series exist-ed over the years, including a number that became household names: *Zadkiel's*, *Old Moore's*, *Poor Robin's*, and *Raphael's*; others went for more fancy-sounding titles such as *Vox Stellarum* or *Merlinus Liberatus*.

Between about 1640 and 1700, almanac writers entered enthusiasti-cally into the raging religious and political controversies of the day, but mostly their sights were set on much lower things. We can dis-tinguish three different types of information in the typical almanac, although in reality they were not as distinct as these categories imply. The one that principally concerns us here was a full calendar of the year, which marked the saints' days and other festivals, with the major ones printed in red (hence 'red-letter days'). As so much of the rural year was organized by the veneration of saints, this was an essential aide-memoire for both farmer and farmworker. The second section included a rather miscellaneous collection of 'useful facts', such as tide tables, lists of kings and queens, birthdays of the current royal family, and a historical chronology of the world starting with 'the Creation'. It is impossible to know whether this information was valued or not by the average almanac reader, but the third section certainly was. The latter took up much of the publication and contained simplified astro-nomical tables, details of eclipses, phases of the moon, and their ac-companying astrological meanings, along with other prophecies and predictions of a generalized political and social nature. The fact that much of this planetary material was couched in such pseudo-scientific language probably added to its attraction. An extract taken at random

We see this fluid rises from the earth into the atmosphere, and is probably going off from thence, when it appears in the Aurora Borealis: And as this electric matter, from its vast subtilty and velocity, seems capable of making great excursions from the planetary system, the several comets in their long excursions from the sun, in all directions, may overtake this matter, and, attracting it to themselves, may come back replete with it.

The information about the phases of the moon was also vital to the farmer. It was very widely believed that the moon had a direct effect on various aspects of agriculture and needed to be carefully monitored. From at least the sixteenth to the nineteenth centuries, few farmers would willingly kill a pig when the moon was on the wane, as they believed that the meat would be sure to shrink in the cooking if they did so, and some were equally convinced that certain crops should always be planted on the waxing of the moon, and others when it was on the wane.

However useful the calendar and the other tables could be, it was the diet of popular astrology, prophecy, and prediction which gave the almanac a bad name with the more educated section of the population. The old radical William Cobbett, for example, writing in 1813, was scathing about the hold that almanacs seemed to have on the minds of semi-literate rural workers:

His standard book will, in all likelihood, be Moore's Almanack, *that universal companion of the farmers and labourers of England. Here we will find a perpetual spring of knowledge; a daily supply, besides an extra portion monthly. Here are signs and wonders and prophesies, in all which he will believe as implicitly as he does in the first chapter of Genesis . . . To keep a people in a state of profound ignorance, to make them superstitious and slavish, there needs little more than the general reading of this single book.*

Saints' Days: Real and Invented

In rural areas especially, everybody had a good working knowledge of the saints' days and church festivals throughout the year, and for those who were unsure of the dates, many homes had a copy of the year's almanac to guide them. Despite the fact that the reformed English Church refused to recognize the power of saints, it is clear that for most of the population these days were far more important than those of the official calendar. In the mid seventeenth century, for example, Henry Best, gentleman-farmer of Elmswell in the East Riding of Yorkshire, noted down in his manuscript account of farming practice (published by the Surtees Society as *Rural Economy in Yorkshire in 1641*) all the fairs in his locality, over two dozen in all. In every case, he named the fair-day in terms of its nearest religious festival or saint's day, and only sometimes gave the calendar date as secondary information:

> *On St. Peters day there is a fair at Frodingham . . . Malton horse fair begins now of late three days before St. Mathew Day . . . On St. Luke day there is a fair at Hunmanby . . .*

Saints' days were so central to the popular notion of calendrical time that people made up their own to describe a particular day, often facetiously: St Distaff's Day (7 January) was the day that women went back to their spinning; St Monday was the extended weekend regularly taken by workers in the shoe trade (*see* p. 582); and Mother Shipton's Day was celebrated by washerwomen in Cambridge (*see* p. 272). Some of them entered everyday language. 'St Monday' was often used to describe any unauthorized holiday, and another fictitious character, St Tibb, only existed in such phrases as 'You'll get your money on St Tibb's Day', which meant 'never'. Any far or mythical time could be referred to as St Tibb's Eve or St Tibb's Day, and sometimes it even meant what one hopes is the most distant day of all, the evening of the last day, or the Day of Judgement.

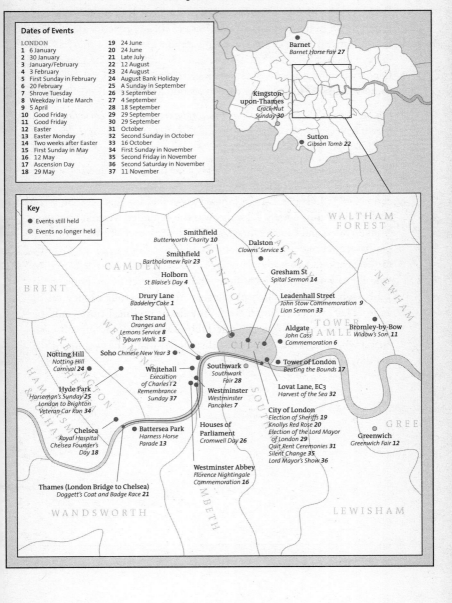

Dates of Events

LONDON
1 6 January
2 30 January
3 January/February
4 3 February
5 First Sunday in February
6 20 February
7 Shrove Tuesday
8 Weekday in late March
9 5 April
10 Good Friday
11 Good Friday
12 Easter
13 Easter Monday
14 Two weeks after Easter
15 First Sunday in May
16 12 May
17 Ascension Day
18 29 May
19 24 June
20 24 June
21 Late July
22 12 August
23 24 August
24 August Bank Holiday
25 A Sunday in September
26 3 September
27 4 September
28 18 September
29 29 September
30 29 September
31 October
32 Second Sunday in October
33 16 October
34 First Sunday in November
35 Second Friday in November
36 Second Saturday in November
37 11 November

Barnet
Barnet Horse Fair 27

Kingston-
upon-Thames
*Crack-Nut
Sunday 30*

Sutton
Gibson Tomb 22

Key
● Events still held
◐ Events no longer held

WALTHAM
FOREST

Smithfield
Butterworth Charity 10

Dalston
Clowns' Service 5

Smithfield
Bartholomew Fair 23

Holborn
St Blaise's Day 4

Gresham St
Spital Sermon 14

CAMDEN

Drury Lane
Baddeley Cake 1

Leadenhall Street
John Stow Commemoration 9
Lion Sermon 33

BRENT

The Strand
*Oranges and
Lemons Service 8*
Tyburn Walk 15

Aldgate
*John Cass
Commemoration 6*

Bromley-by-Bow
Widow's Son 11

TOWER HAMLETS

Soho *Chinese New Year 3*

CITY

Notting Hill
*Notting Hill
Carnival 24*

Whitehall
*Execution
of Charles I 2*
*Remembrance
Sunday 37*

Southwark
*Southwark
Fair 28*

Tower of London
Beating the Bounds 17

Hyde Park
Horseman's Sunday 25
*London to Brighton
Veteran Car Run 34*

Westminster
*Westminster
Pancakes 7*

Lovat Lane, EC3
Harvest of the Sea 32

City of London
Election of Sheriffs 19
Knollys Red Rose 20
*Election of the Lord Mayor
of London 29*
Quit Rent Ceremonies 31
Silent Change 35
Lord Mayor's Show 36

GREE

Chelsea
*Royal Hospital
Chelsea Founder's
Day 18*

Battersea Park
*Harness Horse
Parade 13*

Houses of
Parliament
Cromwell Day 26

Greenwich
Greenwich Fair 12

Thames (London Bridge to Chelsea)
Doggett's Coat and Badge Race 21

Westminster Abbey
*Florence Nightingale
Commemoration 16*

WANDSWORTH

LAMBETH

LEWISHAM

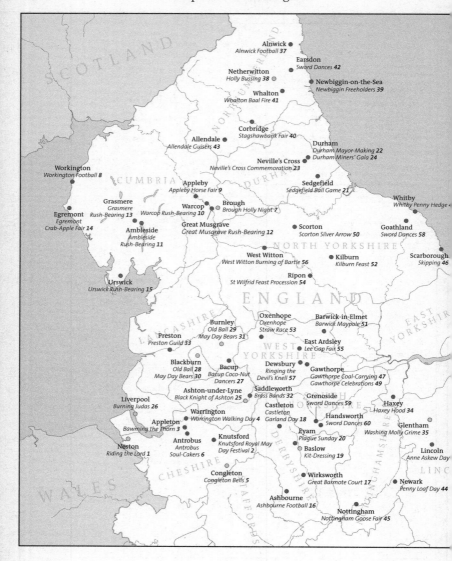

Key

● Events still held
◐ Events no longer held

Dates of Events

CHESHIRE
1 Easter
2 First Saturday in May
3 29 June
4 First Friday in July
5 12 August
6 31 October

CUMBRIA
7 6 January
8 Good Friday
9 First week in June
10 29 June
11 First Saturday in July
12 First Saturday in July
13 5 August
14 Third Saturday in September
15 29 September
Note: Friday following Ash Wednesday – Pully Lug Day (Cumbria) – no longer held, Pace Egg Plays (Cumbria)

DERBYSHIRE
16 Shrove Tuesday
17 April
18 29 May
19 4 August
20 Last Sunday in August
Note: Christmas – Old Horse (Derbyshire) – no longer held, Christmas – Old Tup (Derbyshire) – no longer held

DURHAM
21 Shrove Tuesday
22 Mid May
23 29 May
24 Second/Third Saturday in July

LANCASHIRE
25 Easter Monday
26 Good Friday
27 Easter Saturday
28 Easter
29 Easter
30 May Day
31 May Day

32 Whit Friday
33 29 August
Note: Pace Egging (Lancashire), Pace Egg Plays (Lancashire), 31 October – Mischief Night (Lancashire)

LINCOLNSHIRE
34 6 January
35 Good Friday
36 16 July
Note: Plough Plays (Lincolnshire), Straw Bears (Lincolnshire),

NORTHUMBERLAND
37 Shrove Tuesday
38 Easter Tuesday
39 18 May
40 4 July
41 4 July
42 Christmas
43 31 December

NOTTINGHAMSHIRE
44 11 March
45 First Wednesday in October

YORKSHIRE
46 Shrove Tuesday
47 Easter Monday
48 Ascension Eve
49 First Saturday in May
50 Mid to late May
51 Spring Bank Holiday
52 6 July
53 Sunday in early July
54 July/August
55 17 August
56 24 August
57 Christmas Eve
58 Christmas
59 Christmas
60 Christmas
Note: Pace Egging (Yorkshire), 31 October – Mischief Night (Yorkshire), Easter Monday – Legging Day (Yorkshire) – no longer held

NSHIRE

NORFOLK

Dates of Events

BEDFORDSHIRE
1 Rogation

BERKSHIRE
2 Hocktide
3 March
4 Whitsun
5 30 November
6 13 December

BRISTOL
7 Easter Tuesday
8 Whitsun
9 A Sunday in October

BUCKINGHAMSHIRE
10 Shrove Tuesday
11 May
12 11 November

CAMBRIDGESHIRE
13 Whit Tuesday
14 14 September

CORNWALL
15 3 February
16 Shrove Tuesday
17 May Day
18 8 May
19 7 July
20 25 July
21 Boxing Day
Note: May Day – Ducking or Dipping Day (Cornwall) – no longer held

DEVON
22 Spring Bank Holiday
23 Spring Bank Holiday
24 Late May
25 Second Wednesday in July
26 August Bank Holiday
27 Second Wednesday in October

28 Last Thursday in October
29 5 November
30 5 November
31 Second Saturday in November
32 Fourth Tuesday in November
Note: May Day – Ducking or Dipping Day (Devon) – no longer held

DORSET
33 Shrove Tuesday
34 13 May (Old May Day)
35 14 September
36 10 October

ESSEX
37 New Year
38 Easter Monday
39 Third Thursday in May
40 Early July
41 Early September
42 20 October

GLOUCESTERSHIRE
43 May Day
44 Second Saturday in May
45 Whitsun
46 Spring Bank Holiday
47 Spring Bank Holiday
48 19 September
49 Boxing Day

HAMPSHIRE
50 25 March
51 First Wednesday in August
52 10 October
53 21 October

HERTFORDSHIRE
54 May Day
55 2 October

KENT
56 Easter
57 First Saturday in July
58 25 July
59 24 August
Note: Christmas – Hooden Horse (North Kent Coast)

LEICESTERSHIRE
60 Shrove Tuesday
61 Easter Monday
62 Easter Monday

LINCOLNSHIRE
63 13 November

NORFOLK
64 Third Thursday in September
Note: Norfolk Shrovetide Cookeels (or Coquilles) – no longer held

NORTHAMPTONSHIRE
65 May

OXFORDSHIRE
66 14 January
67 10 February
68 May Day
69 May Day
70 Ascension Day
71 Spring Bank Holiday
72 20 June
73 24 June
74 June/July
75 6 July

SHROPSHIRE
76 Shrove Tuesday
77 Last Sunday in May

Key

● Events still held
◉ Events no longer held

Aston-on-Clun
Arbor Day 77

Kiddermins
Brecknell Bequest

Ludlow
Ludlow Rope-Pulling 76

St Briavels
St Briavels Bread and Cheese Dole 45

Randwic
Randwick Cheese-Rolling 4
Randwick Wap 4

Marshfie
Marshfield Paper Boys

Bristol
Tuppenny Starvers 7
St Mary Redcliffe Rush Sunday 8
Redcliffe Pipe Walk 9

Bridgwater
Bridgwater Carnival 83

Minehead
Minehead Hobby Horse 81

Stoke St Gregory
Egg Shackling 78

Tatworth
Tatworth Candle Auction 80

Shepton Beauchamp
Egg Shackling 79

Sherborne
Pack Monday Fair 36

Hinton St George
Punkie Night 82

Combe Martin
Hunting the Earl of Rone 22

Shebbear
Devil's Stone 29

Bampton
Bampton Fair 28

Holsworthy
Pretty Maid's Charity 25

Hatherleigh
Hatherleigh Carnival 31

Ottery St Mary
Ottery St Mary 30

Kingsteignton
Kingsteignton Ram-Roasting 23

Abbotsbury
Abbotsbury Garland Day 3

Padstow
Padstow Hobby Horse 17
Padstow Mummers' (Darkie) Day 21

Tavistock
Tavistock Goosie Fair 27

Bodmin
Bodmin Riding 19

Ashburton
Ashburton Court Leet 32

Marldon
Marldon Apple Pie Fair 26

St Columb
St Columb Hurling 16

St Ives
St Ives Hurling 15
John Knill Charity 20

Brixham
Blessing of the Sea 24

Helston
Helston Flora Day 18

DEVON

SOMERSE

DO

Abbots
Bromley
*bots Bromley
rn Dance 86*

Tutbury
Tutbury Bull-Running 85

Lichfield
*Samuel Johnson
Commemoration 87*

Hallaton
*Hallaton Hare
Pie and Bottle-
Kicking 62*

Stamford
*Stamford
Bull-Running 63*

Oxford
*Hunting the Mallard 66
St Scholastica's Day 67
Magdalen College Singing 68
Beating the Bounds 70
Magdalen Outdoor Sermon 73*

*alsall
oseley's Dole 84*

Leicester
*Whipping Toms 60
Leicester Hare Hunt 61*

Corby
Corby Pole Fair 65

St Ives
Dicing for Bibles 13

Diss
Chalk-Back Day 64

Atherstone
Atherstone Football 97

Knightlow Hill
Wroth Silver 99

Arden
Woodmen of Arden 98

Olney
Pancake Races 10

Cambridge
Sturbridge Fair 14

Bury St Edmund's
Jankyn Smith's Charity 88

SUFFOLK

Weston-sub-Edge
Robert Dover's Olimpick Games 47

Fenny Stratford
Fenny Poppers 12

Baldock
Lords and Ladies 54

Harwich
*Harwich Kichel-
Throwing 39*

*inswick
nswick
urch-
pping 48*

Charlton-on-Otmoor
*Charlton-on-Otmoor
Garland 69*

Braughing
*Braughing Old
Man's Day 55*

Colchester
*Colchester Oyster Fishery 41
Colchester Oyster Feast 42*

Yarnton
*Yarnton Lot
Meadow 74*

Leighton Buzzard
Wilkes Walk 1

Epping
Epping Stag Hunt 38

ESSEX

*roud
oper's Hill
eese-
lling 46*

Abingdon
*Mayor of Ock
Street 72*

High Wycombe
Weighing the Mayor 11

Maldon
Maldon Mud Race 37

Grove
Duck-Racing 75

Ufton Nervet
*Dame Elizabeth
Marvyn Charity 3*

Eton
*Eton School Montem 4
Eton Wall Game 5*

Fairlop
Fairlop Fair 40

GREATER

London is shown in
further detail overleaf

Bampton
*Bampton Morris
Dance 71*

BERKSHIRE

Aldermaston
*Aldermaston
Candle Auction 6*

Wotton
Forty Shilling Day 89

Rochester
Medway Admiralty Court 57

Whitstable
Whitstable Oyster Festival 58

Hungerford
*Hungerford Hocktide
Court 2*

SURREY

Biddenden
Biddenden Maids Charity 56

Sandwich
Sandwich Bun Race 59

Great Wishford
*Wishford Auction 100
ovely Ceremonies 101*

Weyhill
Weyhill Fair 52

Guildford
Maid's Money 90

Tinsley Green
Tinsley Green Marbles 91

KENT

*shaftesbury
haftesbury Byzant 35*

Tichborne
Tichborne Dole 50

Ebernoe
Ebernoe Horn Fair 95

Hartfield
Hartfield Dole 92

Lewes
Lewes Bonfire Night 96

Rye
Rye Mayor-Making 93

EAST SUSSEX

Southampton
*Knighthood of the
Old Green 51*

Portsmouth
Trafalgar Day 53

Piddinghoe
Little Edith's Treat 94

Corfe Castle
*Purbeck Marblers and
Stonecuttters 33*

SOMERSET
78 Shrove Tuesday
79 Shrove Tuesday
80 6 April
81 May Day
82 Late October
83 First Friday in November

STAFFORDSHIRE
84 6 January
85 16 August
86 4 September

87 18 September

SUFFOLK
88 29 June

SURREY
89 2 February
90 May

SUSSEX
91 Good Friday
92 Good Friday
93 23 May
94 19 July
95 25 July

96 5 November
Note: *Good Friday Skipping
(East Sussex Coast)*

WARWICKSHIRE
97 Shrove Tuesday
98 First week in August
99 10 November

WILTSHIRE
100 Rogation
101 29 May

WORCESTERSHIRE
102 21 June

JANUARY

New Year Customs and Superstitions

New Year's Day has always been rife with meaning for the superstitious person, and the potential problems start the moment the clock has struck midnight. One of the key underlying principles of superstition is that the *beginning* of any enterprise, journey, or period of time is of vital importance and largely determines future success or failure. Good or bad luck can therefore be predicted and influenced by ensuring that one does the right things and avoids the wrong things at the start. This principle can influence people's actions at a variety of levels: how one gets out of bed in the morning to start the day, how the first steps of a journey proceed, how good the first sale of the day is, what to do when one sees a new moon or hears the first cuckoo, and so on. Many wedding superstitions are based on the same principle, as the day marks the beginning of the couple's new life.

New Year's Day is the most obvious starting point of all, and most of us still have a vague feeling that what happens on the day is somehow predictive, as recorded by Jonathan Couch in his *History of Polperro* (1871):

The character of the coming twelve months, for good or bad fortune, is foretold by the appearance of things on the morning of the new year. A trivial mishap, or the slightest instance of good luck, has now more than its usual significance, inasmuch as it predicts, in a general way, the course of events through the coming year.

One of the widespread ways in which a glimpse of the future could be obtained was by 'dipping' into the Bible for guidance, either late on New Year's Eve, or first thing on New Year's morning. A contributor to the *Folk-Lore Journal* of 1886 reported:

Parties are general in Cornwall on New Year's Eve to watch in the New Year and wish friends health and happiness; but I know of no peculiar customs, except that before retiring to rest the old women opened their Bibles at haphazard to find out their luck for the coming year. The text on which the forefinger of the right hand rested was supposed to foretell the future.

Obviously, the randomly selected verse needed some interpretation, and it was quite common for people to discuss its symbolic meanings among themselves during the day. Any religious scruples about fortune-telling were allayed by the knowledge that the Holy Bible could not mislead you, and respectable people, including clergymen's families, were known to indulge in the practice. But there was also a long tradition of using other books opened at random for similar divinatory purposes, although not necessarily at New Year. There is some indication that this was regarded as an acceptable substitute for those who were worried about using the Bible. Oddly enough, the works of Virgil are often quoted in this context, and the use of poetry as a divinatory tool has an even longer history. In their *Dictionary of Superstitions* (1989), Iona Opie and Moira Tatem provide a quotation from St Augustine of Hippo's *Confessions* (*c.* AD 397):

When a man by hap-hazard opens the pages of some poet, who sang and thought of something wholly different, a verse sometimes fell out, wonderfully agreeable to the present business.

Not content with simply observing or predicting the coming year, many people in the past took active steps to ensure their short-term prosperity. A number of customs and beliefs were based on the notion of luck potentially flowing *into* or *out of* the house in the coming year, luck that could be influenced by symbolic activity on New Year's Day. Householders were therefore keen to ensure that the predominant activity on the day was inward, and this is most clearly seen in the widespread custom of **first-footing** (*see* p. 5). Most were content with ensuring that the first *movement* was inward, as Llewellyn Jewitt recorded in 1853:

On this day it is considered unlucky to remove anything from a house until something has been brought in; and therefore each member of the family carries some trifling thing in early in the morning. In the neighbourhood of Newark [in Nottinghamshire] *I have heard the rhyme:*

> *Take out, take in*
> *Bad luck is sure to begin*
> *Take in and take out*
> *Good luck will come about.*

But there were also many who believed that nothing – not even the ashes from the fire or the waste from the kitchen – should leave the house on New Year's Day.

The one thing that no superstitious nineteenth-century householder would allow to leave the house under any circumstances at this time of year was fire. At any other time they would be quite happy to let a neighbour or stranger take a live coal or taper to light their lantern or house fire, but not at New Year. For many, this ban was also in force throughout the Christmas period (*see* **Christmas: Superstitions** for another example), while for others it was only on New Year's morning. A correspondent to *Notes & Queries* wrote in 1862:

My maid, who comes from the neighbourhood of Pendle [in Lancashire], *informs me that an unlucky old woman in her native village, having allowed her fire to go out on New Year's Eve, had to wait till one o'clock on the following day before any neighbour would supply her with a light.*

On symbolically charged days such as New Year's Day, a number of everyday activities could take on additional meanings, and as superstition is primarily negative, these were to be avoided on the day, as here in Devon in 1896:

On New Year's Day one of our maidens (not a Devonshire one) was going to do the family washing, when our West-Country girl exclaimed in horror: 'Pray don't 'ee wash on New Year's Day, Or you'll wash one of the family away'. On inquiry I find the belief widely spread hereabouts, that if the year commences in domestic circles with a washing day, one of the occupants of the house is washed out (i.e. dies) during the year.

The same was said about Good Friday, Holy Innocents' Day (*see* **28 December**), and occasionally Ascension Day, and for obvious reasons this superstition was particularly strong in fishing and other seafaring families.

See also **31 December: New Year's Eve**.

Bank Holiday

English people of middle age and over will remember that New Year's Day was only designated a bank holiday in 1974. Before that date, people still celebrated New Year's Eve, but most workplaces exhibited a decidedly sorry workforce on 1 January every year.

Burning the Bush

In December 1877, the Revd Francis Kilvert, who had just taken up the living of Bredwardine in Herefordshire, stayed up to see in the New Year, and then retired:

After I had gone to bed I saw from where I lay a bright blaze sprung up in the fields beyond the river and I knew at once that they were keeping up the old custom of Burning the Bush on New Year's Day in the morning . . . the whole valley can be seen early on New Year's morning alight with fires.

This custom of 'Burning the Bush' seems to have been unique to Herefordshire, and was only reported from the second half of the nineteenth to the early twentieth centuries, when it was clearly on its last legs. Local folklore-collector Ella M. Leather provided a description in 1912:

This custom was generally kept up all over Herefordshire until about forty years ago, and survives here and there, in the Leominster and Kington districts. The 'bush' is a globe made of hawthorn, which is hung up in the kitchen of the farmhouse, with the mistletoe, after the bush-burning ceremony each New Year's morning; it hangs there till the day comes round again, when it is taken out to be burnt and a new one made. Mistletoe is never brought into the house before New Year's Day; to do so would be most unlucky.

At five o'clock in the morning the workmen fetch the old 'bush' . . . It is carried to the earliest sown wheat field, where a large fire is lighted, of straw and bushes, in which it is burnt. While it is burning a new one is made; in making it, the ends of the branches are scorched in the fire. An old man, who had lived all his life in the Pembridge district, told me that at Shobdon, in his time, they poured cider over it afterwards, 'to varnish and darken the bush like' he said.

Mrs Leather also gives further examples, on similar lines. This is clearly allied to the Twelfth Night fires (*see* **6 January: Twelfth Night**

Fires), which were lighted in the fields elsewhere in the same region, and also connected with wassailing (*see* **Christmas: Wassailing**).

Cream of the Well

In line with the widespread superstitious principle that everyday things take on a special significance at the beginning of a key time-cycle, water drawn soon after midnight on New Year's Eve had a similar reputation to the dew that fell on May Day morning (*see* 1 **May: May Dew**). In 1912, Ella M. Leather recorded:

It was formerly the custom in Herefordshire farmhouses for the servants to sit up to see the New Year in, and at midnight to rush for the 'Cream o' the well', the first water drawn from the well in the year, which was thought to be beautifying and lucky. The maid who succeeded in getting it would take it to the bedroom of her mistress, who would give a present for it. 'My missus always had the cream o' the well to wash in on New Year's morning', said Mrs. M., 'and she always put a shilling under the basin for me, too'.

This first water went by various local names, such as the cream, flower, crop, or ream of the well, and although the idea was widely reported in the north of England and Scotland, the earliest definite reference is from Herefordshire in 1804.

First-Footing and Letting In the New Year

The idea that the first person over the threshold on New Year's Day brings luck to the household is regarded as particularly Scottish, but it was in fact widely practised all over England in the nineteenth and twentieth centuries. Nevertheless, there is no doubt that it was more common, and taken more seriously, the closer one approached Scotland. 'There can be few, if any, houses in our district where the custom of first-footing is not respected,' wrote Rosalie Bosanquet about the village of Cambo, Northumberland, in 1929.

The modern standard of 'a dark-haired man' bringing luck has effectively erased a wide range of local variations. Many early reports did not mention the hair colour of the first-footer and occasionally a fair-haired person was preferred, but in the vast majority of cases a male was acceptable and a female was not. In 1895, C. J. Billson recorded:

Mrs. Billson, native of country near Bagworth [in Leicestershire], *assures me that she has a vivid recollection of her mother and her grandmother not permitting anyone to cross their threshold on New Year's morning until a dark man had first entered the house. They regarded it as particularly unlucky for a woman to be the first visitor.*

It was similarly unusual for both sexes to have a role, although in Lincolnshire in 1908 Mrs Gutch and Mabel Peacock recorded:

You must see first of all on a New Year's morning, one of the opposite sex (not a member of your own family). Boys go round and wish the women a Happy New Year, adding, 'and I've brought you a bit of stick'. Girls do the same to the men, and both expect rewards in the shape of current coin.

Not only does the first-footer need lucky characteristics himself, but he must also carry certain items, or perform certain tasks, to ensure the luck. First-footers often carry symbolic items into the house, such as coal, bread, or whisky; they might say something symbolic – wish luck and joy; or do symbolic things – stir the fire, cut a cake, and so on. The details vary considerably from house to house, but the principles of luck-bringing are the same almost everywhere.

Other superstitions based on the same principle also existed, such as who one first met in the morning or when going to work or when starting on a journey, and these are also classed as first-foot beliefs. They have been identified from at least the fourteenth century, but the earliest record of first-footing at Christmas or New Year is surprisingly late, and is not from Scotland, or even the north of England, but from Herefordshire in 1804:

On Christmas Day it is deemed an omen of ill fortune . . . when a female first enters the house in the morning.

A number of other relatively low-key activities performed at this season were designed to welcome the New Year physically into the house and to allow the Old Year to depart. In Herefordshire in 1912:

As the clock struck twelve it was customary to open the back door to let the old year out, and then the front door to let-in the new year.

This was sometimes combined with the first-foot, so that the first-footer entered by the front door and left by the back. This, incidentally, broke the widespread rule that held for the rest of the year that it was extremely unlucky for someone to enter and leave a house by a different door.

Long before Christmas presents were invented, people were accustomed to exchange gifts at New Year. This tradition was widespread across Europe, and the ancient Romans also indulged in it. Numerous records survive from Tudor times of sumptuous gifts presented to the ruling monarch by the nobility, higher clerics, members of the court and the royal household, and the sovereign reciprocated, mostly with money. Outside the court, other important people could expect gifts from their subordinates, and similar arrangements existed further down the social scale. Indeed, throughout the documentary record until the later eighteenth century there is a definite air of currying favour, if not actual bribery, in the custom. Samuel Pepys, for example, mentions New Year gifts many times in his diary between 1660 and 1669, in a number of contexts, including between him and his wife and friends. But even he was astonished at the number of 'gifts' he was expected to pay out for in his work at the Navy office.

There were many unwritten rules and traditions on the subject. Country tenants were expected to give a capon to their landlord every year. In the eighteenth century, the rector and antiquarian John Brand printed an extract from an untitled volume in the British Library, of the time of Queen Anne (1707–14), which indicates that the tendency for gifts to be given to superiors extended right down the age range:

On the first day of [January] *will be given many more gifts than will be kindly received or gratefully rewarded. Children to their inexpressible joy, will be drest in their best bibs and aprons, and may be seen handed along streets, some bearing Kentish pippins, others oranges stuck with cloves, in order to crave a blessing of their godfathers and godmothers.*

Apart from money and jewellery, gifts ranged from the useful, such as gloves or papers of pins, to the ornamental gilt nutmeg, and often included food of various kinds. Urban middle-class families were certainly exchanging small gifts among themselves, and to friends, throughout the Victorian era. There was a strong tradition for children to make the presents they gave to parents, but popular magazines also ran advertisements for New Year gifts and continued to do so right up to the turn of the twentieth century. But by that time, the new fashion for giving presents at Christmas had made serious inroads into the New Year custom, prompted by the arrival of Santa Claus and the Christmas stocking in the 1860s.

See also **Christmas: Father Christmas/Santa Claus; Christmas: Stockings**.

Mad Maldon Mud Race

Future folklorists and cultural researchers will need to create a new category of custom origin called 'it started with a discussion in the pub', as so many of our modern customs seem to have been born this way. A case in point is the Mad Maldon Mud Race in Essex, a 400-yard dash across the River Blackwater and back, at low tide, which started with a pub dare in the mid 1970s. The event is now organized by the local Lions and Rotary Clubs in conjunction with Maldon District Council, and raises thousands of pounds for charity each year. The 2005 event attracted 180 competitors and about 6,000 spectators, including many journalists and TV camera crews. Fancy dress is a standard feature of modern customs, and the Maldon competitors are suitably attired in a variety of costumes, although it matters little what they are wearing after a few seconds in the Blackwater mud. The day and time vary a little, according to tidal conditions.

Pop (Pope) Ladies

Pop (or Pope) Ladies were cakes, made and sold every year on New Year's Day, and apparently unique to St Albans in Hertfordshire. A contributor to the *Gentleman's Magazine* in 1820 reported:

I happened to sleep at St Albans on the night of the 31st December [1819] and was awakened the next morning by a confused noise of boys and girls in the street crying for sale 'Popladys! Popladys!' . . . a plain cake, like the cross-buns sold on Good Friday but, instead of being circular, was long and narrow rudely resembling the human figure, with two dried raisins or currants to represent eyes and another for the mouth, the lower part being formed rather like the outer case of an Egyptian mummy.

The custom is mentioned occasionally during the nineteenth century, but was said to be dying out in 1896 and does not seem to have survived much into the twentieth century.

6 January

Epiphany

In the Christian calendar, 6 January is Epiphany, named after the Greek word for 'manifestation'. It was originally celebrated in the Eastern churches as the day of Christ's baptism, but after it had been introduced into the West in the fourth century AD it developed into the feast of the manifestation of Christ to the Magi ('wise men'). On the Continent, the day was marked by dramatic representations in church: clergy were dressed as the three Magi, a large star was suspended from the rafters, and a depiction of the nativity scene was revealed by drawing a curtain as the Magi approached. These religious dramas also existed in pre-Reformation England, although it is not clear how widely practised they were here. The churchwardens' accounts for St Mary's, Cambridge, for example, include the following entries for 1557–8:

> *For make of a star*   20d.
> *For painting and gilding the same star*   20d.

As the Magi were later identified as kings, it was appropriate for real monarchs to take particular note of the day; a royal offering of gold, frankincense and myrrh is still made every year at Epiphany. The custom may date back to the Norman kings, and until the reign of George II the sovereign performed the duty in person, but since that time it has been carried out by proxy. Nowadays, the offering is made during Holy Communion in the Chapel Royal, St James's Palace, by two ushers to the Queen, escorted by the Queen's Body Guard of the Yeoman of the Guard.

But 6 January is also **Twelfth Night** (*see below*), and although kings did feature in the secular celebrations of the day, they were play-acted rather than real ones. The duration of the Christmas festival was officially set at twelve days by the Council of Tours in AD 567, when it was laid down that the whole period should be spent in celebration and thanks, and that no one should be made to work during that time.

Old Christmas Day

When the Gregorian calendar was introduced in September 1752 (*see* p. xxix), there was much grumbling about the change, and also much confusion. Many people refused to change the habits of generations, and continued to celebrate major festivals on their equivalent Old Style dates. Most of these temporal anomalies sorted themselves out over the following generations, but the one date on which a significant minority of traditionalists refused to budge was Christmas Day. In 1912, the folklore-collector Ella M. Leather recorded the following words from a Herefordshire man:

'My grandfather always kept up Christmas on Old Christmas Day,' said W.P. of Peterchurch, 'none of your new Christmas for him; it must be the real Christmas, too, for the Holy Thorn blossoms, and the cattle go down on their knees at twelve o'clock in remembrance.' I have talked to many people who firmly believed this; though they have not seen it, their parents or grandparents have.

This tendency continued in some rural families right up to the turn of the twentieth century, one hundred and fifty years after the official change, and even then some folk were still grumbling about it, although they had finally been forced to hold their celebrations on the New Style date.

Twelfth Night

Twelfth Night (or Twelfth Day), the secular aspect of **Epiphany** (*see above*), is one of the three really important festivals of past eras that have almost completely lost their meaning in the modern world (Shrovetide and Whitsun being the others). For centuries, Twelfth Night was a universal time for merrymaking and indulgence by rich and poor alike and was second only to Christmas Day. But with changing fashions, and the restructuring of Christmas carried out by the Victorians, the festival rapidly faded into the vague 'end of Christmas' feeling that is prevalent today. Even its position marking the end of Christmas is now being usurped by New Year's Day.

The very definition of Twelfth Night is problematic. In trying to document the older seasonal customs, there is the problem of Old and New Style dates, created by the change of the calendar in 1752 (*see* p. xxix). The introduction of the New Style calendar removed eleven days from the calendar, and this was particularly confusing over the Christmas/New Year period, as the 'lost' eleven days almost coincided with the traditional twelve days of Christmas, and the Old Style Christmas Eve became entangled with the New Style Twelfth Night. Many people continued to celebrate Old Christmas Day on 6 January, and some diehards even celebrated Old Twelfth Night on 17/18 January. Given the general decline in Twelfth Night celebrations, this confusion is now only important to historians and folklorists, but a further dating difficulty is now apparent. In earlier times, 'Twelfth Night' meant 5 January, i.e. the *Eve* of Twelfth Day, in the same way as Christmas Eve precedes Christmas Day. But nowadays most people regard 'Twelfth Night' as meaning the evening of Twelfth Day (6 January).

For the aristocracy and nobility of Tudor England, Twelfth Night and Day were marked by elaborate masques, plays, pageants, and expensive gifts to and from each other, and for the members of the courts of Charles II to George II heavy gambling was the order of the night. Lower down the social scale, parties and family gatherings were the norm, and the two long-standing features were the Twelfth Night cake and games in which those present took on the fantasy roles of King and Queen. These roles were chosen at random by items placed in the cake; in earlier times a bean and a pea were used: whoever found the bean became the King and whoever found the pea, the Queen. The game was so common that 'King of the Bean' became a phrase used to denote any temporary or play-acted ruler. A clove was also used, and whoever found it in their slice was designated 'the Knave'. Other items that were sometimes used were coins, thimbles, and rings, and those present could be given other characters to play. From the moment they were appointed, the King and Queen presided over the rest of the evening's entertainment.

Samuel Pepys often mentioned Twelfth cakes in his diary. In 1666 he admitted to finding the clove, but he secretly put it into his neighbour's piece. Three years later he recorded a change in the way the characters were chosen:

I did bring out my cake, and a noble cake, and there cut into pieces with wine and good drink, and, after a new fashion, to prevent spoiling the cake, did put so many titles into a hat and so draw cuts; and I was the Queen and The Turner, King; Creed [was] Sir Martin Marrall; and Betty [was] Mrs. Millicent. And so we were merry till it was night.

Marrall and Millicent were characters in John Dryden's *Sir Martin Marrall*, a popular comedy of the period. One hundred years later, things had not changed a great deal, according to the *Universal Magazine* (1774):

I went to a friend's house in the country to partake of some of those innocent pleasures that constitute a merry Christmas; I did not return till I had been present at drawing King and Queen, and eaten a slice of the Twelfth Cake ... A noble cake was produced, and two bowls, containing the fortunate chances for the different sexes. Our host filled up the tickets; the whole company, except the King and Queen, were to be ministers of state, maids of honour, or ladies of the bedchamber. Our kind host and hostess, whether by design or accident, became King and Queen. According to Twelfth Day law, each party is to support their character till midnight.

Neither Pepys nor this anonymous writer says who made their 'noble cake', but the tradition of cakes on this day was so strong that it was the bakers' and confectioners' busiest time of year, and it was a point of honour to rise to the challenge. William Hone's *Every-Day Book* (1827) describes the tradition at its height:

In London, with every pastry-cook in the city, and at the west end of the town, it is 'high change' on Twelfth-day. From the taking down of the shutters in the morning, he, and his men, with additional assistants, male and female, are fully occupied by attending to the dressing out of the window, executing orders of the day before, receiving fresh ones, or supplying the wants of chance customers. Before dusk the important arrangement of the window is completed. Then the gas is turned on, with supernumerary argand-lamps and manifold wax-lights to illuminate countless cakes of all prices and dimensions, that stand in rows and piles on the counters and sideboards, and in the windows. The richest in flavour and heaviest in weight and price are placed on large and massy salvers; one, enormously superior to the rest in size, is the chief object of curiosity; and all are decorated with all imaginable images of things animate and inanimate. Stars, castles, kings, cottages, dragons, trees, fish, palaces, cats, dogs, churches, lions, milkmaids, knights, serpents, and innumerable other forms, in snow-white confectionery, painted with variegated colours, glittering by 'excess of light', reflected from mirrors against the walls, festooned with artificial 'wonders of Flora'.

Lamb's Wool is frequently mentioned since at least the sixteenth century as a drink for special occasions, particularly winter celebrations such as Christmas, Twelfth Night, New Year, and it was often offered by wassailers (see **Christmas: Wassailing**). Its ingredients vary, but its base was hot cider, ale, or more rarely wine. Sugar and spices such as nutmeg, ginger, or cinnamon were added, along with the essential element, apples; the latter were baked or roasted until their pulp fell apart in the liquid, giving the appearance of lamb's wool.

However, as the people gathered round the windows to admire the confectioners' art, another traditional pastime came into play: boys and youths in the crowd took the opportunity to nail bystanders' clothes surreptitiously to the shop window-frames, or to pin them to their neighbours. A really successful prankster could pin several people, male and female, in a chain of trapped humanity. This game could be played at any crowded gathering, and often took place at country fairs, but it was particularly popular in the earlier nineteenth century on Twelfth Night, and, as with all such behaviour, then and now, the joke was appreciated by perpetrators and onlookers but not by those on the receiving end.

By the second half of the nineteenth century, however, Twelfth Night was beginning to lose ground, and its popularity continued to wane as the new 'Victorian' Christmas began to take shape. The Twelfth cake was replaced by the Christmas cake, the coins and thimbles started turning up in the Christmas pudding, the post-Christmas parties began to take place on New Year's Eve and Day, and to most people nowadays, Twelfth Night, while still marking the 'end of Christmas', is simply the day on which we take down the decorations.

See **Baddeley Cake** (*below*) for perhaps the last remnant of the Twelfth Night cake tradition. *See also* **Christmas: Wassailing** for another custom that regularly took place on Twelfth Night.

Baddeley Cake

As already noted, Twelfth Night was traditionally associated with fancy cakes (*see* p. 11); it is therefore perhaps unsurprising that the actor

Robert Baddeley (1732–94), who had previously been a pastry cook, hit upon the idea of an annual cake in his name when thinking of something to do for his fellow-performers. When he died while dressing for a part in Sheridan's *School for Scandal*, his will revealed a bequest for impoverished actors, together with £100 to finance a Twelfth Night cake and wine feast for the company of Drury Lane. They still keep up the tradition at the Theatre Royal by gathering after the performance on that evening, still in costume and make-up, for the Baddeley cake.

Brough Holly Night

This Twelfth Night custom, which involves a lighted tree, seems to have died out in the later nineteenth century but was formerly practised at Brough in Westmorland (now Cumbria). There are several references to the custom from the mid nineteenth century, the fullest being in William Hone's *Table Book* (1827), which also prints an illustration:

Formerly the 'Holly-tree' at Brough was really 'holly', but ash being abundant, the latter is now substituted. There are two head inns in the town, which provide for the ceremony alternately, though the good townspeople mostly lend their assistance in preparing the tree, to every branch of which they fasten a torch. About eight o'clock in the evening, it is taken to a convenient part of the town, where the torches are lighted, the town band accompanying and playing till all is completed, when it is removed to the lower end of the town; and, after divers salutes and huzzas from the spectators, is carried up and down the town, in stately procession, usually by a person of renowned strength, named Joseph Ling. The band march behind it, playing their instruments, and stopping every time they reach the town bridge, and the cross, where the 'holly' is again greeted with shouts of applause. Many of the inhabitants carry lighted branches and flambeaus; and rockets, squibs, &c. are discharged on the joyful occasion. After the tree is thus carried, and the torches are sufficiently burnt, it is placed in the middle of the town, when it is again cheered by the surrounding populace, and is afterwards thrown among them. They eagerly watch for this opportunity; and, clinging to each end of the tree, endeavour to carry it away to the inn they are contending for, where they are allowed their usual quantum of ale and spirits, and pass a 'merry night' which seldom breaks up before two in the morning.

The village of Haxey, historically in Lincolnshire but now in Humberside, is found in the strange area of land called the 'Isle of Axholme', which was once surrounded by such wet land until it was drained by Dutch immigrants in the seventeenth century that it was almost an inland island. Haxey hosts the annual Haxey Hood, one of the best-known and most intriguing customs in England, and the locals are fiercely proud of it.

There are thirteen officials connected with the game: the Lord of the Hood, who is in charge, a Chief Boggin, ten other Boggins, and a Fool. The Fool is dressed in clothes covered in shreds and patches, and has a painted or blackened face; the rest wear red jackets or jumpers, and the Lord and Chief wear impressive hats that are decorated with flowers. The Lord carries a 'wand' made of thirteen willow sticks, which are four or five feet long and bound tightly together into a compact bundle. The 'Hood' itself, which is hotly contended for in the game, is a tightly rolled piece of leather about eighteen inches long and three inches in diameter. Ostensibly, the struggle is between the men of Haxey and the men of Westwoodside, and the two goals are the King's Arms and the Carpenter's Arms respectively. The two teams can be of any size.

On New Year's Eve, the thirteen officials meet to retrieve the Hood from the safekeeping of the pub in which it had ended up the previous year. In the following week they visit numerous pubs and houses in neighbouring villages, sing their three traditional songs, 'Farmer's Boy', 'John Barleycorn', and 'Drink England Dry (Cannons)', pass a hat round, to help defray the costs of the game, and move on.

On Plough Monday itself, the Lord and the Boggins make one more round of the village pubs, settling down in one of them to paint the Fool's face, mostly in black and red. They then process towards the church, but on the way the Fool tries to escape and is caught and carried back, shoulder high, by the other Boggins, and he is finally placed on the mounting stone (the base of an old cross) in front of the church. From this vantage point, he makes his speech of welcome, but the Boggins light a fire of straw behind him, to 'smoke' him. When the flames or smoke get too much, the Fool finishes his speech with the traditional words:

Hoose agen hoose
Toon agen toon
If a man meets a man
Knock 'im doon
But do'ant 'ot 'im [But don't hurt him]

This last line was probably added in the late 1920s. The crowd then follows the Fool up to Haxey Hill, where the game takes place. The first phase of the game is the 'Running Hood', in which the Lord throws up a series of twelve sacking Hoods, one at a time, and the players try to escape from the field with the Hood without being touched by one of the Boggins, who are strategically placed to stop them. About an hour before sunset, however, the main game begins when the real Leather Hood is thrown up. Whoever catches it is immediately surrounded by a heaving mass of people, the 'sway', as each side tries to force it towards their goal. The sway can include anything up to 300 people and at first can seem to the outsider to be immovable. But move it always does, either inching its way forward, or swinging and spiralling violently, occasionally collapsing in a tangled heap of bodies. Sometime during the evening it is clear which way the sway is going, and progress is made towards the winning pub in what local writer Jeremy Cooper describes as a 'triumphant trudge'. The game is officially over when the landlord of the relevant pub touches the Hood. It is then kept safe behind the bar until needed again next year.

The origins of the custom are unknown, and the early history and development are still unclear. The local story tells how Lady de Mowbray – the wife or daughter of a powerful local landowner – was out riding one day when a sudden gust of wind blew off her red silk hood. Twelve or thirteen labourers working in the neighbouring fields attempted to catch the recalcitrant hood, but the wind kept thwarting their attempts. Lady de Mowbray was so amused by their antics that she granted land to the men to provide for a commemorative event every year. The story continues with details which were probably added later: it is said that she called one of the men a 'fool' because he was too shy to hand the retrieved hood to her, and another a 'lord' because he did so. She is even said to have used the word 'boggined', meaning 'trapped or bogged down', which explains the names of the Hood officers.

Thus, suspiciously, all the main words, characters, and actions are explained in a story which, although it has the charm of a fairy tale, is

gestion is that the game is held annually to keep up common rights, or
rights of tenure to certain lands.

The earliest known description dates from 1815, and there are several other published references from the first half of the nineteenth
century which confirm the game's existence and that it was roughly
the same as it is now. It is difficult to be sure, but the earliest accounts
appear to be describing the more open-style game, referred to above
as the 'Running Hood' game, rather than the mass sway. Three important broad conclusions emerge from these early descriptions: firstly,
that a similar game was also played at other nearby villages until at
least the late nineteenth century; secondly, that the de Mowbrays were
already being cited as the custom's founders in the earliest reference;
and thirdly, that the Plough Bullocks, who also went round the village
at this season (*see* **Plough Monday**, p. 19), were also called 'Boggins'
and also took part in the Hood.

There are dozens of similar mass games, usually described as **football** (p. 64), but including other local names such as **hurling** (p. 50)
and **camping** (*see* **Games and Sports**, p. 35). The common elements of
these games are the unlimited or large teams, the lack of detailed rules,
and the great distance between goals, but, as examined in the entry for
'football', the key determinant for the style of play is whether the game
takes place in the streets of the town, or in an open space. Apart from
the shape of the Hood, which is apparently unique, what differentiates
Haxey from other football games are the elaborate ceremonies which
surround it (e.g. smoking the Fool), and the characters involved, but
these may well have been part of a Plough Bullocking custom that was
left behind when the latter faded away.

Moseley's Dole

Moseley's Dole, which formerly took place at Walsall in Staffordshire
on Twelfth Night, provided every man, woman, and child in that town
and some neighbouring villages (including visitors) with the gift of
one penny. The legend which explains this charity tells how Thomas
Moseley, owner of the local Bascote Estate during the fifteenth century, was walking through Walsall on Twelfth Night and heard a child
crying for want of bread. His heart was troubled, and he immediately
founded this charity to ensure that at least on this night of the year
nobody in the area would be without even a loaf of bread. Moseley was

real enough, but the actual origin of the charity lies most probably in the custom of distributing money to encourage people to attend church and pray for the souls of the departed, in this case for Thomas and his wife. By the early nineteenth century, penny loaves were distributed in lieu of cash, and in 1825 the dole was discontinued and the money put towards the maintenance of eleven almshouses.

See also **Doles**, p. 115.

Twelfth Night Fires

This custom, allied to the idea of wassailing the fruit trees, and some-times even going by the same name, involved lighting fires out in the fields on Twelfth Night, or Eve, to bring luck to the crops in the coming year. It was reported a number of times from Gloucestershire, Herefordshire, and Worcestershire in the late eighteenth and nine-teenth centuries, and although it was by all accounts quite common in those areas, it does not seem to have been known elsewhere. The *Gentleman's Magazine* of 1791 provides details of an example from Herefordshire:

At the approach of evening, on the vigil of Twelfth Day, the farmers, with their friends and servants, meet together, and about six o'clock walk out to a field where wheat is growing. In the highest part of the ground, twelve small fires and one large one, are lighted up. The attendants, headed by the master of the family, pledge the company freely in old cider, which circulates freely on these occasions. A circle is formed round the large fire, when a gen-eral shout and hallooing takes place, which you hear answered from all the adjacent villages and fields. Sometimes fifty or sixty of these fires may be all seen at once. This being finished, the company return home, where the housewife and her maids are preparing a good supper. A large cake is always provided.

Twelve fires (or thirteen if the bigger one is counted) are usually specified, but it is not clear whether they represent the twelve days of Christmas, or the twelve Apostles, or even the twelve months of the year. In one account, one of the fires, representing Judas Iscariot, is stamped out early, while there are also hints that the nature of the coming year can be predicted by the behaviour of the twelve fires.

See **New Year Customs and Superstitions: Burning the Bush** for a similar fire-in-the-fields custom from Herefordshire; *see also* **Christmas: Wassailing**.

Plough Sunday

The first Monday after 6 January was widely known as **Plough Monday** (*see below*), and there was a tendency for the name to spread to adjoining days to give us Plough Sunday and Plough Tuesday. Given the religious origin of most Plough Monday festivities, it is likely that in arable areas the church services on the day before would have included some direct reference to ploughs and farming, but there is little evidence that the Sunday was celebrated in any other way. Nevertheless, soon after the Second World War a deliberate combined attempt by members of the Royal Agricultural Society and leaders of the Church of England to revive what they thought of as the 'old Saxon feasts of Plough Sunday, Rogation Sunday, Lammas-tide, and Harvest Thanksgiving' resulted in a number of churches featuring plough blessings in their services. *The Times* (11 January 1954) reported the movement:

Plough Sunday was commemorated at several churches yesterday. At Heddenham, Norfolk, the rector blessed a plough which had been placed in the chancel, and offered prayers for all engaged in agriculture. In the City of London a ceremonial plough which 24 men and women who work in the fields of Dorset brought up with them from Springfield, near Dorchester, was blessed at St Helen's, Bishopsgate. After the service, 12 Dorset men dressed in traditional costume performed the plough dance play in the churchyard.

These celebrations do not seem to have taken permanent hold, and few lasted beyond the 1950s.

Plough Monday

Plough Monday was the first Monday after Twelfth Day, and in rural areas the effective start of the new agricultural year, as Thomas Tusser advised in 1580:

> *Plough Monday, next after that Twelfth tide is past*
> *Bids out with the plough, the worst husband is last*

The commonest early references to customary behaviour on Plough Monday are records from the fifteenth century onwards of 'plough lights' in local churches. These were candles that were kept burning in the church specifically to bring the Lord's blessing on the efforts of farmers and farmworkers. The 'common' or 'town' plough was also kept there, to be loaned out in turn to villagers who could not afford one of their own, and its presence presumably gave the opportunity for services based on blessing the plough and praying for success in the coming year. Some parishes had plough guilds, dedicated to raising money to maintain the lights, and by the early fifteenth century there is evidence of ploughs being moved around for symbolic or fund-raising purposes. *Dives and Pauper* (*c*.1405–10) complains of people 'Leading the plough about the fire as for good beginning of the year', and in 1413, in Durham, there is a record of 4d being given 'to the people who were drawing a plough'. From the 1460s onwards there are numerous references to lights and to ploughs being taken round the parish to raise money for church purposes, but this custom seems to have been restricted geographically, being found only in the eastern midland counties of Lincolnshire, Northamptonshire, Cambridgeshire, Essex, Norfolk, and Suffolk, and not even in every church in these areas. With the Reformation, plough lights were banned along with other 'superstitious practices', and as the raising of money by celebratory and festival customs also began to lose favour, the plough perambulation on behalf of the church soon faded away.

Nevertheless, from the late eighteenth century onwards, there are again numerous references to ploughs being taken round the parish on Plough Monday, but this time the activity was on behalf of those in the party, and the whole affair was, by all accounts, far from godly. It is not entirely clear whether this new plough activity was a direct survival of the old practice, a conscious revival, or a 'new' idea, but the custom of taking a plough round the neighbourhood on Plough Monday was widely reported. Again the activity was concentrated in the eastern counties, but was also found in a wider area, including the neighbouring counties of Yorkshire, Derbyshire, and Northumberland. The men who carried out this custom went by a variety of names – Plough Stots, Plough Jags, Plough Witchers, and Plough Bullocks – and what they did also varied widely: some simply took a plough round the parish, some danced and sang, others performed an elaborate play (*see below*), and some even dispensed with the plough altogether. Recurrent features included Fools of various descriptions, men dressed as women, blackened or reddened faces, white shirts and coloured ribbons, and straw inside clothes, but the one constant aspect was the request for money. In his *Memorials of Godmanchester*, F. W. Bird remembered that around 1850:

Plough Monday was a great institution at Godmanchester [in Huntingdonshire]. *Farming men, many of them dressed as women, and having their faces besmeared, paraded the streets. Not content with assuming grotesque costumes, and bedaubed faces, they stuffed bundles of straw between their shoulders, which gave them a hunch-back appearance . . . They dragged a wooden plough behind them, and men, all more or less hideously attired, accompanied the procession with money boxes. They halted at all the principal houses of the town and asked for 'toll', pedestrians being solicited as they were encountered. If nothing was forthcoming from a call, rumour said that the plough witchers made no more ado but forthwith ploughed up the front part of the houses and departed, but no such damage was remembered in Godmanchester.*

The attitude of the people who were visited, or caught passing by, also varied enormously, from the amused tolerance of those who liked to see old customs perpetuated, to vociferous opposition on the part of those who only saw the drunkenness and potential menace of these visitors. Of all the house-visiting customs in the traditional calendar in the nineteenth century, the Plough Jags excited the most local controversy, perhaps owing to the size of the gangs, which could often exceed twenty, or because they were predominately young men. Even without overt threats of retribution if nothing was forthcoming (which certainly did happen), there was always the covert threat posed by a group of young men in disguise who had already had plenty to drink and wanted more. By the later nineteenth century, local newspapers, magistrates, police, Anglican clergy, Nonconformist ministers, and many other pillars of society began to object, and the Plough Jags either cleaned up their act or were suppressed. The custom survived well into the twentieth century in some parts, but usually in relatively tame forms, as the journal *Folk-Lore* reported from Bedfordshire in 1926:

Plough Monday – All the boys and men at farm work disguise themselves with odd costumes and masks and patrol the streets singing and shaking tins and saying – 'Give poor ploughboy a halfpenny or a penny'. They knock

*at doors and, on being admitted, sing and sometimes dance, and expect
money and beer or wine.*

As mechanization and agricultural depressions drastically reduced
the numbers of men working on the land, the Plough Jags' days were
inevitably numbered.

Plough Plays

The most spectacular and highly developed entertainment provided
by the ploughboys in their Plough Monday perambulations was the
'plough play' or 'wooing play', which is regarded by folklorists as one
of the three main sub-genres of English traditional drama. This play,
which could be performed at any time over the Christmas period, is distinguished from other types of play by a range of characters – the Fool,
the Farmer's Man, Dame Jane, Lady Bright and Gay, the Ribboner,
and the Recruiting Sergeant – and a longer, more complex storyline
than the more basic hero-combat or St George type found elsewhere
(*see* **Christmas: Mummers**). Much of the dialogue was clearly designed
to be sung, and the basic plot involves the courting of a Lady by the
Farmer's Man, who is persuaded to enlist by the Recruiting Sergeant
when the Lady rejects him. The Lady then accepts the Fool's offer instead. In some versions, a character called Dame Jane appears, with a
baby, and accuses the Fool of being the father, which he denies.

JANE: *Tommy, take your bastard.*
FOOL: *Bastard, Jinny? It's not like me and none of mine.*
JANE: *Its nose, eyes, and chin as much like you as ever it can grin.*
FOOL: *Who sent you here with it, Jinny?*
JANE: *The overseer of the parish, who said I was to bring it to the biggest
    fool I could find so I thought I'd bring it to you.*

There are also introductory verses, and lines requesting money at the
end. A short, fairly typical 'hero-combat' play with fight, doctor, and
cure is usually embedded in the plough-play action, although it seems
to bear little or no relation to the rest of the play. An examination of
plough-play texts reveals that they are a pastiche of elements from
other parts of popular culture. There are, in fact, two semi-distinct
types of plough play: in one, the wooing sequence is central to the
plot, and comprises a series of suitors who the Lady rejects in turn until she finally chooses the Fool; while in the more common type, there

is what the play expert Peter Millington calls 'a three-way operatic scene between the Recruiting Sergeant, the Farmer's Man, and the Lady Bright and Gay'.

As with other traditional plays, the performers wore a range of costumes. Some dressed as near to character as they could – the Doctor in a top hat, the Recruiting Sergeant in red uniform – but others wore streamers or patches on their clothes, a style which is found across a whole range of traditional performances. As with all such plays, the female parts were played by men, and these 'females' always dressed in women's clothes, with the Lady Bright and Gay always better dressed than poor old Dame Jane.

Plough plays were found only in the East Midlands – Lincolnshire, Nottinghamshire, Leicestershire, and Rutland – and the earliest known versions only date from the 1820s. The inclusion of a wooing sequence excited some earlier folklorists enough to suggest an origin in an ancient fertility ritual, but as there is no evidence that the plays existed before the early nineteenth century, this is improbable. A glance at a typical plough-play text reveals no sense of ancient ritual, but is pure late eighteenth-century stage song:

> LADY: *What care I for your gold and silver*
> *What care I for your house and land*
> *What care I for your rings and diamonds*
> *All I want is a handsome man.*
> FOOL: *A handsome man will not detain you*
> *For his beauty will decay*
> *The finest flower that grows in the summer*
> *In the winter fades away.*

Historians Alun Howkins and Linda Merricks have argued persuasively that these plays emerged exactly when changes in farming practices were introducing large farms and 'high farming' to the areas where the plays have been reported. These farms needed a large workforce of young men who lived in, mainly in rough and ready conditions, and who formed a semi-distinct group with its own values and culture within the broader society. It is this group of young 'ploughboys' who made up the gangs who went round with the plough or with a play over the Christmas period, and it is to the culture of these men that we should look for questions of origin rather than to the remote but romantic past.

Ploughboys and Maids

Another Plough Monday custom had little to do with ploughs as such, but involved some horseplay between plough lads and farm maids. It was one of those game customs that highlighted the very different spheres allotted to men and women in farm work in the past, and playfully pitted the sexes against each other. In Northamptonshire in 1854, Ann Elizabeth Baker wrote:

When the ploughman returned from his labours in the evening, the servant maid used to meet him with a jug of toast and ale; and if he could succeed in throwing his plough hatchet into the house before she reached the door, he was entitled to a cock to throw at the next Shrove-tide, but if she was able to present him with the toast and ale first, then she gained the cock.

And in Warwickshire in 1930, J. Harvey Bloom recorded:

It was customary for the farm-girls to race from the house to the nearest furrow, snatch up a clod of earth and scamper back again, chased by the plough-boys with their whips. If the girls reached the farm in time to stick a few feathers in the clod of earth before the boys could place their whips upon the kitchen table, then the boys lost their ration of plum pudding.

Such games were reported from various parts of the country in the nineteenth century, but were also known in earlier periods. A version from Leicestershire is included in Thomas Tusser's rustic poetry of 1580, in which the maid had to get the kettle on to boil before being caught:

> *If ploughman get hatchet or whip to the skreene*
> *Maid loseth their cock if no water be seene.*

Plough Monday/
Plough Tuesday

Straw Bears

The annual custom of the 'straw bear' seems to have been confined to the fenland area of Ramsey and Whittlesey in Cambridgeshire,

account from the journal *Folk-Lore* in 1909 clearly relates to street
performances:

*When I was at Whittlesey (Cambridgeshire) yesterday (12 Jan 1909), I had
the pleasure of meeting a 'straw bear', if not two, in the street. I had not
been at Whittlesey on the day for nearly forty years, and feared the custom
had died out. In my boyhood the straw–bear was a man completely covered
in straw, led by a string by another, and made to dance in front of people's
houses, in return for which money was expected. This always took place on
the Tuesday following Plough–Monday. Yesterday the straw bear was a boy,
and I saw no dancing; otherwise there was no change. I was told that two
years ago a zealous inspector of police had forbidden straw bears as a form
of cadging, and my informant said that he thought that in many places they
had been stopped by the police.*

However, in Sybil Marshall's *Fenland Chronicle* (1967), the well-known
evocation of her parents' lives at Ramsey, her mother describes the
bear being brought into houses, and capering about inside. The earliest references to the custom date from about the 1850s, and it seems
to have faded away with the First World War. The straw bear was
successfully revived at Whittlesey in 1980.

There is no indication that the straw-bear performance was anything other than a simple entertainment carried out, like so many
other customs, simply to raise money for the performers, and based
on the real dancing bears that toured the country every year until well
into the twentieth century. Although straw features in other customs
– it was the main ingredient of various effigies such as **Jack-a-Lent**
(*see* p. 86), and was stuffed into clothes to make humpbacks for characters in plough plays; moreover, similar straw-clad figures also featured
in customs in Ireland, Germany, and Austria – the closest analogy to
the straw bear in Britain is not linked to straw but to bears. In certain
parts of Lancashire, it was customary on May Day for a boy to dress
up in a sack and be led by other boys, from house to house, pretending
to be a dancing bear (*see* **1 May: Bears**).

7 January

St Distaff's Day or Rock Day

St Distaff's Day was traditionally the day on which women resumed their spinning after the Christmas period, and was the female equivalent of **Plough Monday** (*see* p. 19). In a custom which, like many others, pitted the sexes against each other, on this day young men would try to steal the women's flax and tow, and burn it, while the women retaliated by soaking them with water. Robert Herrick's poem 'St Distaff's Day or the Morrow After Twelfth Day' (1648) details the tradition:

> *Partly work and partly play*
> *Ye must on S. Distaff's day*
> *From the plough soon free your team;*
> *Then come home and fother them.*
> *If the maids a spinning go,*
> *Burn the flax, and fire the tow:*
> *Scorch their plackets, but beware,*
> *That ye singe no maiden-hair.*
> *Bring in pails of water then,*
> *Let the maids bewash the men.*
> *Give S. Distaff all the right,*
> *Then bid Christmas sport good night;*
> *And next morrow, every one*
> *To his own vocation.*

It is not clear from existing records how widespread this custom really was, or even how long it lasted. Although it is mentioned by several of the leading nineteenth-century antiquarians, their accounts have a vagueness and an underlying similarity which suggests that they were all extrapolating from one source – presumably the Herrick poem.

The 'distaff' and the 'rock' were implements used to spin yarn before the invention of the spinning wheel and were so closely associated with women's work that the phrase 'distaff side' was widely used to describe the female sphere, as opposed to the 'spear side' of the male. The word 'spinster' took on a much wider meaning in the same way. St Distaff did not exist, but the name was formed as a sort of joke, on the same lines as other fictitious saints such as **St Monday** (*see* p. 582) and St Tibb (*see* p. xxxiv).

13 January

St Hilary's Day

St Hilary (*c*.315–*c*.368) may have been Bishop of Poitiers, and he may have produced some influential theological writings, but he would hardly be remembered in England if not for the accident that his feast day occurred around the beginning of one of the four terms of the Law Courts and some older universities. This legal session has therefore been traditionally called Hilary Term.

St Hilary's Day is also reputed to be the coldest day of the year.

14 January

Hunting the Mallard

Few institutions can feel secure enough in their longevity to host a custom which takes place once every hundred years, but Oxford colleges can certainly do so. Hunting the Mallard, a custom which was formerly practised annually but now takes place once a century, takes place at All Soul's College, on 14 January. The Fellows, who are gathered for their Gaudy on that night, elect a Lord Mallard and six officers, who carry white staves and wear special medals on which the bird is depicted. Led by the officers, the whole company sets out at midnight on a torch-lit procession that proceeds to 'hunt the mallard', a mythical bird, all over the college (including the roof), a performance that can take several hours. They sing a special mallard song, of which the chorus runs:

> *O by the blood of King Edward*
> *O by the blood of King Edward*
> *It was a swapping, swapping mallard.*

The age of the custom is not known, but it certainly existed as early as 1632 when it was mentioned in a letter written by Archbishop Abbott. After complaining of gross misconduct such as tearing down doors, the Archbishop writes, 'civil men should never so far forget themselves under pretence of a foolish mallard, as to do things barbarously unbecoming.' The connection between the bird and the college is explained by the legend that a mallard of great size was discovered when the foundations were laid in 1437, but it seems more likely that the custom stemmed from what originally had been a students' joke. The most recent hunt took place in 2001.

17 January

Old Twelfth Night

When the calendar changed in 1752 (*see* p. xxix), many customs were wrenched from their traditionally sanctioned dates and were left dangling on apparently meaningless ones. Clearly, those who organized some events felt a strong attachment to the original night, and were determined to keep to it whatever the government said. So it was that at many farms around Exmoor, and probably elsewhere, wassailers did their rounds of the local orchards on 17 January, as their forebears had done on Twelfth Night (*see* **6 January: Twelfth Night**).

See also **Christmas: Wassailing**.

19 January

St Wulfstan's Day

Wulfstan (*c.*1008–95), appointed Bishop of Worcester in 1062, was one of the leaders of the Anglo-Saxon church at the time of the Norman Conquest, in 1066. Most unusually, he kept his position under the new Norman regime, and continued to serve until his death nearly thirty years later. He was buried in Worcester Cathedral, the rebuilding of which had been one of his favourite projects, and his fame was soon enhanced by news of the miraculous cures that took place at his tomb, leading to his canonization in 1203.

Wulfstan was a very popular saint in the Middle Ages, and King John thought enough of him to request to be buried between his and St Oswald's tomb, at Worcester; pilgrimages in his name persisted at least until the turn of the eighteenth century. His day is almost completely

20 January

St Agnes' Eve

In English tradition, St Agnes' Eve was a very popular night for young women (and occasionally men) to try to predict or control their future marriage prospects. Such love divinations often took place at night, on the eve of the saint whose aid was being invoked – presumably because so many of them involved going to sleep and dreaming. *See* **21 January: St Agnes' Day** for further details.

21 January

St Agnes' Day

Agnes was a Christian martyr who died in Rome *c*.350. Very few facts are known about her life, but later legends describe her as a particularly good-looking thirteen-year-old girl who refused all talk of marriage because she wished to remain a virgin and dedicate her life to Christ. She confounded all attempts to persuade and intimidate her, and despite being placed in a brothel and thrown into roaring flames, she is said to have survived with her virginity intact. She was finally killed by a dagger through the throat. Stories of cures and miracles at her tomb, and visions in which she figured prominently, spread her fame across the Christian world, and she became one of the most popular 'virgin martyrs' of the Middle Ages. In religious pictures, she is often accompanied by a lamb, no doubt because her name resembles the Latin *agnus*, meaning 'lamb', and the animal is a widely accepted symbol for meekness and innocence. The Roman Catholic Church formerly included a ceremony on her day in which newly shorn wool was presented and blessed.

In England, at least from the seventeenth to the nineteenth centuries, Agnes was one of several female saints invoked by young women who wanted to predict or influence their future love life, and St Agnes' Eve was the traditional time for carrying out divinatory practices. It may seem strange that a person who was famous for preferring death to marriage was called upon in this way, and we may think it would be more effective to appeal to someone who had shown some success in this area by having numerous husbands, but superstition doesn't follow such logical patterns. This connection between love divination and St Agnes' Eve was proverbial for seventeenth-century writers, who often mention it, and it was still well known in Victorian times and into the twentieth century. Its popularity was given a distinct boost by the publication of John Keats' famous dramatic medieval poem 'The Eve of St. Agnes' in 1820, which has more than a touch of *Romeo and Juliet* about it. The dashing hero finds out that the object of his affection, whose family is at war with his, plans to carry out a divination ceremony:

> *They told her how, upon St Agnes' Eve,*
> *Young virgins might have visions of delight,*
> *And soft adorings from their loves receive*
> *Upon the honey'd middle of the night,*
> *If ceremonies due they did aright.*

So he sneaks into her bedroom to make sure that she dreams of him. She wakes, and they elope.

Many different love divinations have been recorded as popular on St Agnes' Eve, including the well-known ones of making of the **dumb cake** (p. 302), and the sowing of hemp seed, which was thrown over the shoulder at midnight to conjure up the wraith of the future lover; however, these ceremonies could be undertaken on other nights, such as Hallowe'en, St Mark's Eve, or even Christmas Eve. Other procedures specifically invoked Agnes's name and were thus particular to her night. The following, from Derbyshire, was printed in the magazine *Long Ago* in 1874:

The girl who wished to test her future, on St Agnes' Day, prepared herself by a twenty-four hours' fast, beginning at midnight on the 20th and ending at midnight on the 21st. During this time she took nothing but pure water and she would not, on any account, speak to anyone about the divination and not even mention it aloud to herself. At midnight, on the 21st, she retired to bed, without breaking her fast, and rested on her left side, saying three times the following lines:

Saint Agnes is a friend to me
In the gift I ask of thee
Let me this night my husband see

Her dreams ought to be about her future husband. If she should dream of more than one man, she would marry an indefinite number of times; if she does not dream of a man, she will never marry. The divination was very popular.

22 January

St Vincent's Day

Little is known of Vincent of Saragossa apart from the fact that he was martyred for his faith in AD 304, but he was a widely popular saint across Europe and in Anglo-Saxon England. In English tradition, his day is only remembered in weather predictions, most of which agree that sunshine on the day augurs well for the year. A Northumberland version, quoted in 1904 by local folklorist Mrs Balfour, makes the point:

Remember on St. Vincent's Day,
if the sun his beams display
Be sure to mark the transient beam,
which through the casement sheds a gleam
For 'tis a token bright and clear
of prosperous weather all the year

24 January

Eve of Conversion of St Paul

As noted under **25 January**, St Paul has more than one feast day, and 24 January is the Eve of his Conversion to Christianity. Late January was not a popular time for traditional festivals, presumably because it was too soon after the Christmas/New Year period, but a range of related customs, each concerned in some way with broken crockery, was reported from Cornwall in 1886 by the *Folk-Lore Journal*, including the following:

St Paul's Eve is a holiday with the miners, and is called by them Paul Pitcher Day, from a custom they have of setting up a water-pitcher, which they pelt with stones until it is broken in pieces. A new one is afterwards bought and carried to a beer-shop to be filled with beer.

In other examples, but from a similar period, children roamed the streets throwing broken crockery at people's doors, or into their hallways. The *Western Antiquary* records:

On entering a house, I have, more than once, stumbled over the broken pieces of a 'Paul's pitcher'.

The motif of throwing broken crockery at doors, which has no obvious rational explanation, is more commonly recorded as a Shrove Tuesday custom (*see* **Shrove Tuesday: Shroving and Lent-Crocking**, p. 82).

25 January

St Paul's Day

St Paul was important enough in Church history to receive more than one feast day; **29 June** is his main day, which he shares with St Peter, while 25 January commemorates his conversion to Christianity on the road to Damascus.

In the secular sphere, it was said that the weather on this day was an excellent guide to the prevailing character of the coming year. In most cases, the prognostication simply refers to weather and harvest – 'If St Paul's is fair and bright the harvest will be good' – but some took the prediction into weightier realms, as in the following Cornish example recorded in the *Western Antiquary* in 1884:

> *If Paul's Fair be fair and clear*
> *We shall have a happy year*
> *But if it be both wind and rain*
> *Dear will be all kinds of grain*
> *If the winds do blow aloft*
> *Then wars will trouble this realm full oft*

This predictive nature of St Paul's Day was already well known in the early seventeenth century, but no one has yet suggested any explanation for the day's reputation.

30 January

Execution of Charles I

The execution of Charles I in January 1649 sent shock waves through English society that continued to reverberate for centuries. Almost immediately after his death he was portrayed as a martyr, and the day of his execution was included in the calendar of saints' days in the Anglican Prayer Book from 1662; the special prayers that marked this day were only removed from the official service in 1859. A number of churches in England and abroad are dedicated to him, and it was the custom in many places to commemorate his martyrdom with a muffled peal of bells.

The Society of King Charles the Martyr was founded in 1894, in part to protest against the removal of Charles's feast from the calendar of the Prayer Book, but also to 'work for the preservation and furtherance of the Catholic inheritance within the Church of England'. The Society is still very active, and holds commemorative events for Charles's birth (on or near 19 November) and the Restoration of Charles II (Saturday nearest 19 May), but its main celebration is on 30 January at the Banqueting Hall in Whitehall, London – the site of the execution – with laying of wreaths, prayers, and a special sermon. Other organizations that hold annual commemorative events include the Royal Martyr Church Union (founded 1906) and the Royal Stuart Society.

January/February

Chinese New Year

There have been small groups of Chinese-born residents in Britain for centuries, but the first identifiable communities became established in England in the early nineteenth century, when increasing numbers of Chinese nationals were employed on merchant ships. The first 'Chinatowns' were therefore found in major ports, particularly East London and Liverpool, as shops and other businesses catering for the immigrant seamen were created. British-Chinese residents continued to work largely in the merchant navy until the turn of the twentieth century, but the first Chinese laundry opened in 1901, and the first known Chinese restaurant in 1908. By 1921, over a quarter of the Chinese residents in Britain were employed in laundry-work.

Chinese communities in Britain continued to grow slowly until the Second World War, although it was only after the war that significant numbers of wives and children began to settle, and Chinatowns became truly viable communities. Chinese restaurants, in particular, rapidly became a major feature of mainstream British culture, and could soon be found in nearly every town in the country. The 2001 census revealed 247,403 Chinese people living in the UK.

By the 1960s, the focus for Chinese residents in London had shifted from the East End to Soho, and by the next decade Chinese communities across the country felt confident enough to begin to celebrate their culture in the public arena. The famous Chinese New Year celebrations that take over the local streets started, on a small scale, c.1973, but in London especially they rapidly became an essential part of the local scene, drawing enthusiastic crowds from far and near. Dancing dragons and lions, firecrackers, music, and a range of colourful performers became the instantly recognizable trademark of the Chinese community. The organizing body is the London Chinatown Chinese Association (founded 1978), and at the recent instigation of the Greater London Authority, the celebrations are being drawn further into the orbit of the official London tourist trade, with wider participation, the movement of the public displays into Leicester Square and Trafalgar Square, and the inauguration of an annual China Week. Some locals fear, however, that what they gain in official backing and recognition they may lose in the authentic feel of a home-grown local event.

The Chinese calendar is primarily lunar and does not synchronize well with the purely solar Gregorian calendar of the West. The New Year, or Spring Festival, therefore falls on a different day each year, sometime between 21 January and 21 February. In traditional Chinese culture, the New Year season lasts fifteen days, and everyone is expected to visit their families and friends. As a concession to the western milieu, public celebrations in Britain usually take place on the nearest Sunday.

The one fact that all Westerners know about the Chinese calendar is that each year has an animal name and character. There are twelve of these, and a full Chinese astrological cycle takes sixty years, passing through each of the animal signs five times, although each has one 'golden' year in each cycle. The origin of the animal signs is obscure, but a number of simple fables explain how it came about:

Buddha, on the turn of a new year, summoned all the animals to come to him before his departure from earth. Only twelve came to bid him farewell, so Buddha honoured them each with a year. The order was taken from the sequence that they appeared to him: first the Rat, who is said to have ridden on the back of the Ox and jumped off in front of the Ox when they arrived, then the Ox, the Tiger, Rabbit, Dragon, Snake, Horse, Sheep, Monkey, Rooster, Dog, and Pig.

Other versions of the story mention the Jade Emperor, ruler of the heavens; in one legend, he sent an aide down to earth to bring back the twelve most interesting animals; in another, he held a swimming race and told the animals that the first twelve across a fast-flowing river would each have a year of the zodiac named after them. The absence of the Cat is usually said to be due to the Rat's trickery, which explains those two animals' traditional antipathy. It is worth remembering that 'the year of' does not equate exactly with any particular western year, because of the moveable nature of the New Year.

Games and Sports

In the many possible definitions of the words 'play' and 'recreation', the essential element would seem to be 'choice'. While 'work' is what we have to do, 'play' is what we *want* to do. Play is non-utilitarian, amateur, for pleasure rather than gain. But on another level, we now know that play is necessary for both the individual and society at large. It is essential to our development and to our psychological, physical, and social well-being. Through play we learn teamwork, respect, and community spirit; and, depending on our personal choice, we keep fit, mentally agile, or at least out of mischief.

These theoretical concepts have been developed in relatively modern times, although there have always been a few enlightened individuals who understood the value of a release from the daily grind. 'All work and no play makes Jack a dull boy' has been a well-known proverb since at least the 1650s, although Samuel Smiles, the doyen of Victorian hard-work philosophy, added, 'but all play and no work makes him something greatly worse'. There were also those in a position of authority who were well aware that one way to oil the wheels of local community was to supply the wherewithal for the people's games or festivities. Many squires and local dignitaries made a habit of donating an occasional bull to be baited or an ox to be roasted, or granted the use of their park for an annual fête, or provided some prizes for the children's sports. Such paternalistic gestures were not resented but were seen on all sides as an essential function of the social hierarchy. Local publicans often made similar gestures, although with more commercial motives.

On the other hand, there was also a long tradition of opposition to traditional games, and sustained attempts to control what the people did in their spare time. The religious authorities, in particular, were never happy to let the masses organize their own leisure, and consistently sought to control it. At different times, religious qualms focused on drunkenness, violence, the unsupervised mixing of the sexes, gambling, and other moral dangers, and a long-running battle raged over what people were allowed to do on Sundays, a battle that has still not quite gone away. There were also many other, more utilitarian concerns exercising the minds of those in authority. If folk chose to play bowls instead of practising their archery, the defence of the realm could suffer; if they were injured playing football they might not be able to do the work needed to feed their families. Games were a distraction from more important activities, as in the following example quoted by L. A. Govett in his treatment of *The King's Book of Sports* (1618 and 1633), decrees that were in themselves attempts to defuse the growing concern over Sunday games:

In the records of the county of Surrey it is stated that in 1671 a man was severely punished for bull-baiting, not on account of the cruelty of the sport, but because it was harvest-time, and he caused thereby 'divers labourers and other poor persons to leave their work'.

Attempts to reform popular leisure pursuits were battles for physical space as well as for morals. Modern sports normally take place in dedicated venues – sports centres and stadiums, playing fields, and so on – but this has only been the case for the past hundred years or so. In the earlier Middle Ages, games were played in the churchyard, or even in the church itself, and one of the first campaigns for control saw religious leaders successfully striving to move secular celebrations away from Church property, and to prevent clergy themselves from taking an active part. In rural areas, the games moved to the village green if there was one, or on to nearby common land, or even to any suitably broad stretches of highway. But in urban areas, fairs, bull-runnings, and mass gatherings for football or Guy Fawkes Night took place in the narrow streets of town centres. As the rural areas became enclosed, and land ownership more tightly controlled, and as the town centres developed important business, retail, and civic functions, traditional activities began to be squeezed out. Trespass, civic pride, the danger to property, the effect on trade and the town's reputation, all became factors in this new battle for control.

The history of popular recreation is therefore a chequered one – of attempted control on the one hand and a determination to remain uncontrolled on the other. The documentary evidence of this struggle is, however, potentially misleading. Over the centuries, the voices of the reformers and critics of popular recreation have often been recorded, while those of the ordinary people and their supporters usually have not. We must not be too hasty in assuming that the reformers had it all their own way. Indeed, broadly speaking, most attempts at control were largely unsuccessful, except during the mid seventeenth century when Puritan control was at its height. For the most part, the people continued to play their games, and hold their ales, feasts and fairs, often in spite of the disapproving looks and Sunday sermons of their social betters. Folklorist Christina Hole was quite categorical in her contention that the people had not been beaten:

The favourite pastimes of a country are amongst the toughest plants in the national soil, as uprooting governments have constantly found to their cost. Legal enactments have been made from time to time to restrict or abolish various forms of amusement, yet many of the latter are still with us, and those which are not have quite as often fallen victim to changing public taste as to the power of the law.

This may have been true for earlier periods, but the whole scene began to change for good at the turn of the nineteenth century. That era saw a real sea change in the way traditional recreations were viewed, and they began to be criticized, challenged, and attacked with renewed vigour on a variety of new fronts. This latest climate of opposition was first aimed at the banning of animal sports such as throwing at cocks, bull-running, and bull-baiting, on the grounds of animal cruelty, but it soon graduated to other mass customs such as football, Bonfire Night celebrations, mock mayors, and fairs. After a short, often bitter, struggle, most were suppressed or altered beyond recognition.

A few sports survived in recognizably traditional forms. Regional forms of wrestling, for example, are still popular in Cumbria and Cornwall, and isolated versions of street football and hurling still take place each year. Others were taken in hand by middle-class supporters, cleaned up, codified, and turned into modern professional sports such as cricket and rugby, and in this way the brutal prizefighting was turned into the slightly-less-brutal boxing. Some, like stoolball, have been revived, while others, such as cockfighting and dog-fighting have never quite gone away, despite being illegal for over 150 years

Many of the major pastimes such as **football** (p. 64) and **bull-baiting** (p. 480) have their own entries in this book, but there are dozens of other games and sports that could be investigated if space permitted. What follows is a small sampling of these other, less well-known traditional games.

See also **Shrove Tuesday: Cock Throwing and Threshing**, p. 71; **Shrove Tuesday: Cockfighting**, p. 73; **Shrove Tuesday: Skipping**, p. 84; **Good Friday: Tinsley Green Marbles**, p. 148; **Baiting Bears and Other Animals**, p. 400; **Goose-Riding**, p. 420; **Hurling**, p. 50; **Sparrow-Mumbling**, p. 369.

Camping

One of several old-time games, roughly equivalent to the early mass football but apparently only found in the eastern counties of Norfolk, Suffolk, Essex, and Cambridgeshire. The earliest references to camping as a game date only from the fifteenth century, although 'camp' and 'kemp' are found in Old English and cognate languages such as Dutch and German, meaning 'to fight' or 'to contend', which neatly sums up the impression given of a particularly rough kind of ball game. Robert Forby's *Vocabulary of East Anglia* (1830) gives a good description:

Of the sport itself, however, two varieties are at present expressly recognised: *rough-play* and *civil-play*. In the latter, there is no boxing. But the following is a general description of it as it was of old, and in some places still continues. Two goals are pitched at a distance of 120 yards from each other. In a line with each are ranged the combatants; for such they truly are. The number on each side is equal; not always the same, but very commonly twelve. They ought to be uniformly dressed in light flannel jackets, distinguished by colours. The ball is deposited exactly in the mid-way. The sign or word is given by an umpire. The two sides, as they are called, rush forward. The sturdiest and most active of each encounter those of the other. The contest for the ball begins, and never ends without black eyes and bloody noses, broken heads or shins, and some serious mischiefs. If the ball can be carried, kicked, or thrown to one of the goals, in spite of all the resistance of the other party, it is reckoned for one towards the game; which has sometimes been known to last two or three hours. But the exertion and fatigue of this is excessive. So the victory is not always decided by number of points, but the game is placed against time, as the phrase is. It is common to limit it to half an hour . . . The prizes are commonly hats, gloves, shoes, or small sums of money . . .

It seems clear that camping and the various mass football games have a common ancestry, but by the time written descriptions are available they were at least theoretically distinguishable. In 1892, S. Arnott, writing about the 1780s in *Notes & Queries*, stated quite categorically that 'camping is not football', although in 1823 Edward Moor wrote, 'At times a large football was used, and the game was then called "a kicking camp".' However, Arnott claims that the ball was about the size of a cricket ball, and if the size of the ball is a determining factor, camping should perhaps be compared to Cornish hurling rather than football. By the time of Forby's report, despite the fact that camping seems a very rough game still, the teams were restricted in number and equal to each other, and presumably some sense of order prevailed. In several eastern villages, a piece of land or area called 'Camping Close', or 'Camping Pightle' lived on in memory of the game.

Pell-Mell

Pell-Mell, or Pall-Mall, was a game introduced to England from France, probably during the reign of James I (1603–25), and was very popular with royalty and the nobility. It needed a long flat narrow avenue, along which wooden balls were propelled by hitting them with a mallet. At each end was a ring, suspended from a pole, and players had to hit their ball to the end and through the ring in as few strokes as possible. Samuel Pepys recorded his first encounter with the game in his diary on 2 April 1661:

So I into St. James parke, where I saw the Duke of Yorke playing at Peslemesle – the first time that I ever saw that sport . . .

He also records a conversation with the Pell-Mell keeper on 15 May 1663. The street Pall Mall, in London, is named after the game.

Shuttlecock

The forerunner of the modern sport of badminton (codified in the 1870s), 'battledore and shuttlecock', or simply 'shuttlecock', was very popular in England in the seventeenth century. In February 1602/3, John Manningham's diary records its popularity at the time:

The play at shuttlecocke is become soe much in request at Court, that the making shuttlecocks is almost growne to a trade in London.

'Battledore' was another name for a horn-book, much used in teaching children to read, and consisted of a flat board made of wood and horn with a handle, something like a squared modern table-tennis bat, with text affixed. It is easy to see how this may have been used as a bat, or given its name to something shaped like it. The word 'shuttlecock' goes back at least to the sixteenth century, as the poet John Skelton uses the phrase 'I trow all wyll be nought, Nat worth a shyttel cocke' in his *Why come ye nat to Courte?* of 1522, an invective against Thomas Wolsey; and in his *Sports and Pastimes of the People of England* (1801), Joseph Strutt reprints a scene of two boys playing the game from a fourteenth-century manuscript.

The game passed into the hands of children, although adults could be known to take part on occasion: in nineteenth-century Leicestershire and Yorkshire, for example, Shrove Tuesday was known as Shuttlecock Day, and both children and adults played it. In 1863, *Notes & Queries* recorded:

On the day itself the streets in the lower part of the town (Leicester) literally swarms with juveniles, and even grown men and women, engaged in the pastime . . . Passing through a by-street the other day, I heard a little girl singing –

Shuttlecock, shuttlecock, tell me true
How many years have I to go through.

Stoolball

This ball game was first mentioned in 1475 and regularly reported from then onwards, often as a game played particularly by women, but also by young men, as evidenced by Thomas D'Urfey's *Don Quixote* (1694):

Down in a vale on a summer's day
All the lads and lasses meet to be merry
A match for kisses at stool-ball to play
And for cakes, and ale, and sider, and perry
(Chorus) **Come all, great small, short tall, away to stool-ball.**

There are numerous literary references to the game in the seventeenth century, including in Robert Herrick's *Hesperides* (1648) and John Aubrey's *Natural History of Wiltshire* (1671). The latter writes that it is solely a west of England game, but this is not borne out by other references.

Stoolball is generally regarded as one of the precursors to cricket, although this was questioned by John Goulstone in *Sussex Archaeological Collections* in 1998 and elsewhere. There are wide variations in the equipment and method of play. In the basic, and presumably earliest, form, a milking stool was placed on the ground. A bowler threw a ball and tried to hit the stool, which was defended by another player, using his or her hand. If the bowler hit the stool, or caught the ball when hit by the defender, they changed places. The humble stool was eventually replaced by a purpose-made flat wooden board, mounted on a stake about four feet high, and the batter's hand by a flat round bat. The game then developed along the lines of cricket, with runs, fielders, and so on, but with a softer ball and under-arm bowling. Lowerson details how Major W. W. Grantham championed stoolball as useful for convalescent troops during the First World War, and attempted its revival as part of a Merrie England movement (p. 510). Meanwhile, the game was also being played by predominantly middle- and upper-class women, especially in Sussex and adjoining counties, and the two groups vied for control of the game throughout the interwar years.

Modern-day stoolball is still found mainly in Sussex, where there are dozens of active women's and mixed teams, and many people from the county believe that it originated there. This is not so, but Sussex has had this reputation for some considerable time, as shown by a comment in *Notes & Queries* (1867):

Stool-ball: This game, so often mentioned in old writers, is still played in almost every village in Sussex, and is for ladies and girls exactly what cricket is to men.

Major Grantham's Stoolball Association for Great Britain folded in 1942, but the current National Stoolball Association was formed in 1979.

Joseph Strutt also described a circular form of the game in his *Sports and Pastimes of the People of England* (1801):

. . . a certain number of stools are set up in a circular form, and at a distance from each other, and every one is occupied by a single player; when the ball is struck, which is done as before with the hand, every one of them is obliged to alter his situation, running in succession from stool to stool.

Tipcat

Tipcat was once an internationally popular game with children and adults alike, but is now largely forgotten in England. The 'cat' was a piece of wood, placed on the ground, so shaped at the ends that when a player hit it with their bat (or catstaff) it would fly into the air. As it came up, the player tried to hit it as far as they could. A large ring had been marked out, or agreed, and if the player failed to hit the cat out of the ring they were out. If they succeeded then a score was awarded, depending on the distance the cat had travelled. Variant names for the game are 'Cat', 'Trippet', 'Nipsy', 'Piggy' or 'Peggy'.

The earliest reference to the game so far discovered in Britain is in an Anglo-Latin lexicon of *c*.1440, but wooden 'tipcats' were found in the ruins of Rahan, Egypt, dating from about 2500 BC. In a variant form, a number of evenly spaced holes were made round the circumference of a circle, and a player was placed by each hole, armed with a stick. The cat was thrown to the nearest batsman and if they hit it the players ran on from hole to hole until the cat was retrieved, scoring a point for each hole reached.

Trapball / Knurr and Spell

Trapball was once a popular game, particularly associated with Shrovetide, which has never quite died out. A ball is placed in the bowl of a spoon-shaped piece of wood, on a stand – this is the 'trap'. It is so contrived that when the player hits the handle of the spoon, with their bat, it pivots and throws the ball into the air. The player then has to hit the ball. The other team tries to catch it or bowl the batsman out by throwing the ball and hitting the trap from where the ball has landed. William Hone reports regular games of trapball played at Shrovetide, Easter, and Whitsun, by twelve old women of Bury St Edmunds. In his *Sports and Pastimes of the People of England* (1801), Joseph Strutt prints an illustration from a fourteenth-century manuscript clearly showing an early version of the game, and Iona and Peter Opie give this and other illustrations of the game through the centuries. Young people in rural areas who could not afford to buy or make a trap had to be content with a hole in the ground and an ox bone or piece of wood as a lever.

Knurr and Spell (there are numerous variations on the spelling) is a very similar game, played mainly in the north of England, and first mentioned by name c.1760. The ball was usually made of wood, and in some areas the playing season started at Easter. Later versions of the trap included a spring, which helped to ensure that the ball was released in the same way each time. Frank Atkinson provides some good illustrations and distribution maps of the game in his article 'Knur and Spell and Allied Games' in the journal *Folk Life* (1963).

FEBRUARY

Trial of the Pyx

This annual custom, which originated with Henry II's currency reforms in the twelfth century, is designed to check the composition and weight of newly minted coins. The 'pyx' is the box which contains sample coins put aside throughout the year from the Royal Mint, and every February or March a party of freemen of the Goldsmith's Company meet at Goldsmith's Hall in Gutter Lane, London, to carry out the trial, which is followed by a banquet. The ceremony is not open to the public.

First Sunday in February

Clowns' Service

The annual Clowns' Service, held in Dalston's Holy Trinity church, east London, on the first Sunday in February, must have the most colourful congregation in the country. On this day, dozens of professional and amateur clowns, all dressed in their best costumes and make-up, gather to commemorate the life of Joseph Grimaldi (1779–1837), the comic actor who did much to create the modern clown tradition. Grimaldi's tomb is at St James's church, Pentonville Road, which is where the first commemoration service was held in 1946, but when that church was decommissioned in 1956, the service moved to Holy Trinity. The service includes a prayer which starts, 'Dear Lord, I thank you for calling me to share with others your most precious gift of laughter. May I never forget that it is your gift, and my privilege.'

1 February

St Bridget/St Bride's Day

In Ireland, Brighid, who died around the year 525, is second only in popularity to St Patrick, and her feast is a day of widespread celebration. She was of humble origins, was baptized by St Patrick himself, and later became a nun and first abbess of Kildare. Little is known of her beyond this, but numerous legends about her pious acts and miracles spread her fame across Ireland and on to the Continent by the early Middle Ages. On her day, children in Ireland would go from house to house and display an effigy or doll that represented the saint. Brighid's Crosses, made from straw, would also be hung up to protect the house from evil in the coming year.

In England, her popularity in pre-Reformation times is evidenced by the nineteen ancient churches dedicated to her, including St Bride's in Fleet Street, London, as well as a number of places called 'Bridewell', most probably derived from wells dedicated to her. The most famous of these Bridewells was a palace built between Fleet Street and the River Thames for Henry VIII (r. 1509–47), which eventually became a house of correction; the word 'Bridewell' later became a generic term for a prison.

Nevertheless, except where people of Irish extraction have settled, this saint's day does not seem to have been celebrated much in England since the Reformation, and no widespread customs have been reported, although there are some indications of a belief that dew gathered on St Bride's Day was considered to be particularly good for the complexion (*see also* 1 **May: May Dew**).

2 February

Candlemas (Purification of the Blessed Virgin Mary)

The second of February is dedicated to the Purification of the Virgin Mary (which in Jewish law had to take place forty days after a birth) and to her presentation of the infant Jesus in the temple at Bethlehem, as described in Luke 2:22–39. Celebration of the day was slow to spread across the Christian world, but in the early eighth century the Northumbrian cleric the Venerable Bede recorded that the day was being celebrated in Britain, and he calls it the 'Feast of St Mary'. The vernacular English name 'Candlemas' is not recorded until the year 1014. The day has always had something of a dual aspect, depending on whether the emphasis was placed on the purification of Mary, or the presentation of Christ, and those Christians who were uncomfortable with the 'Jewish' notion of purification after a birth ('churching' in everyday English) naturally tended towards the latter interpretation.

The key element, which gives the day its popular name in English, was the preponderance of candles. These were blessed in the church and were carried in procession around the parish; they could also be seen blazing all around the building itself. This custom is based quite simply upon the idea of Christ lighting the way, shedding light on our darkness, and it is linked in particular to the words of Simeon, who held the baby Jesus and called him 'A light to lighten the Gentiles, and the glory of thy people Israel' (Luke 2:32).

The day was extremely popular in England in the Middle Ages, and ceremonies included dramatic presentations of the scene in the temple; however, Protestant reformers attempted to discredit the blessing of candles and the processions, and by the 1540s many churches had given up the festival. Nevertheless, candles could hardly be eradicated from churches completely, and a special connection between them and the day remained fixed in the popular mind. Despite the efforts of the reformers, the official line in former times that blessed candles banish Satan was widely interpreted by parishioners to mean that candles used in church had protective and magical powers against various illnesses, and thunder and lightning, or could be placed in the hands of the dying to protect their souls.

Apart from superstitions connected with candles, Candlemas did not last well in the festive calendar and there are hardly any recorded customs linked to the day in modern times. One notable exception is the 'cradle rocking' at Blidworth in Nottinghamshire, which takes place on the Sunday nearest to 2 February, but this is a special case as the parish church is dedicated to St Mary of the Purification and therefore has a particular interest in the day. During the afternoon service, a baby boy, born as near as possible to the previous Christmas Day, is laid in a cradle to symbolize the original presentation of the baby Jesus, and is rocked by the vicar while the thanksgiving is said by the congregation. A plaque in the church records the names of all the babies who have been so honoured since the custom was inaugurated in 1922. Many authorities state that this is a revival of an ancient practice, but they offer no evidence to support the claim.

In shoemaking and other indoor trades, Candlemas was deemed to be the day on which candles could be dispensed with during working hours until the autumn – 'At Candlemas throw candle and candle-stick away' was a widely known saying. From at least the mid seventeenth to the late nineteenth century, Candlemas was also considered the end of the Christmas period. Robert Herrick's poem 'Upon Candlemasse Day', published in the collection *Hesperides* in 1648, declares not only that greenery should be taken down but also that all feasting and fun should cease:

> End now the white-loaf, and the pie
> And let all sports with Christmas die.

In Scotland, Candlemas was a full quarter day, and in various parts of England, particularly Cheshire, Lancashire, and Cumbria, it was held as a day for commencing or terminating farm tenancies, and for settling accounts, well into the twentieth century.

Candlemas also had an important part to play in traditional weather-lore, and the most common view was that the prevailing weather of the day predicted the opposite to come, as in this somewhat contrived rhyme from Devon in 1900:

> If Candlemas day be dry and fair
> The half of the winter is to come, and mair
> If Candlemas day be wet and foul
> The half of the winter is gone at yule.

In another report from Huntingdonshire, recorded by the local historian C. F. Tebbutt, we seem to have a pre-echo of the American Groundhog Day:

Candlemas Day was also known as Badgers' Day, in the belief that the supposedly hibernating badger woke up and came to the entrance of his sett on that day. If he found that it was sunny, and he could see the shadow of his tail, he went back to sleep . . . There used to be a stuffed badger at the Chequers public house at Glatton, specially set up because Badgers' Day was also the landlord's birthday.

Forty-Shilling Day

The will of William Glanville the younger, dated 1717, provides for five poor boys under the age of sixteen from Wotton in Surrey to be given forty shillings each on the anniversary of his death, if they fulfil certain conditions. To qualify, they must stand by his white marble tomb, with both hands on the stone, and recite the Lord's Prayer, the Apostles' Creed, and the Ten Commandments, from memory. They must then read a chapter from the Bible, and write out a section of it. If insufficient boys can be found in Wotton, it is permitted to include those from neighbouring parishes. In the past, it was occasionally necessary to erect a tent over the tomb to shelter the boys from the February weather, and in particularly bad winters the whole event was moved to later in the year. The annual event ceased during the later twentieth century, and attempts to revive it failed to attract enough boys to take part.

3 February

St Blaise's Day

St Blaise (also Blaize, Blaze) was widely popular in Britain from the eighth century to beyond the Middle Ages, although nothing is known for certain of his life. He is believed to have been Bishop of Sebaste in fourth-century Armenia (and he is still regularly referred to as 'Bishop', rather than 'St', Blaise), but stories of his martyrdom and miracles are later inventions. According to these stories, while hiding from persecutors in a cave he healed sick people and animals and, in particular, saved the life of a boy who had a fishbone stuck in his throat. He was also said to have been tortured by being torn with iron combs, and these combs became his recognized symbol.

In English tradition, Blaise was adopted as the patron saint of woolcombers – an important and widespread occupation before machinery wiped it out. Every year on or around his feast day, the woolcombers organized a trade procession, which even in small towns was an impressive event, and in larger centres of the wool industry these processions became truly spectacular affairs. The following description,

[3 February 1777] *This day, Munday, being the anniversary of Bishop Blaze, the same was observed in this town in a manner far surpassing anything of the kind ever seen. The cavalcade consisting of between 2 and 300 woolcombers, upon horses in uniforms, properly decorated. Bishop Blaze, Jason, Castor and Pollux, a band of musick, drums, colours, and everything necessary to render the procession suitable to the greatness of the woollen manufactory. The following lines were spoken by the Orators:*

> *With boundless gratitude, illustrious Blaze*
> *Again we celebrate, and speak thy praise, etc.*

The diarist Parson Woodforde recorded a trip to Norwich on 24 March 1793 especially to see the parade there, and even copied out details from the printed leaflet produced on the occasion. These processions presented a curious pastiche of a romanticized Bishop Blaize and characters drawn from the Greek story of Jason and the Golden Fleece, combined with local pride and national patriotism. As the trade disappeared into the factories, the processions gradually faded from the local scene.

Blaise is still remembered, however, for his aid in cases of throat ailments, and in some Catholic churches one can get one's throat blessed on 3 February. The priest holds two lighted candles, tied with ribbon to form a cross, to the throat of the sufferer, and says a blessing along the lines of 'May the Lord deliver you from the evil of the throat, and from every other harm.' The most famous example of this annual blessing takes place at St Etheldreda's church in Holborn, London, where it has been a regular event since 1876.

St Ives Hurling

St Ives, in the far west of Cornwall, maintains one of only two surviving traditional **hurling** games (*see* p. 50). The key feature of hurling is that it is played with a ball about the size of a cricket ball, made of wood or cork, with a silver coating, which is thrown or carried, but not kicked. In the other surviving game, at the Cornish town of St Columb, play takes place in the streets, but in St Ives it is played on the beach, and children and young people are now usually the main participants. The two goals are basketball nets. As is usual with this type of game, the

continued on page 52 ☞

Hurling

Hurling is a fast-moving game played with a small, hand-held ball, made of cork or wood with a silver or occasionally gilt coating. It seems to be unique to Cornwall, although similar games are found elsewhere under different names, and it used to be played throughout the county but now only takes place regularly at St Columb at Shrovetide, and at St Ives on their Feast Monday (the day after the nearest Sunday to 3 February).

In Richard Carew's *Survey of Cornwall* (1602), we are fortunate to have what must be the most detailed explanation of any game in the period. He distinguished two forms of the game – 'to goals' and 'to the country' – and whereas the former was relatively civilized, the latter was an inter-parish match with few restrictions for as many as wanted to play. Carew wrote that hurling 'to goals' took place mostly at weddings, and other accounts mention the game being played at other gatherings, such as at Helston after beating the bounds in 1851 (*see* **Rogationtide**, p. 243, for a description of this custom). In Carew's description, the game was surprisingly well organized. The two teams, of fifteen, twenty, or thirty players, were evenly matched, and they lined up against each other at the start of the game so that individual players knew who they were to mark on the other side; two players were not allowed to set on the same opponent at the same time. Players could not pass the ball forwards, nor could they 'butt or hand-fast under the girdle' (presumably striking or grabbing below the belt).

Hurling to the country was 'more diffuse and confuse' and followed few rules. The goals could be two or three miles apart, and there was no matching of teams:

. . . a silver ball is cast up, and that company which can catch and carry it by force or sleight to their place assigned, gaineth the ball and victory. Whosoever getteth seizure of this ball findeth himself generally pursued by the adverse party, neither will they leave till (without all respects) he be laid flat on God's dear earth.

By all accounts, hurling was a pretty rough game, but no worse than any of the street-football-type games played elsewhere. Carew's final judgement was somewhat ambivalent:

**The ball in this play may be compared to an infernal spirit, for whoso-
ever catcheth it fareth straightways like a madman, struggling and
fighting with those that go about to hold him, and no sooner is the
ball gone from him but he resigneth this fury to the next receiver, and
himself becometh peaceable as before. I cannot well resolve whether I should more commend this game for the manhood and exercise,
or condemn it for the boisterousness and harms which it begetteth.**

However, later writers, especially those from outside the West Country,
were more decided in their opinion, and used their distaste for the game
to dismiss Cornish society in general. Daniel Defoe, in his *Tour through
the Whole Island of Great Britain* (1724–6), writes for example:

**The game called the Hurlers, is a thing the Cornish men value
themselves much upon; I confess, I see nothing in it, but that it is a
rude violent play among the boors, or country people; brutish and
furious, and a sort of an evidence that they were, once, a kind of
barbarians.**

Even before Carew's account, we have an unusual number of references
to the game, which in combination show that it was already well known in
the 1580s. 'The Hurlers' is a group of standing stones arranged in circles
on Bodmin Moor, near the village of Minnions. Thirty-nine of the stones
still survive, and they are the subject of two traditions, versions of which
are told of standing stones all over the country. One tradition is that they
cannot be counted; the second, which gives the stones their name, is
that they were originally people who were turned to stone for hurling on
a Sunday. This latter tradition was already in circulation *c*.1584, when the
antiquarian John Norden first described the stones. A silver ball is also
mentioned three times in 1594 and 1595 in the book of parish accounts
called the *St. Columb Green Book*.

The *Oxford English Dictionary* explains that 'hurling' did not only
mean 'throwing', but back in 1528 it also meant 'struggling' or 'conflicting'. 'Hurling' was also the name of a hockey-type game in Ireland, first
recorded in 1527.

See also 3 February: St Ives Hurling; Shrove Tuesday: St Columb Hurling, p. 81; *compare* Football, p. 64; Games and Sports: Camping, p. 38.

☞ continued from page 49 two teams have traditionally been drawn from different parts of the town – 'uplong' and 'downlong' – although there is a local story that formerly one team was composed of men named Tom, Will, or John, and one of men with other names.

During the rest of the year, the ball is in the keeping of the mayor. On the Feast Monday (the day after the nearest Sunday to 3 February) at 9.30 a.m., the mayor carries the ball to the well of St Ia at Porthmeor, where it is blessed, then back to the churchyard, where he throws it from the wall to the players on the sands below, to the accompaniment of the game's motto, 'fair play is good play'. The game ceases at noon when the ball is returned to the mayor. Coins are later thrown from the balcony of the Guildhall for the waiting children.

See also **Shrove Tuesday: St Columb Hurling**, p. 81.

10 February

St Scholastica's Day

St Scholastica (*c.*480–*c.*543) established a convent at Plombariola in Italy and was the sister of Benedict, the founder of the Benedictine monastic order. Brother and sister met regularly to discuss spiritual topics, and it is said that when Benedict wanted to go home after one such meeting, Scholastica successfully prayed for a storm to prevent his leaving. Her power over storms has meant that she has been invoked against them by her followers ever since. Her name, and her penchant for intellectual debate, ensured that she was remembered by the academic community, and there are numerous schools and colleges named after her. Her festival was traditionally remembered at Oxford, where long-standing rivalry between 'town' and 'gown' exploded into violence on St Scholastica's Day in 1354. In February that year, some students objected to being served 'bad wine' in the Swindlestock tavern by breaking the vessel over the landlord's head. The landlord (who happened to be the town mayor at the time) summoned help from neighbours, the students mobilized their forces, and a pitched battle raged for several days. The townsmen were victorious, ransacking the university buildings and killing over sixty students.

The King expressed his wrath by depriving the town of various privileges, such as control over the price and quality of bread, ale, and wine sold in the neighbourhood, and jurisdiction over both criminal and civil cases where students were involved, bestowing them instead upon the university. He also forced the citizens to acknowledge their guilt by processing to the university for a service of penitence every 10 February, and paying an annual fine of sixty-three pence (one for every student killed in the riot). This continued until 1825, when university and town agreed to drop the custom.

14 February

St Valentine's Day

St Valentine's Day is one of the few festivals which have increased in popularity in recent decades, and it shows no sign of going out of fashion. Despite having an undisputed history spanning at least 600 years, the origins of the festival are still obscure, and the only certainty is that it has nothing to do with the saint from which it gets its name. The dominant feature has always been, as today, the giving of gifts, letters, or cards to a lover, but there have been wide variations within the basic framework. There have also been other customs on the day: children visited their neighbours and sang special rhymes in exchange for pennies; special buns were made and sold; and, not surprisingly, Valentine's Day was one of the times when love-divination procedures were thought particularly effective.

St Valentine and the Romans

There were numerous Valentines who achieved sainthood in the early years of Christianity, but the two who were famous enough to be widely known in late medieval England were a bishop from Terni and a priest from Rome. According to the popular books of saints' lives compiled centuries after these events, they were both martyred by beheading during the reign of the Emperor Claudius sometime around AD 269–73; however, their true histories will probably never be known. The key point for present purposes is that in neither case does the saint's legend offer the slightest hint of a connection with love and romance, or spring, or birds, or anything related to the later customs and beliefs. The only conclusion we can draw is that the martyrs happen to have been assigned a date that, falling in the period traditionally viewed as the start, or precursor, of spring, provided later writers with a convenient day on which to place their new notions of the romantic consonance between nature and the ideal of courtly love.

Although it is also common to explain the origin of Valentine's Day by citing the annual festival of Lupercalia in ancient Rome, which took place on 15 February, again there is no basis for this assumed connection. The Lupercalia was primarily a purification festival and, apart from the coincidence of the date, bore no relationship to any of the later Valentine customs. It seems to have been the Revd Alban Butler who, in his enthusiasm for classical antecedents, first claimed a connection between Valentine and the Lupercalia, in his *Lives of the Saints* (1756). Many writers have followed suit, and have gradually convinced themselves that the Lupercalia was really a love festival in disguise, and that St Valentine was a fertility figure. Some go even further and claim that the Romans chose future partners by lot at this festival, but this detail is not included in any classical writings, and seems to have been invented by the antiquarian Francis Douce, in his influential *Illustrations of Shakespeare* (1807), simply to claim a direct line of descent from the ancient world to the modern custom.

The fourteenth century

The record really begins with Geoffrey Chaucer and his contemporaries in the fourteenth century, although precise dating in this period is not possible and clear precedence cannot therefore be set. Chaucer's 700-line poem *Parlement of the Foules*, written some time between 1376 and 1382, relates how birds choose their mates on St Valentine's Day every year. His friend, John Gower, used the same theme in his *Cinkante Ballades*, written in French, possibly as early as 1374, as did the author of *The Cuckoo and the Nightingale* (probably Sir John Clanvowe, who died in 1391), and the Savoyard soldier-poet, Oton de Grandson, who spent much of the 1370s in England. These writers were almost certainly working within an existing tradition that held Valentine's Day to be the first day of spring, but it is not clear whether they invented the idea of birds mating on that day. Their key achievement was therefore simply in cementing the connection between this particular day and love and romance, albeit in the avian sphere. Most tellingly, however, they did not extend the mating motif in their poems from birds to people, and this negative evidence is the strongest indication we have that they were unaware of any connection between

St Valentine and human romance. It is therefore most unlikely to have
existed before their time.

The connection with humans was soon made, however, in both
France and England, and John Lydgate's poem 'A Valentine to her
that Excelleth All' (*c*.1440) includes several verses that describe people
choosing their loves on this day. It commences:

> *Saint Valentine, of custom year by year*
> *Men have an usaunce* [usage] *in this region*
> *To look and search Cupid's calendar*
> *And choose their choice by great affection*
> *Such as been pricked by Cupid's motion*
> *Taking their choice, as their sort* [lot] *doth fall*
> *But I love one which excelleth all.*

Development of the custom

From that time on, the connection between St Valentine and human
romance was a commonplace for poets and playwrights, including
Shakespeare, Ben Jonson, John Donne, Michael Drayton, and Robert
Herrick, although many of them still emphasized the connection with
birds. Moreover, there is plenty of evidence that Valentine's Day was
not merely a literary conceit but had a place in real people's lives. The
famous series of letters belonging to the Paston family, now in the
British Library, includes three letters from Dame Elizabeth Brews to
John Paston in February 1477 in which she calls him her 'ryght wele-
beloved Voluntyne' and also refers to birds choosing their mates on
the 14th. A year later, the two were married. Nearly two hundred years
later, on 19 February 1654, 27-year-old Dorothy Osborne wrote to her
absent sweetheart, Sir William Temple:

I'll tell you something that you don't know, which is, that I am your Valentine
and you are mine. I did not think of drawing any, but Mrs. Goldsmith and
Jane would need make me write some for them and myself; so I writ down
our three names, and for the men, Mr. Fish, James B., and you. I cut them
all equal and made them up myself before they saw them, and because I
would owe it wholly to my good fortune, if I were pleased, I made both
them choose first that had never seen what was in them, and they left me
you. Then I made them choose again for theirs, and my name was left. You
cannot imagine how I was delighted with this little accident . . . I was not
half so pleased with my encounter next morning. I was up early, but with

no design of getting another Valentine and going out to walk in my night-clothes and night-gown, I met Mr. Fish going hunting, I think he was; but he stayed to tell me I was his Valentine . . .

Dorothy and William were married on Christmas Day the same year.

From about the same period come the deservedly well-known and oft-quoted entries in Samuel Pepys's diaries. Pepys mentions the custom at least twenty-four times between 1660 and 1669, and his descriptions provide the most detailed picture of the custom available before the modern period. The picture that emerges from these early references is of a custom which already had several strands. The theme was romantic love, but in stark contrast to the modern way, the choice of partner was left to fate and the whole thing was treated as an elaborate game. At a party or family gathering, names were written on pieces of paper, which were drawn at random, and people were thus paired up, to play at being lovers. Even married people like Samuel and Elizabeth Pepys took part and had their 'valentines', and they were expected to pay each of them little compliments for the next few days, while the men were required to buy presents. Pepys's entries often display a characteristic concern with how much the whole business would cost him, and he usually bought gifts for his valentine (for example, six pairs of plain and one of embroidered gloves) and for his wife. The higher up the social scale, the more lavish the gift. In February 1556, for example, Queen Mary's Secretary of State, Sir William Petre, gave a present of six yards of black satin (worth 60 shillings) to his valentine, Lady Bulkeley, even though he took no further part in the game, asking his wife to buy the material for him. Adults also sometimes made pretend valentine arrangements with their friends' children.

Fate could dictate your choice of valentine in another way, as it was widely believed that the first eligible person you saw in the morning was the one for you. This notion prompted Elizabeth Pepys to keep her eyes covered for much of the morning in February 1662, in order to avoid seeing the painters working in the house.

The play-acting could, of course, be taken more seriously if the participants wished. Real lovers like Dorothy Osborne were pleased when fate confirmed their choice, and there is some evidence that the result of pairing by lot or chance was regarded as genuinely predictive of future romance between the individuals involved, as expressed by Ben Jonson in Act I, scene 1 of his *Tale of a Tub* (1640):

Last night did draw him for her valentine;
Which chance, it hath so taken her father, and mother,
(Because themselves drew so on Valentine's Eve
Was thirty yeare) as they will have her married
Today by any meanes.

It should also be noted that Samuel Pepys appears to use the valentine custom as a euphemism for some of his extra-marital affairs (see, for example, the entries for March and April 1668).

Letters and cards

Valentine letters were presumably a feature of the day from quite early on, but commercially produced valentine cards did not appear until the early nineteenth century. They rapidly became the norm for potential lovers, and they ranged from simple and unpretentious engravings or lithographs, to expensive handmade concoctions involving embossed card, real silk, feathers, and lace, which feature strongly in many extant collections. They often had spaces for hand-written messages, and the sender who could not compose his or her own verses could fall back on the many traditional verses of the 'roses are red' variety, or one could buy 'valentine writers', small books of suggested rhymes, suitable for all occasions. However, the commercial cards sowed the seeds of their own downfall by providing an all-too-easy means of insulting someone with humorous or offensive parodies of traditional greetings, and despite the huge popularity of card-sending in mid Victorian times, the custom declined markedly as the twentieth century drew near. Many writers in the 1890s took it for granted that valentine-sending was almost dead: on 17 February 1894, the *Graphic* records, 'St. Valentine's Day . . . attracts very little attention nowadays in England, but across the Atlantic the Saint is still honoured', while in 1896 the *Ludgate Illustrated News* remarks, 'Take the undeniable fact that St. Valentine's Day is a day of usages almost wholly neglected.' Many commentators blamed the widespread use of the offensive anti-valentines, although these had already been available for some decades. But the custom did not die, and it struggled on into the twentieth century, albeit a mere shadow of its former self.

After the Second World War, it underwent a major revival, under heavy influence from the USA and the watchful eye of the commercial card manufacturers. There is certainly no stopping it now, and, apart from cards, devotees can choose from a range of staple items such as chocolates, roses, romantic dinners, sexy underwear, and any and everything that can be represented in the shape of a heart or coloured red. One of the developments *c.*1980, which seems destined to become permanent, is the newspaper-column messages on the day.

Visiting customs

Cards and gifts were not the only traditions for which Valentine's Day was notable for previous generations. Several other customs existed, mostly in rural areas, such as a widespread visiting custom, undertaken mainly by children. This was recorded from most parts of the country but was apparently most popular in the eastern counties, particularly Norfolk. Anne Elizabeth Baker included a valentine song in her Northamptonshire glossary of 1854:

Valentining: Children going from house to house, the morning of St. Valentine's Day, soliciting small gratuities. The children of the villages go in parties, sometimes in considerable numbers, repeating at each house one or other of the following salutations, which vary in different districts:

> *Good morrow, Valentine!*
> *First it's yours, and then it's mine,*
> *So please give me a valentine.*
> *Morrow, morrow, Valentine!*
> *First 'tis yours, and then 'tis mine,*
> *So please to give me a valentine,*
> *Holly and ivy tickle my toe,*
> *Give me red apple and then let me go.*
> *Good morrow, Valentine!*
> *Parsley grows by savoury,*
> *Savoury grows by thyme,*
> *A new pair of gloves on Easter day,*
> *Good morrow, Valentine!*

The same author also reported a family custom, whereby the first child to say 'Good morrow, Valentine' on the morning of the 14th could claim a small present from their parents. The children's visiting custom could also include elements of scrambling for coins and eatables (for **Scrambling Customs**, *see* p. 172).

The majority of references to these visiting customs come from the nineteenth and twentieth centuries, but proof of their existence before 1800 can be found in the diary of Parson James Woodforde, of every child under fourteen in the parish who could say 'Good morrow, Valentine', on 14 February almost every year between 1777 and 1802, although when it fell on a Sunday, the children came the following day.

A few nineteenth-century sources, from Leicestershire, Rutland, and Northamptonshire, record that special cakes were made for the day, and called valentine buns or 'plum shuttles'. The latter (pronounced 'shittles') were named after the weaver's shuttle, which they resembled in shape, but further details are not given.

A combination of the visiting custom and gift-giving was also reported in the nineteenth century, in which anonymous gifts were left on the doorstep (although again, the cruel and vindictive could leave empty or worthless parcels). In 1832, the Northamptonshire poet John Clare wrote:

> *Young girls grow eager as the day retires*
> *& smile & whisper round their cottage fires*
> *Listning for noises in the dusky street*
> *For tinkling latches & for passing feet*
> *The prophecys of coming joys to hark*
> *Of wandring lovers stealing thro' the dark*
> *Dropping their valentines at beautys door*
> *With hearts & darts & love knots littered oer.*

Love divination

Last but not least of valentine traditions, the day (or its eve) was considered one of the key dates in the year on which love-divination procedures could properly be carried out. Many of these divinations were well known, such as sowing the hemp seed, in which unmarried girls threw hemp seed over their shoulders at midnight in hopes of seeing the forms of their future lovers following them. The following, as published by James Orchard Halliwell in 1849, is less common, but it is typical of the style for the day:

On Valentine's day, take two bay leaves, sprinkle them with rose water and place them on your pillow, in the evening. When you go to bed, put on a clean night-gown turned inside out and, lying down, say softly:

> *Good Valentine, be kind to me*
> *In dreams let me my true love see.*

Then go to sleep as soon as you can, in expectation of seeing your future husband in a dream.

20 February

John Cass Commemoration

Sir John Cass (1666–1718) was a London merchant and one-time alderman, sheriff, and Member of Parliament for the City. He is remembered as a major benefactor of east London, in particular in the educational sphere. He founded the Sir John Cass School in Aldgate – one of three educational institutions that now bear his name – and the pupils and staff of the school attend a founder's day service at nearby St Botolph's church every year on or near 20 February. Those attending the service carry or wear red feathers in his memory, supposedly because Sir John suffered a major haemorrhage as he sat writing his will and the quill pen he was holding was dyed red with his blood; it is more likely, however, that the red feathers are a reference to the one that is featured in his coat of arms.

Shrovetide and Lent

The period of Lent comprises the forty days immediately preceding Easter (excluding Sundays), starting on Ash Wednesday and finishing on Holy (Easter) Saturday. Ash Wednesday can therefore fall anywhere between 4 February and 11 March. This period was decreed by the early Church as a season of strict fasting, penance, and piety, in preparation for the major festival of the year which culminated in the Resurrection of Christ, although the exact number of days of fasting has varied considerably since that time. During Lent, all meat, eggs, cooking fat, and cheese were strictly forbidden, as were marriage ceremonies and sexual intercourse, and solemn rituals took place in parish churches in which all images, and even parts of the churches themselves, were covered with veils.

In 1538, as leader of the new English Church, Henry VIII softened the official line by allowing dairy products to be eaten; somewhat surprisingly, subsequent Protestant monarchs did not abolish Lent completely but kept the ban on meat-eating in place and continued to enforce the fast. Nevertheless, the official explanation for the fast became increasingly secular and centred on the idea that eating fish supported the fishing industry, which in turn bolstered shipping and thus supported the Royal Navy. Lent was abolished by the Puritans in the 1640s, was reinstated by Charles II in 1664 but never really enforced, and began to fade from English society. By Victorian times, Lent had lost most of its power, as the local historian John Fisher recorded in 1865 in this example from Yorkshire:

At the beginning of Lent the most inveterate of card-players (and their number was legion) used to lay aside their packs of cards, and would not on any account so much as touch them during the whole season of Lent; but now, however, the practice is very different.

In the twenty-first century, only Roman Catholics and particularly devout Anglicans take any real notice of Lent, and even they are usually expected to do little more than give something up during the period.

In terms of the traditional calendar, the most lasting effect of Lent was the concentration of games and customs at Shrovetide, the days just before the season of Lent commenced. It is difficult for us nowadays to understand the almost desperate merrymaking that took place, in the face of six weeks of enforced restricted diet and best behaviour. In England, celebrations did not seem to coalesce into the extended bacchanalia that took place in many European cities, where the whole period between Christmas and Shrove could be devoted to feasting, drinking, and playing, in one long street festival, but there was still plenty of scope for extra food – particularly in the form of pancakes, eggs, and meat – and the playing of vigorous sports such as football, cockfighting, and throwing at cocks.

The former importance of Shrovetide in the traditional calendar is demonstrated by the huge range of customs that are recorded for the time, and the main examples, past and present, are each considered separately below.

See also **Games and Sports,** p. 35.

Egg Saturday

The Saturday preceding Shrove Tuesday; *see* **Shrove Tuesday: Egg Shackling**, p. 75.

Hall Monday

See **Shrove Tuesday: Shroving and Lent-Crocking**, p. 82.

Shrove Tuesday

Shrove Tuesday, the last day before the start of Lent, was named after the 'shriving' (confession and absolution) necessary on the day. Most of the secular festivities of Shrovetide also took place on this day, but the preceding days had their own traditions, which were mainly concerned with food. Collop Monday, for example, the day before Shrove Tuesday, was so called because of the custom of eating 'collops', a word that varies in meaning from place to place but usually means 'slices of meat', or what we would call 'eggs and bacon' or even 'ham and eggs'.

From medieval times onwards, the most enthusiastic of the Shrovetide revellers were apprentices and schoolchildren, and they are the ones who are often named as taking part in the street football, and other seasonal games. In 1890, John Nicholson records in his *Folk Lore of East Yorkshire*:

. . . the children expect to be able to leave school, and have a half holiday, in which to play games with ball. As 'keppin' (catching) balls is the favourite game, the day is called Keppin Day.

Apprentices also had a tradition of wrecking any brothels in the neighbourhood, as described in *Pasquils Palinodia* (1619):

> *It was the day, of all days in the year,*
> *That unto Bacchus hath his dedication,*
> *When mad brained prentices, that no men fear,*
> *O'rethrow the dens of bawdy recreation.*

It is not clear why they should have done this; as a group they are not normally known for their moralistic beliefs or behaviour. More modern apprentices may not have vented their animosity on particular targets, but the feeling that the day should be a holiday survived into surprisingly recent times. As late as March 1954, *The Times* reported this as a potential problem:

The custom of apprentices taking the afternoon off on Shrove Tuesday is dying, but some still carry it on. When all but twenty-five of those at Chadderton, Manchester, left as soon as they had clocked on yesterday morning, the firm felt that they must check a tendency to establish a full day's holiday.

See also **Shrovetide and Lent**, p. 60.

Alnwick Football

Alnwick, in Northumberland, keeps alive one of the few Shrovetide football games, which has survived mainly as a result of a willingness to compromise, but also because it had a powerful ally in the Duke of Northumberland. In 1884, the *Folk-Lore Journal* recorded:

Before the Alnwick Improvement Act came into operation, over fifty years ago, the game was played in the streets of the town, a custom which resulted in much damage to windows, etc., the reparation of which was defrayed by the lord of the manor. The magistrates, after the passing of the Act, prohibited the playing of the game in the streets, and in consequence the Duke of Northumberland instituted an annual match between the married and unmarried freemen, also a match for the townspeople, and this custom went on until 1847, when the Duke of Northumberland died at Alnwick Castle in the month of February, and no game was played the following year. Subsequently, however, the game was resuscitated, the players to be the parishioners of St Michael's v. the parishioners of St Paul's. And so it has continued until now, on Shrove Tuesday, in the 'Pasture' or north demesne, by permission of his Grace the Duke of Northumberland.

Nowadays, the ball is brought from Alnwick Castle, in a procession headed by the Duke's piper, and thrown up at 2 p.m. Unlike other traditional games, the ball is kicked, not carried or thrown, and the goals, which used to be 400 yards apart, are now set at 200 yards. The teams are also much smaller than the 150-a-side that used to be common. The winning team has to score three goals (called 'hales'), and the wooden goals vaguely resemble soccer goals but are only 4 feet 6 inches wide and are decorated with an arch of greenery. After the game, whoever manages to get the ball off the pitch and over the River Aln keeps it.

Tradition has it that the game started after some bloody altercation with the Northumbrians' neighbours, as the jubilant Englishmen kicked a Scotsman's head around. This was said of many other football games, although it is more often a marauding Dane who unwillingly supplied the ball. The earliest known reference to football at Alnwick is in 1762, but there were many other football games in the area and it is probably much older than that.

See also **Football**, *below*.

Ashbourne Football

Ashbourne Royal Shrovetide Football in Derbyshire is one of a handful of matches that preserve something of the flavour of the medieval game. Like the less well-known game at Atherstone in Warwickshire (*see* p. 70), the play takes place mainly in the town rather than in an open space, but at Ashbourne there are at least teams and goals which give it some semblance of an organized game. The teams, however, can be of any size, and are traditionally comprised of those born to the north of the River Henmore (the Up'ards), and those born to the south (the Down'ards).

The game is played on Shrove Tuesday and Ash Wednesday, and starts each day at about 2 p.m., when the ball is turned up at Shaw Croft by a local dignitary. If a goal is scored before 5 p.m., a new ball is

continued on page 70

Football

Football – whether Association or Rugby – is so much part of everyday life that we often forget that in the codified and structured forms we now know the game it is less than 150 years old, and for centuries before that time, 'football' meant something completely different. The early history of traditional 'football' games is clear enough in outline, but it is confused by the lack of precision in the early sources, and there are recurrent problems of definition. Most of the earlier writers only mention the game to rail against its violence and ungodliness, or to report on attempts to suppress it altogether.

The earliest mention of such a game is in William Fitz Stephen's account of London, written *c.*1180, but it is ambiguous, speaking of a 'game of ball', although the other details make it very likely that 'football' is being described:

Moreover, each year upon the day called Carnival . . . [he describes cockfighting in the morning]. **After dinner all the youth of the City goes out into the fields to a much-frequented game of ball. The scholars of each school have their own ball and almost all the workers of each trade have theirs also in their hands. Elder men and fathers and rich citizens come on horse-back to watch the contests of their juniors, and after their fashion are young again with the young; and it seems that the motion of their natural heat is kindled by the contemplation of such violent motion and by their partaking in the joys of untrammelled youth.**

It is clear from this description that this ball game was already a well-established custom at the time. The next reference is also unclear, primarily because it was written in the Anglo-French of the time and is therefore open to questions of translation. It occurs in the *Writ for Preserving the Peace According to the Articles of the Statute of Winchester*, issued on 13 April 1314, in the reign of Edward II, and designed to ban unruly behaviour in the city. The document uses the term *grosses pelotes de pee,* which some have translated as 'foot balls':

And because of the great disturbance in the city by some players of large foot balls thrown in the meadows [or crowds] **of the people, from which many evils might arise . . .**

We have to wait until the fifteenth century for the first clear use of the word 'football'. In Scotland in 1424 it was decreed that 'The Kinge forbiddes that na man play at the fut balle under the payne of iiiid [i.e. fourpence].'

From then on, references come thick and fast, although detail is rarely given, presumably because the game was so common and everyone knew all about it. Sir Thomas Elyot's sparse comment is typical of many from the sixteenth to seventeenth centuries: 'Foote balle wherin is nothinge but beastly furie and exstreme violence'; although the vociferous Puritan

Football

Philip Stubbes can be relied upon, as usual, to give a fuller account (*see* p. 69).

Apart from the violence – which almost all writers emphasize – the picture that emerges is of games with few if any rules, large unrestricted teams of players, and based upon territories (one parish versus another, or the 'uppies and downies' of a town) or played specifically by apprentices or schoolboys. Games could be played in city streets, or in open fields, and the goals could be hundreds of yards or even a couple of miles apart. In the early periods, Shrovetide was clearly the most common time for such games, but they were by no means confined solely to that season.

The annual football at Derby achieved something of a national fame in its time, and in most features was typical of the game in the first half of the nineteenth century. It was described by Stephen Glover in his history of Derbyshire of 1829:

In the town of Derby the contest lies between the parishes of St. Peter and All Saints, and the goals to which the ball is to be taken are Nun's mill for the latter, and Gallow's balk on the Normanton Road for the former. None of the other parishes in the borough take any direct part in the contest, but the inhabitants of all join in the sport, together with persons from all parts of the adjacent country. The players are young men from eighteen to thirty or upwards, married as well as single . . . The game commences in the market-place, where the partisans of each parish are drawn up on each side; and, about noon, a large ball is tossed up in the midst of them. This is seized upon by some of the strongest and most active men of each party. The rest of the players immediately close in upon them, and a solid mass is formed. It then becomes the object of each party to impel the course of the crowd towards their particular goal. The struggle to obtain the ball, which is carried in the arms of those who have possessed themselves of it, is then violent, and the motion of this human tide heaving to and fro, without the least regard to consequences, is tremendous. Broken shins, broken heads, torn coats and lost hats, are among the minor accidents of this fearful contest, and it frequently happens that persons fall in consequence of the intensity of the pressure, fainting and bleeding beneath the feet of the surrounding mob. But it would be difficult to give an adequate idea of this ruthless sport: a Frenchman passing through Derby remarked, that if Englishmen called this playing, it would be impossible to say what they called fighting.

Some Frenchmen would not have been so surprised, however, as such games were not unique to Britain. Many European countries had similar pastimes, including, for example, the game of *soule* in northern France and *calcio* in northern Italy. Indeed, it is often suggested that the game was introduced into Britain from France, presumably by the Normans, although there is no documentary evidence to support this idea.

Local names for the sport – **camping** in the Eastern counties (*see* p. 38), or **hurling** in Cornwall (*see* p. 50) – may reflect different rules, but on present evidence there seems to be little intrinsic difference between these games. Nevertheless, some local factors must have made a real difference to the method of play: a game in a field is more likely to develop 'open' play than one held in the confines of a town, and a small, hard ball the size of a cricket ball is better for throwing distances than a pig's bladder filled with air.

It is appropriate that the first mention of the word 'football' in 1424 appears in an attempt to ban it, as the whole history of the game is littered with attempts at national and local level, mostly unsuccessful, to suppress the game entirely. As with many other mass working-class customs, it was in the mid nineteenth century that its opponents began to succeed in stamping it out. The traditional game at Beverley in Yorkshire was suppressed in the nineteenth century by the local authorities, aided by the militia, after the town's mayor was accidentally caught in the middle of the melee and trampled by the players. **Alnwick football**, in Northumberland (p. 63), is an excellent example of how the game survived by adaptation rather than confrontation, although in this case it helped tremendously that it had the active support of the Duke of Northumberland. The game there was played through the streets and was banned by local magistrates, but was saved from extinction by the grant of a nearby field by the Duke, and a redefinition of the rules.

At the same time as mass football was being suppressed by local authorities, developments in the major public schools were beginning the process of turning street football into modern rugby and soccer. By the early nineteenth century, some kind of football was being played in most of the biggest schools in the country, and from the 1820s to the 1840s there were various moves to codify rules of play within each school, and eventually to reach a national standard. Rugby School was the most influential in this movement, and gave its name to the emerging sport, especially after 1845, when its own rules were codified. But the oft-quoted story that rugby was founded in 1823 when a pupil at Rugby School, William Webb

Ellis, astonished his teammates by picking up the ball and running with it must be apocryphal. The story depends for effect on the idea that the 'football' was previously always kicked, but in any village game of the time the ball would have been handled and run with as well as kicked. The year 1863 saw the beginning of the separation between rugby and soccer, when, in a dispute of rules, certain clubs formed a Football Association; the Rugby Football Union was founded in 1871.

Attempts to suppress the traditional games continued well into modern times. The successful campaign against the game at Chester-le-Street in County Durham, for example, where the game took place at Shrovetide between the Up-streeters and Down-streeters, followed the same pattern of opposition from tradespeople and the local authority that was familiar in the nineteenth century, although apparently without the same level of violent confrontation. On 10 February 1932, *The Times* reported:

The old custom of playing football in the main thoroughfare of Chester-le-Street, Co. Durham, was observed yesterday, but with less enthusiasm than in former years. For 600 years the game has been played in the town on Shrove Tuesday, necessitating tradesmen barricading their shop fronts. Two years ago they unsuccessfully appealed to the town council for assistance, and finally sought police protection. Last year only a few shops were barricaded and the police seized any ball that was thrown into the street. This year not a single shop front in the mile-long main street was barricaded . . . The tradesmen feel that this old custom should be abolished in view of the thousands of pounds vested in their modern shop fronts.

Games which have something of the flavour of traditional football have survived in a handful of places on Shrove Tuesday, including the Alnwick football in Northumberland, the Ashbourne football in Derbyshire (p. 64), the Atherstone football in Warwickshire (p. 70), and the Sedgefield ball game in County Durham (p. 82), while other customs, such as the Haxey Hood in Lincolnshire (*see* 6 January: Haxey Hood), the St Ives Hurling (*see* 3 February: St Ives Hurling), the St Columb Hurling (p. 81) and the bottle-kicking at Hallaton in Leicestershire (*see* Easter Monday: Hallaton Hare Pie and Bottle-Kicking, p. 171), are clearly derived from the same roots. *See also* Good Friday: Workington Football, p. 151.

'Playing at football upon the Sabbath and other Days in England' by Philip Stubbes (1595)

Any exercise, which withdraweth us from godliness, either upon the Sabbath Day, or and other day else, is wicked and to be forbidden. Now, who is so grossly blind, that seeth not, that these aforesaid exercises not only withdraw us from godliness and virtue but also hale and allure us to wickedness and sin: for as concerning football playing, I protest unto you, it may rather be called a friendly fight, than a play or recreation. A bloody and murdering practice, than a fellowly sport or pastime. For, doth not every one lie in wait for his adversary, seeking to overthrow him, and to pick him on his nose, though it be upon hard stones, in ditch or dale, in valley or hole, or what place soever it be, he careth not so he have him down. And he that can serve the most of this fashion he is counted the only fellow, and who but he? So that by this means, sometimes their necks are broken, sometimes their backs, sometimes their legs, sometime their arms, sometime one part thrust out of joint, sometime another, sometimes their noses gush out with blood, sometimes their eyes start out of their heads, and sometimes hurt in one place, sometimes in another. But who soever scapeth away the best, goeth not scot free, but is either sore crushed and bruised, so as he dyeth of it, or else scapeth very hardly. And no marvel for they have sleights to meet one betwixt two, to dash him against the heart with their elbows, to hit him under the short ribs with their gripped fists, and with their knees to catch him upon the hip, and to pick him on his neck, with an hundred such murdering devices: and hereof groweth envy, malice, rancour, chollour, hatred[,] displeasure, enmity, and what not else? And sometimes, fighting, brawling, contention, quarrel picking, murder, homicide, and great effusion of blood, as experience daily teacheth. Is this murdering play now an exercise for the Sabbath Day? Is this a Christian dealing, for one brother to maim and hurt another, and that upon prepensed malice, or set purpose? If this to do to another, as we would wish another to do to us, God make us more careful over the bodies of our brethren.

☞ *continued from page 64*

turned up to start a new game. The centre of town is well boarded up and protected, and only unsuspecting tourists park their cars anywhere nearby. There are few rules, although play cannot continue after midnight (introduced in 1955), and transport of the ball in a vehicle has not been allowed since 1957. The special balls are made in the town and are slightly bigger than a normal football. They are made of leather, with ground cork inside, and are attractively painted. Whoever scores a goal keeps the ball.

The two goals are three miles apart, at Shurston Mill and Clifton Mill. When the mills were still going concerns, the ball had to touch the mill wheel, but now there are purpose-built concrete goals, with a board on which the ball must be tapped three times. The ball is rarely kicked but can be thrown or run with, although often the players have little chance to do so. Most of the time the ball is in the middle of the 'hug' – a huge mass scrum (similar to the 'sway' at Haxey; *see* **6 January: Haxey Hood**), which inches its way in one direction or another, literally steaming in the cold February air. The ball, and the more intrepid players, always goes into Henmore Brook.

Games like this have been widespread in England since medieval times (*see* **Football**, p. 64), but the first specific mention of the game at Ashbourne is in 1821. It is likely to be much older, but, unfortunately, earlier references do not make it clear whether they are referring to Ashbourne or nearby Derby, which also had a long-standing and widely known street-football game. There have been many times in its history when the game has been under threat from reformers, who wished to move it out of the town streets, and abolitionists, who wished to suppress it altogether, usually on grounds of public safety and civic pride. The game got its 'Royal' epithet in 1928, when the then Prince of Wales (later Edward VIII) turned up the ball, and Prince Charles did the same honour in 2003.

Atherstone Football

The 'football' game at Atherstone, in North Warwickshire, preserves many of the reported features of medieval Shrovetide games. The whole play takes place in the town streets, there are no teams, no goals, virtually no rules, and the purpose of the game seems to be simply to get hold of the ball and to be holding it when the game finishes.

The ball, made by Gilbert of Rugby, is much bigger than an ordinary football, being twenty-seven inches in diameter and weighing four pounds. It is made of leather, and filled with water – allegedly to prevent it being kicked very far. The players gather in Long Street, the main shopping street of the town, and the game commences at about 2 p.m., when an invited celebrity throws the ball into the crowd from an upstairs window. All the shopkeepers wisely board up their windows and doors, as up to a thousand people will throng the street during the game, which stays in Long Street and does not spill into other parts of the town. The game finishes at about 5 p.m. when the klaxon sounds.

Attached to the ball are four ribbons – red, blue, white, and gold – and anyone who is in possession of one of these ribbons at the end of the game wins a small amount of money and an inscribed ribbon, but the real winner is the one who is holding the ball when the klaxon sounds, and he gets to keep the ball.

Newspaper cuttings in Warwickshire county libraries reveal that in the 1930s and 1940s the real winning trick was to smuggle the ball out of the street, and it was often stabbed to deflate it and make it easier to conceal.

Websites, newspapers, and local publications proudly state that the game has been played here in an unbroken tradition for over 800 years, but this cannot be proved. The assumption is based on the story that in the twelfth century King John put up a bag of gold for a football game between the lads of Warwickshire and the lads of Leicestershire, but this is unlikely to be true. Moreover, there is no evidence that it became an annual event, or that it was played at Atherstone all those years. Nevertheless, the game is certainly alive and well, and engenders fierce loyalty in its supporters. Some of the townspeople dislike the potential violence of the game, saying that it smacks of mob rule and is out of place in a modern town, but these are exactly the arguments that have been made against street football all over the country for at least 700 years. It seems that even if the game at Atherstone cannot claim its existence for that length of time, the opposition certainly can.

See also **Football**, p. 64.

Cock Throwing and Threshing

Shrovetide was a particularly bad time for cockerels. It is not clear why, but several of the games played on the day involved cocks being maimed or killed, whether by each other in a cockfight or by being beaten to death with flails or sticks thrown at them. 'Throwing at cocks' was a hugely popular pastime, found in urban and rural settings alike all over the country from at least the fifteenth century and probably a good deal longer. Several foreign visitors mentioned it in their journals, including the Dutchman William Schellinks. On Shrove Tuesday 1662, he wrote:

Their entertainment then is to throw at the cock. In London one sees in every street, wherever one goes, many apprentice boys running with, under their arms, a cock with a string on its foot, on which is a spike, which they push firmly into the ground between the stones. They always look for an open space and, for a penny, let people throw their cudgel from a good distance at the cock, and he who kills the cock, gets it. In the country or with countryfolk they bury a cock with only its head above ground, and blindfold a person and turn him two or three times round himself, and he then tries to hit the cock with a flail.

As described here, the usual game was to tether a live bird and charge onlookers for the privilege of throwing pieces of wood at it, to kill or maim it. In some cases, a rule was followed whereby if the thrower who knocked a bird down could run and grab it before it regained its feet, he could claim it, while in others one simply had to kill the cockerel outright to win it. There were many other variations on the game, such as the one mentioned by Schellinks, usually called 'cock threshing', in which the cock was buried, and another in which the live bird was tied to someone's back and the threshers were again blindfolded.

Throwing at cocks was the first popular blood sport to fall victim to the inexorable changes in public taste that led to the suppression of animal baiting and fighting. Whereas cockfighting, although barbaric, could always be explained in sporting terms of a 'natural' fight between equals, so that it enjoyed support from many in the higher classes, throwing at cocks became a symbol of popular pastimes that were based on gratuitous cruelty and violence. There had been sporadic condemnations on both moral and public order grounds since Tudor times, but a sustained campaign began to take shape in the 1730s, with letters to the local and national press calling for its suppression. For the rest of the eighteenth century, suppression was piecemeal, as magistrates, encouraged by local reformers, began to ban the game in their areas. The following example from the *Warwick & Warwickshire Advertiser* of 19 February 1814 was typical:

All our readers, whose breasts are not utterly inaccessible to every just feel-

ing of humanity towards the inferior creation, will rejoice to hear that the Magistrates of this county have determined to suppress the base and brutal custom of throwing at game cocks on Shrove Tuesday. We earnestly hope that the magistrates of other counties will follow such a commendable an example by exerting their authority to prevent at once this cruel oppression of the brutish, and this shocking degradation of the human species.

By the end of the eighteenth century, the game was definitely on the wane, and the last place in which it was reported as taking place was Quainton, Buckinghamshire, in 1844. A pale imitation of the pastime survived for much longer in a fairground game, still called 'throwing at cocks', in which people threw sticks at lead figures.

Cockfighting

Cockfighting could take place at any time of year, but in the medieval and early modern period it was especially popular at Shrovetide. Oddly enough to modern eyes, the sport was particularly associated with schoolchildren and young people, and it was written into the rules of some schools that pupils must pay their schoolmaster a regular sum – termed a 'cock-penny' – to provide the birds for the traditional game on Shrove Tuesday. The earliest reference to cockfighting in England, written by William Fitz Stephen *c.*1180, makes this connection clear:

Each year upon the day called Carnival – to begin with the sports of boys (for we were all boys once) – boys from the schools bring fighting-cocks to their master, and the whole forenoon is given up to boyish sport for they have a holiday in the schools that they may watch their cocks do battle.

Although this is the first written evidence of cockfighting in this country, it was well known in ancient Greece and Rome, and may even have been introduced to Britain by the Romans.

Cockfighting developed into a well-organized professional sport, with well-defined rules and traditions, and a literature and terminology all of its own. Fighting birds were carefully bred and documented; beaks were sharpened, tails clipped, silver or steel spurs attached to their legs, alcohol was placed in their feed, and all the care and attention lavished on them that one would expect for a potentially valuable commodity. Cockfights at local level took place in barns, inns, or fairgrounds, but in London and other major centres there were purpose-built cockpits at which well-advertised professional meetings took place. Dutch visitor William Schellinks visited one in June 1662:

*In the afternoon we went to the cockpit and saw there several cock fights.
There a great deal of money is won and lost by betting. The place is well
laid out for the purpose, a circle with a table or round stage in the middle is
covered with mats, with the devotees sitting around it, with the seats rising
up so they can see above each other.*

Like horse-racing and prizefighting, cockfighting brought together
men from all the social classes, from the roughest to the highest, each
having their part to play. The rich subsidized the sport by organizing
the events, providing funds and premises, owning the cocks, and betting heavily on games, with huge sums of money regularly changing
hands. But there was also a strong working-class tradition of cockfighting all over the country, particularly among certain occupational
groups such as miners.

Samuel Pepys recorded two visits to cockfights, and both times
commented on the 'rabble' he encountered. On 21 December 1663 he
recorded:

*Did go to Shoe Lane to see a cock-fighting at a new pit there – a sport
I was never at in my life. But Lord, to see the strange variety of people,
from Parliament-man . . . to the poorest prentices, bakers, brewers, butchers,
draymen, and what not; and all this fellows one with another in swearing,
cursing and betting. I soon had enough of it.*

Pepys and Schellinks were recording their thoughts at a time when
cockfighting was enjoying a resurgence of popularity after the
Restoration of the monarchy. Cockfighting had, in fact, been banned
only nine years before, by the *Ordinance for prohibiting cock-matches*
(31 March 1654). This order was not concerned with cruelty to animals
but with the question of public order and private morality:

[They] *tend many times to the disturbance of the public peace, and are commonly accompanied with gaming, drinking, swearing, quarrelling, and
other dissolute practices, to the dishonour of God, and do often produce the
ruin of persons and their families . . .*

It is unlikely that this made much difference, as the people involved
were hardly likely to be bothered about their immortal souls, but it
drove the sport underground for a short while and explains its sudden high profile in Pepys's time. The sport's popularity continued
unabated until the turn of the nineteenth century, when public opinion turned decisively against such activities. In the 1830s, intense

for abolition. It was finally made illegal in 1849.

Nevertheless, cockfighting still takes place, on the quiet, all over the country. A joint raid by police and RSPCA officers at a disused warehouse in Lancaster in 2001 found a fight in progress and evidence of others having taken place. As reported in the *Guardian* on 29 May of that year, the RSPCA claimed not only that cockfighting is popular with the travelling community and in mining areas, but also that 'anyone you care to think of can be involved, regardless of wealth, job, or social status'.

Cookeels (or Coquilles)

This was a localized seasonal food, popular in Norfolk and the surrounding area at Shrovetide. It is described in nineteenth-century sources as akin to what we would now call a hot cross bun, but without the cross. There is no agreement as to spelling, and cookeels, coquilles, cockerells, and others were used indiscriminately. The most likely derivation is from 'cockerel', because these birds were so widely connected with Shrovetide for centuries, in the form of **cock throwing and threshing** (p. 71) and **cockfighting** (p. 73). All the written references to the buns stem from the nineteenth century, and there is no indication how old the custom of selling cookeels may have been.

Dough-Nut Day

Dough-Nut Day was a local name for Shrove Tuesday, reported in the nineteenth century from Baldock, Hertfordshire. Here, instead or perhaps as well as, the more usual pancakes, William Hone records in his *Year-Book* (1832) that mothers 'make a good store of small cakes fried in hog's lard, placed over the fire in a brass kettle or skillet, called "dough-nuts"'.

Egg Shackling

One of the staples of everyday diet that was banned during Lent was eggs, and it is no surprise that these feature in customs and food traditions of the Shrovetide season. The Saturday preceding Shrove Tuesday was sometimes called Egg Saturday, because of the number of eggs eaten on the day, and during Shrovetide there were also egg-based customs that mirror those carried out at Easter, as described in

Marianne Dacombe's collection of material from Women's Institutes in Dorset, published in 1935:

In the 19th century at Powerstock there was a curious Shrovetide custom called 'egg shackling' which took place in the school. The children elected a committee and a judge, and there were prizes for the whitest, the brownest, the biggest, and the smallest eggs. Then all the eggs were gently shaken in a sieve. As each egg got a little crack, it was taken out, until the strongest one remained – and this one received the biggest prize.

Egg shackling still takes place at two schools in Somerset – at Stoke St Gregory and Shepton Beauchamp.

Compare **Easter Day: Eggs**, p. 153.

Ludlow Rope-Pulling

This Shrovetide competition formerly took place at Ludlow in Shropshire and involved an immense tug-of-war. According to an account of the custom in 1826, published by William Hone, the 36-yard rope was supplied by the corporation and passed out of the Market Hall window at four o'clock on Shrove Tuesday. The two contesting parties were made up of different halves of the town, and nearly 2,000 people could take part. It was traditional for the losing side to make a collection and buy back the rope for a second contest, and sometimes a third. The overall victors would sell the rope and use the money to entertain themselves. The event began to get out of hand with so many people taking part, and it was suppressed in 1851. Two theories of origin were current: the first was that the corporation knew how the custom started but were keeping it secret; the second was that it commemorated the struggles between the respective supporters of Henry VI and the Duke of York, whose base was at Ludlow Castle, in the Wars of the Roses during the fifteenth century.

The old custom was the inspiration for an annual tug-of-war contest started in the early 1980s between customers of two Ludlow pubs, The Bull and The Feathers, which takes place on Boxing Day (or the day after if Boxing Day falls on a Sunday).

Pancakes

It is somehow appropriate that the last surviving Shrovetide custom for most of us is that we still try to eat pancakes on this day. The connection between Shrove Tuesday and the pancake is a genuinely old one, and *Pasquils Palinodia* (1619) shows that the fun of tossing was well understood from early times:

> *It was the day whereon both rich and poor*
> *Are chiefly feasted with the self same dish,*
> *Where every paunch, till it can hold no more,*
> *Is fritter-filled, as well as heart can wish;*
> *And every man and maid do take their turn,*
> *And toss their pancakes up for fear they burn;*
> *And all the kitchen doth with laughter sound,*
> *To see the pancakes fall upon the ground.*

Three hundred years later, essentially the same scene was repeated in cottages up and down the country. In *A Kind of Magic*, Mollie Harris remembered a telling incident from her Oxfordshire childhood in the 1920s:

The excitement of pancake day in our house had to be seen to be believed, for no other day in the year could afford such luxuries. The fun began as soon as our mother brought her big wash-stand jug from the bedroom and set it on the kitchen table. Into it went a quart of skimmed milk that one of us fetched from Sarah Clarke's, and several eggs from our own hens, all whipped up together with plenty of plain flour into a creamy frothy mixture. A new frying pan – another annual event for the great day – and a pound of best lard to cook the pancakes in, and we were all set to begin. Our mother's face was flushed and happy, her hair untidily wispy as she bent over her task. The fire burnt fiercely, so that she had to hold the pan above the flames. As each pancake was cooked it was doled out to the members of the family in turn, according to one's age, the eldest first.

The room was filled with squealing and laughing as our mother skilfully tossed each pancake high in the air. Blue smoke rose from the boiling fat and there was a strong smell of lemon as she slipped the long-awaited treat on to each plate. At last, it was Ben's turn, he was last-but-one on the list. He had waited patiently for almost an hour, and as she tossed the pancake mother cried, 'Whose turn is it this time?' 'Mine,' Ben shouted excitedly, and he rushed forward, plate in hand and tried to catch it as it came down – our mother tried to do the same thing. She gave him a quick shove, and he went backside first into a bucket of water and she herself, slightly off balance, stumbled a couple of steps sideways onto the sleeping cat. The hot pancake landed right on top of the squealing animal who made a bee-line for

*the door. Someone rushed to open it and the cat streaked out, completely en-
veloped in the cooked batter. 'That's yours boy, go and get it,' Mother yelled
to him above the din as Ben heaved himself up from the bucket; with water
dripping from his trousers he rushed out into the garden. Minutes later he
came back, stuffing lumps of fluff-covered pancake into his mouth, having
cornered his quarry in the wash-house.*

The midday bell which, before the Reformation, had called the faithful
to be 'shriven' on **Shrove Tuesday** (p. 62) continued to be rung in many
places, and was popularly called the 'pancake bell', being regarded as a
signal for the housewife to get the pan on the fire, and schoolchildren
and apprentices to stop work for the day. In 1950, the journal *Folk-Lore*
recorded that in Bedfordshire:

*The 'pancake bell' is still rung, from 11.50 till noon, and the local schoolchil-
dren run to nearby Conger Hill to put their ear to the ground to 'hear the old
lady frying her pancakes' underground.*

As with all feast foods, it was held by many to be inadvisable to
neglect the custom. Robert Forby's *Vocabulary of East Anglia* (1830) contains the advice: 'Shrove Tuesday: Ill luck betides the family in which
pancakes are not served up on that day.'

There seems to be no deep symbolic reason why pancakes should
have been so firmly connected with Shrovetide, and the practical reason that it used up the remaining milk, eggs, and fat before the Lenten
fast makes perfect sense. The words 'pancake' and 'fritter' (the latter
from the French and related to the word 'fry') are both first recorded
in the mid fifteenth century, but there is no reason to believe that the
delicacy itself was new at that time.

Pancake Races

All over the country, in the dull days of February, one of the standard
ways that come to mind when a quick charity or fun event is needed
is a pancake race. One place can claim to be the originator of this
custom: the town of Olney in Buckinghamshire. For many years, in
unbroken tradition, the women of Olney have run in their annual
Shrove Tuesday race, tossing pancakes as they go, and since 1950 have
even competed with the town of Liberal in Kansas for the world title. Competitors at Olney must be over eighteen and residents of the
town. For the race they must wear the traditional 'housewife' costume
of skirt, apron, and headscarf or hat, although this dress code still

leaves plenty of scope for parody and/or fancy dress. The race route has changed a little over time, and now starts from the Bull Hotel, in the market square, and runs alongside rather than through the churchyard, but the length remains at the original 415 yards and the fastest time stands at 58.5 seconds.

The modern race was founded in 1948 by the Revd R. W. Collins, newly appointed vicar of the church of Sts Peter and Paul. He set the course, laid down the rules, and was the presiding presence for many years, an involvement that set the pattern for a strong church element in the custom. But Revd Collins always claimed that he revived the custom, rather than invented it, and he presented as evidence some cuttings from the 1920s that show women (hatted and aproned and holding frying pans) posing with the vicar and the sexton. However, in Graham Lenton's recent book on the custom, local resident Mrs Ivy Perkins remembers that in the 1920s there was no race, and states that they simply walked to the church with their pancakes. An article in *The Times* on 22 February 1939 is the first to describe the race, and claimed that it had been revived fourteen years previously but had recently lapsed.

Despite this confusion, it seems on present evidence that a church-based custom – not necessarily a race – was invented in the 1920s, which was embellished into a race before the Second World War and revived again soon after it. A further search of the local newspapers of the time would probably provide the details. This is very different to the widely accepted story, which claims that the race dates back to 1445 when a harassed housewife heard the Shrove bell and rushed to the church still holding her frying pan. Others have embellished the tale, stating that housewives tried to bribe the churchwarden with pancakes to ring the bell so that the Shrovetide festivities could begin earlier. However, these stories, interesting though they are as traditional tales, are not supported by the documentary evidence. As Graham Lenton points out, standard histories of the area and other pre-twentieth-century writers from the village make no mention of the custom, and nor does anyone anywhere else.

Westminster Pancakes

A custom which is unique to Westminster School in London but which combines the traditional Shrove Tuesday elements of **pancakes** (p. 76) and rough **scrambling customs** (p. 172) is the 'Pancake greaze'.

The latter word is also apparently unique to the school, meaning a 'scrum' or 'crowd'. On Shrove Tuesday morning, the school cook is brought in procession to the middle of the old schoolroom, carrying a frying pan that contains an oversized pancake, which he tosses, straight from the pan, over a high metal bar that runs across the middle of the room, to the waiting boys on the other side. Margaret Brentnall, in her *Old Customs and Ceremonies of London* (1975), writes:

Then, suddenly, the frying pan was swung and up soared the pancake – up and (good throw!) over the bar. At once pandemonium broke loose and the boys became a scrambling mass of bodies where the pancake fell. Then, from the whirl of legs and arms, several triumphant figures emerged, each clutching a piece of mangled pancake. These were duly weighed and the winner, overcome with glory, was presented with the award.

The boy who gets the biggest piece is presented with a sovereign by the Dean of Westminster.

The game was first mentioned as an established event in the 1750s, and since then it has undergone only two changes: in 1885 the participation was restricted to a representative of each form rather than the whole school, and in the late twentieth century fancy dress for the players was introduced.

Purbeck Marblers and Stonecutters

The Company of Marblers and Stonecutters was probably formed in medieval times, to protect the monopoly rights of workers in the lucrative Purbeck marble industry in Dorset. The rules that regulate the Company were laid down in 1651, but they were already then described as 'ancient'. The Company meets annually on Shrove Tuesday at Corfe Town Hall and, although fewer in number than in former times, it continues to regulate the business of the trade, which is still in the hands of certain local families. The members are summoned by the tolling of a bell to meet at noon. After a short service, various ceremonies are carried out, including the induction of apprentices, who, having reached the age of twenty-one, are accepted as freemen on payment of 33 pence (6s. 8d.), one penny loaf, and two pots of beer. In addition, the last married man in the Company brings a football, which is kicked along the streets from Corfe Castle to Owre, to preserve the right of way, essential in the past for getting the stone to the quay.

St Columb Hurling

The Cornish town of St Columb is one of only two places that have retained an annual hurling match, a game that was formerly very widespread in the county. The game here is still played in the streets, and begins at 4.30 p.m. in the market square on Shrove Tuesday and again on the following Saturday. Local traders barricade their premises for protection, as the game can involve hundreds of players and there are few rules to control them.

Hurling (p. 50) is played with a silver ball, about the size of an orange, made of wood or cork and coated in silver. The game begins when the ball is thrown up by last year's winner, or a local celebrity, standing on a stepladder in the market square, with the cry of the game's motto, 'Town and country do your best. But in this parish I must rest.' The ball can be thrown or carried but is rarely kicked, and while sometimes it is lost in a scrum, at other times the play moves fast through the streets with the ball frequently changing hands. For the first hour of the game, play traditionally stays in the streets around the town centre, but after that it can break in any direction. The game is ostensibly between town and country, and each goal is about two miles apart. Each team tries to get the ball to their goal, or to carry it across the parish boundary in any direction. The first to do either of these feats wins the game and is carried shoulder-high back to the square. Play often pauses as the ball is deliberately passed to an elderly or disabled person, or even into one of the adjoining properties, and before women started joining in it was not unknown for young men to try to gain the ball to impress the young women, as recorded in 1972 by A. Rabey, author of an informative booklet on the game:

Many a young hurler has endeavoured to find favour with the young lady of his choice by obtaining the ball for her, often at great personal risk to life and limb, or so it appears, which when handed to the fair one, causes the great mass of hurlers to stand gallantly back as she re-starts the game by throwing the ball back to her would-be sweetheart.

The winner may keep the ball, which is made locally in a traditional manner, but she or he must pay for a replacement.

St Columb can claim to be the home of Cornish hurling in the sense that the earliest written record of the game that can be assigned to a particular place is found in the *St. Columb Green Book*, which includes references to silver balls in 1594–5.

See also 3 **February: St Ives Hurling**.

Sedgefield Ball Game

The annual ball game at Sedgefield in County Durham is one of the survivors of the old Shrove Tuesday football, played in this case with a ball about the size of a cricket ball, which can be kicked, carried, or thrown. At the start and finish of the game, the ball is passed through the metal bull-ring on the village green. Traditionally, the game was played between the tradesmen and the countrymen, as in this account from 1884:

The ball was put through the bull-ring in the middle of the village green exactly at 1pm on Tuesday . . . and was then in for play. Both sides were determined to win or die, as it were, and more reckless play we have not witnessed. No rules were adhered to, and scraped shins became the order of the day. After play lasting three hours and fifteen minutes, the tradesmen were declared the victors, they having succeeded in passing the ball over the pond.

In the modern game there are still no real rules and play is fairly rough, but the action stops occasionally to let a child or pensioner in the crowd have a lucky kick at the ball.

It is not clear how old the Sedgefield game is, as records only go back to the nineteenth century, but confident assertions of 900 years or more, regularly made in the local press, can be discounted.

See also **Football**, p. 64.

Shroving and Lent-Crocking

Shrove Tuesday was one of several days in the year on which parties of children or young people went from house to house, recited a rhyme, and expected gifts of food or money from the householder. The custom went under various names: 'shroving' was the usual term, but Lent-crocking, Nickanan Night, Lansherd Night, and others were also recorded. The rhyme also varied considerably, but it always included a request for gifts, as here from Oxfordshire in 1903:

> *Pit-a-pat! the pan's hot,*
> *I be come a-Shroving;*

> *A bit of bread, a bit of cheese*
> *Or a cold apple dumpling*
> *Up with the kettle! Down with the pan!*
> *Give me a penny, and I'll be on.*

In some cases, however, there could be retaliation if they were not satisfied. The shrovers carried broken crockery or stones, which they threw, or at least threatened to throw, at the doors of anyone who refused to contribute. In other instances, the visitors did not request largesse at all, but simply went round at night and threw the sherds or stones at the door of anyone who had displeased them in recent months, or who they thought needed punishing for some reason. It is not entirely clear whether these two forms are facets of the same custom, or were distinct customs that happened to share some characteristics. Two experts on the subject, Peter Robson and Ronald Hutton, both argue for two separate customs, but the matter is not yet closed.

In some reports, there is more than a hint of what is elsewhere called Mischief Night (*see* 31 **October: Mischief Night**). In 1871, the physician and author Jonathan Couch recorded the following example from Polperro in Cornwall:

On the day termed 'Hall' Monday, which precedes Shrove Tuesday, about the dusk of the evening, it is the custom for boys, and in some cases for those above the age of boys, to prowl about the streets with short clubs, and to knock loudly at every door, running off to escape detection on the slightest sign of a motion within. If, however, no attention be excited, and if any article be discovered negligently exposed, or carelessly guarded, then the things are carried away; and on the following morning are seen displayed in some conspicuous place, to expose the disgraceful want of vigilance supposed to characterise the owner. The time when this is practised is called 'Nicky-Nan-Night'.

Like many other house-visiting customs, shroving appears to have been restricted to certain areas of the country, in this case the South and West; the custom has been reported from Hertfordshire, Buckinghamshire, Oxfordshire, Berkshire, Wiltshire, Hampshire, the Isle of Wight, and especially all the counties of the West Country. The earliest references to shroving customs come from the turn of the nineteenth century, although Hutton quotes a similar stone-throwing custom on the Scilly Isles in the 1740s.

See also 24 **January: Eve of Conversion of St Paul** for another variation on the 'crockery-throwing' theme.

Skipping

Several places in the country had an annual long-rope skipping custom on **Good Friday** (*see* p. 146), but at Scarborough in Yorkshire it was, and still is, carried out on Shrove Tuesday. Hundreds of people turn out with their old washing lines and skipping ropes and, weather permitting, spend the afternoon on the foreshore, which is closed to traffic. With someone at each end doing the turning, and others of all ages and abilities doing the jumping, a lively and energetic afternoon is spent in the seaside air. The mayor rings a bell at noon to signal the start of the session. This official sanction is not a new thing, according to the *Dalesman* (April 1994):

[A previous article] *brought back memories of the 1920s and 30s, in particular of Johnny Jackson, a gents tailor and outfitter whose shop was at the bottom of Queen Street. A small dapper man in morning suit, homburgh hat, military moustache and spats who during his term as mayor rang the starting bell and then skipped in every rope from the Spa to sand-side.*

As at Brighton in Sussex, tradition links the skipping with the local fishing industry, who, it is claimed, finished their line-fishing season at this time of year and after sorting out their ropes gave any worn-out ones to local children.

Mass skipping is a well-entrenched local custom at Scarborough and needs no ancient legend to keep it going. However, theories that it is an ancient magical rite to make the crops grow are not helped by the fact that it cannot be proven that it was carried out here before 1903.

Whipping Toms

An apparently unique custom took place in Leicester every Shrove Tuesday until suppressed in 1846. At the annual fair that was held in the area of the town called the Newarke, various traditional sports such as **cock throwing** (p. 71), shinty (akin to hockey), and **football** (p. 64) were played, but later in the day the 'Whipping Toms' appeared, who claimed the right to use a cart-whip on anyone still in the area. This licensed attack was not without rules, however. The Toms wore a blindfold over one eye, and they were not allowed to whip above the knee,

Scambling Days

In most parts of the country, to 'scamble' signified the action of indulging in a makeshift meal; hence the term 'Scambling Days', which were the Mondays and Saturdays in Lent. On these days, no regular meals were prepared, and people had to make whatever shift they could to keep from going hungry. 'Scambling' (often spelled 'skambling') has an interesting history. It pre-dates the word 'scrambling', to which it is closely related, and meant both 'to scatter', and 'to struggle', often in the sense of contesting for money, sweets, or food thrown to a crowd, as the *Oxford English Dictionary* puts it, 'in an indecorous and rapacious manner'.

or anyone who was kneeling down or who was willing to pay a small fine. When the Toms appeared, most of the people who remained in the Newarke did so specifically to play the game of dodging the whips, and they wore stout boots and carried sticks to help in their defence. Nevertheless, as often happened with such customs in the mid nineteenth century, many local worthies objected to the rough play and in 1846 they sponsored a private Act of Parliament that banned playing at 'Whipping Toms, shindy, football, or any other game' on the Newarke on Shrove Tuesday. Attempts by the locals to continue the custom in 1847 were thwarted by the police.

Ash Wednesday

Compared to the wild abandon and activity of **Shrove Tuesday** customs (p. 62), Ash Wednesday was a universal day of penitence, and the first day of Lent. Its date depends on the timing of Easter, and it can fall anywhere between 4 February and 11 March. Ash Wednesday gets its name from the pre-Reformation rite that was carried out on the day, in which a priest would bless ashes (sometimes made from burning the 'palms' used in the previous year's Palm Sunday service), sprinkle them with holy water, and place some on the foreheads of the kneeling congregation. Words were intoned while this was carried out, which can be translated as 'Remember, man, that thou art dust and to dust thou shalt return.' The use of ashes was abolished in England in 1548 as one of Edward VI's Protestant reforms, but the name 'Ash Wednesday' has lived on in popular parlance to the present day and it is given in the *Book of Common Prayer* as a subtitle for the First Day of Lent.

At least a memory of the old Ash Wednesday survived into the Victorian era and beyond, in the form of which foods were deemed suitable for the day. In 1865, John Fisher recorded in his *History and Antiquities of Masham and Mashamshire* (Yorkshire):

On Ash Wednesday the good people of Masham certainly do not put on sackcloth and ashes. Our fathers and grandfathers used so far to observe this day as to dine upon salt-fish; but we, of the present generation, dine on what we like best or rather upon what some of us can get, and the day is not now otherwise observed.

And the journal *Folk-Lore* reported in 1929 that in Cumberland:

On Ash Wednesday, many folks mek tatie ash, tul t' dinner' (i.e. meat, potatoes, and an onion stewed together).

Jack-a-Lent

One of the most fascinating, but elusive, figures of this season was Jack-a-Lent, sometimes spelled 'Jack o' Lent', who was particularly associated with Ash Wednesday:

An old custom, now quite defunct, was observed here not long since in the beginning of Lent. A figure made up of straw and cast-off clothes was drawn or carried round the town, amid much noise and merriment, after which it was either burnt, shot at, or brought to some other ignominious end. The image was called Jack o'Lent, and was, doubtless, intended to represent Judas Iscariot. A dirty slovenly fellow is often termed a Jack o' Lent.

This appearance in Cornwall in 1871 is a very late example of a figure that had existed in England since at least the 1550s, and was clearly a proverbial character by the seventeenth century, when poets and playwrights often used the name to signify a worthless, empty person, or someone who was attracting universal opprobrium, as in Francis Quarles's *Shepheards' Oracles* (1646):

> How like a Jack a Lent
> He stands, for boys to spend their Shrovetide throws,
> Or like a puppit made to frighten crows.

The Jack figure was made of wood and straw and dressed in old clothes, and could be hung up in public for the duration of Lent, for all and sundry to throw things at ('three throws a penny', according to a line in Act IV, scene 2 of Ben Jonson's play *Tale of a Tub* (1640)), or he could be paraded around the town streets and then attacked and destroyed. Either way, he was there simply to be mistreated – pelted with sticks, stones and filth, shot at, torn apart, and finally burnt.

As in the Cornish example quoted above, some writers thought that our Jack represented Judas Iscariot, but this seems to have been a later idea. It was more widely assumed that he was the target of people's aggression because he signified Lent. Although there is little evidence that English people indulged in the extended bacchanalian festival of Carnival so well known in medieval times on the Continent and portrayed in paintings like *The Fight Between Carnival and Lent* (1559) by Peter Bruegel the Elder, the Jack-a-Lent figure certainly provides some cross-channel parallels. Among other things, the continental festival usually involved street theatre with personifications of Carnival and Lent, and the earliest reference to Jack-a-Lent in England indicates at least the germ of a dramatic representation. Henry Machyn recorded a sheriff of London's parade in his diary on 17 March 1552/3, which involved numerous characters, including minstrels, giants, hobby horses, morris dancers, and a priest shriving a Jack-of-Lent. He was followed by Jack-of-Lent's wife, who was offering a thousand pounds to a physician to save Jack's life.

In later years, the English traditional calendar included a number of very similar customs where a figure was mistreated, reviled, and destroyed, although they had no recorded connection with Lent (*see* **Rough Music**, p. 95; **Easter Day: Riding the Lord**, p. 164; **Easter Monday: Black Knight of Ashton**, p. 167; **24 August: West Witton Burning of Bartle**; and **5 November: Guy Fawkes Night**). A detailed study of these 'stuffed figure' customs may possibly help to illuminate the nature of Jack-a-Lent himself, and vice versa.

Friday following
Ash Wednesday

Pully Lug Day

Two reported customs involve the belief that, at certain sanctioned times, one can pull another's ears with impunity. In nineteenth-century Cumberland and Westmorland, the Friday following Ash Wednesday was Pully Lug Day or Nippy Lug Day for schoolchildren, at least until midday. A correspondent to *Notes & Queries* wrote in 1878:

I have a recollection . . . of one of the day-scholars coming up to me one day, and, exclaiming 'Pully-lug day', forthwith proceeding to pull my 'lugs'.

But in Carlisle, and possibly elsewhere, there existed the idea that one could pull ears on mayor-making day, which in Carlisle was held on 9 November. This is a localized example of a belief that between the retirement of the outgoing mayor and the installation of the new one, normal laws and social conventions do not apply (*see* **Lawless Hours and Days**, p. 412).

29 February

Leap Year Day

The concept of the leap year was introduced by Julius Caesar in his reform of the calendar in 45 BC, in order to correct a small but irritating discrepancy in calculating the length of the solar year, which is 365 days and 6 hours rather than a conveniently round figure. An extra day every four years brings us more or less back in line. But even this is not really accurate enough, which is why centennial years are only leap years if they are divisible by 400 (e.g. the year 1900 was not a leap year, but 2000 was).

By far the most widespread feature of the leap year in British tradition has long been that it is only in that year that women are allowed to propose marriage, and some even go so far as to argue that this 'ladies' privilege' only existed on Leap Year Day itself. It is often confidently asserted that this notion was enshrined in Scottish law at the time of Queen Margaret, in 1288 (or 1228 in other versions), and that if a man did not accept the proposal, the penalty was a fine of one hundred pounds (although some versions say 'one pound'). But this in itself is a myth, and no one has yet produced any evidence of such a law's actual existence. It is also declared, with a similar lack of evidence, that in England a man who refused such an offer could only redeem himself by buying his proposer a new silk gown. The woman herself had to wear a red petticoat when making the proposal. If this were true, every unmarried woman throughout history could have had a wardrobe full of silk gowns simply for the asking and for the price of one cheap petticoat.

The real origin of the 'ladies' privilege' idea is not known, and its early history is not easy to pin down. It was certainly in existence by 1606, when it was described in the book *Courtship, Love and Matrimony*, but a couplet attributed to Chaucer by Vincent Stuckey Lean in his mammoth *Collectanea* (1905) has so far proved impossible to verify:

> *In Leap Year they have power to chuse*
> *The men no charter to refuse*

Nevertheless, in the legendary sphere, a well-known story explains that the leap-year privilege is an early example of feminist agitation for reform of a patriarchal society. The right was reluctantly conceded by St Patrick, in answer to St Bridget's complaint that it was unfair that women were not allowed to propose. Patrick made the offer of allowing women to propose once in seven years, but Bridget bargained him down to once every four years. But the face of matrimony, and relations between the sexes, have changed so much in the last few decades that if the newspapers did not make a feature of the belief every four years, it is unlikely that many of today's young women would know that there ever had been any objection to their initiating a proposal.

There have probably been other notions about the leap year which have not survived. For example, a glimpse of how things were seen over a thousand years ago was provided by R. T. Hampson in 1841, who included the following extract from a 'Saxon document' in his book on the medieval calendar:

Some priests assert that the bissextus [Leap Year Day] comes through this, that Joshua prayed to God that the sun might stand still for one day's length when he swept the heathens from the land, as God granted him.

The incident in question is detailed in Joshua 10:12–14. The natural world apparently cares little about human proposals, but is nevertheless well aware of the existence of the leap year. It was widely thought that broad beans, and other plants, 'grow the wrong way' in a leap year. This idea is still regularly mentioned in gardening circles, although nobody seems to know exactly what the 'wrong way' actually means in this context.

MARCH

Dame Elizabeth Marvyn Charity

This annual dole emanates from the will of Dame Elizabeth Marvyn, who died in 1581. She was buried at St Peter's church in Ufton Nervet, Berkshire, and a tablet there gives the following details:

Lady Marvin in 1581, gave 10 bushels of Wheat to be made into good household bread, 12½ ells of canvass at 1s per ell for shirts and smocks, and also 12½ yards of narrow blue cloth at 1s 3d per yard for coats and cassocks. She did by her will charge divers lands and hereditaments at Ufton and elsewhere with the payment of a sufficient sum of money to purchase the said wheat, canvass and blue cloth. To be annually distributed about the middle of Lent.

A loaf of bread is now given to local people from a window of Ufton Court, in March. The linen has been transmuted into a pair of sheets given to each of nine old-age pensioners who must have lived in the parish at least ten years.

1 March

St David's Day

St Dewi, anglicized as St David, was a sixth-century monk and bishop. He was the only Welsh saint to be officially recognized in the wider Christian community, and was adopted as patron saint of Wales in the twelfth century. Little is known for certain about his life. As Wales's patron saint, his legendary exploits, and customs of his feast day, are largely the province of Welsh folklore, and perhaps this is why St David's Day seems to have had a very low profile in English lore, except insofar as it is reflected in relations between the two neighbouring nations.

There are several recorded instances in the seventeenth century of members of the royal court, including the monarch himself, wearing leeks on St David's Day. At a more popular level, however, traditional antipathy and derision have been more evident, most famously described by Shakespeare in *Henry V* (1599), in which the English braggart Pistol makes fun of the Welsh captain Fluellen's wearing of a leek on St David's Day, and is forced to eat the vegetable, skin and all (Act V, scene 1). Here, it is the English captain, Gower, who supports his Welsh colleague and berates Pistol for mocking 'an ancient tradition, begun upon an honourable respect and worn as a memorable trophy of predeceased valour'. Nevertheless, there was also a custom of hanging Welshmen in effigy on their day, as recorded by Samuel Pepys in his diary for 1 March 1667, and also by visiting Dutchman William Schellinks in his journal in 1662:

. . . being St. David's Day, the day of the patron saint of Wales, when according to ancient tradition, all people born in that principality put a leek in the band of their hats. That is supposed to be in memory of a battle fought and won by them on St. David's Day, in which they wore them in a mark to distinguish themselves from their enemies. So his Majesty and many great Lords and gentlemen, common people, and even lackeys, coachmen, porters, and all kinds of riff-raff and layabouts wear one in their hats. We saw some countryfolk carry such large leeks on their hats that their heads hung almost sideways because of them. And so on this day the Welshmen are greatly teased by the English, not only by calling after them Taffey, Taffey, or David, David, but also by hanging out all kinds of dolls and scarecrows with leeks on their heads, and as they celebrate the day with heavy boozing, and both sides, from the ale, strong beer, sack and claret, become short-tempered, obstinate and wild, so it is not often that this day goes by without mishaps, and without one or the other getting into an argument or a blood fight. It happened this year that near Westminster a Welsh nobleman stabbed an Englishman. So too an English cook who, for fun, stuck a leek on his hat and addressed, as a fellow countryman, a great lord, a Welshman, who passed by with his suite, who responded in Welsh, which is as different

from English as French is from Dutch. When the cook replied sneeringly in English, the lord went for him, the cook fled into his shop and grabbed a spit from the fire and with this attacked the Welshman, who, supported by his servants with their rapiers, all turned against the cook, who was immediately helped by all sorts of rabble, throwing dirt and other things, so that in the end he was compelled to retreat, and the furore getting greater, he was forced to take to the water, and, although he had got help, the mob, fighting furiously, got into the boat, and if his Majesty had not sent help quickly by water, they could easily have been killed . . .

Nearly one hundred years later, the *Poor Robin's Almanack* for 1757 confirmed that the custom still continued: 'But it would make the stranger laugh / To see th' English hang poor Taff'; and English bakers offered gingerbread figures for sale, fixed on skewers and called 'taffies'.

The connection between St David's Day and the leek has never been satisfactorily explained, although the most often quoted story is that St David prompted his countrymen to wear the plant in their hats while in battle with the invading Saxons, in order to distinguish themselves from the enemy, a story that imbues the leek with a defiantly anti-English symbolism. But another legend, also referred to by Shakespeare in *Henry V*, held that Welsh archers, doing service alongside their English brethren at Crécy in 1346 or Poitiers in 1356, started the fashion.

The only other relatively widespread English tradition about St David's Day, reported from late Victorian times, was the warning to housewives that this was the day that fleas appeared, to plague humans for the rest of the year, as in the following example from Devon c.1890:

A house-maid advised Mrs. Hewett not to open her bedroom window on 1st of March, and said that she had heard that the black army always come down Exeter Hill, in swarms, on that day.

The arrival of the 'black army' was sometimes said to be the work of Satan; in a common saying, 'The Devil shakes a bag of fleas at everybody's door on 1st March.'

On a different note, the well-known weather proverb 'March comes in like a lion and goes out like a lamb', has been a commonplace since at least the second half of the seventeenth century, when several writers included it in their books. But some proverb authorities since that time have reported different versions with rather obscure imagery, which have never been properly explained. These sayings preface the well-known words 'comes in like a lion' with phrases such as 'March black ham' or 'March hack ham'. The only version that seems to make any sense is 'March black ram', which some have seen as a reference to the astrological ram of Aries, although the case remains open.

For a rhyme about the weather in the first three days of March, *see* **3 March: St Winwaloe's Day**.

2 March

St Chad's Day

Ceadda or Chad (died 672) was the first bishop of the newly converted kingdom of Mercia, and he made his seat at Lichfield. No major customs seem to have been attached to his feast day, although there were a fair number of churches dedicated to his name, and he achieved lasting fame in the sphere of medicinal wells. A number of wells with a healing reputation bore his name, including one in Lichfield which was claimed in the eighteenth century to be the very one in which the saint himself had bathed. A more famous one in Gray's Inn Road near King's Cross, London, developed into a popular spa and then a pleasure garden; it lasted until 1860, when it was swept away during the building of the Metropolitan Railway.

According to the Venerable Bede, Chad's reputation for healing emerged immediately after his death, and his first wooden shrine had an aperture into which the devout could put their hands to gather pinches of dust to drop into water in order to make medicinal drinks for sick men and beasts.

3 March

St Winwaloe's Day

A somewhat obscure Breton saint of the sixth century; so obscure, in fact, that even the spelling of his name is uncertain: Winwaloe, Winneral, Winnold and Winnal are just some of the variations.

continued on page 99 ☞

Rough Music

'Rough music' customs were an unmistakable way for a community to condemn the behaviour or moral failings of particular individuals in their midst. They usually took place after dark and could involve scores of protesters, mostly men but including some women and even children, who processed around the locality and then mounted a prolonged demonstration outside the home of the object of their disapproval. These demonstrations took various forms across the country, but a constant feature was the deafening cacophony of noise: cooking pots were banged with spoons; stones were rattled in tins; shovels were beaten with hammers; horns, rattles, and drums were used; and people shouted, screamed, and bayed. 'Rough music' is thus a useful generic term for the basic element of the custom, but in reality the activity had a wide number of local names, including 'lew-balling', 'skimmington (skimmity) riding', 'riding the stang', 'ran-tanning', and 'stag-hunting'.

A well-organized rough music usually included lifelike effigies of the guilty parties, which were mounted on a pole (a 'stang'), a cart, or a donkey (facing its tail) and paraded around the neighbourhood. The climax involved the mistreatment and destruction of these figures, which could be torn to pieces, shot at, burnt, or thrown in the river. If the crowd could get hold of the real victims, male or female, they were very roughly handled, forced to take part in the procession, thrown in a pond, and almost murdered, but most accounts stress the symbolic, rather than the actual, violence.

The demonstrators followed some informal rules, which they believed made their activities perfectly legal. In the majority of cases, the affair lasted for three nights, and there was a set-piece verbal accusation, or 'nominy', which was often in rhyme and was shouted out as part of the proceedings. Many believed that anything could be said in the nominy as long as the actual names of the accused were not mentioned, so the declaration often started with an anonymous formula, as in this one from Effingham, Surrey, in 1869:

> **There is a man lives in this place**
> **He brought his servant to disgrace**
> **He beat her black, he beat her blue**
> **And beat her till her bones came through.**

It is clear that local police rarely took any action to prevent rough-music demonstrations. They made themselves scarce while it was going on, or sometimes maintained a discreet presence in the background, as if to ensure that the proceedings did not get out of hand. But this very presence gave the demonstrators a veneer of legitimacy. Rough music could be adapted to suit any sort of community disapproval, but the overwhelming number of documented cases focus on sexual or marital behaviour. Adultery, illegitimacy, overtly 'loose' sexual behaviour, ill-matched marriages, such as a young person marrying an old one, or a widow(er) marrying too soon, were regular motives, as in a case from Croydon in 1881:

A thrice married man has been getting it warm in the Leslie Park Road, where he lives. It is said that he has married his third wife six weeks after the death of the second, and his neighbours and friends have thought fit to demonstrate their disapproval of this proceeding in a very marked manner. They have smashed his windows, discharged fireworks outside his house, treated him and his bride to rough music, and indulged in various other manifestations of ill-feeling.

Men who beat their wives or neglected their families, women who beat or henpecked their husbands, and habitual scolds were all potential targets. A correspondent contributed a note to the *Folk-Lore Journal* in 1884 on the subject:

A few months ago, in a village not far from Stratford-on-Avon, I noticed a quantity of chaff before a house door; on my return home I mentioned that I supposed so-and-so was moving; when I was at once met with the reply, 'Because of the chaff at his door? Oh no, that is the way our people show their feelings for wife-beaters.

The chaff announced publicly that the man had been 'threshing' his wife.

Among the numerous published accounts of rough music, there are few written by participants, and this makes the diary entries of George James Dew, a young carpenter from Lower Heyford in Oxfordshire, particularly interesting. Dew was twenty-one when he recorded his impressions of a 'lew-belling' in his neighbourhood in 1867. Most of the usual elements – the discordant noise, the effigies, the general popular support, and the escalation over three nights – are present in his account. Dew is quite enthusiastic about the affair, but he does at least have second thoughts about the effects of his actions on any innocent parties involved. His account, edited by the historian Pamela Horn, is worth quoting in full:

[14 February 1867] **'Rough music' was heard tonight although not an organised band, on account of some misdeeds in the train between a married woman of Aston and George Coggins, baker, of Lower Heyford . . . the man in question is a drunkard.**

[15 February 1867] **This evening there was a regular organised band both at Aston and Heyford of 'rough music'. The Heyford party went down to George Coggins', and the Aston party following them. Afterwards they came back together and the rattle was most noisy; all the old tin and iron utensils I should think to be found in both parishes were rattling. George Coggins went to Banbury and came back by the last train. The musical party was awaiting his arrival at the station, but he popped into the waiting room, and they did not know he was there, else he would have had the honour (or rather the disgrace) of having a vast number of musicians to play to him in that strain which would have been suitable for the occasion – This has been the practice, in all occasions of known adultery or a man beating his wife. The punishment to the offenders must I am sure be very sharp. I somehow approve of it because it is a manifestation of the hatred of the public to such acts. They call it a 'skimmington' or 'lewbelling' . . .**

[16 February 1867] **A most tremendously noisy lew-belling tonight again for George Coggins. Our Heyford chaps went to Aston and played all round there, and then both came to Heyford to play. They had effigies of Mrs. Thomas and George Coggins; she with a large crinoline and bonnet, and he a stout fellow with his baking apron on. They were mounted on poles and were kissing each other at every short interval. They shot at these effigies when they got to the Bell Inn, and again as they passed George Coggins' house, but when they returned to here again they were both in flames and they burnt them, throwing about the flaming crinoline and apron and making such a rattle for the offender to hear as one would not easily forget. The place was swarmed with people and the old kettles rattled to a high pitch. I enjoyed it very much, because I never saw one carried out so well before – To look at the other side of the affair, although the discordant music was cheering and pleasing, is somewhat sad. This George Coggins, baker, has a wife faithful in every respect and such as a wife ought to be, but how dreadfully annoying must this disturbance be to her.**

There is no doubt that such activities had widespread popular support and were based on a feeling that they could reach those parts of community life that the law could not, and this underlying approval has been reaffirmed in the writing of many modern social historians. But the custom carried such a potential for sheer vindictiveness and moral fascism that a close reading reveals rough-music events to be as potentially dangerous and morally dubious as any other manifestation of mob rule. They were certainly open to a charge of hypocrisy. One wonders how many men in the rough-music band also knocked their wives around, or how many had committed adultery, or would do so, given half the chance. One wonders also how often the actions were prompted by inaccurate or spiteful rumour. A modern analogy might be drawn with those who recently attacked a paediatrician because they thought the word meant 'paedophile'. In many cases of rough music, it is implied that the crimes attracted attention because they were habitual, but in some instances, where we have unusually detailed information, there are indications of other underlying motives, such as disputes over money or property, and suggestions that the events were expressions of malice and naked aggression rather than pure moral indignation.

A particularly pointed version of rough music, called the 'Stag Hunt', existed in Devon and Somerset. In this, one of the villagers was chosen to be the 'stag', and dressed accordingly, complete with horns, if some could be procured. The others in the crowd acted as huntsmen and hounds, and 'pursued' the stag all around the town, accompanied by the usual rough-music sounds as well as a cacophony of hunting horns and baying dog noises. The chase studiously avoided approaching too close to the home of the victim until the climax of the affair, when he was finally 'caught' on the very doorstep and a bladderful of blood spilled. The symbolism of the Stag Hunt appears to be even more horrific than the usual rough-music antics of skimmingtons and stang-ridings elsewhere.

There are numerous historical accounts of rough-music events. Real-life examples occur in the diaries and memoirs of people such as Henry Machyn (for example on 22 February 1562/3) and Samuel Pepys (on 10 June 1667), as well as court records and newspaper reports from the seventeenth to twentieth centuries and folklore and local history publications from the mid nineteenth to the mid twentieth centuries. They were regularly mentioned in plays and poems of the sixteenth and seventeenth centuries, and well-known fictional treatments can be found in Hogarth's *Hudibras Encounters the Skimmington* (1726), and Thomas Hardy's *Mayor of Casterbridge* (1886).

His cult was quite popular in medi-eval England, particularly in Cornwall and East Anglia, and his day was regularly listed in almanacs. But except for the few places where churches were dedicated to him, or fairs held on his day, any lasting fame rested on the fact that his feast came third in the widespread rhyme which predicts stormy weather in the first days in March:

> First comes David, then comes Chad,
> And then comes Winneral as though he was mad.

5 March

St Piran's Day

One of Cornwall's most popular saints, and also known in Brittany and Wales, Piran (or Perran) probably originated from Ireland and died in Cornwall sometime around the year 480. Details of his life are decidedly sketchy, mainly because of the mistaken identification of him as the Irish saint Ciaran, which has all but destroyed any facts that might have otherwise survived. Piran was claimed as the patron saint of Cornish tin-miners, and they regularly took this day off work in his honour, although the only detail that has survived of their celebrations is that they always got roundly drunk.

6 March

See **14 December: St Tibba's Day**.

9 March

St Constantine's Day

Tradition has it that St Constantine was a Cornish chieftain, of un-certain date, who later became a monk, but the name is so common in early Britain that it is impossible to disentangle one figure from another. There is even some doubt about whether his feast day should be 9 or 11 March. One legend told of him (and of others) is that he was out stag-hunting when the chase drove the quarry into the vicinity of a holy hermit, who took the animal under his protection. When Constantine moved to strike the hermit in anger, Constantine became frozen to the spot and was unable to move a muscle until the holy man's prayers released him. Constantine was naturally so impressed that he immediately converted to Christianity.

A chapel dedicated to him existed at St Merran, and his feast day was celebrated with a game of **hurling** (p. 50). A holy well nearby had the useful attribute of allowing anyone to bring rain if they drew water from it and poured it out on the stone.

10 March

In many collections of traditional lore, the character of the days of middle and late March predict the weather for the rest of the year, although the sayings are often contradictory. At the turn of the twentieth century, for example, Sarah Hewett recorded in her *Peasant Speech of Devon* that 'If it does not freeze on the 10th of March, a fertile year may be expected.' But the *Shepherd's Kalendar* of c.1680 maintained that 'Mists or hoar frosts on the 10th of March betoken a plentiful year.' Perhaps we can blame the change of calendar in 1752 for the discrepancy (*see* p. xxix).

11 March

Penny Loaf Day

During the English Civil War, when the Nottinghamshire town of Newark was under siege from Parliamentary forces, local merchant and alderman Hercules Clay dreamt on three separate nights that his house was on fire. He took this as a warning and moved his family out, and, sure enough, his house was destroyed by artillery fire soon afterwards. Hercules was so impressed that he left money to the town corporation and the vicar to commemorate his escape with a special sermon and the distribution of penny loaves to the poor every year on 11 March, the very day of his deliverance. Clay died soon afterwards, in December 1644, and at least part of his bequest is still carried out.

By the late nineteenth century, the distribution of penny loaves was so popular with locals that the police were put under severe strain trying to keep order. Nottinghamshire writer J. Potter Briscoe recorded in 1876 that the distribution was then carried out at the town hall, and applicants had to enter in single file and were then locked in until the ceremony was over, to stop people coming up more than once for a loaf. In 1894, 2,000 children turned up, many of them from villages outside the town, and the trustees began to think of alternative ways to help the poor in the spirit of Clay's bequest. In 1899, instead of a general handout of loaves, poor local children were given boots, through the schools. The special service and sermon still continues each year at Newark parish church, attended by the mayor and members of the corporation, and a small loaf is now given to each of the members of the choir in remembrance of their benefactor.

For St Constantine's Day, *see* **9 March: St Constantine's Day**.

Second Monday in March

Commonwealth Day

Empire Day was inaugurated in 1901 and celebrated on 24 May, to mark the achievements of the British Empire. It was a day of popular festivity, but as the empire gradually disintegrated during the twentieth century, the patriotic fervour of the day became increasingly anachronistic. In 1958, it was renamed Commonwealth Day, and in 1977 the Commonwealth nations chose a new day for the celebrations – the second Monday in March – which is now celebrated in each country of the Commonwealth. The way in which the day is celebrated is deliberately left to each country to decide, although common themes are education, the benefits of democracy, and international links and cooperation. The Queen gives a special Commonwealth Day speech.

See also **24 May: Empire Day**.

12 March

St Gregory's Day

Pope Gregory the Great (*c.*540–604) holds a key position in the history of Christianity in England, as it was he who sent Augustine to convert the Anglo-Saxons. His feast day was thus given a high profile and celebrated in the early English Church, but this popularity does not seem to have translated into secular regard, and no known traditional customs took place on his day. Nevertheless, in the late 1930s, A. R. Wright and T. E. Lones reported from Lancashire:

The farmer and the cottager deem it necessary, in order to obtain a good crop of onions, to sow the seed on St. Gregory's day, which is called 'Gregory-gret onion'.

17 March

St Patrick's Day

St Patrick (*c.*390–*c.*461), the patron saint of Ireland, is enthusiastically celebrated wherever Irish people have settled. He was formerly famous all over the English-speaking world for bringing Christianity to Ireland, although the heroic, almost single-handed nature of his ministry has been greatly exaggerated and his two most famous exploits – banning all snakes from Ireland, and using the shamrock to explain the doctrine of the Trinity to doubting heathens – are much later accretions to his legend.

The key feature of his day has long been the wearing of the symbols of Irishness: the shamrock, the harp, the colour green, and, previously, a St Patrick's cross. The first mention of the shamrock as a national symbol is found in the early 1680s. The same source also describes the wearing of crosses on St Patrick's Day, and for centuries the two symbols existed side by side. Jonathan Swift, for example, wrote to his 'Stella' (Esther Johnson) from London in 1713:

The Irish folks were disappointed that the Parliament did not meet today, because it was St. Patrick's day; and the Mall was so full of crosses that I thought all the world was Irish.

Pudding-Pies

A number of different special or festive dishes went by the local name 'pudding-pies' in various parts of the country. In 1869, for example, *Notes & Queries* recorded that at Deddington Fair in Oxfordshire, principally a livestock mart held on St Cecilia's Day (22 November):

. . . woe betides the farmer when he gets home from the gathering, if he has not brought home some 'pudding-pies' . . . These are made by setting up a crust composed of flour mixed with milk or water, and mutton suet melted and poured into it hot. These crusts, which are set up like meat pie-crusts, are then placed in the sun for a day or two to stiffen. They vary in size from about three to four inches in diameter, and are about one inch deep. When thoroughly hard they are filled with the same materials as plum puddings are made of, and when baked are sold at twopence, threepence and fourpence each.

But in Kent in 1912, pudding-pies were quite different:

Throughout Lent the shops at Gravesend (Kent) sell 'pudding pies' (tartlets containing custard sprinkled with currants), and some people call the first Sunday in Lent 'Pudding-pie Sunday'. But I have been told that the pudding-pies should be eaten on the Sunday nearest the middle of Lent, i.e. Mothering Sunday.

Many other sources state that 'pudding-pies' were appropriate to Lent.

The sight of Irish children wearing crosses made of coloured paper or card, decorated with silks and ribbons, on this day was a regular occurrence until the early twentieth century. However, shamrocks and harps eventually took over. In her *Lincolnshire Calendar*, Maureen Sutton records that in the 1940s:

My grandmother would send my brothers and I a little Irish harp made from cardboard and covered in green, white and gold silk, it was lovely. We wore it to school on the day, or a bunch of shamrock pinned to our coat.

Today, in urban areas with large Irish populations, grand St Patrick's Day dances are held, although even in Ireland these major celebrations of St Patrick's Day appear to be a relatively recent phenomenon.

Beyond these celebrations by Irish communities, the day does not seem to have been marked by any other traditional customs in England. Indeed, John Brand's *Popular Antiquities* (1849) and A. R. Wright and T. E. Lones's *British Calendar Customs: England* (1936–40), which are the key texts for customs research, list no English events for the day at all. Perhaps the 'Irish' nature of the day was simply too strong to warrant any competition. Nevertheless, as with the wearing of Welsh leeks on 1 **March**, donning the Irish national emblem in England has frequently caused friction by bringing local tensions to the fore, and latent anti-Irish feelings, one of the least-attractive traits of English society, can often be seen below the surface. On 17 March 1944, two English women working in a munitions factory in Croydon recorded in their diary:

St. Patrick's Day today and a great many Irish melodies on Music While You Work [a BBC radio programme]. *Poor Moroney says that since the banning of travel to Ireland the people in the factory who don't like him make his life a burden to him by jibing at Ireland and the Irish.*

In an unrelated tradition, recorded in Robert Chambers' *Book of Days*, it was reported that 'The early English calendars pretend that on the 17th of March Noah entered the Ark (*introitus Noae in arcam*) and they add, under 29th of April, *Egressus Noae de arca*' (Noah left the Ark).

Braggot Sunday

'Braggot Sunday' is a colloquial name for Mid-Lent or **Mothering Sunday** (*see* p. 105), in recognition of one of the popular drinks of the day, variously spelled 'braggot', 'bragget', and 'bracket'. The precise composition of the drink varied, but it usually consisted of fermented honey and ale, and was therefore akin to mead or metheglin, and a byword for sweetness; in *The Miller's Tale*, Chaucer wrote 'Hir mouth was swete as bragot or the meeth.'

Wiggs

'Wigg' is a dialect word for a cake or bun, known virtually all over the country but meaning quite different things in each area. Correspondence on the subject published in *Notes & Queries* in 1874 includes descriptions as diverse as: an ordinary tea-cake (Durham and Northumberland); an elongated bun with carraway seeds (Lincolnshire); a plum bun (Lincolnshire); an oval cake with honey in the middle (Hampshire); and a plain half-penny bun (Bristol). The word has a long and respectable lineage, with the *OED* providing citations from 1376, including one from Good Friday (8 April) 1664, when Samuel Pepys ate a Lenten supper of 'wiggs and ale'.

Mothering Sunday

Mothering Sunday occurs on the fourth Sunday in Lent, otherwise known as Mid-Lent Sunday, and can fall anywhere between 1 March and 4 April. It was one of the few vernacular customs which was universally regarded as a good thing, and which therefore attracted no reformers who wanted it abolished. On this day, young people (usually women) who were working away from home would try to get back to visit their families, and, typically, bring them presents and share a family meal.

The two earliest references show that the custom was already well established in the mid seventeenth century. The first is from the diary of Richard Symonds, published in 1644:

Every mid-Lent Sunday is a great day in Worcester, when all the children and god-children meet at the head and chief of the family and have a feast. They call it the Mothering-day.

The second is from *Hesperides* (1648), the well-known collection of poems by Robert Herrick:

> *I'll to thee a simnell bring*
> *Gainst thou go'st a mothering.*

These and almost all the other references to Mothering Sunday come from either the western counties of England, or from Wales, and it seems likely that it was a regional custom that gradually spread across the rest of the country; however, it was apparently never universal, as a correspondent to the *Gentleman's Magazine* of 1784 commented:

I happened to reside last year near Chepstow in Monmouthshire, and there for the first time heard of Mothering Sunday.

In its traditional form, it just about lasted into the twentieth century. The folklore collector Ella M. Leather commented that in Herefordshire in 1912:

The pretty custom of going a-mothering on Mid-Lent Sunday was generally kept up until a few years by the country people, and is now by no means forgotten, but declining. The confectioners' shops in Hereford are well stocked with Simnel cakes during Lent; they have an inscription in sugar icing, 'For my dear mother', or 'Mother'. Formerly these cakes were always made by the donors.

Various special foods have been recorded as traditional Mothering Sunday fare, including veal, rice pudding, and **frumenty** (p. 536), but by far the most common delicacy was the simnel cake, mentioned by Herrick in 1648 and again by Mrs Leather in 1912. Unfortunately, there seems to be no agreement on what constitutes a proper simnel, and Shrewsbury, Devizes, and Bury each claimed to have the *real* one. Folklorist Charlotte Burne described one version from her own experience in Shropshire in 1883:

They are very rich plum-cakes, encased in a crust of flour-and-water, coloured with saffron. They are made round, and rather flat, with a curiously-scalloped upper edge, and are first boiled for several hours, then brushed over with egg, and baked. Simnels are made in other towns besides Shrewsbury – notably Bury, in Lancashire – but the curious saffron crust and the singular manner of preparing the cake seem to be peculiar to our county.

She reprinted her grandmother's recipe for Bury simnels in the journal *Folk-Lore* in 1909:

To 3 lbs of flour add 3 lbs of currants, ½ lb of butter rubbed into the flour, 2 oz of candied lemon, 1½ oz of bitter almonds, ½ oz of cinnamon, ¾ lb of loaf sugar, the rinds of 2 large lemons, ½ lb of yeast, 5 eggs, the whites and yokes beaten separately, and a pint of cream. Mix it together and make it up immediately into simnels (i.e. in the shape described above). Let them stand to rise well on the tins, and bake in a moderate oven.

The word 'simnel' is attested in English at least from about 1300, coming to us from the French, but ultimately deriving from the Latin *simila* or 'fine flour'. Nevertheless, the traditional tale which explains the name is more colourful, as in this version from Shropshire, printed in Robert Chambers' *Book of Days* in 1864:

Long ago there lived an honest old couple, boasting the names of Simon and Nelly, but their surnames are not known. It was their custom at Easter to gather their children about them, and thus meet together once a year under the old homestead. The fasting season of Lent was just ending, but they had still left some of the unleavened dough which had been from time to time converted into bread during the forty days. Nelly was a careful woman, and it grieved her to waste anything, so she suggested that they should use the remains of the Lenten dough for the basis of a bake to regale the assembled family. Simon readily agreed to the proposal and further reminded his partner that there were still some remains of their Christmas plum pudding hoarded up in the cupboard, and that this might form the interior, and be an agreeable surprise to the young people when they made their way through the less tasty crust. So far, all things went on harmoniously; but when the cake was made, a subject of violent discord arose, Sim insisting that it should be boiled, while Nell no less obstinately contended that it should be baked. The dispute ran from words to blows, for Nell, not choosing to let her province in the household be thus interfered with, jumped up and threw the stool she was sitting on at Sim, who on his part seized a besom, and applied it with right good will to the head and shoulders of his spouse. She now seized the broom, and the battle became so warm, that it might have had a very serious result, had not Nell proposed as a compromise that the cake should be boiled first, and afterwards baked. This Sim acceded to, for he had no wish for further acquaintance with the heavy end of the broom. Accordingly, the big pot was set on the fire, and the stool broken up and thrown on to boil it, whilst the besom and broom furnished fuel for the oven. Some eggs, which had been broken in the scuffle, were used to coat the outside of the pudding when boiled, which gave it the shining gloss it possesses as a cake. This new and remarkable production in the art of confectionary became known by the name of the cake of Simon and Nelly, but soon only the first half of each name was alone preserved and joined together, and it has ever since been known as the cake of Sim-Nel, or Simnel.

The festival of Mothering Sunday was somewhat hijacked by Christian writers who declared, on no evidence other than the word 'mother', that the day had originally been the day on which people went home to visit their 'mother' church. Nevertheless, it is the churches that have kept its memory alive into recent times. In post-war Britain, child- and mother-centred services became customary, as a letter to *The Times* (4 April 1954) makes clear:

I should like to point out that Mothering Sunday in our village has not died out, but is a great occasion for the children. The older children go as a family to Holy Communion in the early morning, and in the afternoon the Sunday School children take their mothers to the Parish Church. Each takes its mother to the altar to receive a posy. A large iced cake made especially for the occasion by young wives of the church is blessed and a piece given to each parent. The Mid-Lent service is a red-letter day for the children.

But in the same timeframe, for non church-goers, Mothering Sunday has been almost completely eclipsed by the imported **Mother's Day** (*see below*).

See also **Shrovetide and Lent**, p. 60; **Braggot Sunday**, p. 104.

Mother's Day

Mother's Day was first suggested in 1907 by Miss Anna Jarvis, a schoolteacher in Philadelphia, who wished to do something to commemorate her own mother and, by extension, mothers everywhere. As a direct result of her energetic lobbying, Congress recognized the new day in 1913 and set it at the second Sunday in May.

In 1916, there were attempts by Mr J. A. Whitehead of Richmond, director of Whitehead Aircraft Ltd, and his friends, to introduce a similar day in Britain. The idea was enthusiastically supported by many celebrities of the day, including the Queen, the Bishop of London, and Lady Haig, and for a few years *The Times* made an annual announcement of the chosen date, in early August. There is little doubt that the new initiative was a symptom of the rise in national sentiment occasioned by involvement in the First World War, and little is heard of the idea after 1920. However, it appeared again in Britain soon after the Second World War, probably as a result of a

Its real success this time was due to commercial interests in the following decades, when the opportunity was taken to create a new market for cards and other gift items. In Britain, the new Mother's Day got tangled up with the existing **Mothering Sunday** (*see* p. 105), which was also undergoing a strong revival at the time, encouraged by the Church of England, and for decades the two existed side by side. But Mother's Day rapidly gained the upper hand, and it is probably true to say that except in church-going families, where Mothering Sunday is still enthusiastically kept up, Mothering Sunday is forgotten. If the wording on the cards available in shops is anything to go by, Mother's Day wins hands-down.

19 March

St Joseph's Day

As the husband of the Virgin Mary, St Joseph has naturally featured in numerous legends, and he has had plenty of devotees over the centuries; however, his day does not seem to have attracted any widespread traditional lore in England. Nevertheless, in her *Lincolnshire Calendar* (1997), Maureen Sutton did report the following advice: 'On St. Joseph's Day throw away the warming pan.'

21 March

St Benedict's Day

Benedict, founder of the influential Benedictine monastic order, was born around the year 480 and died on 21 March, around 550. His feast was therefore traditionally celebrated on the day of his death, but in the Roman Catholic Church it has been moved to 11 July. As with the other saints whose feast days fall at this time of year, Benedict's name is usually invoked in regard to weather and crops. The *Transactions of the Devonshire Association* (1973) recorded:

Where the wind is on 21 March it will prevail for the summer.

And in John Ray's *English Proverbs* (1670):

> *Saint Benedick*
> *Sow thy pease or keep them in thy rick.*

Weekday in late March

Oranges and Lemons Service

The church of St Clement Danes, which sits on a traffic island in the middle of the Strand in London, was built by Sir Christopher Wren in 1682, although the tower and spire were added by others at a later date. The first church on the site was believed to have been built by Danes, who settled nearby; hence the church's name. The church was very badly damaged by bombing in the Second World War, and when restored in the 1950s it became the official RAF church, dedicated to the memory of Allied airmen killed serving their country.

St Clement Danes has laid strong claim to be the church mentioned in the famous 'Oranges and Lemons' nursery rhyme, and a carillon that was installed in 1920 plays the tune every day at 9 a.m., 12 noon, 3 p.m. and 6 p.m., for all to enjoy. An annual children's service began that same year, and this still takes place in late March, attended by the pupils of St Clement Danes Primary School, which is itself over 300 years old. At the end of the service, the children are each given an orange and a lemon.

The 'Oranges and Lemons' rhyme is first recorded *c.*1744, but it is not unique, being simply the best known of several rhymes based on local church bells reported in various parts of the country. There is no way of knowing whether St Clement Danes is the one mentioned in the rhyme, as there is another London church dedicated to the same saint not far away in Eastcheap.

See also **23 November: St Clement's Day**.

25 March

Annunciation/Lady Day

This feast, commonly called Lady Day, celebrates the day on which the Angel Gabriel visited Mary and announced the conception of Christ (as related in Luke 1:26–38). Once the birth of Christ had been fixed at 25 December, it was a simple matter to count back nine months to set the date of the conception. For early Christians, the Annunciation, rather than the Nativity, was seen as the start of the Christian era, and 25 March was therefore viewed as the real New Year's Day. This had serious long-term repercussions on the way the calendar developed in England (*see* p. xxx).

Since at least late medieval times, Lady Day has been regarded as one of the key 'rent days' in the year – the time when rents and other legal payments were due, contracts were made, and periods of employment began or ended; although not always counted as one of the official 'quarter days', it retained this feature in many communities up and down the country. It was also a particularly popular time for **hiring fairs** (p. 470) and the merrymaking associated with such gatherings. In 1926, the *Transactions of the Devonshire Association* recorded:

Although servants are hired from Lady Day, they would not think of going to a new place until after the following Tuesday, which is known as 'Burgening [Bargaining] *day'. On that day they go to Bideford market* [in Devon]*, meet each other and, if they have not already done so, make their 'burgens' with their future employers.*

Tichborne Dole

One of the most famous surviving charity doles in the country takes place every year at Tichborne in Hampshire. Each year, on Lady Day, the inhabitants of Tichborne and Cheriton, near Winchester, are entitled to visit the big house at Tichborne Park to collect a gallon of flour for each adult (half a gallon for children), provided by the descendants of the Tichborne family, who have been prominent in village affairs since at least 1166. The flour is first blessed, and a short prayer said to remember Lady Mabella, the supposed originator of the dole. The flour is then dispensed from a large wooden hopper into the sacks and pillowcases brought by the locals.

Doles like these were common in England in the past, and many villages had similar distributions, but few have survived. Like the similar custom in Biddenden in Kent (*see* **Easter Monday: Biddenden Maids Charity**, p. 165), the Tichborne Dole is particularly memorable because of the unique, and suitably romantic, story of its origin.

In the time of Henry II (1154–89), as the much-loved Lady Mabella lay on her deathbed, she piously requested that her husband, Sir Roger Tichborne, should inaugurate an annual distribution of flour in her name to the poor. We know that he was not pleased with the suggestion, but we are not told the reason for his extreme response. He pulled a burning brand from the fire, and said that she could have as much land for her charity as she could walk around before the brand went out. As she was bedridden, this must have seemed a safe bet, but she called her servants to carry her outside and she managed to crawl round twenty-three acres before the flame went out. This land was thereafter known as 'The Crawls'. But Mabella was not finished yet. Not trusting her husband to keep his promise, she laid a curse on anyone who interfered with the annual dole, stating that if they did so, there would be a generation of seven sons, followed by one of seven daughters, the family would die out, and the house would fall down.

Needless to say, effective as this story is, it is almost certainly a fabrication and was quite possibly invented to explain why the fields were called 'The Crawls'. No serious discussion can begin until some basic questions are asked: when was the dole itself, the Lady Mabella story, and the field name 'The Crawls' first recorded? It would also be interesting to know if an alternative origin was recorded before this story became current. At present the Mabella story cannot be shown to go back very far. It was already in circulation by 1855, when Francis Baigent published his article on Mabella's genealogy, 'On the Family of de Lymerston', in the *Journal of the British Archaeological Association*, where he rightly calls the story 'the traditionary legend', but no earlier written version has yet come to light. Nevertheless, there is evidence that the dole itself is much earlier, as a painting of the event carried out by the Flemish painter Gillis van Tilborgh in 1671 shows the family dispensing basket-loads of loaves.

There is another aspect of Tichborne history that has a strong bearing on the survival of this dole, and it explains why this little village in Hampshire was very much a household name in the middle years of Victoria's reign. In 1862, when the current baronet, Sir James

Tichborne, died, the search began for his son and heir, Roger, who had travelled abroad nine years before. Roger's mother refused to believe him dead, advertised for information, and employed investigators in Australia to find him. In 1866, a man appeared who claimed to be the missing Roger, and although he had some supporters, and Lady Tichborne herself seemed to believe him, civil court proceedings were commenced to prove the claim, followed by criminal court proceedings against the claimant, which lasted until 1874. The man was revealed as a complete impostor – he was actually a man named Arthur Orton – and he was sentenced to fourteen years for perjury. The story of 'the Tichborne Claimant', or, after a while, simply 'the Claimant', was hugely popular in newspapers and magazines of the time, and was one of the most celebrated stories of the late nineteenth century. Countless articles, pamphlets, books, stories, and even songs were written about the case, and everybody in the country knew all the intimate details of the affair. In their search for something interesting to say about the village, journalists of the time also printed the story of the charity and its supposed origin with Sir Roger and Mabella in the twelfth century, thus ensuring that this explanation for this dole gained widespread publicity.

See also **Doles**, p. 115.

Care or Carling Sunday

Care or Carling Sunday is the fifth Sunday in Lent, also known as Passion Sunday. The name 'Carling Sunday' is derived from the custom most often reported for this day, the eating of 'carlings', as in the following record from Yorkshire in 1810:

The rustics go to the public house and spend each their carling-groat in drink, for their carlings are provided for them gratis.

'Carlings' were usually grey peas steeped overnight in water, then fried in butter the next day and seasoned with pepper, although at least one account describes them as being served with sugar and rum, a more interesting variation. Eating carlings on this day was common across the northern counties of England and in lowland Scotland, but it does not seem to have been found south of Cheshire or Lancashire.

The serving of peas and beans during Lent is no surprise, as pulses were an important staple when meat was forbidden, and it is most likely that the name 'carling' is derived from 'care' and not, as many other writers have presumed, that 'care' is derived from 'carling'. As the period of Lent progressed towards Holy Week, leading up to Good Friday and the commemoration of the Crucifixion, it was a time of increasing gloom for devout Christians, and various days in the sequence took on the term 'care'; thus 'Care Friday' and 'Care Week', in addition to 'Care Sunday'. The derivation of the word has excited much debate, but it seems quite clear that it is ultimately derived from Germanic roots in which 'kar' signified 'mourning' and was strongly attached to Holy Week in the same way as 'Care' was in this country. In English, the meaning of the word 'care' has changed over the years, but in its older form it signified sorrow, trouble, and grief, and was thus appropriate for the season.

See also **Shrovetide and Lent**, p. 60.

March/April

Borrowed Days

A widespread traditional saying, reported from all quarters of the British Isles since at least the mid sixteenth century, maintains that March borrowed three days from April; the last three days in March are therefore called the 'Borrowed Days' or 'Borrowing Days'. There is much confusion about the precise nature of this interchange and its result, however. If March had borrowed days from April, it would seem logical for the last three days in March to be warmer and milder than they should be for that time of year, and for three days in April to be unseasonably cold. Indeed, some of the recorded examples are clearly based on this reading of the situation:

[North of Ireland, 1852] *Give me (says March) three days of warmth and sunshine for my poor young lambs whilst they are yet too tender to bear the roughness of my wind and rain, and you shall have them repaid when the wool is grown.*

Another assessment of the relative mildness of the months in question, as quoted in *Notes & Queries* in 1852, has a similar positive outlook:

continued on page 119

Doles

Charity has always been a Christian obligation, and there have always been people who took this duty very seriously. Although there were particular days when charity was expected from the living (*see*, for example, **21 December: St Thomas's Day**), there was also a strong and long-lasting tradition for people of means to make wills in which they left money or provisions to the local poor or some other deserving group. Most of these bequests consisted of a single donation, but some people opted to set up a long-term 'dole' in which something – money, food, clothes, or fuel – was distributed to local people on a regular basis, usually annually. Most doles were set up with a mixture of motives, but often the testator wished simply to be remembered. None of us like to think that we will be forgotten after death, and in a belief system that incorporated the idea that souls lingered in Purgatory instead of going straight to Heaven, the thought was particularly frightening. Souls could be helped on their way by the masses and prayers of the living, and much ingenuity was therefore spent in devising ways to ensure that the deceased was brought to people's minds at least once a year, for evermore. Nevertheless, it would be too cynical to imply that the testators' motives were always purely selfish and only concerned with the fate of their own soul. Bequests such as money, food, coal, and blankets made a real difference to the poor, and although a penny loaf a year does not sound much to modern ears, if there were several such doles in a parish, the cumulative effect could be impressive. For those living close to subsistence level, a little goes a long way.

After the Reformation, masses and obits were banned, and in many cases they were replaced by commemorative sermons. A graveside dole is a particularly effective way of ensuring that the recipients connect the gifts with the name of the donor (*see*, for example, **Maundy Thursday: Henry Travice Charity** (p. 133) and **Good Friday: Hartfield Dole** (p. 144)), while other benefactors requested that the first charge on the charity be the cleaning and repair of their tomb. However, those who wished to set up such a charity had to ensure that there remained sufficient money to cover both the dole itself and the costs of its administration over a long period. Some simply left a sum of money to be invested, so that the profits could be used to support the charity, but a safer method was to leave land that could be rented out year after year, and the rent used to support the purposes of the charity. Generally, the only institution that existed to serve the whole community, and was likely to continue to do so in perpetuity, was the Church, and it was common for legacy-writers to name the local vicar as administrator or chief trustee.

The recipients of charity doles varied considerably, according to the whim of the deceased. Some simply stipulated 'the poor', but many named specific groups such as twelve widows, four old men, six women who had lost their husbands by drowning, those born in a particular street (*see* **21 June: Brecknell Bequest**), or the current cast at Drury Lane Theatre (*see* **6 January: Baddeley Cake**). Yet others sought to help the young by sponsoring apprenticeships, rewarding good behaviour in certain trades, or encouraging pious education; and some tried to provide a service to the community in the form of a field on which the rushes could be grown to be strewn in church, or money to repair the church, to provide new bell ropes, or to repair the town bridge.

Many thousands of these charities were created from the early modern period up to the early nineteenth century. Some were straightforward and sensible, others were eccentric, but over the generations they often evolved in peculiar ways, accumulating and losing details as circumstances changed. In many cases, the original documents were lost and the doles developed into traditional customs, acquiring legends to explain their origin.

But what looks like a completely random set of traditions can be seen on closer inspection to display recurrent details and patterns, which may help to chart the development of doles. One regular motif is the moving of a dole from the church to the churchyard, as religious sensibilities changed or the dole became too rowdy. Sometimes the dole was moved off church premises entirely. Another common element is the distribution of items by throwing them to crowds of people, to be scrambled for (*see* **Scrambling Customs**, p. 172; **Easter Monday: Hallaton Hare Pie and Bottle-Kicking**, p. 171; and **Whit Sunday: St Briavels Bread and Cheese Dole**, p. 269). Charities so often specify bread and cheese as the fare to be distributed, that land set aside for such purposes often became known locally as 'Bread and Cheese Land', as at Biddenden in Kent (*see* **Easter Monday: Biddenden Maids Charity.** p. 165).

Many simply gave out bread or buns, without gimmicks; for surviving examples of these doles, *see* **March: Dame Elizabeth Marvyn Charity** at Ufton in Berkshire, **Easter Tuesday: Tuppenny Starvers** in Bristol (p. 180), and **24 August: Sandwich Bun Race** in Kent. In more than one instance, the local vicar was expected to provide food and drink on a particular day. At Drayton Beauchamp in Buckinghamshire, for example, a long-standing custom developed in which anyone who wished could present themselves at the rectory on St Stephen's Day (26 December) and consume as much bread, cheese, and ale as they wished, at the vicar's expense. When the custom began to get out of hand in the early nineteenth century, the incumbent replaced it with a money dole (which the locals called 'Stephening money'), which in turn was abused. No evidence could be found to explain how it had started or if there was any legal obligation involved, and the whole affair was stopped c.1827.

There is no doubt that some of the bequests were eccentric, even by the standards of the time. But some of the bizarre details make some sense on closer inspection. Thomas Gray, for example, who composed his will in 1691, left money to buy land at Castle Donnington, so that the profits of that property could be used:

. . . to lay out six nobles yearly to buy six waistcoats of grey cloth, edged with blue galloon lace, and 40s to buy three coats of grey cloth, to be faced with baize; and that four of the said waistcoats should be given yearly to four poor widows . . .

It is clear that he wished his recipients to be distinguished by wearing a kind of uniform, and he specified its basic colour as a pun on his name.

Not everyone was in favour of such charity. Even as early as the mid seventeenth century, Sir William Petty (1623–87) wrote in his will:

As for legacies to the poor, I am at a stand; as for beggars by trade and election, I give them nothing; as for impotents by the hand of God, the public ought to maintain them; as for those who have no calling or estate, they should be put upon their kindred; as for those who can get no work, the magistrates should cause them to be employed, which may be well done in Ireland, where is fifteen acres of improvable land for every head; prisoners for crimes, by the king; for debts, by their prosecutors; as for those who compassionate the sufferings of any object, let them relieve themselves by relieving such sufferers – that is, give them alms *pro re nata*, and for God's sake, relieve the several species above mentioned, if the above-mentioned obligees fail in their duties. Wherefore, I am contented that I have assisted all my poor relations, and put many in a way of getting their own bread, and have laboured in public works, and by inventions have sought out real objects of charity; and I do hereby conjure all who partake of my estate, from time to time,

to do the same at their peril. Nevertheless, to answer custom, and to take the surer side, I give £20 to the most wanting of the parish, in which I may die.

By the late nineteenth century, many doles had disappeared. The money had run out, the trustees could not be bothered to administer them, or the original terms were forgotten; sometimes, more honourably, the money had been put to more relevant charitable causes. But enough doles survived for them to be regarded as major nuisances, and some even argued that they were counter-productive. A writer in *The Times* in 1889 complained of a woman who had received a sixpence dole in church and gone straight to a public house to spend it on gin. The problem that exercised Victorian minds – and one that can still be heard in the rhetoric of politicians today – is how to help the 'deserving poor' without subsidizing the idle and wicked. A correspondent to *The Times* in 1898 spoke for many on this point:

In the course of 30 years' ministry in a rural parish, overdone with dole charities, of 1300 souls, it has been my duty as trustee to take part in distributing no less a sum in the aggregate than £7000 in gratuitous doles of money, flour, and clothing, of which it may be affirmed that as far as the conferring of any substantial and permanent blessing on the beneficiaries is concerned, it would have been much better to have thrown this money into the sea; the only apparent result being to raise unduly cottage rents . . . I cannot recall in my long experience an instance of gratitude on the part of any receiver of a dole, which is invariably regarded as a due, while nothing develops more quickly than the latent suspicion that the poor are being robbed of their rights, or breeds more fruitfully mutual jealousy and uncharitableness than any effort which may be made to deal with those doles so that the deserving and thrifty may be assisted and the shiftless and undeserving excluded.

Only a handful of doles remain today. There is a daily dole at Winchester in Hampshire (*see* **Daily Customs: Wayfarers' Dole**, p. 580) and a weekly one at Woodbridge in Suffolk (*see* **Weekly Customs: John Sayer Charity**, p. 582). Some struggle to find enough recipients, while others such as the one at Biddenden in Kent and Tichborne in Hampshire (*see* **25 March: Tichborne Dole**) are nationally known, having become part of our folk heritage, and are in little danger of disappearing.

[c.1709] The three last days of March are called 'the Borrowing Days' in Scotland, on account of their being generally attended with very blustering weather, which inclines people to say that they would wish to borrow three days from the month of April in exchange for the last days of the month of March.

But these views of the March/April swap, which are perhaps down to wishful rewriting or simple misunderstanding, are completely out of step with the vast majority of recorded versions. Most state unequivocally that the three borrowed days bring bad weather, as in John Brockett's *Glossary of North Country Words* (1846):

> *March borrowed of April*
> *Three days, and they were ill*
> *The one was sleet, the other was snow*
> *The third was the worst that e'er did blow.*

An alternative version of the third day was that it 'froze the birds' legs to the trees'. In addition to being the commonest reading, the extreme nature of the three days is found in all the earliest known versions, from the *Complaynt of Scotland* of 1548, onwards, and it is most probably the original meaning.

A motive for this deal between the two months is not usually provided, but some versions state that it is to kill or frighten some sheep, as in another Scottish example from Chambers' *Book of Days* (1864):

> *March said to April*
> *I see three hoggs* [young sheep] *upon a hill*
> *And if you'll lend me days three*
> *I'll find a way to make them dee.*

In most cases a reason for the need to kill the sheep is not given, but occasionally it is implied that the sheep were the bribe in the deal between the months.

To complicate matters still further, some versions of the story say that March borrowed three days from February, or even that February borrowed them from January. And in other accounts, it was not simply a question of bad weather on these days, as noted in R. T. Hampson's *Medii Aevi Kalendarium* (1841):

They who are very superstitious will neither borrow nor lend on any of those days, and if any should propose to borrow from them, they would esteem it an evidence that the person wished to employ the article borrowed for the purposes of witchcraft against the lender.

Moreover, H. P. Whitcombe records in his *Bygone Days* (1874):

The first three days in March were formerly called 'blind days', and the farmer considered them unlucky; they would never sow any seed at that time . . .

According to *Notes & Queries* of 1903, France and Spain have similar beliefs about Borrowed Days.

APRIL

Great Barmote Court

Once a year, at the Moot Hall in Wirksworth, right in the centre of the Derbyshire lead-mining district, a court is held that is claimed to be the oldest surviving industrial court in Britain, possibly even the world. The Great Barmote Court, set up by Edward I in 1288, is the official body that regulates the previously lucrative lead-mining industry. Lead-mining had already been carried out for centuries when the lead-rich area of Derbyshire was granted to Edmund, first Earl of Lancaster, in 1265. To encourage exploitation of the natural resource, and make significant money for the Crown at the same time, it was decreed that any man might mine for lead, without hindrance, but a duty would be payable on the extracted ore. There were a few exceptions to the areas that could be mined – churchyards, gardens, orchards, and highways – but every other part of what was known as 'The King's Field', extending over some 115 square miles of the Peak District, was open to all-comers. Even landowners could not stop someone mining their land. The minerals under the ground belonged to the Crown, and only the Crown could forbid people from getting at it.

The Great Barmote Court had widespread powers over those in the industry and even acted as coroner in the event of a fatal accident in a mine; however, the industry began to decline in the late eighteenth century and never recovered its former glory. The court's jurisdiction is now confined to upholding regulations and collecting fees. Nevertheless, it is still regulated by a Barmaster and a Steward, appointed by the Chancellor of the Duchy of Lancaster, and both must be an experienced barrister or solicitor. These officials are aided by a jury of twelve members (previously twenty-four), who hold office un-til the next meeting. Before the business of the court is carried out, it is customary to provide beer, bread and cheese, clay pipes, and tobacco for those attending.

There were previously two Great Barmote Courts, one at Monyash for the High Peak, and the one at Wirksworth with jurisdiction over the Low Peak, but these are now combined and the one Great Court meets once a year, although Small Barmote Courts can be convened at any time, as necessary.

1 April

All Fools' Day

The first of April is the day it is traditional to play tricks on peo-ple. Nowadays universally called April Fool's Day, in earlier sources it was almost always given as 'All Fools' Day', parodying the Christian Church's All Souls' Day and All Saints' Day. There have been various local names for those fooled, such as April gowk (cuckoo), or April noddy or noodle.

The origin and development of April Fool's Day remains a mys-tery. The earliest mention we can find is in John Aubrey's *Remaines of Gentilisme and Judaisme* manuscript (*c*.1686), where he simply states: 'Fooles Holy Day – We observe it on ye first of April . . . and so it is kept in Germany everywhere.' But the complete absence of references to the custom in the plays and poems of the sixteenth and seventeenth centuries, and in the diaries and letters of people like Samuel Pepys, suggests that it was introduced to Britain sometime in the late seven-teenth century, not long before Aubrey was writing, and it probably came from France or Germany, where it is known to have existed ear-lier. However, the custom certainly caught on quickly enough, and it is recorded throughout the eighteenth century in terms which show that everyone was familiar with it.

By the late nineteenth century, writers were beginning to claim that the custom of fooling people was dying out, at least for adults, and since then its demise has been regularly predicted. The tradition was still vigorously followed by children in the 1950s when Iona and Peter Opie were researching their influential book *The Lore and Language of*

up and down the country detailing how much fun they could still get
from simple traditional jokes. Adults, too, had not entirely given it
up at that time, as recorded in the recently published diary of two
women working in a wartime aircraft factory in Croydon, edited by
Sue Bruley:

Thursday 1 April 1943 – April Fool's Day, which was driven home to us
because we found on arrival that the night shift had coated all the handles
of the machines with grease! A simple-minded not very funny joke. After
this Nancy roamed round the shop, her eyes sparkling and sending about a
dozen people, one after the other, on a fool's errand to the time office. She told
each one so gravely that they were wanted in the time office, that everyone
was taken in and there was quite a procession and the clerks in the time
office got quite hysterical.

Nevertheless, local observance seems to have gradually faded in recent
decades, and we can probably agree with Maureen Sutton, writing on
calendar customs in Lincolnshire in 1997, that 'The custom now seems
to be losing some favour, but is still a favourite with the national media.' Newspapers, local and national, do certainly seem keen to keep
the game alive, and their seasonal jokes often spoof officialdom and
bureaucracy. Examples taken at random from a huge file include: the
Guardian of 1 April 1986, which carried a number of spoof job advertisements on their Public Appointments page for, among other
things, a fund-raiser for the charity 'Aid to the Ambiguous', a 'Senior
Rhubarb Consultant' for West Midlands County Council, and four
'Assistant Generic Complaints Postulators' for South Yorkshire; and
the *Croydon Post* of 1 April 1998, which carried a front-page story under the bold headline 'Colour Cars Face Green Ban', written by one
April-Fay Solod, who reported that the local council had agreed a
plan to alleviate town-centre traffic problems by decreeing that streets
could be used on particular days only by cars of a certain colour. These
media jokes are following their own tradition, perhaps started by the
famous occasion in 1957 when the normally strait-laced BBC broad-
casted a report about spaghetti growing on trees in the current affairs
programme *Panorama*. Public hoaxes are not new, however. Robert
Chambers' *Book of Days* (1864), for example, recorded the following
incident:

. . . in March 1860, a vast multitude of people received through the post a

card [saying] . . . *'Tower of London – Admit the bearer and friend to view the annual ceremony of washing the white lions, on Sunday April 1st, 1860. Admitted only at the White Gate . . .' The trick is said to have been highly successful. Cabs were rattling about Tower Hill all that Sunday morning, vainly endeavouring to discover the White Gate.*

A correspondent to *Notes & Queries,* however, claimed that this story had been in the newspapers in the mid 1850s, and in his *The Rise and Fall of Merry England* (1996), Ronald Hutton claims that the story appeared in 1698. Certainly, 'Washing lions in the Tower' became something of a saying in its own right, meaning a hoax or wild goose chase.

Apprentices and newcomers in various occupations were particularly likely to be the butt of April Fool's jokes, and they could be sent to fetch items such as straight hooks, left-handed screwdrivers, striped paint, or whatever was relevant to their particular trade. An italic full-stop was popular in the print trade. When the 'fool' asked for each item, the trick was to treat the request seriously, claim not to have it, and to send him/her on to another old hand – 'to hunt the gowk another mile', as the Scots put it.

Since the first descriptions, the core of April foolery was usually this sending of people on fruitless, or sleeveless, errands ('sleeveless', meaning 'futile' and of uncertain origin, has been around since at least 1387, but has long been obsolete). Pigeon's milk, hen's teeth, and a book about Eve's mother are other traditional items that fools were regularly sent to find. The simpler tricks, such as gluing a coin to the floor, leaving a purse or parcel in the street with string attached, pulling coat-tails, and pinning signs or tails to backs, seem to have been a later development, perhaps from the mid nineteenth century onwards, although, as the Opies point out, jokes such as 'Your shoelace is untied!' or 'Your buckle's undone!' have a history of at least 200 years.

As with other children's customs, there is a strict rule that any trickery must cease at midday (*see,* for example, **29 May: Royal Oak Day**), and anyone who fails to observe this time-limit is themselves the fool:

> *April first has gone and past*
> *And you're the biggest fool at last.*

This rule has been in place at least since the 1870s.

Over the years, there have been a number of interesting but groundless claims about the origin of April Fool's Day. It has been posited that 1 April was the one day of the year when lunatics were let out of their asylums; it has also been suggested that it was the day that Noah foolishly sent the dove on its fruitless search for dry land, and that it was the day the Romans fooled the Sabine men into bringing their women to town. Tricks are not, of course, restricted to 1 April. In some parts of northern England, May Day was the day for playing tricks (*see* **1 May: May Goslings**), while certain tricks, such as pinning people's clothes together, were traditional on particular days (*see* **6 January: Twelfth Night**). Mischief Night (*see* **31 October: Mischief Night**) also shared some characteristics with April Fool's Day.

Palm Sunday

Palm Sunday is the sixth Sunday in Lent, the start of Easter or Holy Week, and can fall anywhere between 15 March and 18 April. It commemorates Christ's triumphant entry into Jerusalem on the donkey, when, according to the Gospel of John (12:12–13), the people spontaneously gathered to welcome him, 'Took branches of palm trees, and went forth to meet him, and cried, "Hosanna: Blessed *is* the King of Israel that cometh in the name of the Lord."'

By the Middle Ages, the day was celebrated with elaborate ritual: 'palms' were gathered beforehand, blessed in church, and then waved or strewn in front of a procession of clergy, which could include a wooden donkey on wheels or a picture of Christ riding one. Churches were decorated, and the day was one of joyful celebration, which contrasted markedly with the congregation's deepening gloom as Good Friday approached. At the Reformation, Palm Sunday celebrations were so entrenched that they escaped the reformers' zeal for a while, and in the 1530s they were specifically named as one of the few ceremonies to be spared the axe; however, in 1549 they were suppressed under Edward VI, then reprieved by Mary, and banned again by Elizabeth in 1559. In Catholic countries, and in Catholic churches in Britain, Palm Sunday continued to be celebrated with palm-bearing processions, and this probably helped to keep the original attributes of the day in the public's mind even while the established Church took no official notice.

The key features of the many secular Palm Sunday customs reported from most parts of the country in the nineteenth and twentieth centuries were trips into the countryside, called 'going a-palming' or something similar, to collect catkins, flowers, or other plants, in order to decorate the house or church, make crosses out of them, and wear pieces in buttonholes for the day. The problem for English people, of course, has always been that palms do not grow here, and although some churches have imported the real thing from Spain, several other plants have traditionally been used instead. Box, cypress, hazel, yew, and willow are mentioned in early records as being gathered to decorate homes and churches, but, as Maureen Sutton's *Lincolnshire Calendar* (1997) makes clear, the plant that many held in particular affection was the 'pussy willow', with its attractive catkins:

We always went out for our Sunday walk, the whole family. Mother liked to take home some pussy-willow, especially for Palm Sunday. Father used to tell us a little rhyme that went: 'I have a little pussy, Her coat is silver grey, I found her in the meadow, Not very far away, My little silver pussy, Will never be a cat, 'Cause she's a pussy-willow, Now what do you think of that?'

Fond memories of a similar custom were included in Flora Thompson's evocation of an Oxfordshire childhood in the 1880s, published as *Lark Rise* in 1939, but earlier accounts, such as the almanac *Time's Telescope* (1826), show that the event was not necessarily so innocent:

[On the Saturday night] *several hundreds of the workers of East London go with their families to the Sluice House at Hornsey, where, and in the adjacent fields, they carouse till daybreak. Soon afterwards, they collect their 'palm branches' and, to the best of their ability, make their way home.*

Along the Welsh border, the day was called 'Flowering Sunday', after the custom of decorating graves of deceased friends and relatives with flowers on the day, described by Charlotte Burne in 1883:

Popularly, Palm Sunday appears to have been regarded as a sort of anticipatory Easter and [they] *are both celebrated in the once (no doubt) common custom of strewing the graves of departed friends with sweet spring flowers. Albrighton churchyard yearly presents a touching sight on Palm Sunday, when all the graves are decked with daffodils and other flowers gathered in the woods and meadows about Boscabel and Whiteladies. I learn from an eye-witness that the display in 1879 was especially brilliant.*

In other places this was done on Easter Sunday. Superstitions gathered round the plants used on Palm Sunday, as they do at all traditional festivals. The plants strewn in the church processions, for example, were eagerly collected afterwards as they were reputed to preserve the house from thunder and lightning.

In the later twentieth century, while Catholic churches were simplifying their Palm Sunday rites, many Anglican churches were busy re-introducing palms into their celebrations for the day, and many church-going people still take note of Palm Sunday, although in a much more restrained way than in previous times.

Caistor Gad-Whip Ceremony

A very odd ceremony formerly took place at Caistor church in Lincolnshire every Palm Sunday. A sale document of 1845 relates how a man would bring a 'gad-whip' into church while the service was in progress:

The whip is taken every Palm Sunday by a man from Broughton to the parish of Caistor, who, while the minister is reading the first lesson, cracks it three distinct times in the porch, then folds it neatly up, and retires to a seat. At the commencement of the second lesson, he approaches the minister, and kneeling opposite to him with the whip in his hand, and [a] purse at the end of it, held perpendicularly over his head, waves it thrice, and continues in a steadfast position throughout the whole of the chapter. The ceremony is then concluded. The whip has a leathern purse tied at the end of it, which ought to contain thirty pieces of silver.

A 'gad-whip' was a heavy cart-whip, and the one used in Caistor was substantial: according to a contributor to *Notes & Queries* in 1901, the whip-stock was 5 feet and 8 inches long, with a heavy lash of white leather of 7 feet and 9 inches.

This custom was described and dissected by many antiquarians in the first half of the nineteenth century and by others since then, but has puzzled them all, particularly as there is no documentary evidence of its origin or early history – there is no sign of it in the property deeds of the manors concerned, and nobody seems to have mentioned it in print before the late eighteenth century. It appears to be a service owed by the Lords of the Manor of Broughton to the owners of Hundon, and presumably it was some sort of condition of tenure, but this is based on supposition. In the absence of any real information regarding its origin, there have been the usual attempts to explain it from internal evidence. One story is that the ceremony was imposed on some early lord of the manor as penance for killing a boy with a whip. Others point to connections between the money in the purse – which some accounts describe as 'thirty pence' – and the thirty pieces of silver paid to Judas in Matthew 26–7, which were the passages traditionally read in church on Palm Sunday, although the biblical verses make no mention of whips or anything similar. Other details are similarly treated, so, for example, the three cracks of the whip have been equated with Peter's three denials.

By the mid nineteenth century, the days of the gad-whip custom were clearly numbered. In 1836, Sir Culling Eardley Smith was Lord of the Manor of Broughton and therefore responsible for maintaining the custom. He petitioned the House of Lords and the Bishop of Lincoln for help in identifying why the custom took place and what would happen to him if he failed to carry it on, with the clear intention of discontinuing it. Moreover, local newspapers began to comment that such antics in church were disgusting and irreverent, although the publicity they gave the ceremony brought crowds to the church to see it. It seems to have faded away *c.*1850.

For another custom that probably owes its existence to manorial obligations, *see* **Ascension Eve: Whitby Penny Hedge**, p. 248.

Figs

Palm Sunday was one of the days also called 'Fig Sunday' in parts of the country, as recorded in the *Folk-Lore Journal* (1885):

This day is called 'Fig Sunday' in Northamptonshire. A girl from Syresham in that county, living in service in Shropshire, received a present of a box of figs and a box of sweets from her mother last Palm Sunday.

Similarly, in *Folk-Lore* (1929), in Oxfordshire:

Palm Sunday is called Fig Sunday and people make fig puddings, 'in remembrance of the barren fig-tree'. Miss Christian remembered one family where the children used to have bags of figs or dates given them on the morning of Palm Sunday.

See **Fig Sunday** (p. 131) for further examples.

Martinsell Hill

Any prominent hill near a village is likely to have been the site of a fair or other gathering, often on 1 May or another special spring day. Martinsell Hill, at the southern end of the Marlborough Downs, overlooking the Vale of Pewsey, was no exception. The site of an impressive 32-acre Iron Age hill fort, it had a fair that took place on Palm Sunday which, apart from fighting and other field sports, was affectionately remembered for the custom of rolling oranges down the slopes, sliding down the hill, and a game that involved hitting a ball up and down the hill with a hockey stick. The annual gathering faded away c.1860, and A. G. Bradley, a Wiltshire writer who was born in 1850, was just too late to remember it at first hand:

In the eighteenth and nineteenth centuries, great sports were held up here on Martinsell. The custom still, I believe, survives in picnics for children. But at the original function a part of the programme consisted in sliding down the almost perpendicular face of the hill seated on the jawbones of horses . . . I can myself remember as a child the well-worn mark of a slide traced down this three or four hundred feet of precipitous turf . . . All trace, however, of the historic slide has long vanished. But within the memory of men only elderly, the pugilists of the neighbouring villages used to take advantage of what was left of the ancient festival, and fight out their battles on the top of Martinsell. These encounters were sometimes so ferocious that unsuccessful efforts were made to stamp out the festival, which, however, died a natural death.

See also **Fairs, Feasts, Wakes, and Revels,** p. 341.

Pax Cakes

In three Herefordshire churches – those of Sellack, Hentland, and King's Caple – a custom that may be 500 years old takes place every Palm Sunday. After the normal service, round shortbread biscuits called pax cakes are handed by the vicar to each of the congregation, with the spoken blessing, 'Peace and good neighbourhood'; these words are also stamped on the cakes, along with an image of a lamb. The custom is said to date from the will of Thomas More in 1484, or of Lady Scudamore in 1570, or both, which provided for a feast to be held in the church each year, to promote peace and friendship. The feast may have dwindled to a biscuit, but the principle is still the same.

See also **Doles,** p. 115.

Water

Palm Sunday was one of several days on which children customarily collected water from a certain well in the neighbourhood and mixed it with ingredients such as sugar, broken sweets, or liquorice in order to make it into a drink, as in Oxfordshire in 1929:

On Palm Sunday, which is often referred to as Spanish Sunday, an old custom still survives. Just over the boundary, in the parish of Wilcote, is an old well of beautiful clear water, surrounded by a wall, with stone steps going down to it. It is called the Lady's Well, and on Palm Sunday the girls go there and take bottles with Spanish juice (liquorice), fill the bottles, walk round the well, and drink.

See also **Easter Monday: Water** (p. 177) for further examples.

Holy Week Monday

Bourne Running Auction

By the terms of Matthew William Clay's will of 1742, a piece of land in Bourne, Lincolnshire, was bequeathed to the town, the rent from which was to be used to buy bread for the local poor. The original land was swallowed up by the local Enclosure Award of 1770, but another field of just over an acre, now called Whitebread Meadow, just north of Bourne, was set aside to satisfy the terms of Clay's bequest. On the Monday before Easter, the auction for the grazing rights on the field is still held, at Queen's Bridge at the end of the Eastgate area of the town. It follows a rather unusual procedure, set down in the will: two boys (or, nowadays, girls) start to run a 200-yard race and the bidding commences; the last bid made before the first runner's return is the winner. The money raised is now given to charity and has not been used to buy loaves for distribution since the late 1960s.

Although the exact nature of this auction is peculiar, it was not unusual in the past for auctions to have definite ending points dictated by a semi-random occurrence. **Candle auctions** were particularly common (*see* p. 138), and at Wishford in Wiltshire the 'midsummer tithes' auction ends when the sun disappears over the horizon (*see* **Rogation Monday: Wishford Auction**, p. 247).

See also **Doles**, p. 115.

Fig Sunday

In many parts of the country, regional dishes with figs as the main ingredient were eaten in great quantities on Palm Sunday, which was often called 'Fig Sunday' as a result. The dishes were sometimes called 'figsue' and could be in the form of pies or puddings, varying considerably from place to place. *Notes & Queries* (1856) records that in Staffordshire:

The fig-pies are made of dry figs, sugar, treacle, spice, etc. They are rather too luscious for those who are not 'to the manner born'.

The reasoning behind this custom is not entirely clear. Fig trees are not native to this country, but English people would have been long familiar with imported figs and the many mentions of the plant in the Bible: Adam and Eve used fig leaves to cover their nakedness, and in his parables Jesus speaks of cursing a fig tree which bore no fruit when he was hungry (Matthew 21:19–21) and of the barren tree which the gardener offered to save with manure (Luke 13:6–9). The most plausible explanation of the strong link between the fig and Palm Sunday is that, as related by Matthew, Christ had wanted to eat figs on his way into Jerusalem. Nevertheless, in many parts of the country, the customary day for indulging in figs was Mid-Lent Sunday or even Good Friday, so this explanation may not be as convincing as it first appears. According to C. F. Tebbutt, folklorist of Huntingdonshire, fig puddings were still popular in St Neots in 1950.

Traditional recipes for fig pie and fig pudding can be found in Florence White's *Good Things in England* (1932), which includes the following, entitled 'Mrs. Hart's Fig Pudding (Worcestershire)':

½ lb breadcrumbs; ½ lb figs; ½ lb moist sugar; 6 oz suet; ½ nutmeg; 2 eggs; wine sauce. Time to boil 4 hours. 1) Mince the figs very very small; 2) Mince the suet very very fine; 3) Mix bread-crumbs, figs, sugar, suet, nutmeg, all together very well; 4) Moisten with the eggs which should first be well beaten; 5) Put in a greased mould or basin, cover well with greased paper and steam, 4½ hours; 6) Turn out and serve with wine sauce.

Maundy Thursday

Maundy Thursday, the day before Good Friday, was also known as Holy Thursday or Shere Thursday. 'Shere' was a technical term, now obsolete, used in the manufacture of coins, and signified 'the deviation from the standard weight of coins permitted by law' (*OED*); its use in this context probably refers to the special coins minted for the day.

On Maundy Thursday, the ruling monarch (or his/her representative if they are away) presents Maundy gifts to as many elderly people as there are years in their reign. The custom takes its origin from an incident in the life of Christ, recorded in the Gospel of John (13:4). Immediately after the Last Supper, Jesus laid aside his garments, girded himself with a towel, and, taking a basin of water, washed the feet of the Disciples. He delivered to them a command for his followers to love one another, saying, 'I have given you an example that ye should do as I have done to you.' This command, or *mandatum*, is the origin of both the name and the custom of Maundy. Most branches of the Christian faith formerly carried out a foot-washing ceremony, and England was no exception. Indeed, foot-washing ceremonies were quite common in abbeys and cathedrals around the country from about the sixth century until the Dissolution of the Monasteries (1536–40), and could be performed at any time during the year, sometimes daily. It is not clear when ruling monarchs started taking a regular personal role in the Maundy ceremony, but the earliest definite reference relates to King John in 1210. The present custom is properly called the Royal Maundy because, at least in earlier days, other nobles and high-ranking churchmen also gave out Maundy doles.

In earliest times, the poor people who received the foot-washing numbered twelve or thirteen, and it is not clear when the figure was increased to match the years in a monarch's reign. Somewhat sumptuous robes were given to the poor people as well, but Queen Elizabeth I stopped this custom and instituted the more practical gift of money instead; it was also customary to give food. The last king to perform the foot-washing himself was James II, in 1685. Until the mid eighteenth century, when the foot-washing was abolished, the Lord High Almoner then carried out this part of the ceremony, and he also sometimes gave out the money on the monarch's behalf.

A description of the ceremony in 1731:

On the 5th April, 1731, it being Maundy Thursday, the King then being in his 48th year, there was distributed at the Banqueting House, Whitehall, to 48 poor men and 48 poor women, boiled beef and shoulders of mutton, and small bowls of ale, which is called dinner; after that, large wooden platters of fish and loaves, viz, undressed, one large ling and one large dried cod; twelve red herrings and twelve white herrings; and four quartern loaves. Each person had one platter of this provision; after which was distributed to them, shoes, stockings, linen and woollen cloth, and leathern bags, with onepenny, twopenny, threepenny and fourpenny pieces of silver, and shillings, to each about £4 in value. His Grace The Lord archbishop of York, Lord High Almoner, also performed the annual ceremony of washing the feet of the poor in the Royal Chapel, Whitehall, as formerly done by the kings themselves.

The custom has changed a great deal over the years, and both the food and the clothes have long been commuted into money. Since 1971, the ceremony has taken place at a different cathedral each year, and the recipients are chosen from the surrounding area for their contributions to the local community.

See also **Doles**, p. 115.

Henry Travice Charity

This Maundy Thursday dole was founded by Henry Travice, who died in 1626. In his will, he stipulated that £10 from the annual rent charge on a property in Widnes, Manchester, should be distributed to forty poor parishioners, on or near his grave. The charity itself takes place in the place of his burial, St Mary's church in Leigh, by his pew. A brass plaque in the church reads (with spelling modernized):

Here near adjoineth the burial place belonging to the house of Mr. Henrie Travice late of Light Oaks, who departed this life the 7th of August Anno Doi 1626 aged 64 and give by his last will unto forty poor people of this parish five shillings apiece yearly to be delivered them near his gravestone hereunder placed, on Thursday in the Passion Week forever.

Recipients have to walk the length of Henry's pew to be eligible, and as £10 gives forty people very little worth having, the number of recipients has been reduced.

See also **Doles**, p. 115.

This was one of the many customs in which coins or food were thrown to children to be 'scrambled for'. James Cossins reported in his *Reminiscencs of Exeter Fifty Years Since* (1878) that in Devon in the 1830s:

At Exeter Cathedral on this day, after service, 'Peter's Pence' were given to children, distributed by the vergers, standing at the door under the north tower; the exit being the entrance near Southernhay, giving the alert ones time to come round again. The confusion and noise were so great, the vergers were desired to throw the pence in the yard for a general scramble. The custom ceased many years since.

No other information is given, but the interesting detail here is the name for the money. 'Peter's pence' was the vernacular name for a tax of one penny per household (in Latin, *denarii S. Petri*) that was sent to Rome specifically to support the Pope, instituted by King Offa in the eighth century and renewed after a lapse by William the Conqueror. The custom spread to Europe, but was abolished in England by Act of Parliament (25 Henry VIII cap. 21) in 1534. In later years, the phrase denoted a voluntary contribution to the clergy paid by Roman Catholics.

See also **Scrambling Customs**, p. 172.

5 April

John Stow Commemoration

John Stow was born in London in 1525. The son of a tailor and apprenticed to his father's trade, he would hardly be remembered today if he had not branched out into a very different field. What set him apart from other master tradesmen of the time was that he somehow acquired a taste for books and historical scholarship, and he began to collect materials to support his interest in historical study. His first book, published in 1561, was *A Summarie of Englysh Chronicles*. Only one copy of the first edition survives, but the book was popular enough to go through eleven editions in his lifetime. Sometime in the early 1560s, Stow took the very bold step of giving up his tailoring business to concentrate on research and writing, a decision that resulted in his lasting fame but ensured that he himself suffered an old age dogged by poverty. He was even granted a licence to beg the year before he died.

Elizabethan England may have seen a flowering of literary talent, but it was also a period of political and religious intrigue, and anyone who spent their days with books was considered highly suspect. Stow was reported to the authorities as 'a suspicious person, with many dangerous and superstitious books in his possession', and was duly investigated by Edmund Grindal, the Bishop of London, who sent his henchmen to inspect Stow's library. He must have been exonerated, as he continued to amass historical materials, and his most famous publication, the *Survey of London*, was published in 1598, with a revised edition in 1603.

This immensely readable book was the first real study of London and is one of our best sources of information on Elizabethan life. One of the pleasures of the *Survey* is that Stow does not confine himself to the lives of the great and the good, or to buildings and institutions, but also notices the daily doings of the common people around him, and the book contains numerous vignettes of real Elizabethan life; he writes of maypoles, and streets decorated with evergreens for Christmas, and provides one of the first descriptions of **rough music** justice (*see* p. 95), writing of one John Atwod, a draper of the parish of St Michael's, who one day discovered a priest paying amorous attentions to his wife. He describes how the priest was:

... on three market-days conveyed through the high streets and markets of the city with a paper on his head, wherein was written his trespass. The first day he rode in a carry, the second on a horse, his face to the horse tail, the third led betwixt twain, and every day rung with basons, and proclamations made of the fact at every turning of the street, and also before John Atwod's stall, and the church door of his service ...

Stow's *Survey* is still in print today, over 400 years after its first publication.

When Stow died on 5 April 1605, he was buried in St Andrew Undershaft church on Leadenhall Street, and his wife erected a terracotta monument in his memory; this was replaced by a marble monument in 1905. This later monument includes an effigy depicting him in characteristic writing pose, and every year, on or near the date of his death, a commemorative service takes place. As befits the memory of the first chronicler of the capital city, the service is formally attended by the Lord Mayor or one of the aldermen. During the service, they place a new quill pen in the hand of the effigy, which remains there until the following year.

6 April

Flitting Day

The sixth of April was one of several regular 'flitting days' recorded in various parts of the country. As farm and domestic workers were often employed by the year, a set pattern arose, agreed by long local custom, by which the coming and going of staff was regulated: a hiring fair, or set market day, would take place, during which employers and workers could meet and make a bargain (*see* **Hiring Fairs**, p. 470); on another day their old employment officially ended; on another, the new position started, and there was usually a few days of free time built into the system when the workers could have something of a holiday. For single people the whole procedure was relatively simple, as a tin trunk usually held most of their belongings, but for families living in tied accommodation it was quite an operation moving from one place to another.

For many, the term ended at Michaelmas (29 September) and moving day was therefore in early October, but in those areas where the employment year ran to and from Lady Day (25 March), 6 April was the usual day for removal. It was a matter of fierce pride that you left the place in good order. In her *Lincolnshire Calendar* (1997), Maureen Sutton remembers that:

We always had to move on 6th April. It was a big job for mother as she had to leave everything spick and span for the new family moving in. You had to leave the fire grate spotless, white-wash the walls, and leave the fire ready to light. It was also the day when you paid up the year's rent.

Another widespread term for Flitting Day was 'Pack Rag Day' (*see* **14 May**).

Tatworth Candle Auction

The Tatworth Candle Auction is one of several **candle auctions** (p. 138) that survive in England, whereby the right to use a piece of common land is auctioned off while an inch of candle burns. In the Somerset village of Tatworth, the auction takes place on the Saturday after 6 April (Old Style Lady Day); a short business meeting is held on the same day. The property in question is a six-acre field called Stowell Mead, which, being wasteland left over after the enclosure of land in the parish in 1819, is owned by the villagers. The procedure is as follows: a short candle is placed on a square board suspended by chains from the ceiling of a room in a local inn, and whoever is the highest bidder when the flame dies is the winner; anyone who leaves their seat while the candle is burning is fined, a rule designed to prevent anyone from interfering with the flame, and the whole procedure takes about twenty minutes. The annual money raised at the auction is divided among the sixty or so locals who have 'rights', or shares, in the meadow, after deductions are made for the traditional bread, cheese, and watercress supper.

Easter

Easter is the oldest feast of the Christian Church, and although the celebration of Christmas now eclipses all other festivals, both religious and secular, the earlier Christian churches regarded Easter as by far the most important of the year. Easter celebrates the central mystical miracle of the faith, the death and resurrection of the Saviour Jesus Christ, an event that for Christians proves Christ's divinity; and it was this that was commemorated in church in complex ritual over the Easter period.

In the pre-Reformation Church, Easter was marked by a series of impressively dramatic and emotional set pieces of religious symbolism, which were popular with clergy and congregation alike. First, the cloths that had veiled parts of the church and the saints' images during Lent were removed. Then, on Good Friday, both clergy and parishioners crept barefoot and on their knees to kiss the foot of the crucifix, in a ceremony usually called 'creeping to the Cross'. A model sepulchre was

Candle Auctions

Although nowadays we assume that an auction continues until no one present will bid any further, there have been many other ways of organizing sales to bidders in the past. Several earlier methods were based on having a definable end-point at which the highest standing bid won the purchase, and the most widespread way of calling time on the auction was to light a candle and allow people to bid until the flame went out. Clearly, a short piece of candle was necessary, and it was customary to use an inch; hence the phrase 'selling by inch of candle'. It is not always easy to define the exact moment a flame goes out, and in a later refinement a pin was inserted into the candle one inch from the top, with the bidding continuing until the pin dropped out – a much more dramatic, and precise, method. In some cases the candle was hidden out of sight of the bidders.

There is plenty of evidence that auction by candle was an officially sanctioned way of organizing such affairs. The *Act for Settling the Trade to the East Indies* of 1698, for example, stipulated that goods be 'sold openly and publicly by inch of candle', and even redundant Navy ships were disposed of in the same way, as recorded in Samuel Pepys's diary entry for 3 September 1662:

built, usually from wood and canvas but of more substantial form in the larger institutions, to represent the cave in which Christ's body was laid, and an elaborate pyx, containing the Host, was placed inside, along with a crucifix. Some parishioners sat up all night to watch, in memory of the soldiers who guarded the original tomb, and to tend the candles that were kept burning around it. On Easter Sunday, the clergy approached the sepulchre in procession, and 'raised up' the host and crucifix, returning them to their proper places in the church. On Easter Saturday, all lights and fires had been extinguished, and a new fire kindled by the clergy, using flints, from which holy flame all candles and fires were re-lit. The church was then ablaze with light, including a very large candle called the Paschal candle. References in churchwardens' accounts show that some sort of performance often took place, presumably re-enacting the principal events of the Easter story. All these rituals were swept away with the Reformation, and for those who lived through these changes, the new Easter must have seemed bleak indeed.

After dinner by water to the office; and there we met and sold the *Weymouth*, *Successe*, and *Fellowship* hulks. Where pleasant to see how backward men are at first to bid; and yet when the candle is going out, how they bawl and dispute afterward who bid the most first. And here I observed one man cunninger than the rest, that was sure to bid the last man and to carry it; and enquiring the reason, he told me that just as the flame goes out the smoke descends, which is a thing I never observed before, and by that he doth know the instant when to bid last – which is very pretty.

Nevertheless, candle auctions are slow and inefficient, and only useful for sales in which not more than a handful of large lots are on offer. For a modern-day sale in which hundreds of lots are rattled through, candle auctions would be completely inadequate, and it is not surprising that the candle method lost favour in the eighteenth century and was gradually replaced by the open-ended ascending bid system. However, candle auctions have survived in a handful of places, nearly always concerned with the letting of common land; *see*, for example, 6 April: Tatworth Candle Auction; 13 December: Aldermaston Candle Auction; and Occasional Customs: Chedzoy Candle Auction, p. 585. For other unusual surviving auctions, *see* Holy Week Monday: Bourne Running Auction, p. 130; and Rogation Monday: Wishford Auction, p. 247.

Unfortunately, the Scriptures do not make it clear when the resurrection of Christ occurred, and arguments about the correct method of calculation led to some of the bitterest controversies that Christianity has ever seen. Unfortunately, too, the Church Fathers of yesteryear opted for a complex moveable festival, based on full moons and equinoxes rather than a fixed date, and this has caused havoc with the calendar ever since. The following explanation printed in *Whitaker's Almanack* is about as simple as one can find on the subject:

Easter Day is the first Sunday after the full moon which happens on, or next after, the 21st day of March; if the full moon happens on a Sunday, Easter Day is the Sunday after . . . The moon referred to is not the real moon of the heavens, but a hypothetical moon on whose 'full' the date of Easter depends, and the lunations of this 'calendar' moon consist of twenty-nine and thirty days alternately, with certain necessary modifications to make the date of its full agree as nearly as possible with that of the real moon, which is known as the Paschal Full Moon. At present, Easter falls on one of 35 days (22 March to 25 April).

Parliament took the bold step of passing a bill in 1928 that fixed Easter to the first Sunday after the second Saturday in April, but with the proviso that the churches agreed. They have not yet done so, and the act remains unimplemented.

English is unique in calling this festival 'Easter'; nearly all the other European languages use a word derived from the Latin *pasch*, as is to be expected of a Christian festival. The origin of the word 'Easter' is obscure, and is not helped by the ubiquitous uncritical acceptance of an otherwise unsupported comment by the Venerable Bede (673–735) in his *De Temporum Ratione*:

Eosturmonath has a name which is now translated 'Paschal month', and which was once called after a goddess of theirs named Eostre, in whose honour feasts were celebrated in that month. Now they designate that Paschal season by her name, calling the joys of the new rite by the time-honoured name of the old observance.

He similarly offered a deity as a derivation for the Anglo-Saxon name for March, stating, 'Hrethmonath is named for their goddess Hretha.' However, there is no other evidence that either goddess existed, and we have to face the possibility that Bede was wrong. It is with due trepidation that one questions not only the scholarship of such a pivotal figure but also the host of etymologists since who have accepted his word, and it can indeed be argued that as Bede was writing so soon after the conversion of the Anglo-Saxons to Christianity, he should have known what he was talking about. Nevertheless, it seems quite possible that Bede, as a Latin speaker and writer, simply expected months to be named after mythological or historic figures, and, faced with unknown words, fell prey to what is nowadays an extremely common trait – the construction of word origins based on present-day expectations and assumptions rather than on real evidence from the past. It is distinctly odd that only the months of April and March are given divine names. All the other months are named for the activities that went on in them; so, for example, Blodmonath (November) is 'blood month', named after the slaughter of animals for winter, and Solmonath (February) is 'cake month'. What seems clear is that, goddess or not, the English word 'Easter' is derived from the word 'east', and therefore probably from 'dawn'.

The general holiness of the Easter season made it a favourite time for charitable **doles** (p. 115). The **Biddenden Maids Charity**, in Kent (*see* p. 165), still survives, but most have long since disappeared. It was common for food provided by such bequests to be consumed in the church itself, but this offended emerging Puritan sensibilities. The poor parishioners of Clunganford, Shropshire, for example, complained to Archbishop Laud in 1637 that they had been accustomed to eat their annual Easter feast of bread, cheese, and beer in the church, but it had been moved to the parsonage a few years ago, and now the parson wanted to do away with it altogether. However, in 1647, the Puritans specifically banned Easter:

An Ordinance for Abolishing of Festivals (8 June 1647). Forasmusch as the feasts of the Nativity of Christ, Easter, and Whitsuntide, and other festivals commonly called holy days, have been heretofore superstitiously used and observed. Be it ordained by the Lords and Commons in Parliament assembled, that the said [feasts] *... be no longer observed as festivals or holy days within this kingdom.*

It never regained its former ritual glory in English churches, but by the nineteenth century the attractive custom of decorating churches with flowers at the season, which still continues, was widespread. A correspondent to *Notes & Queries* reported in 1850:

In the village of Berkley, near Frome, and on the borders of Wiltshire, the church is decorated on Easter Sunday with yew. Flowers in churches on that day are common, but I believe the use of yew to be unusual.

Other mid-century reports from around the country show that the use of yew, box, and other evergreens was not so unusual as this correspondent thought.

Good Friday

The Friday before Easter Saturday is the day on which Christians commemorate the crucifixion of Jesus Christ. It has been called 'Good Friday' in England since at least 1290, and it is usually assumed to be derived from 'God's Friday', but the citations given in the *Oxford English Dictionary* do not bear this out, and it seems that in earlier times 'good' was added to various other words to denote holiness. 'Holy Friday' and 'Long Friday' were among other recorded names, the latter probably referring to the long fasting required on the day. Whatever its derivation, the 'good' in the name has long perplexed believers and non-believers alike, who have never been quite sure why it should be 'good' at all.

Before the Bank Holiday legislation of 1871 (*see* **Bank Holidays**, p. 373), Christmas Day and Good Friday were the only holidays granted to most workers, and it is hardly surprising that they regarded the latter as an opportunity for fun and pleasure. But the Church dictated that it be a day of solemnity and fasting, a sort of super Sunday, on which no work should be done. It was a popular day for Christian charity, and many annual **doles** (p. 115) were distributed on the day. In the secular sphere, however, the popular ambivalence surrounding the day is demonstrated in various superstitions: many of these were concerned with everyday activities considered unlucky on the day, such as washing clothes, cutting hair and fingernails, and baking bread; while others suggested that bread baked, and eggs laid, on Good Friday had excellent medicinal and protective properties, and it was also supposed to be a particularly good day for planting in the garden. Game customs such as marble-playing and skipping were also common (*see separate entries, below*).

Bread and Eggs

An extremely widespread belief, found in every part of England throughout the nineteenth century, maintained that bread or buns baked on Good Friday would never grow mouldy. They were also believed to have curative powers for a range of complaints, including those of the stomach or digestive system. The usual way to preserve this Good Friday bread was to hang it by a string from the kitchen ceiling, and when needed a piece would be grated or soaked in water to be drunk by the patient (*see* **Good Friday: Widow's Son** (p. 150) for a surviving example).

A parallel superstition, less commonly reported but still widespread, held that eggs were similarly incorruptible, and a letter in *Notes & Queries* (1921) confirmed it:

Last Christmas, a lady told one of my nearest relations that if an egg, laid on Good Friday, is kept without being disturbed, it will generally be per-

fectly fresh at the time when the Christmas pudding is made. She stated that she had proved this. Out of pure curiosity my relation placed, on Good Friday last (March 25) an egg, laid by one of her hens on that day, in an egg-cup and put it in a cupboard in her drawing-room, where it remained untouched until Dec. 1, when it was broken and used in the Christmas pudding. I can avouch that when the egg was broken there was no smell, except that of a fresh egg, which in all one could judge of, it appeared to be.

These superstitions appear to be very old, but cannot be traced earlier than the eighteenth century. They are in line with other beliefs that edibles associated with Christian ceremonies, such as the wine and wafers of communion, and the water used in baptism, also possess similar medicinal powers.

Burning Judas

An example of a custom that only seems to have existed in this country in one small area is that of burning the Judas on Good Friday. An excellent account published in the journal *Folk-Lore* in 1954 is worth quoting in full:

A custom that is peculiar to one part of Liverpool only is one that happens every Good Friday. For weeks before the children collect wood, paper, straw, shavings, etc., anything that will burn. The boys get one of their father's old suits and stuff it with straw, etc. They get a comic mask to complete the job and this dummy is carefully looked after till the Day. At the first sign of daylight on Good Friday morning, all the children of the neighbourhood congregate round the particular guy which they now call Judas. The children's ages range from five years up to twelve and fourteen, and being a densely populated area close to the docks there are many children. The fun starts as the sun rises and the leader hoists the Judas on a pole and knocks at the bedroom windows and all the children join in the chorus, 'Judas is a penny short of his breakfast and until you throw some coppers to them they won't give you any peace'. When they have combed the neighbourhood they begin the serious part of burning the Judas, and out come all the combustibles they have been collecting. For some reason the burning of the Judas must take place by 11 o'clock a.m. Now the police intervene as the fires are lit in the middle of the street, and scores of children whooping for joy and throwing wood and straw on it. To prevent accidents the police scatter the fires and seize the Judases and take them to the police station at Essex Street and destroy them there. It is comic to see a policeman with two or more Judases under his arm striding off to the Bridewell and thirty or forty children of all ages crowding after him, shrieking, 'Judas', and by this time the younger children are thinking the policeman is Judas. By 12 noon the excitement is all over. This custom only occurs at the South End of Liverpool, never up North or anywhere else along the eight miles of Dock Estate. I was told the idea originated many years ago when the old Spanish sailing ships docked and discharged their cargoes of wine and citrus fruits in the South End Docks.

The idea that the children learned the custom from continental sailors is quite feasible. An illustration published in the *Graphic* on 15 April 1876, for example, shows Portuguese sailors in Liverpool Docks involved in hanging an effigy for the custom of 'flogging Judas', a custom that was widely practised in Portugal, Spain, and South America.

Butterworth Charity

This annual charity, carried out at the priory church of St Bartholomew the Great, in Smithfield, the City of London, is named after Joshua Butterworth, although it was already in existence before he gave money in 1887 to perpetuate the custom. It is believed to have been founded in 1686, but it is not known by whom. Every Good Friday, money and hot cross buns (presumably bread was used in earlier times) was distributed to poor widows of the parish, on a conveniently flat tombstone in the churchyard. In 1973, no poor widows presented themselves, which, while being bad for the tradition, is a good thing for society as a whole, and the children who were present were invited to eat the bun instead. They were not reluctant to do so, and the tradition continues with this new audience, every Good Friday, after the morning service.

See also **Doles**, p. 115.

Hartfield Dole

This graveside dole takes place every Good Friday at Hartfield church in Sussex, at the tomb of Nicholas Smith, who died in 1631. Smith left money to be invested and the interest to be divided among the poor of the parish. There is no reason to believe that there is more to this than a straightforward alms bequest, but a story explaining the dole tells how Smith was a rich man from East Grinstead who went about dressed as a beggar, asking for food and shelter, in order to test the true character of the people of Sussex. At every turn he met with contempt and refusal, until he came to Hartfield, where he was treated with kindness and generosity. He therefore asked to be buried at Hartfield, and founded the charity in his name.

See also **Doles**, p. 115.

Hot Cross Buns

Two festive foods – pancakes on Shrove Tuesday and hot cross buns on Good Friday – have survived into the present day, even though most traditional aspects of their special days have long ceased to have any widespread resonance. Although hot cross buns can be bought in supermarkets all year round, many English families try to eat them on Good Friday, and some baker's shops still open specially on the day to serve freshly baked buns.

The development of the 'cross bun' is not very clear, as there were apparently various types of cake that were special to Good Friday. Some nineteenth-century sources refer to triangular cakes, and others to 'cakes' of unspecified shape or size. However, the earliest specific reference to a 'hot cross bun' occurs in *Poor Robin's Almanack* (1733):

> *Good Friday comes this month, the old woman runs*
> *With one or two a penny hot cross buns.*

Further confusion arises as the marking of food with a cross was not confined to Good Friday buns. Right up to the early years of the twentieth century, it was normal practice when baking bread to mark the dough with a cross before putting it into the oven, and this practice is well documented from the mid thirteenth century. Indeed, in pre-Reformation England it would have been commonplace to make the sign of the cross over all food, in preparation and before eating.

Many festive foods, such as goose at Michaelmas and mince pies at Christmas, attract superstitions which maintain that good luck will accompany those who follow custom, but that bad luck will result from a failure to partake, and the hot cross bun is no exception. *The Testimony, Trial, Conviction, Condemnation, Confession, and Execution of William Smith*, an account detailing the story of a man who was executed in 1753 for murdering several people by giving them arsenic-laced cake, provides a good example:

I am a butcher, and I have had dealings with Mr. Harper . . . and he invited me to dine upon a Good Friday Cake as we call it; for he was a right good neighbourly man and he invited five other neighbours ... to eat of this cake ... We have a notion ... in our country, that if we do eat of a cake made purposely on Good Friday we shall never want money or victuals all the year round, which for as many years as I can remember has always fallen out true.

In recent times, the poor old hot cross bun has come under pressure from a variety of directions. On 17 March 2003, *The Times* reported that four local councils have decided to ban them from their schools, because they might offend children of other religions. However, the bun has attracted ingenious but nonsensical speculation about its ancient pagan origins, despite its bearing the overtly Christian symbol of a cross and being sold on the day of Christ's crucifixion, and this has prompted some devout Christians to refuse them. Perhaps the wildest fancy that seeks to prove the hot cross bun's remote origins is based on the similarity of the word 'bun' to the Ancient Greek word *boun*, which, we are told by the eighteenth-century antiquarian John Brand, was a cake with two horns, offered to the gods at Arkite temples every seventh day. In fact, 'bun' is of uncertain derivation and has only been recorded in English since 1371. As the *Oxford English Dictionary* explains, although the word has various shades of meaning in different parts of the country, a basic definition for usage in England is 'a sweet cake (usually round), not too large to be held in the hand while being eaten', which sums it up perfectly.

Skipping

In several parts of the country, people would gather in a convenient open space on Good Friday to take part in an orgy of communal skipping. This was not the solo skipping of the type still done by girls in the school playground, but the version with two people turning a long rope, which could accommodate several skippers at the same time. The best known examples of Good Friday skipping customs were at Cambridge and along the Sussex coast. A correspondent to *Notes & Queries* reported in 1863 that:

In Brighton on this day the children in the back streets bring up ropes from the beach. One stands on the pavement on one side, and one on the other, while one skips in the middle of the street. Sometimes a pair (a boy and a girl) skip together, and sometimes a great fat bathing-woman will take her

place, and skip as merrily as the grandsire danced in Goldsmith's Traveller.
They call the day 'Long Rope Day'. This was done as lately as 1863.

Twenty years later, Brighton antiquarian Frederick Sawyer commented
further:

The custom continues to be observed with vigour, and burly navvies may
also be seen skipping actively; whilst on the Level at Brighton on Good
Friday, 1883, there were scores of skippers. Mr. Rolf says the name is 'Long
Line Day'.

The custom continued at Brighton until the outbreak of the Second
World War, but the closing of the beaches in anticipation of inva-
sion finally killed it. Good Friday skipping was also reported from
Hastings, Hove, Southwick, Patcham, Lewes, Alciston, and other
Sussex locations.

At Cambridge, local people gathered with ropes and picnics on the
open ground called Parker's Piece. In her *Cambridgeshire Customs and
Folklore* (1969), Enid Porter records that:

Until early in the evening the skipping went on, the men traditional-
ly turning the ropes and the women jumping, although this . . . was not
always strictly followed because children often skipped with the adults.
Tradesmen selling sweets, ice-creams, toys, lemonade, etc., set up stalls along
the Parkside.

The Cambridge skipping also faded away at the outbreak of the
Second World War, but Porter's informants referred to similar
activities in other nearby villages earlier in the twentieth century.

There have been sporadic revivals of Good Friday skipping in various places in Sussex, but the one place that has continued its skipping without need of revival is Scarborough, in Yorkshire, where it is
done on Shrove Tuesday (*see* p. 84). Communal skipping was probably
much more widespread in the past than present evidence indicates.
There are isolated reports, for example, from London, Leamington
in Warwickshire, Pontypool in Monmouthshire, and Guildford in
Surrey, and further research will probably turn up many more examples. One such is the remarkable film made by the firm Mitchell
and Kenyon, of Preston egg-rolling in 1901, published by the British
Film Institute as *Electric Edwardians*. In the massed crowd scenes, it is
difficult to see any egg-rolling taking place, but in among the throng

there are at least a dozen long skipping ropes in action, with men, women, and children taking part.

The origins of communal skipping on Good Friday are still uncertain. Although skipping is nowadays regarded as an activity for young girls, in the past it was done by boys and by adults as well; however, it does not seem to be as old as is usually assumed. Child-lore experts Iona and Peter Opie have found no earlier reference to skipping with ropes before the seventeenth century, although skipping through hoops is a little older. In Sussex, local tradition links the custom with fishing families, saying that the ropes were supplied by the fishermen, which may be true at these locations but can hardly be relevant at inland places. Another widespread tradition is that the custom celebrates the death of that unpopular figure Judas Iscariot, with the skipping rope symbolizing the rope he used to hang himself; however, any Good Friday custom is likely to attract a Judas Iscariot story. The problem with all these explanations is that such communal skipping customs cannot be shown to be any older than the mid nineteenth century.

Tinsley Green Marbles

Every Good Friday, the Greyhound pub at Tinsley Green, near Gatwick Airport in Sussex, plays host to teams of marble-players from far and wide for the World Marbles Championship. Marble-playing has a venerable history, which is hardly surprising given the essential simplicity of rolling round items along the ground, and evidence from the ancient world shows that analogous games were played with fruit stones, nuts, and clay balls, while in later years marble, alabaster, glass, and metal were used to make more effective missiles.

The first evidence of the game in Britain appears surprisingly late, in the mid seventeenth century, with references to 'bowling-stones', but from that time on there are numerous descriptions and illustrations to prove its popularity. It is clear that the game was played by people of all ages until the earlier twentieth century, when it became essentially a children's game.

The organized annual championship matches that take place at Tinsley and other places in Britain date only from the 1930s and 1940s, although they seem to have started a little earlier in America, in the 1920s. Marble-players are famous for having their own language: tolleys, alleys, and taws are types of marbles, while fudging, fubbing,

fulking, and fullocking are dialect terms for leaning forward too far,
or otherwise trying to cheat. There are also numerous arcane rules and
traditions. The order of play is traditionally determined at Tinsley by
a 'nose-drop', whereby contestants hold a marble at nose height, and
drop it. The owner of the marble that lands nearest to a line drawn on
the floor goes first.

The game at Tinsley takes place on a well-sanded raised concrete
circle, six feet in diameter, between two teams of six. Forty-nine marbles are placed at the centre (four for each player, plus one). The rules
are relatively simple, but appear complex, even in the words of expert
observer Iona Opie:

*First player knuckles down at edge of ring and shoots his tolley to knock one
or more marbles right out of the ring. If he succeeds, and his tolley remains
in the ring, he shoots again. If he fails, but his tolley remains in the ring, it
stays there until his turn comes round again, when he shoots from wherever
it happens to be. If in the meantime his tolley has been knocked out of the
ring by his own or the opposing side, he is 'killed' and is out of the game.*

In 2005, twenty-three teams took part, necessitating a series of heats
leading up to the final. As the date of Good Friday varies from year
to year, weather conditions and, in particular, the all-important light
can vary considerably. The game itself may not have altered in the
seventy-five years since its inception, but the event certainly has,
and over twenty-five years ago there were worries about wider fame
affecting the day: 'Some of the original atmosphere has been lost with
the influx of TV crews, foreign tourists and the like,' wrote Sussex
expert Tony Wales in 1979.

No self-respecting annual custom can exist without a historical legend to explain its origin, and at Tinsley it is said that the game originated when two young Elizabethans contended for the hand of a local
maiden. This must be such a recently invented story that it may not
be too late to pin down its actual origin with some in-depth local research. There is no reason to think that Sussex was particularly known
for marble-playing in the remote past, but in recent years the county
has certainly earned that reputation, and another well-known Good
Friday match has taken place at Battle since it was revived in 1948.

Washing Molly Grime

A strange charity, which formerly took place at Glentham in Lincolnshire every Good Friday, was popularly known as 'washing Molly Grime'. A rent-charge laid on a local estate provided the annual sum of seven shillings, which was used to reward seven poor spinsters of the parish provided they fetch water from Newell Well (about two miles away) and duly wash a stone statue on one of the tombstones, which was called 'Molly Grime'. The origin of the custom is still unknown, but it lapsed in 1832 when the estate was sold, and no provision was made for the money to continue.

See also **Doles**, p. 115.

Widow's Son

The pub called the Widow's Son (sub-titled 'the Bun House') in Devons Road, Bromley-by-Bow, has a mass of blackened, dust- and cobweb-laden hot cross buns hanging from its ceiling. Every Good Friday they add another one. The story behind this custom tells how a widow lived in a cottage on the site. Her only son went to sea, and, expecting his return at Easter, she baked a hot cross bun for him as she had always done before. By next Easter, he still had not returned, but, ever hopeful, she baked another, and so on each year until she had quite a collection hanging from a beam in the kitchen. After she died, a pub was built on the site, and the proprietors continued the tradition of hanging up a new bun every Good Friday.

Oddly enough, the strangest part of the tale – the hanging of buns from kitchen ceilings at Easter – is the part of the custom that is the most commonplace. It was very widely believed, from at least the mid eighteenth century, that bread or buns baked on Good Friday would never go mouldy and possessed marked medicinal powers, for animals as well as humans. Pieces of 'Good Friday bread' that had hardened over the months, or years, were grated and put into food and drink to cure a wide variety of complaints, including stomach upsets and bowel problems. The accumulated bread was usually hung up in the cottage kitchen until needed. Less well known, but still widespread, was the idea that the bread was also 'protective', as recorded in William Hone's *Every-Day Book* (1827):

In the houses of some ignorant people, a Good Friday bun is still kept 'for luck', and sometimes there hangs from the ceiling a hard biscuit-like cake of open cross-work, baked on a Good Friday, to remain there till displaced on the next Good Friday by one of similar make ... and [it is] affirmed that it preserves the house from fire, and 'no fire ever happened in a house that had one'.

Others maintained that the bread protected against shipwreck, which may be more relevant to the Widow's Son story. The pub has been called 'The Widow's Son' since at least 1851, but it is not known how far back the bun-hanging goes. It is tempting to assume that the pub is so named because of the existing story, but it is equally likely that the story was invented to explain the unusual pub name.

For many years, the new bun was hung up by a sailor, and while the locality remained linked to the docks, it was not difficult to find one, but the area has changed dramatically, and in recent years it has been the custom for a serving member of the Royal Navy to do the honours. The event is now officially sponsored and has gained something of the air of a publicity stunt, but it still continues.

See also **Good Friday: Bread and Eggs**, p. 142.

Workington Football

At Workington in Cumberland, they have a surviving example of the 'mass' football games that were previously widespread in the country but can now only be found in a handful of places. The game is played on three days over the Easter period – Good Friday, Easter Tuesday, and the following Saturday, although the Easter Tuesday game is claimed to be the original one, and local records show it has been in existence since at least 1779.

The game is played with a leather ball, slightly smaller than a regular football, and teams can be of any size. Ostensibly, the contest is now between the 'Uppies and Downies', defined by which part of the town the player lives in, but most accounts state that it was previously between sailors and miners. Each game starts in the evening, between six-thirty and seven o'clock, and can last well into the night. Play starts when the ball is thrown up on the bridge over the beck, roughly halfway between the two 'hails', or goals, which are situated at Workington Hall and the harbour, respectively, about a mile and a half apart.

As is the case in many of these mass football customs, the ball spends much of its time in a huge unwieldy 'scrum', and the players have the reputation of being no respecters of property, regularly tramping over allotments, gardens, and cricket pitches, and spilling into the town's streets; however, the game was certainly rougher in the past. At least two players have been drowned during a game (in 1882 and 1932), and numerous serious injuries were regularly recorded. As elsewhere in similar circumstances, there was a local belief that players could not be prosecuted for anything that happened during the game (*see* **Lawless Hours and Days**, p. 412). Although the local police have traditionally tried to control the game and prevent its worst excesses, there does not seem to have been any serious attempts to suppress it outright.

See also **Football**, p. 64.

Easter Saturday

Bacup Coco-Nut Dancers

Every Easter Saturday, the Britannia Coco-Nut Dancers spend all day touring the streets of the Lancashire mill town of Bacup, dancing to the sound of a silver band, which trudges along in their wake. To the outsider, the dancers' costumes are colourful and distinctive, although somewhat bizarre. They wear a black long-sleeved jumper, crossed diagonally by a white sash, black breeches, white socks, fancy black clogs, a short white 'kilt' with red and blue horizontal stripes, and white hats decorated with rosettes and a feather of red or blue. They also have blackened faces. Strapped to their hands, knees, and waist are round pieces of wood, the 'coconuts' that give the dance its name, and that are struck together in set rhythmic patterns during dancing. There are eight men in the team, including a leader who is called the 'Whipper-In'. He uses a whistle, to communicate when the other dancers should stop and start, and he carries a whip, with which he can theoretically control the crowd.

The dancers progress along the street in two files of four on each side, with a kind of running dance step, stopping every now and then to perform a static dance in single file. Each dancer bends forward to strike his hands against his waist and knees, stands up to strike hands with his neighbour, and turns on the spot. Then they continue down the street. At certain locations they stop to perform their 'garland dances', of which there are five variations. They form up in couples in a square formation, each pair carrying a hooped garland between them, and they perform simplified quadrille movements. These garland dances have their own tunes, but the rest of the time the band plays the same melody over and over again, which, like other traditional tunes played all day at public customs, is more hypnotic than monotonous.

As Theresa Buckland suggests, the origins of the custom may lay in other local customs that involved 'blacking up'. The blackening of faces was formerly found in various traditional customs all over England, including pace-egging and versions of the mumming play, but its origin and meaning is obscure. In some cases, it is almost certainly directly descended from the blackface minstrelsy that was hugely popular in Britain in the nineteenth century (*see*, for example, **26 December: Padstow Mummers' (Darkie) Day**), and this has led some modern commentators to condemn the practice outright, as racist. But in many cases this link seems inappropriate, and it has often been suggested that blacking the face was originally a form of disguise. It is certainly an effective camouflage, and there are plenty of references to those who have blackened their faces for precisely this reason when involved in social disturbances, or when performing mass customs under threat from the police.

Easter Day

Eggs

The egg seems to have been one of the most adaptable symbols in myth and ritual across Europe and Asia, and most religions have some egg symbolism or other. It is often connected with spring, and in the Christian festival of Easter an egg can symbolize new life, birth, regeneration, or other qualities, depending on the context required. The emergence of a chick from the egg can be symbolic of Christ rising from the tomb, or the egg can even be seen as the stone rolled away from the tomb. It is perhaps this symbolic versatility rather than any intrinsic properties that has ensured the egg's enduring attraction to people looking for metaphor.

On a more prosaic level, eggs were an essential part of the staple diet of rich and poor alike, but were banned for the forty days of Lent. This enforced abstinence goes a long way to explaining why eggs should feature so widely in Shrovetide customs, just before Lent, and at Easter when the people celebrated their return. Eggs were often given as gifts, or as tribute, or as payment in kind for rent or service to a superior in a social hierarchy, such as a medieval manor. In farming communities, eggs acted as a minor currency, and, being under the control of the women of the household, provided a modest but steady income for the family, in addition to much-needed protein at mealtimes.

See also **Easter Day: Pace-Egging**, p. 158; *compare* **Shrovetide and Lent**, p. 60; **Shrove Tuesday: Egg Shackling**, p. 75.

Greenwich Fair

Greenwich Fair is an excellent example of a fair that had no founding charter or official standing, but just grew on the spot by sheer weight of visitor numbers. From at least the early eighteenth century, Londoners had been in the habit of going out to Greenwich for day trips in spring and summer, and by the 1760s the Easter and Whitsun holidays had become the favourite days for these excursions. Among other simple pleasures, it was traditional for young people to run down the grassy hill, hand-in-hand in couples, or in long linked lines, but wherever there are people in holiday mood, providers of food, drink, and entertainment are never far behind. The attractions on offer soon grew from one lone gingerbread-seller to an impressive annual gathering of stalls, booths, rides, and sideshows. Nationally famous travelling outfits such as Richardson's Circus and Wombwell's Menagerie started making regular appearances, and by the turn of the nineteenth century a full-blown pleasure fair was in operation every year on both holidays.

The fair attracted the attention of many of the London-based writers and artists of the day, and there are many good descriptions and pictures of the event in the first half of the nineteenth century. Most other fairs were burdened by the lingering feeling that they were being held for more important business than fun, something that stemmed from the days when the buying and selling of sheep, horses, or cheese had been their *raison d'être*. But Greenwich had no such baggage, and was devoted entirely to pleasure. By all accounts, it was particularly popular with London servant girls and their young men, and the dancing booths, where couples paid a small sum for each dance they took part in, did very good business. One of the crazes, noted by the social commentator Nathaniel Hawthorne in the following account from 1863, reflected their holiday mood:

What immediately perplexed me was a sharp, angry sort of a rattle, far off and close at hand, and sometimes right at my back. By-and-by, I discovered that this strange noise was produced by a little instrument called 'The Fun of the Fair' – a sort of rattle, consisting of a wooden wheel, the cogs of which turn against a thin slip of wood, and so produce a rasping sound when drawn smartly against a person's back. The ladies draw their rattles against the backs of their male friends (and everybody passes for a friend at Greenwich Fair) and the young men return the compliment on the broad British backs of the ladies; and all are bound by immemorial custom to take it in good part and be merry at the joke.

This description helpfully elucidates an obscure passage in Douglas Jerrold's immensely popular comic tales *Mrs. Caudle's Curtain Lectures*, first published in *Punch* in 1845. In one of the chapters of this series, Mrs Caudle berates her husband for sneaking off to Greenwich Fair, and one of her particular complaints was:

Then you must go in the thick of the fair, and have the girls scratching your coat with rattles . . . Don't tell me people don't scratch coats unless they're encouraged to do it.

Probably the most famous description of the fair is by Charles Dickens, in his capacity as journalist rather than novelist. His lively account appeared in *Sketches by Boz*:

Half the private houses are turned into tea-shops, fiddles are in great request, every little fruit-shop displays its stall of gilt gingerbread and penny toys; turnpike men are in despair, horses won't go on, and wheels will come off; ladies in 'caravans' scream with fright at every fresh concussion, and their admirers find it necessary to sit remarkably close to them, by way of encouragement; servants-of-all-works, who are not allowed to have followers, and have got a holiday for the day, make the most of their time with the faithful admirer who waits for a stolen interview at the corner of the street every night, when they go to fetch the beer – apprentices grow sentimental, and straw-bonnet makers kind.

Nevertheless, the fun sometimes got out of hand, and without the protection of any kind of official status the fair was vulnerable to the displeasure of the local authorities. After serious rioting took place at the Easter gathering in 1850, it was rapidly suppressed.

New Clothes

In these days of cheap imported clothes, it is easy to lose sight of the tremendous importance of *new* clothes for people on restricted budgets, and it is no surprise that they take on a symbolic meaning above and beyond their practical use. In Britain, there were several widespread superstitions about new clothes, and one feature of these beliefs was that on certain days one was expected to wear at least one item of new clothing, for luck and future prosperity. If one did not, it was said, the birds would mess on you. Whitsun and New Year were two of these key times, but the superstition was most widespread at Easter. In 1909, Hastings M. Neville recorded that in Northumberland:

Whether from respect for the chief Sunday in the year, or simply from the following of old custom, every woman and child who comes to church on Easter Day wears some new article of clothing.

This idea was found in all parts of the British Isles, well into the twentieth century, but in England it was probably most widely known in the northern counties, where other Easter customs were also concentrated. In *Cumbria Within Living Memory* (1994), it was reported that:

After leaving the Sunday School we then set out on our favourite part of the day, calling on all the houses in the village to show off our new outfits and receive yet more pasche eggs and oranges. Sometimes after being told how smart we looked we would be given a little pinch and told 'that's a nip for new!'

The 'pinch for luck' was also widespread, and if done cruelly (as at school) could take much of the child's pleasure in their new clothes away; however, an alternative, kinder verbal benediction was available in the form of: 'Health to wear it, strength to tear it, and money to buy another.'

Given the importance of Easter in the religious calendar, the emphasis on looking your best probably goes back a long way. It was certainly proverbial in the sixteenth century, as noted in Thomas Lodge's

Wits Miserie (1596): 'The farmer that was contented in times past with his russet frock and mockado sleeves, now sells a cow against Easter to buy him silken gear for his credit'; and in Act III, scene 1 of William Shakespeare's *Romeo & Juliet* (1597), 'Didst thou not fall out with tailor for wearing his new doublet before Easter'. Over half a century later, Samuel Pepys provides some nice examples of the idea:

[9 February 1662] . . . *was all day in my chamber – talking with my wife about her laying out of £20; which I had long since promised her to lay out in clothes against Easter for herself* . . .

[30 March 1662] *Easterday: Having my old black suit new-furbished, I was pretty neat in clothes today – and my boy, his old suit new-trimmed, very handsome.*

Pepys's diary entries also demonstrate that Easter had been formalized as the time of year when new fashions were set, at least for the gentry who had the means to worry about such things:

[15 February 1667] *She did give me account of this wedding today, its being private being imputed to its being just before Lent, and so in vain to make new clothes till Easter, that they might see the fashions as they are like to be this summer – which is reason good enough.*

See also **Whitsun: Superstitions**, p. 266.

Old Ball

Old Ball was an Easter house-visiting custom, reported only from the area around Blackburn and Burnley in Lancashire. A real horse's skull, or a wooden replica, was mounted on a pole, with glass bottle bottoms for eyes, a jaw that could open and close, and nails for teeth. The operator would bend forward and grasp the pole in both hands, and was covered by an old sack or cloth, which formed the horse's body. Lancashire folklorists John Harland and T. T. Wilkinson described Old Ball's antics in 1867:

He runs first at one then at another, neighing like a horse, kicking, rising on his hind legs, performing all descriptions of gambols, and running after the crowd; the consequence is, the women scream, the children are frightened, and all is one scene of the most ridiculous and boisterous mirth . . . Sometimes a doggerel song is sung, while Ball prances about and snaps at the company. As soon as the song is finished, Ball plays his most boisterous pranks and frequently hurts some of the company by snapping their fingers between his teeth when they are defending themselves from his attacks. The writer has seen ladies so alarmed as to faint and go into hysterics.

This was a localized form of the 'mast' version of the hobby horse, similar to others found elsewhere such as the **Hooden Horse** of Kent and the **Old Tup** in Derbyshire and Yorkshire (*see* **24 December**). There are no records of Old Ball before the nineteenth century and he did not survive into the twentieth. Harland and Wilkinson imply that it was Ball's rough behaviour that prompted his downfall and disappearance.

See also **Hobby Horses**, p. 226.

Pace-Egging

Until the modern era succeeded in wiping out nearly all vestiges of regionalism in traditional culture, the strong connection with eggs made Easter one of the times at which the northern counties of England had more in common with lowland Scotland than with midland or southern England. The 'pace-egg' customs described below were widely reported in Lancashire, Cheshire, parts of Yorkshire, Cumbria, Northumberland, and County Durham, and many were also recorded in Scotland, but the standard nineteenth-century folklore collections from elsewhere in England make little reference to eggs at Easter. Indeed, they hardly mention the season at all as a time for traditional custom. In those northern areas, a series of varied but overlapping customs, concerned with collecting eggs and using them in various ways, existed throughout the nineteenth and well into the twentieth century. They could be rolled on the ground, bashed together like conkers, kept for show, made into special Easter cakes, or simply eaten then and there. They might be decorated, grandly or simply, by the donors or the recipients, or they might feature, somewhat marginally, in an Easter version of the mummers' play (*see* **Easter Day: Pace-Egg Plays**, p. 162). Any of these customs could be called 'pace-egging', although this was often rendered as 'peace-egging', 'pash-egging', or 'paste-egging'. This term is clearly derived from *pasch* (the Latin for Easter), a word that would presumably have been familiar to English people from church services, and it has been used with this meaning in English since at least 1385. The word 'pace-egg' does not appear until 200 years later, in the *Beehive of the Romishe Churche* (1579), in a context superstition, to be derided and discarded:

Fasting days, years of grace, differences and diversities of days, of meats, of clothing, of candles, holy ashes, holy pace eggs, and flames, palms and palm boughs, staves, fools' hoods, shells and bells, paxes, licking of rotten bones, etc.

However, there is no record of a secular visiting or egg-decorating custom until 1778, when William Hutchinson wrote in his *History of Northumberland* that 'The children have dyed and gilded eggs given to them, which are called "Paste eggs".' In its most basic form, pace-egging resembled numerous other house-visiting customs in which parties (usually children or young people in this case) went from house to house singing a song and asking for money or food. Similar visiting customs took place at other seasons and in other areas: *see* **2 November: All Souls' Day**, **23 November: St Clement's Day**, and **Christmas: Wassailing** for examples. The song regularly used in this form of pace-egging also usually accompanied the pace-egg play, and versions varied considerably. One collected in Westmorland in 1909 commences:

> *Here's two or three jolly boys all of one mind*
> *We've come a-pace-egging if you will prove kind*
> *If you will prove kind with your eggs and strong beer*
> *We'll come no more nigh you until the next year*
> *Fol de roodle di diddle dum day*
> *Fol de roodle di diddle dum day.*

There were also numerous variations on the basic house-visit theme, as indicated in the standard collection of Lancashire folklore by John Harland and T. T. Wilkinson in 1882:

Young men in groups varying in number from three to twenty, dressed in various fantastic garbs, and wearing masks − some of the groups accompanied by a player or two on the violin − go from house to house singing, dancing, and capering. At most places they are liberally treated with wine, punch or ale, dealt out to them by the host or hostess. The young men strive to disguise their walk and voice, and the persons whom they visit use their efforts on the other hand to discover who they are; in which mutual endeavour many and ludicrous mistakes are made. Here you will see Macbeth and a fox-hunter arm in arm; Richard III and a black footman in familiar converse; a quack doctor and a bishop smoking their pipes and quaffing their 'half and half'; a gentleman and an oyster-seller; an admiral and an Irish umbrella-mender; in short every variety of character, some exceedingly well-dressed, and the characters well sustained . . .

Children, both male and female, with little baskets in their hands, dressed in all the tinsel-coloured paper, ribbons, and 'doll-rags', which they can command, go up and down from house to house; at some receiving eggs, at others gingerbread, some of which is called hot gingerbread, having in it a mixture of ginger and cayenne, causing the most ridiculous contortions of feature in the unfortunate being who partakes of it. Houses are literally besieged by these juvenile troops from morning till night. 'God's sake! A pace egg', is the continual cry.

Something of the feeling of these customs survived well into the twentieth century, as recorded in the Lancashire Federation of Women's Institutes' *Lancashire Lore* (1971):

Around Easter, at Overton and Middleton in the 1930s, we would go pace-egging. I remember one year putting on a dress inside out and covering my face with flour – it was then the custom to go round knocking on doors and be given decorated hard boiled eggs. We used to take little milk cans round the hedges collecting gorse flowers for my mother to colour our own home-produced eggs.

What the recipients did with the eggs varied enormously, but one recurrent feature was rolling them. In Northumberland in 1909, Hastings M. Neville related that:

The children all assemble in a field having a steep slope and bowl the eggs uphill with as much force as they can. The object is to try whose egg will hold out longest without breaking; and sometimes who can throw the egg furthest.

This account is only unusual in that the eggs were rolled uphill. More usually they were rolled downhill, or along flat ground, and some suitable slopes gained a reputation that has lasted for generations. In 1880, a correspondent to *Notes & Queries* reported:

On Easter Monday, the singular custom of rolling oranges and dyed eggs down the slopes of Avenham Park, Preston, Lancashire, was adhered to by all the youngsters of the neighbourhood. The grounds . . . were covered by a dense multitude of people, who come annually in the vicinity to witness and take part in this unique festivity.

While on 4 April 1988, *The Times* announced, 'This afternoon, up to 40,000 will take part in the ancient custom of Easter egg-rolling in Avenham Park, Preston.' Egg-rolling could also be done competitively, with the eggs deliberately aimed at each other, like bowls, and with broken or cracked eggs being claimed by those whose eggs stayed whole. This could also be done in single combat, like conkers, and this was called 'egg-dumping' or 'jarping'; antiquarian John Brand described the game in the mid nineteenth century:

Holding his egg in his hand, he challenges a companion to give blow for blow. One of the eggs is sure to be broken, and the shattered remains are the spoil of the conqueror, who is instantly invested with the title of a cock of 'one, two, three', etc, in proportion as it may have fractured his antagonists' eggs in the conflict. A successful egg in a contest with one which had previously gained honours adds to its number the reckoning of its vanquished foe. An egg which is the 'cock' of ten or a dozen is frequently challenged.

The Opies found that egg-rolling was still popular in Scotland, and in England 'north of the Trent', in the 1950s. They also reported that egg-decorating, as mentioned by Hutchinson in 1778, was still prevalent. In 1849, John Brand also commented on this custom:

In the North of England, it is still the custom to send reciprocal presents of eggs at Easter to the children of families respectively betwixt whom any intimacy exists. The eggs being immersed in hot water for a few moments, the end of a common tallow candle is made use of to inscribe the names of individuals, dates of particular events, etc. The warmth of the egg renders this a very easy process. Thus inscribed, the egg is placed in a pan of hot water, saturated with cochineal, or other dye-woods; the part over which the tallow has been passed is impervious to the operation of the dye; and consequently when the egg is removed from the pan, there appears no discoloration of the egg where the inscription has been traced, but the egg presents a white inscription on a coloured ground. The colour of course depends upon the taste of the person who prepared the egg; but usually much variety of colour is made use of. Another method of ornamenting 'pace eggs' is, however, much neater, although more laborious, than that with the tallow candle. The egg being dyed, it may be decorated in a very pretty manner, by means of a penknife, with which the dye may be scraped off, leaving the design white, on a coloured ground.

Many other natural dyes were used, including onion skins, saffron, and the afore-mentioned gorse flowers, while ribbons, tinsel, and other items glued to the shell could be used to make presentation pieces. In middle-class Victorian homes, egg-decorating was often a complex craft, if not actually high art, and in this way the custom finally broke free from its regional confines and spread across the rest of the country in the later nineteenth century. The story of the 'Easter Eggs and How the Girls Made Them', for example, published in the *Girls' Own Paper* of 12 March 1881, explains how three teenagers made a range of pretty presentation eggs for their families, including ones with painted and etched shells and some with little dolls or sweets inside. But although the girls 'knew of' the tradition of decorating eggs, they had to look up how to do it in books.

By this time, shops had begun to sell professionally decorated eggs, and in 1875 John Cadbury had launched the first commercial chocolate egg, which eventually revolutionized the connection between eggs and Easter. On 10 March 1894, *Chambers's Journal* noticed the trend:

Year by year the season of Easter has attained increased importance in our midst, giving an opportunity to those so inclined of displaying feelings and affections towards relatives and friends by the distribution of little presents in the various forms of 'Easter Eggs'.

See also **Easter Day: Eggs**, p. 153; *compare* **Shrovetide and Lent**, p. 60; **Shrove Tuesday: Egg Shackling**, p. 75.

Pace-Egg Plays

A number of customs that took place at Easter were called **pace-egging** (*see* p. 158), but one of the best-known was a version of the mummers' play (*see* **Christmas: Mummers**). As with many other egg customs, pace-egg plays were found only in Lancashire, Yorkshire, and Cumbria (where they were called 'Jolly Boys'). They were often performed by children rather than adults, and from the 1930s onwards there was a strong tradition of performances organized by local schools. The play performed annually at Midgley in West Yorkshire by teenagers from Calder Valley High School since 1932 is the best known and longest-lasting of these. School-based teams normally performed in the street, for everyone present, rather than acting privately during house visits, and this pattern has been continued by modern revival teams.

Most pace-egg versions are at heart a fairly typical 'hero-combat'

play in which two 'heroes' (typically, the King or Saint George, and
Bold Slasher) boast and fight; one is injured or killed and is revived by
a doctor. On the whole, the text is similar to other mumming plays,
as in the extract here from Greenodd, Lancashire, published in Alex
Helm's *The English Mummers' Play* (1980):

> *In steps I, Prince of Paradise, black Morocco King*
> *My sword and buckle by my side and through the woods I ring*
> *And through the woods I ring*
> *I'm brave, lads, and that's what makes us good*
> *And through thy dearest body, George, I'll draw thy precious blood.*

However, small details are different: a calling-on song is included, for
example, which introduces characters such as Tosspot, Lord Nelson,
Paddy from Cork, and a female called Molly Masket (with eggs in her
basket) or Dirty Bet:

> *So the first to come in is old Tosspot you see*
> *A jolly old fellow in every degree*
> *He wears a top hat and he wears a pigtail*
> *And all his delight is in drinking mulled ale.*

Those named in the song do not normally take part in the play itself, and these songs also often accompanied the 'pace-eggers' who
did not perform a play but simply went from house to house begging
money and/or eggs. In general, performers in pace-egg plays dress
'in character' (i.e. with some attempt to depict their character realistically), although in earlier sources they often wore little more than
distinguishing sashes over their ordinary clothes.

The question of the role of print in the development and dissemina-
tion of mummers' plays is still a vexed one, but chapbook texts were
certainly influential in the spread of pace-egg plays, although even here
the full extent of that influence is open to debate. Chapbooks were
small cheap booklets that provided the texts of the plays and rudimen-
tary instructions for performance, and were available from travelling
chapmen and in stationers' and toyshops a few weeks before Easter,
from the mid eighteenth century up to the First World War; one edition was even reprinted in 1959. The typical chapbook, like its cousin
the broadside, was decidedly at the lower end of the printing trade, and
was roughly printed on cheap paper. Pace-egg plays, with titles such
as *The Peace Egg, or St. George's Annual Play for the Amusement of Youth*,

were printed mainly in the area where the plays were later collected by folklorists, but they were also printed as far afield as Glasgow. One of their major attractions for children was the inclusion of several crude but lively woodcuts depicting the characters.

Since the 1960s, many enthusiastic revival teams have been founded, a number of which, having acquired sufficient stability and longevity, can now claim to have founded new traditions in themselves.

Riding the Lord

A problematic description of a custom, written by George Gleave of Manchester in 1895, describes a unique custom at Neston in Cheshire:

The morning's interlude usually began with the hidden but grotesque custom of what was called 'Riding the Lord' . . . [which] consisted in a man such as 'Ned Fabb,' who was not over scrupulous with regard to his employment, riding for some small pecuniary consideration on a donkey from the top of what is now called High-street to Chester-lane; and, in his burlesque progress, encountering, not only the ribald jeers of the holiday spectators, but also the more formidable and unsavoury bespatterment of a continuous fusillade of rotten eggs.

The Local Studies librarian at Cheshire Record Office confirms that no other independent source seems to mention this custom at all, although many subsequent writers, including the influential folklorist Christina Hole, repeat Gleave's account, often without acknowledgement. This being so, it would normally be safest to discount the custom completely, except for the fact that it appears to share interesting connections with other customs in which a person or effigy is similarly mistreated, including widespread **rough music** (p. 95) and Guy Fawkes events (*see* **5 November**), and particularly those surrounding **Jack-a-Lent** (p. 86), the Riding of the Black Lad (*see* **Easter Monday: Black Knight of Ashton**, p. 167) and the Burning of Bartle (*see* **24 August: West Witton Burning of Bartle**).

Easter Monday

Biddenden Maids Charity

One of the most widely known charity doles in the country is the annual distribution of bread and cheese at Biddenden in Kent, on Easter Monday. Recipients are handed a large loaf of bread, half a pound of cheese, two pounds of tea, and a commemorative 'cake', which is actually a hard, inedible biscuit. A colourful story explains the origin of the custom. The cake bears an embossed image of two women, standing very close together, and the words 'Elizabeth and Mary Chulkhurst'; on the dress of one is written 'A 34 Y', and on the other, 'IN 1100', which is usually taken to mean 'Aged 34 in the year 1100'. The story relates that Eliza and Mary Chulkhurst were conjoined twins, joined at shoulder and hip, who were born (or died) in 1100. They lived until the age of thirty-four, when one of them died. The other twin refused offers to attempt a surgical separation, saying that 'they had come into the world together, and they would leave it in the same way', and she died soon after. As was common in those days, the sisters left a legacy, in the form of twenty acres of land, sufficient to fund the annual distribution of bread, cheese, and ale to poor parishioners.

The story of the Chulkhurst sisters is central to the village's heritage. They are depicted on the sign in the centre of the village and on at least one other property nearby; there is also a new development called Chulkhurst Close, and the dole itself is officially called the 'Chulkhurst Charity'. However, there is a problem with the story. Although the dole has certainly existed for a long time, and the 'Bread and Cheese Land' is real enough, there is no evidence of when the legacy was founded, or who it was founded by, although 1100 is probably far too early. There is also no independent evidence that Eliza and Mary Chulkhurst even existed, let alone that they were responsible for the Biddenden dole. The whole story of the Siamese twins seems to have been invented to explain the illustration on the biscuit. The evidence to support this idea comes from two early written sources, and the key witness is Edward Hasted, whose *History of Kent* was published in 1790:

There is a vulgar tradition in these parts that the figures on the cake represent the donors of this gift, being two women, twins who were joined together in their bodies and lived together so, till they were between twenty and thirty years of age. But this seems to be without foundation. The truth seems to be that it was the gift of two maidens of the name of Preston, and that the print of the women on the cakes has taken place only within these fifty years, and was made to represent two poor widows as a general object of a charitable benefaction.

Hasted may be referring to the second edition of Dr Ducarel's *Repertory of the Endowments and Vicarages in the Dioceses of Canterbury and Rochester*, published eight years before, in 1782. This short account mentions that the women were conjoined, and lists their age as twenty or thirty years, and Ducarel provides an engraving of the illustration on the cakes. In this picture, the two women do indeed seem to be joined at the arm, but although their dresses meet, they are clearly not joined 'at the hip'. The only word on the cakes is 'Biddenden', and there is none of the lettering on which the 'Chulkhurst' story is based.

We are also fortunate that in 1656, the rector of the parish, William Horner, attempted to prove that the Bread and Cheese Land formed part of his own glebe lands. He was unsuccessful, but his action resulted in documentation of the charity being preserved in the parish records, which are now available in the Centre for Kentish Studies in Maidstone. As is the nature of such cases, the officials took evidence from elderly people in the parish, to establish what was known of the charity's history. In the surviving papers, the land is referred to throughout as the 'bread and cheese lands', and there are several mentions of the charity being instituted by 'two sisters', but there is no mention of the name Chulkhurst or any of the other colourful details of the modern story. Indeed, it seems that the names of the benefactors had already been forgotten in 1656, and how Edward Hasted came up with the name 'Preston' is at present unclear. Nevertheless, even if the story itself is full of holes, it is remarkable that the dole still continues each year.

The Biddenden dole is not unique, however, and in fact seems to be part of a long tradition of 'bread and cheese' charities, although the only other one still going is at St Briavels in Gloucestershire (*see* **Whit Sunday: St Briavels Bread and Cheese Dole**, p. 269), and that has taken a very different shape. A detailed comparison with these other doles may well shed some light on Biddenden's history. See, for example, the following piece taken from the Charity Commissioners' Reports:

Bread and cheese lands: the lands thus denominated are said to have been given by two maiden gentlewomen, for the purpose of supplying the poor with a donation of bread and cheese on the Sunday before Christmas. Neither the names of the donors nor the date of the gift are known, but it is a very ancient one.

Apart from the time of year, this description fits Biddenden exactly, but it was actually written about a custom that took place at Paddington, in London, until the mid nineteenth century. Similarly, a dole in which bread and cheese was thrown from a church tower existed at Twickenham, Middlesex, up to the turn of the nineteenth century. The custom had originally taken the form of breaking two large cakes in church on Easter Monday, but the Puritan parliament of 1645 decreed the cake to be superstitious and insisted it was replaced with bread and cheese for the poor. This is an excellent example of the way in which customs sometimes undergo abrupt alteration in response to changes in the prevailing religious or cultural atmosphere of the period, rather than being subject to the slow organic evolution that we often assume has always been the norm.

For another example of cakes being distributed in church, *see* **Palm Sunday: Pax Cakes**, p. 129. *See also* **Doles**, p. 115.

Black Knight of Ashton

The former celebrations at Ashton-under-Lyne in Lancashire are an excellent example of how a long-term local working-class custom can become a disreputable and discouraged event, but when taken by the ruling elite, and cleaned and prettied up, can be made the centrepiece of a new custom that celebrates and supports the town's prosperity and bolsters local pride.

Until late Victorian times, the inhabitants of Ashton-under-Lyne would be treated on Easter Monday to the spectacle of the Riding of the Black Lad (or Knight, or Boy). An effigy of a knight in black armour and black cloak was mounted on a horse, paraded around the town, and shouted and jeered at by the waiting crowds. At an appointed place, the Black Lad was dismounted, pelted with mud and stones, verbally insulted, and finally shot to pieces with any guns the townsfolk could muster. An eyewitness account from 1870 reveals the carnival nature of the proceedings:

It was easy to see that it was a gala day. In the market ground was the usual spectacle of a Lancashire fair. Once or twice we heard sounds of music in the distance and saw crowds hurrying off in search of the sounds which they knew heralded the approach of the Black Knight. We joined one of these parties and soon saw, marching down the middle of the street, a motley crowd. After the musicians came the figure of the Black Knight, in grotesque costume and mounted on some kind of a horse, followed by his retainers, who were busy collecting coppers from the crowd. The figure of the Black Knight, provided with a dragoon's helmet, a cuirass having the arm-holes stuffed with bunches of heather, and red trowsers apparently stuffed with sawdust, was held in place by a youth riding behind it. It turned out, however, that this was not the true Black Knight; we found that there were three Black Knights, so we paid to each.

The tale that explains the Black Knight's fame tells of one Sir Ralph de Assheton, a fifteenth-century lord of the manor, who was exceptionally cruel to everybody in his power, including his wife, servants, and subjects. He pillaged and murdered at will, and had a habit of placing his victims in a spike-lined barrel and rolling them down a nearby hill. He also had a particular antipathy for those who allowed corn marigolds and other weeds to grow on his land. After murdering his wife, he was finally shot down in the street by one of her relatives, or by one of his disgruntled tenants. In a further incongruous detail, he (or his descendant) is reputed to have left money to fund the annual celebration of his life and death. Unsurprisingly, this story is not only historically inaccurate, with a mistaken chronology, but there is also no evidence that any of the Assheton family had a reputation for being cruel or despotic. The whole thing appears to have been invented simply to explain the *Black* in 'Black Knight', as that epithet, in popular parlance, refers to character as well as appearance.

The first known reference to the custom, in 1795, already cited Sir Ralph as the basis for the Black Lad, and this idea was developed by Dr Samuel Hibbert, of the Society of Scottish Antiquaries, in 1822. Hibbert's theory was recycled in William Hone's immensely influential *Every-Day Book* (1827), and from then on became the accepted story, accruing details along the way. Folklorists such as Christina Hole have offered a different interpretation, that the effigy, so reviled and mistreated, symbolized winter and was ritually destroyed each year to welcome the spring. Unfortunately for this explanation, however, there is no evidence that the custom even existed before the 1790s, or that it had a ritual basis.

A letter published by Hone in 1827 claimed 'it is the most thronged, and the most foolish, day the Ashtonians can boast of.' As indicated by William Axon in 1870, by his time there were several effigies parading the town, some more respectable than others, and the feeling grew that the 'real' custom had degenerated into a form of begging for money to spend on drink. It is a familiar story that was played out in towns all over the country, as such customs gradually lost the support of the important middle classes who increasingly ran local public affairs.

By the late nineteenth century, the old custom of Riding the Black Lad had virtually died out, unlamented by most of the respectable inhabitants of Ashton. By the time increasing prosperity and civic pride brought about the idea of a historical pageant to celebrate the town's heritage in 1910, the reality of the old celebrations was safely in the past, and the organizing committee chose the Black Knight of Ashton as the pageant's centrepiece. The unofficial historical story with which the figure had been associated became the official text, and was taught to schoolchildren and recounted in countless pageant programmes, local histories, town guides, and, nowadays, Internet sites. The Ashton pageant was on a large scale, and it became one of the best-known in the area. It included, over the years, all the usual waving dignitaries, trade floats, tableaux, marching children, banners, bands, collectors rattling tins, and individual and group efforts in fancy dress, in addition to, at various times, a May Queen, Rose Queen, Harvest Queen, Civic Queen, Pageant Queen, and Cotton Queen. The Rose Queen was prompted by the move of the pageant to Alexandra Rose Day, in 1928.

The real centrepiece, however, which the crowd waited eagerly to see, was always the Black Knight himself, an imposing figure on horseback, and usually dressed completely in black on a black horse. His costume changed over the years and was the subject of much comment and debate, but it always approximated the current idea of a knight, with helmet, cloak, and sword. He was attended by a large retinue, including wife, servants, and guards, all in period costume, and often some boys carrying a barrel with spikes inside.

The annual pageants increased in scale, complexity, and popularity for the next few years, but, as with many other celebratory events, the First World War put an end to it. Nevertheless, the Black Knight Pageant was successfully revived in 1928, lapsed in 1935, staged again in 1939, and 1947 (for the town's centenary celebrations), and finally lapsed in 1954. Over the years, the pageants provided immense pleasure for participants and onlookers, and raised significant amounts for local charities, particularly, in the early years, for the local hospital. In recent years, ideas for large-scale events in Ashton, as elsewhere, have taken the form of carnivals rather than pageants, and the Black Knight has lost his opportunity for an airing. But he has a new lease of life as emblem for the Arcades shopping centre in the middle of town, where his statue can be seen every day by the people of Ashton.

The Black Lad is not alone in English tradition. The mistreatment of an effigy or particular person is a motif that appears in a number of contexts, most widely as an essential element of **rough music** activities (p. 95), but also in other, specific customs: *see* **Easter Day: Riding the Lord**, p. 164; **Ash Wednesday: Jack-a-Lent**, p. 86; **Spring Bank Holiday: Hunting the Earl of Rone**, p. 286; and **24 August: West Witton Burning of Bartle**.

Epping Stag Hunt

An annual occasion at Epping, in Essex, until 1853 was a stag hunt held on Easter Monday, in which hundreds of Londoners joined, to their own peril and the chagrin of the real hunting fraternity in the area, who largely stayed away from the event. Later accounts stress the comic effect of hopelessly inexperienced men and women, gaudily dressed for the hunt, chasing an 'old fat one-eyed stag' released from a cart. Thomas Hood's comic poem 'The Epping Hunt' (written in the 1820s) sums it all up. It commences by introducing its 'hero' grocer:

> *John Huggins was as bold a man*
> *As trade did ever know,*
> *A warehouse good he had, that stood*
> *Hard by the church of Bow.*

And goes on to relate, in over a hundred verses dripping with puns, how Huggins and his co-hunters, in pursuit of the stag, get lost, thrown off their horses into ditches, and overturn their carts.

In previous times, however, the hunt had been much more respectable, with the Lord Mayor, aldermen, and the Corporation of London in attendance. It was reputedly inaugurated as long ago as 1226.

Gawthorpe Coal-Carrying

Gawthorpe, a small West Yorkshire village that lies between Dewsbury and Wakefield, hosts the World Coal-Carrying Championship. This annual race was started in 1963, apparently after a 'discussion' in the pub between two locals on the subject of how fit each one was. Contestants have to cover a course around the village of just over a thousand metres, carrying a sack of coal weighing fifty kilos across their shoulders. There is also a ladies' race, with competitors carrying twenty kilos. The current world record for men is four minutes and six seconds, while for women it is five minutes and five seconds. The winners receive money, vouchers, and so on, depending on the sponsor, which at present is the local brewery, H. B. Clarke & Co. The event has changed somewhat in its time, as the local coal-pits have closed and the racers are less likely to be local miners and more likely to be from outside the immediate area; but it still remains a well-loved event in the village, and raises money for local charities.

See also **First Saturday in May: Gawthorpe Celebrations**.

Hallaton Hare Pie and Bottle-Kicking

The Leicestershire village of Hallaton carries out an annual hare-pie scramble and bottle-kicking, which probably combines two previous customs joined into one – the first a traditional 'dole', and the second a form of mass 'football'. The two are now intertwined on Easter Monday, but either could quite logically stand alone.

The 'dole' part of the day involves the hare pie and some 'penny loaves', which are distributed to the people. After a church service at about 11 a.m. at St Michael's, the rector cuts up the hare pie, and distributes some pieces, but most of it is placed into sacks for later. In the afternoon, a procession takes place up to Hare Pie Bank, where the rest of the pie is flung to the crowd. The hare pie is not made of hares' meat, and as hares are out of season at Easter and have never been a popular food with English people, it possibly never was. It now contains beefsteak, although earlier sources mention mutton, veal, and bacon. Most **scrambling customs** (p. 172) involve hard or at least durable substances such as pennies, sweets, or oranges, and pieces of meat pie do not seem to be ideal for throwing to the crowds. It is often reported that people do not actually try to eat the pie, but photographer and author Brian Shuel commented in 1985 that '[t]he scramble was a

token affair for the young, not taken very seriously. The pie was delicious, far from inedible like many early reports complain.'

The 'bottle-kicking' part of the day then takes place at Hare Pie
Bank. The 'bottles' are actually three small wooden kegs, two of which
contain beer, while one is empty. They are blessed in the morning
church service, and are prominently carried in the procession by three
men, each holding one at arm's length above his head. The contest

continued on page 174 ☞

Scrambling Customs

A very common feature in a range of customs was to throw things to a
waiting crowd to be 'scrambled for'. Coins were one of the staple items,
but food such as buns, oranges, nuts, and even bread and cheese were
regularly distributed in this way, and although in the twentieth century
the scramblers were usually children, in previous times the method was
also used with adults and even the elderly. The throwing could take place
from any convenient vantage point, but balconies, upstairs windows, and
even church towers were regularly used in this way.

Scrambling could form part of another custom (*see*, for example,
Easter Monday: Hallaton Hare Pie and Bottle-Kicking, p. 171), or as
the favoured method of distribution in a charity dole. It could also feature
in well-to-do rural weddings, where the bridegroom might throw handfuls
of coins to the village children, or it could provide the popular climax to
a civic ceremony like a mayor-making. As late as 1956, a reporter in *The
Times* took this civic connection for granted:

**It was truly reviving to the spirits to read of the aldermen and other
civic dignitaries of Abingdon on the occasion of the Queen's visit, in accordance with their ancient custom, throwing buns . . . As
there were some 2000 buns, at least the enjoyment was not done
for some while. In a short time on November 9 mayors in other bor-
oughs will be throwing down hot coppers to children in the street,
but there is about that gesture none of the fine venomous aiming
that there can be with a bun.**

At Harwich, Essex, where the bun-throwing is still part of the mayoral
celebrations, there were worries about hygiene in the 1960s, and the
decision was made to wrap the buns in cellophane first.

The whole idea might seem strange or even reprehensible to modern eyes, especially if perishable food is being flung, but there were two different trains of thought behind the procedure which were probably in action at different times. If children were the recipients, there was a definite emphasis on the 'fun' involved, not only for the children themselves, but also for the adult organizers and watchers. When coins were used, there was a strong tradition of heating them first, and there can be no other explanation for this procedure beyond the extra enjoyment it provided. But in cases where the scrambling was part of a charity dole, the throwing seems to have been a deliberate policy to ensure random distribution that showed no favour, and was therefore deemed to be 'fair'. There was also the added advantage that such a method needed little administration. It was only when the proceedings became too boisterous, or even riotous, that scramblings were replaced by more controlled methods of distribution. Oddly enough, however, there is some evidence that the scrambling element may not necessarily have been an original feature of any particular custom at all. In a case described by Daniel Lysons in his *Environs of London* (1792), it was introduced to replace much more sedate proceedings:

There was an ancient custom at Twickenham, of dividing two great cakes in the church on Easter Day among the young people; but it being looked upon as a superstitious relic, it was ordered by Parliament, 1645, that the parishioners should forbear that custom and, instead thereof, buy loaves of bread for the poor of the parish with the money that should have bought the cakes. It appears that the sum of £1 per annum is still charged upon the vicarage for the purpose of buying penny loaves for poor children on the Thursday after Easter. Within the memory of man they were thrown from the church steeple to be scrambled for; a custom which prevailed also, some time ago, at Paddington, and is not yet totally demolished.

Scrambling customs still survive in a number of places.

See also 14 February: Valentine's Day; Shrove Tuesday: Westminster Pancakes, p. 79; Maundy Thursday: Peter's Pence, p. 134; Hocktide: Hungerford Hocktide Court, p. 183; Mid May: Durham Mayor-Making; Third Thursday in May: Harwich Kichel-Throwing; Ascension Day: Oxford Beating the Bounds, p. 252; 23 May: Rye Mayor Making; Whit Sunday: St Briavels Bread and Cheese Dole, p. 269; 29 September: Michaelmas/Feast of St Michael and All Angels.

☞ *continued from page 172* then begins, and is between the people of Hallaton on one side and those of neighbouring Medbourne on the other, with any outsiders joining the latter team, which gives them a distinct advantage. Each team tries to get the bottle to their goal, one of two streams, which are a mile apart.

As with other traditional games subsumed under the name **football** (p. 64), there is no limit to the number of players and virtually no rules, but because this game takes place in the fields rather than the village streets, the style of play is more open and more akin to a very rough rugby match than some other games are. Despite the name, the bottles are rarely kicked. The game begins when a bottle is thrown up three times, and play only starts when it lands after the third throw. Whoever first grabs it is immediately surrounded by a mass of players of both sides. John Morison and Peter Daisley write in their recently published book on the custom:

The scrum writhes and churns as combatants strive to get hold of the bottle. The whole throng struggles forward, backwards, and side to side in no clear pattern. The crowd presses all around until suddenly there is a break. A combatant emerges with the bottle. Scattering onlookers, he is oblivious to resistance and charges through such minor obstacles as barbed wire fences and hedges . . . Such breaks rarely last long. Soon the man with the bottle is dragged down and becomes the nucleus of another scrum.

After a goal is scored, a second bottle is thrown up, and if there is a tie after the second game, the third is brought into play as a decider. The game changes character as the day wears on: participants become tired, some drop out, the scrums get smaller, and play becomes more open.

Certain aspects have been revived or introduced in recent years, as the usual tendency towards making an event a more family-friendly (or perhaps tourist-friendly) carnival or pageant has taken place. Many traditional customs were perfunctory and even dull for the outsider to watch, but a little imaginative tinkering can bring a sense of cohesion, as well as colour, to the day. There is now a children's parade in the morning, and some of the adults have recently started to dress up in medieval costume. The penny loaves have been re-introduced after having been dropped for many years, necessitating a 'bread lady' to carry the basket, and the carrying of a hare as a sort of standard in the procession revives an element mentioned in earlier descriptions, although nowadays it is a brass replica rather than a dead animal on the pole. Nevertheless, these improvements have made no difference to the bottle-kicking, which still remains one of the roughest, toughest customs in the English calendar.

It is nowadays suggested that the bottle-kicking aspect of the day developed from the scrambling custom. The argument is that the hare pie, penny loaves, and ale were all designed for distribution by scrambling, and that local youths, as is the nature of youths everywhere, were primarily interested in the drink, and banded together to ensure that they captured the prize. This idea is certainly supported by one of the earliest descriptions of the custom, found in a letter from John Tailby to local historian John Nichols in 1796 (reprinted in Morison & Daisley (2000)) that speaks of scrambling for the ale but not of any organized 'game'. But it is just as likely that the original dole was for food and drink – some of the food to be scrambled for, the rest distributed or consumed on the spot, and the ale would be in the latter category.

Much also has been made of the 'sacred' nature of hares for Ancient Britons, the ancient connection between hares and Easter, and a supposed pagan origin of the Hallaton custom, all of which are extremely dubious. The scrambling custom is clearly the result of a Christian dole that distributed food, a form of bequest common from medieval times onwards. The only mystery is why it is called a *hare* pie, and as we only have second- and third-hand reports of the nature and contents of the original bequest at present, which are already heavily coloured by later assumptions, this will only be solved if the original can be found.

See also **Doles**, p. 115.

Harness Horse Parade

The Harness Horse Parade takes place in London's Battersea Park every Easter Monday, although it was previously held in Regent's Park. The parade dates back to 1886, when it was inaugurated to encourage commercial horse owners to take a pride in their animals, but the current series came into being in 1965, when it amalgamated with the London Van Horse Parade. The event starts at 10 a.m. and attracts scores of entries, including a wide range of horses and vehicles.

Legging Day

The following report can be found in John Nicholson's *Folk Lore of East Yorkshire* (1890):

At Easter, boys and girls try to catch each other by the ankles and trip one another up, or 'leg them down', as they say. Hence Easter Monday is known as 'Leggin Day', but if you trip any one up at any time, you offer as excuse 'It's leggin day ti-day!'

Unfortunately, no other information is forthcoming.

Leicester Hare Hunt

This former calendar custom, with civic overtones, took place in Leicester on Easter Monday until about 1767. The mayor, corporation, and officers would proceed to a piece of land called Black Annis' Bower Close, at the edge of Leicester Forest, to witness the annual 'hare hunt'. In this hunt, a dead cat that had been treated with aniseed water was trailed on a rope around the town, through streets and alleys, by a rider; the hounds and huntsmen were then let loose to follow the trail. The first documentary evidence for the custom occurs in the town records for 1668, but it was then described as an ancient custom, and it is more than likely that the hunt originally involved a real hare.

Sun Dancing

One of the most widespread Easter beliefs, reported from all over England, and in Ireland and Wales as well, was the idea that the sun literally danced for joy at the Resurrection on Easter Monday morning. The notion was already proverbial in the mid seventeenth century, as it is included in John Suckling's 'Ballade Upon a Wedding' (1646):

> *But oh! she dances such a way –*
> *No sun upon an Easter day*
> *Were half so fine a sight . . .*

It was recorded several more times before 1700, and numerous times from then on. There were a few variations; in some families, for example, it was said that you could see a lamb in the sun as it rose on that morning.

Educated people usually smiled condescendingly when reporting the idea, but there is no doubt that many believed it literally. The majority presumably took it on trust from hearsay, but there were plenty who made an annual trip to the nearest high hill to try to see it, as with this gentleman in Devon in 1876:

I was awoke at daylight by gravel being thrown against my window, and on lifting the blind found that it proceeded from old John, who had come to call me to see the 'sun dance' . . . On mounting the side of Corndon Torr old John would occasionally turn round toward 'sunrise' and remark how fortunate we were in having so favourable a morning for our observation. We did not follow his example, reserving ourselves for the coup d'oeil at the summit; and in a few moments we were amply repaid, for a scene of unparalleled splendour broke upon our view, through a cloudless sky and rare atmosphere. 'How long will this continue, John?', 'Why, maister, up along ten o'clock; but not so strong when the sun has more power. I saw it Good Friday morning preparing; but on this morning it is ordained to dance to remind us of the Saviour's rising from the grave. See how red it is at the edges!' And so the old man, with uplifted eyes, had his gaze fixed upon the now bright morning sun.

But the 'maister' reported only that 'there was the same flickering, radiating effect that is seen at sunrise from any high summit.' He clearly lacked sufficient faith, or perhaps it was the Devil at work, as was said in Sussex at a similar time:

There is a tradition that the sun always dances on the morning of Holy Sunday, but nobody has ever seen it because the devil is so cunning that he always puts a hill in the way to hide it.

Compare 24 **December: Cattle Kneeling; Christmas: Holy Thorn(s).**

Water

A children's custom, which went under various local names, involved the collection of water from a specific well, and mixing it with sugar, broken sweets, peppermint, or liquorice, to make a special drink. A correspondent to *Notes & Queries* wrote in 1870:

Elecampane on Easter Monday: During a recent visit to the little village of Castleton in Derbyshire, I noticed every child without exception had a bottle of this mixture – the younger ones having one tied around their necks – all sucking away at this curious compound of Spanish juice, sugar and water, with great assiduity. I was informed by a very old man that this custom had always obtained in Castleton on Easter Monday as long as he could remember.

The traditional day for this activity varied from place to place, but it usually took place on Easter Monday, Ascension Day, or Palm Sunday, and its names included Elecampane (a herb), Spanish Sunday, Sugar-Cupping Day, Sugar-and-Water Day, Rinsing Day, and Shakking Monday. Derbyshire seems to have been the centre of the custom, where it is frequently reported from *c.*1830 well into the twentieth century, but it does not seem to have been much known in England outside the Midlands.

See also **Palm Sunday: Water**, p. 130.

Easter Monday and Tuesday

Lifting

This custom, also called 'heaving', was widely reported in eighteenth- and nineteenth-century sources from the western side of north and middle England (Lancashire, Cheshire, Shropshire, Staffordshire, Worcestershire, and Derbyshire) and the northern half of Wales. A Manchester correspondent to the *Gentleman's Magazine* of 1784 describes it in the following way:

The men lift the women on Easter Monday, and the women the men on Tuesday. One or more take hold of each leg, and one or more of each arm, near the body, and lift the person up, in a horizontal position, three times. It is a rude, indecent, and dangerous diversion, practised chiefly by the lower class of people. Our magistrates constantly prohibit it by the bellman, but it subsists at the end of the town; and the women have of late converted it into a money job. I believe it is chiefly confined to these northern counties.

The basic procedure was very similar from place to place, although there were differences in detail. Charlotte Burne, for example, re-corded that in part of Shropshire the men carried posies that were dipped in water to sprinkle on the feet of the women, and whereas men were usually lifted in the way described, women and elderly people were more often placed in a chair, which was usually decorated with ribbons and bows. There was also a wide variation in the amount of 'rough handling' allowed. Nearly all the descriptions stress that it was very much a working-class custom, and several say that women and timid men avoided going out on the day if they could. But staying at home was not always sufficient protection, as the *Folk-Lore Journal* (1883) indicates:

> . . . *a case heard before Norton Magistrates the other day. The prosecutor, William Pullen, charged Thomas Lawton for being in his house for an unlawful purpose. Defendant entered Mr. Pullen's house, and said he had come to lift his wife, and two men followed defendant to the garden-gate. Prosecutor told defendant to get out, or he would kick him out. He would not allow any one to take such liberties. Defendant thereupon became very abusive. It was stated that defendant was endeavouring to carry out an old Cheshire custom. The men lifted the women on Easter Monday, and women lifted men on Easter Tuesday. The magistrates informed defendant he must apologise and pay the costs.*

On the other hand, an old bookseller, over eighty years of age in 1881, told Charlotte Burne, 'It was a very pretty, pleasant old game . . . and I never heard that there was any harm in it.'

Owing to the Easter setting, it has been assumed on all sides that the custom celebrated the resurrection of Christ, and one report mentions that the lifters sang, 'Jesus Christ is risen again.' It is possible that this is true, but there is no real evidence either way. Nor is it clear how old the custom might be. It was certainly widespread by the second half of the eighteenth century, but it seems to spring into being at that time fully formed. It is tempting to assume a direct development from the much earlier custom of Hocktide binding (*see* **Hocktide**, p. 182), which also involved men and women trapping each other on alternate days, and again this is a distinct possibility. Binding and lifting were done at different times, but only a week apart, and it is possible that as Hocktide had lost most of its meaning by the Restoration, a revival could have moved the custom to the previous week to bring it into the Easter holidays, and the alteration from binding to lifting made at the same time in reference to the Resurrection. Occasional examples involving both ropes and chairs, as here from Worcestershire in 1856, might be evidence of a direct link:

At Kidderminster . . . the women decked themselves gaily for the occasion, dressed a chair with ribbons, and placed rope across the street; any man bold enough to come within yards of them was caught, placed in the chair, which was lifted up and turned round three times, and finally set down; the terms of release were then settled.

However, this is speculation, and one factor that can be used to argue against the theory is the geographical evidence. As stated, lifting was recorded almost exclusively in the western midland counties of England and in North Wales. Hocktide binding, on the other hand, was heavily concentrated in the South and East. Moreover, there were other variations on similar themes, less commonly reported, that pitted men against women on adjacent days, often concerned with shoes and hats. In 1865, in his *History and Antiquities of Masham and Mashamshire*, John Fisher recorded that in Yorkshire:

On Easter Sunday, young men and boys, by prescriptive right, take the liberty of taking the shoes from off young women's feet, and of keeping them till redeemed by a payment of money; and on Easter Monday, the young women in exercise of the same right, possess themselves, as best they can, of the hats of the young men and retain them until they are redeemed by a like payment.

Lifting survived in a few places until the turn of the twentieth century, but faded away soon after.

Easter Tuesday

Holly Bussing

This Easter Tuesday practice was reported only from the Northumberland village of Netherwitton in the mid nineteenth century, although it was claimed to be a 'very ancient custom'. The young people of the village, accompanied by the parish clerk 'with his violin', gathered holly in the local woods and decorated a stone cross that stood in the village, after which they spent the rest of the day dancing.

Tuppenny Starvers

This annual dole takes place at the church of St Michael-on-the-Mount Without, in Bristol, on Easter Tuesday. After a children's service, those attending are given large buns called 'Tuppenny Starvers', although they were previously only given to children. The custom dates from at least 1739, when local inhabitants Peter and Mary Davis took steps to perpetuate it; they left a legacy to support it when they died in 1748. Incidentally, 'tuppenny' is the pre-decimal pronunciation of 'twopenny'.

See also **Doles**, p. 115.

Low Sunday

Low Sunday is the first Sunday after Easter, and can fall anywhere between 29 March and 2 May. It goes by various names, including Little Easter Sunday, White Sunday, and Quasimodo Sunday. The latter refers directly to the first words of the Latin anthem chanted at the beginning of the mass for the day, 'Quasimodo geniti infantes' ('Like newborn babes'). Similarly, 'Low' is not intended to belittle the day in relation to Easter, but probably stems from *laudes*, 'praise'.

Few secular customs seem to have adhered to this day, perhaps because it was too close to the celebrations of Easter. But one apparently unique ceremony calls for special notice. The Cornish historian Richard Carew (1555–1620) provided an interesting description of an annual 'mock prince' ceremony at Lostwithiel, which in 1602 was 'only of late days discontinued':

Upon little Easter Sunday the freeholders of the town and manor, by themselves or their deputies, did there assemble: amongst whom one (as it fell to his lot by turn) bravely apparelled, gallantly mounted, with a crown on his head, a sceptre in his hand, a sword borne before him, and dutifully attended by all the rest on horseback, rode through the principal street to the church; there the curate in his best beseen solemnly received him at the churchyard stile and conducted him to hear divine service, after which he repaired with the same pomp to a house foreprovided for that purpose, made a feast to his attendants, kept the table's end himself, and was served with kneeling, assay, and all other rites due to the estate of a prince: with which dinner the ceremony ended and every man returned home again.

There seems to be no direct parallel between this custom and any other, although it is tempting to link it to the numerous mock mayors found up and down the country (*see* **Mock Mayors and Courts**, p. 298). However, this comparison is not convincing: these mayors were invariably play-acted by the roughest elements in the community, with great parody and burlesque, whereas Carew's prince was drawn from the higher strata of society and treated with respect, even by the clergy.

Hocktide

Hocktide is the Monday and Tuesday after Easter, and can therefore fall anywhere between 30/31 March and 3/4 May. Its origin is a real mystery, although it was already being cited as a quarter or term day by *c*.1175, and was often paired with Michaelmas to divide the year in two; from the early fifteenth century it was a minor church festival. Even the word 'Hocktide' has excited controversy, with the *Oxford English Dictionary* remarking, 'Few words have received so much etymological and historical investigation . . . but the origin has not yet been ascertained.' There is no trace of it in Old English or in other Germanic languages, although there have been numerous unsuccessful attempts to link it to words meaning 'high holiday' or even 'high wedding'.

By the early fifteenth century, Hocktide was almost synonymous with the custom of 'binding' that took place at the season, in which men and women tried to capture and bind each other with ropes that were only released on payment of a small fee. The men attempted to bind the women on one day, and the women tried to catch the men on another. The earliest sources to mention the custom – in London in 1406 and 1409 – condemn the practice, but by the 1450s church accounts begin to include regular entries for money raised in this way at Hocktide, and it is noteworthy that where the takings of two sexes are separately accounted, the women always gathered far more:

> *St. Mary-at-Hill (London) parish accounts*
> *1497*
> > *Gathered by the women on Hob Monday*   *13s. 4d.*
> > *By the men on Tuesday*   *5s.*

It is clear from these records that the Hocktide games gathered significant sums of money for the Church, and there is also evidence that the participants were treated to a feast on the day, presumably to reward their efforts. But the later history of the custom is chequered, as it again fell foul of changing religious morality. It disappeared *c.*1549 under Edward VI, was revived under Mary, and continued into the reign of Elizabeth I, but gradually dwindled until it again disappeared with the Puritan rule of the mid seventeenth century. It is not clear how far Hocktide binding was revived after the Restoration, but by the eighteenth century it had been eclipsed by the custom of 'lifting' or 'heaving' at Easter, which also pitted men against women on alternate days (*see* **Easter Monday and Tuesday: Lifting,** p. 178).

As already indicated, the origins of both custom and festival remain a mystery. Popular explanations are that the binding custom commemorated the massacre of the Danes in 1002, or that it celebrated English freedom when the last Danish king, Hardicanute, died in 1042, and Edward the Confessor gained the throne. Neither of these explanations holds water, but the massacre story was already in circulation in the fifteenth and sixteenth centuries, and it is interesting to note that spurious historical explanations are not simply a modern manifestation.

Hungerford Hocktide Court

The people of Hungerford, in Berkshire, are probably the only ones in the country who still care about Hocktide. They have a unique surviving manorial court, with colourful characters and customs attached, which meets each year at this season. The owners of about one hundred properties in the High Street are commoners of the Court and have certain rights of common, and of fishing in the River Kennet, which were formerly economically significant and are still important to the local community. They were reputedly granted by John of Gaunt in 1364, although this cannot be proven as the supposed charter has been lost. Despite numerous attempts over the centuries to challenge these rights, they still exist and they are administered and upheld by the Court.

At 8 a.m. on Hock Tuesday, the commoners are called to attend the Hocktide Court by a man ringing a bell in the street and blowing a hunting horn from the balcony of the town hall; there is a fine for non-attendance. The Court sits at nine o'clock to consider business relating to the town's commons, and to elect officers, including the Constable (equivalent to a mayor), Portreeve, Bailiff, Water Bailiffs, Aletasters, and four Tithing men. Two of the latter are designated

'Tuttimen', and they set off along the High Street, ostensibly to collect dues from each inhabitant, but whereas the men have to pay in coin, the Tuttimen extract a kiss from the women. The Tuttimen wear top hats and morning dress, and carry poles decorated with ribbons and flowers. They are accompanied by the Orange Scrambler, who carries a bag of oranges to give in return for the kisses and to children they meet on the way. Their progress is traditionally impeded, rather than assisted, by the hospitality they receive in many houses. As the *Independent* reported in 1993:

> *'Basically all we do', said one of the Tuttimen, 'is turn up, kiss a few girls, hand out a few coins, and get plastered.'*

Strangely enough, the word 'tutty' is in the *Oxford English Dictionary* and has a respectable lineage back to at least the sixteenth century, meaning 'a nosegay, a posy, a tuft or bunch of flowers'.

After the traditional luncheon following the Court's business, any newcomers are likely to be seized for the ceremony of 'Shoeing the Colt'. The Colt is grabbed by the Official Blacksmith and assistants, who commence to hammer a nail into his/her shoe, until s/he cries, 'Punch!' and thereby agrees to pay for more drinks.

The Hocktide Court is now a registered charitable trust, and those involved are fiercely proud of it. According to the same piece in the *Independent* from 1993:

> *'This is the sort of thing we English have gone to war to protect,' said Andrew Sawyer, the local vicar . . . 'This, and the right to gather watercress from the marsh.'*

Two weeks after Easter

Spital Sermon

'Spital' comes from the same root as 'hospital', but in late medieval times the word already meant a charitable institution dealing with beggars and those afflicted with 'foul diseases', and it never lost its low-class status. Annual sermons given in aid of these institutions were usually held outdoors, although visiting dignitaries would have shelters in which to sit. The sermon that now takes place at St Lawrence

Jewry church in Gresham Street, London, has had a number of venues, and was originally held at the priory church of St Mary Spital, where the outdoor pulpit was destroyed in 1642. After the Restoration, the sermons were held in other London churches until they settled at St Lawrence's after the Second World War. The Lord Mayor of London still attends in state, with his retinue, but the date of the sermon is sometimes rearranged to suit his/her busy schedule. Traditionally it occurs on the second Wednesday after Easter, but in 2006 it took place in March.

Another outdoor spital sermon takes place at Magdalen College, Oxford, in June every year (*see* **24 June: Magdalen Outdoor Sermon**).

19 April

Primrose Day

The Primrose League was formed in 1883 to perpetuate the political ideals of Benjamin Disraeli (Prime Minister in 1868 and 1874–80), who died on 19 April 1881. Although nowhere near as strong as it used to be, the League was until recently still a presence in the modern Conservative Party, and sympathizers wear primroses, or primrose badges, on the day of Disraeli's death. It is clear that in the first half of the last century this was a popular feature of the day, and in her *Lincolnshire Calendar* (1997) Maureen Sutton includes reminiscences of several people who remember trips to the woods just before the day to gather primroses for sale to the general public.

It is usually stated that the spring flower was Disraeli's favourite, but Sutton also reports a tradition that this was a misunderstanding. She claims that Queen Victoria sent a wreath of primroses to Disraeli's funeral, with a note that read, 'His favourite flowers', by which she meant those of her late husband, Albert, but this was naturally taken to refer to Disraeli himself.

21 April

Queen Elizabeth II's Birthday

Queen Elizabeth II's real birthday is on 21 April. The day is marked by gun salutes in Hyde Park at 12 noon, and at the Tower of London at 1 p.m.

See also **Second Saturday in June: Queen Elizabeth II's Official Birthday**.

23 April

St George's Day

St George is the patron saint of England, but he has always proved something of a problem for the English. He may not even have existed at all, but it is possible that he was one of several candidates in early Christianity, none of whom had anything to do with England, dragons, or damsels in distress; these legends were not developed until the Middle Ages. Modern English people have proved notoriously unwilling to do anything to celebrate his day, despite periodic campaigns in the national press, and there are regular calls for his replacement by a home-grown real-life saint such as St Edmund, St Alban, or St Cuthbert.

The main contender for the real St George was a Christian, born in Cappadocia, who served with distinction in the Roman army. When Emperor Diocletian began his persecution of Christians, George publicly declared his faith, was tortured in just about every way imaginable, and finally beheaded in AD 303. The legend of his fight with a dragon was added in the thirteenth century, and was a masterstroke in public relations for the saint's image. It not only gave him a spectacular backstory, but also provided an instantly recognizable trademark, which made him a popular figure for all kinds of illustrations and effigies.

St George was introduced to Britain by returning Crusaders, who had come across his cult in their Middle Eastern campaigns. It was mainly his reputation as 'soldier saint' which attracted them, and he famously appeared in the sky to encourage the Christian troops at Antioch in 1098. St George's Day was officially recognized at the Synod of Oxford in 1222, and by the mid fourteenth century he had ousted Edward the Confessor as putative patron saint of England. George fitted well with the prevailing fashion for chivalry, and it is no accident that the most exclusive mock-chivalric institution of all, the Order of the Garter, was founded about the same time, with St George as patron.

George rapidly became widely popular with rich and poor alike. One of the most obvious manifestations of this popularity was the proliferation of guilds, or fraternities, dedicated to him, which existed in many areas as associations devoted to religious and charitable works. These guilds were particularly strong in Leicester, Norwich, Coventry, York, Stratford, and Chester, but not, it seems, in London, and their primary concern was to provide and maintain effigies of the saint in local churches; some were even wealthy enough to build chapels dedicated to him. The effigies were carried in procession around the parish every April – as near to St George's Day as possible – and these events became one of the most spectacular and extravagant affairs in the local church calendar. Even more popular for the crowd than the saint himself was the figure of the dragon. This could be a small one made of wood and mounted on a pole (with snapping jaws worked by a string), or a more elaborate basket-work affair that men could carry from inside or wheel along. George also appeared in civic pageants, celebrating the election of a new mayor, for example, and 'riding St George' was an annual excuse for the local great and good to ride in state around the town.

Nevertheless, the adoration of saints came under severe attack in the reform of the church in the mid sixteenth century. Much to the surprise of many people, St George's status as national patron did not save him from the reformers' zeal. Effigies and statues of George, along with all the other saints, were destroyed, and most of the processions which featured him simply faded away or became purely secular events; the scene was set for the long period of official neglect of the national saint, which still continues. At any given time, at least since the restoration of the monarchy in 1660, St George's Day could have been declared a national holiday – for patriotic if not religious reasons – and there have been plenty of unsuccessful campaigns to bring this about.

There has been no shortage of debate about why the English take so little interest in their patron, but no definite conclusion is ever reached, and perhaps cannot be. The main argument of the pro-St George lobby is that neglect of the saint is evidence of a lamentable lack of patriotism on the part of the average English person, and that the English do not care enough about its great history and traditions. But this ignores the complexity of national identity. An apparent lack of interest can certainly be seen negatively, as apathy and indifference, but it can also be viewed positively, as inner strength and confidence. There is no doubt that the attitudes of many English people are based on assumptions of cultural supremacy, and many take an inverted pride in the fact that they do not need to make such a fuss to demonstrate their patriotism. In the words of an *Express* headline, 'If you're truly English, who needs St. George?' (6 April 1998). This trait, of course, is often seen as infuriating arrogance by England's neighbours, but it is a useful line of thought. It follows that the more fuss other nations make of their patriotic symbols, the more they show that they are trying too hard – always proving that they have something to prove.

At a more rarefied level, it can also be argued that the apparent disinterest in patriotic symbols is largely because the English have never felt particularly under threat as a nation (at least since 1066), and England has therefore never needed to assert its distinctiveness like many other nations have. Certainly, England has not been invaded or needed to tear itself away from another dominant nation, although the decline of international power and loss of empire in the last century certainly gave some patriots pause for thought. In the 1990s, plans for political devolution in Britain, and vague fears of being subsumed in a federal European Union, brought another upsurge of St George mania, which was fed by a new craze for supporters of England's sports teams to display St George flags on their houses and mini flagpoles on their cars. The broadsheet newspapers were full of articles debating concepts of 'Englishness', and the tabloids equated a love of St George with patriotism; in April 1997, the *Sun* gave away a 'cut-out-and-keep red and white flag of St. George', which they 'urged every Englishman and woman to wave with pride'.

The conspicuous display of the flag bearing the red cross of St George seems to be a relatively recent phenomenon, but there have been outbreaks of these flags before, as an integral part of attempts to 'bring back' St George's Day, for example at Kidderminster, Worcestershire, in 1914, and various places in 1936.

Nevertheless, a few scattered customs for St George's Day in latter years have been reported across the country. In 1997, the folklorist Maureen Sutton reported that some Lincolnshire people remembered school-based celebrations taking place on 23 April, and that some wore bluebells or other blue flowers to school on that day. One also commented, 'my mam used to say it was the day to pick dandelions to make your wine, but only if the sun was full on them.' And in his *Folklore of Gloucestershire* (1994), Roy Palmer describes a customary gift, made to successive sovereigns by the people of Gloucester, of a pie made from lampreys caught in the River Severn. The custom is reputed to have been started in the time of Henry I, and continued until 1917.

24 April

St Mark's Eve

In English tradition, St Mark's Eve is one of the key nights on which to divine the future, but there is no clue as to why this particular date was chosen. Certainly, there seems to be nothing in the life or writings of the Evangelist St Mark that would deserve this reputation, but the idea was extremely widespread. Love divinations were the common forms of attempted prediction, and they come in a wide variety of forms, ranging from the relatively safe ('you will dream of your future lover') to the genuinely frightening ('the wraith of your future lover will be summoned to your side'). The most striking feature of St Mark's Eve divinations is that they frequently tend towards the scary end of this range. Girls would wash their chemises, in ritual silence, and hang them in front of the fire, waiting for their future husband to appear and turn them; or they would sit in the barn and wait for the figure to walk through at the stroke of midnight, or pluck grass from a grave at midnight and place it under their pillows to encourage prophetic dreams. The venue and timing combined with the prescribed actions to guarantee the frisson of trepidation that surrounded the whole proceedings. The climax nearly always occurred at midnight, when the house was still and silent, or was in a deserted barn, churchyard, or other scary place, as in the following Lincolnshire example from 1891:

A youth or girl walks round the church, at dead of night ... looking into each window in succession, in expectation of seeing, in the last window, the face of his or her partner in life.

'Porch-watching' was another very widespread custom, but this was designed to reveal more serious matters than who would marry whom. Anyone who wanted to know who would die in the parish in the coming year could stand in the church porch at midnight on St Mark's Eve, and they would see a ghostly procession of figures approaching and entering the church. Those who were destined to die would not come out again, while those who were to be seriously ill would leave the church after a short stay; in some versions, another procession, consisting of couples to be married, would also appear. In most cases, if the watcher fell asleep it was believed to be a sure sign that they would be one of the doomed, but occasionally they would simply sicken and die as a result of the shock of seeing themselves. It was also occasionally reported that anyone who 'watches' once must do it again every year, as for example in the following piece from Yorkshire, recorded by local writer Richard Blakeborough in 1898 (here translated from his colourful but almost unreadable attempt to render deep Yorkshire dialect on the page):

I never watched myself, but one James How used to watch the dead go in and come out at Bon'iston church every St. Mark Eve as it come around. He had to; he was forced to it; he couldn't help himself ... Aye, and he saw the spirits of all of them that were going to die that year, and all of them dressed in their natural clothes, or else how would he have known who they were? They all passed close to him, but none of them ever gave him a nod, or anything of that sort. But them as does it once have to do it. They can't hold themselves back. They're forced to go every time St. Mark's Eve comes round. Man! it's a desperate thing to have to do, because you have to go. Whah! at the last end you see yourself pass yourself and then you know your time's come and you'll be laid in the cold ground before that day twelvemonth.

The belief in porch-watching was reported from most parts of England, but it seems to have been particularly well known in East Anglia, the Midlands, and the northern counties. The earliest known reference is from Nottinghamshire in 1608, and the belief lasted well into the late nineteenth century, but became much rarer as the twentieth century advanced.

25 April

St Mark's Day

St Mark's Day does not seem to have made any great impression on English tradition, and there are no widely reported customs special to the time – in marked contrast to the huge popularity of his eve for divinatory practices (*see* p. 189). Nevertheless, in places where the parish church was dedicated to the saint, there would certainly have been celebrations on the day.

One annual custom, which took place in Alnwick in Northumberland from at least *c.*1645 to the mid nineteenth century, was 'leaping the well', although 'scrambling through the pond' would have been a more appropriate name. Men who were to be made Freemen of the Borough assembled early on St Mark's Day and paraded the town on horseback. At a certain point in the day, they were obliged to dismount and make their way through the Freeman's Well, a large dirty pool about twenty yards long, as best they could. The background to this custom is unknown, but the local origin story includes the traditional motif, familiar from many other places, that King John found himself mired in the pond one dark night and set the freemen the task to punish them for neglecting to repair the town's roads.

At Morpeth, also in Northumberland, 25 April was the day for 'riding the boundaries of the common'. It was recorded in 1892 that:

After meeting in the market place the corporation, on horseback, proceeded to the Common, the waits going first, then the serjeant carrying the purse on a staff, after him the Bailiffs, and lastly the mob; they passed round the boundaries of the Common till they reached a well, east of the road to the High House, when the younger ones raced up to the winning post. There was then a race for a silver cup.

The custom of riding the bounds of the common continued until 1974, when local government reorganization wiped it out. But the similar custom of riding the boundary of the whole borough is still practised every year, on or near to St Mark's Day. This is administered by a board of trustees, which means that the tradition should continue in the future.

George Dew, of Lower Heyford in Oxfordshire, recorded in his diary in 1866 a personal custom instituted by the local miller: Thomas

Rose's Great Day. Rose kept it in commemoration of the day he won a lawsuit against Judge Page concerning the height of the water in the mill head. On his 'Great Day', his millers and other men dined at his house, business ceased, and cakes or buns were distributed among the children. This is an excellent example of how people feel the need to mark particularly important days in their life, and the way that personal celebrations often took exactly the same form as traditional public ones.

29 April

According to early English calendars, on 29 April, '*Egressus Noae de arca*' (Noah left the Ark), having entered it on 17 March.

30 April

May Day Eve

Eves are often overshadowed by the activities of the days that follow them, and May Day Eve is no exception. In times when the predominant May Day custom was decorating buildings with greenery and flowers, many people spent much of 30 April out in the woods and fields gathering the materials for their celebrations (*see* 1 **May**). Nevertheless, those living in Lancashire, Yorkshire, and neighbouring counties had at least one widely practised custom on the day, in the form of Mischief Night, when young people believed they had the traditional right to play tricks. In 1896, P. H. Ditchfield recorded in his *Old English Customs*:

At Oldham, the Eve of May Day is known as Mischief Night when it was the custom for people to play tricks on their neighbours. My informant remembers seeing a thatched house, in a village near Oldham, adorned with mops, rakes and brushes, on the tops of which were stuck mugs, tubs, and pails.

Mischief Night itself has proved strangely schizophrenic. Not only did some people celebrate it on 4 November rather than 30 April, but sometime in the mid twentieth century it began to gravitate to Hallowe'en, which is when many young folk in Yorkshire now celebrate it (*see* **31 October: Mischief Night** for further details).

On a much grander scale, 30 April is also known in Germanic countries as *Walpurgisnacht*. St Walburga, or Walpurgis, was an eighth-century Anglo-Saxon nun who was sent to Germany to help Boniface in his missionary work; she became abbess at the key religious centre of Heidenheim, and died there in AD 779. Her lasting fame, however, was prompted nearly a century later, when her remains were removed (to join the relics of her brother St Winnibald), and medicinal oil started to flow from her new tomb. Walburga's feast day is 25 February, but the eve of the date of her translation (1 May) became widely known as *Walpurgisnacht*, and in local tradition became the greatest night for witches to ride and meet. This tradition does not seem to have taken root in England, although the name has been familiar to literate Britons at least since the translation of Goethe's *Faust* in 1823, in which it featured.

Shakespeare set his play *Midsummer Night's Dream* on May Eve, and although one would expect to find the connection between the date and the fairy world to be evident in English folklore collections, this is not the case. If such a tradition existed, it has left only the faintest of echoes in occasional isolated examples, such as that recorded by Ella M. Leather in Herefordshire about the turn of the twentieth century:

On the Eve of May Day, at Kingstone and Thruxton, folk used to put trays of moss outside their doors for the fairies to dance upon.

MAY

Corby Pole Fair

Two thousand people at Corby New Town, Northamptonshire, were clapped in the stocks yesterday, the day of the ancient village Pole Fair, which is held every 20 years. To be released from the stocks, a toll – a coin of the realm – had to be paid. The 'victims' did not go willingly but were taken by groups of men patrolling the streets, and carried to the stocks in a chair on a wooden pole. The money goes to charity.

The strange procedure described in this extract from *The Times* (12 June 1962) explains the name of 'Corby Pole Fair', which is indeed held only once in twenty years. It is not known why it is held so infrequently, or whether it previously occurred more often, as the town's charter, granted by Elizabeth I in 1585, does not mention a fair at all. It is claimed locally that the charter was granted in gratitude when Elizabeth was helped out of a bog by Corby people (although similar stories exist in many other places).

If townsfolk can only hold a fair once every two decades, it is inevitable that they will want to pack as much entertainment into the day as possible, and the 2002 programme included processions, bungee-jumping, a fireworks display, archery, tug-of-war, a pageant, maypole dancing, a Pole Fair Queen, and numerous other attractions, as well as the men with the pole. Although unusual at a fair, this pole activity is simply a version of the 'riding the stang' custom found in many other places, often in the context of **rough music** (p. 95).

Maids' Money

At Guildford in Surrey, local resident John Howe left money in his will, dated 27 January 1674, to buy land, the profits of which would pay for an annual gift to a deserving maidservant. The trustees should first find:

. . . two poor servant-maids, within the said town, of good report, who should have served masters or mistresses there two years together . . . and that no maid should be chosen that should live in any inn or alehouse . . .

The two women then had to throw dice to decide who should get the money. The loser could try again for the following three years, but if she was still unsuccessful she had to retire from the field. The money was worth trying for – in 1900, the sum given was £12, less expenses. Nevertheless, many maids were happy to lose. It became the custom to use the income from another Guildford fund, John Parsons' charity, to give to the losing maid as a consolation prize. The Parsons' money formerly went to finance an apprenticeship, but there was often no suitable candidate. Ironically, this fund often generated a higher sum than the Howe charity, so the loser got more than the winner.

Remarkably, the ceremony is still carried out, every May, at the guildhall in Guildford, in the presence of the mayor. It forms part of the annual general meeting of the administering body, Guildford Poyle Charities, and the candidates, who are nowadays domestic helpers rather than live-in maids, still throw dice to win what now amounts to about £60 each year.

Weighing the Mayor

A unique civic custom takes place at the guildhall in High Wycombe High Street, Buckinghamshire, every May, when the newly elected mayor takes office. The new mayor is publicly weighed on a tall brass tripod balance fitted with a seat. His or her weight is then recorded, and the macebearer calls out the figure to the assembled crowd. A year later, the outgoing mayor is weighed again, but instead of the actual weight being announced, the macebearer declares the previous recorded weight, adding 'and some more' if it has increased, or 'and no more' if it has stayed the same or fallen. 'And no more' is greeted with cheers and applause, as it signifies that the incumbent has been diligent and active in pursuing mayoral duties, but the cry of 'and some more' is taken as evidence of too many civic dinners, and is greeted with good-natured jeers and barracking. The weighing-in ceremony can only be shown to date from Victorian times.

1 May

Judging by the range of traditional customs that took place on May Day, it was second only to Christmas in popularity with the English people. The day was celebrated, in one way or another, all over the country, and a wide range of customs has evolved since the Middle Ages, which provide a complex pattern of interlocking custom and regional difference. It is therefore difficult to give a lucid chronological account in short order, except on a very simplistic level. We desperately need a full-scale historical study of the day in all its manifestations.

The most obvious point to be made is that in a northern country like England, it is not at all surprising that previous generations thought the coming of spring and summer a cause for joy and celebration. Without being overly romantic or needing to invent ancient ritual origins, we can agree with folklorist Charlotte Burne's comment, made in 1883, that:

We, with our coal fires, our plate-glass windows, our lamps and gas-lights, and all our many appliances for indoor comfort and amusement, can hardly appreciate the misery of the cold dark days of winter to our forefathers, their keen enjoyment of the light and warmth and freedom of summer, and the delight with which they greeted the returning spring . . .

If that was true in Victorian England, it is doubly so in the twenty-first century.

May celebrations took place at all levels of society, and evidence comes from a wide range of documentary sources, including royal, municipal, ecclesiastical, literary, antiquarian, and folkloric records. Kings and queens went maying; town corporations and guilds put on shows; the clergy took sides in supporting or vociferously condemning the people's activities; poets and playwrights, from Chaucer onwards, developed May Day into a potent arcadian symbol; nineteenth-century antiquarians and folklorists documented surviving customs in admiring or nostalgic detail; and twentieth-century enthusiasts revived and invented May customs with gay abandon. But there is confusion in this mass of information. Changing vocabularies and imprecise definitions often make it difficult to be sure what is going on. 'Going a-maying' and 'bringing in the May' originally meant going out of town or village into the countryside, to fetch greenery or flowers back for decoration, but either phrase was used in later times to cover any traditional May activity including, for example, bathing the face in May dew. A 'maypole' can be a seventy-foot pole set in the ground on the village green, or a portable six-foot pole for children to dance around, or a two-foot decorated stick carried from house to house by boys and girls accompanying their May garland. A 'garland' can be the pyramid of shiny metal carried on the head of a dancing milkmaid, a small nosegay sold in the street for luck, a huge wreath of flowers hung on a maypole, or a bell- or globe-shaped construction of greenery carried round the village by children or worn on the head of the King on Castleton Garland Day (*see* **29 May: Castleton Garland Day**).

May Day certainly roused strong feelings, for and against. In his *Survey of London* (2nd edn, 1603), John Stow writes:

In the month of May, namely, on May-day in the morning, every man, except impediment, would walk into the sweet meadows and green woods, there to rejoice their spirits with the beauty and savour of sweet flowers, and with the harmony of birds, praising God in their kind.

Compare Stow's sweet meadows with Philip Stubbes' famous diatribe against setting up maypoles, in which he claims that only a third of the maids who went a-maying came back 'undefiled' (*see* **1 May: Maypoles**). The earliest known reference to May Day customs, in 1240, is already a criticism – Robert Grosseteste, Bishop of Lincoln, complained of priests who took part in 'games which they call the bringing-in of May' – but by the fifteenth century, local authorities in Kent and Devon are recorded as giving money to people coming 'with their May', and in the following century even the royal family were involved. An oft-quoted account included in Edward Hall's *Chronicles* (1542) tells how King Henry VIII and Catherine of Aragon went a-maying in 1515 to Shooters Hill, and there played at being Robin Hood with a picnic banquet in flower-decked arbours.

This notion of going into the countryside and bringing back foliage was the core of May Day activity for centuries, even if only on a theoretical level, but what happened to the plants once they had been brought in varied widely. The earliest descriptions simply indicate that houses and public buildings were adorned with 'birch boughs' and the like, but by the nineteenth century there was a wide range of traditions, all based on the same simple principle. The following selection of extracts demonstrates something of this variety, but there were many more ways of using branches and flowers:

[Lincolnshire, ?1820s] *A woman from the extreme north of Lincolnshire . . . said that when she was a girl at Winteringham, she and other girls always dressed the lugs (ears or handles) of their milk kits with leaves on May-day morning.*

[Herefordshire, ?1850s] *When . . . I lived at Kington, no house was without its bough of green birch in the doorway.*

[Derbyshire, 1860s] *When she was young, every house in Abney had a garland hung above its door on the first day of May. She had helped to make these garlands; they were round, like hoops, and made of bits of green things, Mary blobs, and so on. People would plod through snow to get flowers for them. The garlands were about a foot in diameter and were left hanging over doors till the flowers were withered.*

[Leicestershire, 1895] *It hath been a custom, time out of mind, for children to scatter flowers before people's doors in towns, on May Day.*

[Cheshire/Lancashire, 19th century] *It was formerly a custom . . . for young men to place birchen boughs on May-day over the doors of their mistresses, and mark the residence of a scold by an alder bough. There is an old rhyme which mentions peculiar boughs for various tempers, as an owler (alder) for a scolder, a nut for a slut, etc.*

If Puritan critics like Stubbes are to be believed, people also had a great deal of fun that had little to do with greenery while out in the woods overnight, and another characteristic feature of bringing in the May was noise. The returning Mayers announced their arrival with loud jubilant cheering, firing of guns, and, particularly, the blowing of horns.

Particular aspects of May customs – garlands, dolls, maypoles, and so on – are detailed below. Although the arrival of May Day itself was the catalyst for all these activities, it is clear that the celebrations spread into the rest of the month. This was particularly so after the Restoration, when Royal Oak Day was added to the calendar (*see* **29 May: Royal Oak Day**).

Bank Holiday

Normally quite consensual, the timing of bank holidays occasionally hits the headlines, especially when the idea of celebration or commemoration is mixed with that of 'holiday' pure and simple. August Bank Holiday causes no problems because it is simply an arbitrary late summer day, but the adoption of May Day as a new bank holiday in 1978, by the Labour Government of the day, created a major furore. The Conservative opposition claimed that May Day's international socialist nature made it an unsuitable choice, and *The Times* ran a suitably thunderous leader suggesting that the British public should use the day to commemorate innocent people murdered in the Soviet Union.

Many people countered by pointing out that much of the long history of May Day celebrations was devoid of any political content, but the Conservative politicians remembered the Labour Day rallies of the interwar and immediate postwar years, such as recollected by Jessica Mitford in her autobiography:

On May Day the entire community turned out, men, women, and children, home-made banners proclaiming slogans of the 'United Front against Fascism' waving alongside the official ones. The long march to Hyde Park started early in the morning, contingents of the Labour Party, the Co-ops, the Communist Party, the Independent Labour Party marching through the long day to join other thousands from all parts of London in the traditional May Day labour festival.

When the Conservatives returned to power in 1979, they planned to scrap the May Day holiday and to replace it with a more patriotic 'Trafalgar Day' in October. This in turn was criticized, as it would disrupt manufacturing output in the important run-up to Christmas, and it met with a lukewarm response from the public who, not surprisingly, preferred a day off in early summer to one in late autumn. The plan was quietly shelved in 1993, but the principle of patriotism is still regularly cited when the question of the timing of new bank holidays is discussed, and many Conservative rank and file members still grumble about May Day every year. The edge is somewhat blunted by the fact that the holiday is now on the first Monday in May, which seldom falls on the first of the month.

Bears

A May Day custom that seems to have been restricted to the Burnley and Blackburn areas of Lancashire was a sort of mock dancing bear enacted by boys while the girls were out with their garlands and may-poles, as described in the *Burnley Express* (11 February 1983):

One went to the grocer's shop and begged an old sugar sack. The boy chosen would have it put over his head, the position of his eyes and mouth located, and holes would be cut into the sack to allow him to see and breathe. Then the boys wanted a staff as the real bear man had. So a broom handle would be obtained . . . then a length of clothes line to keep the 'bear' at a safe distance from the public.

The 'bear' would dance, turn somersaults, and catch the pole, as in-structed, just like a real dancing bear, and his attendants would keep up a constant chatter in imitation of the real bear-wards, who were normally Eastern or Southern Europeans, on the lines of 'Addy-om-pom-pay', or 'Addy-addy-on-kon-kay'.

The boys' bear was clearly well known within its restricted area from the First World War to the 1940s, but it is not clear whether it goes back any earlier. Real dancing bears were surprisingly common in late nineteenth-century England, and they could still be seen occasionally in both village and town streets in the 1920s.

Casting Clouts

The well-known phrase 'Cast ne'er a clout [or 'Ne'er cast a clout'] till May is out' cautions people not to cast off their winter clothes until they are sure that summer is with us. In recent years it has been commonly stated that the phrase does not refer to the month of May but rather to the blossoming of the hawthorn, which in many parts is referred to as 'may', but many earlier references to the phrase make it perfectly clear that the month is what is meant. The saying was of-ten extended to include other months, as in a Devon version noted in 1932 – 'Till April is dead, change not a thread' – and a rhyme printed in *Notes & Queries* in 1870 but claimed to be current in Yorkshire a hundred years before:

> *Don't change a clout*
> *Till May is out;*

The earliest known reference in English dates from 1732, but a Spanish version, which translates as 'Do not leave off your coat till May', was known at least a hundred years before that.

Charlton-on-Otmoor Garland

In the parish church of Charlton-on-Otmoor, dedicated to the Virgin Mary, there is a large image in the shape of a cross, or possibly of a person with outstretched arms, perched on top of the rood screen. The figure is made of wood, entirely covered with evergreens, and is therefore usually referred to as 'the garland', although some also call it 'the lady'. The garland greenery is replaced twice a year by the church-wardens, on 1 May and 19 September (the patronal festival), and on the first of these dates the local schoolchildren bring a long garland made of bunches of flowers joined together by a 'rope' of evergreens to the church for a special service. Others carry small crosses of wood or flowers, which are placed around the church, and the long garland is placed across the front of the screen. After the service, the children perform maypole and country dances to entertain the crowds who always flock to the church on this day. It is altogether a charming and relatively low-key community celebration.

This direct school involvement only dates back to 1963, and indeed the customs surrounding the 'garland' have undergone an astonishing degree of change, even within its 200-year recorded history. Our first reference is in fact an illustration, published in Dunkin's *History of Bicester* (1816), which shows two garlands of far more open construction than the present solid one, and although still basically cruciform in shape, looking more like John Wyndham's triffids than a person. A second illustration, from 1846, shows only one garland, of similar shape and still of openwork. We are told that in 1854 the local vicar, the Revd George Bliss, objected to the garland and had it removed, but it was restored as soon as he left the village. Up to about 1857, the garland(s) were carried in procession around the village on May Day, accompanied by music, morris dancing, and singing, and were taken to visit the principal houses of the area. By 1890, however, the custom had lapsed so far that nobody even bothered to replenish the greenery on the garland, and it took a deliberate effort on the part of local church officials to re-introduce it.

It is confidently stated by virtually all writers on the subject that the garlands are direct remnants of the statues that adorned parish churches before the 1540s. The view of folklorist Christina Hole in her *Dictionary of British Folk Customs* (1976) is typical:

During the upheavals of the Reformation, the statues were destroyed, and the people of Charlton erected two green garlands in their place.

Certainly, prior to the Reformation, English churches were alive with saints. They were carved into the fabric, painted on walls and other flat surfaces, and stood as statues of painted wood or stone, often with their own candles burning and a small altar at their feet. The most impressive group of images was on the rood screen, with a huge crucifix, flanked by Mary and St John, which would have been in constant sight of the congregation. The removal of images did not happen overnight, but from the 1530s onwards saints gradually disappeared from the church, and all images, in every church and chapel, were ordered to be removed in February 1548, and again by Elizabeth I in 1559 after the reversal of policy during Mary's reign (1553–58).

To the average parishioner, little concerned with doctrinal niceties, the church must have seemed unbelievably bare and impersonal after the saints' removal, and we know that at least some images were hidden, or quietly spirited away to be stored in safety, in case they were ever allowed to return. In some places, there was violent opposition, but the reformers had all the power, and their orders were eventually carried out everywhere. The crucifixion scenes on roods were particularly disliked by reformers. If anything did escape their reforming zeal, it would certainly have been swept away by the further draconian Puritan repression of the seventeenth century.

The idea that the Charlton garlands are direct descendants of the rood screen group must therefore be regarded more as wishful thinking than serious reflection, based on the idea that the authorities did not mind, or somehow did not notice, the simple subterfuge. It is almost inconceivable that the garlands could have been tolerated for the next 300 years. Moreover, we do not have any indication that the garlands even existed before the early nineteenth century, and if they did so it is distinctly odd that no one thought them worthy of mention until 1816.

A possibly more fruitful avenue of investigation is to pursue the similarity between the Charlton garland and other garlands that were carried around on May Day. Oxfordshire had more than its fair share of garland customs, and they varied widely in detail, but mostly followed a similar overall pattern. They were nearly all made in a way similar to the Charlton garlands shown in the nineteenth-century illustrations, and they were all taken round the village and shown to local residents at the doors of their houses. Many included a doll, usually called 'my lady' or something similar. Admittedly, it was not usual for the perambulation of the village to be formalized into a procession with music and dancing, and nor was it common for the garland to be stored in the church, although garlands featured in other church-based customs. The case is therefore far from closed, but on present evidence it seems likely that rather than being a religious symbol that was later treated in a secular way, the Charlton garland is a secular May garland that later became incorporated into an ecclesiastical setting. Nevertheless, a possibly analogous custom took place at Bodmin, in Cornwall, which further research may show had relevance to the Charlton Garland. At Bodmin, a 'riding' or procession took place each year in July, and at least one account mentions the participants carrying flowers and decorated poles (*see* **7 July: Bodmin Riding**).

Children's Garlands

One of the prettiest and most characteristic of rural spring customs was the carrying of garlands around the village by children on May Day morning and singing or dancing at people's doors. By far the most famous account of May garlanding is the delightful description in Flora Thompson's *Lark Rise*, first published in 1939, which recalls her Oxfordshire childhood in the last decades of the nineteenth century, but there are many other detailed descriptions and May garlanding is one of the best documented of all calendar customs. The following was published in *Notes & Queries* in 1854:

In Huntingdonshire, the garland is of a pyramidal shape, in this respect resembling the old 'milk-maid's garland'... The crown of the garland is composed of tulips, anemones, cowslips, king-cups, meadow-orchids, wallflowers, primroses, crown-imperials, lilacs, laburnums, and as many roses and bright flowers of all descriptions as can be pressed into the service. These, with the addition of green boughs, are made into a huge pyramidal nosegay; from the front of which a gaily dressed doll... stares vacantly at her admirers. From the base of the nosegay hang ribbons, pieces of silk, handkerchiefs, and any other gay-coloured fabric that can be borrowed for the occasion. The garland is borne by the two maids-of-honour to the May Queen . . . who place their hands beneath the nosegay, and allow the gay-coloured streamers to fall towards the ground. The garland is thus from four to five feet in height . . . The sovereignty of the Queen o' the May is not hereditary, but elective; her majesty being annually chosen by her school-fellows in the morning . . . Her chief symbol of sovereignty is a parasol, which she bears with grace and dignity. Moreover, she weareth white gloves, and carrieth a bag that displayeth a pocket-handkerchief. She has a white veil too; and around her bonnet is her crown, a coronal of flowers. In front of her dress is a bouquet . . . You may be quite sure that her majesty is dressed in her very best, and has put on that white frock for the first time since last summer.

Preceding the maids-of-honour, and followed by her attendants, both male and female, her majesty makes the tour of her native place, and, at the various homes of her subjects, exhibits the charms of Flora [the doll] and her garland. If, as is commonly the case, the regal procession is composed of school-children, they sing such songs as may have been taught them. It is then usual for loyal subjects to make a pecuniary present to the May Queen, which is deposited in her majesty's handkerchief-bag, and will be expended on the coronation banquet; a feast which will take place in the school-room, or some large-roomed cottage, as early as three o'clock in the afternoon, when her majesty will be graciously pleased to sit down in the midst of her subjects, and will probably quaff at least ten of those cups that cheer but not inebriate, and will consume plum-cake and bread-and-butter in proportion.

Taken altogether, published accounts show a wide variety of detail, especially as regards the shapes and sizes of the garlands, but there is an overall similarity in what the children did at each door. In the journal *Folk-Lore* (1900), a correspondent wrote:

I was at Wilton [Wiltshire] on the first of May 1896. There I saw many parties of little girls, one of whom would carry a short stick, at the top of which was a garland or bunch of flowers. The girls would stand at the doors of houses and sing a song, the last line of which was, 'Please give a penny for the garland.' Wilton is a small town and the garlands were numerous, so I suppose the house-to-house visitation was soon done, as when I left, soon after nine a.m., the girls were either wandering aimlessly about with their garlands or sitting on doorsteps counting their gains. I was told that the pence are collected in order to be afterwards spent at Wilton Fair, which is held on the first Monday in May. The same day I reached Salisbury about eleven o'clock. Although it is only three miles from Wilton, the fashion of the May observance was different. The girls, instead of being in parties of four or five, went about in couples, each member of which held the end of a short stick, to the middle of which the garland was tied, and hung between the two girls as they walked along. The garland (as I suppose I must call it) was in the form of a crown, whose circlet and bows were covered with flowers. I did not hear any singing, and the girls went from shop to shop, within which they would wait until they received either money or a dismissal.

Children carrying portable maypoles almost always danced (*see* **1 May: Maypoles**), those with garlands usually sang, and the songs varied considerably from simple traditional ditties to somewhat trite poems taught to them by schoolteachers. But the main difference was the degree of adult involvement in the proceedings. Scholars have labelled the customs where the children acted on their own initiative as 'independent' garlanding, to distinguish them from those in which adults – usually the local school staff – took control of making the garland and organizing the children's activities. Even in so-called 'independent' garlanding, it is unlikely that adults were ever completely excluded, but there is strong evidence that by about the 1880s adult involvement was increasing rapidly, with children still carrying the garlands but school, church, or parents taking on the essential planning and organizational roles. Adults oversaw the construction of the garland, taught the children more 'refined' songs, and even controlled how the money that the children collected was spent – often on a tea or other treat. Many took this patronage even further, and sought to encourage the custom by offering prizes for the best garlands.

The most trustworthy writers on the subject, such as Roy Judge and Ronald Hutton, agree that children's garlanding customs increased strongly as the nineteenth century progressed, especially in the southeast of England. Adult intervention is likely to be the main cause of this increase, and was often based on the fashionable ideas of a romantic **Merrie England** (p. 510) that were affecting traditional customs across the country. But not all places in England had children's May Day garlands, and the geographical pattern of the custom is puzzling. Numerous examples were documented in the South, South-East and Midlands, and along the southern coast of the West Country, but none in the North and few in East Anglia.

There is little evidence of children's garlanding before the early nineteenth century, but it certainly existed before that time. Gideon

Mantell, for example, pioneer surgeon and geologist, was born in Lewes, East Sussex, in 1790, and he often noted in his journal the presence of garlands in the town on 1 May:

[1819] *The garlands of this year are more beautiful and numerous than I ever remember;* [1821] *The annual custom of exhibiting garlands on this day was but partially observed;* [1829] *The garlands very numerous, but shabby in the extreme;* [1830] *But a sorry display of garlands, altho' flowers are very abundant; this, like every other cheerful innocent custom, is dwindling away;* [1846] *Went to Tunbridge Wells and returned in the evening . . . Children were carrying about garlands; the first I have seen since leaving Lewes. Well do I remember my childhood's garlands!*

These entries seem to indicate a tradition in decline, although this may simply be a facet of the diarist's increasing age. However, the last comment is particularly interesting, as it proves the existence of the garlanding custom in the area before 1800.

Ducking or Dipping Day

For some, 1 May (or 2 May in some accounts) was 'Ducking' or 'Dipping Day'. The Cornish historian Jonathan Couch recorded in 1871:

On May morning the children, and even the adults, go out into the country, and fetch home branches of the narrow-leaved elm, or flowering boughs of the white-thorn, both of which are called 'May'. At a later hour, all the boys of the village sally forth with bucket, can, or other vessel, and avail themselves of a licence which the season confers, to 'dip', or well-nigh drown, without regard to person or circumstance, the passenger who has not the protection of a piece of 'May' conspicuously stuck in his dress, at the same time that they sing, 'the first of May is dipping day' . . . There is a great deal of fun on the occasion, for many an unfortunate body who has failed to comply with an ancient custom is seen slinking home like a drowned rat.

The custom seems to have been unique to Devon and Cornwall, but it has definite echoes of the more widely known Royal Oak Day, when anyone not wearing an oak leaf was punished (*see* **29 May: Royal Oak Day**). Naturally, not everybody found the custom a bit of harmless fun, as in the following example from Devon:

In 1894 the practice resulted in the death of one Dr. Twining, when his horses were frightened by the water thrown over a fence by William John Luscombe (13) and Samuel George Hine (16), and in bolting overset his carriage. He sustained an injury to the ankle, which later necessitated amputation of his leg, from which he died. The boys were charged with manslaughter at Exeter Assizes, but were later discharged.

Fighting

People in the past seem to have taken their feeling of home territory very seriously, and to have readily used it as an excuse for a good punch-up. Even such a staid and decorous affair as 'beating the bounds' could result in fights if parties from one parish met another on their rounds (*see* **Rogationtide: Beating the Bounds**, p. 243). Yarleton Hill, in Gloucestershire, formed the intersection of several parishes, an opportunity too good to miss. In 1779, county historian Samuel Rudder described the events that occurred there:

Annually, on the first day of May, there is a custom of assembling in bodies on the top of this hill, from the several parishes, to fight for the possession of it, upon which account it is sometimes called May-Hill.

A similar affray took place at another hilltop May fair every year at Wrekin Wakes, in Shropshire, according to folklorist Charlotte Burne in 1883. Here, the local colliers and countrymen fought for possession of the ground after the pleasure-seekers had enjoyed the sideshows and gingerbread stalls.

Such fierce territoriality existed in both town and country. Many urban working-class autobiographies touch upon the author's childhood fear of venturing into another area, or even down the wrong street, while Richard Jefferies, the immensely popular chronicler of the late Victorian rural scene, described a similar scenario in Wiltshire:

Every hamlet used to have its representative fighting-man – often more than one – who visited the neighbouring villages on the feast days, when there was a good deal of liquor flowing, to vaunt their prowess before the local champions . . . There was a regular feud for many years between the Okebourne men and the Clipstone 'chaps'; and never did the stalwart labourers of those two villages meet without falling to fisticuffs with right goodwill.

The same pattern was repeated all over the country, and, as at Yarleton Hill, the rivalry could be formalized into a regular custom or even game. Many of the recorded mass football games, for example, were also ostensibly played between inhabitants of two different parishes, or parts of a town (*see* **Football**, p. 64).

See also **Palm Sunday: Martinsell Hill** (p. 129) for a similar affair.

Horse Decorations

The feeling that May Day should be celebrated with decoration and finery was not confined to rural areas, and there existed a strong tradition of decorating horses and vehicles, particularly in Manchester but also in towns in Lancashire, Yorkshire, and Cheshire, as well as in London. May Day decorations seem to have been first apparent in the coaching fraternity, and the earliest description so far unearthed occurs in the *Gentleman's Magazine* of 1754, although it is clear that it is a well-established custom even at that date:

They took places in the waggon, and quitted London early on May morning; and it being the custom in this month for the passengers to give the waggoner at every inn a ribbon to adorn his team, she soon discovered the origin of the proverb, 'as fine as a horse', for, before they got to the end of their journey, the poor beasts were almost blinded by the tawdry party-coloured flowing honours of their heads.

By the time the coaching industry collapsed in the face of competition from railways, the custom was already entrenched in other horse-based occupations. Drivers of delivery vehicles, mail vans, cabs, and omnibuses all felt it their duty to put on a good show on the day. A correspondent described the scene in Manchester in the *Pall Mall Gazette* in 1880:

There was on May-day the usual annual procession through the streets of Manchester of dray and cart horses, every trade, from machinery and cotton down to beer, being represented. The animals were literally covered with decorations of flowers, ribbons, garlands, flags, and small coloured balloons; the brass trappings shone like burnished gold, and the hoofs are first blacked, and then topped with white – to represent top-boots, I suppose. Many of these horses are simply perfection of their kind.

Perhaps inevitably, these spontaneous and individual forms of customary decoration soon became organized into parades and formal processions, with rules and prizes. In 1890, the *Stockport Advertiser* commented:

Everything that went on wheels from a mourning coach to a doll's carriage was more or less ornamented . . . [but] the display would have been infinitely better and more imposing had there been an organised competition and procession.

The same suggestions were also being made in other towns. The London Cart Horse Parade Society was set up in 1886 for just this purpose, while animal welfare pressure groups of the time openly used parades to improve the treatment of animals, by fostering pride in the animals' appearance.

For modern horse parades, *see* **Easter Monday: Harness Horse Parade**, p. 175; **A Sunday in September: Horseman's Sunday**, p. 391.

International Labour Day

The first of May was adopted as International Labour Day at the first congress of the Second Socialist International in Paris in 1889, to proclaim and celebrate the potential economic and political power of a united working class. It is often assumed that this was a deliberate move to take advantage of the long-standing traditional popularity of May Day across Europe, but it seems that the choice of day was largely fortuitous. In their eagerness to forge a truly international workers' movement, European organizers were keen to ally themselves with developments in the United States, where 1 May was already associated with strikes in support of the agitation for an eight-hour working day. But it was an inspired choice all the same, and the previous history of the day provided an immediate legitimacy to the new celebrations.

In the early days of the labour movement in Britain, and into the Edwardian era, a combination of socialism and romantic utopianism proved a heady mixture for an extremely wide range of individuals and organizations on the fringes of socialism and left-wing causes. Ideologies and projects as diverse as William Morris's Victorian medievalism, the Arts and Crafts movement, Garden Cities, folk song and dance, and countless brotherhood and utopian movements and experiments contributed to the new May Day. In retrospect, most of these smacked of well-meaning middle-class romanticism, and were a far cry from the realities of industrial toil, mass unemployment, and squalid urban living conditions, but the images conjured up by these movements had a powerful effect at the time. The iconography of labour publications often depicted a romantic view of May Day, harking back to a supposed utopian past, and a popular feature at labour gatherings was the presentation of maypole dances by the children of the local Socialist Sunday schools. As the *Oxford Chronicle* commented, in 1906:

The idea of a May-day festival took us a long way back, to the days when men and women led simpler and more natural lives, when the air was purer and food was unadulterated, when the people had a pride and pleasure in their work and felt glad to be alive.

But all this changed after the First World War. Between the wars, May Day labour gatherings lost their romance and, particularly in large industrial towns, the day was celebrated with processions of bands, banners, and speeches, and demonstrations of class solidarity and strength, rather than maypole dancing. The soft edges of utopia had given way to the hard edges of interwar political struggles.

Jack-in-the-Green

Up to the turn of the twentieth century, a very odd-looking character called Jack-in-the-Green could be regularly seen dancing in the streets of certain towns every May Day. He was an integral part of the seasonal celebrations put on by chimney sweeps, and would play his part in collecting money to help see them through the summer, the lean period of the trade. A. R. Bennett, writing of his childhood in south London in the 1860s, provides a good description of the custom:

A lusty sweep – for strength and endurance were necessary for the due performance of the part – covered himself down to the boots with a circular wicker frame of bee-hive contour, carried on the shoulders, and terminating in a dome or pinnacle above his head. This frame was entirely concealed by green boughs and flowers. May blossoms preponderating if the season was propitious. A small window gave egress to his gaze, but was not very obvious from without, and one seldom caught a glimpse of the perspiring countenance within. Women and girls, one to each corner, and two or three men and youths, sometimes with sooty faces, mouth-organs and tambourines, formed his escort, the females being in short dresses, white stockings and gaudy shoes, like sorry May Queens. The verdure-clad sweep pranced, twirled, jumped and capered to the music while the others danced around.

At this time, the Jack was just starting its slow decline, and thirty years later he had become a rarity. Because of this, he still had the power to surprise:

Walking along Jamaica Road I saw what looked like a big bush hopping from one side of the street to the other, and bobbing up and down . . . This being the first time I had seen a Jack-in-the-Green, it scared the life out of me.

This was again in London, about 1900.

Jack-in-the-Green rarely appeared alone. He was first seen as an addition to the existing milkmaids' garland dancing (*see* 1 **May: Milkmaids' Garland**), and although he himself would certainly need at least one musician and someone to collect the money, he invariably had other companions to increase the entertainment value of the performance. Early on these were sweeps' boys or apprentices, who played percussion on shovel and brush, but these went out of favour as the tide of indignation against the treatment of 'climbing boys' swept through the nation's conscience. A character dressed as a Lord, and another as a Lady – the latter sometimes a real woman and sometimes a male parody of one – as well as various kinds of clown, were his most common companions. They all danced and were no doubt very funny and charming, or tedious and grotesque, depending on their individual skill and the mood of the beholder.

There is a surprising amount of information on the Jack from the late eighteenth and nineteenth centuries, much of it pictorial, and we must be eternally grateful for the detective work of the late Roy Judge, whose study *The Jack-in-the-Green* (2nd edn, 2000) presents all the available evidence in a scholarly and accessible way; he commented that 'A reasonable conclusion from this evidence would seem to be that the Jack-in-the-Green appeared in the last thirty years of the eighteenth-century in the context of the May Day activity.' The mass of available evidence also shows that the custom was an urban one, found most often in London but also regularly in the southern counties of Hampshire, Sussex, and Kent, and in Buckinghamshire and Oxfordshire, and comparatively rarely outside this restricted area. Nevertheless, even with all this evidence, it is not totally clear how the Jack developed his distinctive leaf-clad garb. The most likely explanation is that the costume is an extension of the May garland theme which, in the form that featured in the milkmaids' dance, was carried on the head, probably in combination with a costume that had greenery or ribbons attached to various parts of the body. But this, at present, is speculation.

Jack-in-the-Green has certainly proved popular with modern audiences, and he can be seen again in the streets taking part in many revived spring celebrations, such as the annual Rochester Sweeps Festival in Kent. However, his history and reputation have been sadly misrepresented. Despite the fact that Jack dates from the late eighteenth century, lasted for little more than 150 years, and was an urban rather than rural custom, he is routinely claimed as an ancient pagan tree-spirit, or as a personification of a vegetation god who dances to welcome the spring. He has also become inextricably tangled up in the complex modern persona of 'the Green Man', that powerful symbol used by the romantic wing of various eco-friendly and New Age groups. He has thus been absorbed into the amorphous blend of foliate heads (as the Green Man carvings in churches were previously called), medieval wildmen, Robin Hood, Gawain and the Green Knight, and anything or anyone else 'green', who are all now equated with vegetation and nature spirits. Needless to say, there is not the slightest evidence that Jack-in-the-Green has any connections with these other characters, but it is probably impossible now to rescue him from such dubious company.

Lords and Ladies

A May Day calendar custom, apparently unique to the village of Baldock in Hertfordshire, was described by a correspondent to William Hone's *Year-Book* (1832). Female inhabitants in the poorer areas were in the habit of making effigies 'of rags, pasteboard, old masks, old canvas, straw, etc.', which they dressed up in their own and their husbands' clothes, and set on chairs by their front doors, with a hat to collect money from passers-by. The figures were called 'my lord and my lady', and were sometimes arranged as a domestic tableau beside a table with pipe, mug, newspaper, and so forth, and they were profusely decorated with flowers. The account is in the past tense, and the writer comments that he could not say whether the custom still continued.

Magdalen College Singing

Early on May Day morning, the choir of Magdalen College, Oxford, along with officials and invited guests, ascend to the top of the college's

Huge crowds of revellers have already gathered in the street at the base of the tower and on the river, and as soon as the songs (which are nowadays amplified) are over, the bells are rung and a noisy street party commences with jugglers, acrobats, morris dancers, sideshows, and fancy dress, to welcome in the month of May.

The ceremony on the tower is impressive in its simplicity, but even this relatively straightforward event has changed over the years, and, thanks to the thorough research of folklorist Roy Judge, we know a great deal about how and why these changes came about. What happened here can be taken as a model for changes imposed on numerous traditional calendar customs by reformers up and down the country in the nineteenth century.

The actual origin of the Magdalen singing is unknown, but the most likely explanation is that it commenced as a celebration of the tower's completion in 1509. Seventeenth-century sources describe it as a secular event, and the choir probably sang popular songs of the day, but from about 1800 it became widely believed that the singing had started as a requiem mass for the repose of the soul of Henry VII, probably because he had also died in 1509. This theory of origin dictated the way the custom was to change a few decades later. In the eyes of the college authorities, the occasion was clearly ripe for reform, and the key instigator of the reforms was Magdalen fellow Dr John Rouse Bloxam (1807–91), who first took note of the ceremony in the early 1840s. He found that it was:

. . . more like a Baccanalian song than sacred hymn. The choirmen and choristers went up the Tower in their usual garb and kept their hats and caps on during the singing. The principal function of the choristers seemed to be to throw down rotten eggs on the people below.

In other reports, those in the street below seemed mostly intent on drowning out the singing by blowing their traditional May Day tin trumpets, and the whole affair was viewed as an example of the long-standing antipathy between town and gown. Bloxam drastically reformed the occasion by introducing a new atmosphere of simple piety. He made the choir dress and behave appropriately, and insisted that the assembled crowd removed their hats. Most importantly, as Roy Judge commented, he made 'the ceremonial a self-conscious occasion, aware of its own tradition'.

Reformers such as Bloxam based their efforts on a combination of the currently accepted ideas of origin, which, as in this case, were usually spurious, and the preoccupations of the cultural milieu in which they themselves lived. What was in the air in mid-century Oxford was a heady combination of church reform (including the revival of ceremonials associated with the Oxford Movement) and a romantic medieval antiquarianism. Customs reformed in this way therefore possessed the dual power of contemporary resonance and an apparent historical legitimacy.

However, the story has another twist. In the 1870s, when scholars started looking at the documents preserved in Magdalen's archives, the Henry VII story was quickly discredited. But just as this new rigour in antiquarian research had finally laid Henry's soul to rest, a new explanation was being formulated that claimed – on no evidence – that the May Day singing must be a relic of pagan times. The Christian element, it was said, had been 'grafted on some pagan rite of the worshippers of nature', the custom being 'Druidical by origin and Christian by conversion'. The spread of this new orthodoxy was typified, and greatly assisted, by Holman Hunt's well-known painting *May Morning on Magdalen Tower* (1888–91) with its unashamedly romantic Druidism. Fortunately, this new interpretation, which is still rampant, has not yet been allowed to affect what happens on the tower, but it is quite feasible that it will one day, with the singers dressed in pseudo-Druidic robes and singing newly written anthems of sun worship.

The Magdalen singing gets all the headlines, but it is not unique, and there have been many other examples of tower-top singing, such as the event at Sidney Sussex College in Cambridge, detailed by Enid Porter in her *Cambridgeshire Customs and Folklore* (1969). Most of these are clearly copies of the Oxford event, but there are indications of a more complex history. Christine Bloxham, for example, relates how, in the early seventeenth century, singing on the New College tower was moved to Ascension Day precisely because the 'Magdalen College men and the rabble of the towns' dominated May Day morning.

May Dew

For at least 200 years, it was widely believed that bathing the face in dew early on May Day morning was excellent for the complexion, and in particular helped to whiten the skin and eradicate freckles.

[28 May 1667] *After dinner my wife went down with Jane and W. Hewer to Woolwich in order to a little ayre, and to lie there tonight and so to gather May dew tomorrow morning, which Mrs. Turner hath taught her as the only thing in the world to wash her face with, and I am contented with it.*

Two years later, he was not so contented:

[10 May 1669] *Troubled, about 3 in the morning, with my wife's calling her maid up, and rising herself, to go with her coach abroad to gather May-dew – which she did; and I troubled for it, for fear of any hurt, going abroad betimes, happening to her.*

But she returned safely before he was up. Elizabeth Pepys's morning jaunts are the first recorded examples of the belief in May dew, and the wording of the first extract seems to imply that the idea was new to her. It is quite possible that it was new to England at the time, perhaps introduced from the Continent. It is noteworthy that Elizabeth clearly believed that the efficacy of the dew lasted all the month of May, and not simply on 1 May; the latter date was most definitely the norm in later years.

The idea was still around in the twentieth century, but in some circles only just. In Gloucestershire, 1906:

I overheard this conversation between two Minchinhampton girls: 'They do say that if you wash your face in the May dew, early in the morning, you'll have a good complexion.' 'Oh, you silly, they only tell you that to make you get up early!'

May dew was also occasionally reported as generally medicinal, especially for weak limbs, and some also claimed that you could 'make a wish' while gathering it.

May Dolls

Dolls were often included as an integral part of the May garlanding custom (*see* 1 **May: Children's Garlands**), but sometimes the doll took the central role itself. 'May Dolls' and 'May Babies' were carried from door to door in exactly the same way as the 'vessel cup' visitors at Christmas (*see* 24 **December: Vessel Cups**), except that spring flowers took the place of winter evergreens. A Miss Pinchard of Torquay,

Devon, contributed the following description to the Devonshire Association in 1876:

At a very early hour every little cottage girl in whose family there is a doll is astir, completing preparations that have been begun days before. The doll, whether large or small, is dressed in her best, and laid in a long cardboard box. She is then decorated with the best flowers the little ones have been able to procure from field or garden . . . The doll herself is nearly hidden by flowers, and her bed and pillow also. She is then covered carefully over, and the owner, accompanied by a following of little sisters and friends, all neat and in their best, sallies forth. The little party call at every gentleman's house, with, 'Please to see the May doll?' as their appeal. Sometimes they succeed in getting them carried to the mistress, and sometimes not. It depends in part on whether the leaders are known to the family. I myself always now leave word with my servants whose dolls may be brought in; but in former days I used to be overwhelmed by their number. I have known as many as thirty carried to the bedside of a sick child, to whom the day was quite a delight. Of course the children expect, and receive, a few pence; and I am told that this is faithfully and equally divided between the seven or eight children who usually accompany each doll; the whole being collected in a little bag, and then shared at the close of the day.

Enid Porter recorded that 'May Dolling' survived in Cambridgeshire until at least the 1960s.

May Goslings

Everybody knows that 1 April is the day for playing tricks, but in the northern counties of Cumbria, Lancashire, and parts of Yorkshire and Northumberland, people had a second chance to make fools of each other on 1 May. The victim was called a 'May gosling' or 'geslin' in the local pronunciation. Iona and Peter Opie found the custom alive and well in the 1950s, and reported that the traditional tricks were the same as those recorded for 1 April, and that the trickery had to stop at 12 noon:

> *May gosling's dead and gone*
> *You're the fool for thinking on.*

It is not clear how old the May gosling custom was. It was certainly widespread by the late eighteenth century, as the *Gentleman's Magazine* (April 1791) included a mention:

A May gosling on the 1st of May is made with as much eagerness in the north of England, as an April noddy (noodle) or fool, on the 1st of April.

But this is over a hundred years after the first mention of April Fool's Day.

May Queens

One of the most widespread elements of the modern May Day is the election and crowning of the May Queen, sometimes as a ceremony in its own right but more often as a key element in a larger event such as a village fête or procession. May Queen ceremonies vary considerably in complexity, but the core remains remarkably similar. A young woman or girl is chosen (elected or appointed) to personify the season or event and to be the Queen for the year. She is dressed in suitable garb, in which elements of royal, bridal, and fairy traditions combine, and is topped with flowers or a crown, and attended by a few similarly dressed companions. She rides in state in the procession, or sits in similar state at the village fête. The age of the May Queen varies considerably from place to place, but where she is old enough, she often acts as a minor celebrity throughout the year of her reign, appearing at a variety of local events. The popularity of the basic idea is demonstrated by the numerous variations on the theme, created to suit local circumstances, such as the Rose Queen, Harvest Queen, and Dairy Queen, but the principle is always the same.

Like the plaited maypole, the May Queen is so much part of England's accepted May Day iconography that we assume it to be an ancient institution, but it is, in fact, almost entirely another nineteenth-century invention, and was an integral part of the Victorian remodelling of May Day on Merrie England lines (*see also* **Merrie England** (p. 510) and **1 May: Maypoles**). A key feature of such nineteenth-century antiquarian innovations was that their creators invariably believed that they were bringing back the real spirit of a lost golden age, blithely billing their inventions as 'ancient traditions', and we have naturally inherited this notion.

The germ of the idea for a May Queen probably came from the May Lord and Lady characters who presided over Whitsun Ales (*see* **Church Ales**, p. 258) and other spring gatherings, but the genre was largely created from scratch by the usual suspects in the Merrie England movement – Washington Irving's *Sketch Book* (1820) and

Bracebridge Hall (1822), articles in the *Examiner* and other campaigning periodicals by Leigh Hunt and others, and, most important of all, Tennyson's poem 'The May Queen' (1832), with its insistent refrain, 'For I'm to be queen o' the May', which provided the romantic literary backdrop to countless May Day recreations. The interest in May Queens gathered pace throughout the century, and was given another huge boost with the foundation of the world-famous May Queen ceremony at Whitelands College, in London, inspired by John Ruskin in 1881.

There is no doubting the widespread popularity of the May Queen idea in communities across the country, or that it was entirely appropriate to the image of May Day that local event committees wished to create. But it was nearly always too tightly controlled and circumscribed by its romantic origin to become a true folk custom. Time and again in Victorian and Edwardian accounts of May Day, it is clear that the celebrations had been introduced, shaped, and organized by the local elite, including vicars, schoolteachers, stalwarts of temperance societies, and the Sunday school movement, all working to the same blueprint. As Charlotte Burne wrote in 1883:

At Albrighton, near Shiffnal [Shropshire], *a May-day festival is yearly held under the superintendence of the venerable Vicar, whose custom it has been for many years past to gather the boys of his parish about him for a treat on the 5th of November, and the girls on the 1st of May, on which occasion a very pretty ceremony has gradually grown up. After morning service in church, almost the whole congregation go to the Vicarage, where presently the chosen May Queen, in pretty gala dress, her hair garlanded with flowers, is brought forth and mounted on a horse gaily caparisoned with wreaths of flowers and greenery. The Volunteers' band heads the procession, then come two little boys on horseback, as the Queen's herald and champion, and her page riding on a donkey, all gaily dressed in appropriate fancy costumes. Next follows her Majesty; the Vicar walking beside her, and four little girls as her maids of honour, holding a canopy over her head, while eight or ten others, all dressed alike in white frocks and coloured ribbons, follow two and two behind. The girls of the national schools come next, and the general company, wearing or carrying flowers, bring up the rear of the procession . . . They walk the whole length of the village, and then return to the Vicarage, where the Queen is enthroned beside a Maypole, and the children spend the afternoon in games and dancing.*

their hundreds every year, but there is a small but discernible shift in
the general view of such events. In an increasing number of cases, girls
and young women appear much less willing to be dressed in white
satin and flowers, and paraded around billed as the 'prettiest girl' in
town. They are less willing to volunteer or to feel it an honour, and
it is quite possible that over the next fifty years the May Queen will
become largely a thing of the past – and ripe for re-invention in the
next century.

See also **First Saturday in May: Knutsford Royal May Day Festival**;
Rose Queens, p. 328.

Maypoles

For most English people, mention of a maypole will conjure up a picture of schoolchildren dressed in white, dancing round a short pole,
and holding ribbons that make pretty patterns as they weave in and
out of each other. This type of 'ribbon dance' maypole has been around
for little more than 170 years, however, having been introduced to this
country by professional choreographers in numerous romantic theatrical pieces, organized fêtes, and revived or created May Day customs
from about the 1830s. In the classic **Merrie England** mould (p. 510),
it was immediately billed as an 'old English custom', despite its lack
of historical roots. By the later nineteenth century, it was being dis-
seminated through the English school system by enthusiastic schoolteachers, and although it can now claim to be 'traditional' in its own
right, for many it will always have an air of official culture rather than
genuine folk tradition, precisely because it is perpetuated by teachers
rather than by the people themselves. It has little in common with the
English maypole as it has existed since the late Middle Ages.

The older maypole tradition involved no plaited ribbons, although
it was always the focal point of dancing. The pole could be anything up
to one hundred feet tall, and was usually brightly painted and decorated with garlands, rosettes, and hanging ribbons, but there was nothing
for the dancers to hold on to, except each other. Surviving illustrations
of village celebrations almost invariably show adult dancers holding
hands in a circle round the pole. If they remained in this linked circle,
there would have been little else to do than go forward and back, and
round to left or right. But if they let go their hands, they could thread
in and out of each other, or undertake more complex movements,

and more than one seventeenth-century maypole description refers to 'turning and kissing'. When dancing in couples became generally fashionable from the early nineteenth century, it is likely that most of the dances round the maypole became indistinguishable from dances round the village hall or ballroom.

Maypoles were almost always set up on the village green, or other appropriate open space, and became the true focal point for seasonal celebration. As Lincolnshire folklorist Ethel Rudkin recorded of the village of Hemswell in 1936:

Feast week was in Maytime (i.e. first week in May) and there used to be stalls in the street round the Maypole. There was 'good-stuff' stalls, and 'sweet-meat' stalls and 'aunt Sally' – a rare fine show it was! As a little 'un I remember it – and I'd 4d to spend, so I spent it all in halfpence – and I did buy a lot with that 4d! We danced at nighttime round the maypole, but only just ordinary round dances, none of these dances with ribbons attached to the pole – I never heard tell of that being done.

But there were other types of maypole around on May Day, especially in the hands of children. A variety of children's May customs included a portable maypole, or at least a decorated stick called by the same name, and, ever-resourceful, some twentieth-century children adapted the ribboned school model, as described by a contributor to the Opies' *Lore and Language of Schoolchildren* (1959):

On May 1, 1952, I visited the recent building estates in the Monkmoor area [of Shrewsbury] and found four separate groups of children performing a maypole dance . . . The maypoles consisted of a pram wheel decorated with crepe paper and streamers set on top of a pole so that it would revolve. The pole (varying from about 3 to about 5 feet high) was held in position by the Queen seated upon a wooden stool. The number of dancers (all girls) varied from four to ten . . . The performers seemed aged about 5–11 and were dressed in crepe paper finery, the queen usually wearing a crown of some sort.

The early development of the maypole is unclear. There is no evidence that the pole was a development of the pagan worship of trees, or was seen as a fertility-based phallic symbol. The first definite references are in the fourteenth century; one in a Welsh poem, although the word is in English, and the second in another poem, 'Chaunce of the Dice', a decade or so later. The latter concerns the permanent pole at Cornhill in London, reputedly taller than the steeple of the nearby church, which was generally known as St Andrew's *Undershaft* as a result. John Stow's *Survey of London* (1598) explains that this maypole was taken down for a while after 'Evil May Day' of 1517, when apprentices rioted against foreigners, and was finally attacked and chopped up by a zealous Protestant preacher in 1549. From this time onwards, the maypole had a chequered career, being used as a potent symbol by both sides in the protracted battle between religious reformers and conservative supporters of popular pastimes.

Real maypoles need regular replacement. The part that is underground quickly rots, and poles are regularly blown down or damaged in winter storms. The fetching and setting up of a new pole was always an occasion for celebration and merriment, and this was one of the grounds on which the reformers sought to ban the custom. The famous diatribe against maypoles, penned by Puritan Philip Stubbes in 1583, is worth quoting in full, as it not only demonstrates the depth of feeling against such events but also provides our best description of the custom at this period:

The manner of May games in England: . . . Against May day, Whitsunday, or some other time of the year, every parish, town, and village assemble themselves together, both men, women, and children, old and young, even all indifferently, and either going all together, or dividing themselves into companies, they go some into the woods, and groves, some to the hills and mountains, some to one place, some to another, where they spend all night in pleasant pastimes, and in the morning they return bringing with them birch boughs, and branches of trees, to deck their assemblies withal. And no marvel, for there is a great Lord present amongst them, as superintendent and lord over their pastimes and sports: namely, Satan Prince of Hell: But their chiefest jewel they bring from thence is the may-pole, which they bring home with great veneration, as thus: they have twenty, or forty yoke of oxen, every ox having a sweet nosegay of flowers tied on the tip of his horns, and these oxen draw home this May-pole (this stinking idol rather) which is covered all over with flowers and herbs, bound round about with strings from top to the bottom, and sometimes painted with variable colours, with two or three hundred men, women, and children following it, with great devotion. And thus being reared up, with handkerchiefs and flags streaming on the top, they strew the ground round about, bind green boughs about it, set up summer halls, bowers, and arbours hard by it. And then fall they to banquet and feast, to leap and dance about it, as the heathen people did, at the dedication of their idols, whereof this is a perfect pattern, or rather the thing itself. I have heard it credible reported (and that viva voce) by men of great gravity, credit, and reputation, that of forty, threescore, or a hundred maids, going to the wood overnight, there have scarcely the third part of them return home undefiled. These be the fruits, which these cursed pastimes bring forth. Assuredly, I think neither Jews nor Turks, Saracens, nor Pagans, nor any other people how wicked, or barbarous soever, have ever used such devilish exercises as these; nay, they would have been ashamed once to have named them, much less to have used them. Yet we that would be Christian, think them not amiss. The Lord forgive us and remove them far from us.

Maypoles were banned by Parliament in 1644, and although some royalist centres were slow to comply, before long the country was devoid of maypoles for the first time in at least 300 years. Nevertheless, the symbolic nature of the maypole was again in evidence at the Restoration, as they sprang up all over the country in deliberate defiance of the Puritan rule of the Commonwealth. The one difference at this time, however, was that Royal Oak Day began to rival May Day as the time for celebration (*see* **29 May: Royal Oak Day**). Maypoles continued to be evident in English villages and towns through the next centuries, but after the peak of popularity at the Restoration, they gradually faded away – this time from neglect and changing fashion rather than opposition. A few places still have maypoles on traditional lines, including: Barwick-in-Elmet in Yorkshire (*see* **Spring Bank Holiday: Barwick Maypole**, p. 283), Hemswell in Lincolnshire, Ickwell in Bedfordshire, and Padstow in Cornwall.

Milkmaids' Garland

[1 May 1667] *Thence to Westminster in the way meeting with many milkmaids with their garlands upon their pails, dancing with a fiddler before them.*

Samuel Pepys here shows no surprise about seeing milkmaids dancing, as it was a common sight in urban streets on May Day. The 'milkmaids' dance', or 'milkmaids' garland', was for many a symbol of spring, and there are numerous published approving descriptions and illustrations that demonstrate that the custom was a welcome diversion of the season. It should be explained that 'milkmaids' in this context are not necessarily those who milked the cows, but those who delivered the milk to urban houses. Ostensibly, the maids danced in the streets in front of their customers' houses, and collected money from them, but no doubt they solicited contributions from passers-by as well. On 2 May 1710, a correspondent to the *Tatler* reported:

I was looking out of the parlour window this morning and receiving the honours which Margery, the milkmaid to our lane, was doing me by dancing before my door with the plate of half her customers on her head.

In Pepys's time, the 'garland' was usually the maid's ordinary milk-pail, colourfully decorated with flowers and ribbons, and carried on her head, while she danced to the music of an accompanying fiddler. The poise and dexterity necessary to dance thus encumbered added to the charm of the scene. Later illustrations, however, indicate that the 'garland' developed rapidly through various stages to become a veritable pyramid of silver plate and utensils, borrowed or hired for the occasion, and heavy enough to need to be carried on the head of an attendant male, or even on a litter between two men, leaving the maid to dance more freely. The typical milkmaid's May Day entourage thus grew to include various supernumeraries, including even a policeman, or some other responsible person, to guard the valuable silverware on show.

There was also a bunters' garland, which parodied the milkmaids' custom. 'Bunters' were low female rag-pickers or, in some parlance, prostitutes, who danced accompanied by predominately brass garlands, rather than silver and gold. They were no doubt amusing or grotesque, according to the perspective of the beholder.

The heyday of the milkmaids' garland custom was the eighteenth century, and it seems to have faded away quite rapidly in the early nineteenth. By this time, the May Day streets were becoming quite crowded, as other trade groups also put on displays and collected money. The chimney sweeps and Jack-in-the-Greens (*see* p. 210), in particular, regarded this as their special day, and one that marked the end of the lucrative winter season, and illustrations show sweeps' boys and apprentices joining in the milkmaids' dance, providing percussion with the tools of their trade, the brush and shovel. The inherent ambiguity of this juxtaposition of summertime, milk-white, female grace, and winter soot-black male grotesquery was not lost on contemporary observers, and although it cannot be proved that the sweeps' involvement drove the milkmaids from the streets, the temporal coincidence of the decline of the one and the rise of the other is certainly suggestive.

Minehead Hobby Horse

The Minehead hobby horse, in Somerset, has the dubious distinction of always being compared unfavourably with the more widely known **Padstow Hobby Horse** (*see below*), but this is unfair. The two traditions are quite similar in outline, but whereas the Padstow 'Oss is predominately black, and it seems as if the whole town is celebrating the custom, the Minehead horse is colourful and mobile, playful and mischievous, and the undoubtedly charming festivities follow a simpler approach. The Minehead horse comes out briefly on the evening of 30 April, and then on the first three days of May. He tours the streets of the town and neighbouring area, to the music of accordions and drum. There are usually two or three horses at any given time, including, at present, the Sailors' Horse, which is generally regarded as the original, and the Town, or Show, Horse.

The basis of the horse is a boat-shaped wooden frame about eight feet long and three feet wide, supported on a man's shoulders. The frame is covered in a cloth, which hangs down to the ground and is decorated with coloured roundels and other shapes. Across the top are multicoloured ribbons, and the carrier is hidden by a mask and hood, which is also covered with ribbons. As with other hobby animals, the Minehead horse can run, dance, sway, or jump as the mood takes it, and, as Herbert W. Kille notes in his 1931 article on West Country hobby horses, it regularly pays 'obeisance to onlookers, especially if they be affluent-looking ones, or, if they be otherwise, flutters its hundreds of ribbons with a wicked shake and rushes affrightingly at them'.

The horse used to carry a ladle in its mouth to collect money, but nowadays this is done by attendants; its mouth could also be made to snap at people, but this too has been removed. If people refuse to give money they can be 'booted'. The victim is seized, held face down, and struck ten times on the posterior by the front of the horse (in previous times by a boot), to shouts of 'Oh one! Oh two! Oh three!', and so on. If anyone offends the horse it metes out a more summary punishment by suddenly whipping round and catching the unwary bystander with its rope tail.

Herbert Kille's account of the custom speaks of the horse being attended by fantastically dressed men known as 'gullivers', 'up to about fifty years ago' (i.e. about 1880), whose task was to collect money by knocking on doors and accosting passers-by. They were armed with clubs, and local legend maintains that they were suppressed because they got involved in a fight with someone who would not contribute, and ended up killing him, but no evidence has yet been found to support this story. Numerous photographs of the custom in the twentieth century do not show any attendants, apart from musicians, but around 1970 one team re-introduced the gullivers, whose costume of ribbons and masks deliberately echoes that of the hobby horse itself.

The earliest known reference to the hobby horse custom is in James Savage's *History of the Hundred of Carhampton* (1830), but his comment that 'this custom has prevailed for ages' implies a much longer history that had gone unrecorded.

See also **Hobby Horses**, p. 226.

Padstow Hobby Horse

Unite and unite and let us all unite
For summer is a-come unto day
And whither we are going we all will unite
In the merry morning of May.

The town of Padstow, on the north coast of Cornwall, has the most famous hobby horse in the country, and the locals are fiercely proud of their tradition. On 30 April the town is decorated with greenery, bunting, and flags in preparation for the big day, and on May morning the 'Oss emerges from his long sleep to spend the day dancing through the streets among the huge crowds of tourists and visitors, who outnumber the locals several to one. It is a mark of Padstow's independence that they not only still continue the tradition, but also do it on their own terms. Like other community customs, the celebrations at Padstow on May Day are so important to the community that those who live away try to get home for the day; and if they cannot, we are told, they make sure to sing the May Day song to themselves to compensate a little.

The 'Oss is difficult to describe adequately, but it comprises a circular frame, about five feet in diameter, which is carried on straps on the shoulders of a man inside. Covering the frame and hanging down all round, almost to the ground, is a black cloth. The carrier's head pokes up through a hole in the centre, and is covered with a tall conical hat and a grotesque mask. Attached to the front of the frame is a small

continued on page 228

Hobby Horses

For many centuries, hobby animals have been a popular feature of a number of traditional customs, and although it is usually a horse that is impersonated, other animals, such as rams and bulls, are occasionally made on similar lines. The animals can appear on their own (*see* 24 **December: Hooden Horse**) or as part of another custom (*see* **Whitsun: Morris Dance**, p. 263), and they come in a variety of guises. There are two basic forms of construction, dubbed the 'tourney' horse and the 'mast' horse, although the best-known existing hobby horse customs, at Padstow in Cornwall, and Minehead in Somerset (*see* 1 **May: Minehead Hobby Horse**; 1 **May: Padstow Hobby Horse**), are not typical, and are made on different lines.

For the tourney horse, a man stands inside an oval frame, which is fixed round his waist, usually by straps over the shoulders. The frame is covered with a cloth that hangs down all round, partly obscuring the rider's legs, and a small replica horse's head is fixed at the front, with a tail at the rear. The man appears to be riding the horse, and refinements such as reins for him to hold, and dummy rider's legs sewn on the horse's sides, greatly enhance the illusion. In skilled hands, a tourney horse can run, jump, skip, and dance; its rider can see perfectly well, and it is the most mobile of the hobby horse types under consideration.

The mast horse is decidedly more primitive-looking than the tourney horse. A real horse's skull, or a wooden replica, is mounted on a pole about three or four feet long. A man bends forward and grasps the pole near the top in both hands, and he and the pole are completely covered by a cloth fixed to the underside of the horse's head. The result is somewhat formless, and hardly horse-like at all, but it can be extremely effective, and frightening, in the right hands (*see*, for example, 24 **December: Old Horse**).

Within these basic designs, either type of horse can have refinements. Particularly popular are snapping jaws worked by a string, bells, pieces of metal that jangle, and glass for reflective eyes. The tail might be realistically fashioned from horsehair or rope, which fetches the unwary onlooker a blow as the horse wheels round, or it can even be full of sharp tacks or fish hooks to make sure no bystanders try to catch hold of it.

The tourney horse has been known for many years as an accompaniment to the morris dance, but it has also featured in processions and other customs, such as the Horn Dance at Abbots Bromley (*see* 4 **September:**

ied history. He turns up as the Hooded Horse in Kent, the Wild Horse in
the Cheshire version of the mummers' play (*see* **31 October: Antrobus
Soul-Cakers**), in the plough plays of the East Midlands (*see* **Plough
Monday**, p. 19), as the **Old Tup** and the **Old Horse** in the Midlands (*see*
24 December), and in the well-known Welsh custom of the Mari Lwyd.

The earliest documentary evidence is found in a fourteenth-century
Welsh poem by Gruffud Gryg, and a later Cornish play, *Beunas Meriasek*
(1504). Although these were written in Welsh and Cornish respectively,
in both the phrase 'hobby horse' appears in English. Sandwiched in time
between these references is an entry in the churchwardens' accounts
for St Andrew Hubbard in 1460/1: 'To Mayers child for dancing with the
hobby horse'. From the early sixteenth century onwards, references to
hobby horses abound, and a reasonable picture of its style and activities can be formed. Whenever contextual details can be found in these
early references, it is clear that the hobby horse's primary task was the
collection of money, often for the Church but also for other institutions,
and it was probably used in this way because it was an immensely popular entertainment with the people. There is little doubt that the tourney
horse, at least, owes its existence to its entertainment value rather than
any supposed ritual or ceremonial function. But the real paradox for the
hobby horse historian is that the apparently primitive mast-horse only
starts to make an appearance in documentary records from the mid
nineteenth century onwards.

This fact puts into serious doubt any supposed direct link between
hobby horse customs and the prehistoric cave paintings found in some
European sites, which appear to represent humans impersonating animals. The enormous gulf in time and geography between these primitive representations and our modern hobby horses make it impossible
to draw any connections without a huge leap of faith. Similarly, the occasional prohibitions by early continental Church authorities against
people dressing as animals, which themselves need re-analysis, are
separated from our historical examples by over a thousand years.

The one comparison that might save our mast horses from the igno-
miny of being mere Victorian inventions is the Scandinavian evidence
most recently presented by Terry Gunnell in his *Origins of Drama in
Scandinavia* (1995). He describes a range of animals, including the widely
known *Julebukk* or *Julegeit* (Christmas goat), which were found across
most of Scandinavia, from the first known mention in Denmark in 1543,

until the late nineteenth century. Apart from the fact that these creatures were decorated with fur and wore horns, they were constructed in a very similar way to our mast horses, and behaved in corresponding ways. They too were used primarily as part of a winter house-visiting custom, and could be found alone and with other dramatic forms. The British evidence has been ably collected by Dr E. C. Cawte in his *Ritual Animal Disguise* (1978), but thirty years later there is still much more work to be done on the subject.

See also **Easter Day: Old Ball**, p. 157; **24 June: Midsummer's Day/St John the Baptist's Day**.

☞ *continued from page 225* stylized horse's head, and at the rear a tail. It is surprising how versatile and lifelike such a strange monster can be. It walks, sways, dances, swings, and swoops – not much like a horse, admittedly, but like a live creature all the same. There is a Teaser, previously called the Dancer, who holds a flat painted club and dances in front of the 'Oss, encouraging, leading, and teasing it, as well as musicians and drummers, lots of them nowadays, and young people, some of whom collect money from the onlookers, while others dance. The musicians play the same hypnotic tune all day, as the 'Oss dances all around the town, but every now and then it sinks to the ground, whether pretending to be dead, asleep, or from simple exhaustion is not clear. The music and song changes to a slow dirge, the dancers crouch, and those close enough might reach out and gently stroke the 'Oss, but as the slow verse ends, and with a triumphant cry of "Oss 'Oss!' he springs back on to his feet and is off again.

There are two 'Osses at present, which to the untrained eye look identical, but their attendants are easily distinguished as they are dressed in either red or blue. There have been many 'Osses over the years, as reported to collector Doc Rowe:

Well we had all sorts of Osses at one time. Old Baker had one and the . . . Lion had one; Albert Giddy had a horse called 'Princess Mary' . . . Didn't Sussex Langford have one? Then there was Rosie Walker's 'Oss . . . the striped one. We had a white 'Obby 'Oss for a year or two. Oh yes, I remember that one. It was all white.

The musicians and attendant singers, dancers, and collectors wear a white costume, but their hats, sashes, and ribbons are brightly coloured. The red team wear headscarves and sashes and look like stage pirates, while the blue team look more like stage sailors. The two 'Osses wend their separate ways around the town, and while you are following one it seems as if the other does not exist. But they both return to the middle of town for the evening climax, and sometimes they will dance together.

The red team claim that theirs is the original 'Oss, as the blue one descends from an 'Oss that came out after the First World War, but although the respective lineage is well documented in the twentieth century, the earlier period is less clear, and some even say that the blue one is really the oldest. Hundreds of photographs, dating back to around the First World War, provide evidence for changing styles and fashions, although they do not reveal much about the actions of the 'Oss and the attendant dancing. In the earlier pictures there are far fewer onlookers, but also fewer musicians (only one or two melodeons, and one or two drums), fewer white costumes, and more hats decorated with flowers, like May Day customs elsewhere. The musicians and Teaser often seem to be in fancy dress, and the latter sometimes appears dressed as a woman.

The origin of the custom is not known. The popular historical story is that one day, when all the men were out fishing, a French ship appeared off Padstow and the women feared an invasion. So they dressed up as the 'Oss and the French were so perplexed at the sight that they promptly sailed away. The earliest known reference appears in the Revd R. Polwhele's *History of Cornwall* in 1803, but as he describes it as a 'man drest up in a stallion horse's skin', it is not clear whether he actually witnessed a performance. Two decades later, however, F. Hitchins and Samuel Drew's *History of Cornwall* (1824) refers to 'canvas being extended with hoops, and painted to resemble a horse', which is certainly akin to the present-day form.

The Padstow Mayers also have a night-visiting custom on 30 April, when they go round to selected houses singing their 'night song':

> *Arise up Mrs. ——, and gold be your ring*
> *For summer is acome unto day*
> *And give to us a cup of ale the merrier we shall sing*
> *In the merry morning of May.*

Other verses serenade the Mr and Miss ——, together with the 'young men', who are exhorted to go to the greenwood to fetch the

May. Padstow also has a minstrel-inspired singing custom on Boxing Day (*see* **26 December: Padstow Mummers' (Darkie) Day**).

See also **1 May: Minehead Hobby Horse; Hobby Horses**, p. 226.

Randwick Cheese-Rolling

Randwick, near Stroud in Gloucestershire, was home to an apparently unique annual custom involving large, round cheeses. Unlike the other Gloucestershire cheese-rolling at Cooper's Hill, where they were chased down a hill (*see* **Spring Bank Holiday**, p. 284), at Randwick they were treated far more respectfully. William Hone records in his *Table Book* (1827) that:

Three large cheeses (Gloucestershire, of course), decked with the gayest flowers of this lovely season, are placed in litters, equally adorned with flowers, and boughs of trees waving at the corners. They are thus borne through the village, accompanied by a joyous throng, shouting and huzzaing with all their might and main, and usually accompanied by a little band of music.

The cheeses were then rolled three times around the church, carried back through the village, and then cut up and distributed. This account is the first mention of the custom, and it was probably originally a dole, or the distribution of food as a result of a local bequest, which often featured seemingly bizarre characteristics (*see* **Doles**, p. 115).

The cheese-rolling was revived in 1972, and incorporated into the local festival called Randwick Wap (*see* **Second Saturday in May: Randwick Wap**).

3 May

The Day of the Invention of the Holy Cross

According to one version of the legend, St Helena, the mother of St Constantine, discovered the three crosses on which Christ and the two robbers had been crucified, in the Holy Land in the early fourth century AD. The day is sometimes called St Helena's, although her real feast day is 18 August, and to complicate things further, some early British writers confused matters by claiming her as English-born.

Presumably unrelated to these ecclesiastical connections, 3 May was known as 'Sting-Nettle Day' in Devon. In 1880, the Devonshire Association recorded:

> The first of May is 'May-doll day'
> The second of May is 'kissing day'
> The third of May is 'sting-nettle day'.

On the 3rd of May this year I was passing through the village [Bovey Tracey] *and was struck with the peculiarity of all the children being provided with a nettle, or bunch of nettles, with which they were flogging each other. Having never seen the like before, Mr. B. thought there must be some meaning in this demonstration, and on enquiring of some of the children, he was informed that it was 'Sting-nettle Day'.*

This does not seem to be reported as a separate custom anywhere else in the country, although one of the common punishments for not wearing an oak leaf on Royal Oak Day (*see* **29 May: Royal Oak Day**) was to be attacked by nettle-wielding children.

First Saturday in May

Gawthorpe Celebrations

Gawthorpe, the Yorkshire village famous for its World Coal-Carrying Championship contest every Easter Monday (*see* p. 171), also holds impressive May Day celebrations on the first Saturday in that month. A procession involving themed floats, bands, children in fancy dress, and the local May Queen takes place, and there is also plaited maypole dancing, of which Gawthorpe is particularly proud, performed by schoolgirls from the village. The event has been organized by the Maypole Committee since 1874, but this was merely a formalization of an older tradition of maypoles in the village.

Earlier May celebrations were not always so well disciplined as the current ones. In 1850, for example, inter-village rivalry got out of hand when men from nearby Chickenley undertook a raid and sawed partway through the pole; in the ensuing fight, one man died and many were injured. The wind finished off that particular pole not long after, but there have been others since.

Knutsford Royal May Day Festival

Knutsford, in Cheshire, offers one of the best-known and largest modern May Day celebrations; hundreds of people take part, and even more line the streets to watch and admire them. The main event is the procession through town, which manages to preserve a local homely feel by featuring local children dressed as 'figures from the pages of fable and history', as the local paper described them. There are also morris dancers, brass bands, a town crier, a Jack-in-the-Green, and a Chinese dragon, among others, as well as a May Queen and her court of attendants. Knutsford takes its May Queen very seriously, and her crown is a replica of Queen Elizabeth's. A new one is provided each year, because the May Queen is allowed to keep hers as a souvenir of the day.

The present series of celebrations commenced in 1864, which makes it probably the longest-running May Day in the country. It is an excellent example of how the Victorians remodelled May Day (as they did Christmas), to remove the less salubrious aspects and create a new, respectable, family-friendly festival that lasted for generations to come. The word 'Royal' was added to its title in 1887, in honour of a visit from the then Prince and Princess of Wales.

Knutsford also has a unique custom called 'sanding', in which coloured sand is used to decorate the pavements on May Day and in honour of other special occasions, and the town was the model for Mrs Gaskell's popular novel *Cranford* (1851–3).

First Sunday in May

Tyburn Walk

A procession or pilgrimage takes place in London every year to commemorate Catholics martyred for their faith during the sixteenth and seventeenth centuries on Tyburn gallows. The route roughly follows that taken by prisoners from Newgate Prison to Tyburn, and it has been undertaken every year (including the War years) since its inauguration in 1910. The Walk was under severe threat in the year 2000 when pressure was put on the organizers to avoid busy shopping centres such as Oxford Street, but it has continued, albeit more informally and with fewer participants, and it now approaches its centenary. The Walk is normally now held on the first Sunday in May (except when this coincides with May Day Bank Holiday, in which case it is held on the second Sunday), and commences from the Church of the Holy Sepulchre, on the Strand (almost opposite the Old Bailey), at 2 or 2.30 p.m.

8 May

Helston Flora Day

The town of Helston, in Cornwall, maintains what must be the most famous traditional dance custom in Britain. Every May, the participants form up in couples and dance through the town, in and out of houses and shops, to a lively tune played by the town's silver band. The dance takes place four times during the day, each time involving a different section of the town's population.

In the case of most traditional customs, the earliest recorded references are vague and ambiguous, but we are lucky to have an unusually detailed account of the festivities at Helston in our first reference, which shows that all the essential elements of the day, as recently observed, were already in place in the late eighteenth century. The account was published in the *Gentleman's Magazine* of 1790 and signed by 'Durgan', and it is worth quoting in full:

At Helstone [sic], *a genteel and populous borough town in Cornwall, it is customary to dedicate the 8th of May to revelry (festive mirth, not loose jollity). It is called the Furry-day, supposed Flora's day; not, I imagine, as many have thought, in remembrance of some festival instituted in honour of that goddess, but rather from the garlands commonly worn on that day. In the morning, very early, some troublesome rogues go round the streets with drums, or other noisy instruments, disturbing their sober neighbours, and singing parts of a song, the whole of which nobody now recollects, and of which I know no more than that there is a mention in it of the 'grey goose quill' and of them going to the 'green wood to bring home the summer and the May-O' and, accordingly, hawthorn flowering branches are worn in hats ... About the middle of the day they collect together to dance hand-in-hand round the streets, to the sound of the fiddle playing a particular tune, which they continue to do till it is dark. This is called a 'faddy'. In the afternoon, the gentility go to some farmhouse in the neighbourhood to drink tea, syllabub, etc., and return in a morris-dance to the town, where they form a faddy, and dance through the streets till it is dark, claiming the right of going through any person's house, in at one door and out at the other. And here it formerly used to end, and the company of all kinds to disperse quietly to their several habitations, but latterly, corruptions have in this, as in other matters, crept in by degrees.*

Already in 1790 he is writing of 'corruptions' creeping in, although the sum total of the changes that he mentions are that the 'gentility' go on to a ball, and faddy their way home at the end of the evening, while the 'mobility', as he calls the lower classes, have a similar evening's entertainment at the local pubs. Already, too, there is confusion over the name. It is clear that 'furry day' is the older term, and all serious researchers accept that it is derived from a Cornish or English dialect form of 'fair day'. This is supported by the fact that 8 May is St Michael's Day, to whom the parish church is dedicated, and therefore the logical day for a local fair or feast. The names 'floral' and 'flora' may well have been introduced by some eighteenth-century antiquarian in his quest for classical origins, but even if that is so, they have become so entrenched, and are used by both locals and outsiders, that there is no shifting them now. Indeed, 'Floral dance' fits the May-time scene so well that its acceptance was perhaps inevitable.

On Flora Day, the town is decorated with bunting, greenery, and blossoms, and people wear lily-of-the-valley buttonholes and other flowers. The streets are crammed with spectators, allowing only a narrow passageway for the dancers to make their way through. Nowadays, there are four dances, at seven, ten, noon and five in the afternoon. The first one, previously for servants and others who would be on duty later in the day, is mostly now for young people, the men wearing ties and white shirts, the women in smart summer dresses; the second is the children's dance (introduced in 1922), and the dancers are all in white. The most famous – probably because it photographs well – is the Principal Dance, which begins at noon at the guildhall. This dance used to be restricted to the gentry, but participation is now by invitation of the organizing committee. The men wear grey top hats and black tails and the women are in gaily coloured dresses and impressively wide-brimmed summer hats, which looks more like a scene from Ascot than one in a Cornish town. The last dance is a relative free-for-all, when anyone is allowed to join in. Each dance takes its own route, which can take over an hour to complete and is very tiring for participants. Douglas Kennedy, former long-time Director of the English Folk Dance and Song Society, described how he and his wife fared when they were invited to take part in the Principal Dance in 1957. The night before, they were schooled in dancing 'with gaiety combined with dignity', but on the day they faced the last stretch up a steep hill to the town hall with decidedly flagging energy and stiff limbs.

One of the main reasons for the widespread fame of the event is the song 'The Floral Dance', composed in 1911 by a professional concert singer from London, Katie Moss, after she had visited the Helston Floral Dance that year. Her words, which are little short of twee, and her tune, which differs significantly from the way it has always been played in Helston, has been regularly performed as a pseudo-folk song by concert artists ever since. It was later arranged for brass band and became a staple of that repertoire all over the world. It is unfortunate that this later version is now more widely known than Helston's original, but it is encouraging that the people of Helston have remained resolutely unaffected by this.

Equally regrettable, but now firmly incorporated into the celebrations, is the 'enactment' of the 'Hal-an-Tow', the song that was sung by Durgan's 'troublesome rogues'. This part of the day was suppressed in the nineteenth century but was re-introduced in 1930, in suitably sanitized form, by the Helston Old Cornwall Society, when someone also decided that the song should not merely be sung but acted out in costume. The text is nothing if not eclectic, but it makes no real sense and speaks of Robin Hood and Little John, the Spaniards, St George, and Aunt Mary Moses in successive verses. However, its chorus makes perfect sense in the context of the day:

> *Hal-an-tow, jolly rumble O*
> *For we were up as soon as any day O*
> *And for to fetch the summer home*
> *The summer and the May O*
> *For summer is a-come O*
> *And winter is a-gone O.*

The phrase 'Hal-an-Tow' has generated a few fanciful derivations, but it probably means the dance 'Heel and toe'.

12 May

Florence Nightingale Commemoration

It takes a special kind of celebrity to become a lasting icon in the public's eye, but Florence Nightingale (1820–1910) fits that role perfectly. Nightingale was born to well-off parents, but at a relatively early age she decided to eschew the usual middle-class woman's path of marriage and family to dedicate herself to God's service. To this end, she decided to train as a nurse, and at the outbreak of the Crimean War in 1854 Nightingale used her connections, notably with Sidney Herbert, Secretary of War, to get permission to take a party of nurses to the front to care for wounded combatants. What she found there appalled her. The army offered the wounded no real care, and the hospitals were unhygienic and badly organized; above all, the military hierarchy seemed oblivious to the needs of sick and wounded soldiers. Nightingale was a formidable presence and completely reorganized hospital care, lobbying for improved conditions in health and welfare, and continuing to do so when back in Britain. She is credited with laying the foundations of modern nursing.

Florence Nightingale is still remembered at an annual service at Westminster Abbey, on or near her birthday, 12 May. Although her life and work is the focal point of the event, the service also celebrates nursing and healthcare work in general, and members of the different professions take an active part. Nightingale was famously dubbed 'the lady of the lamp', and the National Army Museum in Chelsea possesses one of the original lamps used in the Crimean hospital. In the Westminster Abbey service, the lamp is carried to the altar by a nurse, escorted by student nurses, and passed from hand to hand between representatives of the different branches of healthcare work and then to the officiating clergyman, who places it on the altar.

The May

Hastings Neville, writing of life in rural Northumberland just before the end of the nineteenth century, described the importance of 12 May to local families:

Our May Day is not the first of the month with its romance of maidens going forth to bathe their faces in the early dew, nor is it the 29th, the oak apple day of the South ... We have no May Day of this sort ... With us the 12th of the month is so important a crisis in the life of our agricultural families that it is always called by them 'The May'. It is well if that day dawns brightly and with good omens, for it is the great day which terminates and begins the annual term for which our farm workers are hired ... above all it is the day of 'flitting' from farm to farm of those who for various reasons find it desirable to make a change of place and master ... There they go, cart after cart, passing up the bank, as we call our hill, the furniture in one cart, piled to a dangerous height, with the grandfather clock lying lengthwise and risking its life on the top. The people themselves consider the flitting a sorrowful time.

This day is, of course, close to Old May Day.

A different custom, reported in the early twentieth century in Lancashire, dictated that on this day children had to wear a particular flower. *Lancashire Lore*, published by the Lancashire Federation of Women's Institutes, recorded that the 'children wore a May gollen (marsh marigold) ... Those without had their hair pulled.' *See* **29 May: Royal Oak Day** for a similar custom.

See also **6 April: Flitting Day; 14 May: Pack Rag Day.**

Second Saturday in May

Randwick Wap

Randwick Wap is the local name for this Gloucestershire village's annual feast or revel, which was formerly held on Low Sunday (the Sunday after Easter), and which stood out from other such village festivals by featuring the election of a mock mayor. The *Gentleman's Magazine* of 1784 published the following account of the proceedings:

One of the parish is ... elected mayor, and carried in great state, colours flying, drums beating, men, women, and children shouting, to a particular horse-pond, in which his worship is placed, seated in his arm-chair; a song is then given out line by line by the clerk, and sung with great gravity by the surrounding crowd ... The instant it is finished the mayor breaks the peace by throwing water in the face of his attendants. Upon this much confusion ensues.

However, the ensuing horseplay – and the generally drunken nature of the goings-on – was enough to get the event suppressed in 1892. A medieval origin is claimed for these festivities, although printed records mentioning them can only be traced to *c*.1703. Nobody has yet come up with a convincing etymology for the word 'Wap' in this context.

The event was revived in 1972, and is now held on the second Saturday in May every year. The focal point is a procession of villagers, all in costume, from the war memorial to the Mayor's Pool, led by a 'mop man' who carries a wet mop to clear the crowds out of the way. Various officials are elected for the day, including a mayor and mayoress, who are carried shoulder-high in the procession, and the mayor is dunked in the pool, as before. The afternoon is spent in the usual village fête manner. A cheese-rolling custom, formerly carried out on 1 May (*see* 1 **May: Randwick Cheese-Rolling**) is now incorporated into the revived Wap.

See also **Mock Mayors and Courts**, p. 298.

Second Sunday in May

Mother's Day (US)

In the USA, Mother's Day occurs on the second Sunday in May, but in Britain it is celebrated on Mid-Lent Sunday.

See **Mothering Sunday**, p. 105; **Mother's Day**, p. 108.

13 May (old May Day)

Abbotsbury Garland Day

In Abbotsbury, a small village on the coast of Dorset, the children have a May garland custom that has survived despite many changes in village life that would normally have wiped out such a thing years ago. Several villages along the Chesil coast previously had garlands in May, but all these traditions disappeared by 1950; at Abbotsbury, the custom has been kept going simply because the local people have been determined not to let it die. Flowers and greenery are fixed to a frame of wire, plastic, or wood, which is then mounted on a pole and carried between two children. The garlands are carried around the village and shown to each householder, and the children are usually given a small sum of money for their trouble.

The custom is first mentioned in John Hutchins' *History of Dorset* (1867), and at that time it was in the hands of families involved in fishing. Each family made a garland, which was paraded around the town by the children, and a party was then held on the beach. Some of the garlands were rowed out to sea and thrown overboard, and the whole event was respectable enough to include a special church service. After the First World War, the garlands began to be placed on the village war memorial rather than being cast on the waves. The local fishing industry virtually disappeared after the Second World War, and the garland custom was kept alive by increasing school involvement. As the children in the village all went to the local school, they could be granted the day off on 'Garland Day'. Later, the older children were bussed to school in Weymouth, so the young ones took their garlands round during the day, and the older ones in the evening. However, the local school closed completely in 1981, and as the education authorities outside the area could hardly be expected to honour Garland Day in the same way, again there had to be changes. During these years, the number of garlands has gradually declined; eight was the norm in the 1920s, but there have been only two or three in recent years. For some time, it has been the custom to make one garland of wild flowers and one of garden flowers. In 2005, two garlands were made for the children to take round separately when they returned from school in the evening, but only eight children actually took part.

Cowslips

Some time in May, although at least one Victorian informant specified the 13th, country girls turned to the humble cowslip for a game and a marriage divination. Mollie Harris remembered doing so in Oxfordshire in the 1920s:

When spring had really come and the warm sun had brought out more meadow flowers, we would pick baskets of cowslips so that our mother might brew some home-made wine. We used to keep some of the best blooms ourselves to make what we called a 'tisty tosty ball'. Taking off the main stalk we would bunch up the thick flower-heads together, tying them in the middle with wool, and this made a lovely soft sweet-smelling ball. Then for hours we would play a game called 'Tell me true', each girl tossing a ball in the air, keeping in time with this jingle

> *Tisty tosty tell me true*
> *Who shall I be married to?*
> *Tisty tosty, cowslip ball*
> *At my sweetheart's name you'll fall.*

Each of us had our favourites where the boys were concerned and we'd chant them – Percy, Charlie, Jimmy, Tom, Billy, Frankie, Bob and Bert, and, strange as it seemed, the ball always managed to fall at the name we wanted it to.

Miners' Holiday

In the first third of the nineteenth century, Derbyshire miners had their own May Day celebration – on *old* May Day. In 1829, county historian Stephen Glover wrote:

On the 13th of May the miners dress their coves or cowes (the places in which they deposit the ore) with oak branches, garlands and other rural decorations. This is called the 'miners' holiday'. A dinner of beef, pudding and ale is provided on the occasion, and, when the weather is favourable, the festivities are conducted in the open air. The Bar-masters preside and music and old songs conclude the proceedings . . .

Rook Sunday

According to Maureen Sutton, the nearest Sunday to 13 May was termed 'Rook Sunday' in parts of Lincolnshire well into the twentieth century, because rook pies were traditionally eaten on the day. The pies were made from baby rooks (called 'squabs'), which are easily obtained at that season and apparently taste like a cross between chicken and turkey. The outside edge of the pastry was marked with the rooks' feet, and although some informants commented that people would eat anything if they were hungry enough, it is clear that some regarded the rooks as a local delicacy. Florence White includes a traditional Nottinghamshire recipe for rook pie in her *Good Things in England* (1932).

14 May

Pack Rag Day

This day was one of the key dates in the farmworkers' calendar in Lincolnshire, as it was two days earlier in Northumberland (*see* 12 **May: The May**). The folklore collectors Mrs Gutch and Mabel Peacock recorded in 1908 that:

Bank holidays pass almost unnoticed, but May 14th, or Pag-rag day, is a great event, when the single farm servants, male and female, leave their places, or at least take a week's holiday, and spend the time visiting their friends and going round to different markets. The married men decide whether they will remain with their masters at Candlemas; they have the privilege of attending what is called the labourer's market soon after that date, when they hire themselves again and leave their old places April 6th.

See also 6 **April: Flitting Day; Hiring Fairs**, p. 470.

Mid May

Durham Mayor-Making

The Mayor of Durham is elected at the council's annual meeting, usually in mid May. After taking the oath of acceptance and being given the mayoral seal, he or she later appears on the town hall steps and throws a handful of coins (nowadays 5p pieces) to the waiting crowds. 'Scrambling' customs like these were not uncommon at mayor-making ceremonies, and similar actions still take place at Harwich in Essex (*see* **Third Thursday in May: Harwich Kichel-Throwing**) and at Rye in Sussex (*see* 23 **May: Rye Mayor-Making**).

See also **Scrambling Customs**, p. 172.

Mid to late May

Scorton Silver Arrow

The Society of Archers was formed in 1673, at a time when archery had already seen a long decline in popularity, as it changed from a military necessity to a sport. The first meeting of the new society took place at Scorton in Yorkshire on 14 May 1673 and, apart from understandable breaks during wartime, this annual meeting has taken place every year since, a feat that leads the society to claim it as 'The world's longest established and oldest recorded sporting event'. The modern meetings are always held in mid to late May, but the venue varies from year to year. The current rules state that it must take place in Yorkshire, although for a while it was allowed to wander into Lancashire on occasion.

As befits a sporting event with such a long history, there are plenty of strange rules and customs. The competitors clearly enjoy themselves, but the archery remains very serious indeed. Shooting takes place for two hours in morning and two hours in the afternoon, with a splendid lunch in between, followed by the Society's annual general meeting.

The targets are the standard four feet in diameter, and are one hundred yards apart, with shooting in both directions – alternating from one end to the other. The most coveted prize of the day, from which the event gets its name, is the Antient Scorton Silver Arrow, which is won by the first archer to hit the gold centre. In addition to the prestige of gaining the arrow, the winner becomes Captain of the Antient Scorton Silver Arrow for the year, and organizes the next meeting. The idea of a 'silver arrow' is itself traditional: it was the most common prize offered in early modern times when archery contests were common. There are also several other prizes, including a gold embroidered belt, a silver bugle, and a horn spoon.

15–18 May

These dates are sometimes known as 'Franklin Days' in Devon. *See* **19 May: St Dunstan's Day** for an explanation.

Third Thursday in May

Harwich Kichel-Throwing

The throwing of coins by newly elected mayors, for people to 'scramble for', is a fairly regular motif across the country, but at Harwich in Essex they throw 'kichels' instead. These are small torpedo-shaped, spiced fruit buns, which are made specially by a local baker, and are eagerly sought by the waiting children. The throwing takes places about midday, from the window of the council chamber, in the guildhall.

See also **Scrambling Customs**, p. 172.

Rogationtide

Beating the Bounds

Rogationtide is the Monday, Tuesday, and Wednesday immediately preceding Ascension Day, the fortieth day after Easter Sunday, and can occur any time between 27/29 April and 31 May/2 June. It was traditionally the time for the faithful to go in procession around the parish, led by the clergy, carrying crosses and banners, giving thanks to God, and blessing the fields, crops, and animals. This three-day festival was inaugurated in Gaul, in the late fifth century, ostensibly as a direct response to a period of earthquakes, crop failures, and other disasters, and from there it spread to Rome and on to other parts of the Christian world. It was introduced to the English Church in 747, and came to be known as Rogation, from the Latin *rogare,* 'to ask or beseech'.

The division of the country into parishes also took place about this time, and, although it is not clear when it happened, the procession to bless the fields came to include the notion of checking the parish boundaries, and what is now called 'beating the bounds' was born. The latter is one of the longest-running festivals in the English calendar, although it has changed considerably over the years, and in particular the relative weight given to sacred and secular aspects of the custom has fluctuated widely. Checking parish boundaries was not an entirely secular activity, as local church finances (based on tithes, taxes, and rates) were calculated on a parish basis, and the clergy thus had a keen interest in preserving their rights. Nowadays the custom is universally called 'beating the bounds', but previous generations had a variety of names, such as ganging (=going), processioning, bannering, and crossing.

By the time of the Reformation, the overtly Catholic practices of carrying crosses and images and blessing the crops were banned, but the local clergy were instructed by decree of Elizabeth I to continue to be actively involved in the perambulations, to provide appropriate prayers, sermons, and the giving of thanks to God. In the absence of effective record-keeping, the extent to which local officials were forced to rely on the memories of old people for evidence in local matters and legal disputes cannot be overstated, and this was especially true in the area of custom and tradition. An example from Tudor Cheshire is included in a 'boundary roll' of a court leet at Congleton in 1593. The boundaries are described, followed by the testimony of three local men, each over eighty years old, which detail how things had been in the past and how they had changed in their lifetimes: watercourses and ditches had been altered; a barn had been built straddling the boundary; and people had been accustomed to cut turf on a certain common and had been responsible for repairing a certain road.

By the time of the Puritan revolution of the 1640s, there was little that even the strictest religious reformers could object to, and in most places the custom continued throughout the Interregnum. The secular importance of boundary-keeping is clear in the description preserved in the journal of visiting Dutchman William Schellinks, in 1662:

On the 16th [May], *Ascension Day, we saw the minister taking procession, as is done in London every year as follows: The minister, the churchwardens, and all who depend on the parish inspect all the wards of their parish to see whether any new houses or dwellings have been built, which should have been registered by them for the payment of tax and record these, and also renew the old markers, which are painted on the wall on many different corners and quarters, to mark the boundaries of the parishes. For this purpose all the youngsters of the parish, great and small, assemble, each with a stick or rod in his hand, and walk two and two ahead, and when a marker is put up or renewed with the date of the year they make a loud noise all together and then go on to the next. This is done to impress on the young memories of the children the extent of the parish, so that they preserve it in the future*

without loss, and everyone gets a loaf of white bread from the minister. If it   245
happens that two such parties meet, a fight usually ensues.

Rogationtide

In rural areas, the boundary markers were often stones, crosses, or prominent trees. On its way around the parish, the procession would stop at some of these key points, for a prayer, hymn, or sermon, and these activities often gave a lasting name for the locality. Many local maps still show a 'Vicar's Oak' or 'Gospel Oak' in memory of these customary points. In a detailed account of the two-day perambulation of Purton parish, in Wiltshire, in 1733, the regular phrase occurs, 'where a Gospel was read, and a cross made' and it is clear that crosses were cut into the trunks of trees.

The day was also one of community festivity: food and drink were provided at certain points in the perambulation, and many customs developed that were far from solemn. The wands carried by participants were often used to literally 'beat' the boundary markers, and other seemingly bizarre activities took place, designed to fix these locations in people's memories. Boys were turned upside down, bumped on stones, whipped, beaten, or otherwise mistreated, and items were thrown to be scrambled for. In Yorkshire in 1890:

At Beverley, 'Rammalation Day' is Rogation Monday. What a day of merriment it is to the boys! At certain places, money, nuts, and oranges are scrambled for, and, as ditches form the boundary here and there, great fun is caused by throwing the money and oranges into the water, the youngsters jumping in and splashing about in the water. He who knows the boundary stones will run on ahead; and, if found sitting there alone, receives a shilling.

There were also traditional ways of dealing with first-timers, although not all victims of this horseplay were willing ones, as the *Graphic* reported on 28 November 1874:

Mr. Checkley, a farmer, has recovered £10 as compensation for injuries he received at the hands of a party of officials, headed by the Mayor of Maidenhead, who, chancing to meet with him while they were beating the bounds of the borough, picked him up and bumped him against a post so severely that he was unable to go about his work for a week. One plea for the defence was that all the respectable members of the party, including the Mayor and Town Clerk, were bumped. The judge remarked that such horseplay was detestable.

Schellinks' comment about fighting, quoted above, is also borne out in many other descriptions, and however respectable most beating-the-bounds customs may have been, the underlying impulses of territoriality that inform them also had a much less civilized aspect, as here in Exeter in the 1830s, recorded by James Cossins in his *Reminiscences* in 1878:

If, by chance, any of the different parishes met in their perambulations, there was a desperate struggle to disarm each other; but the great event was to wait in the New London Inn Square, as the parishes of St. David's and St. Sidwell's generally finished the rounds at the same time at this point. Then commenced, not a sham fight, but an earnest one, many of the combatants being young men. The parishioners were at times obliged to interfere, there being no police to force them.

(*See also* 1 May: Fighting.)

The nineteenth century saw a long, slow decline in boundary customs, mainly because more efficient mapping and record-keeping made them obsolete. But although the original *raison d'être* for beating the bounds has long disappeared, the custom is still carried out in some places and regularly revived in others, for a variety of reasons. Apart from the nostalgic notions of continuing ancient customs, perambulating the boundaries is often seen as an effective way of engendering local knowledge and community spirit, and is also used to raise money for church repairs or other charitable purposes, by combining the tradition with the more recent idea of 'sponsored walks'. In the 1990s, groups set up to safeguard dwindling common land and public open spaces deliberately encouraged boundary perambulations as a way of raising local consciousness on the subject.

However, even such a solidly Christian custom such as beating the bounds has not escaped the modern assumption that all traditional activities are pagan fertility rituals. Julia Smith reported in her *Fairs, Feasts and Frolics* (1989) that in Yorkshire:

One vicar said there was no longer provision in the Church of England liturgy for such a service; the blessing was regarded as the remains of a pre-Christian ritual, and with modern maps it was no longer necessary for the people to be shown the physical boundaries. He dissociated the Church totally with any boundary walking that may still take place.

See also **Ascension Day: Oxford Beating the Bounds**, p. 252; **Ascension Day: Tower of London Beating the Bounds**, p. 253; **18 May: Newbiggin Freeholders**.

247

Rogation Monday

Rogation Monday

Wilkes Walk

Edward Wilkes, who died in 1646, was a substantial benefactor to the Bedfordshire town of Leighton Buzzard, and among other projects founded the local almshouses. But it was his son, Matthew (who died in 1693), whose will stipulated a ceremony in his father's name that continues to this day. On the Monday of Rogationtide, at around midday, a procession including the charity's trustees, and the clergy, churchwardens, and choir of All Saints church, led by a garland-bearer, makes its way through the town to the almshouses in North Street. A short service takes place, and while an extract from Edward's will is read out, a member of the choir is stood on his or her head (on a cushion), 'in order that those watching may understand and retain the words better'. This detail clearly stems from the same idea as the bumping, suspending, and whipping that went on during beating-the-bounds perambulations, where the victims were meant to remember the location at which they were so dealt (*see* **Rogationtide: Beating the Bounds**, p. 243). But it could be seen to be counter-productive in the case of the Wilkes ceremony. It is quite likely that those watching are so amazed at what is happening to the poor upside-down youngster that they take no notice at all of what is being said at the time.

Matthew also left money to be given to residents of the almshouses and for refreshments at the end of the procession, but the latter had to be discontinued in the late nineteenth century because too many people used to turn up for them. They have now been reintroduced.

Wishford Auction

One of several unusual forms of auction in the country takes place every Rogation Monday at Wishford in Wiltshire. The auction is for the right to the summer grazing on two water-meadows, which is called the 'midsummer tithes' but runs from Rogationtide to old Lammas Day (12 August). Buyers are summoned by the church bell, about fifteen minutes before sunset, and the parish clerk walks up and down between the church porch and gate while the bidding takes place. As soon as the sun dips below the horizon, he strikes the church key on the gate, and the auction is over.

For other unusual auctions, *see* **Candle Auctions**, p. 138.

Ascension Eve

Whitby Penny Hedge

Early on the morning of the day before **Ascension Day** (p. 251), two local residents make their way across the mud on Whitby's upper harbour to construct the 'penny hedge' – in reality a mere apology for a fence of hazel and willow twigs – which must be strong enough to withstand three tides. When they have finished, a third man, who represents the Abbot of Whitby's steward, blows three blasts on an old horn and shouts, 'Out on ye! Out on ye! Out on ye!', which, we are told, means 'Shame on you!'

The custom itself is unique, impressively simple, and is carried out in such a matter-of-fact manner that onlookers are sometimes disappointed that there is not more to it. The temptation to jazz it up a bit must have been very strong in recent years. Indeed, Julia Smith reports that in 1982 the town council discussed the idea that the custom and accompanying legend should be annually re-enacted by actors or local schoolchildren. It is a tribute to the good sense of the people of Whitby that this suggestion was not accepted and the hedge is still constructed in the old way, without fuss, and without pseudo-historical costume. Long may it continue so.

Despite its simplicity, however, and the fact that numerous writers have spent considerable time analysing its history, the origin of the penny-hedge custom remains obscure. One problem is that commentators have not always succeeded in separating the custom, the accompanying legend, and the historical facts.

The legendary explanation relates that in 1159, in the reign of Henry II, a group of nobles, including one with the splendid name of Lord Ugglebardeby, were out boar-hunting in Eskdale Forest, which

1 Two scenes from a recent Mad Maldon Mud Race:
early in the day (above) and a short while later (below) [*New Year*]

2 Haxey Hood, Humberside: the Chief Boggin holding the 'hood' that will soon be hotly competed for [*6 January*]

3 The new straw bear parading the streets of Whittlesey, Cambridgeshire (above) [*Plough Monday/ Tuesday*]
4 Cupid's arrows are the dominant theme for George Cruickshank's take on Valentine's Day in 1837 (below) [*14 February*]

5 In the Ashbourne (Derbyshire) football game (above),
the ball always ends up in the river [*Shrove Tuesday*]
6 Contestants prepare for the pancake race at Olney, Buckinghamshire (below),
dressed in regulation housewife costume [*Shrove Tuesday*]

7 April Fool's Day (above): the famous spoof 'spaghetti harvest' broadcast by the BBC in 1957 [*1 April*]

8 Coco-Nut Dancer at Bacup, Lancashire (below): probably the strangest dance costume in the country [*Easter Saturday*]

9 George Cruickshank's comic view of Beating the Bounds in 1837 (above): an innocent bystander gets beaten by mistake [*Rogationtide*]
10 Bampton morris dancers, Oxfordshire (below): the morris team with the strongest claim to 'traditional' status [*Whitsun*]

11 Cousins Florence and Mary Nutter in their best finery for
the Whit Walk in Manchester, around 1905 [*Whitsun*]

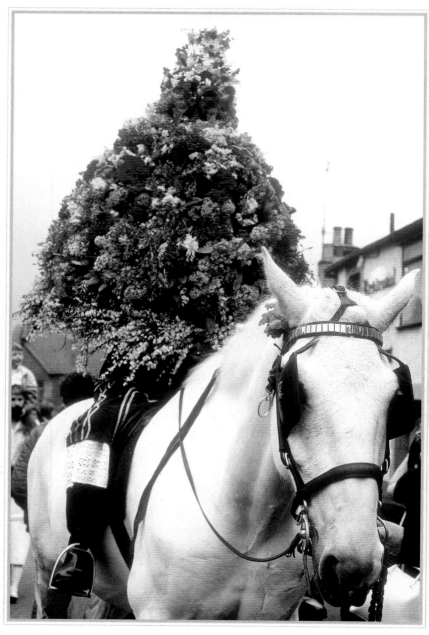

12 Garland Day at Castleton, Derbyshire:
the king being led around the streets [*29 May*]

belonged to the Abbot of Whitby. They and their hounds were in full chase of a great wild boar, when the exhausted animal ran into an isolated hermitage. Some say the boar dropped dead at the hermit's feet, others say that the hermit barred the door and refused to let the hunters in. Either way, the noblemen were so angry at being deprived of the best bit of the chase that they took their vengeance on the hermit by beating him almost to death. He only lived long enough to tell the Abbot to pardon the huntsmen if they agreed to pay penance every Ascension Eve by building the hedge (and, considering that he was dying, he went into impressively precise detail about the timing of the ceremony, where it should take place, and exactly how much wood they must cut – 'with a knife of one penny price'). According to early writer Lionel Charlton, this tale was already circulating in printed form before 1779, but while it may be no mere modern legend, it is clearly a romantic fiction. All the internal details of dates and names are incorrect, and very similar tales are told of other hermits in other woods.

All serious writers agree that the hedge-building custom is a survival of a medieval service, or obligation, called a *horngarth*, which was owed by tenants to the lord of the manor. In this case, the lord was the Abbot of Whitby, who was an immensely powerful figure in the local area. The abbey was founded by St Hilda in AD 651, destroyed by a Viking raid in 867, revived about the year 1078, and finally dissolved by Henry VIII in 1539. A great deal of evidence about the business affairs of the abbey has survived in two volumes of *Cartularies*, or registers of events and transactions, compiled in Latin by scribe monks, which cover the period from about 1170 to the early sixteenth century. The horngarth is mentioned many times in the *Cartularies* as a service owed to the Abbot of Whitby by holders of certain lands, and it was presumably important enough to warrant this continued reference, but its exact nature is never explained. The word *garth* is Anglo-Saxon for 'a fence or enclosure', but the *horn* element is open to debate. Most writers take it to mean 'cattle or oxen' (i.e. *horned* animals), but others assume that it signifies those who were responsible for constructing or repairing the *garth*, who were summoned by blasts of a horn. This has a spurious ring of authenticity only because the hermit tale and the later custom feature a horn.

Whatever its function, it is unlikely that the horngarth dates back to St Hilda's time, but it was definitely in existence by 1148. An important entry in the *Cartularies* of about 1315, reveals that the materials for the construction were taken from the Abbot's woods, and that 'Alexander's men' were taking too much and selling the surplus to people in the town. It was therefore decreed that the wood should be supplied by the Abbot's men rather than being collected by those about to use it. An even more detailed entry also exists, but its nature is highly ambiguous, being written on the flyleaf of the first volume, in a later hand. From internal evidence, this addition may possibly be as early as the 1540s (i.e. just after the dissolution of the abbey) but it could be much later. It presents a description of the horngarth service 'to be done on Holy Thursday even', saying that the men who were 'bound to this service' met at sunrise and, after cutting wood under supervision of the Abbot's bailiff, they carried it on their backs:

... so coming to the water at the town end they made the hedge which should stand three tides, and then the officer did blow out upon they.

The crux of the matter is how much credence can be placed on this flyleaf addition.

It may, for example, be a contemporary agreement on the form of the custom now that the abbey had been dissolved, or it could simply be an addition by a later writer who was already familiar with the custom and the legend.

On balance, the most likely conclusion is that the horngarth service was indeed a commitment owed jointly to the lord of the manor, for erecting or maintaining a fence or other enclosure. There are verifiable examples of such obligations elsewhere in the country, for example in response to the annual need to erect a temporary fence to protect the land set aside from the open fields for the purpose of growing hay. It must be said, however, that the one major problem with this explanation is the riverside location, and the detail of the three tides, which are a prominent feature of the current custom, and were already in place when the flyleaf addition was made. This does not seem to fit with the idea of keeping farm animals in or out of a particular place, which has led some writers to propose that the horngarth was not an animal fence at all but something to do with the loading and unloading of boats – a jetty, for example, or a protective enclosure for goods in transit to and from the manor.

In theory, it is easy to see how a medieval obligation such as the horngarth could become an apparently 'meaningless' custom over time. There was a marked trend throughout the later medieval period for services to be commuted into cash payments. Given that several tenants were obliged to contribute their time and labour to the work, there may well have been a time when the majority had commuted to cash while a few continued to offer physical service. Even when changing circumstances had rendered the service itself unnecessary or superfluous, the tenants would be forced to continue to comply, because the custom of the manor dictated that failure to do so would result in a fine, loss of rights, or even loss of land. Similarly, it was in the lord of the manor's interest to hold the tenants to their obligation, in the expectation that they would eventually pay good money to be relieved of the burden.

For another bizarre custom, seemingly based on manorial obligations, *see* **Palm Sunday: Caistor Gad-Whip Ceremony**, p. 127.

Ascension Day

Ascension Day commemorates the ascension of Christ into Heaven, forty days after he had risen from the dead, and is therefore held on the fifth Thursday after Easter, falling anywhere between 30 April and 3 June. Often referred to as Holy Thursday, it is one of the major festivals of the Christian Church and has been around in one form or another since at least the fourth century. In secular English tradition, the visual image of Christ ascending to the heavens resulted in a strong connection between the day and all things pertaining to the sky, such as clouds, rain, and birds. This underlying connection is manifested in a variety of customs, including **well-dressing** (p. 312) and beliefs in the medicinal properties of any rain that falls on the day. In 1882, the Folklore Society's journal *Folk-Lore Record* reported:

At daybreak on Ascension morning, two men, and a woman carrying a child, were seen hurrying towards the celebrated well at North Molton, each trying to outrun the others, so as to be the first to bathe, and to be cured of some ailment. Later in the day merry groups of children and picnic parties enlivened the glen in which the well is situated . . . Every year pilgrims, full of faith in the miraculous power of the water, visit the spot for bathing; and jars of the water were carried by some of them to their homes; indeed, believers prize this water which they carry back with them, as much as ever did pilgrims of old value the leaden bottle of liquid obtained from Beckett's tomb at Canterbury.

More obscurely, but still based on the same principle:

[1584] *To hang an egg, laid on Ascension Day in the roof of the house, preserveth the same from all hurts.*

[In Worcestershire, 1909] *If you hang clothes out to dry on Holy Thursday there will be a death in the family, and the corpse will be laid out in some of the clothes.*

[In Devon, 1787] *Hailing the Lamb: It is the custom in many villages in the neighbourhood of Exeter 'to hail the lamb'. That the figure of a lamb actually appears in the east upon this morning is the popular persuasion; and so deeply is it rooted that it had frequently resisted (even in intelligent minds) the force of the strongest argument.*

The latter should be compared to the 'sun dancing' belief (*see* **Easter Monday**, p. 176).

Ascension Day follows Rogationtide, and there is often an overspill of beating-the-bounds ceremonies, sometimes even with the addition of a water feature, as in the following example from James Cossins' *Reminiscences of Exeter Fifty Years Since* (1878):

The parochial bounds were beaten on Ascension Day, by parishioners, accompanied by the clergymen, wardens, etc., who afterwards dined together at one of the hotels or inns in the parish. On this day it was considered lawful to throw water over any parties passing, and in many streets a pond would be made, and unless some pence were thrown in, the boys would splash the water over passers-by, and such dread was there of these customs that parties in the country would not come into the city on that day, unless necessity compelled.

Hunting the Earl of Rone

See **Spring Bank Holiday**, p. 286.

Oxford Beating the Bounds

Beating the bounds is still carried out in two adjoining parishes in Oxford on Ascension Day: St Michael in the Northgate, and St Mary the Virgin. At both events, there is a procession of the choir, various dignitaries, and numerous onlookers, led by the vicar. After a short service, they seek out the boundary markers, following a long-established route, mark them with chalk, and beat them with the long white canes that they carry. When thinking of beating-the-bounds ceremonies, most people probably imagine the typical rural scene of beaters locating boundary stones in fields and hedgerows, and being 'bumped on them', but in urban settings it is very different. The boundary markers in Oxford can be set into walls, high or low, or even into the floor, and can be down narrow alleys, in basements, and behind or inside buildings. The routes take in the college buildings within the parish as well as shops and pubs, much to the surprise of the people they meet on the way. They stop for refreshments at various locations, and at one point students throw coins and sweets for the choristers to scramble for.

See also **Rogationtide: Beating the Bounds**, p. 243; **Scrambling Customs**, p. 172.

Tower of London Beating the Bounds

Most beating-the-bounds customs are concerned with ecclesiastical parishes, but the need to maintain boundaries is equally important for many other bodies. Every third year, in the evening of Ascension Day, the boundaries of the Liberty of the Tower of London are perambulated, and literally beaten. After a short service in the Chapel Royal of St Peter ad Vincula, a colourful procession forms up, led by the Tower's Chief Yeoman Warder, in full state dress and carrying his mace. Others include the Yeoman Gaoler, with his axe, two Yeoman Warders, the Resident Governor, and a group of children carrying willow wands.

There are thirty-one markers bearing the letters 'WD' (War Department), and as the procession reaches each one the Chief Yeoman Warder calls out, 'Cursed be he who removeth his neighbour's landmark – whack it, boys, whack it!', and they beat it to death with their wands. One innovation first tried in the 1980s in the interests of safety is that if a marker is situated on a busy road, the Chief points to it with his mace and shouts, 'Mark it well', and those in the procession answer loudly, 'Marked!' The perambulation is completed when the procession re-enters the Tower by the East Gate, and the National Anthem is sung on Tower Green. Refreshments are then served to the participants.

See also **Rogationtide: Beating the Bounds**, p. 243.

18 May

Newbiggin Freeholders

Newbiggin-on-the-sea, in Northumberland, was at one time a very important port, and to be a freeholder was a prized position, carrying the right, for example, of collecting tolls from ships loading and unloading in the harbour. Little of that right now remains, but the freeholders own Newbiggin Moor, from which they derive income from rent paid by a golf course, and others. On the Wednesday nearest to 18 May, the freeholders perambulate the boundaries of their land, distributing peanuts and collecting any monies due to them. If there is a new freeholder to initiate, they are lifted bodily and bumped gently ('dunted') on the dunting stone.

See also **Rogationtide: Beating the Bounds**, p. 243.

19 May

St Dunstan's Day

St Dunstan (909–88) took an extremely active part in the political and religious life of tenth-century England at the highest levels, serving as adviser, bishop, and archbishop to successive kings, including Eldred, Edgar, and Edward the Martyr. One of Dunstan's particular achievements was the revival of monastic life, and the introduction of the Benedictine rule, which lasted until the sixteenth century. After his death, he was credited with great wisdom and a number of miracles, and a nationwide cult grew up, which lasted for centuries. He was reputed to be an expert craftsman, and metalworkers such as goldsmiths, jewellers, and locksmiths adopted him as their patron saint. The most persistent of his legends, first recorded *c.*1120, tells how he was busy making a chalice when the Devil appeared, in the guise of a young woman, to tempt him. Dunstan grabbed the Devil's nose with his red-hot tongs, and kept him trapped for some considerable time. You can still see the very tongs at Mayfield in Sussex. (A similar story is told of St. Eligius; *see* **1 December**.)

Despite his popularity, no widespread customs or festivals on his day seem to have been recorded, although parish churches dedicated to him would have held celebrations in his honour. One calendar tradition, however, reported widely in Devon in the nineteenth and twentieth centuries, comes close to slandering his good name by implicating him in a shady business deal with the Devil. Three days in May, locally termed 'Franklin Days', were reputed to be prone to cold weather and sharp frosts. The particular days varied, but were often the 17th–19th, or the 19th–21st, and however they were counted, they usually included Dunstan's feast day. The story was told as follows in *Notes & Queries* (1861):

St. Dunstan bought a quantity of barley and therewith made beer. The Devil, knowing that the saint would naturally desire to get a good sale for the article which he had just brewed, went to him and said that if he would sell himself to him, the latter would go and blight all the apple trees; so that there would be no cider, and consequently there would be a greater demand for beer. St. Dunstan, wishing to drive a brisk trade ... accepted the offer; but stipulated that the trees should be blighted in three days ... 17th, 18th and 19th May, the last named date being St. Dunstan's Day ... About the middle of May, consequently, as the three fatal days are approaching, many anxious allusions are made to St. Dunstan, and should a sharp frost nip the apple-blossoms, they believe they know who has been at the bottom of the mischief.

Sometimes the same story was told of a man named Franklin, or even of the anonymous and presumably infamous 'brewers from North Devon', but poor Dunstan was the most commonly cited villain of the piece.

One more aspect of the day was recorded in Yorkshire in the 1890s by Richard Blakeborough: 'No luck will follow a declaration of love if made on St. Dunstan's Day'; however, no explanation is given for this pronouncement.

In addition, the Society of King Charles the Martyr holds events on this day to commemorate the restoration of Charles II; *see* **30 January: Execution of Charles I.**

20–21 May

Reckoned by some people as two of the three 'Franklin Days'; *see* **19 May: St Dunstan's Day.**

23 May

Rye Mayor-Making

On or near 23 May, the town of Rye in East Sussex chooses its new mayor, and his or her first task in office is to throw pennies from the town hall window to the crowd of waiting children outside. Scrambling customs like this were formerly quite common, and just to add to the fun the pennies at Rye were heated before throwing.

The first of two stories told to explain the custom is that at one time the mayor was also the local Member of Parliament, and in the habit of bribing voters. The second says that Rye was previously the site of a mint, and once, when coins were in short supply, new pennies were brought still hot from the foundry. Neither of these explanations is true, or even necessary, as throwing coins for scrambling was common at a variety of celebrations, including civic events such as mayor-making, weddings, and whenever someone rich enough to have coins to spare wanted the fun of seeing the children scramble.

See also **Scrambling Customs,** p. 172.

24 May

Empire Day

The idea for Empire Day originated in Ontario, Canada, where the Education Department there set aside a day in 1899 to celebrate the achievements and glory of the British Empire, and Canada's place in it. According to *The Times* on 20 March 1899:

The morning shall be devoted chiefly to familiar talk about Canada's

relation to the Empire, and readings from Canadian and British authors, 257
while patriotic recitations, songs, and speeches will occupy the afternoon.

24 May

The idea was soon being enthusiastically discussed in Britain, and after the death of Queen Victoria in 1901, Empire Day was formally adopted in 1903. It was also known as Victoria Day, because the date chosen was the late Queen's birthday. Following the Canadian precedent, it was mainly a school event, although in many villages there was also strong church involvement. The school day was given over to dressing up, processions, marching, speeches, tableaux, patriotic singing, and usually a tea or other festive gathering. One of the contributors to *East Kent Within Living Memory*, published by the East Kent Federation of W.I.s in 1993, reported that:

When I was at school at Cliftonville in the 1930s, we celebrated Empire Day every year. We practised for weeks before, then the day arrived. We started with the raising of the Union Jack and singing God Save the King. First came the top infants class, who danced, each representing the four corners of the British Isles, with a flag for each. They would finish by standing back-to-back, then a child would step up onto a chair holding a Union Jack. Next was the tableau. A senior pupil would come first and sit on the dais as Britannia, reciting a verse about Britain, followed by a girl in the costume of each country of the Empire, reciting a verse about each one and carrying produce they provided. I remember New Zealand carried a toy lamb and Australia a basket of apples. When the tableau was complete we all sang with gusto Land of Hope and Glory, Land of our Fathers, Londonderry Air, Jerusalem, and Ye Banks and Braes, ending with God Save the King and saluting the flag.

Such overtly imperial rhetoric was completely out of place in the postwar period, when the Empire was fast disintegrating, and in 1958 Empire Day was replaced by Commonwealth Day, on 12 June (Elizabeth II's official birthday), which was moved again in 1977 to the second Monday in March.

For many, 24 May is also Wesley Day, celebrating the lives of the Christian evangelists John Wesley (1703–91) and Charles Wesley (1707–88), with a special commemorative service at Lincoln Cathedral

See also **Second Monday in March: Commonwealth Day**.

Church Ales

In some areas of medieval and early modern England, before church rates and taxes were widely adopted, a common way of raising money for the upkeep of the parish church was to hold a fund-raising event called an 'ale'. As the name suggests, this was a day of merrymaking, with food, drink, dancing, and games. Ales were particularly common across the south of England and the South Midlands, but were only sporadically reported elsewhere in the country.

Many church ales took place at Whitsun or early May, taking the generic name 'Whitsun ales', but church ales could also be held at any time in the spring or summer, while some places held more than one in a year. Some became fixed annual events, but more often they were organized only when need arose. A group of neighbouring parishes might pool their resources and take it in turns to organize the event. In earlier reports, it is clear that the event took place in the church or churchyard, but changing notions of propriety forced it out of sacred ground and into the parish. Some parishes had a 'church-house' – the forerunner of the village hall – in which they could hold their festivities, while others made do with a barn or temporary building.

As they were organized by, and for, the Church, expenses for the ale were usually recorded in churchwardens' accounts, and a wealth of useful information has survived. The accounts for the parishes of Seal and Elstead in Surrey, transcribed by William Hart in the *Surrey Archaeological Collections*, vol. 2 (1864), are an excellent example. The accounts for 1592 include the following items:

3 bushels of wheat (14s.); 9 barrels of beer (40s.); Veal and lamb (22s. 9d.); A load of wood and the carriage (5s.); Spice and fruit (7s. 1d.); Butter, cream and milk (4s.); Cleats and nails to the smith (14d.); Gunpowder (4s.); More wheat (8s. 2d.); Paid to the musician for 5 days play (20s.); To the drummer (2s.); For more butter and cream (2s. 3d.); More spice and fruit (4s. 2d.); To Goodman Shrubbs' wife for helping all the time (12d.); Meat and beer for the musicians and other helpers (13s. 4d.).

It is interesting to note that they underestimated the butter, cream, spice and fruit, and had to order more, but the beer apparently lasted well enough. Four shillings' worth of gunpowder was presumably used for fireworks or some similar entertainment. The accounts for 1611 include

similar items, including another payment to 'Shrubbs' wife' and payments to the musicians; however, one additional entry – 'paid the Vice,
otherwise the Fool' – hints at a different form of entertainment.

Many church ales were discontinued in the early decades of the seventeenth century, while others struggled on amid increasing calls for their
suppression. They had long attracted the vociferous disapproval of the
religious reformers, who seemed bent on eradicating all forms of enjoyment, but increasing opposition came from those who argued that such
gatherings created too many opportunities for drunkenness and public
disorder, and it is probably these latter concerns that prompted local
magistrates to start taking action.

Nevertheless, ales had their supporters among those who cherished
old customs and traditions or who were opposed to the new puritanical
religion. Richard Carew, the Cornish historian, took an optimistic view of
the benefits of social gatherings, in 1602:

**. . . entertaining of Christian love, conforming of men's behaviour
to a civil conversation, compounding of controversies, appeas-
ing of quarrels, raising a store which might be converted partly to
good and godly uses, as relieving all sorts of poor people, repairing
of churches, building of bridges, amending of highways, and partly
for the prince's service, by defraying at an instant such rates and
taxes as the magistrates imposeth for a country's defence. Briefly,
they tend to an instructing of the mind by amiable conference, and
an enabling of the body by commendable exercises.**

And King James himself listed 'Whitsun ales' as suitable for Sunday
entertainment in his *Book of Sports* of 1618 (*see* p. 354). However, once
Parliament got the upper hand, church ales were specifically banned
by the *Ordinance for the better observation of the Lords Day*, passed on
8 April 1644.

Some ales were revived after the Restoration, particularly in
Oxfordshire, and continued into the nineteenth century, organized by
publicans or other local individuals rather than the Church authorities.
Eating, drinking, and dancing were still the main activities of the day.
Published descriptions from the time show a remarkable similarity in
how these later ales were organized. A Lord, Lady, and various attendants
were elected to rule the festivities, which took place in a suitable barn or
shed, or in a 'bower', which was created with greenery or tarpaulin. In an
elaborate running joke, strangers were asked to name items displayed

around the bower and were punished when they said the wrong thing. A wooden horse had to be referred to as 'my Lord's gelding', a stuffed owl as 'my Lady's canary', a flail as 'my Lord's nutcrackers', and so on. Offenders were forced to pay a forfeit of a shilling, and if they could not, they were manhandled and carried around the field on the wooden horse, or 'married' to 'his Lordship's cook', an ugly, dirty creature who wielded a dirty dishcloth and a sharp toasting fork.

Whitsun

Whit Sunday is the seventh Sunday after Easter, and commemorates the descent of the Holy Spirit upon the disciples, in the form of tongues of fire, as promised by Christ before his ascent into Heaven. The official name for the festival is 'Pentecost', meaning 'fiftieth', and it is derived from an existing Jewish festival that celebrated the first fruits of the corn harvest, and the giving of the Law of Moses, fifty days after the Passover. It is still not entirely clear why the English call the festival 'Whitsun'. The most plausible explanation (though still not very convincing) is that it was named after the white clothes worn by people being baptized on the day. In the mid nineteenth century there was still vigorous debate about whether it should be written 'Whit Sunday' or 'Whitsun Day', but we now use both terms. Being tied to Easter, the actual date varies from year to year, but is always between mid May and mid June.

Whit Monday was officially recognized as a bank holiday in 1871, which gave a boost to its already considerable popularity, but it lost its status in 1971 when the **Spring Bank Holiday** (p. 282) was created. Some religious Whitsun events cling tenaciously to the real day, but most secular customs associated with the season have now moved to the bank holiday.

Whitsun's position in early summer made it one of the favourite times in the traditional calendar, and a range of open-air events took place on the day or during the following week. Whitsun ales and morris dancing in the South, and Whit walks and wakes in the North, were characteristic of the season, along with countless fêtes, fairs, club walks, pageants, parades, and excursions, all over the country. In many

places, Whitsun was much more important than May Day. A poster   261
advertising Whitsun attractions at Sunbury in Middlesex in 1758 gives

Whitsun

a flavour of the season at the time:

*On Whit Monday, in the morning, will be a punting match . . . The first
boat that comes in to receive a guinea . . . In the afternoon a gold-laced
hat, value 30s. to be cudgell'd for . . . On Whit Tuesday, in the morning,
a fine holland smock and ribbons, value one guinea, to be run for by girls
and young women. And in the afternoon six pairs of buckskin gloves to be
wrestled for.*

Nevertheless, in Victorian and Edwardian times, the festivities of
Whitsun were often decidedly less spontaneous than May Day, being
organized by church or chapel, school or club, or other worthy institution. Olive M. Philpott records in the *Dorset Year Book* (1961/2) that in
Wiltshire, about 1910:

*Whit week, however, was the highlight of the whole year. It was the Sunday
School Anniversary at the Chapel on Whit-Sunday when, dressed in our
smartest summer frocks and suits, we gabbled our recitations and lustily
sang our Anniversary hymns. That was followed on Whit Monday by the
excitement of the Sunday School tea (what memories of slabs of delicious
plum cake, thin bread-and-butter and sugary small cakes, washed down
with sweet milky tea). We thought this a cut above the Church children's
lemonade and buns on the Rectory lawn. Tea was followed by sports and
games until sunset. But all that excitement paled before Whit-Wednesday,
when we had the village Club-walking.*

In the newly industrialized towns of the Midlands and the North, the
tradition of the whole town closing down for a week rapidly became
a widespread feature, and Whitsun was often the convenient time.
John Harland and T. T. Wilkinson report in their *Lancashire Folk-Lore*
(1882):

*It is customary for the cotton-mills, etc., to close for Whitsuntide week to
give the hands a holiday; the men going to the races, etc., and the women
visiting Manchester on Whit-Saturday, thronging the markets, the Royal
Exchange, the Infirmary Esplanade, and other public places; and gazing in
at the shop windows, whence this day is usually called 'Gaping Sunday'.*

See also **Easter Day: Greenwich Fair**, p. 154.

Eton School Montem

Eton School Montem was a well-known custom in its day, perhaps based on the Boy Bishop ceremony (*see* **6 December: Boy Bishop**), but with military rather than ecclesiastical trappings. The day of the custom changed over time, occurring in January, Whitsun, December, sometimes once a year and sometimes every two years. It was already well known in the seventeenth century, when it was mentioned in John Aubrey's *Remaines of Gentilisme and Judaisme* (1686).

The main event of the day was a procession by the boys, who dressed as sumptuously as possible (many hired costumes for the day). The senior boys were given military rank for the occasion – Marshal, Captain, Chaplain, Lieutenant, and Ensign, the latter carrying the flag with the motto *Pro More et Monte* – and the procession formed up in strict order. The younger boys carried white poles and acted as servants. They marched round the school and out to Salt Hill (*ad montem*, meaning 'to the hill', gives its name to the custom), near Slough, where the Chaplain led a service and speeches were made. Some of the boys were designated as 'Salt Collectors', whose job it was to collect money from the boys and from any passers-by, visitors, or tourists. On more than one occasion the visitors included royalty, and the money collected, which could be a substantial sum, went to the Head Boy. The Salt Collectors carried bags of salt, either to exchange for the contribution, as some sources specify, or to stuff into the mouths of any enemies they might meet. The day ended with a general feast. The ceremony was a mixture of serious pomp and pointed parody, and could at times be rough. Successive schoolmasters made attempts to tame it, and it was finally suppressed *c.*1876.

Food

As with all the major festivals, Whitsun was associated with particular sorts of food. Tea and buns were consumed at countless Whitsun gatherings, but other foodstuffs varied from place to place. Earlier records mention milk and cream products as being particularly linked to Whitsun, and there are references to children going from house to house collecting these, while several others mention gooseberries, as in the following example from Enid Porter's *Cambridgeshire Customs and Folklore* (1969):

The village policeman of Manea said in 1936 that 'veal is always eaten here at Whitsun'. In many Cambridgeshire families Whitsunday is the day for eating the first gooseberry pie of the year with, if possible, the first home-grown new potatoes.

On the question of seasonal cakes, many localities settled for a variation of the simnel, better-known elsewhere as Mid-Lent Sunday and Easter food (*see* **Mothering Sunday**, p. 105), and cheesecakes are also regularly mentioned. However, one unique example can be found in *Traditional Food East and West of the Pennines* (1991):

Goosnargh cakes can be bought at Goosnargh [Lancashire] Post Office and in surrounding towns. It was estimated that at one time over 50,000 were sold during Whitsuntide at one shilling per dozen. No one can agree on the origin of these distinctive biscuits, which resemble a shortbread, flavoured with caraway and coriander and with a thick sugary crust.

Morris Dance

The morris dance is one of the most widely known forms of traditional display dance in England, and everybody knows roughly what morris dancers look like: usually male, they dress in white (or at least in a white shirt), with crossed baldrics, or rosettes and ribbons, and, most importantly, with pads of bells strapped to their shins, which ring loudly when they move. They wave white handkerchiefs or clash short sticks together as they dance, and we might expect them to be accompanied by a Fool with a bladder on the end of a stick, and a hobby horse. Many people picture a morris dance as taking place on a spring morning on the village green, with all the local folk gathered *en fête* around the maypole. However, while the costume of modern-day morris dancers certainly retains many features that were present as far back as the 1580s, and the village green was indeed one of the dance's natural habitats, the morris also existed in other contexts, many of them urban, for example in civic processions, at court, and in the theatre.

Our view of the morris dance has been heavily influenced by the wealth of material gathered by Edwardian folk-dance collectors when the traditional morris was on its last legs. Their evidence referred largely to the second half of the nineteenth century, and they present-ed a picture of numerous village teams, across the South Midlands, each with their own traditional dances, tunes, and steps, which varied from each other but clearly drew from a shared pool. These forms were labelled the 'Cotswold Morris', because of the area in which they were found, but further research identified quite different styles of morris in other regions. 'North-West Morris', for example, found in Lancashire and Cheshire, features much larger teams, and dances designed for processional performance.

Over 300 years ago, the morris dance was popular with playwrights and poets, who used it as a symbol of simple rustic pleasures. It was clearly already proverbial in Shakespeare's time: in Act II, scene 4 of *Henry V*, the Dauphin urges France to make war with England insouciantly:

> *And let us do it with no show of fear*
> *No, with no more than if we heard that England*
> *Were busied with a Whitsun morris dance.*

And in Act II, scene 2 of *All's Well That Ends Well*, a clown remarks, 'As a pancake for Shrove Tuesday, a morris for May Day'. At about the same time, Thomas Dekker also featured the morris in his plays *Shoemaker's Holiday* (1599/1600) and *Witch of Edmonton* (*c*.1623). Others, however, saw the morris as yet another example of the depravity of the peasantry's traditional pastimes, declaring that this ungodly behaviour should be reformed or suppressed outright. As is often the case, Philip Stubbes, the Puritan reformer, provides one of the earliest descriptions of the morris. It is included in his *Anatomie of Abuses* (1583), in the section on 'Lords of Misrule', by which he meant the May or Summer Lord appointed to oversee the spring celebrations:

Then every one of these his men, he investeth with his liveries of green, yellow, or some other light wanton colour. And as though that were not gaudy enough, I should say, they bedeck themselves with scarfs, ribbons and laces, hanged all over with gold rings, precious stones, and other jewels; this done, they tie about either leg twenty or forty bells, with rich handkerchiefs in their hands, and sometimes laid across their shoulders and necks, borrowed for the most part of their pretty Mopsies or loving Bessies, for bussing them in the dark. Thus all things set in order, then have they their hobby horses, their dragons, and other antiques, together with their bawdy pipers, and thundering drummers, to strike up the Devil's dance withal: Then march this heathen company towards the church and churchyard, their pipers piping, their drummers thundering, their stumps dancing, their bells jingling,

their handkerchiefs fluttering about their heads like mad men, their hobby 265
horses and other monsters skirmishing amongst the throng . . .

Whitsun

The early history of the morris dance is still under debate, but it is clear that it was already widely known in the second half of the fifteenth century. At least nine references are known from that period, with the two earliest dating from 1448.

Some of these early references refer to representations of morris dancers on fine art objects, such as silverware and tapestry, but there are others in contemporary account books that detail payments for actual performances. The spelling of the word varies considerably, including 'moryshh', 'morys', and 'moruske', and it is significant that these words had already been in circulation for at least a hundred years to describe 'Moorish' things. The etymological evidence seems to point quite conclusively to a connection with 'Moorish', but this only gets us part of the way. We do not know, for example, whether the dance was so called because it came from North Africa, or because people thought it looked like something that they would expect to see performed there. There are similar words, meaning both a dance and 'Moorish', in other European languages, so it is quite possible that the dance was introduced from another country – perhaps Spain, because of its close connection with Moorish culture, or the Low Countries – but if so, it is still not clear whether that country invented or inherited it. Despite the wealth of new material uncovered by the latest generation of morris-dance researchers, the origins of the dance still elude us, partly, perhaps, because we have been searching for one specific origin rather than several.

Various antiquarians and early folklorists showed some interest in the morris dance over the years, primarily because of its literary reputation, but it was not until the turn of the twentieth century that serious research got underway. A number of collectors were involved, but the leading light was undoubtedly Cecil Sharp (1859–1924), who deliberately set out to create a folk-dance revival, in which the morris was to play a central role. Sharp and his disciples were reasonably successful in spreading the word, and a number of morris-dance clubs were formed in the interwar years; however, the real explosion of interest came with the postwar folk revival in the 1960s, and there are still several hundred clubs in Britain.

See also: **Spring Bank Holiday: Bampton Morris Dance**, p. 282.

Superstitions

Whitsun does not seem to have engendered as many superstitions and beliefs as other festivals. The only one that was at all widespread was that it was one of the main times of year when new clothes were particularly prized (others were Easter and New Year), and, indeed, if one ventured out without wearing at least one new item, the birds would be sure to mess on you. New clothes were also a marked feature of those taking part in Whit Walks and Whit Sings (*see below*), and brought about their own traditions when children visited family and neighbours. In 1998, a member of the East Yorkshire Women's Institute remembered the custom in her childhood:

It was traditional on Whit Monday to go to grandma's and show her my new clothes. Nearly all children got some, if not all, new clothes at Whitsuntide. My cousins and I were all taken off to grandma's house in the morning, and on arrival we paraded and twirled before her and Auntie V.

See also **Easter Day: New Clothes**, p. 156.

Whit Walks

As indicated in the entry for **Whitsun** (p. 260), this festival was a favourite time for outdoor events, and particularly popular at this season was any type of walk, parade, or procession. In the South, it was common for local benefit clubs to choose this time of year for their annual parade and dinner, and for Sunday schools and church organizations to hold their treats. But further north, the real feature of the season was the Whit Walk, organized by the different churches and involving the whole clergy and congregation in an impressive procession through the town, with everyone in their best clothes, holding large banners and other symbols, and led by a brass band. These walks made a great feature of the children, who were usually dressed up in white for the occasion, and it was second only to Christmas as the high spot of the juvenile year. This focus on children was one of the earliest features of the walks, as they grew directly from the active Sunday school movement founded by Robert Raikes (1735–1811), which swept across the country in the early nineteenth century. In Manchester and other nearby towns, the Whit Walks quickly became large affairs and grew as the century progressed, with Anglican, Nonconformist, and Roman Catholic churches vying to put on the best show. In the mid twentieth

century, they were still very popular events, as *The Times* of 7 June 1949
indicates:

At Manchester, after a dull start, the weather brightened up for the 143rd Whit-walk. More than 12,000 children, representing 34 Church of England Sunday schools, were gaily dressed for the walk, which was led by the Bishop of Manchester, Dr. Greer, to the marching tunes of nearly 40 bands.

On the *Have Your Say Magazine* website recently, Lillian Barlow remembered the thrill of taking part in the Whit Procession in Manchester forty years ago, and her description highlights all the key points of the occasion: the chance to dress up in new clothes; the close connection between local pride, school, church, and community; the colour, banners, music, crowds, and noise; and a nostalgia for the simple pleasures of a bygone age:

It was 1958, and I was 11 years old. In preparation for Whit Monday my sister and I had a bath, washed our hair, had our supper and were sent to bed early. We had to be up at 6am the following morning. I remember lying in bed feeling nervous and excited. My sister and I had both been confirmed that year, and this meant we would be walking with the banner representing our church. The Confirmation Banner always led the procession, behind the brass band, of course. The banner was huge, and had ten white ribbons hanging from it, five at the front and five at the back. Ten girls who'd been confirmed that year were chosen to walk with the banner, both my sister and I had been chosen.

Mam had made our dresses. Though it was dark I could see the outline of them hung on the wardrobe door. The bodices were made of white satin and the skirts were ballerina length, made up of layers and layers of white net. They were lovely. Mam had made our head-dresses too. They were made in the same materials as our dresses, and were sort of a banana shape, rather like a headband but much more fancy. Our shoes were flat, white ballerina type and we had new white socks. And to complete the outfit a posy of flowers which had been made by my aunty. I closed my eyes and tried to imagine what we would look like. I finally drifted off to sleep.

Morning came and the house was buzzing with excitement. I remember mam making toast which I couldn't eat because of the butterflies in my stomach. My sister and I were finally ready. Together with mam, dad, our younger brothers and sister, who were all dressed up in their best clothes, we made our way to St. James' Church, Collyhurst. It was a beautiful church. It was the church in which my mam and dad were married. It was the church where I was baptised, and it was the church in which I was confirmed . . .

As we approached the church, I could see all the children assembled, dressed in their lovely outfits. The teachers from the school were trying to organise them. My sister and I were spotted by Mrs. Gaskell, one of the teachers from the school, and were ushered by her to the front of the procession. I remember my mam asking if my sister and I could walk at the back of the Confirmation Banner down to Albert Square. I wondered why. I realised later, if you walked at the back of the banner going down to Albert Square, you walked at the front of the banner coming back!

Eventually we were organised and ready. My sister and I stood together holding the long white ribbons that draped from the back of this awesome banner. We spoke not one word to each other. The band struck up with Onward Christian Soldiers. To this day I will never forget how overwhelmed I felt, I almost burst into tears. We followed the band down Rochdale Road making our way to Albert Square. The road was lined with people threefold. All my aunties, uncles, friends and neighbours were there, shouting and clapping as we walked by. 'Hold your Lily up,' they shouted. We reached Albert Square and my dad was there waiting to take us for a drink. The square was packed with children and adults from all the different churches in Manchester. I remember feeling intimidated and frightened and hoping I wouldn't get lost. I held onto my dad's hand tight. After our drink we found our way back to our assembly point and prepared for the walk back to church.

On the return journey, my sister and I walked in front of the banner, by this time the crowds were even greater. I remember seeing a mass of red, white and blue flags and shakers. Everyone was wearing red roses and there was red, white and blue bunting all along the roads and streets where we walked. The leader of the brass band periodically threw his stick up in the air and caught it, and everybody went wild, cheering and clapping him on. As the band marched on they played songs like There'll Always Be an England, Sons of the Sea, Pack Up Your Troubles in Your Old Kit Bag, and best of all Land of Hope and Glory. Now and again two or three women would come out of the crowd into the middle of the road in front of the brass band and dance and sing, kicking their legs in the air and waving their flags. It was a joy to see everyone so happy.

About twelve thirty in the afternoon we arrived back at the church. My mam, dad, brothers and sister were all there to meet us, we made our way back home chattering excitedly about the events of the morning. My nana *would have a big potato pie ready for us at home. I was hungry now and looking forward to my potato pie. As we approached our house nana was on the veranda looking out for us. That was the last year I walked in the Whit Procession, but I continue to watch them every year. In fact I'm fifty now and I have not missed a Whit Monday yet.*

Declining congregations in the later twentieth century caused the demise of many of the walks, but some still survive, and usually take place now on Spring Bank Holiday. Other related customs have developed, like the Saddleworth Brass Band Competitions (*see* **Whit Friday: Brass Bands**, p. 272), and 'Whit Sings'. In 1996, a member of the West Yorkshire Federation of W.I.s remembered the 'Mollicar Sing':

This annual event on Whit Sunday was first held in 1900. It was started by the Zion Chapel, Almondbury, later amalgamated with the Wesleyan Methodist church, and now simply the Methodist church. The walk always started at 7.30 am, mainly through the Mollicar . . . with the singing of hymns at allotted places through the walk. The woods were at their best, with new green foliage and birds in full song. The sing finished about 9 am, and in earlier years Mr. and Mrs. Gostridge of Farnley Hey boundary provided the breakfast – ham and eggs for the grown-ups and bantam eggs for the children.

Whitsun Ales

See **Church Ales**, p. 258.

Whit Sunday

St Briavels Bread and Cheese Dole

In 1779, Gloucestershire historian Samuel Rudder wrote that at St Mary's church in the village of St Briavels in the Forest of Dean:

They have a custom of distributing yearly upon Whitsunday, after divine service, pieces of bread and cheese to the congregation at church, to defray the cost of which, every householder in the parish pays a penny to the church-wardens; and this is said to be for the liberty of cutting and taking the wood in Hudnolls. The tradition is, that the privilege was obtained of some Earl of Hereford, then lord of the forest of Dean, at the instance of his lady, upon the same hard terms that Lady Godiva obtained the privileges for the citizens of Coventry.

No earlier record of the St Briavels custom has yet come to light, which is strange because one would expect a church-based custom to leave some evidence in church records. A further account published in 1807 adds the detail that the bread and cheese was cut into inch-square pieces and thrown to the congregation from the church gallery, resulting in a great 'tumult and uproar'. As a result, the annual distribution moved out of the church into the lane. Folklore writer Phyllis Crawford witnessed it in the 1930s:

So after Evensong is finished you may see them, a mixed crowd of country people, tourists, colliers from the Forest of Dean, farmers, small shopkeepers, maids. They gather in the lane by a high stone wall, from which, like a spasmodic shower of too, too solid snow, the pieces of bread float down. Everyone grabs for the same piece, fingers get scratched, arms get bumped, hats get knocked askew. The polite apologise and get nothing, the eager snatch, hastily rejecting dry bits of bread for more succulent morsels of cheese. Finally with one devastating hurl the last fragments are flung to the crowd, the empty hamper overturned. Laughing and munching, the crowds slip away.

The bread and cheese is still thrown to the congregation every Whit Sunday, although the 'scrambling' is now more sedate. A local tradition holds that because the bread and cheese is blessed by the vicar before being distributed, it will not go bad and is particularly wholesome, which is a localized example of a previously widespread belief that bread baked on Good Friday, or the wafers and wine used in Holy Communion are similarly incorruptible (*see* **Good Friday: Bread and Eggs**, p. 142).

This would seem to be a simple example of a food dole, set up by a benefactor's bequest in aid of the poor, if it were not for the detail given by Rudder that all the householders paid money to finance the distribution. This strongly suggests the maintenance of a local right, and supports his assertion that the whole affair was linked to the liberty of cutting wood. Social historian Bob Bushaway draws parallels between the St Briavels custom and that of Great Wishford in Wiltshire, which was similarly concerned with wood rights (*see* **29 May: Grovely Ceremonies**).

See also **Doles**, p. 115; **Scrambling Customs**, p. 172.

St Mary Redcliffe Rush Sunday

The Rush Sunday service at St Mary Redcliffe church was instituted by the will of William Spenser, Mayor of Bristol, in 1493, and it originally commemorated an earlier mayor, William Canynge, who did much to rebuild and support the church, and even gave up his considerable wealth to become a priest. The Rush Service takes its name from the rushes and herbs strewn on the floor for the occasion, and as one of the official Civic Services of the year, it is attended by all the dignitaries of the City of Bristol in full regalia. The City can certainly put on a good show, and the procession to the church is led by the City Swordbearer, who carries the Pearl Sword and wears his Elizabethan Cap of Maintenance, followed by the Lord Mayor and Lady Mayoress, the city councillors and aldermen in their scarlet robes, and no less than eight macebearers carrying the City Maces. Everyone not carrying something else carries a posy of spring flowers in their hands. They enter the church to a fanfair of trumpets.

See also **Rush-Bearing**, p. 322.

Whit Tuesday

Dicing for Bibles

In a curious juxtaposition of the instruments of gambling and religion, the custom of dicing for Bibles takes place every Whit Tuesday in St Ives, Cambridgeshire, in accordance with the will of Dr Robert Wilde, who died in 1678. Wilde, who was a somewhat unconventional Puritan minister, left £50 to be invested in land to buy six Bibles, for which six boys and six girls (of good repute, over twelve years of age, and able to read) would contest by throwing dice. The land bought with the money became known as Bible Orchard. A report of an enquiry into the charity in 1879 reports that the vicar thought it a scandal that dice-playing should take place in church. The dicing was originally carried out on the altar of All Saints, but was moved to a table in the church c.1880, then to the local school, and then, in 1936, back into the church once more.

Whit Wednesday

Mother Shipton's Day

A former Cambridge resident, aged eighty-two in 1964, told folklorist Enid Porter that in her youth the washerwomen in the many small laundries in the town used to drink rum in their tea on the Wednesday in Whitsun week. They called the day 'Mother Shipton's Holiday'. Another informant confirmed this description, and added that 'Mother Shipton was the patron saint of laundresses'.

'Mother Shipton' was a fictional character, given a spurious biography in a series of chapbook publications from 1641 onwards, which included her hugely famous prophecies. These prophecies have probably been in print in some form or other ever since, and new generations of prophecy lovers continue to find 'amazing' predictions therein. The best-known example of public credulity occurred following the publication of a new edition of her sayings, by Charles Hindley in 1862, which included not only a prediction of steam trains ('carriages without horses shall go') but also a prophecy that the world would end in 1881. These caused a great deal of consternation at the time, forcing Hindley to admit that he had simply fabricated them.

Whit Friday

Brass Bands

The Whit Friday brass band contests, which take place in the Pennine villages around Saddleworth, where Lancashire meets Yorkshire, are one of the high spots of the bandsman's year, and are quite unique in the musical calendar. Far from being a static competition, contests are held in various villages, and bands rush from one to another to compete in as many as they can. The Saddleworth contests grew directly from the bands' involvement in the Whit Walks, which were tremendously popular in the area (*see* p. 266). By the 1880s, so many churches and chapels wanted to hold a Whit Walk that bands were brought in from well outside the immediate area in order to satisfy demand. Alec

*The Black Dyke Mills Band . . . were the first to arrive. They came by the
train due at 7.42 am. There was a pretty large crowd assembled to welcome
them and they marched away looking very smart in their Hussar uniform
and playing a lively quickstep. The next train brought with it no less than
six bands and by this time all the approaches to the station were besieged by
the townsfolk and there was a very lively scene until the last of the bands
had marched to its destination.*

The concentration of a number of bands in one area led to inevitable
fraternization between musicians and friendly rivalry between bands,
and as the walks took place in the morning, the afternoons and evenings were free for musical pursuits. The year 1884 saw the first organized contest between bands, but the competitions stayed local and low
key until an explosion of interest in the 1890s, as word of the contests
spread and they took on a life of their own. At a local level, they still
remained essentially an adjunct to the walks, but as the popularity of
the walks began to decline, and the band contests continued to grow,
the balance between the two gradually shifted. As with all public
events, tensions sometimes occurred, as the *Stalybridge Reporter* (1926)
commented:

They [the churches] *take this one day in the year to have their processions,
they spend combinedly hundreds of pounds in bringing the bands into the
town, thereby making the band contest possible and then a certain number
of people abuse the privilege of hearing good music by making it a day for
drinking too much.*

The modern competitions start in the afternoon and are open to all-
comers, so that local bands can compete against world-famous outfits;
they are funded and organized by local volunteers in aid of charity.
The contests now take place in twenty different locations and over a
hundred bands take part. In most cases, each band plays two pieces
at a contest, which is judged 'blind' (the adjudicator cannot see the
bands), and then they move on swiftly by coach to the next venue, not
knowing how well they have done until much later.

Late May

Blessing of the Sea

'Blessing the Sea' or 'Blessing the Fleet' ceremonies take place in a number of locations around the coast, but many are one-off or short-lived events, prompted by one person's enthusiasm. The ceremony at Brixham in Devon, however, has managed to survive through several revivals, and is a good example of just such an event. The earliest reference we have to the ceremony is from 1926, when the Revd George Gordon, of St Peter's church, conducted a special service at the pier on Rogation Sunday. It was particularly appropriate because at that time the congregation of St Peter's was mainly drawn from fishing families. Gordon led the choir and congregation in procession down to the pier, where they sang hymns, chanted Psalm 130, and offered special prayers for the blessing of the fishermen and fleet. Gordon left St Peter's in 1928, and it is unlikely that the special services continued as an annual event, but they certainly took place in 1937, 1947, and 1953, and throughout the 1980s. The service now takes place in late May, as part of the Brixham Heritage Festival, and features two local choirs and the town band.

The service held every May in Hastings is another example. An interdenominational service is organized by All Saints church, and includes the local Salvation Army band; the clergy addresses the congregation from the deck of the local lifeboat.

See also 25 July: Whitstable Oyster Festival.

Last Sunday in May

Arbor Day

In the Shropshire village of Aston-on-Clun, close to the Welsh border, a unique annual tree-decorating custom is carried out on the last Sunday in May (but formerly on **Royal Oak Day**, for which *see below*). The tree, which stands prominently in the middle of the village, was once a large black poplar, reputed to be over 300 years old; however, this was blown down in 1995 and was replaced by a 28-year-old sapling.

The villagers decorate it with gaily coloured flags.

The story behind the custom tells how local landowner John Marston married Mary Carter in May 1786, and the tree was decorated to welcome the newlyweds to the village. Mary was so pleased with this gesture that she laid down the rule that the Marston family would provide the flags and manpower to decorate the tree every year on their anniversary. This explains why the tree is often called 'the Bride's Tree'. Nevertheless, some people argue that the villagers already had an old tree-decorating custom, or that they were simply celebrating Royal Oak Day, and young Mary Marston simply misunderstood and no one had the heart to tell her the truth. Nowadays, the tree is the focal point for a fête and a day of community celebrations, including a charming children's wedding pageant in eighteenth-century costume, but these cannot be proved to be any older than about 1912.

So the matter would rest, but unfortunately an idea has taken hold that the custom is linked to fertility rites, and the Arbor Tree Festival Committee's official website boldly states that it dates back to the Iron Age:

. . . a tree . . . was decorated for the fertility rites practised by the pastoral shepherds living in the hills of Clun Forest . . . These pastoral tribes worshipped Brigit, the Celtic Goddess of Fertility. Her shrine was a tree on which the tribal emblems and prayer flags were kept: fertility for the people and the land being invoked.

Needless to say, this is completely fanciful.

29 May

Royal Oak Day

29 May 1661 – This was the first anniversary appointed by Act of Parliament, to be observed as a day of general thanksgiving for the miraculous restoration of his Majesty; our vicar preaching on Psalm 118:24, requiring us to be thankful and rejoice, as indeed we had cause.

John Evelyn's diary here records the introduction of a new special day into the English calendar. When Charles II rode into London on his birthday, 29 May, in 1660, and restored the monarchy to England, the people were provided with a festival date which would continue to resonate for centuries and which, in a few isolated cases, is still celebrated today. As John Evelyn noted, the day was officially declared one of national joy and celebration, and was marked with the bonfires, bells, and special services common on such patriotic occasions. There was certainly no shortage of biblical references to provide religious legitimacy to the Restoration, and Samuel Pepys noted that in his church on that day the sermon was based on the phrase 'Nay, let him take all, since my Lord the King is returned' (2 Samuel 19:30). Nevertheless, despite this religious backing, Royal Oak Day was part of the gradual trend of secularization that saw political and patriotic festivals (such as Guy Fawkes Night) replacing religious ones.

Three things ensured that Royal Oak Day was immediately accepted by the general populace. Firstly, the Restoration was genuinely popular and was seen as a welcome return of the 'merry England' that had been so harshly put down by the Puritan revolution. Secondly, the new king rapidly acquired a recognizable trademark – the oak leaf, which symbolized the story of his hiding in an oak tree after defeat at the Battle of Worcester had quashed any hopes of a royalist comeback in September 1651. Thirdly, the timing of the new celebration brought it into the ambit of existing May Day celebrations, which already had a tendency to spread through the month, and Royal Oak Day quickly rivalled May Day and Whitsun as the key day in early summer for time off work in pursuit of pleasure. Royal Oak Day even stole some of the main features of May Day, such as the erection of maypoles. Houses and churches were also decorated in the same way as at the beginning of the month, with the only real difference being the preponderance of oak boughs for the King's day. The habit of leaving boughs at people's doors also transferred from the 1st to the 29th, as in this account of customs in Charlbury, Oxfordshire, in the early twentieth century, published in *The Listener* in 1957:

. . . *going round to the houses of the gentry very early on the morning of May 29 and decorating the knocker or lintel with oak-apple sprays. The decorators would call later on the day for a gift of money. If none were forthcoming, they would stand and chant:*

> *Shig-shag – penny a rag*
> *Bang his head in Cromwell's bag*
> *Bad cess to this house come to stay*
> *Before next twenty-ninth of May.*

However, the dominant custom, which really came to symbolize the day, was the wearing of sprays of oak leaves (preferably with a gall or apple attached, and often gilded or otherwise enhanced) in lapels and hats, and by all accounts this was done by almost everybody, high and low, male and female, adult and child, throughout the eighteenth and early nineteenth centuries. John Byng (later Lord Torrington) recorded in his diary in 1789 that when passing through Barnet, in Hertfordshire, 'every horse, carriage and carter was adorned with oaken boughs and apples, in memory of this once-famous day'. Schoolchildren were given a day (or at least a half-day) off school, and all over the country it was reported that whoever did not wear such an emblem was attacked unmercifully by their schoolfellows, and could be pinched, stung with nettles, kicked, or pelted with birds' eggs (sometimes rotten ones). 'These pinches are no common ones; they hurt pretty well and a kick is generally administered with it,' complained (Sir) Alfred Lyall, who was at Eton in 1845, and it was not only rough public-school boys you had to watch out for, as a correspondent to *Bye-Gones* (1889–90) showed:

I was travelling from Crewe to Runcorn [Cheshire] *on the 29th of May. There were six girls in the carriage with me all wearing oak leaves and two of them carrying bunches of nettles. On being asked what the nettles were for, they said, 'To beat those who have no oak'.*

In common with several other children's customs (e.g. April Fool's Day, and 'pinch-punch' rituals), the persecution of non-participants usually had to end at noon, and indeed many removed their oak symbols at that hour. One completely unexplained development, however, was that in many villages the children substituted ash for their oak leaves and wore those in the afternoon.

Oak-wearing by adults was probably already declining when the special prayer of thanksgiving was removed from church services in 1859, and by Edwardian times many writers were mourning its demise. However, Iona and Peter Opie found it was still alive and well in the children's calendar in a number of places in the 1950s, particularly in midland and northern counties. It is certainly dead and forgotten now.

Numerous local dialect names for the day have been recorded, based on particular features of the custom, including: Oak Apple Day, Shick-Shack Day, Shig-Shag Day, Yak-Bob Day, Bobby-Ack Day, and Nettling Day.

Castleton Garland Day

The High Peak village of Castleton in Derbyshire plays host to a unique garland custom every 29 May. The famous garland is constructed on a heavy bell-shaped framework, large enough to envelop a man's body down to his waist, which is then completely covered in greenery and flowers. The man who 'wears' the garland is called the King, and he is seated on a horse, which must be led because his hands are busy supporting and controlling the garland. He is accompanied by a Queen, or Lady, also on horseback, and both are dressed in Stuart-style costumes. Before the garland is placed on his head, the King leads a procession, which includes a team of girl morris dancers dressed in white, a silver band, other attendants, and the Queen, who brings up the rear, around the village. The garland is then put into place, and the procession again tours the village, stopping at various places for the girls to dance. The King is then led to St Edmund's church, where the garland is hoisted by rope to the top of the church tower; it then remains on show for a few weeks until all the flowers have died. The special topknot of the garland, also called 'the Queen', is removed before the hoisting, and is laid on the village war memorial. The pubs in the village take it in turns to host the garland.

Until the early years of the twentieth century, the whole affair was the responsibility of the village bell-ringers, and had been so for some time; the earliest known reference to the custom is in the churchwardens' accounts of 1749: 'paid for an iron rod to hang ye ringers garland in 8d.'.

The garland custom is deservedly well known, and very photogenic, so we are blessed with numerous descriptions and photographs from the post-Second World War period; however, we are doubly fortunate that Sheffield-based folklorist Sydney Oldall Addy visited Castleton in 1900 and published the results of his fieldwork in a detailed paper in the journal *Folk-Lore*, which remains a model for how to report on traditional customs. Addy's work is particularly important because he interviewed local people rather than just watching the event from the sidelines, and he took note of details that were often ignored by other collectors, such as the costumes worn and who was taking part. When Addy visited Castleton, he noted the changes that had recently been made in the way the custom was carried out, and there have been many more alterations since his time. Although the essential parts of the custom – the two horseback figures, the garland on the man's head, the procession with dancers, the hoisting of the garland – have remained the same, almost all the details have undergone radical change: the dancers used to be men but are now young girls dressed in white; the 'Queen' was a man dressed as a woman, and is now a real woman; the 'Queen' part of the garland was given to a local dignitary, then to a recently married couple, and is now laid on the village war memorial; the costumes of the King and Queen have become more overtly historical; and the King and Queen themselves were previously simply known as the 'man' and the 'woman'.

The most important lesson to learn from these changes is the folly of basing explanations of a custom's origin on the details of the way it is now carried out. The origin and earlier history of the custom are very much open to speculation, and many theories have been put forward, including the idea that it developed from the story of Sir Gawain and the Green Knight, the Jack-in-the-Green (*see* 1 **May: Jack-in-the-Green**), and foliate heads, or is linked to numerous spring gods and sacrificial beheadings. But May garlands of similar construction (although not of the same size) are common all over England, and even the hoisting of greenery to the top of the church tower is not unique, as a similar activity formerly took place at Membury, in Devon. On the current evidence, the custom appears to be the result of moving a May garland to Royal Oak Day and giving it 'royal' trappings in honour of Charles II (*see* **29 May: Royal Oak Day**, p. 275). Local folklorist Georgina Boyes, however, has suggested a connection with the custom of **rush-bearing** (*see* p. 322), which was particularly widespread in Derbyshire.

Grovely Ceremonies

In many traditional customs, details that seem strange to the modern eye might be the result of accretions over the years, or they might have been part of the conditions stipulated in bequests, charters, or other founding documents. Rarely do we have direct evidence either way, but in the case of Great Wishford's 'Grovely' Ceremonies in Wiltshire, we can see that some of the picturesque, even bizarre, details were laid down 400 years ago. In this case, the day's events are direct survivals of conditions stipulated in charters of 1597 and 1603, which confirm and delineate existing rights for villagers to gather wood in nearby Grovely Wood, a former royal forest. The charter specifically states that the inhabitants must go to the cathedral 'in a dance' and that they 'there made their claim to their customs in the Forest of Grovely in these words "Grovely! Grovely! And all Grovely!"'

In earlier times, the right to gather wood for fuel and other domestic uses was an extremely important one to the rural population, and it involved complex definitions of the type and size of wood that could be gathered, and the method of its taking, as well as strict regulations on who could demand access to woodlands and when access could take place. But there was also tension between villagers and landowners as the latter increasingly came to regard woodland as a commercial asset that required improved management and severely controlled access. The majority of the rural population lost any rights to gather wood centuries ago: most rights simply lapsed as they became unnecessary or meaningless, while others were legislated out of existence; however, the inhabitants of Great Wishford have managed to keep their rights alive, and are determined to continue to do so.

The celebrations that surround their declaration of rights used to take place in Whit week, but at some point they were moved to 29 May. It is not unusual to find customs gravitating to **Royal Oak Day** (*see* p. 275), and in this case the link between the 'oak' motif of the day and the wood-gathering theme of the custom make it a particularly logical development. This day is now the major festival day of the year for the village, organized by the Oak Apple Club, which was set up in 1892 to ensure the survival of the rights. At the crack of dawn there is a visit from the Tin Can band, who make a cacophonous noise to wake people up. Many people rise early to go in procession to the forest, dressed in old-fashioned clothes and bonnets, under a banner bearing the words 'Grovely! Grovely! And all Grovely!' along with their other motto, 'Unity is strength'. They return with branches to decorate houses, and a large bough to hoist to the top of the church tower. Representatives go to Salisbury Cathedral to lay branches on the altar, and a dance is still performed, by four women wearing period costume, bonnets, and aprons. A village fête and other entertainments round off the day.

Neville's Cross Commemoration

On the Saturday nearest to 29 May every year, the choir of Durham Cathedral sing anthems from the top of the tower after evensong, facing east, south, and north. Tradition has it that they have done so almost every year since the mid fourteenth century, and that it has nothing to do with the month of May but commemorates a battle fought in October 1346. In that year, while King Edward was away besieging Calais, the Scots army, led by King David, took the opportunity to invade England. They were stopped and beaten back at the decisive battle of Neville's Cross, near Durham. The Cathedral monks are said to have watched the battle from the tower and to have broken into a triumphant singing at its successful outcome. In a further legend, it is said that the Prior of Durham, John Fosser, had a dream the night before the battle that prompted him to go to the Cross and take with him as a banner the sacred cloth which St Cuthbert had used to cover the chalice while saying mass. The Prior and some of his monks did so, and this act was said to have provided the spiritual assitance necessary for the Scots' defeat. To this day, it is also said that if you walk nine times round the Cross, and then put your ear to the ground, you will hear the sounds of the fighting.

The connection between the tower singing and the battle has never been proved, and it is unlikely that the custom has survived in an unbroken line for nearly 700 years. Two alternative theories put forward the idea that the tower singing once formed part of a guild procession, or that the singing was started to celebrate deliverance from a great fire on 25 May 1429.

Royal Hospital Chelsea Founder's Day

The Royal Hospital Chelsea was founded by Charles II in 1682, as a retirement home for army veterans who had served for twenty years or who had been invalided out of the service. He borrowed the idea from a similar institution founded in France by Louis XIV in 1670. Residents wear a distinctive red coat and black tricorn hat, based on the army uniform worn in the time of the first Duke of Marlborough (1650–1722), and are known colloquially as Chelsea Pensioners.

It is appropriate that the Hospital's Founder's Day celebrations should take place on 29 May, Charles II's birthday and the anniversary of his Restoration in 1660, although they sometimes now take place in early June, for convenience. At present there are about 400 residents, termed 'in-pensioners', who occupy 'berths' within the building, and it is these men who parade in their best uniforms on Founder's Day. Since 1980 they have been inspected by a member of the royal family. The statue of Charles, which stands in the South or Figure Court, is draped with oak leaves, and all the participants also wear a sprig of the same. The grounds of the Hospital, and some of the buildings, are open to the public most of the year.

Spring Bank Holiday

Spring Bank Holiday (the last Monday in May) was created in 1971 to replace the moveable Whit Monday holiday, and formed part of the gradual shift from religious to secular holidays. For centuries, **Whitsun** (p. 260) had been a major marker of the onset of summer, and was thus a favourite day for outdoor events. Countless fairs, fêtes, walks and club feasts were held on the day, and it was natural that those that had survived into the 1970s should gravitate to the new day.

Bampton Morris Dance

At Bampton in Oxfordshire, every Spring Bank Holiday morning, one of the classic scenes of the English village idyll can be found, with the performance of the local morris dance. Of all the morris dancing that takes place in the country, the Bampton men have the strongest claim to being 'traditional', in the sense that they perform their local dances in their own style, and have performed every year since before the folk-dance revivals of the early twentieth century created a new nationwide interest in the subject. Nevertheless, it is certainly true that the interest created by these revivals has played a significant part in keeping the local tradition alive. Morris dancing was traditionally performed at Whitsun, but at Bampton, as elsewhere, it has gravitated to Spring Bank Holiday. The dancers perform all round the village and its environs on the day itself, but they also dance at other times of the year at special events, or when invited elsewhere.

Six dancers dressed in white, wearing black bowler hats decorated with flowers, bells round their legs, and holding handkerchiefs in their hands, go through the evolutions of the dances, to the sound of a fiddle or melodeon. There is also a Fool or clown to entertain the crowd with antics and banter, and a 'Cake-Bearer', who carries a whole fruit-cake impaled on a sword. Pieces of this cake, which are considered lucky, are presented to members of the audience if they give a donation. Nowadays there are three sides, but they all use the same repertoire, and at its best the dancing is unhurried, almost perfunctory, but with the indefinable grace that revival teams never seem to be able to manage. It is no wonder that visiting romantics have thought they have seen pagan rituals to welcome the spring, or visions of a golden age of **Merrie England** (p. 510).

The first published account of morris dancing at Bampton is found in the Revd J. A. Giles's history of the village, published in 1847, but he was apparently not very keen on it:

Another season of festivity is Whitsuntide, when the Morris dancers exhibit their saltatory powers for the amusement of the people, and to gather a few shillings for their own private emolument. As these functionaries do nothing but dance, and thoroughly fatigue themselves before nightfall, they must be considered to have earned the hot suppers and mulled ale, which probably terminate the festival, but they have no farther claim to delay the progress of this history.

This confirms that the dancing was already an established tradition by this date, and there has probably been an unbroken series of annual performance since that time, apart from during the First World War. Further research undertaken by dance historian Keith Chandler, based on the evidence of the continued involvement of particular local families, demonstrates that the local tradition can be traced back to the early nineteenth, or perhaps even late eighteenth, century. However, claims of a 600-year tradition – probably based on the fact that the earliest references to morris dancing in this country are from the fifteenth century – are groundless.

See also **Whitsun: Morris Dance**, p. 263.

Barwick Maypole

Barwick-in-Elmet may not have the only traditional maypole in the country, or even in Yorkshire, but it does vie with other places for the tallest example, and once every three years it steals the limelight by taking the pole down – by hand – and putting it back up again a few weeks later.

The pole is taken down on Easter Monday, repainted, re-garlanded, and then re-erected on Spring Bank Holiday, amid much rejoicing. The whole operation was previously carried out through a combination of brute strength and skill, with ropes and ladders, and scores of men providing the muscle, all coordinated by an elected Pole Master shouting his orders. But modern safety rules now insist that cranes and hard hats are the order of the day, which is organized by the Barwick-in-Elmet Maypole Trust. Once down, the pole is transported to a field on the shoulders of a hundred volunteers, where the renovation is carried out: it is repainted white, with two parallel stripes, red and blue, spiralling around from top to bottom; a stainless-steel weathervane in the shape of a fox is fixed to the top; and the four large garlands are renewed. The latter are constructed by members of different local women's organizations and are fixed on the pole about fifty feet from the ground. Each garland weighs a hundredweight, and is decorated with coloured cloth rosettes (over 6,000 of them), artificial flowers, and ribbons of red, white, and blue that have little bells attached to them. The garlands are paraded around the neighbouring villages before being hung. Every so often, the maypole needs to be completely replaced, as happened in 2005. The new pole is a Scots pine from Finland, ready spliced in two sections and nearly eighty-six feet tall.

Spring Bank Holiday in a maypole year is a major celebration for the villagers, especially for the children, and the day is taken up with a procession of floats and bands, maypole and morris dancing, and the crowning of the Maypole Queen. At about 6 o'clock in the evening, however, the climax of the day is the placing of the newly painted pole back in its hole and hauling it upright again. A local climbs up the pole to release the ropes and, if he is brave enough, he ascends to the top and gives the weathervane a swing.

Cooper's Hill Cheese-Rolling

Every Spring Bank Holiday, at Cooper's Hill, between Brockworth and Painswick in Gloucestershire, a large round Gloucester cheese, weighing about 8 lbs and specially made for the occasion, is set rolling down a hill. A dozen or so young men launch themselves headlong down the steep slope in pursuit, most of whom are sent sprawling, rolling, and tumbling within a few steps. They have little hope of catching the cheese, but the first to the bottom wins it. During the day there are three races for men, and one for women, and although there are numerous bruises, dislocations, concussions, and occasional broken bones, it is rare that anything more alarming occurs.

A description from the journal *Folk-Lore* in 1912 shows that little has changed:

The master of the ceremonies, Mr. W. Brookes, who has officiated in this capacity for thirty years, appeared wearing, as usual, a brown top-hat which his parents won in a dancing contest many years ago, and with a chemise over his coat. He stood by the maypole and repeatedly called to the crowd to form 'the alley' down the slope. The course being clear, the Vicar opened the ball by sending the first 'cheese' (a disc of wood wrapped in pink paper) rolling down the hill. Helter-skelter ran nine young men after it, and most of them pitch-poled. The first to secure the disc, stopped at the bottom by a hedge, had to trudge uphill again, and there exchange it for the prize cheese.

The 'cheese-rolling' custom is all that remains of the Cooper's Hill wake, which was once held on top of the hill every Whit Monday and included many other standard features of annual gatherings, such as wrestling, shin-kicking, girning, smock races, a maypole, and plenty to eat and drink. The cheese-rolling itself, far from being an ancient ritual, is therefore simply the sole survivor of an activity that routinely took place at fairs and wakes up and down the country – providing, of course, that they had a suitable hill nearby. Thomas Hughes mentions the custom in his *Scouring of the White Horse* (1859), stating that it was a feature of the fairs that took place at Uffington in Berkshire at the scouring of the chalk hill-figure there in the eighteenth and early nineteenth centuries. The cheese-rolling at Cooper's Hill certainly dates back at least to the early nineteenth century, but there is no record of it before that time.

In the early 1990s, the cheese-rolling custom came under fire from the local authorities over fears of crowd and participant safety, and in 1999 it was even banned by Gloucestershire County Council, who own the land. A small group of stalwarts defied the ban and chased a cheese early on the day, and it was back the following year, at an earlier time of day (to try to ensure that the contestants were sober), and with some safety netting to protect the spectators from the bounding cheeses and runners. Oddly enough, this was just the time when the custom was becoming popular with the national press, who now report on it each year, usually accompanied by a piece on the eccentricities of the English. Now that its fame has spread, the event attracts entrants from far and wide, and seems in little danger of being allowed to lapse.

See also **Fairs, Feasts, Wakes, and Revels**, p. 341.

Hunting the Earl of Rone

On Spring Bank Holiday, the people of the North Devon coastal town of Combe Martin present their own unique ceremony, 'Hunting the Earl of Rone', a colourful revival and extension of a custom that was last performed in town around the time Queen Victoria came to the throne.

We have no accounts that date from when the original custom was active, but several good descriptions were published while it was still in living memory. It ceased *c.*1837, apparently suppressed because of the drunkenness and disorder that characterized the day. In these earlier accounts, the characters included: the Earl of Rone, who wore a grotesque mask, clothes stuffed with straw, and a string of twelve sea-biscuits around his neck; a hobby horse; a masked and gaudily dressed Fool; a donkey, decorated with flowers and another sea-biscuit necklace; and a troop of grenadiers, wearing tall hats covered with ribbons. The day for the full performance was **Ascension Day** (p. 251), but during the preceding fortnight the hobby horse and Fool had already toured the neighbourhood, collecting money to defray the costs of the custom. At 3 p.m. on Ascension Day, the grenadiers would march to nearby Lady's Wood, and after much searching, discover the Earl of Rone hidden there. They would fire a volley of shots and set the prisoner on the donkey, facing its tail. The hobby horse, Fool, and all the spectators would form up into procession to escort the prisoner back to town. At certain points, the grenadiers fired further volleys and the Earl fell from the donkey. The soldiers expressed their joy at this, but the hobby horse and Fool lamented the goings-on, and the latter would revive the Earl and set him back on the donkey. The procession halted at every pub and collected money from bystanders, but disbanded when it finally reached the sea.

Hunting the Earl of Rone provides a pleasant puzzle for would-be experts on traditional customs. Taken as a whole it is unique, but every single element, apart from the Earl himself perhaps, can be found in another custom. **Hobby horses** (p. 226) appear all over the country (most notably, for present purposes, in Minehead and Padstow), and Fools often accompany plough plays, morris and sword dancers, and many other performances. Guns fired in the air were a standard feature of a range of customs, including Guy Fawkes Night, the Padstow 'Obby 'Oss celebrations, and weddings, at least until the passing of the

Firearms Act of 1835. A character placed backwards on a donkey was a regular feature of **rough music** activities (p. 95), and a character stuffed with straw appeared in several customs, including **Jack-a-Lent** (p. 86) and the Burning of Bartle (*see* **24 August: West Witton Burning of Bartle**). The grenadiers sound like South Country mummers, with their tall beribboned hats, and even the motif of someone falling down dead or wounded and then being revived is a commonplace of the mummers' play (*see* **Christmas: Mummers**). As for the Earl himself, most commentators, now and in the nineteenth century, have assumed that he is based upon the Irish 'outlaw' Hugh O'Neill, Earl of Tyrone (1540–1616), who fled to Rome in 1607. However, there is no evidence linking him with North Devon, or any of the other features of the custom, nor is there any indication that the story of his flight and adventures were well known enough at the time to influence any village customs.

The custom was researched and 'reconstructed' by local enthusiasts in the 1970s, and was performed as part of the town's carnival, but in 1978 the real revival came about, and the event has been staged successfully every year since. The 'Hunting' is now one of the most important features of Combe Martin's year, with scores of locals taking part, and hundreds of onlookers. All the known details of the old custom have been preserved, and a few additions have been made: more people are now allowed to take part, new features such as dancing and children's processions have extended the festivities, and many dress in old-fashioned costumes.

Kingsteignton Ram-Roasting

The ram-roasting fair at the Devonian village of Kingsteignton (a village billed on the parish council's website as the biggest in England), formerly took place on Whit Tuesday but is now held on Spring Bank Holiday Monday. It takes the usual form of a local fair, with stalls, bands, and May Queens, but a special feature is the roasting of a sheep on a spit, which is then shared out to the fair-goers. The event itself has not changed much since 1883, when a contributor to *Notes & Queries* described it in the following way:

A lamb is drawn about the parish on Whitsun Monday in a cart covered with garlands of lilac, laburnum, and other flowers, when persons are requested to give something towards the animal and attendant expenses; on

Tuesday it is killed and roasted whole in the middle of the village . . . The lamb is then sold in slices to the poor at a cheap rate.

However, the participants have not always behaved very respectably. Phyllis Crawford, who visited the fair *c.*1936 in preparation for her book *In England Still*, reported a conversation with the ninety-year-old widow of a former vicar, who explained how the custom had been tidied up and tamed:

My husband started the procession, dear, and all the sports and fancy dresses; you see, before that when they had roasted the ram they used to go to the public houses and I am afraid they used to get drunk. Yes, my dear, it was very rough, you wouldn't have liked it at all. He let them go on with the ram-roasting, dear, they had always done that, but the rest he had to stop. And you see how nice it is now. Quite a fine old ceremony.

It has been said that the custom started at some remote period before Christianity was introduced to Devonshire when there was a terrible drought, and that a ram was sacrificed to the gods to bring a stream by the village – and so by rights the local river should be diverted and the ram roasted in the riverbed once more. However, there is no evidence that the custom is older than the nineteenth century, and it is standard fare for any custom involving dead animals to be linked to sacrifices. Rather more prosaically, it was once far from unusual for animals, usually sheep or oxen, to be roasted at local fairs and other gatherings, in order to feed the hundreds of people that attended them.

See also **Fairs, Feasts, Wakes, and Revels**, p. 341.

Robert Dover's Olimpick Games

Robert Dover (?1582–1652) was a lawyer who settled in the Cotswolds in 1611, and sometime soon afterwards organized the first of what became known as Robert Dover's Olimpick Games, on an open hillside called Kingcombe Plain (later renamed Dover's Hill), above Weston-sub-Edge in Gloucestershire. It is possible that he based his games on an existing local feast or ale, but it is equally possible that the idea was his own.

Dover seems to have been quite the extrovert and very skilled in self-promotion, and his Games soon achieved a much higher profile than most local events ever do. Based on contemporary publications, the early events included a range of activities, from horse-racing, harecoursing, and hunting, to more modest field events such as running, jumping, throwing the sledgehammer, wrestling, fencing, dancing, and even board games such as chess. His Games were founded at the very time a national debate was raging over the propriety of such sports, and this can hardly be accidental. This controversy focused particularly on what should be allowed on Sundays, but an increasing number of Puritans wanted all such gatherings banned (*see The King's Book of Sports* 1618 and 1633, p. 354).

With the onset of the Civil War in 1642, Dover's Games ceased, but they were re-introduced after the Restoration by his grandsons John and Thomas Dover. The event continued to be held until 1852, when enclosure of the area again killed it. Dover's Hill became the property of the National Trust in 1929, and the Games were again held as a one-off event in May 1951 for the Festival of Britain. Meanwhile, at nearby Chipping Campden, a smaller Whitsun celebration occurred every year, known as the Scuttlebrook Wake. By the mid twentieth century, this event included all the usual May Queens, processions, fancy-dress competitions, and funfair rides expected of such affairs, and in 1966 Dover's Games were revived on Dover's Hill as part of the celebrations. The Games are now played on the Friday night and the Wake is celebrated on Saturday. At the Games, many of the traditional field sports of the earlier periods have been revived, coupled with spectacular events such as hot-air balloons, parachute jumps, and motorbike scrambling.

See also **Fairs, Feasts, Wakes, and Revels**, p. 341.

JUNE

Trinity Sunday

Trinity Sunday is celebrated eight weeks after Easter, the first Sunday after Whitsun, and can fall between 10 May and 20 June. The Christian doctrine of the Trinity, which developed in the earliest period of the Church's existence, caused a tremendous amount of discussion and dissension that rumbled on for centuries. By the Middle Ages, the idea of a special day devoted to the Holy Trinity existed in various parts of the Christian world, and it was particularly popular in England, probably because Thomas Becket, who was consecrated on that day in 1162, actively promoted its use. However, it was not fixed as a universal feast day until 1334. In Britain, after the Reformation, churches were widely dedicated to the Holy Trinity as a way of avoiding references to specific saints, and this tendency continued into the late nineteenth century. According to publisher William Chambers, writing in 1864, one-fifth of all new churches in his time were dedicated to the Trinity.

Nevertheless, the day does not seem to have attracted many traditional customs, and the few that are recorded are single local observances rather than widespread traditions. Seventeenth-century antiquarian John Aubrey described an apparently unique garland custom that took place at Newnton, in Wiltshire, in his time: a local girl would wear a garland round her neck, and then place it on a young man's neck, who returned it, with much saluting and kissing. Whenever possible during this custom, things were done three times (three knocks on the door, three kisses, and so on), in keeping with the day's name. This ceremony was reputed to commemorate the granting of some common land to the parish by King Athelstan, and the story goes that he had noticed their need for such land when he happened to be passing and met a milkmaid who was feeding her cow on the roadside verge.

Other customs are clearly linked to the dedication of the parish church, as at Old Clee in Lincolnshire, where they strew grass in the aisles of the Saxon church of the Holy Trinity and St Mary every Trinity Sunday. According to C. Ernest Watson, who wrote up the history of the area in 1901, stuffed chine and cheesecakes must be eaten on this day.

The time of year in which Trinity Sunday falls made it a favourite day for feasts, wakes, and other local gatherings. In the mid 1880s, Charlotte Burne described the Caradoc Wakes, which took place at the summit of one of the Stretton Hills and offered all the usual feast-day attractions, including stalls selling beer and food, gingerbread hawkers, foot-races, wrestling, rolling cakes down the side of the hill, fiddling, and dancing. This wake faded out in the mid nineteenth century, but in Burne's time parties of young people still spent at least some of Trinity Sunday on the hill.

See also **Fairs, Feasts, Wakes, and Revels**, p. 341.

Thursday after Trinity Sunday

Corpus Christi

This is one of several major Church festivals which were extremely important public events in their day, but are now virtually forgotten. Corpus Christi (meaning 'Body of Christ') was a relative latecomer to the festival calendar, being introduced by Pope Urban IV in 1264 and relaunched by Pope John XXII in 1317. It was created to honour the body of Christ, and to commemorate the central mystery of the Eucharist, in which Christ is believed to be truly present in the wine and bread of the mass.

The new feast was enthusiastically adopted by some English churches almost immediately, and in a very short time specialist guilds were being formed. By the middle of the fifteenth century, Corpus

Christi guilds were so common as to be the third most popular subjects for such groups (after the Virgin and the Trinity), and their primary task was to organize processions of the host through the streets. These processions involved not only the Corpus Christi guild members but also the local clergy, officials of the town, and members of trade guilds, and by Tudor times the processions had grown into huge affairs, particularly in urban areas such as York, Shrewsbury, Durham, Coventry, and Lichfield, which could support lavish productions. Houses and churches were decorated, streets were strewn with rushes and flowers, and the members of the procession carried torches, banners, crosses, garlands, pictures of saints, and even models of beasts. In pride of place at the front of the procession, the host, enshrined in a pyx of crystal, silver, or even gold, was carried on the shoulders of the clergy. Onlookers were required to kneel, bareheaded, as the procession passed.

As they developed in size and complexity, the processions began to include tableaux and pageants, which eventually turned into plays on biblical themes, enacted on carts both moving and stationary. It is generally agreed that these Corpus Christi plays performed an important role in the development of drama in Britain. An extract from a nineteenth-century description of proceedings in York, as presented by folklorists A. R. Wright and T. E. Lones, gives a flavour of the day:

On the day before and the morning of the day itself, thousands of spectators streamed into the city. On Corpus Christi morn, artisans and tradesmen rose early, spending an hour or two completing the arrangements of their large stages. At 9 a.m. the procession started, beginning to play first at the gates of the priory of the Holy Trinity; then it proceeded so every street had a pageant, 'all at one time playing together'. Scaffolds and stages were erected in the streets, in those places where they determined to play their pageants . . . their Mystery Plays bearing titles such as, for example, 'Cain and Abel', 'Slaughter of the Innocents', and 'Deliverance of Souls from Hell'. In the year 1415, fifty-four distinct dramas were represented on fifty-four stages . . . The Corpus Christi plays were kept up till 1584 at York.

It is no surprise that the ceremonial carrying of the host through the streets was abolished at the Reformation. In many places the processions also lapsed, but in others they simply took on a new secular role, and were transformed into trade guild affairs or town pageants, such as the Shrewsbury Show, which survived until the 1860s.

First week in June

Appleby Horse Fair

The fair at Appleby-in-Westmorland, twelve miles south-east of Penrith and now in Cumbria, is probably the best-known surviving horse fair in the country and – not coincidentally – also the best-known gathering of travellers and Gypsies in the year. Those who still travel in horse-drawn vans, and those who for generations have driven cars and lorries, still congregate at Appleby in the old-fashioned way.

Nominally restricted to the Fair Hill just outside the town, the trading spills over in all directions, and for horse lovers the fair is an exciting event. The running of horses through the crowded streets of the town has been banned by the local council for safety reasons, but there are plenty of other places where they can be put through their paces; in addition there is horse-racing, much voluble bargaining and trading, business for the farrier, fortune-telling, and stalls selling crafts and horse-related equipment. A set piece, most popular with photographers and tourists, is the riding of horses into the River Eden for a good wash (with washing-up liquid) and a swim. The banks of the river are lined with spectators, and if the weather is good it is hard to find a place to watch the free show. Many of the visitors do not trade in horses, and the number of tourists and would-be travellers grows each year, but of all groups in England, Gypsies are the ones who have resisted being turned into quaint tourist attractions, and Appleby retains much of its old atmosphere.

It is often claimed that Appleby Horse Fair was founded by a charter granted by James II in 1685; however, that charter was for a fair in April and was soon rescinded. The present fair has a more prosaic origin: by resolution of Appleby Borough, in 1750.

8 June

In June, farmers are already anxiously looking forward to the harvest, and they could choose from any number of traditional weather predictions. In 1869, Richard Inwards recorded in his classic *Weather-Lore* collection:

If on the 8th of June it rain
It foretells a wet harvest, men sain'.

Let us hope its accuracy was more impressive than its poetry.

Second Saturday in June

Queen Elizabeth II's Official Birthday

It is not entirely clear when British sovereigns started to have two birthdays, but from at least the twentieth century it was the custom to name an 'official birthday' for each ruler in addition to their natural one. The reason is simple. Many of the celebrations that surround a monarch's birthday are held outdoors, and it is far more pleasant for those involved, and the crowds watching, if the events can take place on a summer's day. Until 1959, the Queen's official birthday was on the second Thursday in June, but it now takes place on the second Saturday in June. The day is celebrated by the Queen's Birthday Parade, which takes place on Horse Guards Parade, Whitehall, at 11 a.m., and by gun salutes in Hyde Park and the Tower of London.

See also **21 April: Queen Elizabeth II's Birthday.**

10 June

Duke of Edinburgh's Birthday

The birthday of the Duke of Edinburgh is marked by gun salutes in Hyde Park and the Tower of London.

11 June

St Barnabas' Day

Barnabas (martyred AD 71) was an early Christian disciple, but not one of the twelve Apostles. A one-time companion of St Paul, he was active in spreading the word of the new religion, especially in his native Cyprus. A dozen or so ancient churches in England were dedicated to him, which indicates that he was known here but was not particularly popular. Nevertheless, according to the evidence supplied by the churchwardens' accounts of St Mary-at-Hill, London, in the fifteenth and sixteenth centuries, St Barnabas' Day was an important feast day. Churches were decorated with garlands of roses, woodruff (a woodland herb with sweet-scented leaves and small white flowers), and lavender. Maidens went 'gathering' for church funds, and money was paid out for 'bread, wine and ale for the singers of the King's Chapel and for the clerks of the town'. Later periods show no evidence of such customs on the day. A possible clue to the basis of these activities is a rhyme, reported fairly regularly in later years:

> *Barnaby bright, Barnaby bright,*
> *The longest day and the shortest night.*

These words only make sense if account is taken of the adoption of the Gregorian Calendar in 1752 (*see* p. xxix): old St Barnabas' Day fell eleven days later, so the customs could possibly be seen as celebrating midsummer. The midsummer date also made St Barnabas' Day a popular time for fairs.

Third Sunday in June

Father's Day

Father's Day was first suggested in 1909 by Sonora Dodd of Washington, in appreciation of her own father, and in direct imitation of the new Mother's Day, which was beginning to gain support at the time. It took much longer to catch on than Mother's Day had done, but was finally recognized by a joint resolution of Congress in 1956, and received Presidential support in 1966 and 1972. In the latter year it was officially set as the third Sunday in June. Father's Day entered British popular culture in the wake of Mother's Day sometime after the Second World War, not without opposition, and many still regard it as a 'card-day' too far.

20 June

Mayor of Ock Street

One of the few surviving mock-mayor ceremonies in England, albeit in extremely attenuated form, is the election of the Mayor of Ock Street in Abingdon, Oxfordshire, each June. The mayor has no duties or powers, but serves as the squire of the local morris team.

In the nineteenth century, Ock Street was the proverbial 'rough end' of town, which is exactly the kind of place one would expect to find a mock-mayor custom, but the history of the ceremony has proved surprisingly difficult to chart with any certainty. Indeed, there is no record of a mock mayor before the 1860s, and its history is inextricably bound up with other, much older traditions: the local horse fair, which was formerly held each year in Ock Street on 20 June, until it was moved in 1876; and the local morris team, which claims to have been in existence for nearly 500 years. However, although there is a record of a payment for morris bells in the churchwardens' accounts for St Helen's church in Abingdon, in 1560, this does not prove the continuous existence of a morris team until the next evidence of one, in 1783. For much of its recorded history, the position of mayor has been held by members of the Hemmings family, who were also stalwarts of the morris team, and the holder of the office is now always a morris man. The modern morris side carries a pair of ox horns, mounted on a pole, on which is painted the date '1700', and this is often given as the date of foundation of both the dancing and the mayor-making. Keith Chandler, in his paper delivered at the Calendar Customs conference in 1984 (published in 1993), ably presents such conflicting and confusing evidence as is available.

See also **Mock Mayors and Courts**, p. 298.

21 June

Brecknell Bequest

Charity doles often include seemingly bizarre details, which may once have had a rational basis or may simply have stemmed from the whim or sense of humour of the benefactor. The Brecknell bequest is an example of the latter, and is described in John Noake's *Guide to Worcestershire* (1868):

[Kidderminster] *A bachelor named Brecknell, in 1778, bequeathed a farthing loaf and twopenny cake annually to every single person, born in Church Street, who would apply for it on the 21st of June. The mere residents of that street, if not born there, are also entitled to a cake, but their claim is forfeited when they leave the street. The recipients make themselves truly 'jolly' on the night of the distribution.*

For those born in the street, the right to this dole lasted for life, and tradition has it that it was once claimed by someone living in America. Bequests such as this would have done little to relieve real poverty, but if the purpose was primarily to perpetuate the benefactor's name, then this was duly achieved for a century or so.

   See also **Doles**, p. 115.

23 June

Midsummer Eve/St John's Eve

See 24 June: Midsummer's Day/St John the Baptist's Day.

24 June

Midsummer's Day/St John the Baptist's Day

Midsummer was undoubtedly one of the high spots of the festival year in medieval times, but the widespread modern idea that it was formerly regarded as one of the times of year when fairies and sprites were abroad is wrong. This notion is based solely on a literal reading of the title of Shakespeare's comedy *A Midsummer Night's Dream*, but the text makes clear that the play's action takes place on May Day Eve, which in European folklore is certainly the time when fairy and mortal worlds were believed to intermingle. In England, there is little folkloric evidence of a connection between midsummer and

continued on page 300

Mock Mayors and Courts

In towns and villages up and down the country, the pomp and ceremony that surrounded local government and politics was deliberately parodied in raucous ceremonies which appointed a mock mayor, or occasionally a mock Member of Parliament or even a mock king. These burlesque officers often had traditional names that matched their sham status (for example the Mayor of Bartlemas (Newbury), the Lord Mayor of Pennyless Cove (Tenby), and the Mayor of Shamickshire (Bideford)), and were appointed in ways that poked pointed fun at the real dignitaries. Although many details varied widely, the basic structure of mock-mayor ceremonies was remarkably similar from place to place. He was invariably 'chaired' around the neighbourhood, or he rode a 'charger' (usually a donkey) around the town; he might carry a mace made of a cabbage stalk, in order to ridicule official regalia, and he often made preposterous speeches, promising food and drink for all, or gave out ludicrous summary judgments to punish imaginary transgressions by bystanders. He was often accompanied by his 'mayoress', a man dressed in women's clothes, which greatly increased the scope for ribald and coarse humour.

Before the passing of the 1836 Municipal Reform Act swept them away, there were indeed many civic and manorial customs and offices that had clearly outlived their usefulness and these were ripe for parody. A description of a real mayor-making in Exeter in the 1820s shows what the mock ones were satirizing:

The Mayors were nominated by the body, the freemen being nominally the electors. I never remember any opposition. On the day of the election, the members of the body and freemen assembled in the Guildhall; the intended Mayor was proposed, with the other officials; after taking the oath and duly signing the documents, on the cheering subsiding, the Hall echoed with the sound of various drawings of bottled wine corks . . . A procession was then formed to perambulate the city walls, headed by the tradesmen's corps or constables, about twenty-four in number; then the staff and mace-bearers, sword-bearer, the Mayor elect walking uncovered, with his hat in hand; Aldermen, with scarlet robes and three-cornered hats, followed by members and officials; in the rear being three tradesmen's sons, named Mayor's stewards (the outside one called gutter steward), wearing long black robes, with tufts and three-cornered hats.

If this had survived to the present day we would cherish it as a piece of traditional pageantry, but at that time it must have struck a sour note with those who had no say in the way their community, or even their country, was governed. Nevertheless, the idea that mock mayors were an overt protest by a politically aware but disenfranchised underclass is hardly sustainable, although there must have been elements of this in some instances. Most of the evidence points to the parody as being just a bit of fun.

It is no surprise that Exeter had its own regular mock mayor. When china-dealer 'Sir Osborn China' was 'elected' and paraded round the town in the 1830s, he wore a chamberpot on his head, which he removed when ladies were present, and his election speech included something for everybody:

And that you may be enabled to have tea cheaper, I will order a canal to be cut, that the largest ships from China shall come close to your doors; your mill stream shall be turned into milk, beer shall be pumped from your wells, made from the finest malt and hops that can be procured.

Mock-mayor ceremonies could be held at any time of year. Where there was a real mayor, the burlesque usually took place on or near the day of the mayor-making, but others gravitated to coincide with the local feast, such as at Oswaldkirk, in North Yorkshire, where the mock mayor presided over the annual three-day fair in July. Some, like the famous one at Garratt, in Wandsworth, south London, were timed to coincide with national elections.

In some places, the joke was extended, and a mock corporation or mock court had a more permanent existence. At Walton-Le-Dale in Lancashire, the mock corporation grew from a Jacobite Club, founded in 1701, while the mock court of Halgavor in Cornwall, as recorded by Richard Carew in 1602, had less exalted aims:

The youthlier sort of Bodmin townsmen use sometimes to sport themselves by playing the box with strangers, whom they summon to Halgavor. The name signifieth the Goat's Moor, and such a place it is, lying a little without the town, and full of quagmires. When these mates meet with any raw servingman or other young master who may serve and deserve to make pastime, they cause him to be solemnly arrested for his appearance before the mayor of Halgavor, where he is charged with wearing one spur, or going

untrussed, or wanting a girdle, or some such felony; and after he hath been arraigned and tried with all requisite circumstances, judgment is given in formal terms and executed in some ungracious prank or other, more to the scorn than hurt of the party concerned. Hence is sprung the proverb, when we see one slovenly apparelled, to say, 'He shall be presented in Halgavor court'.

Most mock-mayor customs had disappeared by the late nineteenth century, although a few lasted until the early twentieth, and one or two still survive in one form or another. Civic pride was no doubt piqued by these parodies, which must have played a part in their demise, but in truth they were also drunken and riotous affairs, openly organized or supported by local publicans, and often shamelessly using 'dim-witted' locals to play the part of mayor. There was also a local notion that normal laws were suspended on mayor-making day, when people believed they could get away with anything (*see* Lawless Hours and Days, p. 412). The 'ceremonies' were thus mostly attacked on public order grounds, and put down by the police – although suppression was not always a simple matter, as demonstrated by the mayor-making on the annual club day at Chipping, Lancashire, in 1881, reported by the *Antiquary*. Here, '[t]he police interfered and summoned ten of the men before the Clitheroe magistrates for being drunk', but the court 'dismissed all the cases, one of the justices remarking that he approved of old customs being carried out'.

See also Second Saturday in May: Randwick Wap; 20 June: Mayor of Ock Street; 6 July: Kilburn Feast; 26 July: Mace Monday.

☞ *continued from page 297* the supernatural, except in the limited sense that it was one of the favourite times for love **divination** (*see* p. 304). Another factor that has contributed to our mistaken view of midsummer is the unfounded belief that at this time of year Druids used to worship the rising sun at Stonehenge, for which a string of romantic antiquarians are at fault. As Stuart Piggott commented in his classic book on Druids, 'In [John] Aubrey's tentative association of Stonehenge and other prehistoric stone circles with the Druids is the germ of an idea which was to run like lunatic wildfire through all popular and much learned thought, and particularly emotive feeling, until modern times.' In fact, from the time of the earliest records, midsummer in England was celebrated with bonfires, processions and parades, and by decorating houses and churches with greenery.

By many accounts, it seems that the whole period between St John the Baptist's Eve (23 June) and St Peter's Day (29 June) was regarded as one festival, loosely termed 'midsummer', and many customs and celebrations could be found throughout that time. The flavour of the season is indicated in John Stow's famous description of midsummer in London in the 1590s:

In the months of June and July, on the vigils of festival days, and on the same festival days in the evening after the sun setting, there were usually made bonfires in the streets, every man bestowing wood or labour towards them; the wealthier sort also, before their doors near to the said bonfires, would set out tables on the vigils, furnished with sweet bread and good drink, and on the festival days with meats and drinks plentifully, where-unto they would invite their neighbours and passengers also to sit and be merry with them in great familiarity, praising God for His benefits be-stowed on them. These were called bonfires as well of good amity amongst neighbours that being before at controversy, were there, by the labour of others, reconciled, and made of bitter enemies loving friends; and also for the virtue that a great fire hath to purge the infection of the air. On the vigil of St. John the Baptist, and on St. Peter and Paul the Apostles, every man's door being shadowed with green birch, long fennel, St. John's wort, orpin, white lilies, and such like, garnished upon with garlands of beautiful flow-ers, had also lamps of glass, with oil burning in them all the night; some hung out branches of iron curiously wrought, containing hundreds of lamps alight at once, which made a goodly show.

Churches, too, were bedecked with birch boughs. The records of St Mary-at-Hill church in London, for example, include many referenc-es to payments for 'birch at Midsummer' nearly every year throughout the fifteenth century, and it is interesting to note that they refer to the season by that secular name rather than St John's Day.

Stow rightly stressed the dual purpose of the bonfires – peace and good neighbourhood on the one hand, and on the other the belief that the smoke of bonfires was medicinal, and purified the air. For this rea-son, sixteenth-century religious reformers branded midsummer fires as 'superstitious' and they were finally suppressed. However, the im-pulse to build bonfires is too strong, especially on a summer's evening, to be laid aside to order. Even Henry Bourne, curate of All Hallows

Dumb Cake

One of the earliest descriptions of the dumb cake was included in an anonymous chapbook published in London in 1685, entitled *Mother Bunch's Closet Newly Broke Open*. Every page of this little book is devoted to ways in which young women can divine their future love life, and in particular how they can determine who their future husband will be. These divinatory procedures range from the simple to the complex, and one of the latter is to make what is here headed the 'Dutch Cake', although every other source calls it a 'dumb cake', on Midsummer Eve.

Three, or four, or more of you are to make a cake of half flour and half salt (no matter what flour it is) and some of every one of your own water, make this cake broad and thin, then every one of you either make a mark that you know or set the first two letters of your name on it with a pin or bodkin, but leave such distance that it may be cut; then set it before the fire to bake, but all this while speak not a word. Turn it every one of you once, then let it bake a little more, and then throw on every one a little salt, and she that turn'd it first let her turn it again, then the person to be her husband will cut out her name and break it in two and give her one half, and so the next, till the last. If there be any so unfortunate to hear a bell, I wish I had them to my bedfellows this night to prevent leading apes in hell . . .

Although it is underplayed here, it is the wraith of her future husband who will appear and break the cake with the girl, not the real person, and it is this that gave the procedure the thrill of the supernatural. The key principle in this type of ceremony is that it has to be difficult, both as a test of the participant's resolve and as a way of ensuring that any perceived failure can be blamed on some tiny deviation from the rules rather than a failure of the underlying principle. The dumb cake therefore has to be made by several people in co-operation, in total silence from start to finish, and the ingredients are so unpleasant that it is a real trial to eat. The high concentration of salt, and the frequently recorded use of soot or urine, would certainly test anyone's determination. Mother Bunch does not actually stipulate that the girls must eat the cake, but in nearly all the other recorded versions they do, and this resulted in the participants making tiny, thimble-size cakes, which stuck to the letter of the rules but were far easier to cope with.

in Newcastle, and not usually one to tolerate any hint of popishness in popular custom, seemed loath to condemn the bonfire outright in his *Antiquitates Vulgares* (1725):

But whatever reason the heathens had for kindling these fires . . . it was certain that the custom was invented and practised by them; and because of the superstition attending the observation of it, was very justly forbidden by the Council. And undoubtedly was the making of such fires now attended with any such superstition, it would be equally criminal to observe them, but when they are only kindled as tokens of joy, to excite innocent mirth and diversion, and promote peace and good neighbourhood, they are lawful and innocent, and deserve no censure. And therefore when on Midsummer-Eve, St. Peter's Eve, and some other times, we make bonfires before shops and houses there would be no harm in doing so, was it not that some continue their diversion to too late hours, and others are guilty of excessive drinking.

Later folklorists found, or thought they found, lingering remnants of fire customs at midsummer in various parts, and the tradition of lighting bonfires seemed particularly tenacious in the West Country, but even these faded out until revived by the self-conscious inventions of the Old Cornwall Society in the 1930s. (For an event that retains the atmosphere of the communal fires of olden times, *see* **4 July: Whalton Baal Fire.**)

The other main feature of Midsummer was the processions. These had their ultimate origin in urban areas in the musters of the local watch, who were charged with policing the city at night, and were commanded to accompany the mayor and aldermen in procession on Midsummer and St Peter's Eve, as much as a show of strength as of civic dignity and pride. Trade guilds also had their parades, and in towns that could muster the necessary manpower and resources, these processions became spectacular torch-lit affairs, with giants, devils, hobby horses, drummers, trumpeters, armed mounted and marching companies, and tableaux depicting famous scenes. Something of the flavour of the late medieval midsummer processions can be gleaned from visiting the one processional giant to have survived – now safely housed in Salisbury Museum. This splendid giant belonged to the local Tailors' Guild, and was an essential feature of their annual midsummer processions until the Reformation declared such figures 'superstitious'. He may have been repaired, remade, reclothed, and repainted many times, but to all intents and purposes he is still the same giant.

The Tailors' Guild had been chartered in 1447, and had been staging pageants and processions for many years before the Giant was first mentioned in its records in 1570, when they planned to 'sett goinge for the accustomed pageant of Mydsomer feaste, the Gyant, the thre black boyes, the bearer of the gyant and one person to play the Divell's part'. As the same entry speaks of making repairs to the Giant's coat, he was presumably not new at the time. St John the Baptist was the patron saint of tailors, so it was particularly appropriate for them to parade on 23 June, the eve of his feast. At some point, however, the giant became known as Christopher – presumably because that saint was the most famous giant in Christian legend, and many other processional giants were also associated with him in the popular mind.

When acquired by the museum in 1869, the Salisbury Giant was fourteen feet tall, but he was shortened a little to fit his new accommodation. His head is a piece of solid wood, but his body is a hollow open woodwork frame, light enough to be carried on the shoulders of one person hidden inside. He can therefore turn, sway, and tilt in a much more lifelike way than if he were simply wheeled along, although this brings the danger of accident, and in at least one photograph (from 1911) he can be seen lying flat on the ground. His attendants are called 'Whifflers' ('whiffler' is a name for an armed attendant in a procession, and dates back to at least the early sixteenth century), and carry his huge two-handed sword, and his 'mace', a rhomboid shape made of canvas on the end of a long pole. The museum also possesses Hobnob, a hobby horse, which has accompanied the Giant on his outings since the sixteenth century. Morris dancers also featured regularly in the processions. From the eighteenth century onwards, the Salisbury Giant has only been brought out on special occasions, usually royal events such as coronations and jubilees, or to celebrate major military victories.

Finally, commenting on the weather around midsummer, Devon folklorist Sarah Hewett wrote in 1900, 'Before St John's Day we pray for rain, after that we get it anyhow.'

Divination

Midsummer's Day and Eve may not have been particularly well known for fairy activity, but they were regularly cited as times when particular divinations could be successfully carried out, such as watching in the church porch at midnight to see who in the parish would die in the coming year (*see* **24 April: St Mark's Eve**). Love divinations, such as sowing the hemp seed – whereby girls threw hemp seed over their shoulders, out of doors at night, in the hope of seeing the form of their future husband – and making a **dumb cake** (*see* p. 302), were also popularly carried out at this time, although they too could also be performed on other nights of the year. Two divinatory procedures, however, were only carried out at midsummer. The most widespread was a simple procedure called 'Midsummer Men', mentioned by John Aubrey in his *Remaines of Gentilisme and Judaisme* (1686) as being performed in Wiltshire in his day:

I remember, the maids (especially the cook-maids and dairy-maids) would stick up in some chinks of the joists, etc., Midsummer-men, which are slips of orpines. They placed them by pairs, one for such a man, the other for such a maid his sweetheart, and accordingly as the orpine did incline to, or recline from ye other, that there would be love, or aversion; if either did wither, death.

The same procedure was being tried right into the twentieth century. Orpine was so often the plant used for this ceremony that it was called 'Midsummer men' in local dialects across the country. The other midsummer love-divination also involved plants, but this one needed better preparation, as described by Mrs Bray in Devon in 1838:

It is said here that if a young woman, blind-folded, plucks a full-blown rose, on Midsummer day, while the chimes are playing twelve, folds the rose up in a sheet of white paper and does not take out the rose until Christmas, it will be found fresh as when gathered. Then, if she places the rose on her bosom, the young man to whom she is to be married will come and snatch it away.

Election of Sheriffs

The two Sheriffs of the City of London are elected by the City Livery Companies on 24 June, to serve for one year. They take office on 28 September, the day before the new Lord Mayor does so. The sheriffs' primary function is to support the Lord Mayor in carrying out his duties, which includes presenting petitions to Parliament and attending sessions at the Central Criminal Court. Candidates for Lord Mayor must have previously served as sheriff, and while the latter are mentioned as early as the seventh century, the title of Lord Mayor only came into being in 1189.

This ceremony, revived in 1924, involves the presentation of a red rose to the Lord Mayor of London every 24 June at the Mansion House in London. The story behind this custom tells of how Lady Constance, wife of Sir Robert Knollys, built a footbridge in 1381 connecting two of her properties in Seething Lane, London, without first obtaining the Lord Mayor's permission, for which she was fined one rose each year. That custom fell into disuse in the seventeenth century, and the present ceremony was revived by the Revd 'Tubby' Clayton (founder of the organization Toc H), who entrusted its continuance to the Company of Watermen and Lightermen.

Magdalen Outdoor Sermon

In medieval times, a 'spital' was a charity hospital that catered for the poorest people in society, and therefore usually had the reputation of being a foul and pestiferous place. One of the ways in which money was raised to support these institutions was for a special annual church service, with sermon, to be given, attended by local dignitaries. Given the nature of these hospitals, however, it was traditional to hold these meetings out of doors. One surviving example, which lapsed in the nineteenth century, but was revived in 1896, is the sermon preached at Magdalen College, Oxford, on a Sunday morning near 24 June. The pulpit is built into the outside wall of the College, on the site of which the Hospital of St John the Baptist previously stood, and the congregation includes the President, Vice-Chancellor, and senior Proctors, seated in state on the lawn.

Another 'spital sermon' takes place two weeks after Easter at St Lawrence Jewry church, Gresham Street, in London, but this one is nowadays held indoors; *see* **Two weeks after Easter: Spital Sermon**, p. 184.

Midsummer Cushions

A picturesque custom, reported by M. A. Denham as common in northern England in the late eighteenth century but which had died out by his time in the 1850s, was the making and displaying of Midsummer Cushions:

The young lads and lasses of the town or village having procured a cushion . . . and covered it with calico, or silk of showy and attractive colour, proceeded to bedeck it with every variety of flower which they could procure out of their parents' and more wealthy neighbours' gardens, displaying them in such a manner so as to give it a most beautiful appearance. All this done, they placed themselves, with their cushion of Flora's choicest gems, in the most public place they conveniently could, soliciting of every passer-by a tri-fling present of pence, which in numerous cases was liberally and cheerfully bestowed . . . This custom prevailed from Midsummer Day to Magdalene Day [22 July], which latter has long been corrupted to 'Maudlin Day' . . .

Unfortunately, Denham never managed to obtain the rhyme that accompanied this display custom. In 1778, John Hutchinson reported a similar custom from Northumberland, but explained that the cushions were made out of stools, with a layer of clay smeared on top, and flowers stuck into the clay. A similar custom of the same name was reported by the Northamptonshire poet John Clare: in preparing a manuscript collection of his poems for publication in 1832, which he proposed to call *The Midsummer Cushion*, he wrote in explanation of the term, 'It is a very old custom among villagers in summer time to stick a piece of greensward full of field flowers & place it as an ornament in their cottages which ornaments are called Midsummer Cushions.'

26 June

St Anne's Day

For many years, the rush-bearing custom at Ambleside in Westmorland was held on the nearest Saturday to St Anne's Day, but it now takes place at the beginning of July; *see* **First Saturday in July: Ambleside Rush-Bearing**.

28 June

St Peter's Eve/St Paul's Eve

See **29 June: St Peter's Day/St Paul's Day.**

29 June

St Peter's Day/St Paul's Day

Considering the pre-eminence of Sts Peter and Paul in early Christian history, and their continued popularity ever since, it might seem strange that no particular festivals and few customs have been recorded for this day. However, they were simply too close to St John's Eve and Day to acquire many customs of their own, and instead became incorporated into a midsummer festival season that lasted until the end of the month (*see* **24 June: Midsummer's Day/St John the Baptist's Day**).

In some areas it was said that the weather on St Peter's Day was crucial to the apple crop, as in this example from Herefordshire in 1886:

Unless the apples are christened on St. Peter's Day the crop will not be good; and there ought to be a shower of rain when the people will go through the orchards, but no one seems to know for what purpose exactly.

But similar things are also said of St Swithun's Day (*see* **15 July**), and sometimes of St James's Day (*see* **25 July**).

Bawming the Thorn

In the Cheshire village of Appleton, they have a seemingly unique custom called 'Bawming the Thorn', which is performed on or near 29 June each year. Local primary-school children decorate a hawthorn tree with ribbons, garlands, and flags, then dance round it singing their 'bawming song', and later have a tea, some sports, and a fancy-dress parade. The tree stands in the middle of the village, and is protected with railings; the present one dates from 1967, when its predecessor blew down. It is not known how many trees have come and gone on the site before, but the original is said to have been an offshoot of the famous Glastonbury thorn, and was brought to Appleton by Adam de Dutton, lord of the manor in the twelfth century. Local tradition maintains that the bawming custom also dates back to that time but was allowed to lapse in Victorian times and was revived in the 1930s – although there must have been other lapses, as the current series commenced in 1973. Some have stated that it goes back even further to times of pagan tree-worship.

The bawming song was composed by a local man named Rowland Eyles Egerton Warburton (1804–91), probably in the 1860s:

Up with fresh garlands this midsummer morn
Up with red ribbons on Appleton thorn
Come lasses and lads to the Thorn Tree today
To bawm it and shout as ye bawm it 'Hurray!'

The word 'bawm' is no help in tracing the custom's development. It is usually glossed simply as 'decorating', and is always assumed to be an ancient word, but the *Oxford English Dictionary* does not include it. Joseph Wright's *English Dialect Dictionary* does, and he gives several examples of its use, but all refer to the Appleton custom, except one later example from Cumberland, so we have no earlier use of the word than the custom itself. The earliest written description so far found is in Roger Wilbraham's *An Attempt at a Glossary of Some Words used in Cheshire* (1817), and this shows that the custom and name were already in existence in the early nineteenth century:

At Appleton it was the custom at the time of the Wake to clip and adorn an old hawthorn which till very lately stood in the middle of the town. The ceremony is called the Bawming of Appleton Thorn.

The real clue to the origin of the custom is Wilbraham's mention of the local wake, and in the absence of any other evidence it seems likely that the bawming is simply the survival of general village wake decorations (*see* **Fairs, Feasts, Wakes, and Revels**, p. 341). The dating of the tree to the twelfth century is highly questionable, and we can dismiss the tree-worship theory without hesitation. As regards the idea of the Glastonbury thorn, which nowadays seems to be said about nearly every plant-based custom in the country, it is interesting to note that although local author William Beament includes the story in his book *An Account of the Cheshire Township of Appleton Thorn* (1877), in his unpublished diary entry for 30 July 1844 he makes it clear that at that time he was in complete ignorance as to the origin of the custom.

A piece in the *Warrington Guardian* of 29 July 1912, shows that the 'Fête at Appleton Thorn' was alive and well at that time and that the celebrations then were much as they are now, except there is no mention of fancy dress. Children and officials paraded the village, led by a band, the children danced round the tree carrying bouquets and singing Warburton's song, and then hung their flowers on the fence. There was a tea, and then sports and games – including tug-of-war, climbing the greasy pole, and men's and women's slow bicycle races.

Jankyn Smyth was a major benefactor to Bury St Edmunds in Suffolk, founding almshouses and building the town's guildhall. When he died, in 1481, he founded a charity that would ensure that he was remembered. He instructed that on the anniversary of his death a requiem mass should be said, for the benefit of his soul, attended by the town's officials and the residents of the almshouses. After the mass, the participants would be treated to cakes and ale. He could not have known, of course, that the Reformation was just around the corner, when masses for the dead would be abolished. Fortunately, the Bury officials substituted sermons for the masses, and it continues to this day, attended by civic dignitaries and schoolchildren. It is said to be the oldest endowed service in England, and usually takes place on the Thursday before 29 June.

Warcop Rush-Bearing

Warcop is one of the five places in Cumbria that have existing rush-bearing ceremonies, and the distinctive feature of its celebrations is the ornate floral crown worn by each girl, as recorded in the *Cumbrian* magazine (1995):

The girls of the village wearing their best dresses are crowned with garlands made of rushes, ferns, mosses and flowers and the boys carry symbolic crosses made of rushes bound with red ribbon. To the sound of the brass band, all the villagers, young and old, walk from village to church where a special service is held to bless the rushes.

The ornate crowns contrast well with the simple crosses. The procession takes place on St Peter's Day, although the church is dedicated to St Columba (whose feast day is on 9 June), and the clergy meet the children at the church gate, and lead them into the church, which is also decorated with flowers.

See also **Rush-Bearing**, p. 322.

June/July

Yarnton Lot Meadow

In earlier forms of farming, villages often had open hayfields, held in common, in which various villagers had rights to a share of the yield. Rather than simply getting all the hay in and dividing it, complex systems usually evolved whereby parcels of land within the field were allotted to each individual. As the quality of the land and crop varied, lots were drawn to determine who got the hay from which plot. At Yarnton, four miles from Oxford, the three meadows of Pixey, Oxhay, and West Mead were formerly treated in this way, but only the latter remains. The field is divided into thirteen lots. An auction is first held to sell the rights to the hay, and those who have bought rights assemble at 8 a.m. on the meadow on the Monday after St Peter's Day, where the two Head Meadsmen are in charge of drawing the lots. The thirteen individual strips of meadow are marked with wooden pegs, and the Meadsmen draw small wooden balls from a bag to determine who gets which strips. The balls bear names such as Boat, Freeman, Gilbert, and Watery Molly, which were presumably the names of previous tenants. Once the hay is cut, those with rights can also graze cattle or horses on the field.

Previously, the hay was cut on one day, but this necessitated the influx of a large number of temporary workers, whose bad behaviour gave the event a bad name, and it was decided to spread the haymaking over three days so that local workers could manage it themselves. There were also celebrations after the haymaking, with decorated wagons, morris dancing, races, and a prize garland, but this too was suppressed in 1840 when the local vicar complained to the landlord.

See also 5 July: Old Midsummer's Day for a similar open field procedure at Congresbury and Puxton in Somerset.

Well-Dressing

Without doubt the prettiest and most artistic of English customs, well-dressing is now found in many villages across the country; however, its real home is in Derbyshire, where it can be found in over eighty villages, including Youlgreave, Wirksworth, Tideswell, and, the most famous of them all, Tissington. Different villages undertake their dressing when convenient to themselves, at any time between May and August, but at Tissington it is usually carried out on Ascension Day. Many villages decorate a well or spring, but some bedeck another form of water feature, and a few decorate something that has no connection with water at all.

A simplified description of what is involved in well-dressing is as follows. One or more boards with a raised edge are prepared, depending on the size of the project. Hundreds of nails are driven into the board, to help keep the other materials in place, and it is then covered with a smooth layer of well-puddled clay, half an inch to an inch thick. The basic design has already been marked out on large sheets of paper, which are laid across the board, and the lines of the picture are pricked out through the paper on to the clay. The outlines of the design are then filled out, using hard objects such as small cones, berries, seeds, or pieces of wood. The full picture is then coloured in, painstakingly, using moss, leaves, and individual flower petals, all pressed into the clay by hand. The work is hugely labour-intensive, and requires patience, dexterity, and skill in equal measure. Many of the villages pride themselves on using nothing but natural organic materials.

The frames are then transported to the site, where they are set up, the largest often needing a scaffolding frame to keep them in position. Some consist of a simple flat screen, while others have side and top panels. Biblical scenes are by far the most common, but sometimes local scenes, or a topical reference to some national celebration, are depicted.

Most present-day well-dressings have a relatively short history, either originating in the last few decades, or being revivals of traditions from the nineteenth or early twentieth century. However, the earlier history of well-dressing is not at all easy to ascertain, and the picture is considerably distorted by extravagant claims that well-dressing has been carried out, in an unbroken tradition, for 600 or 700 years, or even that the custom stretches in an uninterrupted line back to pagan times. Certainly, archaeological evidence shows that some wells and other water features were the focus of attention or veneration at periods before the Christian era; however, the new Christian Church spent much time and effort both trying to suppress such 'superstitious veneration' and trying to promote its own holy wells, although not necessarily at the same time. Some 'pagan' sites were rededicated to Christian saints, and continued in use, but most, it seems, were not.

Be that as it may, early documentary references to 'decorated' wells refer to them as being adorned with rags, ribbons, garlands, and so on, which may have been personal relics left by those who had attended the well for a cure or to ask a favour, or they may have been decoration as celebration or veneration. With this possible ambiguity in mind, the earliest references to 'well-dressing' become less than clear; as, for example, the following extract, which appeared in the *Gentleman's Magazine* in 1794:

In the village of Tissington . . . it has been the custom, time immemorial, on every Holy Thursday, to decorate the wells with boughs of trees, garlands of tulips and other flowers, placed in various fancied devices.

Nevertheless, not long after this, in 1818, Ebenezer Rhodes provided a good description of the custom, which does follow the modern well-dressing form:

. . . newly-gathered flowers disposed in various boards . . . cut to the figures intended to be represented, and covered with moist clay into which the stems of the flowers are inserted . . .

The first confirmatory picture appeared in *The Mirror* on 20 May 1837.

As the evidence stands, therefore, well-dressing as we know it today cannot be shown to have existed earlier than the late eighteenth century – over a thousand years after Christianity reached these shores. It is also noteworthy that all the pre-1820 evidence for well-dressing relates to the village of Tissington, making it possible that, far from being a widespread ancient custom, it was unique to Tissington and spread to other nearby villages in the early nineteenth century. Tissington is not one of those wells that contain archaeological proof of previous votive use.

JULY

Ashburton Ale-Tasting

See **Fourth Tuesday in November: Ashburton Court Leet.**

Early July

Fairlop Fair

Fairlop Fair, an immensely popular haunt for visitors from east London and Essex, took place in early July around a huge oak tree in Hainault or Epping Forest (about ten miles out of London and two miles from Chigwell). The oak was reputed to be thirty-six feet in circumference, and was clearly centuries old. The fair was founded by Daniel Day (born 1683), block- and pump-maker, who used to visit the area every year to collect rent from land he owned there, and was in the habit of inviting his tenants and friends to an outdoor meal of bacon and beans under the tree. Others apparently started to join in, and before he knew it, a full-blown fair with stalls and sideshows had developed around him. He was well aware of his founding-father status, and revelled in the fair each year until his death in 1767. Day's coffin was made from a branch that had fallen from the tree, and he asked to be buried at its foot, but was actually laid to rest in nearby St Margaret's, Barking.

This story has the rounded contours of an oft-told, oft-copied ac-count, and it may not be strictly true in all details. It is likely, for example, that such an impressive tree had already attracted al fresco gatherings before Day's time, and that he extended or formalized them. The tree continued to be the focal point of the fair, although it was damaged by a fire started by careless picnickers in 1805, until it was finally blown down in 1820. The wood was used to make the pulpit and reading desk of St Pancras church on Euston Road, London, and a number of other commemorative items, some of which still exist.

In its heyday, Fairlop attracted huge numbers of pleasure-seekers and was a regular feature of the Essex calendar, as reported in the *Illustrated London News* on 15 July 1843:

According to ancient custom 'gay Fairlop' was held on 'the first Friday in July on the borders of Hainault or Epping Forest, and drew together an immense number of persons. The block-makers, sail-makers, mast-makers, as usual, proceeded to the forest at an early hour in their amphibious-looking 'frigates', mounted on carriages, rigged out like ships, and decorated with colours. Each of these vehicles was drawn by six horses, gaily dressed out, and the wives of the men in their holiday gear followed in open landaus. The booths and shows were not so numerous as on former occasions, and the restriction of the fair to one day by the Essex magistrates has sadly diminished the profits of those who cater for the public. The Gipsies were uncommonly numerous; but the thimble and pea-riggers were dispersed by the police, and quitted the fair amidst the hootings of the people . . . The conduct of the assembled thousands was marked by the greatest good humour and decorum, and there was not a single police charge arising out of 'the first Friday in July'.

The detail of the trippers' 'frigates' is illustrated in Robert Chambers' *Book of Days* (1864), which shows a horse-drawn cart made up to look just like a sailing ship. The picturesque qualities of the old oak were also much appreciated by artists, and numerous illustrations and prints were produced. In common with many fairs, attempts at restriction and suppression continued through the Victorian era, but the Fairlop Fair struggled on until 1900, when it finally disappeared.

See also **Fairs, Feasts, Wakes, and Revels,** p. 341.

4 July

Stagshawbank Fair

Stagshawbank Fair, held annually at Corbridge in Northumberland, sixteen miles west of Newcastle, was one of the biggest and most popular fairs in the north of England for at least 700 years. It was originally held at midsummer, but 4 July (old Midsummer Eve) became the traditional date after the change of calendar in 1752 (*see* p. xxix). The fair was certainly in existence in 1204, and possibly originated before the Norman Conquest.

As with other villages in the area, on both sides of the border, there was a perennial fear of attack by raiders, right up to the turn of the eighteenth century, but in more peaceful times the fair attracted crowds of buyers and sellers from Scotland as well as all over the north of England. During the Middle Ages, Stagshawbank was particularly known for metalwork products, and in 1314 the King's agent was present, buying up horseshoes and nails to equip the army in the Scottish wars. In later years, the fair became known primarily for the sale of livestock, especially sheep, but as with all big country fairs, the range of goods on sale was wide, as indicated by Robert Forster's description of the fair *c.*1850:

Besides horses, sheep, cattle, and swine, various articles of merchandise were offered for sale consisting of men's hats, boots, and shoes, these articles generally filled several stalls, the former being mostly from Hexham, and a considerable quantity of the latter from Corbridge. Jewellery and hardware stalls were prominent; saddlery and farming goods, such as hay rakes, forks, etc., were always plentiful, and always a large supply of cooperage goods, such as tubs, barrel churns, etc. Webs of cloth coarse and fine were shown to advantage on the green carpet by the side of the pond. The far-famed gloves, known as 'Hexham Tans', suitable for all purposes and for all classes, always formed noticeable articles of sale ... At the south side of the Horse Fair, in the distance you saw a strong made man somewhat elevated, with a crowd around him offering articles for sale; on approaching, we observe that it is Mr. C., from the once famous Dog Bank, Newcastle, selling watches by auction being for the most part forfeited pledges, the auctioneer assuring the public that each watch he offered was far superior to the one just sold, as once belonging to some squire or gentleman whose name was well known in the neighbourhood.

The opening of the fair was accompanied by a certain degree of ceremony, as the officials of the lord of the manor, the Duke of Northumberland, rode out in procession from Corbridge and around the boundaries of the fair site, accompanied by the Duke's piper. A proclamation to declare the fair open was read before any trading was allowed to commence.

Stagshawbank Fair was finally abolished in 1927, under powers of the Fairs Act of 1871, but people still flock to Corbridge every Spring Bank Holiday for the County Agricultural Show, which is traditionally the first such show of the season in the region. Stagshawbank Fair is also still remembered in the title of a traditional tune, popular with pipers from the area.

See also **Fairs, Feasts, Wakes, and Revels**, p. 341.

Whalton Baal Fire

As detailed under **24 June**, one of the dominant features of the traditional midsummer festival was the communal bonfire, and the best modern example of a fire that retains the atmosphere of those old days is the annual 'Baal Fire' at Whalton in Northumberland, just over five miles from Morpeth. The fire takes place on old Midsummer Eve and is built on the village green, close to the local pub; older accounts describe the care with which the young men of the village built the fire each year, and the way locals danced round and jumped through the flames – as young people do with bonfires the world over. It is unlikely that the fire is a direct survival from medieval times, although it could be. The name 'Baal' has excited many writers to flights of ancient fancy, but its origin is still unknown.

5 July

Old Midsummer's Day

In the open field systems that existed before enclosure, much ingenuity was devoted to ensuring that everyone got their fair share of the land and its produce.

Fairness depended largely on allotting scattered parcels or strips of land to those local inhabitants who had rights to a share, and in particular on ensuring that nobody got the best, or the worst, land every year. A relatively well-documented survival of the old system existed in one area of Somerset until 1811, which provides a good example of how such things were managed and the seemingly bizarre local customs that grew up over time. A description published by the county historian the Revd John Collinson while the practice there was still in operation gives a good summary:

> *In the parishes of Congresbury and Puxton are two large pieces of common land, called East and West Dolemoors, which are divided into single acres, each bearing a peculiar and different mark cut in the turf, such as a horn, four oxen and a mare, two oxen and a mare, pole-axe, cross, dung fork, oven, duck's nest, hand reel, and hare's tail. On the Saturday before Old-Midsummer, several proprietors of estates in the parishes of Congresbury, Puxton, and Week St. Lawrence, or their tenants, assemble on the commons. A number of apples are previously prepared, marked in the same manner with the beforementioned acres, which are distributed by a young lad to each of the commoners from a bag or hat. At the close of distribution each person repairs to his allotment, as his apple directs him, and takes possession for the ensuing year. An adjournment then takes place to the house of the overseer of Dolemoors (an officer annually elected from the tenants) where four acres, reserved for the purpose of paying expenses, are let by inch of candle, and the remainder of the day is spent in that sociability and hearty mirth, so congenial to the soul of a Somersetshire yeoman.*

However, nothing was simple is these old field systems. The acres, furlongs, and chains in which the land was measured were not standard sizes but local customary variations, the marks were symbolic rather than pictorial (the 'hare's tail' resembled a circle with a cross inside), and the number of tenants and plots seem to have had little direct relationship. The apples seem an unusually picturesque detail, but are strangely reminiscent of the situation at Yarnton, in Oxfordshire, where common land plots continue to be allotted each year by drawing wooden balls from a bag, each ball bearing a name that corresponds to a particular plot (*see* **June/July: Yarnton Lot Meadow**). Most of the detective work necessary to understand the situation has been recorded by Keith Gardner in *Bristol & Avon Archaeology*, to which article interested readers are directed.

See also **Candle Auctions**, p. 138.

6 July

Duck-Racing

The custom of 'duck-racing' was traditionally carried out in the Oxfordshire (previously Berkshire) village of Grove on the first Saturday after 6 July, as the culmination of the traditional Grove Feast. The village brook was dammed, and a series of ducks released on to the water, one at a time. Contestants had to catch the duck with their bare hands, and the winner kept it as a prize. *John Bull* magazine (1955) reported the words of one competitor:

> *'Duck racing isn't as easy as it sounds', says Albert Cook, who one year won five out of six races, 'I've seen a dozen men take twenty minutes to catch a duck.'*

There are many stories of spectators getting so excited that they jumped in the water fully clothed to join in the fun. According to local belief, the sport had been carried out in the village for over 200 years, which is such a modest figure in comparison with the claims of other customs that it may have been true. By the early 1960s, the RSPCA claimed that the sport was cruel to animals, and it was discontinued.

Kilburn Feast

Kilburn Feast, in North Yorkshire, is a mere shadow of what it used to be. In former times it was primarily a horse fair, with additional sideshows and village sports, although its origin is unclear, as the presumed charter, claimed to be of Charles II's time, is now lost.

The key feature of the present-day feast is the mock mayor and mayoress (the latter played by a man, of course), who are elected to direct proceedings. The couple are dressed in appropriate costumes, and they progress through the village in a handcart, fining people for ridiculous transgressions (in the manner of mock mayors everywhere) and thereby collecting money, food, and drink, which all go towards the feast. The first victim is the local landlord, who is fined a barrel of beer. Much of the fun is provided by the mayoress, who insists on kissing everyone 'she' can catch hold of, leaving bright-red lipstick traces on their faces. It is in the nature of traditional customs that they acquire and lose elements over the years. In the 1980s it was claimed that it was 'unlucky' for the identity of the mayoress to be guessed, but this can hardly have been a permanent feature – in July 1960, for example, the *Yorkshire Post* proudly announced 'her' identity as sixteen-year-old Peter Medhurst.

Locals are pleased to keep this a relatively low-key event. As one participant told author Julia Smith in the 1980s:

Johnny Kirk, whose family had been connected with the mayor-making over the years, said they did not want to make a big production of it or turn it into a tourist attraction; they wanted to keep it as it was, a local event for local people.

See also **Mock Mayors and Courts**, p. 298.

First Friday in July

Warrington Walking Day

Warrington, formerly located in Lancashire but now in Cheshire, is situated between Manchester and Liverpool. It hosts the biggest and best-known of the surviving walking days in the country, on the Friday of the first week in July each year. As with other such walks, church organizations together with groups such as the Guides and Scouts march proudly through the streets of the town, with banners, to the sound of various bands.

The Warrington Walk was reputedly started by local clergyman Revd Horace Powys, in 1834, as a counter-attraction to the local races, although Whit Walks in the Manchester area could have provided a model for it. Until 1857, only the Anglican churches took part, but the Roman Catholics, and, later, other denominations, then started to hold processions on the same day. Each denomination stuck to its own route until 1995, when a terrorist bomb brought a new feeling of solidarity to the local people and the churches started marching together. By tradition, local shops close while the walk is in progress, and although this is not so strictly observed now as it used to be, some still do. Nowadays, the walk attracts about 4,000 participants, from about thirty churches, but this is less than half the number who used to take part in its heyday before the Second World War.

See also **Whitsun: Whit Walks**, p. 266.

First Saturday in July

Ambleside Rush-Bearing

Of the five places in Cumbria that have existing rush-bearing ceremonies, Ambleside and Grasmere (*see* 5 **August: Grasmere Rush-Bearing**) are the most famous and attract the most participants and onlookers. As elsewhere, at Ambleside the main part of the celebration is the procession with band, banners, and villagers carrying rushes, flowers, and 'burdens' of rushes made into symbolic shapes. They parade around the village and up to the church, where a special service takes place, and those taking part are traditionally rewarded with gingerbread. For many years, the ceremony was held on the Saturday nearest St Anne's Day (26 July), as the present St Mary's church replaced one dedicated to St Anne, but it is now held on the first Saturday in July.

Nowadays, the 'bearings' or 'burdens' are mostly made from natural flowers and rushes, but for a time in the past they were primarily made of wood covered with coloured paper. Margaret Nicholson, whose parents ran the local post office in the mid nineteenth century, wrote down her memories of the burdens in 1898, and extracts were included in the 1953 booklet on rush-bearing by E. F. Rawnsley:

The 'burthens' were devices of every imaginable shape made by the carpenter for the great ladies, and by the skilful-handed ones at home during the winter months, covered with coloured papers and coloured flowers . . . Yards of tissue paper must have been used. Aye, we know about that, for we had to lay in a stock of blue and pink and yellow, and Mr. Harrison of Scale allowed us ten shillings to give away to the poor folk in sheets of tissue each year, and we used to cut it into frills for them for the making of rosettes and flowers.

Margaret's mother was in charge of making the collection to cover the cost of the gingerbread, and once they got 'refined' enough to replace the traditional fiddler with a proper band, for them too. The rush-bearing ceremony of half a century ago is depicted in a mural, twenty-six feet long, created by Gordon Ransom in 1944, which can be seen in St Mary's.

See also **Rush-Bearing**, p. 322.

Rush-Bearing

Until 200 years ago, rushes strewn on the floors of buildings for warmth and comfort would have been a common enough sight in many rural areas, and before that in urban settings too. Floor rushes were used extensively in domestic settings, from cottage to royal palace, although there were vast differences in how they were treated. At the upper levels of society the rushes were changed frequently, and herbs and flowers were mixed with them to keep them sweet, but at the lower end, new rushes were simply thrown on top of the foetid mess that had become of the previous ones. In the better houses it was also the custom to honour guests by putting down new rushes; 'Is the supper ready, the house trimm'd, rushes strew'd, cobwebs swept?' asks Grumio in Act IV, scene 1 of Shakespeare's *Taming of the Shrew*, and many other dramatists and poets of the time have referred to the practice. Queen Elizabeth I was probably the last monarch to have her palaces regularly strewn with rushes, but in other circles rush floors could still be found in some areas in the nineteenth century.

Churches were also regularly strewn with rushes. In early modern times, there were no pews and the congregation stood, or knelt, on the floor for the whole service. In unheated churches with earth or stone floors, this could be a serious trial, and a layer of rushes could make all the difference. Provision of rushes was normally the responsibility of the churchwardens, and they were chargeable to the parish, so payments appear regularly in early parish accounts. It was quite common also for devout parishioners to bequeath money to pay for the rushes, or to leave parcels of land from which the rushes could be cut annually.

As churches gradually acquired decent floors, rushes became superfluous and in most cases simply faded from the local scene, but the speed at which these changes took place varied widely from parish to parish. In Lancashire alone, for example, Kirkham church was flagged in 1634, but Saddleworth was not paved until 1826, and the floor of Pilling church was covered with rushes until about 1868. By the nineteenth century, however, rushes on church floors were seen by many as decidedly unhygienic and unbelievably antiquated.

As often happens with church-based events, the annual rush-strewing took on a celebratory aspect, giving a devotional spin to a practical occasion, and bringing the rushes to the church, or 'rush-bearing', became a major festival in which the whole community could join. Again there was wide variety within the custom, but two relatively distinct ways of rush-bearing developed. In Cheshire and Lancashire, the rushes were brought with much celebration on highly decorated carts during the village wakes, accompanied by drummers, musicians, and morris dancers, as in the following memory from Lancashire in the 1830s:

I remember going to stay at Radcliffe to see the rush-bearing . . . We stood out-of-doors to watch the procession coming up the road. The morris-dancers came along dancing, both men and women, and I think there was a clown. They were decked up with ribbons and things; the men had ribbons flying from their caps or hats and their shoulders. The cart (or I think it was a waggon) came after them. On the driving-seat, as I may call it, sat a man and a woman, Robin Hood and Maid Marian, in a green bower arching over their heads. Behind and above this was a tall erection, with straight sides and a pointed gable-ended top, all made of rushes, and against the flat front of it were hung large silver spoons and tankards, shining.

These rush-cart celebrations had taken shape by at least the 1720s, and had a carnival atmosphere. But in other places, the normal rush-bearing festival was a more controlled and dignified religious procession in which women and children took a prominent part, carrying flowers, token rushes, and symbolic devices in various shapes, such as crosses, harps, and crowns; it is this method of rush-bearing that has survived at places like Grasmere in Cumbria (*see* 5 **August: Grasmere Rush-Bearing**). This form of celebration is probably nearer to the original than the noisy extrovert festivities of the rush-carts, and James I's *Book of Sports* (1618), for example, which laid out the sports that were permissible on Sundays (*see* p. 354), specifically names rush-carrying as a female custom:

And that women shall have leave to carry rushes to the church for the decoring of it, according to their old custom.

Similarly, a description of Grasmere in the eighteenth century:

About the latter end of September, a number of young women and girls (generally the whole parish) go together to the tops of the hills to gather rushes. These they carry to the church, headed by one of the smartest girls in the company. She who leads the procession is styled the Queen, and carries in her hand a large garland, and the rest usually have nosegays. The Queen then goes and places her garland upon the pulpit, where it remains till after next Sunday, the rest then strew their rushes upon the bottom of the pews, and at the church

door they are met by a fiddler, who plays before them to the public house, where the evening is spent in all kinds of rustic merriment.

This evidence also demonstrates that it is somewhat simplistic to believe that the routine practice of replacing the rushes on a church floor suddenly became a symbolic ritual once the practical necessity had disappeared. It is clear that the rush-bearing had taken on a range of festival trappings at many churches long before their new flooring made them obsolete. At Grasmere again, where the floor was paved in 1840, a visitor noted in 1818 that:

. . . every part of the church crammed with all sorts of tawdry and ridiculous things stuck upon sticks, hoops, and crosses, and made to stand upright. These sticks were . . . covered with coloured paper, red, green and yellow, flowers of all sorts.

Some further questions still remain, such as why the major rush-cart festival developed in such a restricted area and, indeed, how the transformation from practical to festive actually took place. Some have assumed that the change was planned by the Church authorities, as in an article in *Country Home* magazine in June 1909:

In their wisdom, clergymen and churchwardens turned a matter of necessity into a religious festival, and thus won the interest and co-operation of the laity, which likes to have a prosaic duty glorified into something higher and more attractive.

But in her analysis of rush-carts and wakes published in 1982, Theresa Buckland rightly stresses the community's involvement in the rush-bearing celebrations – the collection of money from the local gentry, the loan of silver items to decorate the cart, and the hours spent embroidering sheets, sewing on ribbons, and constructing 'bearings' to carry – and implies that this was a relatively secularized custom that had been grafted on to a religious base.

Children's rush-bearing processions survive at five Cumbrian villages, and the rush-carts have been revived in recent years at several places, including Saddleworth and Sowerby Bridge.

See also Whit Sunday: St Mary Redcliffe Rush Sunday, p. 271; 29 June: Warcop Rush-Bearing; First Saturday in July: Ambleside Rush-Bearing; First Saturday in July: Great Musgrave Rush-Bearing; 5 August: Grasmere Rush-Bearing; 24 August: St Bartholomew's Day; 29 September: Urswick Rush-Bearing.

Great Musgrave Rush-Bearing

Great Musgrave is one of the five places in Cumbria that have existing rush-bearing ceremonies. Theirs is less well known than similar customs at Grasmere (*see* 5 **August: Grasmere Rush-Bearing**) or Ambleside (*see above*), and therefore preserves a more intimate village community feel. At two o'clock on the first Saturday in July, children form up behind the silver band and the village rush-bearing banner, while adult participants join in behind, and they all march from the village hall to St Theobold's church for a service that includes parts specially aimed at the children. The girls carry posies and wear floral crowns (made the day before to make sure they are still fresh), while the boys carry symbolic crosses made from green rushes bound at the centre and ends with red ribbon. These crowns and crosses are laid at the foot of the altar, but are removed on the following Monday when they are placed on special hooks in an arc above the west door, and there they stay till next year's rush-bearing. A tea is served in the village hall, and games are held in the neighbouring field to round off the day.

See also **Rush-Bearing**, p. 322.

Medway Admiralty Court

On the first Saturday in July, the Mayor of Medway assumes his or her other role as Admiral of the River Medway and in full regalia enters a gaily decorated barge moored on the river, to preside over the Medway Admiralty Court. This court regulates the fishery and oyster beds of the River Medway between Sheerness and Hawkwood Stone, near Snodland, in Kent, and takes its jurisdiction from a charter of Henry VI in 1446, which granted exclusive rights to the citizens of Rochester to take 'fish both great and small' from this part of the river. The court's powers were later codified in the Rochester Oyster Fishery Acts of 1729 and 1865. Daniel Defoe's *Tour through the Whole Island of Great Britain* (1724–6) described the court in the mid eighteenth century:

There is in the River Medway, at Rochester, and in several of its creeks and branches within the jurisdiction of the City, an oyster-fishery, which is free to every one who has served seven years apprenticeship to any fisherman or dredger, who is free of the said fishery, and the Mayor and citizens of Rochester hold a Court, commonly called An Admiralty Court, once a year, or oftener, when occasions have required it, for the regulating of the said fishery, and to prevent abuses committed in it. In these courts they appoint from time to time, when oysters shall and shall not be dredged and taken, which they call 'opening and shutting the Grounds'; also the quantity each dredgerman shall take in a day, which is usually called 'Setting the Stint'. They have power to go on board, and enforce these orders.

The court is still made up of Aldermen of the City, and a jury of free-men, who are the only ones allowed to fish the river. The main quali-fication for freeman is the seven-year apprenticeship to another free-man described by Defoe. In 2004 there were twenty-two Freemen of the River, and that year also saw the first-ever female apprentice in fourteen-year-old Robyn Wadhams.

For many years the Medway fisheries were in decline, but recent initiatives on conservation and water quality are showing results and fish stocks are improving rapidly. Unlike most of the courts that have survived from medieval times, the Admiralty Court still has a genuine function and real teeth: Medway Council and the Rochester Oyster and Floating Fishery continue to take action against poachers and unlawful fishing, and in 2003 they successfully prosecuted an Isle of Sheppey fisherman for encroaching on their stretch of the river.

Sunday in early July

Oxenhope Straw Race

The Oxenhope Straw Race is an excellent example of how a small fund-raising idea, hatched by individuals, can grow into a major com-munity event. The Pennine village of Oxenhope, near Keighley, West Yorkshire, hosts an annual race that started with a few friends in 1975 but now attracts hundreds of contestants from all over the country, and has so far raised over £250,000 for local charities. Each team, of at least two people, has to follow a prescribed route of about two and a half miles around the village, taking in five pubs, carrying a bale of straw, and drinking a pint of beer at each pub. Serious athletes take part and try to get round in record time, but dozens of other teams also enter, often dressed in the most bizarre costumes imaginable: on skis, wearing underwater flippers, as a Chinese dragon, pushing

and for various categories of participant, and the village caters for the
huge influx of people by putting up marquees and providing bands,
dances, and numerous other family activities.

7 July

Bodmin Riding

This day marks the translation of the relics of Thomas Becket (1118–
70), Archbishop of Canterbury, to a new shrine in 1220. Thomas was
famous for his long-running and bitter dispute with Henry II over
the respective powers of Church and State, but is mostly remembered
for his brutal murder in Canterbury Cathedral. Although he was well
known enough across Europe during his life, his death brought him
extreme celebrity, and numerous stories of miracles were soon in circulation, resulting in his canonization in 1173. His major feast day was
celebrated on the day of his death, 29 December.

A well-known event took place on or near Thomas's feast day on
7 July, in Cornwall. Named the 'Bodmin Riding', it involved residents
taking to the streets and processing around the town and into the
countryside, and then gathering for sports and other entertainments.
The earliest documentary evidence to anything called a 'riding' is
found in the parish church rebuilding accounts of 1469–72. These accounts include details of money 'received of the stewards of the Riding
Guilds', and list five such guilds – St Loy's, St Petroc's, St John's, St
Anyan's, and St Martin's. There are indications elsewhere in the accounts that each guild was associated with a particular trade – smiths,
skinners and glovers, shoemakers, and so on. No further details are
given in these early accounts, but a later description is provided by
a letter written by W. R. Gilbert of Bodmin Priory in July 1812, who
claimed to have taken part within the previous twenty or thirty years:

*On Monday, a grand procession of the principal inhabitants, formed into
classes with the emblems of their trades and professions, took place, preceded
by music, drums, etc., and two men, one with a garland, the other a pole ornamented with flowers, ribbons, etc. etc. which they had previously deposited
at the Priory.*

continued on page 330 ☞

Rose Queens

On 1 April 1989, the *Independent Magazine* recorded the following:

A vicar in Bury, Lancashire, has declared all-out war on superstition. The Rev. Ben Turner is the new Anglican incumbent of the Bury parish church, St. Stephen's. Until this year the local Rose Queen has been crowned in the church every May. The honour goes to the girl who has attended Sunday School most often. But it will not happen this year unless Mr. Turner relents. The Rose Queen is a heathen activity, he maintains, 'It is firmly rooted in pagan fertility rites, like dancing round a maypole ... To continue such a practice, outwardly harmless and entertaining as it may be, shows poor theological understanding.'

Unfortunately, the Revd Turner had fallen rather publicly into the trap of believing that all traditional customs must be extremely old, and are therefore linked to pagan activities. The Rose Queen was in fact a late Victorian invention encouraged, and perhaps even created, by clergy and respectable church-goers as a piece of safe and controlled pageantry, and it has continued largely in the same vein ever since.

Like the May Queen on which she is modelled, the Rose Queen is nearly always associated with other events, such as local fêtes, pageants, carnivals, and feasts, but unlike her predecessor, the Rose Queen seems to be a decidedly regional custom. It is very common across Cheshire and Lancashire, and some can be found over the border in Wales, but there are few elsewhere. It is probably no accident that these are the places where the 'Wakes Week' (*see* **Fairs, Feasts, Wakes, and Revels,** p. 341) is more important in the festival year than May Day, and it is likely that the Rose Queen tradition developed simply because it was the wrong time of year for a 'May' Queen. However, beyond the name, there is no discernible difference between the two, and sometimes they exist side by side.

The Rose Queen's main function is to act as a focal point (albeit a relatively inactive one) in the procession or fête to which she is linked, and in some cases to act as a temporary minor celebrity, gracing other local events with her presence during the year of her reign. She also has a more minor role the following year in the crowning of her successor. Most Rose Queens considered it a real honour to be chosen, and remember with pleasure the year they were crowned. Gatherings of 'past queens' in parades are always popular.

Several local Rose Queen traditions have a similar foundation story, based on the spontaneous actions of a group of local girls whose idea was enthusiastically taken up by others, and although this may be true in some cases, it is more likely that the local fête committees made the first decision to have a Rose Queen, and the story has drifted from one location to another. *Lancashire Lore* (1971), which features contributions from the various Women's Institutes in the county, provides a prime example:

The crowning of a Rose Queen on field day is not a very old custom at Wrea Green [Lancashire]. Apparently, rather more than forty years ago, a group of young girls of the village having seen queens walk in procession in neighbouring towns, decided to have a queen of their own. They made their own dresses and had a lace curtain as a train. Then, dressed in their finery, they chose their queen and proceeded to walk round the Green. They carried a banner with 'Dr. Barnardo's Homes' written across it, for they were, in fact, collecting for that charity. A butcher from Ansdell watched them and was so thrilled with what he saw that he gave them half-a-crown. They then had their crowning ceremony in somebody's garden, followed by tea on the front lawn. The second-year children got a length of cloth from the mill at Kirkham for their train. After that the field day committee incorporated the crowning of a Rose Queen into the field day festivities.

Many Rose Queen ceremonies were founded between the 1920s and 1950s, and many of these did not last very long, but a search of the Internet reveals that dozens of Rose Queens are still crowned each year. However, if the following report from the *This Is Lancashire* website (30 May 2000) is indicative of a general trend, their days may be numbered:

An unprecedented royal procession will be parading through the streets of Darcy Lever to mark the end of an era at a Bolton church. More than thirty 'de-throned' queens of the past will join the colourful parade to commemorate the last coronation at St. Stephen's and All Martyrs Church. The Rose Queen tradition has graced the church for more than half a century. But it comes to an end this year because of a lack of teenagers putting themselves forward for the honour. Where once teenage girls fought to be crowned Rose Queen, they no longer see the 'street cred' in the position, refusing to wear the frilly dresses.

See also 1 May: May Queens.

☞ *continued from page 327* Other descriptions vary considerably in detail, and although most writers have assumed that this later celebration was a direct survival of the medieval custom, there is a degree of confusion and misinformation in the documentary evidence, usefully gathered together by Pat Munn in her book *Bodmin Riding* (1975), that requires some careful historical interpretation – particularly as the word 'riding' can be interpreted in a number of ways, relating to several types of event that are all linked together by the idea of processing or parading, but not necessarily (although usually) on horseback. The pre-Reformation religious guilds often called their annual procession around the parish, on which they carried images of their patron saint and other symbols, their 'riding' (*see* **23 April: St George's Day** for the example of the Riding of St George). Trade guilds, which were often closely connected to the Church, could also call their procession a 'riding', and in the civic sphere the annual procession by a town corporation, often at the investiture of a new mayor, could similarly be so named. A riding could also refer to the custom of 'beating the bounds' (*see* **Rogationtide**, p. 243), as in the 'common ridings' of some Scottish towns, and, last but not least, it could mean the parading of a particular effigy or character, such as the Riding of the Black Knight at Ashton-under-Lyne (*see* **Easter Monday**, p. 167).

It is not surprising that the earliest evidence of the Bodmin Riding reveals that trade guilds were involved in raising money for a church rebuilding fund, as support of the Church was one of the main reasons for the guilds' existence, and nor is it unusual that this was organized on a trade-by-trade basis; however, these religious guild-ridings should have disappeared with the Reformation, when they were expressly banned. The carrying of a garland in Gilbert's account is also worthy of note, although other descriptions simply mention that flowers were gathered. This garland brings Bodmin in line with another unexplained custom, which took place on May Day at Charlton-on-Otmoor in Oxfordshire, where a greenery-clad 'garland' was carried around the parish to principal houses (*see* **1 May: Charlton-on-Otmoor Garland**). Garlands on May Day were not unusual, but there is no evidence that the Bodmin Riding ever took place at that time of year. Indeed, it is not clear why the event took place on 7 July, apart from the reason that good weather could generally be expected on that day. The earliest account giving a firm dating of the custom is from 1700 – 'the two Mondays right after St. Becket's Day' – which is well before the confusion of the calendar change of 1752. However, it has also been suggested that the saint King Edgar was far more important to Bodmin than Thomas Becket, and his feast day is 8 July.

The exact relationship between the guild ridings of the fifteenth century and the 'ridings' of the nineteenth century at Bodmin has still to be determined, but it is most unlikely that a thinly disguised religious procession could have survived both the Reformation and the Puritan revolution of the seventeenth century. If there is a connection at all, it is more likely to have been one of revival than survival. The custom was certainly revived again in 1974, and the historical Riding is now used by local enthusiasts in the town as the basis of a popular 'medieval' festival, which is held each year in early July, organized by the Bodmin Riding and Heritage Committee.

10 July

An example of how the practices of the local farming year could dictate a rural community's calendar is provided by Northumbrian writer Hastings Neville, writing of the late nineteenth century:

Twice a year, 'Cheviot's mountain lone' is enlivened with a great gathering of the hill shepherds, and the bleating of many sheep. One meeting takes place on the very top of Cheviot on the 10th of July, the other on 10th November, lower down near the foot of the mountain. There are generally about 30 to 40 shepherds present, and sometimes 400 sheep to be exchanged. The day begins with sports, for our hill shepherd is a great lover of sport. The real purpose, however, of these meetings is to restore lost sheep to their proper owners. Many a stray sheep gets far away from its proper feeding ground to another where it does not belong, and these are looked after by each shepherd until the half-yearly exchange takes place.

Second Wednesday in July

Pretty Maid's Charity

Not all charities date from the distant past. In the North Devon town of Holsworthy, the Revd Thomas Meyrick founded what has become known as the Pretty Maid's Charity when he died in 1841 (Meyrick's brother, Owen, was Rector of Holsworthy at the time, which explains the charity's location). Thomas left money for government stock that would yield an annual interest of £3 10s, and of this, £2 10s was to be given to 'a young single woman resident in the parish being under 30 years of age, and generally esteemed by the young as the most deserving and most handsome, and most noted for her qualities and attendance at church'. He thought that by this example, 'rulers would learn that subjects are better directed and led by harmless amusement and judicious reward than by fear of punishment'. The other pound was to go to a spinster over sixty years old who had similar qualities, but this part of the charity has now been dropped and the whole amount is given to the young person. The identity of the recipient is kept secret until she walks out of St Peter's church door at twelve o'clock on the second Wednesday in July, the first day of the local fair, which she visits in her new official capacity.

Second/Third Saturday in July

Durham Miners' Gala

Durham Miners' Gala, usually held on the second or third Saturday in July, was the biggest trade union gathering in Europe in its heyday, and even today is an impressive event. The Durham Gala was first held in 1871, organized by the Durham Miners' Association, and grew to outshine all other local galas in the North-East, soon becoming known as 'The Big Meeting'. The programme usually involves a grand procession of union lodges, each carrying their huge colourful banners and accompanied by brass bands, which march out to the city's racecourse.

Speeches are then made by visiting unionists and politicians. The afternoon includes a large funfair and a variety of other entertainments, together with a memorial service at the cathedral. The procession then re-forms and marches back through the streets of the city.

The day has always been a major demonstration of worker solidarity and union pride, mixed with all the fun of a family summer outing. The Gala suffered as a result of the gradual wasting away of the coal-mining industry in the late twentieth century, and especially the rapid closure of pits in the 1990s, but in recent years a revival has begun, with the active help of trade unions in other industries. Saturday, 10 July 2004 saw the 120th Gala, and there is every sign that it will continue for many years to come.

15 July

St Swithun's Day

Swithun (or Swithin) was Bishop of Winchester in the ninth century, and a major player in the religious and political life of Wessex at a time when it was becoming the dominant force in the emergence of England as a nation. He died in 862 and would hardly have been remembered in the popular mind had it not been for the miracles that reportedly occurred when his remains were moved on 15 July 971. According to legend, he had requested to be buried in the churchyard, but his remains were later brought into the church, as a matter of respect. Among other marvellous things that then occurred, it rained so hard for forty days that those in authority moved him outside again; hence the only fact that most people know about St Swithun's Day is the weather prediction:

> St Swithin's day, if thou dost rain,
> For forty days it will remain;
> St Swithin's day, if thou be fair,
> For forty days 'twill rain nae mair.

This idea was already current in the early fourteenth century, and has been proverbial ever since.

This connection between the saint and rain engendered other beliefs, including the idea commonly held all over the country till at least the early twentieth century that the day was crucial to the apple crop. In Warwickshire, folklorists A. R. Wright and T. E. Lones recorded that:

You won't have the jam made till the apples are christened ... We never eat or cut apples until St. Swithin has christened them.

Swithun was popular enough in medieval times for many ancient churches to have been dedicated to him, and in these parishes his day will have been marked with celebrations or other events. At Old Weston in Huntingdonshire, for example, a remnant of the annual hay-strewing (*see* **Rush-Bearing**, p. 322) on his day lasted well into the twentieth century. In the Roman Church, the day of his death, 2 July, was deemed his feast day, but in England it is 15 July.

16 July

Anne Askew Day

In the war that raged between Catholic and Protestant factions in Britain and elsewhere in the sixteenth century, both sides told and retold stories of their own martyrs, as evidence that they were in the right and their opponents in the wrong. Anne Askew, Protestant martyr, was born *c*.1520, and took on the Catholic establishment by daring to dispute publicly with Lincoln Cathedral clergy. She was burnt at the stake for heresy in London in 1546, aged only twenty-five. Her case became a major *cause célèbre* in the growing Protestant agitation, and accounts of her 'examination' were published and widely read. She is commemorated by a service at Lincoln Cathedral every 16 July.

19 July

Armada Day

The defeat of the Spanish Armada in July and August 1588 is seen as one of the seminal events in the history of England, and is thus imbued with a considerable weight of nationalist, religious, military, and romantic symbolism that has outlasted its real historical significance. This is not to suggest that the threat of invasion was not very real at the time, but its memory, like that of the Gunpowder Plot of 1605, served a much wider purpose in national consciousness and rhetoric for a long time after the actual event.

The huge Spanish fleet sailed from Lisbon on 29 May 1588, planning to liaise with an army raised in Flanders by the Duke of Parma to invade and occupy England. The plan had been under discussion for several years, and all of Europe (including England) knew that it would soon be carried out. Despite Philip II's overtly religious rhetoric, which described the affair as a crusade to bring England back into the Catholic fold, backed by the Pope's cautious promise of financial aid if the campaign was successful, Philip clearly had ambitious political motives as well. He himself had a claim on the English throne, and there was a great deal for Spain to gain in terms of international influence, military supremacy, and trade. Both sides claimed that God was on their side, and when it was later discovered that an unseasonable storm had struck the decisive stroke against the Spanish, the victory was hailed in England, and other Protestant countries, as divine vindication of the Protestant religion. For centuries afterwards, the defeat of the Spanish Armada was used as a symbol to underpin Britain's claim to greatness.

News of the defeat was slow to circulate, and it was weeks before its decisive nature was fully realized by the English court. Nor was a straggling sea campaign conducive to engendering an official 'Armada Day', and celebrations in 1588 and ensuing years tended to be combined with the festivities that commemorated the accession of Elizabeth I on 19 November, which already had more than their fair share of patriotic and religious symbolism.

Any tributes that have sprung up since, such as those at Plymouth, where most of the English fleet was stationed to await the Armada's arrival, have usually settled on 19 July, as it was on this day that the Armada arrived off the Lizard and the English knew for sure that an invasion attempt was imminent. However, any time in late July would be equally appropriate.

Little Edith's Treat

Elizabeth Croft, a parishioner of Piddinghoe in East Sussex, left a bequest that funded annual gifts of coal, clothes, and money to the local poor, and money to respectable young people, in order to commemorate the lives of her husband, Hugh (d. 1866), and her son Gilmore (d. 1869). She also sought to perpetuate in the following way the memory of her only granddaughter, Edith, who was born on 19 July 1868 and died in October the same year:

The interest arising from £100 of the said stock to be known as 'Little Edith's Treat' to be expended on the 19th of July in each year, in a treat to the children of the National School of the said Parish and in rewards, more especially to the girls who are skilled in plain needlework and to the boys and girls who are neat in their dress, clean in their habits, and regular in attendance at church and school.

These treats followed a regular pattern. On the afternoon of Edith's birthday (or the nearest school day), the schoolchildren were told the story of Little Edith and the bequest, and were then taken to the Hoe (the village open space) for games, races, and a splendid tea. The vicar usually threw a handful of coins into the air for the children to scramble for, and there were prizes and gifts distributed back at the school. After the local school closed in 1952, the treats became intermittent and were based around the Sunday school while it was in operation, sometimes taking the form of children's outings rather than treats. In 2000, some of the money was used to provide a children's Christmas party. The fund is still active, and admirably fulfils the spirit of the original endowment even if actual circumstances have necessitated changes.

See also **Doles**, p. 115.

20 July

St Margaret's Day

Despite the fact that a historical Margaret of Antioch almost certainly never existed, St Margaret was extremely popular in the Middle Ages, and well over 200 ancient churches in England were dedicated to her. Her legend claims that she was the daughter of a pagan priest who threw her out of the house once she became a Christian, so she became a shepherdess. After converting numerous people to Christianity and stoutly refusing marriage, she underwent various tortures and was swallowed by a dragon, emerging unscathed when it burst asunder.

It was said that if pregnant women invoked her name, they would be spared the pain of childbirth, which naturally made her popular. Nevertheless, she does not seem to have had a lasting traditional impact, and no major festivals, customs, or superstitions are reported for her day, although it must have had local significance in parishes where the church was named after her.

In weather-lore, St Margaret's Day was often expected to be wet; if it was, it was termed 'Margaret's flood', or, somewhat confusingly, it was said that St Mary Magdalene (whose feast day was on 22 July) was washing her handkerchief to go to her cousin St James's Fair (25 July).

25 July

St Christopher's Day

The only thing that is known of Christopher is that he was martyred in the third century. His name means 'bearer of Christ', which explains the origin of the immensely popular story of his being instructed to help travellers across a river, and carrying the Christ child. As the patron saint of travellers, his popularity increased tenfold with the rise of mass transportation and tourism in the nineteenth and twentieth centuries, and the immediately recognizable emblem of a giant carrying a child can be found in countless cars, trains, and planes the Christian world over.

Less well known in modern times is the idea that St Christopher protected believers against sudden death, recorded by Samuel Rudder in his *New History of Gloucestershire* (1779):

There was a colossal figure of St. Christopher painted against the wall of Bibury church, in pursuance of an opinion that prevailed in the ages of ignorance and superstition, that whosoever had seen the image of that saint, should not die of sudden or accidental death . . . Accordingly, this figure was opposite to the entrance at the south door of the church; but it hath lately been covered with whitewash, and nothing remains to be seen but the two following lines [in Latin, which translates as]

> *Saint Christopher's fair figure who shall view*
> *Faintness nor feebleness that day shall rue.*

Numerous other churches had similar images, but only a few survived the Reformation.

St James's Day

As befits his position as one of the Apostles, James the Great (martyred AD 44) was a very popular saint in England, with 400 ancient churches bearing his name. The idea that James preached in Spain before his death has now been exploded, but the claim that he is buried at Compostela made it Spain's most popular shrine and one of the best known in Europe, from the twelfth century onwards. So powerful was the connection between the saint and his shrine that his emblems became the hat and scallop shell associated with Spanish pilgrims.

In England, there are occasional printed references to apple trees being blessed on St James's Day, although this is more often said of St Swithun's Day (*see* 15 July). The well-known proverb 'He who eats oysters on St James's Day will not want for money' is slightly puzzling because the English oyster season traditionally started on 4 August, but the proverb may be referring to Old St James's Day (*see* 5 **August: James I**). For another possible connection between St James and oysters, *see* **Early August: Grottoes**.

Ebernoe Horn Fair

This sparsely populated West Sussex village, about four miles from Petworth, is famous for its fair, which is more like a village fête, except that a whole sheep is roasted and eaten during the day. While the sheep is roasting, a cricket match is played between local teams, and the player on the winning side who scores the most runs is presented with the sheep's horns. A special Horn Fair song is sung during the presentation of the horns.

The origin of the fair is unknown. The only concrete date in its history is 1864, when, according to the local press, it was revived after a long lapse, but there is no evidence that it existed before that time. The Horn Fair song was 'discovered' in a nearby village in the early 1950s and enthusiastically taken up by the fair's organizers, but again there is no evidence that it was originally connected with Ebernoe, as its text contains no local allusions and the song is found elsewhere in the country. Nevertheless, after fifty years of singing it, the people of Ebernoe have made it their own. Versions vary, but the following was noted by Mervyn Plunkett from George Tompsett, of Cuckfield,

As I was a walking one morning so fair
So fresh was the lilies and cold blew the air
I spied a fair damsel all on her grey mare
And she was a-riding all unto Horn Fair.
I asked this fair maid if I should ride by her side
Oh no said this damsel my mammy would chide
And besides my old daddy will beat me full sore
He'll never let me ride on his grey mare no more.
You charming fair creature why do you say so
I can hear by your talk you are for a game of play
I can hear by your talk you're for a game of play
And if you don't make haste you won't get there today.
If you would go unto Horn Fair you must walk on your way
I will not let you ride on my grey mare today
You will rumple my muslin and uncurl my hair
And leave me alone all unto Horn Fair.
You charming fair creature how can you say no
With you I intend to Horn Fair to go
We will join the best of company when we do get there
With horns on our heads as fine as our hair.
There's hook-d horns and crooked horns and horns of every kind
Like jolly cockle shells all in a row.

John Knill Charity

John Knill was a man apparently determined to be remembered. A
St Ives worthy, customs and excise man for the district, and mayor in
1767, he first built a strange fifty-foot pyramid (called Knill's Steeple)
on top of Worvas Hill to serve as his monument when he died, which
also provided a useful landmark for ships off the Cornish coast. He
then set up a detailed list of instructions about the celebrations that
were to take place at his Steeple: little girls in white were to dance for
at least fifteen minutes and then sing the Old Hundredth psalm, two
widows were to oversee the proceedings, and prizes were to be given
to the best pilchard packers, knitter of fishing nets, and apprentices.
The first celebrations took place in 1801 while he was still alive, and he
left money in trust for their continuation. Ironically, Knill is buried in
London rather than on his hilltop, but the custom still takes place every

five years, led by the current mayor and town officials, and little girls still dance around the monument as part of the celebrations. Naturally enough, some changes have had to be made, but on the whole the event remembers Knill as he wished. An early account of the proceedings, dated 1826, was published in William Hone's *Every-Day Book* (1827).

See also **Doles**, p. 115.

Whitstable Oyster Festival

Whitstable, a small town gathered around its harbour on the eastern coast of Kent, holds an annual nine-day festival in honour of its most famous product and staple of the local economy, the Whitstable native oyster. The festival usually starts on the Saturday nearest to 25 July, as the trade claims St James as its patron saint. The local oyster fishery was already an established trade in Norman times, but the grounds were leased from the Crown until 1793, when local people formed the Whitstable Oyster Company to buy them for themselves.

The festival is a modern version of the Whitstable Regatta, an annual gathering first recorded in the late eighteenth century, but is now a major spectacle that still manages to retain its local feel. It starts with the ceremonial landing of the first catch of the season, at Long Beach, followed by the 'oyster parade', which accompanies the horse-drawn cart that delivers the fresh oysters to restaurants and cafes in the town. The scene is then set for a week and a half of celebrations, including concerts, family events, and competitions, firework displays, workshops, Miss Whitstable and her entourage, sideshows, and demonstrations, many of which have a maritime theme, and all now organized by Canterbury City Council. The harbour is packed with boats of all kinds, many of which are historic or restored crafts, which gather for the 'Harbour Day'. One of the quieter moments is when a procession leaves St Peter's church for the 'blessing of the waters' service at Reeves Beach one evening during the festival.

See also **Late May: Blessing of the Sea; Early September: Colchester Oyster Fishery; 20 October: Colchester Oyster Feast.**

The English calendar is littered with local festive gatherings throughout the spring, summer, and autumn, which are almost indistinguishable from each other but have a bewildering variety of names – fairs, feasts, fêtes, wakes, revels, ales, treats, mops, and so on. In many cases, these names contain clues about the origins of the particular event, but this cannot be taken for granted because over time the words gradually came to mean simply 'annual festive gathering' and distinctions became blurred. Theoretically, the only one with a strict meaning is 'fair'. An official fair could only be granted by royal charter, which not only gave permission for the gathering to be held, but also assigned an 'owner' who possessed the very lucrative right to collect the tolls, dues, and fines generated by the event. The economic and social impact of a fair was greatly increased by the fact that while it was in operation all trading in the area fell under the jurisdiction of the owner, who in effect took over nearly all local power for the duration. The fair-owner even held his or her own court to try cases and settle disputes arising from the fair.

The economic value of fair-ownership was well understood in medieval times, and charters were often granted to religious and charitable institutions, as a way of giving them long-term funding. But as time went on, this situation almost inevitably led to power struggles with town or parish authorities who naturally resented being pushed aside every year at fair time.

Given that different rules applied while a fair was in operation, it was essential that everyone knew exactly when the fair opened and closed. Public ceremonies, such as the procession of worthies to the site, and the reading aloud of the charter, were therefore carried out, and a symbol was often hoisted aloft, such as the giant gloves at Honiton and Chester, which remained on show while the fair was in operation. Many fairs acquired quaint local names, either named after a saint, such as Barnaby Fair, or after some leading feature, such as gooseberry fair, ram fair, walnut fair, horn fair, pudding-pie fair, and pack Monday fair.

The architects of the calendar change of 1752 fully realized that fairs needed to be carefully handled, especially in cases where the timing of the fair was closely related to a particular produce or natural feature. It was therefore decreed that fairs should retain their place in the natural year by changing their nominal date. Unfortunately, this caused a good deal of confusion, and while some fairs immediately changed their date, others did not, and some even vacillated between the two. It took several years for a regular pattern to be established. By the nineteenth century, however, the trading basis for most fairs had been eroded to such an extent that they had outlived their commercial usefulness, and they continued to exist mainly as pleasure fairs. Some were inconveniently located in the crowded streets of a growing town or on prime building land, and they were increasingly seen as anachronistic, and an affront to local propriety and civic pride. Sometimes the possession of a royal charter made it difficult for local authorities to suppress them, and so the Fairs Act (1871) came into force, to remedy the situation:

Whereas certain of the fairs held in England and Wales are unnecessary, are the cause of grievous immorality, and are very injurious to the inhabitants of the towns in which such fairs are held, and it is therefore expedient to make provision to facilitate the abolition of such fairs.

Local authorities all over the country took the opportunity to close fairs down for good. Others were moved to more convenient open sites on the edge of town, and a stricter control of those that remained was introduced.

Feasts, on the other hand, were originally associated with the local church, and either occurred on the feast day of the saint to which the church was dedicated, or were celebrated on the anniversary of its consecration. Originally, they were therefore occasions of both piety and celebration and were at first held in the church and churchyard, but as the fun started to take precedence the ecclesiastical authorities tried to separate them from the holy ground by decreeing that they must be held elsewhere in the community. In many villages, the feast was the most enjoyable day of the year, but after the Reformation the link with saints, even if tenuous, became embarrassing, as any appearance of the veneration of saints could be construed as continuing outmoded popish habits. Henry VIII tried to bring feasts under control by decreeing that they were to be held on a Sunday in October, but this was widely ignored, and they continued to be held on dates to suit the community concerned.

Wakes were similarly linked to the church. Before the Reformation, the celebration of any major religious festival began the evening before, when the devout sat up in the church to watch through the night. The *Oxford English Dictionary* defines this sense of 'wake' as 'abstinence from sleep, watching, practised as a religious observance . . . a night spent in devout watching (on the eve of a festival . . .)'. Local festivals right across the Midlands and the north of the country were called 'wakes', and this same word was adopted in the early nineteenth century in newly industrialized towns when factory owners found it convenient to give all their workers time off at the same time. 'The Wakes' or 'Wakes Week' soon became generic terms for this annual holiday, even when it later began to last a fortnight.

Ales were organized specifically to raise money, usually for the church, but sometimes for other purposes (*see* Church Ales, p. 258).

Revel is the dialect word for an annual gathering in the south-west of the country, and this meaning of the word is recorded from the fourteenth century.

In our mobile modern world, where entertainment and company are available day and night, it is difficult to comprehend the importance of these gatherings in the lives of working people before the mid twentieth century. This was especially true of rural workers, whose opportunities for socializing were severely restricted by long hours and geographical isolation. When an opportunity did arise, they grasped it enthusiastically, and perhaps uncritically. As late as 1909, Hastings Neville could say in his affectionate account of his fellow rural Northumbrians:

They love a crowd. A crowd is their idea of success, whether the object be a bazaar, a missionary meeting, or a service in church or chapel. If they go away saying, 'What a people there was there!', you may know that your audience is satisfied.

Annual feasts and fairs were not simply seen as opportunities for time off work but also as chances for entertainment, shopping, lots of food and drink, meeting old friends, or old enemies, and as a rare opportunity to mingle with the opposite sex. The following example was printed in the journal *Folk-Lore* in 1912:

A farmer's wife from Offord Cluny has given me the following information . . . The great day of the village year is Feast Sunday, the last Sunday in June, 'when all friends meet' and girls in service take a holiday. Scarce a house in the village but has been 'done up', papered or painted to be ready for the Feast. Plum puddings are made, and fillets of pork prepared. About two weeks beforehand part of the hind leg is put in salt water; these 'fillets' are stuffed and boiled, and everyone reckons to have new potatoes and green peas for the Feast. Things are very backward if they can't have

them ready by Feast Sunday ... On Feast Monday stalls are set up down the village street, and there is dancing in the evening ... On Feast Tuesday the Sunday School children have their treat.

The standard fare of all these events was food and drink, music and dancing, stalls and sideshows, and sports and games, but another popular feature was a procession, and in later times they sometimes included carnivals, pageants, and May Queens. Memories of these times always loom large in the reminiscences of those who grew up before the First World War, as in the following account from Mrs Elie Hilda Williams, born in 1891, who was remembering Hay-on-Wye:

For the children, at May Fair time, they had the ha'penny horses: that was a roundabout with little horses and cockerels, and the man turned the handle in the middle; that was for the tinies, and then you graduated to the 'penny horses', and they were bigger. Then there were coconut shies, and boxing booths, and sideshows of all kinds: there were always 'Fat Lady' shows if I remember rightly.

And in 1966, a Yorkshire woman recalled:

Our village church had a feast day in July when the Sunday School scholars, followed by a large congregation, walked behind the huge banner with a picture of the Good Shepherd embroidered on it. The village brass band led us to different points in the village where hymns were sung. We always had a new frock for this, the biggest day in our calendar. Afterwards there was a tea in the Sunday School.

However, the children may not have noticed everything that was happening in the adult world around them. Nineteen-year-old George Dew, from Lower Heyford in Oxfordshire, recorded in his diary on Sunday, 27 August 1865:

Heyford Feast – The drunkenness of this day has been most abominable. Very few people at church; but public houses full. It would be no loss if there were no feasts.

By all accounts, any of these events could have their rough side, at least until Victorian reformers got hold of them, but some had a particular reputation for regular and almost ritualized fighting. There seems to have fights between different parishes (*see* 1 May: Fighting, for examples).

More respectably, the rise of local friendly societies and mutual clubs in the nineteenth century provided many communities with another opportunity for pleasure, in the form of the 'Club Feast'. Members of these clubs were particularly fond of ceremonial regalia and processions, which they took very seriously. Arthur Wade, born in Rudston, East Yorkshire, in 1900, remembered the Feast Days of the Ancient Shepherds Friendly Society, in his young days:

Because you couldn't go in the Shepherds' procession on Club Feast Day without a staff and a sash like these here. It was a green silk sash, with an orange rosette or an orange and white one – there was a few different kinds; and the officials used to wear white sashes, wi' a white rosette . . . The sashes went over one shoulder, and they fastened wi' tapes; you'd be walking in twos, and one would have it over one shoulder, and one over t'other, so that they both slanted outwards – it looked better that way. And if there was a lad, and he wanted to walk wi' me, we had to change our sashes so they both slanted out – you couldn't have 'em both going one way. Then everybody would have a staff, and that was green too . . . And we used to have a very big banner, wi' Latin on it, and there'd be two strong chaps carrying a pole at each end, and they used to have white gloves on that carried 'em. And they used to have two young lads to hold long tapes from the banner, and when the wind got hold of it, it used to nearly pull them kids off their feet, because it was a terrible big banner.

See also Hiring Fairs, p. 470.

26 July

Mace Monday

A mock-mayor ceremony formerly took place at Newbury, in Berkshire, on the first Monday after St Anne's Day, which apparently followed the normal pattern of such events (*see* **Mock Mayors and Courts**, p. 298). Mock mayors were usually associated with a particular public house – in this case the Bull and Dog, where a feast of bacon and beans was provided, and plenty to drink, as reported in William Hone's *Every-Day Book* (1827):

In the course of the day a procession takes place. A cabbage is stuck on a pole and carried instead of a mace, accompanied by similar substitutes for the other emblems of civic dignity, and there is, of course, plenty of 'rough music'. A 'justice' is chosen at the same time, some other offices are filled up, and the day ends by all concerned getting comfortable 'how come ye so' [i.e. drunk].

This 'justice' was termed the Mayor of Bartlemas, and the day was called Mace Monday. It seems to have died out before the 1890s.

28 July

Old St Kenelm's Day

At Clent, in Worcestershire, the parish church is dedicated to St Kenelm, and presumably the local wake, or feast day, was formerly held on that saint's day (17 July), but slipped to 28 July following the introduction of the Gregorian calendar in 1752 (*see* p. xxix). One bizarre feature of the festivities on this day, or on the Sunday following, was called 'crabbing the parson' and was reported by several writers as having taken place until the mid nineteenth century. In 1856, John Noake recorded:

The custom of crabbing the parson was observed till lately at St. Kenelm's. It was the practice for the villagers and all who chose to arm themselves with crab apples on the wake Sunday, and as the parson approached the church the crabs were thrown at him, until he reached the church porch. The use of sticks and stones in place of crabs led to the suppression of the custom.

No sensible explanation for this custom has been put forward, and it is particularly unclear why the local clergy would put up with such behaviour, but the Clent custom was in fact far from unique. Almost exactly the same procedure was recorded in Victorian times at Hawkridge, Somerset, on Revel Sunday, the nearest Sunday to St Giles's Day (1 September), and at Mobberley, Cheshire, the Sunday after St Luke's Day (18 October). All that can be said is that this custom seems to be associated with the local saint's day rather than with

a civic function such as mayor-making, which also attracted similar 347
'lawless' behaviour, such as throwing cabbage stalks at the officers of
the new corporation (*see* **Lawless Hours and Days**, p. 412).

Late July

Doggett's Coat and Badge Race

Thomas Doggett (*c.*1670–1721) was a popular actor, playwright, and
theatre manager of his time, particularly celebrated for playing 'low
comedy' parts. He was also a staunch Whig, and a particularly enthusiastic supporter of the new Hanoverian dynasty ushered in by
the accession of George I in 1714. He inaugurated a boat race on the
River Thames in the King's honour on the anniversary in 1715, which
continues to this day. Doggett's political motives are quite clear, but
another version of the race's origin was preferred by Dorothea Fisher
OBE, born in 1890, who was steeped in river lore and so well known
in the area that she was popularly called 'Mother Thames'. Her husband Billy had won the event in 1911, and the story she used to tell was
reported in the *Guardian* in 1974:

*Doggett was stranded on the wrong side of the river on a stormy night and
the ferry wouldn't take him across. He was going to be late for the theatre.
A young lighterman came to his rescue and rowed him over, thus earning
gratitude and the first Doggett's coat and badge.*

When Doggett died, he left money to the Fishmongers' Company to
perpetuate the annual race, and it is still held over the same four-and-
a-half-mile stretch of the Thames, from London Bridge to Chelsea.

Originally, the contestants had to row their ordinary wherries
against the tide, which called for immense strength and stamina, and
the race could take up to five hours. By the turn of the twentieth century, however, the decision had been made to row with the tide, and
special racing skiffs were introduced in 1906; nowadays, the race takes
about twenty-five minutes. There have been other minor changes: the
coat is now red, rather than the original orange, and the race is held
on a day in late July when the tide is right rather than the original
1 August. Holders of the coat and badge are expected to assist and
officiate at future races and at ceremonial functions on the river.

Swan-Upping

Since its introduction to Britain in the thirteenth century, the swan has always been a royal bird. It could not be owned by anyone without express permission from the Crown – a right worth possessing when swans were a regular item on the banquet table. Permission to keep swans on the River Thames was granted to the worshipful Company of Vintners in 1473, and about the same time to the Dyers as well. These grants are still in force, and so any swans on the Thames belong to the sovereign or one of these two companies.

Once a year, in late July, the swan keepers for each of the companies meet the Royal Swan Keeper or Master, and together they journey down the river, from London Bridge to Henley, catching and examining around 600 birds. They mark the beaks of all the young birds they find – one nick for the Dyers, two for the Vintners – according to their parentage. Any brood of mixed parentage is split equally. The Queen's swans are left unmarked, on the principle that she owns *all* unmarked swans. This process, known as swan-upping, can take several days to complete, although in past times, when more birds were kept, it could take up to two weeks. The occasion is surrounded by a certain amount of colourful ceremony and pageantry as befits its royal purpose, but also calls for a great deal of skill and stamina.

July/August

Dog Days

Visited the old Merediths at the Bridge Gate. Mrs. Meredith said she was very ill. 'Tis the dog star,' she said, 'I shall not be better till Saturday when the dog days end. 'Tis an evil star.'

This entry in Francis Kilvert's *Diary* for 8 August 1878 refers to the 'dog days', the period in which the dog star rises coincidentally with the sun, which was believed to be the hottest, and therefore the most unwholesome, time of year. It was regarded as an evil time, when malign influences were abroad, dogs ran mad, and people became ill. The actual dates are difficult to pin down, as they can be calculated on the greater dog star (Sirius) or the lesser dog star (Procyon), and they

were calculated as falling between 3 July and 11 August, and many in
the West keep to these dates, even if they are not correct for their own
time or geographical position.

St Wilfrid Feast Procession

Wilfrid (*c*.633–709), Abbot of Ripon and Bishop of York, was one of
the most influential figures in the early English Church, and enjoyed a
stormy relationship with sovereigns and fellow clergy, which resulted
in two trips to Rome to gain the Pope's support. Wilfrid built Ripon's
first church (St Peter's), in North Yorkshire, on the site of the present
cathedral, which is now dedicated to him, and he founded numerous
other churches and monasteries. His cult, which began soon after his
death, was strongest at Ripon, and he is still very much part of the local scene. His feast day is 12 October, but his return from exile to the
city at Lammas is celebrated by the people of Ripon on the Saturday
before the first Monday in August. A man dressed as a bearded Bishop
Wilfrid, in white robes and on a white horse, leads the procession of
floats, bands, and morris dancers that ushers in the two weeks of celebration called the Wilfrid Feast. He is met at the cathedral door by
the dean, the mayor, and the city council, and nominally presides over
the feast. In her book on the customs of Yorkshire, published in 1989,
Julia Smith reported that two feast delicacies bear the Saint's name:
'Wilfrid pies' – apple pies served with cheese, or with cheese cooked in
them; and 'Wilfra tarts', which she describes as:

*Shortcrust pastry base, but the filling consists of butter, ground almonds,
sugar and grated rind of a lemon, together with breadcrumbs which have
been soaked in hot milk, mixed together with a beaten egg.*

As Wilfrid was a popular local saint, his effigy would almost certainly
have been carried through the streets on special occasions before the
Reformation, and it is claimed that when effigies were banned, human
representatives took their place. However, the notion that the custom
at Ripon could have an unbroken lineage of over a thousand years is
highly unlikely.

AUGUST

Early August

Grottoes

In nineteenth- and twentieth-century London, a common cry that greeted pedestrians in summer was 'Please Remember the Grotto!', as an urchin held out a shell or grubby hand in expectation of a small coin. The day on which this occurred was known as Grotto Day. An article in *The Times* (21 November 1957) remembers the Old Kent Road in the early 1900s:

When was Grotto Day? It happened just once a year, but who whispered round Ruby Street that today was Grotter Day? It was a suggestion that sent some to the gasworks to collect clinker, one to the fishmonger to collect scallop shells, and some to beg or steal flowers. Then against the high gable at the end of the street we would build our grotto, clinker upon clinker, to form a mystic rockery with carefully spaced apertures in the fabric that would reveal the candlelight that was ultimately to shine inside. Two feet high and about as wide, the front elevation was finished with an arched doorway. A half-circle of stones for a forecourt, the whole decorated with flowers, mainly marigolds, and the edifice was finished. Then inside went the candles.

The children also chanted a traditional rhyme, which sounds more music hall than ancient folk song, as recalled by Rose Gamble in her autobiography *Chelsea Child* (1979):

> *Please remember the grotto*
> *Me father has run off to sea*

Me mother's gone to fetch 'im back
So please give a farthin' to me.

The custom was reported most regularly from London, but it was also found in places such as Essex, Norfolk, Hampshire, Sussex, and Swansea, and the time of year varies widely from report to report. Early August seems to be the most usual time, but it could be carried out in late July or early September. Nineteenth-century sources link the custom to the start of the oyster season in early August, and describe the grottoes as primarily built of oyster shells. Nowadays, oysters are hardly daily fare and their shells are not so easy to come by, but in earlier times the oyster was a poor person's food, often bought and eaten in the street, and vast quantities were sold. Henry Mayhew estimated in 1850 that 124 million oysters were sold each year in the streets of London alone. Later sources mention such grotto materials as clinker, stones, broken china and glass, beads, ribbons, flowers, and moss, and specify that there was nearly always a candle lit inside.

The earliest known mention of the custom is in the almanac *Time's Telescope* in 1823, and we have no evidence that it was any older than this. If it existed before that time, it certainly cannot have been as well known as it was soon to become, and by the 1840s and 1850s it was frequently mentioned in newspapers and magazines. The custom remained very widespread in the early twentieth century, and it lasted in some places into the post-Second World War period. The last was probably seen in Mitcham, in Surrey, in the 1960s.

Street customs such as these have long excited a range of adult reactions. A *Punch* cartoon of 15 August 1857, for example, urged people, 'Please do not remember the grotto', and seventy years later, in *The Times* of 1 September 1925:

It was recently reported that the Justices of the Juvenile Offenders' Court at Tower Bridge had appealed to the Press to emphasise the nuisance caused by 'grottoes' made by children on the pavement at this time of the year, and by their appeals to 'remember the grotto'.

It is common for writers on the topic to assume a historical connection between the grotto custom and St James, whose symbol from the twelfth century onwards was the scallop shell associated with pilgrims visiting his shrine at Santiago de Compostela, in Spain. But this theory has its problems. St James's Day is 25 July, a little too early in the year for the core grotto season, which was most often reported as occurring in August. The native oyster season also often started in August, despite the traditional advice to only eat an oyster 'when there's an R in the month'. St James's feast day Old Style is 5 August, however, which brings it closer to the grotto season, but the theory is still not very convincing. Indeed, the late appearance of the custom in the documentary record, its variable date, and the close connection with the oyster season, make the St James connection appear to be simply a coincidence of timing, but further research is needed to verify or refute this idea.

First Wednesday in August

Knighthood of the Old Green

Old Green in Southampton, Hampshire, is claimed to be the oldest bowling green in the world, having been reputedly in continuous use since 1299 (despite the fact that for some of that time bowling was illegal for ordinary folk; *see* **The** *King's Book of Sports* **1618 and 1633**, p. 354). This particular tournament, however, known as the Knighthood of the Green, has been staged since 1776.

The winner of the tournament becomes a Knight of the Green and is forbidden to enter again, instead becoming one of the officers who organize and adjudicate the proceedings. The contest is open to all club members, who are referred to as 'Gentlemen Commoners' for the duration of the game, which can last several days. The rules differ from normal bowls. The jack, which has one flattened side so that it can be placed on a penny laid on the green, is placed by the Knights anywhere on the green. Contestants bowl two woods each and try to get as close to the jack as possible. As each wood is bowled, its distance from the jack is measured and recorded and it is then removed before the next wood is bowled. If the jack is knocked from its position, it is put back on the penny for the next contestant to aim at. When all have bowled, the winner of that 'end' is announced, the jack is placed somewhere else, and the contestants bowl from the jack's previous position. The first player to reach seven ends wins, and becomes a Knight. The Knights wear full morning dress, complete with black top hats.

First week in August

Woodmen of Arden

The Woodmen of Arden is an exclusive archery club, based at Meriden, in Warwickshire, which claims to be the exact centre of England. The Woodmen still use traditional longbows made of yew, and wooden arrows with silver tips, and they dress in an antiquated garb of green coat, buff waistcoat, green tie, and white trousers. They hold meetings, called Wardmotes, throughout the year, but their Grand Wardmote takes place over four days in the first week in August and comprises competitions, prizes, and business meetings. Club records date back to 1785, and it may well be even older than this.

1 August

Lammas/St Peter ad Vincula

The derivation of the word 'Lammas', and the ecclesiastical activity appropriate to the day, have exercised many antiquarians down the ages, resulting in some confusion. It was often assumed that the word meant 'lamb-mass', a false etymology that led to some parishes introducing services in which a lamb was brought to church for a blessing, as recorded by John Brand in 1849:

On that day, the tenants who held lands of the cathedral church at York, which is dedicated to St. Peter ad Vincula [whose feast day is also 1 August] *were bound by their tenure to bring a live lamb into the church at high mass.*

However, the true derivation is from the Old English *hlafmaesse*, which means 'loaf-mass', and it is clear from Anglo-Saxon records from the ninth century onwards that it was celebrated in the church as a festival of 'first fruits', with bread and wheat, to celebrate the corn harvest. Some Anglican churches still hold Lammas services in which loaves of bread feature prominently, but these are revivals or re-creations of the ancient festival, and were introduced in the 1940s. In 1945, for example, the Revd D. L. Couper, Chaplain to the Bishop of Chichester, working

continued on page 357 ☞

The King's Book of Sports 1618 and 1633

Before James I (VI in Scotland) had even arrived in London to take up the throne of England in 1617, he was embroiled in a controversy about games and pastimes.

Passing through Lancashire, he was presented with a petition from locals who claimed that they were being prevented from indulging in traditional games on Sundays by zealous clergy and magistrates. James's response was later codified in *The Kinges' Majesties Declaration Concerning Lawfull Sports*, commonly called *The King's Book of Sports*, printed and circulated in May 1618.

Certainly, James I liked his sport (by many accounts he was obsessed with stag-hunting), but *The King's Book of Sports* has to be seen primarily in terms of the religious controversies of the period. One of the main points at issue was the way in which Sunday should be celebrated, and, in particular, what the people at large were permitted and forbidden to do. Leaving aside the in-fighting over whether the 'Sabbath' meant Saturday (as in Judaism) or Sunday (as in Christianity), the growing Puritan faction in the English Church and establishment were increasingly able, at local level, to prevent games and sports taking place on what they regarded as the Lord's Day. It is not presuming too much to speculate that most of the people simply wanted to play games on the one day a week they were not at work, and no doubt wished that their sports had no religious or political significance.

The Sunday games – or at least the laissez-faire attitude that allowed them to take place – were associated in the religious reformers' minds with Catholicism, and it was a widespread conspiracy theory of the time that Catholics encouraged Sunday games specifically to undermine the Protestant church services. However, it was also argued, and believed by the King himself, that a certain measure of fun and relaxation could entice Catholics into the fold. It was no accident that the first decree was made for Lancashire, the county with a reputation for having the highest number of Catholics in England.

The King's Book of Sports explains that the declaration reiterated the decree that was made in response to the people in Lancashire, who had complained that they were being prevented from enjoying their:

. . . lawful recreations, and honest exercises, after the afternoon sermon or service. We now find that two sorts of people, wherewith

that country is much infected (we mean Papists and Puritans) have maliciously traduced and calumniated those Our just and honourable proceedings.

If sports were not allowed, the *Book of Sports* continues, there would be two regrettable 'inconveniences': firstly, as mentioned above, it would deter Catholics from converting to the Protestant Church; and secondly, healthy exercise makes people's bodies 'more able for war, when We, or Our successors, shall have occasion to use them'. The alternative was 'filthy tiplings and drunkenness, and breeds a number of idle and discontented speeches in their ale houses'. Some pastimes were therefore permitted, while others were banned:

And as for Our good people's lawful recreation, Our pleasure likewise is, that, after the end of Divine Service, Our good people be not disturbed, letted, or discouraged from any lawful recreation, such as dancing, either of men or women, archery for men, leaping, vaulting, or any other such harmless recreation, nor from having of May Games, Whitsun Ales, and Morris-dances, and the setting up of Maypoles, and other sports therewith used, so as the same be had in due and convenient time, without impediment or neglect of Divine Service: and that women shall have leave to carry rushes to the church for the decoring of it, according to their old custom. But withal we do here account still as prohibited all unlawful games to be used upon Sundays only, as Bear and Bullbaitings, Interludes, and at all times, in the meaner sort of people, by law prohibited, bowling: and likewise we bar from this benefit and liberty, all such known Recusants, either men or women, as will abstain from coming to church or Divine Service, that will not first come to the church and serve God: prohibiting in like sort, the said recreations to any that, though conform in religion, are not present in the church at the service of God, before their going to the said recreations.

Modern readers might wonder why such an innocuous pastime as bowling should be ranked alongside bearbaiting and banned outright. However, bowling had become such a popular craze that working people were thought to be neglecting their ordinary labour in order to spend time playing, and so, for their own good and the good of the nation, it was believed that it had to be restrained. Notice that the declaration only bans bowling for 'the meaner sort'.

The Book of Sports was not well received by the religious reformers of the day, who denounced it roundly, although some magistrates were pleased to have a clear ruling on what was becoming a major focus of factional confrontation within their communities. The zealots took it as one more sign that the sovereign was not to be trusted in matters of religious policy, and they did not give up the fight. Charles I felt it necessary to reissue the book in 1633, but by this time the reformers had gained so much confidence that it was largely irrelevant, and only eleven years later, not only were the provisions of the declaration rescinded by Parliament but the book itself was publicly burnt. The new statute, *An Ordinance for the better observation of the Lords Day* (8 April 1644) ran as follows:

And be it further ordained, that no person or persons shall hereafter upon the Lords-day, use, exercise, keep, maintain, or be present at any wrastlings, shooting, bowling, ringing of bells for pleasure or pastime, wake, otherwise called feasts, church-ale, dancing, games, sport or pastime whatsoever; upon pain, that every person so offending being above the age of fourteen years, shall lose, and forfeit five shillings for every such offence . . .

And because the profanation of the Lords-day hath been heretofore greatly occasioned by May-poles (a heathenish vanity, generally abused to superstition and wickedness), the Lords and Commons do further order and ordain, that all and singular May-poles, that are, or shall be erected, shall be taken down and removed by the constables, borsholders, tything-men, petty constables, and churchwardens of the parishes and place where the same be: and that no May-pole shall be hereafter set up, erected, or suffered to be within this kingdom of England, or Dominion of Wales . . .

And it is further ordained by the said Lords and Commons that the King's Declaration concerning observing of wakes, and use of exercise and recreation upon the Lords-day; the Book intituled, *The Kings Majesties Declaration to his Subjects concerning lawful sports to be used*; and all other books and pamphlets that have been, or shall be written, printed, or published, against the morality of the fourth Commandment, or of the Lords-day, or to countenance the profanation thereof, be called in, seized, suppressed and publicly burnt by the Justices of Peace . . .

☞ *continued from page 353* with groups such as the Young Farmers'
Clubs and the Royal Agricultural Society, launched a campaign to
revive 'the old Saxon festivals of Plough Sunday, Rogation-Sunday,
Lammas-tide, and Harvest Thanksgiving' (*The Times*, 15 November
1948). He wrote new services for these days, and his ideas were
enthusiastically adopted by many churches across the country.

Although not one of the official quarter days, Lammas was a regular day for paying rents, settling debts, and changing jobs and houses.
Cumbrians, probably under Scottish influence, often divided the business year into two periods, rather than four, with settlements due at
Candlemas (2 February) and Lammas. In an extension of this association with payment and the settlement of outstanding dues, the phrase
'the latter Lammas' was, from at least the mid sixteenth century, applied to the Day of Judgement, and by further extension it could mean
'never', as in the phrase 'I'll pay you at the latter Lammas!'

Its position in the year also contributed to its key role in the organization of rights to common lands. Where common or church land was
rented out by the half-year, or where common strips of land were ap-
portioned annually, Lammas was often the time that the business was
carried out. In agricultural communities, these arrangements often
involved important economic rights, and were jealously guarded and
carefully administered. As A. R. Wright and T. E. Lones, the compilers
of the classic *British Calendar Customs* volumes, recorded:

*Certain lands were used by their owners for the growing of wheat and other
crops, but on a date fixed by custom were thrown open for common pasture and other purposes . . . The lands remained open until the following
spring. The custom was followed in or near Colchester, Coventry, Epping,
Newbury, Staines, Ware, and Watford Fields.*

Lammas was also a very popular day for fairs, for example at Exeter and
York, and local feasts and revels, as at Combe Martin in Devon, where
the church is dedicated to St Peter ad Vincula. Given that temporary
rules and regulations were in force during the time of a fair, it was essential that everybody knew when it opened and closed. Impressive
civic processions and readings of proclamations were therefore often
reported, along with the use of highly visible symbols, which could be
displayed while the fair lasted. Local resident James Cossins remembered that in the 1820s the Lammas Fair at Exeter:

. . . was a pleasure fair, commencing on the Tuesday, by a procession starting

from Westgate, consisting of the head constable, with a roll of parchment (tied with blue ribbons), containing the charter for holding the fair, which was read aloud by him at the site of the old gate. Two staff bearers accompanied him with their three-cornered hats, also two fifers and one drummer, followed by a man carrying a very long blue and white pole, surmounted by flowers and an immense stuffed white glove, and hundreds of children following. After the perambulation, the glove was mounted on the highest part of the Guildhall, until the fair (which lasted three days) was over.

It is not entirely clear why a glove was the chosen symbol, but in other contexts a lord or other high-ranking individual would send an official or messenger with a glove as a token of his authority, and this is presumably an extension of this idea. The phrase 'The glove is up!' was often used to mean that the fair was open.

A further etymological puzzle surrounds 1 August, as in earlier records the day was referred to as 'the Gule of August'. The *Oxford English Dictionary* states that the ulterior etymology of the word is unknown, but that it has been in use at least since 1300, and also existed in Old French and Medieval Latin. It has been suggested that it derives from the Welsh *gwyl*, or 'feast', but it is not clear why or how Norman English (or Old French) picked up such a word, and it is more likely that both the Welsh and English terms are derived from the Latin. It is very unlikely that the phrase meant 'the Yule of August', signifying that the festival was like a summer Christmas.

As already indicated, 1 August is also one of the feast days dedicated to St Peter. He shares his main feast day with St Paul on 29 June, but the feast on 1 August is called Peter Ad Vincula, or 'Peter in Chains', and commemorates the incident in the Acts of the Apostles (12:3–8) when an angel visited him in prison, 'and his chains fell off from his hands'. *See* **12 August: Congleton Bells** for a relevant custom.

See also **Fairs, Feasts, Wakes, and Revels**, p. 341.

Minden Day

Minden Day, important to British army personnel, veterans, and their families, commemorates the Battle of Minden in Germany, which took place on this day in 1759 during the Seven Years War. A column of British infantry, including men of six different British and three Hanovarian regiments, unexpectedly routed eleven squadrons of French cavalry and smashed through the French line, showing unbelievable bravery and coolness in the face of overwhelming odds. Each of the regiments involved (the Suffolk, the Royal Hampshire, the Lancashire Fusiliers, the Royal Welch Fusiliers, the King's Own Yorkshire Light Infantry, and the King's Own Scottish Borderers) still celebrates the day with parades and reunions, and serving and retired soldiers alike wear fresh 'Minden roses' in recognition of the story that while advancing towards the French line, the men passed through some gardens and plucked roses to decorate their hats. In August 2003, the florists Interflora sent 700 fresh red roses to the soldiers of the King's Own Scottish Borderers who were serving in Iraq at the time.

4 August

Kit-Dressing

Since at least the fourteenth century, the word 'kit' has been used in various parts of the country to mean a wooden vessel, with hooped staves and handles, of varying size, but often specifically to denote a milking pail, or receptacle for carrying produce such as butter or fish to customers or to market. In 1829, Stephen Glover wrote of a custom called 'kit-dressing' in his classic history of Derbyshire (1829):

At Baslow the rural festive kit-dressing took place on the 4th of August, in 1829; the procession was attended by the Baslow band, and the decoration of the kits surpassed in beauty and taste any that had been seen before. On one of the kits was this inscription:

> *The farmer, the plough-boy, the fleece and the flail*
> *Success to the milk-maid who carries the pail.*

A beautiful garland and a large pink flag were emblems carried in the procession. Twigs of willow were bent over the tops of the kits and entwined with flowers and ribbons. The garlands were formed upon a framework of woven willow twigs, and were adorned by means of silk, muslin, and trinkets of silver and gold.

As this is the only reference to the custom, it is not clear whether this was widely known or simply a local occurrence, but there is a reference to something similar in Lincolnshire in the 1820s (*see* 1 **May**).

The decorating of trade implements for celebration was not uncommon, and a close analogy to this custom was the milkmaids' dance (*see* 1 **May: Milkmaids' Garland**), but the Baslow procession seems to have been larger and more organized. It is also a mystery why it took place on 4 August.

5 August

Grasmere Rush-Bearing

William and Dorothy Wordsworth lived and died in Grasmere, and the village is now one of the most popular literary shrines in England, besieged by tourists for much of the year. Given their romantic propensities, the Wordsworths were naturally very keen on local traditions, and they took a particular interest in the annual rush-bearing, which they regarded as the prettiest of summer celebrations. This interest helped to protect the custom when attendance was low, and ensured its survival into the twentieth century, when local traditions were appreciated and encouraged once more, as symbols of old-time community.

Grasmere rush-bearing remains justly famous, and is by far the best known of the five existing rush-bearing ceremonies in Cumbria. At present, the ceremony takes place on the Saturday nearest to St Oswald's Day (5 August), to whom the local church is dedicated, but the date seems to have varied over the years. As with other Cumbrian rush-bearings, the key part of the day is the procession, with marching band, banners, clergy, and the congregation, who carry flowers, rushes, and special 'bearings' – rush-covered wood and wire in symbolic shapes such as crosses, hearts, and harps, as well as wreaths, a pole with a serpent coiled round it, and appropriate biblical scenes, such as Moses in the bulrushes. The central focus of the procession is a group of six girls (the Rush-Maidens) dressed in green and white, with flowers in their hair, holding outspread between them a large embroidered sheet on which are placed a few token rushes, and carrying other rushes in their free hand. They all march to the church, where a special service is held, and the rest of the day is spent *en fête*, with wrestling and a dance in the evening.

Since at least the early nineteenth century it has been traditional to give all the participating children a piece of gingerbread and, from

13 Grovely celebrations at Wishford Magna, Wiltshire:
the dance outside Salisbury Cathedral to preserve the right
to gather wood in the local forest [*29 May*]

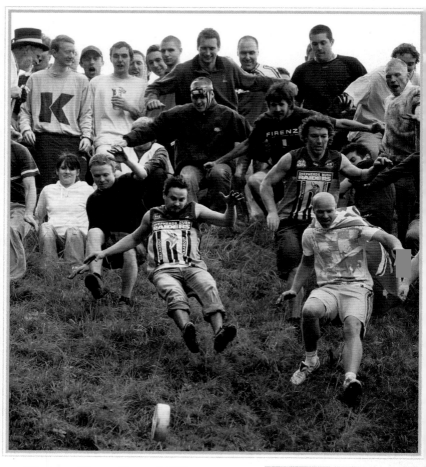

14 Cheese-rolling at Cooper's Hill, Gloucestershire (above), in 2006 [*Spring Bank Holiday*]

15 The 1968 winner (right) shows the difference in costume thought appropriate for the day

16 Schoolchildren Bawming the Thorn at Appleton, Cheshire [*29 June*]

17 Two variations on the theme of children and flowers
for rush-bearing ceremonies: Warcop (above) …

18 ... and Grasmere (above), Cumbria [*July*]
19 Even the swans are well posed (below) for Edwardian photographer
Benjamin Stone at the swan-upping in 1905 [*Late July*]

20 Whoever Bartle was, he must be burnt every year at
West Witton, Yorkshire (above) [*24 August*]
21 Another Benjamin Stone photograph (below): the horn dancers
at Abbots Bromley, Staffordshire, in 1906 [*4 September*]

22 The bonfire boys parade the streets of Lewes, East Sussex (above),
to celebrate Guy Fawkes Night [*5 November*]
23 Sword dancers at Flamborough, Yorkshire (below) [*Christmas*]

24 Father Beelzebub in the Marshfield Paper Boys' version of the mummers' play (left) [*26 December*]

25 Another winter fire festival (below): the Guisers at Allendale, Northumberland [*New Year's Eve*]

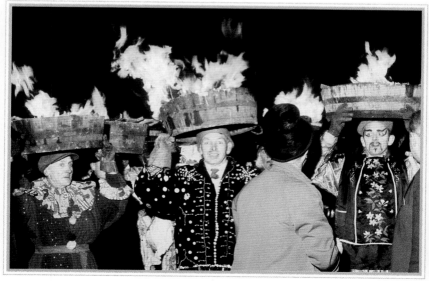

1834, a small coin, which was introduced to encourage attendance after a particularly low point when only seven children turned up. There are numerous accounts of the celebrations from the nineteenth century onwards, which show that in essentials the day has changed little for nigh on 150 years. The following was published in *Notes & Queries* in 1875:

I chanced to be in Grasmere . . . in July 1875 . . . As the children arrived with their standards they ranged themselves along the inside of the wall, resting their rush crosses, etc., on the wall, and holding them so. When more than a hundred of these pretty emblems, each held by a little child, were arranged on the wall, a more pleasing sight could hardly be seen . . . The church bells rang out a merry peal, and soon after six the children set off marching in procession two and two, headed by a band, through the village. The procession was very pretty . . . While the rush-bearers were assembling, a plate was handed round among spectators for the purpose of collecting a little money to pay the band, and to provide each of the children with twopence-worth of gingerbread . . . After marching through the village the children brought their rush standards back to the church where they were fixed upright on the edges of the pews; a nail driven through the wooden square at the foot of the standard seemed to be the mode of attachment. At morning service on Sunday the effect was extremely pretty, and the old church was filled with a most delightful perfume of flowers, ferns, and rushes. The service commenced with the singing of the . . . hymn which has been used for many years in Grasmere church, the Hymn for the Rush-Bearers.

Rush-bearing at Grasmere is first mentioned in the churchwardens' accounts of 1680, when a shilling was paid 'For ale bestowed on those who brought rushes and repaired the church', and similar entries appear regularly until 1841, when the church was paved. A painting of the Grasmere rush-bearing by local artist Frank Bramley, exhibited at the Royal Academy in 1905, now hangs in the village hall.

See also **Rush-Bearing**, p. 322.

James I

During the reign of James I (1603–25), 5 August was one of the days on which church bells across the nation were rung in his honour – in this case to commemorate his escape from the captivity imposed by Lord Gowrie in 1582–3 (known as 'the Gowrie conspiracy').

The fifth of August is also Old Style St James's Day, and regarded by some as the correct day to make grottoes in the street (*see* **Early August: Grottoes**).

10 August

St Lawrence's Day

St Lawrence, Deacon of Rome, was martyred in AD 258 and was an extremely popular saint across Europe; in pre-Reformation Britain, 228 churches were dedicated to him. No widespread customs seem to have taken place on his feast day, but its high summer date made it a popular time for fairs. The fair at Alvechurch, in Worcestershire, for example, included an ox-roasting, while a large gathering at Tan Hill, on the Wiltshire Downs near Devizes, was famous for its salt beef and beans. St Lawrence's is also the local feast day at Whitwell, in Derbyshire, and from 1879 until it lapsed in recent years, this included an open-air service of thanksgiving on the top of High Hill, where the stone for the church was believed to have been quarried.

As with many martyrs of the period, almost nothing is known of Lawrence's real life, but this did not stop the legend-makers, and various vivid stories are told about him. One in particular has been regarded by many as the origin of the term 'Lazy Lawrence', a phrase that was until recently, and possibly still is, regularly used in everyday speech. Legend has it that Lawrence was laid out on an iron griddle and slowly roasted over a fire. After a while, the saint taunted his tormentors and, exhibiting the power of Christian fortitude, asked them to turn him over, as he was quite done on that side. 'Lazy Lawrence' was thus a widespread term for anyone who showed signs of undue indolence. 'He has Lawrence on his back' or 'Lawrence has a hold of him' were similarly reported as meaning laziness personified, while 'St Lawrence weather' was used to describe hot sultry days. In truth, however, these phrases were derived from a popular seventeenth-century story, widely circulated in chapbooks, entitled 'The History of Lawrence Lazy'.

12 August

Congleton Bells

The feast of St Peter ad Vincula (St Peter in Chains) falls on 1 August, but an apparently unique custom that is clearly related to his festival took place at Congleton, in Cheshire, each year on 12 August, because of the eleven days lost at the change of calendar in 1752. The parish church there is dedicated to St Peter ad Vincula, and so the local feast or wake was held on his day. On the Wake Sunday, the following custom, described here by the *Monthly Packet* magazine, was also carried out:

On the Wake Sunday, from time immemorial until several years ago, an extraordinary musical performance aroused the inhabitants from their sleep very early in the morning. The instruments were horse collars hung round with numerous bells of peculiar shape; these collars were placed on men's shoulders and, walking through the streets of the town, the men shake the collars vigorously and thus cause the bells to emit a loud noise. Formerly, a heavy chain was used; the bells were an innovation introduced a few generations ago.

Other accounts relate that the custom was still called 'the ringing of the chains' even when bells were used, and that the noise made was certainly not musical. It was suppressed in the late nineteenth century, apparently because it had long fallen into abuse and degradation. The ownership of the bells, and the right to perambulate the town with them, was said to be hereditary, and had for several generations been in the hands of a family of chimney sweeps named Stubbs. They had taken to profaning the occasion by getting drunk and descending into burlesque. Finally, when two branches of the family were disputing ownership of the bells, and both had been locked in the town gaol for fighting, the town clerk took the opportunity to buy the bells, and from then on they belonged to the town's corporation. They are now on display in the Congleton Museum, and can be seen on the museum's website. Although the symbolism of the chains or bells for the day is clear, it is not known how or when it started, and no reports of similar activities elsewhere have yet come to light.

Gibson Tomb

The eighteenth-century mausoleum of the Gibson family stands in the churchyard of St Nicholas church in Sutton (formerly Surrey but now a London borough) – although there is no evidence that the family, who came from Walthamstow, had any previous connection with Sutton. When Mary Gibson died in 1793, she left money to Christ's Hospital, on condition they ensured that the Rector of St Nicholas undertake an annual inspection of the tomb and carry out any necessary repairs, as well as preaching a memorial sermon. The sermon lapsed in the late nineteenth century, but the unlocking and inspecting of the tomb continues to this day every 12 August, although the exact form of the ceremony has changed several times in its 200-year history. As with other impressive tombs, the Gibson mausoleum has attracted its share of local beliefs and legends, including the idea that if one walks seven times around it, a ghost will emerge from an urn on its roof.

16 August

St Roch's Day

St Roch was born at Montpellier, France, c.1350, and spent his short life as a hermit and on repeated pilgrimages. On one of these religious trips he caught the plague and was kept alive in the woods by food that was brought to him by a dog. He died c.1380, but soon acquired the reputation for healing the disease. His fame was on the wane in the seventeenth century, but was revived in Europe in the nineteenth, as a result of widespread fears over cholera. Although antiquarian John Brand presented evidence in his *Observations on the Popular Antiquities of Great Britain* (1849) that St Roch's Day was celebrated in Britain in the seventeenth century under the name 'Rock Monday', it is not clear what was done on the day, or how widely known it was.

Tutbury Bull-Running

Bull-running was a 'sport' in which a bull was let loose and then chased through streets or fields by the people involved, and should therefore be sharply distinguished from the common **bull-baiting** (p. 480), in which dogs were set to attack a tethered animal. Only a handful of places in England are recorded as having bull-running customs, the most widely known being at Stamford, in Lincolnshire (*see* **13 November: St Brice's Day**).

At Stamford, the bull was forced to run through the streets, but at Tutbury, the chasers had to catch it on open land. In order to make this more difficult, the bull's horns were removed, its ears and tail cropped, and its body was smeared with soap. This latter detail makes it sound like a particularly difficult version of the well-known fairground game of catching the greasy pig. Pepper was blown into the bull's nose to make it angry. If the chasers could hold the bull long enough to cut off a piece of hair as proof, they could keep the animal, to sell, keep, or eat as they thought fit.

Originally, the bull-running was only a small part of the annual celebrations of the 'Court of Minstrels', a sort of trade guild for musicians, granted a charter by Richard II in 1380/1. The bull was originally supplied by the Prior of Tutbury, but after the Dissolution swept away the priory it was provided by the Duke of Devonshire. In former times, only the minstrels did the chasing, but over the years the custom came to include enthusiastic participants from the town and further afield, which brought it into disrepute. It was abolished in 1778.

17 August

Lee Gap Fair

Lee Gap Fair, in the parish of Woodkirk, West Ardsley, near Leeds, is one of the surviving horse fairs that still attract a strong Gypsy presence, and its organizers claim it to be the oldest chartered fair in England. A charter from King Stephen in 1136, confirming an earlier one, does indeed grant two fairs to the parish of Woodkirk, in August and September, and there are still two Lee fairs: Lee Gap Fair on 17 August, and Latter Lee on 17 September.

See also **Fairs, Feasts, Wakes, and Revels**, p. 341.

23 August

St Bartholomew's Eve

John Stow, in his *Survey of London* (1598), recorded an interesting custom in which schoolboys pitted their learning against each other:

I myself, in my youth, have yearly seen, on the eve of St. Bartholomew the Apostle, the scholars of divers grammar schools repair unto the churchyard of St. Bartholomew, the priory in Smithfield, where upon a bank boarded about under a tree, some one scholar hath stepped up, and there hath opposed and answered, till he were by some better scholar overcome and put down; and then the overcomer taking the place, did like as the first; and in the end the best opposers and answerers had rewards, which I observed not but it made both good schoolmasters, and also good scholars.

A contributor to William Hone's *Year-Book* (1832) commented that a similar custom prevailed in Yorkshire until the early eighteenth century at Lee Fair (*see* **17 August**).

24 August

St Bartholomew's Day

Despite being one of Christ's Apostles, nothing is known for sure about St Bartholomew's life, but according to legend he died after being flayed alive and then beheaded. He therefore became, somewhat pointedly, the patron saint of tanners and other workers with knives. In religious illustrations he is often shown holding a knife, or even with his own skin draped over his arm like a cloth. He was very popular in medieval England, and 165 ancient churches were dedicated to him, including Croyland Abbey, in Lincolnshire, where a custom of giving little knives to the congregation in his memory took place on this day until abolished in the fifteenth century. Although his popularity seems to have gradually waned, his day was a regular one for fairs, including Newbury Fair, in Berkshire, and Whittingham Fair, in Northumberland, as well as the famous **Bartholomew Fair**, in London (*see below*). There were also other outdoor gatherings on the day, and presumably the weather at this time of year contributed to their popularity. William Hone's *Year-Book* (1832) includes an example of one such event that took place 'some time ago' at the village of Donnington, in Lincolnshire:

In the morning a number of maidens, clad in their best attire, went in procession to a small chapel, then standing in the parish, and strewed its floor with rushes, from whence they proceeded to a piece of land, called the 'Play Garths', where they were joined by most of the inhabitants of the place, who passed the remainder of the day in rural sports, such as foot-ball, wrestling, and other athletic exercises, with dancing, etc.

Apart from these, only a handful of disparate customs took place on this day (*see below*) each of which seem to have little or no connection with the saint, apart from being associated with an institution dedicated to him.

In the realm of weather-lore, according to Richard Inwards' classic collection on the subject, published in 1869, 'At St. Bartholomew, there comes cold dew.' But this seems more to do with the rhyme than any deep meteorological insight, because exactly the same was said of St Matthew's Day (21 September).

Bartholomew Fair

In its heyday, Bartholomew Fair was one of the four great fairs of England, and for centuries it was famous nationwide as a major place for entertainment of all kinds, high and low (but mainly low). Its charter was first granted in 1133 by Henry I, to the Prior of St Bartholomew's church and priory, Smithfield, but it was taken over by the City of London when the monasteries were dissolved. The fair commenced each year on St Bartholomew's Day, but its duration varied; in Charles II's time it was so popular that it was extended to fourteen days.

All the well-known writers and artists were familiar with it, and it became proverbial for summer fun, laughter, and a somewhat raffish pleasure – or for the depths of its iniquity, depending on your viewpoint. Numerous songs described its attractions or were set at the fair; Ben Jonson published a popular comedy, *Bartholomew Fair*, in 1614; and engravings of the fair appeared on a regular basis. All the major travelling play companies visited the fair every year, and it was famous for puppet plays and religious mystery plays as well as regular drama.

In addition, there were numerous music and dance shows, spectacu-lars, acrobats, tightrope walkers, gingerbread sellers, a menagerie of animals, ballad-singers, bearded ladies, fat men, giants, dwarves, fortune-telling horses, mermaids, and, of course, card-sharps, pick-pockets, prostitutes, pimps, and vagabonds.

Opposition came from many quarters, and there were repeated attempts at suppression in the late eighteenth and early nineteenth centuries, but the fair managed to struggle on till 1855, when it was proclaimed for the last time.

See also **Fairs, Feasts, Wakes, and Revels**, p. 341.

Sandwich Bun Race

Sandwich, one of the medieval cinque ports along the Kent and Sussex coast, has an 800-year-old almshouse called the Hospital of St Bartholomew. The exact date of its foundation is not known, but it was certainly in existence by 1287 and probably dates from the early thirteenth century. The hospital is still home to sixteen elderly 'broth-ers' and 'sisters', who live in cottages grouped around the equally an-cient St Bartholomew's chapel. On St Bartholomew's Day each year, there is a special service at the chapel, attended by the residents and the Mayor and councillors of Sandwich. After the service, children race around the outside of the chapel and are then given buns. Adults are given a hard-baked biscuit stamped with the arms of the town. It has been suggested that the buns have replaced an earlier dole of bread, which is possible, and that this dole was itself a replacement of charity food given to pilgrims. However, the latter is said of every food custom within fifty miles of Canterbury, so is not likely to be accurate.

See also **Doles**, p. 115.

West Witton Burning of Bartle

This unique custom takes place in the North Yorkshire village of West Witton. A few days before the Saturday of the village feast, a larger-than-life effigy, stuffed with straw, with torches for eyes and named Bartle, is made by certain villagers. On the evening of the Saturday, Bartle is carried on the shoulders of two men and paraded through the village, stopping at houses and pubs, and being held up to peer in at cottage windows; the crowd grows as they proceed. Whenever the procession stops, a third man proclaims:

Sparrow-Mumbling

One of the many sports or games in which our forebears indulged at fairs and other gatherings, but which to modern eyes seem cruel and senseless. Exact details vary, but in one version a live cock sparrow, with clipped wings, was placed into a hat, and participants, whose arms were tied behind them, tried to bite off the sparrow's head. The bird, of course, attempted to defend itself by pecking its assailant's face. In another version, to which nineteenth-century Cornish miners were apparently partial, a live sparrow was fastened to a man's teeth by a string, and he had to attempt to pluck the feathers off the unfortunate bird, using only his lips. Sparrow-mumbling dates back at least to George Chapman's *Andromeda Liberata* (1614), which includes the passage: "Twill be most ridiculous and pleasing to sit in a corner and spend your teeth to the stumps in mumbling an old sparrow till your lips bleed and your eyes water.'

> *At Penhill Crags he tore his rags;*
> *At Hunter's Thorn he blew his horn;*
> *At Capplebank Stee he brake his knee;*
> *At Grisgill Beck he brake his neck;*
> *At Wadham's End he couldn't fend;*
> *At Grisgill End he made his end.*
> *Shout, lads, shout. Hooray!*

Everyone joins in the 'hooray'. Once the procession reaches Grass Gill End, Bartle is unceremoniously dowsed in paraffin and burnt, accompanied by the onlookers' cheers and jeers.

At first glance, the name and timing of the custom are easily explained. The parish church is dedicated to St Bartholomew, whose day is 24 August, and the local feast therefore took place at that time. However, it is unlikely that the figure represents the saint, as the mishandling and execution show a disrespect, or even hatred, that would hardly have been tolerated, so this may not be his original name. The dominant local legend is that Bartle was a swine thief who was hunted down and killed by outraged villagers, as detailed in the rhyme, which lists real local places on the moors above the village. Some, however, have claimed that Bartle was a local giant – in the days when giants were common enough – and that this explains why the effigy is usually larger than life. J. Fairfax-Blakeborough included a somewhat unpleasant story that detailed the life and death of 'The Wicked Giant of Penhill' in his book *The Hand of Glory* (1924), which was based on his father's extensive collection of Yorkshire lore. He does not give his giant a name, but the location and the fact that the giant's primary concern is care of his swine-herds indicate a connection with the Bartle. Unfortunately, Fairfax-Blakeborough's stories are usually so embellished as to preclude their being used as evidence of previous tradition, but they may well have influenced later perceptions.

Notwithstanding these legends, many writers have assumed that the custom has ancient origins, and have written of corn gods (because of the straw involved), scapegoats, and the usual fertility rituals, but any dispassionate examination of these theories is hampered by the fact that none of them ventures to say when the custom was first recorded, and so these theories are not supported by any factual evidence.

Although the Burning of Bartle appears to be unique, it does have connections with other customs. The most obvious common element is the production and destruction of an effigy in human form. Such figures are often found in 5 November proceedings, but were also used in a range of other traditions at different times of the year: *see*, for example, **Rough Music**, p. 95; **Ash Wednesday: Jack-a-Lent**, p. 86; **Good Friday: Burning Judas**, p. 143; and, most notably, **Easter Monday: Black Knight of Ashton**, p. 167.

Last Sunday in August

Plague Sunday

Few villages in Britain can claim genuine hero status, but Eyam (pronounced Eem) in Derbyshire is one. In September 1665, while the Great Plague was raging in London, the disease was brought to Eyam, probably in some infected cloth imported by the local tailor. The local rector, William Mompesson, supported by his wife Catherine and the previous incumbent Thomas Stanley (who had been ejected from the living at the Restoration) persuaded the villagers to impose a strict quarantine to contain the disease and prevent it spreading to neighbouring villages. The plan worked, and no cases were reported outside Eyam, but the village itself paid a heavy price. By November 1666, the disease had run its course, but few local families escaped its touch, and 260 of the original 350 inhabitants had perished. Many of their gravestones can still be seen. Since 1905, 'Plague Sunday' has been celebrated on the last Sunday in August, to commemorate the villagers' sacrifice. A procession makes its way to Cucklet Delf, the spot where outdoor services had been held while the plague raged, and a memorial service, with special plague hymn, takes place.

On another note, although it is almost universally believed in Britain that the children's rhyme 'Ring a Ring o' Roses' commemorates the Great Plague of London, this is not supported by any evidence. Rather, it is the best-known example of the way in which modern groundless suppositions about traditional rhymes and customs are invented and take hold – indeed, becoming folklore themselves. The earliest printed reference to the rhyme that has been found to date is in an American source from the 1880s.

29 August

Preston Guild

In medieval times, in Britain and across Western Europe, a local guild merchant wielded a great deal of power over trade and commerce in the area of its jurisdiction, granting privileges to its members and severely circumscribing the commercial activities of outsiders. These restrictions amounted to a monopoly on most areas of commerce, and, apart from during a fair, no non-guild member could trade in the town without express permission, which was rarely granted. Guild court meetings at which new members were admitted and other business was transacted were held periodically, and these events became major celebrations in themselves, with trade processions, triumphal arches, dinners, speeches, balls, concerts, and all kinds of popular entertainment. Many guilds pre-dated the growth of effective local government and provided the basis of the latter when it finally evolved. As guilds also had close connections with the religious establishment, it was common for local business, civic, and religious elites to become inextricably intertwined.

The charter for Lancashire's Preston Guild, granted by Henry II, dates back to *c.*1179. Since 1562 the guild has met every twenty years (except in 1942), to confirm its powers and agree new freemen. Although gradually stripped of its power over the years, and losing all remaining vestiges of it by the Municipal Reform Act of 1835, the meetings are still held, and comprise general celebration and merrymaking in the town. To be elected Freeman of the Guild has no practical purpose any more, but it is still regarded as an honour; and the phrase 'once every Preston Guild', meaning 'not very often', is still current in Lancashire. The next Preston Guild will be held in 2012.

August Bank Holiday

Marldon Apple Pie Fair

Marldon is a village near Paignton, in Devon, which holds an Apple Pie Fair every August Bank Holiday Monday. All the usual trappings of a popular village fête are present, including sideshows, craft tents, sports, demonstrations, and arena events, but the unique local feature is the entrance of a donkey pulling the apple pie cart, and the presence of the Apple Pie Princess. The following account was printed in the *Transactions of the Devonshire Association* in 1935 and is couched in the past tense, but it does not specify which year is being remembered:

The Marldon Apple Pie, which was oval in shape, about the size of a kitchen table, and brought from Marldon to St. Marychurch in the apple season annually by a Marldon countryman who possessed an orchard. This man, George Hill by name, was in the habit of bringing into Torquay weekly a donkey laden with panniers full of apples, and returning home with panniers full of washing to be laundered. During the homeward journey, George was usually asleep, but the donkey would safely convey him home. The Marldon Apple Pie was driven all round St. Marychurch in a cart decorated with flowers and ribands, and drawn by two black donkeys wearing harness and reins decorated with plaited reed (i.e. straw). The pie was afterwards eaten, with cream if desired, by all who cared to pay for a slice, in a playing field by Cary Park, where a fair and sports were being held. The tale of poor George Hill's last days is a sad one. Once when asleep on his homeward journey, his goods were stolen. Not long after this calamity George was found dead, possibly from the effects of his shock.

Village tradition claims that the first fair was held in 1888, but it has certainly not had an unbroken run since that time. Cuttings from the

continued on page 374

Bank Holidays

The current system of official bank holidays was created by the Bank Holidays Act of 1871, which was later incorporated into the Banking and Financial Dealings Act of 1971. The original Act provided for the Bank of England to be closed on certain days in the year, and, most importantly in legal terms, any bills or promissory notes that fell due on those days were payable on the following day without penalty. The days stipulated by the 1871 Act were Easter Monday, Whit Monday, the first Monday in August, and Boxing Day; Good Friday and Christmas Day were already accepted as common-law holidays by virtue of long tradition. It quickly became the norm for other institutions to close on these days, and employees in most sectors became accustomed to take them as holiday. Since that time, two have been added – New Year's Day (1974) and May Day (1978) – bringing the total number of bank holidays for England to eight per annum. In 1971, the moveable Whit Monday holiday was changed to the fixed Spring Bank Holiday, and August Bank Holiday moved from the first to the last Monday in August. There have also been a number of special bank holidays, such as one for the Royal Wedding in 1981 and for the Queen's Golden Jubilee in 2002. Contrary to widespread popular opinion, bank holidays are not 'statutory holidays', and employees are not permitted to refuse to work on those days.

Normally quite consensual, the timing of bank holidays occasionally hits the headlines of political debate, especially when the idea of celebration or commemoration is mixed with that of 'holiday' pure and simple. August Bank Holiday causes no problems because it is simply an arbitrary late summer day, but the adoption of May Day as a new bank holiday in 1978, by the Labour government of the day, created a major furore. The Conservative opposition claimed that May Day's international socialist nature made it an unsuitable choice, and *The Times* ran a suitably thunderous leader suggesting that the British public should use the day to commemorate innocent people murdered in the Soviet Union. When the Conservatives returned to power, they seriously planned to scrap the May Day holiday and to replace it with a more patriotic 'Trafalgar Day' in October (*see* 21 October). This in turn was criticized, as it would disrupt manufacturing output in the important run-up to Christmas, and it met with a lukewarm response from the public, who, not surprisingly, preferred a day off in early summer to one in late autumn. The plan was quietly shelved in 1993, but the principle of patriotism is still regularly cited when the question of the timing of bank holidays is discussed.

A current campaign highlights the paucity of bank holidays in Britain, compared to many other European countries. A short paper by Michael Jacobs, published on the Fabian Society's website, shows that the Netherlands has seven bank holidays; Britain, Ireland, and Finland each have eight, while all the other major European countries have many more, with Italy and Iceland topping the chart with sixteen and fifteen bank holidays respectively.

☞ *continued from page 372* *Western Morning News* show that the fair was revived in 1958 or 1959, after a 'lapse of 70 years'. Since then, however, it has been held every year, and now takes place in the Jubilee Meadow. For a while, the pie was a fake one containing hundreds of individual real pies, but about ten years ago it returned to its former glory and a very real apple pie is now made by a local baker in a stainless steel dish, about 2 feet 6 inches by 2 feet in size, which was donated to the village by the local postman. It is still brought to the fair in a donkey cart, and the Apple Pie Princess makes the first cut.

Notting Hill Carnival

London's Notting Hill Carnival, which takes place over the August Bank Holiday, is often billed as the biggest street party in Europe, or even the world, and attracts up to one and a half million people to its north London locality. From small local beginnings just over forty years ago, the event has grown to such huge proportions that its organization is a full-time operation, undertaken nowadays by the London Notting Hill Carnival Ltd.

Many events and activities are organized in the community in the preceding six weeks, and there are band competitions on the Saturday, and a shorter child-friendly family parade on the Sunday. However, the climax of the celebrations, and the event that steals all the headlines, is the big parade on the August Bank Holiday Monday, which covers a three-mile route around Great Western Road, Chepstow Road, Westbourne Grove, and Ladbroke Grove, and has to be experienced to be believed, consisting of a huge colourful orgy of loud music, dancing in the street, outrageous costumes – which would not disgrace carnival participants in Brazil – and much eating and drinking from the many stalls that line the route.

The Notting Hill Carnival grew from various ad hoc gatherings of immigrants, mainly from the Caribbean, who settled in the area in the 1950s and wished to bring something of their own culture to life in their new home. These events coalesced into a street carnival in 1964, and it has been held every year since, becoming bigger and more audacious every year. In earlier years there were some problems of violence in the crowds, but that is now long gone, and the main problems facing organizers nowadays are how to squeeze a million people safely into the narrow streets of this corner of north London, and provide enough facilities for them. Attempts by the Greater London Authority to spread the carnival into neighbouring areas and Hyde Park have so far met with resistance from local organizers, who fear that the event will lose its vital local base if it moves too far from its roots and becomes too closely identified with official local government tourism initiatives.

See also **First Friday in November: Bridgwater Carnival.**

SEPTEMBER

Harvest Customs

The importance of the harvest in an agricultural economy can hardly be overstressed, and in England in past centuries the whole life of the nation depended on it. Even when the harvest had lost some of its economic edge, it still had a deep psychological impact on rural communities, as the Wiltshire writer Alfred Williams commented in 1912:

The in-gathering of the corn-harvest is by far the most important feature of the farm year, especially where there is much arable land, or perhaps it may be all corn in some places, as on the Downs, for instance. If the weather is wet in hay-time and the crop spoiled, that may not matter very much; but in the harvest, that is truly tragic! Who does not deeply grieve, apart from the monetary loss involved, to see all that is left of the beautiful corn blackening and rotting in the fields, under the dark rainy skies of October and November, as is sometimes the case, utterly useless for anything but litter and manure, and the ground too wet and sodden to admit of collecting it for that purpose even? It seems as though you have lived the year for nothing then; that all the bloom and sunshine of the spring and summer were mockery; that Nature brought forth her beautiful children but to destroy them.

Of all the points of the farming year, it was the time when the farmer needed the full co-operation of his workers. The workers, too, knew that a successful harvest was essential to the economic well-being of the community, and that a bad one would affect their chances of employment the following year. They could also earn double their usual wage during the harvest, and the amount of work doubled too, so it was well within their own interest to make it a successful season.

Embedded in the practical and physical arrangements necessary to 'win' the harvest, a number of customs and usages grew up over the years, which served to keep the workers amused, gain them some monetary advantage, or celebrate their achievements.

Whether a particular custom had its origin in a game, a practical response to a practical problem, or a superstitious impulse, remains to be discovered. However, the idea that harvest customs are direct survivals of belief in corn goddesses and vegetation spirits of pre-Christian times, which has been the ruling orthodoxy for many years, is not supported by the documentary record, and it is time it was discarded.

Farmworkers often tried to enhance their autonomy in their day-to-day work by organizing themselves: the sheep-shearers formed their own autonomous band, who contracted with the farmer for the job; the haymakers organized themselves under an elected captain and lieutenant; and so on. Rules were also created that helped the workers to take control of the process. A very widespread notion, for example, held that they could exact 'largesse' (i.e. money) from any stranger who set foot on the land on which they were working, or even who passed by on the footpath, and if the farmer himself appeared he could expect some rough handling. The following account was written in Northumberland in 1909, but refers to the second half of the nineteenth century:

A practical joke was played on the farmer if he dared to show himself in the field, and this he took good care as a rule not to do. It was called 'putting up the master'. If the farmer by any chance made his appearance, it was a custom for the hands, chiefly the women workers, to set on him, pull him off his horse, and 'grip' him, and toss him in the air, not only once, but three or four times, catching him as he fell . . . It says a great deal for the strength, nerve and dexterity of the harvest maidens of those days, that the farmer was always safely caught after his tossing and suffered no harm.

The harvesters also called on tradesmen and others in the village who had dealings with the farm, and solicited contributions from them.

Many harvesters made a particular game out of cutting the last of the standing corn. A few stalks were left standing and tied together. The men then took it in turn to throw their sickles (sometimes blindfolded or backwards to make the game more difficult) to see who could cut them down. Others made even more of a ceremony of it. In 1903, the journal *Folk-Lore* reported:

A farm-worker from the East Riding of Yorkshire described a harvest custom of 'burning the old witch'. The harvesters twisted together the last few standing stalks of corn, making it into a little sheaf, and then set fire to it. The last time he saw it done was about 1850, but he remembered it being referred to, as for example when a co-worker said 'I think we'd better burn it, if it would bring us better luck next time', as late as the 1880s.

One regular procedure carried out upon the last sheaf, which was sometimes combined with the sickle-throwing, was called 'crying the neck', or something similar. It was most widespread in the West Country, but it existed elsewhere in the country too. This example, referring to Cornwall in 1839, was published in *Folk-Lore* in 1890:

Now, when all the corn was cut at Heligan, the farming men and women come in front of the house, and bring with them a small sheaf of corn, the last that has been cut, and this is adorned with ribbons and flowers, and one part is tied quite tight, so as to look like a neck. Then they cry out, 'Our/My side, my side' as loud as they can; then the dairymaid gives the neck to the head farming-man. He takes it and says, very loudly three times, 'I have him, I have him, I have him'. Then another farming-man shouts very loudly, 'What have ye? what have ye? what have ye?', 'A neck, a neck, a neck'. And when he has said this, all the people make a very great shouting. This they do three times, and after one famous shout go away and eat supper, and dance, and sing songs. The custom passed away with the introduction of machines.

In other accounts, the ceremony was carried out in the field. The earliest, and fullest, description of this ceremony was contributed to William Hone's *Every-Day Book* in 1827 by a Devon correspondent.

A close examination of nineteenth- and twentieth-century descriptions shows that at that time the sickle-throwing, and probably also the 'crying of the neck', were simply games, and they may well have been nothing more than that. However, there may be relevant material in the regulations laid down on medieval manors to regulate the behaviour of the serfs in the harvest field – in particular, in the stipulations concerning the amount of free hay or corn the peasant could take from his lord's field after his labours there. The descriptions included in H. S. Bennett's excellent *Life on the English Manor 1150–1400* (1948) are at least suggestive of a connection with the later customs:

On certain Ramsey manors the peasants were allowed to 'carry home so much hay or straw as they could bind in a single bundle and lift upon their sickle [or scythe] *handle, so that the handle touch not the ground. And, if perchance the handle break, then he shall lose his straw or grass and be at the lord abbot's mercy, and pay a fine, coming to the best accord that he can with the abbot'* . . . [another] *custom which allowed the serf to take from the abbot's courtyard a bundle of as much straw as he could carry, 'but, if the band break he shall lose his straw'* . . . *In the west of England, on a manor of the Abbot of Glastonbury, the size of the sheaf taken by the peasant was measured in a strangely elaborate manner: 'If any sheaf appears less than is right, it ought to be put in the mud, and the hayward should grasp his own hair above his ear, and the sheaf should be drawn midway through his arm, and if this can be done without defiling his garments or his hair, then it is adjudged to be less than is right; but otherwise it is judged sufficient.' In other manors the serfs had the right to medkniche when they mowed the lord's meadow. This was as much hay as the hayward could lift with his little finger as high as his knees.*

It takes no great stretch of the imagination to see these as possible precursors of the harvest games reported in the nineteenth century, and there are many more examples like these tucked away in medieval cartularies and other manorial documents. At present, evidence of a direct connection is hardly more than circumstantial and must be treated with due caution, but the hypothesis is certainly worth further investigation. Another 'game' related by Bennett was as follows:

In connection with the boon services at haymaking, there was a widespread custom whereby the lord released a sheep into the meadow. On some manors it became the property of the serfs only if they could catch it before it escaped out of the field; on other manors it was handed over to them for their feast as part of their reward . . . [Elsewhere] *the ram was brought to the centre of the field; if it remained quietly grazing then the customary tenants claimed it, but if it wandered out of the field they lost it and the abbess had it restored to her* . . .

Once the corn was finally cut down, the last load was brought in with some considerable ceremony. The final cart itself was decorated with flowers, ribbons, greenery, and the like. Women and children would ride on top of the load, and sometimes a male and female were placed on the front of the waggon, to represent the king and queen of the harvest. These characters were not always what they seemed, as in a piece printed in *Folk-Lore* (1902) that referred to Oxfordshire in the 1830s:

> *On the last night of harvest, when the last load was to be carted, it was the custom to send down to the fields a number of band-boxes containing women's dresses and a good deal of finery for the men and horses. Four young men then dressed themselves up, two to represent women, and they sat in couples on the four horses that drew the load. Some of the village children sat on the top of the load (my informant said that she and her sisters had often done so) and on reaching the house were treated to cakes, etc. . . . . After this I believe the men had a supper.*

Whatever else took place, there was always much shouting and cheering, as in this Devon example, also from *Folk-Lore* (1890):

> *At Kingsbridge, the following was formerly recited or sung (at the end of the harvest): 'we've a ploughed, and we've a sowed, we've a reaped, and we've a mowed, we've a sheaved, and we've a bound, and we'll a stood upon the ground'. At the end was 'Hip, hip, hip, hurrah!'*

Several accounts of the last load mention that water was deliberately thrown over the jubilant harvesters:

> *The top of the last load was crowded with reapers – men, not children – who sang lustily as they came through the village 'Harvest home! Harvest home! We wants water and can't get none!' which certainly was not true in fact, as from every house they passed buckets of water were thrown on them . . .*

This was from Oxfordshire in 1872, published in *Notes & Queries*, and a similar account in the same journal describes how, at a Rutland harvest, female servants waited concealed behind a hedge to attack the last load with buckets of water and apples.

The making of some sort of figure out of straw was extremely widespread in the British Isles, although it was not found, according to current evidence, in East Anglia, the south, or the south-east of the country. The figure went by a wide variety of names – 'kern', 'kirn', or 'churn', for example, from Yorkshire to Scotland – and was almost invariably referred to as a baby, or a female, such as 'maiden' or 'old hag'. This in itself has caused some confusion, as a historical account of, say, a 'harvest lady' could be describing a real person or a straw figure. The term 'corn dolly' was not used by farmworkers but was invented *c.*1940 by enthusiasts who developed straw-work into a new and complex craft.

The earliest probable reference to a straw figure comes from the writings of the German visitor Paul Hentzer, who met some harvest workers at Windsor, *c*.1598, and commented that their last load was decorated with flowers and 'an image richly dressed'. In later accounts, the nature of the figure, its size and complexity, what was done with it, and how it was treated, varied enormously and still needs to be fully documented. The figure might be made from the last stalks cut or from the 'best' straw; sometimes the figure consisted of a few stalks twisted together, usually in a cross or a crude human form, and sometimes it was skilfully made up to represent a small human figure, decorated with ribbons, and so on. However, if an elaborate figure was fashioned, it must of necessity have been made some time in advance of the last load if it was to adorn the cart on its way back to the farmyard. In some accounts, it seems to have been simply decorative, but in others it was definitely symbolic and was hung up in the barn, on the principle that some part of that year's luck should be kept until the next year. This principle operated in other customs, such as the Yule Log, of which many householders were careful to keep a piece to be used to light next year's specimen (*see* **24 December: Yule Log**). The straw figure could also be used in a protective way, as in this Lincolnshire example from 1899:

No further back than last September, I saw a veritable 'kern baby' – a largish doll cunningly twisted out of barley straw, and perched up on a sheaf exactly facing the gate of the grand wheat-field in which it stood. I missed seeing the owner, a small freeholder, but mentioning the matter to an old dame (of whom a Marshman would say, 'them as knows all she knows hasn't no need to go to no school'). She made a reply which proves that, whatever else the Marshman has learnt of late to doubt, he still firmly believes in the Devil and his angels: 'Yes, she be there to fey away t' thunder an' lightnin' an' such-like. Prayers be good enough as far as they goes, but t' Almighty must be strange an' throng wi' so much corn to look after, an' in these here bad times we mustn't forget owd Providence. Happen it's best to keep in wi' both parties.'

Finally, it might even be sent to a neighbouring farmer who had not yet finished his harvest as a not-so-subtle jibe at his tardiness. This procedure was sometimes called 'the mare', but 'crying the mare' could also be achieved with a real horse. According to *The Times* (2 October 1934):

[An] *explanation was given me nearly 40 years ago by an old labourer in Staffordshire who remembered the days before the introduction of reaping and threshing machines. The first farmer to finish his harvest, he told me, would dress up one of his horses with ribbons, etc., and send it round in derision to his neighbours who were not so fortunate as himself. This mocking offer of help was, of course, always refused and the rider of the horse generally pelted. For this reason, said Old Dick, they generally put up on the mare the youngest boy on the farm. Such was the custom in Staffordshire in the first half of the nineteenth century.*

Gleaning

On most farms, by long-standing custom, local people were allowed on to the fields after harvest to 'glean' what crops had escaped the harvesters. Gleaning was an extremely important contribution to the domestic economy, and sufficient grain could sometimes be gathered to keep a family in flour for the whole winter. It had been allowed for time out of mind, and was regarded by many villagers as an inalienable right, although in reality it was at the discretion of the farmer unless written into the agreement made with the harvesters.

Gleaning conduct was usually governed by well-understood local rules. Some farmers would leave a single sheaf in the field to signify that gleaning could not yet take place, and in many areas the church bell was tolled to signal the start and finish of the gleaning day. For local mothers gleaning was hard work, but it was not all bad for the children, as Edwin Grey described in his memories of rural Hertfordshire in the 1870s:

The gleaning season was made the most of by many of the cottage women, for the flour obtained as a result of this wheat gleaning was a great asset to the food supply of the household during the autumn and early winter. There were, of course, many women who, owing to home ties and duties, could not go out to glean, but the number who did so, together with the boys and girls, was quite considerable ... The gleaning of the harvest fields was much enjoyed by the youngsters, both boys and girls, for those who attended school were at this season of the year on holiday, and so were, as one might say, free; so that I and many others, though not compelled to glean, went more for the fun. As a rule the children did their bit at gleaning, but it was the games, the romping, and the searching of the hedgerows for nuts, skeggs (a large sloe) etc., which was the lure for most of us boys ... Mrs. Day was recognized as the head of our party. She it was who decided as to our route; to which

farm and to which field we should go; the other women told of informa-
tion obtained from their husbands as to the progress of the harvesting at the
respective farms on which they worked, when such and such a field would
probably be cleared and so on . . .

I so well remember the lively cottager [Mrs Day], *for although past mid-*
dle age, she would sometime indulge in a step-dance for her own and our
amusement. She generally wore a large straw hat with turned-down brim
all round (mushroom shape, I think it was called) with a sort of frilled cap
beneath it. To an outsider from town, these gleaning parties must have
looked a queer company, for most wore their oldest clothes . . . but although
an odd-looking lot of humanity, they were by no manner of means dejected
or miserable, for they moved off to their destination with laughter, chat-
ter, and many snatches of song. They carried their day's rations with them,
generally bread, butter, cheese, or maybe some cold meat, or other homely
fare, together with a bottle or two of cold tea, these provisions being either in
baskets or wrapped in cloths or aprons. The two latter were used later to tie
up the handfuls of wheat into bundles, which were then carried home on the
head . . . It was an unwritten law that gleaning could not commence until
the last shock was carried . . . When at length the time came to start glean-
ing, each donned his 'earbag'. This was made of any material, with strings
or tapes at the top corners to tie round the waist; it was worn in front of the
body, and had the appearance of a small apron nearly all pocket. Into this
pocket during the gleaning were put the short or broken-off ears; we were
told to pick up all of these short ears, and were assured that they were the best
wheat. When the gleaning was finished for the day, the bunches of gleaned
wheat were tied up into bundles in the cloths or aprons, large bundles for the
adults and smaller ones for the youngsters; with those well-balanced on the
head they started for home. I recollect the youngsters used to sing, or shout
as they neared any cottage: 'Wheat, wheat, harvest home, see what great
bundles we bring home.' On arriving at home, the wheat ears would be cut
from the straw, the ears being put into a sack, or tied up into a bundle, the
straw being either burnt or thrown into a neighbour's pigsty.

Harvest Suppers

Soon after the prolonged effort of getting in the harvest, most farmers treated their workers to a celebratory feast in the form of a harvest
supper, although the exact name varied according to locality – harvest
home, mell supper (in the northern counties), or horkey supper (in
eastern England), for example. The event also varied considerably in

scale, depending on the nature and size of the farm, the character of the farmer, and the social structure of the village, but most followed a relatively standard pattern. The successful harvest was a village-wide event, and it was common for key people in the village to be invited along to the supper. Some, like the squire, vicar, and doctor, were invited as a matter of courtesy because of their social position, while others, such as the blacksmith and wheelwright, were there as an acknowledgement of the part they played throughout the year in keeping the farm operational. Descriptions of harvest suppers often stress the classless nature of the proceedings, with master and man attending on equal terms, but although this may have been the ideal, it can hardly ever have been the real situation. Not only was there a sharp division between farmer and worker, but within the farm workforce there was a strict hierarchy in which most workers were extremely jealous of their position. Nevertheless, the huge team effort needed to get the harvest in successfully gave the harvest home at least a temporary foundation of brotherhood and common cause, assisted, no doubt, by the alcohol, which flowed freely.

It goes without saying that the real attraction for the workers was the feast itself. The opportunity to indulge in good food and drink, in large quantity, and at someone else's expense, was too rare to be treated lightly, and there are many tales of the prodigious quantities some men could put away at this one sitting.

[Norfolk, 1845] *Tomorrow the men have a harvest-home dinner, and the next day they put apart to get drunk; such being the invariable custom of the county. I proposed last year that they should get drunk on the day of the harvest dinner, but they scouted the idea – they would have a day for intoxication entirely. Such was the custom. It was true that they would lose a day's wages, but they must do as their forefathers had always done before them.*

From a psychological perspective, this was not simply senseless gluttony. The harvest supper was the official end to an exceptionally gruelling time for most of the workers, who had been toiling hard, against the clock, for weeks on end. It was certainly an emotional and physical release as well as a free meal.

Harvest suppers usually took place in the barn, which had been cleaned up and decorated for the occasion. They tended to begin with the feast, then speeches and toasts would follow – particularly those thanking the farmer and his family – then singing, with contributions from all and sundry. The singing might last for the rest of the evening, or it might be adjourned so that dancing could take place. In many cases, the farmer and his family would stay for the feast, the toasts, and the speeches, but would then withdraw, along with any other 'gentry', to let the workers enjoy themselves in their own way. However, there were many variations on this pattern, and games and other entertainments were sometimes included. The following is a Dorset version of the most widely reported harvest supper song, published in 1935:

> Here's a health unto our Master, the founder of the feast
> I hope to God wi' all me heart his soul in heaven may rest
> And all his works may prosper, whatever he takes in hand
> For we are all his servants, and here at his command
> Then drink, boys, drink, and see you do not spill
> For if you do, you shall drink two, it is our Master's will.
> Here's a health unto our Master, our Mistress shan't go free
> For she's a good provider, provides as well as he
> For she's a good provider, and bids us all to come
> So take this cup and sup it up, for 'tis our harvest home
> Home boys home, home boys home
> Fill it up to the brim and drink it off clane
> For 'tis our harvest home.

The theme of drinking was common in the songs, and in many of the games. In Yorkshire and Northumberland, young men wearing disguises might make a show of gatecrashing the event, as described by veteran folklorist Eliza Gutch in 1901:

Later in the evening a wild cry of fire! or an alarm of some kind would be sprung upon those within the barn. Whatever form the alarm given took, it had but one object in view, to induce those within to open the barn door. This having by some means been accomplished, the 'Guisers', a kind of sword dancers, attempted to force an entrance; and although it was the universal custom to make some show of keeping out these uninvited guests, they were always permitted to join the party, for great was the merriment they created.

The same book includes the text of a traditional dialect playlet that was performed in the 1820s, which comprised a sung dialogue between Polly and, in succession, an old man, an old lady, and a squire; she decides to marry the latter.

Other places had other traditions. In 1896, a Lincolnshire contributor to *Notes & Queries* wrote:

In the first quarter of the present century 'the old sow' used to appear in that county at harvest suppers. To the critical eye this curious animal was nothing more nor less than two men dressed up in sacks to personate a traditional visitor to the feast. Its head was filled with cuttings from a furze-bush, and its habit was to prick everyone whom it honoured with its attentions. 'I used to be very much afraid of it when I was a child,' says my informant.

Despite the show of égalité and fraternity to which the harvest supper aspired, there were many in the nineteenth century who disapproved of the rough humour and potential gluttony and drunkenness involved in such affairs. Even before the suppers were killed by mechanization and the reduction of the agricultural workforce, there was pressure to clean them up. George James Dew, of Lower Heyford, Oxford, recorded in his diary a visit to a combined 'harvest home' for several of the farms in his neighbourhood, in September 1864, when he was eighteen. The event was clearly one of the new-style, respectable affairs, with the vicar, and other local worthies, presiding and giving speeches; entry was by ticket. This was a far cry from the old homely private gatherings of farmer and workers that were now being castigated for their rough and drunken ways. Dew was particularly impressed, as was the reporter from the *Oxford Chronicle* (10 September 1864):

There could be no better proof of the good understanding existing amongst the farmers of Lower Heyford than the unanimity and goodwill which existed among them on this first general gathering, for we believe that all joined in this demonstration with heartiness and goodwill which resulted in most complete success.

Harvest Festivals

On 23 September 2000, the *Telegraph* reported:

Harvest festival is upon us again, a time when churches all over England welcome the fruitfulness of autumn by propping giant marrows against the rails of the altars and singing 'We plough the fields and scatter'.

The harvest festival as we know it today was the single-handed invention of one of the great eccentric clergymen of the nineteenth century, Robert Stephen Hawker (1803–75), who was the vicar of Morwenstow parish in north Cornwall for forty-one years. Despite the isolated position of his parish, Hawker was well known in his lifetime not only for his strange behaviour and colourful clothes, but also for his somewhat unorthodox religious beliefs, which culminated in his being baptized into the Roman Catholic Church on his deathbed. He was an enthusiastic antiquary, a published poet, and intimately involved in the lives of his parishioners. Stories of his antics abounded: he was said to have rescued sailors from wrecks, fought drunken fishermen, smashed up the old pews in his church with an axe, and regularly preached surrounded by ten cats.

Hawker announced the idea of a harvest thanksgiving to his congregation in 1843, and his notion obviously struck a chord with the times because within a decade the idea had been taken up in churches all over the country. Harvest festivals rapidly became widespread, and it became quite normal for churches to be decorated with fruit, flowers, vegetables, and other produce donated by the congregation, on a Sunday in late September or early October. Even in the twentieth century, the harvest festival had for many a slightly unofficial feel about it, as if it belonged to the people rather than the church itself, and it was certainly one of the most popular events in the ecclesiastical calendar.

Hawker was very fond of early Church history, and he almost certainly got the idea from reading about Lammas (*see* 1 **August**), which was probably celebrated as a festival of 'first fruits' in the Anglo-Saxon Church. Some authorities therefore write of him 'reviving' rather than inventing the harvest thanksgiving, and he may well have thought of it in this way himself.

Hop-Picking

The use of hops for making beer was introduced into England from Holland in the early fifteenth century, and the new ingredient turned the traditional English ale into beer. The new bitter drink met with some opposition from traditionalists and gained acceptance only slowly, but hop-growing gradually became a major agricultural industry, so that by the mid seventeenth century hops were grown in fourteen counties in England. Kent claims to be the site of the earliest cultivation in Britain, and certainly it was the most famous of hop-growing areas, accounting for over a third of the national crop.

If left alone, hop bines will grow along the ground and twine around anything they meet, but cultivators soon learned to provide poles and wires for the hops to climb; if tied at regular intervals, they will grow over twenty feet high. The short picking season, and the labour-intensive task of hand-picking, made the use of migrant workers inevitable, and as the work of removing the hops from the bines was suitable for women and children, whole families could be involved, as Arthur Young's *Farmer's Kalendar* (1771) was well aware:

Plenty of hands should, on all accounts, be provided for this important business; women do it as well as men; it is a work rather of care than of labour.

Hop-picking was thus very different from the usual pattern of predominately male migrant agricultural work, and whole families used to move into the area for the season, with the well-known annual exodus of working-class families from East London to go 'hopping down in Kent' mirrored in a smaller way in the Midlands and other hop-growing areas. Hopping was hard work and conditions were rough, but many urban families regarded it as a holiday with pay.

The local people viewed the annual invasion with ambivalence. Country folk have always distrusted townies, and the East London working-class families who descended on quiet Kent villages often seemed like a race of aliens to the locals, although as it happened every year both residents and visitors knew roughly what to expect. The influx brought colour, noise, and excitement, which pleased and frightened some locals in equal measure, but their townie habits were unfamiliar, and they behaved with a remarkable lack of restraint, as people on holiday often do. Country writer C. Henry Warren recorded his memories of village life in his *Boy in Kent* (1938), calling his chapter on hop-picking 'The Gay Invaders':

These were all people from a world I knew nothing about. If I had been suddenly conveyed to the Bermudas, I could not have been more entranced than I was by these gay and vivacious people.

They brought welcome trade to the village, but this too came at a price. The following piece describes the scene in his father's village shop:

In the shop itself the stir and bustle was just as frantic. First of all everything was cleared away until not so much as a jar of sweets or a tin of treacle was left within reach, and even in the windows there was nothing but a swept-up heap of dead wasps in a corner. Then, after the shop had been scrubbed from top to bottom, Horace, the odd-job man, would arrive with planks and poles and hammer and nails and begin erecting a high barricade round the counters. The place rattled with his vigorous hammerings ... 'I think we could do with just a few more nails here, Horace', my father would say, 'or we shall have the hooligans all over us in a trice!'

Many pubs simply refused to serve them. But it was quite common for families to frequent the same farm every year, and in many cases a guarded respect or even friendship was built up over the generations. Many local families also welcomed the chance to earn extra money during the season, which helped with expenses such as winter fuel, or new coats and boots for the children, although locals and Londoners were usually kept apart in the fields. In *East Kent Within Living Memory* (1993), a villager is recorded saying:

Our farm was a small, privately owned farm, where no Londoners were allowed; we were all 'respectable' local families.

The same villager also remembered the four-mile walk to and from the farm, the difficulty getting the brown stains and horrid taste off the hands, and the smell:

The smell of the hops was really overpowering and a few people, my mother and myself among them, were quite badly affected, feeling sick and faint for the first few days, after which we became immune to the smell.

It is easy to romanticize the old hand-picking days. The visiting pickers were often housed in appalling conditions, a state of affairs that lasted well into the twentieth century, and improvements were mainly the result of agitation by interested outsiders. Sending missionaries to the hop-fields was a popular activity for London churches, and even if the visiting philanthropists were overly concerned with the pickers' moral and spiritual shortcomings, they did sterling work in advertising and improving the degrading living conditions and lack of sanitation provided by the hop-growers.

Hop-picking naturally had its own traditional customs, modelled on those of other seasonal agricultural tasks, such as the hop-pickers' feast to celebrate the end of the season, and the election of a king and queen of the hop-fields. A traditional way of greeting a stranger, or punishing some minor transgression of hop-field etiquette, was by 'cribbing' them – bundling them into one of the hop bins.

By the middle of the twentieth century, the great days of hop-growing in Britain were definitely over, and as machines took over from hand-picking, a whole way of life simply faded away.

Early September

Colchester Oyster Fishery

The River Colne and neighbouring estuaries on the Essex coast have been famous for oysters since Roman times and maybe even before. The industry of commercial oyster-growing needs to be carefully organized in order to avoid a local free-for-all, and this was recognized in the first municipal charter granted to the town of Colchester by Richard I in 1189, by which the corporation owns the fisheries, which are then rented out.

The oyster season traditionally opens in September, and runs through to March – quite literally, as the proverb says, when there is an 'R' in the month. Early in September, the Mayor of Colchester, accompanied by other members and officials of the corporation, ventures out in a boat to dredge up the first oysters of the season. The charter is read out, and the company partakes of gin and gingerbread – nobody knows why – and samples the fresh oysters. They also send a loyal message to the Queen. The ceremony does not always go quite to plan, as *The Times* of 22 September 1928 reported:

The company were about to drink a toast in gin, in accordance with ancient custom, when the table containing the tiny glasses, filled with gin, overbalanced and fell, crashing to the deck, together with the small cakes of gingerbread provided for the occasion. Amid hearty laughter fresh supplies were soon forthcoming and the ceremony concluded in the time-honoured fashion.

Later in the year, Colchester holds its annual Oyster Feast (*see* **20 October**).

Commercial oyster fishing is now concentrated in the Mersea Island area, due south of Colchester. According to the *Independent* (30 September 2005), Colchester native oysters are highly regarded abroad, and local producers have applied to the European Union for the delicacy to be granted Protected Geographical Indication (PGI) status, which would recognize its unique qualities and stipulate that it can only be produced in the designated area.

See also 25 July: **Whitstable Oyster Festival**.

A Sunday in September

Horseman's Sunday

On a Sunday in September, horses and their riders gather outside the church of St John and St Michael, in Hyde Park Crescent, London, for a service and blessing conducted by the local vicar, who is also on horseback. The horses all receive commemorative rosettes, and they then parade around the park. The event was founded in 1968, by local resident Ross Nye, who was worried that if local riding stables were closed, horses would disappear from the area. A similar event takes place in the same month on Epsom Downs.

For other horse parades, *see* **Easter Monday: Harness Horse Parade**, p. 175; 1 **May: Horse Decorations**.

1 September

St Giles's Day

Almost nothing is known of the real St Giles, who died about the year 710, except that he founded a monastery in Provence. This did not stop the medieval legend-makers, however, who provided a set of colourful incidents for his life story, including an explanation of how he was given the money for his great foundation. It was said that while he was living as a hermit he was accompanied by a pet doe, which provided milk for his nourishment. Unfortunately, the King's huntsmen loved to pursue this doe and eventually trapped her in the dense thicket in which Giles lived. The doe was protected from harm by Giles's prayers, but he himself was wounded by a huntsman's arrow. The King, on recognizing Giles's holiness, gave him many gifts, which he used to found the monastery. In other parts of the legend, Giles demonstrated remarkable healing powers, along with the ability to obtain pardon for people's sins, however great, simply by prayer.

These stories contributed to Giles's fame, and he was widely popular in medieval England, with many churches dedicated to him. His feast day was conveniently placed in the year for outdoor events, and was particularly popular for local fairs, feasts, and revels. Two of the most famous fairs in the country were held, at different periods, around St Giles's Day: one at Oxford, which still continues, and the other at Winchester. The Oxford fair was described by fairs historian R. W. Muncey in the 1930s:

Probably the greatest features of the fair are the steam roundabouts of various kinds, which are lit up at night by the brightest of electric lights, and stretch along for some considerable distance above the college in nearly one unbroken line and are usually crowded by numbers of visitors. The steam organs and instruments are continually playing and cause the greater part of the din which drowns every other softer sound. The fair occupies all the open space between St. Giles's Church and the Martyrs' Memorial. There are to be seen a circus, midgets, boxing exhibitions, freaks, people fat and people strong; while swings and sausage stalls occupy a place, together with shooting galleries and cocoa-nut shies. Smaller booths and stalls line the pavement of the street on both sides. Here you can buy toys, crockery and fancy articles of various kinds.

Strictly speaking, St Giles's Fair is not a proper fair at all, as it seems not to have been founded by charter but to have grown from a local 'wake', probably based on the feast day of the church (*see* **Fairs, Feasts, Wakes, and Revels**, p. 341). Nor is it nearly as ancient as many writers seem to think: the fashion at one time to describe it as 'eight hundred years old' seems to be based on the date of the foundation of St Giles's church. It is possible that an annual wake commenced at that time, but the earliest known documentary reference dates only from the 1620s, and the event only started to become widely known in the early nineteenth century. Its very shape proclaims its special nature. Not many large fairs now take place in city streets, and those that do are usually squashed into a central circle or square, but this fair stretches out along both sides of St Giles's church and into Woodstock and Banbury Roads.

As with most big fairs, St Giles's Fair came under pressure in Victorian times because of its drunkenness and rowdy behaviour, and came close to suppression at times, but it managed to survive and is still held on the first Monday and Tuesday in September, drawing large enthusiastic crowds. In direct contrast to its rowdy past, however, the Bishop of Oxford and the choir of St Giles's church nowadays open the fair with a blessing and some songs, delivered from one of the large roundabouts.

There is no doubt about the age of St Giles's Fair at Winchester, which flourished and died centuries before its Oxford counterpart. There is some disagreement about whether the oldest fairs in England were founded by the Romans or the Anglo-Saxons, but it was the Normans who were particularly energetic in the granting of charters for new fairs. Grants were often made to religious foundations as a convenient way of raising money for large building projects or the maintenance of monasteries and other institutions, and the great St Giles's Fair at Winchester was a good example of such a grant. It was founded by charter from William Rufus in 1079, primarily to raise money for rebuilding the cathedral, and although originally restricted to three days, it was so popular that in its heyday its term stretched to twenty-four days. The gathering took place on the top of St Giles's Hill, just outside the town, and the stalls on the site were so substantial, and laid out in regular streets, that it was likened to a 'wooden town', surrounded by a large fence to ensure that no traders got in or out without paying the required fees. The fair continued under the strict ownership and control of the Bishop, who opened it each year with much ceremony, and the city had no jurisdiction for the duration, which caused constant friction between the ecclesiastical and secular authorities. This fair attracted traders from all over Britain and Europe, and was one of the four major fairs in the country (the others were St Ives, Northampton, and Boston), but by the fifteenth century it was in decline. The citizens of Winchester petitioned for their own fair in 1449, and were granted a nine-day fair on St Swithun's Day (15 July); however, the days of St Giles's glory were past.

Many other smaller fairs and feasts took place on or around St Giles's Day, but one puzzling custom that is worthy of note took place at Hawkridge, in Somerset, on the Sunday nearest to St Giles's Day, which was their local Revel Sunday: on this day the rector was pelted with apples on his way from the rectory to the church. This bizarre custom was also reported from other places in the country at other times of the year (*see* **28 July: Old St Kenelm's Day**).

3 September

Cromwell Day

The Cromwell Society exists to promote the study and understanding of the life and times of Oliver Cromwell (1599–1658). They commemorate the day of his death, 3 September, with an open-air service in front of his statue outside the Houses of Parliament, and lay a wreath there. The service is only allowed to be attended by members of the Cromwell Association, but the proceedings can be seen and heard from the public pavement.

Merchant Navy Day

In the year 2000, the Merchant Navy Association (founded 1989) declared 3 September as Merchant Navy Day, in commemoration of the sinking by U-boat of the unarmed merchant vessel the SS *Athenia* on this day in 1939 – the first day of the Second World War. All nineteen crew and ninety-three passengers were lost. Merchant seamen have long felt that their service's significant contribution to the war effort has been undervalued, and it is one of the aims of the Society to raise the profile of the Merchant Navy and celebrate its importance to Britain, past and present.

4 September

Abbots Bromley Horn Dance

On the Monday following the local Wakes Sunday (i.e. the first Sunday after 4 September, or Old St Bartholomew's Day), the village and surroundings of Abbots Bromley in Staffordshire are visited by a unique set of dancers. The team comprises six men, each carrying a splendid pair of reindeer antlers, plus a Fool, a Maid Marian (played by a man), a hobby horse, a bowman (who twangs a bow), a musician and a triangle player.

Starting from the parish church at 8 a.m., the team perambulates the parish, visiting key houses, farms, and other places, at every stop forming up to perform their dance. Between visits, they often stroll along, as if 'off-duty', but when approaching any dancing place they fall into single file behind the leader, sometimes weaving in a serpentine form, or form a circle. At each 'station' they form up in two lines, advance and retire a few times, tilting their horns as they meet, and then cross over and repeat. During this dance, the horns are carried at chest height, and although they advance towards each other, they do not make any aggressive movements and they certainly do not clash them together, as some writers claim; nor is there any fancy dance-step, but what has been variously described as an 'easy, matter-of-fact walk', or a 'steady rhythmical plod'. Round about 8 p.m. they return to the village and perform their final dance in the street.

Reliable eyewitness accounts from the earlier twentieth century all stress the unhurried and determinedly unspectacular manner of the whole affair, as in *The Times* of 7 September 1936:

The whole thing is done unassumably and with a quiet purposefulness which is the keynote of the whole proceedings. One feels they are not danc-ing for joy or self-expression, but going quietly about a task which must be accomplished without unnecessary fuss.

Similarly, folklorist Evelyn Wells wrote in 1938:

There was no audience, nor any expected. A small boy carried sandwiches and a flask. A horn dancer's wife straightened their costumes and sent them off . . . The costumes, which they hope soon to renew, were shabby; one or two chewed gum, and the hobby horse had an occasional cigarette. The tunes, a fast one and a slow one, were of a nameless variety.

The costumes worn today do not go back very far. A set of pseudo-medieval jerkins and knee-breeches was designed by Mrs Lowe, the local vicar's wife, in the 1880s, possibly based at some remove on those of the morris dancers shown in the famous early sixteenth-century painted window (usually called the Betley window, but now at Leigh Manor, Minsterley, in Shropshire). The costumes were renewed in 1904, and again in 1951, on similar lines, and this design has now be-come traditional in itself, but they remain as a warning to those who would take things at face value and extrapolate backwards to construct theories of origin. According to *The Times* (7 September 1936), 'The days are still remembered when the dancers wore only their workaday clothes with a few pink and white rosettes fastened to them for the occasion.'

The horns are kept in the church when not in use. They are genuine reindeer horns, mounted on wooden heads, with a handle protruding below to enable the dancers to carry them as they dance. They weigh between 16 and 25 lb, with a span ranging from 77 cm to 101 cm, and they seem to have always been painted three of one colour and three of another, although the colours have changed over the years – from red and white, to blue and white, and at present brown and off-white. One of the horns was carbon-dated in 1976, and the result was a mean date of AD 1065 +/- 80 years, although where they came from, and how they got to Abbots Bromley, remains unknown.

The earliest references are not quite as straightforward as one would like. Robert Plot, in his *Natural History of Staffordshire* (1686), mentions a 'hobby horse dance' accompanied by six men carrying 'rain deers heads', which was performed at Christmas, New Year, and Twelfth Night. Sir Simon Degge (1612–1704), who was brought up in the area, annotated his copy of Plot's book with the comment that he had often seen the dance before the Civil War, which probably takes us back to the 1620s. More recently, morris-dance historian Mike Heaney discovered an earlier reference, which shows that the hobby horse already existed in the parish in 1532, but it does not mention the horns. In Plot's day the season for performance was midwinter, which is certainly the most common time for 'animal disguise' customs elsewhere in the country, and it was transferred to Wakes Week at some later date. Later sources also indicate that the dancers used to go out on several consecutive days.

There has naturally been a great deal of speculation about the origin of the custom, and many have connected it to a pagan fertility ritual, an ancient ceremony to ensure successful hunting, and the assertion of some common right or privilege in regard to the chase, but none of these is supported by any evidence. It may even be that the hobby horse is older than the horn dance. What is clear is that the hobby horse, as at other places, was used in the sixteenth century to collect taxes and dues owed to the lord of the manor (*see* **Hobby Horses**, p. 226); and Plot, straight after describing the dance, writes of money being collected for cakes and ale, and used to repair the church and keep the poor. Whether the horse did the collecting, or simply accompanied the money-collectors to sweeten the event by entertaining the people, is not known. But a significant proportion of early references indicate that this money-gathering was the horse's primary purpose.

On the question of dating, one confident but groundless assertion is that the horn dance was first performed at the founding of the local fair in 1226. This idea is now met with in so many sources that it is probably impossible to eradicate. It apparently started with speculation by Marcia Rice in her 1939 history of Abbots Bromley, and while it is true that Henry III granted a three-day fair for St Bartholomew's Day in 1226, there is no evidence that this had anything to do with the horn dancers.

Barnet Horse Fair

There is something romantic and slightly dangerous about a horse fair, which other livestock marts cannot hope to equal. Perhaps it is simply that Gypsies do not gather to exchange handfuls of money over sheep, or gentlemen wager their families' fortunes on a cow race. This fair was chartered in 1588, and for centuries was one of the busiest livestock marts in the region – although Barnet's real fame was for horse-racing, which drew large unruly crowds from north London until it ceased in 1870. The associated horse fair was similarly patronized by dealers and buyers from the capital, and was so well attended by street traders in mid Victorian times that it was known in some circles as the 'costermongers' carnival'. According to James Greenwood's *Unsentimental Journeys* (1867), it enjoyed an extremely raffish reputation:

My first impression was my last, and still remains – viz, that Barnet Fair is a disgrace to civilisation. I have witnessed a Warwickshire 'mop' fair; I have some recollection of 'Bartlemy'; I was at Greenwich when, on account of its increasing abominations, the fair that so long afflicted that Kentish borough was held for the last time; but take all these, and skim them for their scum and precipitate them for their dregs, and even then, unless you throw in a very strong flavouring of the essence of Old Smithfield on a Friday, and a good armful of Colney Hatch and Earlswood sprigs, you will fail to make a brew equal to that at Barnet. It is appalling.

Given this kind of write-up, it is remarkable that Barnet Horse Fair survived at all, but while the races and the general livestock have long been forgotten, the horse fair persists to this day, albeit somewhat shakily. By the mid twentieth century, the glory days were well over, but it was still a significant date on the horse-lover's calendar, as William Addison indicates in his *English Fairs and Markets* (1953):

Barnet Fair is still the most racy event of its kind near London. Even in 1952, 620 horses were sold, including 74 sturdy Welsh cobs from Glamorgan, most of which changed hands within a couple of hours.

However, the real threat to the fair came not from human opposition but the inexorable march of bricks and mortar, as the area rapidly developed from Hertfordshire countryside into a north London borough. The site of the fair changed many times in the interwar years, and it was increasingly seen as a historical relic. On 6 September 1954, *The Times* commented:

In a 20-acre field which once afforded wider vistas, Barnet horse fair opened today, bringing its annual touch of medieval muddle to what tidy modern planners know as the South Hertfordshire conurbation. New facets of the fair's surroundings add point to the remarkable fact of its survival each year; since last September council flats have risen on waste ground close by and beyond the fairground stands the vitreous contemporary cube of a new school.

A mere shadow of its former self, Barnet Horse Fair is now held at Greengates Stables, on 4, 5, and 6 September, unless one of those dates is a Sunday, in which case it continues on the following day.

14 September

Holy Rood or Holy Cross Day

This day, also known as the Exaltation of the Cross, has a somewhat confused ancestry. A much-revered relic of the True Cross was carried off by the Persians in the year 614, when they occupied Jerusalem, but it was recovered in the spring of 629 and lodged in Constantinople for safety; this event, however, is commemorated as a feast day on 14 September.

In English folk tradition, 14 September has long been known as 'the Devil's Nutting Day'; a phrase that draws together several strands of folklore dating back at least 450 years. Early connections between Holy Rood Day and nutting are shown in a tradition at Eton in 1560, recorded by antiquarian John Brand, in which the boys were allowed a half-holiday on the day to gather nuts, and in the line 'all the youth are now a-nutting gone', which occurs in *Grim the Collier of Croydon*, an anonymous play of the early seventeenth century. 'Going a-nutting' also crops up in songs and plays as a byword for seduction and sex, which gave the activity a particularly risqué air, and a well-known notion, current from at least the 1660s to the late twentieth century, claimed 'a good year for nuts, a good year for babies'. The Devil was also often coupled with the gathering of nuts. Country people were constantly warned not to go nutting on Sundays, as the Devil would be there, disguised as a gentleman, to pull down the upper branches for them. And going nutting on 14 September was believed to be particularly risky, as in the letter written by the Northamptonshire poet John Clare to William Hone, in 1825:

On Holy Rood day it is faithfully and confidently believed both by old and young that the Devil goes a-nutting on that day and I have heard many people affirm that they once thought it a tale till they ventured to the woods on that day when they smelt such a strong smell of brimstone as nearly sti-fled them before they could escape out again.

There is also at least one legend (at Haselor, Warwickshire) that tells how a particular hill was formed when the Devil dropped his nutting bag in fright when he met the Virgin Mary on the road. In a few sources, 21 September is named as the 'Devil's Nutting Day'.

On a different note, passion flowers were traditionally associated with the crucifixion, and by extension with Holy Rood Day, when it was supposed most likely to flower. Believers saw symbolic analogies between parts of the flower and Christ's five wounds, the three nails used, and so on.

Shaftesbury Byzant

As it was built on a hill, the town of Shaftesbury in Dorset was without a water supply of its own, and inhabitants had to collect their water from wells at Enmore Green, in the neighbouring parish of Gillingham. In order to preserve their ancient right of access, the townsfolk processed to Enmore every year on Holy Cross Day, and there performed a dance and presented the monarch's bailiff with a penny loaf, a gallon of ale, a calf's head, and a pair of gloves. This annual excursion to Enmore had already developed into a general holiday by at least 1364, and the celebrations were further formalized by a new agreement between the Mayor of Shaftesbury and the Lord of

continued on page 402 ☞

Baiting Bears and Other Animals

Bull-baiting and bear-baiting were the two most popular 'sports' that pitted dogs against other animals for entertainment. Bull-baiting (p. 480) was more of an everyday occurrence and took place in pub yards and market-places for all and sundry to watch, but bear-baiting was more likely to be staged in more controlled surroundings, where admission could be charged. Both could be seen on a regular basis.

Bear-baiting has a long history. It is often stated that the sport was introduced to Britain from Italy in the twelfth century, and was first seen at Ashby-de-la-Zouche in Leicestershire, but it is likely to have been known here long before that time, as it was on the Continent. The first definite mention of the sport in England is in William Fitz Stephen's *Description of London* (*c.*1180; reprinted as *Norman London* in 1990), where he writes:

In winter on almost every feast day . . . fat bulls with butting horns, or huge bears, do combat to the death against hounds let loose upon them.

Judging by the frequency with which bear-baiting appears in diaries and published accounts, it was a far from unusual spectacle in Britain from the sixteenth century onwards. Royalty was partial to the sport, and Henry VIII and Elizabeth I both kept their own stables of bears and mastiffs, as did several of the country's nobles in the same period. There were also regular venues, particularly in London, where the paying public could see baitings of various kinds; two of the most famous were the bear gardens at Bankside, Southwark, and Hockley-in-the-Hole, Clerkenwell. For the next 300 years, anyone who wished to attend a bear-baiting could usually find one somewhere in London most weeks of the year. The advertisements for these institutions make grim reading for modern eyes, as they often declared how fiercely the different animals would fight, and that the contests would be 'to the death!', as if the spectators felt cheated if no animal was actually killed.

In addition to the weekly spectacles in the big cities, some travelling dancing-bears were also available for 'baiting'. Gordon Home, in his fascinating history of Pickering, Yorkshire, quotes from a manuscript compiled in the early nineteenth century, which includes so many telling details that it is worth quoting in full.

Concerning a case of bear-baiting we have a most detailed account which Calvert heads with 'The Baiting of a Bear at Pickering,

Tuesday, Aug 15th, 1809, which I did myself witness'. Then he begins: 'A week Wednesday senight there did with drum and panpipes parade publickly the streets of this town two mountebanks leading by a chain a monster brown bruin which, as well as it being a good dancer and handing of its pole, its master did acclaim it to be the master of any dog of no odds what be his breed and which they would match for a crown to come off conqueror if given fair play and a fifteen-foot chain. Now it happening that in these parts there be living several sporting men some of which be owners of bull dogs of good courage and nowther dog nor master ever shirking a fight more than one dog was entered to test its skill'.

A day was fixed for the contests which were to take place in the castleyard, and soon the news was so handed from mouth to mouth that the demand for seats in the rough wooden stand, erected for those who chose to pay, was so great that another stand was built and the first one was enlarged.

On the appointed day a huge concourse including 'farmers, butchers, hucksters, badgers, cadgers, horse-jobbers, drovers, loafers, and scamps and raggels of all kinds' assembled in the castleyard. There were 'not a few young sparks and bespurred and beruffled bucks come thither from as far as Hull' who had brought with them certain over-dressed women.

The first dog matched against the bear was owned by one Castle Jack, 'a worthless waistrel'. The bear received the rush of the dog standing on his hind legs and gripped him in his forepaws, biting and crushing him to death. After this no one seemed inclined to let their dogs go to such certain death and the assemblage gradually became disorderly and many quarrels and fights took place before the crowd finally dispersed. Calvert says: 'and so when I did withdraw myself, the whole crowd seemed to be owther cursing, fighting, or loudly proffering for to fight any one. As I took my steps back to my uncle I could not help but consider that those of the Methodist holding, who did as we went towards the green beg and pray for us to be mindful of our sinful pleasures and of the wroth to come and who did pray for us to then turn from our sinful course, and though we who did pass them did so with scoffs and . . . gibes in some cases, yet I could not help but in my own heart consider that they were fully in the right on't'.

This was at the time when the national campaign against animal-baiting was already underway, and would lead to its suppression in 1835, along with other blood sports. But the Pickering manuscript clearly describes a popular event, drawing eager spectators and would-be participants from a wide area, albeit largely from the disreputable end of the social spectrum. There was local opposition, but in the short term this seems ineffectual. The account, however, demonstrates why the attack on blood sports such as these could be made equally on moral and public order grounds, and also how their suppression could be portrayed, by later historians, as a class-based attack on the customs and pastimes of working people.

Before the watershed of the Cruelty to Animals Act of 1835, there seems to have been no limit to the ingenuity some people would use to cater for the public's lust for animal blood, and dog fights, baitings, and matches between various species were a common occurrence. Dogs were set on anything that could fight back, including horses and donkeys, or that could be made to participate in the 'game'. Badgers, for example, were often baited, and the principle there appears to have been to see how many times the dog would draw the badger from its box in a given time. Whereas bull- and bear-baiting are almost certainly extinct, dog-fighting, badger-baiting, and the like have proved more resilient and still continue clandestinely, although to what extent is impossible to say.

☞ continued from page 399 Gillingham manor in 1662. This agreement also speaks of the procession being headed by a 'prize besome', decorated with feathers, gold, rings, and jewels – presumably the forerunner of the curious 'byzant', which is now in Shaftesbury Museum and has been described by researcher George Frampton as:

> . . . a trophy or mace about three feet in height . . . weighing around 40 lbs. Its frame is made of carved wood with gilded gesso, and is liberally decorated with gold coins, peacocks' feathers, and ribbons. In one year, this included a great variety of silver and gold medals, stone buckles, and garnet necklaces, and up the sides a number of diamond rings . . . and four pictures in miniature.

The annual processions continued until the custom lapsed in 1829, but it was revived, in varying degrees of fidelity to the original, on several occasions in the twentieth century.

Sturbridge (sometimes Stourbridge) Fair was the greatest in the land in its heyday, but it began relatively humbly. In 1211, King John granted a charter to the lepers of the Hospital of St Mary Magdalen at Sturbridge to hold a fair on the vigil and feast of the Holy Cross; such a right was at that time a common way of ensuring that religious and charitable institutions had a regular income. By the end of that century the hospital had virtually ceased to function, but the town of Cambridge claimed the profits from the fair and continued to own it until its demise 700 years later. The University of Cambridge also claimed jurisdiction, which resulted in a long-running feud over their respective rights up to the mid sixteenth century.

In 1589, Sturbridge was described as by far the largest and most famous fair in all England, and it maintained its pre-eminence well into the eighteenth century. The best description of the fair at the height of its fame was published by Daniel Defoe in his *Tour through the Whole Island of Great Britain* (1724–6). He was suitably impressed by its sheer size and the huge quantity of business carried out there:

It is kept in a large corn-field, near Casterton, extending from the side of the River Cam, towards the road, for about half a mile square ... The shops are placed in rows like streets, whereof one is call'd Cheapside; and here, as in several other streets, are all sorts of trades, who sell by retail, and who come principally from London with their goods; scarce any trades are omitted, goldsmiths, toyshops, brasiers, turners, milliners, haberdashers, hatters, mercers, drapers, pewterers, china-warehouses, and in a word all trades that can be named in London; with coffee-houses, taverns, brandy-shops, and eating-houses, innumerable, and all in tents and booths.

Such an operation needed a great deal of preparation and organization. The fair traders had the right to enter the field on a set date, whether the farmers had finished their harvest or not, but by the same token the field reverted to the farmer on a set day after the fair, and he could 'throw down' any booths that had not been removed. Defoe commented that the huge quantity of dung, straw, and other litter and waste left behind was ample compensation to the farmer for the inconvenience of the fair, because when ploughed in it made excellent manure.

Defoe identified two staples of the trade there: wool and hops. The wool dealing was carried out in a special area called 'the Duddery', where £100,000 worth of trade was done in less than a week. Much of this was wholesale trade, with merchants using the fair as the main place to meet and restock their chapmen and agents, settle accounts, and place orders. The hop dealers also had their special part of the field, and the trade was so important that, as Defoe said, 'there is scarce any price fix'd for hops in England till they know how they sell at Sturbridge Fair.' In the last few days of the fair the emphasis was more on pleasure, and crowds flocked to the sideshows and entertainments, while a horse fair took place on the last day. The length of the fair fluctuated over the years, from the original two days up to thirty-five days at its peak.

Fairs like Sturbridge were so important to the country's economic well-being for so long because they provided regular and secure opportunities for wholesale dealing in commodities. The huge amount of money that changed hands was largely between manufacturer and the distributor, rather than between retailer and customer. But when the wholesalers found other methods of distributing their stock (by the newly developed railways, for example), the focus of the fair shifted, and while the retail trade was still large, it was not sufficient to maintain the fair on its former scale. While many famous fairs got out of hand and were suppressed, Sturbridge's fate was rather a long lingering decline throughout the nineteenth century. The *Victoria County History* for Cambridge recorded its final demise:

The fair was proclaimed for the last time in September 1933 to an audience of three. By Home Office order, confirming a resolution of the Town Council, it was abolished 5 July 1934.

See also **Fairs, Feasts, Wakes, and Revels**, p. 341.

Third Thursday in September

Chalk-Back Day

Chalk-Back Day was a little-known annual custom recorded in Diss, Norfolk, but with possible connections elsewhere. The earliest record of it goes back only to 1851, in *Notes & Queries*:

It is customary for the juvenile populace, on the Thursday before the third Friday in September . . . to mark and disfigure each other's dress with white chalk, pleading a prescriptive right to be mischievous on 'chalk-back day'.

This account is confirmed by later writers, who show that it was not simply a short-lived craze but survived until about 1900.

The local hiring fair was held on the same day, and this may be a clue to its meaning, as an account from Yorkshire in 1890 makes clear:

At Bridlington, on the Sunday night preceding the fair, which is held on the Monday before Whit Sunday, the boys used to assemble on the Church Green, where the fair was held, each armed with a lump of chalk, and each intent on chalking the backs of as many of the other boys as possible. This often led to quarrels, as the boys then had on their Sunday clothes.

There is also a strange echo of this behaviour in reports of Greenwich Fair in mid Victorian times, where a local craze involved running wooden 'rattlers' down people's backs (*see* **Easter Day: Greenwich Fair**, p. 154). Another possible link comes from further afield: 'Chalk Sunday' (usually the first Sunday in Lent) was widely held in Ireland in the nineteenth century and up to about 1930. As at Diss, Irish children chalked people's backs on the day, but there it was specifically those who were unmarried, which could be a gentle joke or an unpleasant comment on the popularity, or otherwise, of the victim, depending on the circumstances. Further examples from England are needed before we can hope to speculate on its meaning or origin.

Third Saturday in September

Egremont Crab-Apple Fair

Egremont Fair, in Cumbria, consciously preserves many of the traditional games and pastimes of old-time country fairs, such as gurning (and Egremont is said to hold the World Championship competition), climbing the greasy pole, wrestling, tug-of-war, and children's races; but it has also introduced a number of others that are probably unique, including a pipe-smoking contest, ferret show, and the singing of hunting songs. The fine art of pole greasing was described by Egremont locals in *John Bull* magazine in 1955:

We haven't been able to grease the pole properly since before the war . . . Nowadays, wagon grease is used . . . but really it should be soft soap covered by lard . . . A sheep's head or a leg of mutton trailing coloured ribbons is tied to the top of the pole and anyone who can bring down a ribbon wins the prize . . . The greasy pole is the bane of wives and mothers, and the delight of the outfitters.

The fair gets its name from the custom of throwing apples from a slow-moving lorry, to the waiting crowds, at midday. They used to be crab apples, but nowadays ordinary eating apples are thrown. Organizers claim that Egremont's fair has been held every year since its charter was granted in 1267 (except during the two world wars), and this could well be true.

17 September

Latter Lee Fair

See **17 August: Lee Gap Fair**.

18 September

Samuel Johnson Commemoration

Samuel Johnson (1709–84), journalist, critic, essayist, magazine editor, and, most famously, dictionary maker, was the leading figure in the literary world of his day and is still held in high regard. He is buried at Westminster Abbey, where an annual commemoration takes place each December. But on or near his birthday, 18 September, they hold a ceremony in his honour in Lichfield, Staffordshire, the place of his birth. The mayor and corporation, members of the Johnson Society, and pupils from Johnson's old school place a wreath on his statue, and later they hold a birthday supper and a commemoration service in the cathedral.

Warden pies, made with Warden pears, were an autumn and winter delicacy in various parts of the country, up to Edwardian times at least. Sussex writer Lilian Candlin gave one example:

Wardens were not soft like the modern stewing pear. They were quite hard when cooked and needed good teeth to eat them . . . To make a Warden Pie: Peel the pears and quarter them, then simmer them in sweetened water for about two, to two and a half hours. By this time they should be tender and have turned a pale pink colour. Leave them to get cold. Meanwhile line the edge of a pie dish with thin pastry. Fill the dish with the pears, add a little lemon juice, and a wineglassful of claret or port wine. Top with pastry and bake. When serving lift the lid and gently spoon in two or three table-spoonsful of rich thick cream.

Warden pears were particularly prized in Bedfordshire, and hot baked Wardens were a delicacy of the Bedford Michaelmas (Old Style) Fair and were hawked in the streets throughout the season. The *Oxford English Dictionary* gives numerous literary references to Warden pies from the fifteenth century onwards, including one from Shakespeare's Clown in *The Winter's Tale*, who reminds himself in Act IV, scene 3, 'I must have saffron to colour the Warden pies.'

Southwark Fair

Southwark, or Lady, Fair was one of the big fairs of the London area, attracting huge crowds until the mid eighteenth century and second in importance only to Bartholomew Fair (*see* **24 August**). Southwark Fair was founded in 1462, by charter of Edward IV to the City of London, and was opened each year by the mayor and other officials, when they rode in state across London Bridge. Originally it ran from 7 to 9 September, but the change of calendar in 1752 (*see* p. xxix) brought its start date to 18 September, and its original three days were regularly stretched to two weeks, much to the annoyance of the local inhabitants who often agitated to get the fair limited to its statutory duration.

Most ancient fairs followed the same historical pattern, beginning as essential gatherings for buying and selling goods, but gradually changing to those for pleasure only; and Southwark was particularly

famous for its entertainments and show-booths, which drew enthusiastic playgoers from all levels of society in great numbers. The two
great seventeenth-century diarists, John Evelyn and Samuel Pepys,
both recorded visits, and both mentioned the spectacular tightrope
walking and dancing (13 September 1660 and 21 September 1668, respectively). In 1720, John Strype's *Survey of the Cities of London and
Westminster* commented that it was 'noted chiefly for shows, drolls,
puppet-shows, rope-dancing, music booths and tippling houses',
and it was particularly these show-booths that were guilty of staying
longer than the official three days. By the mid eighteenth century, a
combination of locals and reformers had become vociferous in their
condemnation of the fair, claiming that it tended 'only to the destruction of youth of both sexes, and the encouragement of thieves and
strollers', and they succeeded in getting it suppressed in 1762.

See also **Fairs, Feasts, Wakes, and Revels**, p. 341.

19 September

Painswick Church-Clipping

On the Sunday nearest to 19 September, the parishioners of Painswick,
Gloucestershire, gather to 'clip' their church. The church is dedicated
to St Mary, and the patronal feast should therefore be on the Nativity
of the Blessed Virgin (8 September), but owing to the reform of the
calendar in 1752, 19 September is the Nativity Old Style, and the date
of the village feast.

After a procession of the faithful to the church, the children (and
some adults) join hands to completely encircle the building while the
clipping hymn is sung. At the chorus they all walk three steps forward
and back, swaying their arms, which some say represents the beating
of angels' wings. The children are dressed in their best, and have flowers in their hair or in buttonholes and posies, and there is a special
church service. Participating children traditionally receive a bun and
a small coin.

The modern ceremony at Painswick is a charming combination of
simplicity, joyfulness, and solemnity, but its history and development
is confused, and often misrepresented. The first confusion is over
the name. 'Clipping' is an Old English word meaning 'clasping' or

'embracing', and has been used in that sense, in literature and some local dialects, almost to the present day. However, because the Painswick ceremony occurs on the church's patronal festival, some earlier writers suggested that 'clipping' was derived from the Anglo-Saxon word *ycleping*, which meant 'naming', while others thought it was so named because of an allied custom of 'clipping' the churchyard yews for the day.

The survival of the custom is also a little confused. It is clear that it was revived in late Victorian times, by the Revd W. H. Seddon, having last been carried out around 1851. In addition, the Revd Percy Dearmer, while on holiday duty at Painswick in 1908, claimed that he 'gave time to re-organizing the Clipping Service'. However, there is no evidence that it existed in Painswick before about 1820.

Other present-day churches occasionally hold clipping ceremonies, although Painswick rightly gets all the publicity. In past years the custom was by no means uncommon in England, and the list of places that are recorded as having church-clipping ceremonies in the nineteenth century includes: Cradley, Worcestershire; Burbage, Derbyshire; Guiseley, Yorkshire; Wellington and Ellesmere, Shropshire; Beckington and Rode, Somerset; Bradford-on-Avon, Wiltshire; and Sheepscombe, Gloucestershire. The majority of these took place on Shrove Tuesday, but some were held at Easter, and some on the day of the local church's dedication. There were local variations, of course. At Wellington, for example, the participants all carried toy trumpets, which they blew vigorously as they marched round the church, prompting some commentators to presume a connection with the story about the walls of Jericho.

The earliest reference to church-clipping, however, relates to Birmingham. A correspondent to William Hone's *Every-Day Book* (1827) remembered Easter Monday clipping there in his or her childhood, which probably therefore refers to the mid or late eighteenth century. Despite regular confident assertions of the ancient origins of church-clipping, there is thus no evidence at present that it existed earlier than a mere 250 years ago, and talk of direct survival from the Roman festival of Lupercalia must be regarded as nonsense. However, research into the early history and development of church-clipping would be welcome, and one element of that enquiry might be a possible connection between the circling of the church and the game-custom of dancing hand-in-hand through the streets, often called

'Thread the Needle'. An article in *Folk-Lore* in 1912 drew attention to several places where the two customs occurred together, and others where they were separate.

One further aspect of the Painswick Feast was mentioned in the magazine *John Bull* (24 September 1955):

'When I was a girl' says Lucy Hobbs, *'every family in Painswick made a puppy-dog pie for the Clipping.'* Small china dogs were baked in meat and apple pies. The practice died out a few years ago, but Lucy Hobbs hopes to see it revived this year.

These 'puppy-dog' or 'bow-wow' pies are variously described as containing meat, apple, or plum, or even as almond-paste cakes, but the china dog inside is the defining detail. There are several similar traditions regarding their origins. All the stories agree that visitors from a neighbouring town (usually Stroud), or some unwelcome and uncouth navvies, were given pies made out of dog meat – some say because the hosts had run out of proper meat, while others maintain that it was done deliberately to put the arrogant outsiders in their place. Either way, the relations between the two places were not improved by the occurrence, and the traditional rivalry of neighbours was given added point by the mere mention of puppy-dog pies by one side or the other.

21 September

St Matthew's Day

This day was sometimes claimed to be the Devil's Nutting Day, but it was more commonly said of **14 September: Holy Cross Day/Holy Rood Day**. In weather terms, it was recorded by Richard Inwards in 1869 that 'St Matthew brings on the cold dew', but the same was also said of St Bartholomew's Day (24 August).

29 September

Michaelmas/Feast of St Michael and All Angels

The Archangel Michael was extremely popular in England in the Middle Ages, and hundreds of early churches were dedicated to him. He was one of the figures portrayed killing a dragon, and his reputation as 'Captain of the heavenly host' in the biblical 'war in heaven' (Revelation 12:7–9) ensured his popularity with soldiers as well as with the general public.

The one feature of Michaelmas that affected almost everybody in the country but is now almost entirely forgotten was the custom of eating roast goose on the day. The Michaelmas goose tradition was once stronger than the modern traditions of eggs at Easter and turkey at Christmas combined, and as with most festival foods, there was a widespread idea that it was lucky to follow tradition, and unlucky not to. As Robert Forby's *Vocabulary of East Anglia* (1830) says, 'If you don't baste the goose on Michaelmas Day, you'll want money all the year', and Jane Austen was clearly aware of the superstition when she wrote to her sister Cassandra on 11/12 of October 1813 [i.e. Old Style Michaelmas Day], 'I dined upon goose yesterday – which I hope will secure a good sale of my 2nd edition.'

There has never been a satisfactory explanation for the goose-eating tradition, apart from the prosaic reason that geese are at their prime at that time. One widespread, but completely untrue, historical story makes it our patriotic duty to do so. It was said that Queen Elizabeth I was eating goose on Michaelmas Day when she received the news that the Spanish Armada had been defeated, and she declared that henceforth all true English people should eat the same on that day, in thanks and remembrance for our national delivery. The romance of this story notwithstanding, there is evidence that the connection between Michaelmas and the goose was already in place in the fifteenth century. It lasted into the early twentieth century, but then rapidly faded from the national consciousness.

As one of the four quarter days, Michaelmas was an important time in legal and economic affairs from at least medieval times to the late nineteenth century. It was often the day that local courts were held, rents were due, annual employment terms expired, and was one of the days locally called 'Pack Rag Day' because so many families were busy

Lawless Hours and Days

A minor thread running through many traditional customs is the belief that at certain times, or on certain days, normal laws are suspended, and everyone can do as they like without fear of reprisal. These are sometimes explicitly named as 'lawless' hours or days, meaning 'exempt from or outside the law' rather than simply 'illegal', a fine distinction. The times in question vary from place to place, and although some seem to be arbitrary, others are more specific. One regular time was on mayor-making day, apparently on the principle that there was an interregnum between departing and incoming mayor, which resulted in a temporary legal hiatus.

According to the *Staffordshire Advertiser* of 5th February 1910, a woman from Alsager's Bank was summoned to the Newcastle-under-Lyme County Police Court for throwing liquid over a man at Silverdale, and pleaded that it was done on (the mayoral?) election day and that 'there is no law on election day; you may do whatever you like'. She was convicted and fined.

At other times, the lawlessness took a particular form, as recorded in the *Gentleman's Magazine* of 1790:

At Kidderminster is a singular custom. On the election of a bailiff, the inhabitants assemble in the principal streets to throw cabbage-stalks at each other. The town-house bell gives signal for this affray. This is called 'lawless hour'. This done (for it lasts

changing their accommodation at the time (*see also* 14 May: Pack Rag Day). In local government, it was a favourite day for new mayors to be elected (*see* Election of the Lord Mayor of London, *below*) or to take office, and was thus a day of civic pomp and ceremony. James Cossins described the scene in his youth in Exeter in the 1820s:

The election of Mayors for the City of Exeter, under the old Chamber, was about Michaelmas . . . On the day of the election, the members of the body and freemen assembled in the Guildhall; the intended Mayor was proposed, with the other officials; after taking the oath and duly signing the documents, on the cheering subsiding, the Hall echoed with the sound of various drawings of bottled wine corks, the liquor being freely passed around the an hour), the bailiff elect and corporation, in their robes, preceded by drums and fifes (for they have no waits), visit the old and new bailiff, constables, etc. attended by the mob. In the mean time, the most respectable families in the neighbourhood are invited to meet and fling apples at them on their entrance. I have known forty pots of apples expended at one house.

See 28 July: Old St Kenelm's Day for another custom that involves throwing things at otherwise respected persons.

Another lawless day, similarly associated with the appointment of the mayor and civic officers, took place in Exeter, as described by a correspondent to William Hone's *Year-Book* (1832), remembering his time in the town 'more than a dozen years' earlier. He wrote of 'squads of the mischief-loving part of the mobility' taking to the streets on 29 May, damming up the kennels (watercourses) to make deep pools, and expecting passers-by to give money or be drenched with the none-too-clean water. The procedure was also described by James Cossins in his *Reminiscences of Exeter* (1878), but he places it on Ascension Day.

The belief also surfaced on certain days when locals believed they had the right to enter local woods to hunt small animals – sometimes specifically squirrels, but often any small game. Again, the day varied from place to place, including Good Friday, St Andrew's Day (*see* 30 November), and Boxing Day (*see* 26 December: Hunting and Shooting). For other nights that were widely considered to be lawless, *see* 31 October: Mischief Night and 5 November: Guy Fawkes Night.

See also Mock Mayors and Courts, p. 298.

table . . . A procession was then formed to perambulate the walls, headed by the tradesmen's corps of constables, about twenty-four in number, then the staff and mace-bearers, sword-bearers, the Mayor-elect walking uncovered, with his hat in hand; Aldermen, with scarlet robes and three-cornered hats, followed by members and officials; in the rear being three tradesmen's sons, named Mayor's stewards (the outside one being called gutter steward), wearing long black robes, with tufts and three-cornered hats, who had the privilege of dining at the Mayor's banquets. Some of the electors and inhabitants would accompany the procession, and give vent to their feelings by an occasional cheer. At two fixed points on the route . . . apples were thrown about for a general scramble, and at another wine was provided.

The ceremony wound up in the evening with the good old English custom of dinner.

A generation or two before this, Exeter's mayor-making, like many other places, was accompanied by rougher activities than scrambling for apples. It was traditional on these occasions for the incoming mayor to supply a bull to be baited in the street for the people's amusement, and there was a curious local belief that just before the new mayor took office there was a 'lawless hour' when normal laws and regulations had no effect. In Exeter, youths would dam up any streams or gutters to create pools of water with which they could soak passersby if they were not paid a fee; but in Kidderminster, Worcestershire, the people threw cabbage stalks at each other, and then pelted the newly elected corporation with apples.

See also **Hiring Fairs**, p. 470; **Lawless Hours and Days**, p. 412.

Blackberries

An extremely widespread superstition, found all over the British Isles, maintained that blackberries were bad, or even poisonous, after a certain date. This date varied from place to place, ranging from Michaelmas to 10 or 11 October, and as the latter equates to 29 September before the change of calendar in 1752, it is clear that Michaelmas is the key day. The reason for the blackberries' sudden decline was that the Devil interfered on that day. In 1882, the *Western Antiquary* reported:

The belief that it is unlucky to eat blackberries after Michaelmas Day, because 'His Royal Highness' then tampers with them, still lingers in Exeter and neighbourhood. Some time ago, whilst walking in the country round here, a young friend who was with me warned me against plucking any blackberries: 'Because,' said he, grimly, 'it's past Michaelmas Day and the Devil's been at 'em.'

In the polite versions of this superstition, the Devil puts his foot on the berries, or wipes his club or tail over them, but in more graphic versions he defiles them in more earthy ways. The belief certainly dates back to the early eighteenth century, but was particularly well known in the nineteenth, and can still be heard in some areas.

A peculiar custom, which prevailed at Kingston-upon-Thames church in Surrey until the early nineteenth century, involved the cracking of nuts during the service on the Sunday before St Michael's Day. This was not confined to children but was indulged in by all ages, and according to Edward Brayley's *Topographical History of Surrey* (1850), 'the cracking noise was often so powerful, that the minister was obliged to suspend his reading, or discourse, until greater quietness was obtained.' It was thought to be a remnant of a civic custom, having something to do with the choosing of the bailiffs and other members of the town corporation on Michaelmas Day, although it is difficult to understand quite how the two were connected, unless it had something to do with the idea of a 'lawless hour' (*see* **Lawless Hours and Days**, p. 412). The connection between nuts and Michaelmas, however, is shown by other references, such as Oliver Goldsmith's *Vicar of Wakefield* (1766):

They kept up the Christmas carol, sent true-love knots on Valentine morning, ate pan-cakes at Shrove-tide, shewed their wit on the first of April, and religiously cracked nuts on Michaelmas Eve.

Election of the Lord Mayor of London

The Lord Mayor of London is head of the Corporation of London, the local authority that governs the City of London – a position not to be confused with the Mayor of London, created in 2000, who is head of the Greater London Authority. The Lord Mayor's position is somewhat older, dating from about the year 1192.

The Lord Mayor is elected on 29 September, then presents himself to the Lord Chancellor at the House of Lords in October for royal approval, and finally takes office on the second Friday in November (*see* **Second Friday in November: Silent Change**). To be eligible, a candidate must be a serving alderman, and have served previously as a sheriff, of which there are always two at a time, elected annually from their own ranks by the aldermen. The Liverymen of the City put forward eligible names for Lord Mayor to the Court of Aldermen, who make the final decision at a meeting at the Guildhall.

The Lord Mayor of London is still an extremely important personage in the nation, and in many situations is second only in precedence to the sovereign. In addition to the numerous ceremonial tasks, the frequent entertaining of dignitaries, and the foreign trips to represent the City, the Lord Mayor chairs the Court of Aldermen and the Court of Common Council, and serves as Admiral of the Port of London, Chief Magistrate of the City, and Chancellor of City University.

As the Lord Mayor is drawn from the business and social elite of the capital, it is to be expected that the candidate has not always been at the cutting edge of societal change, but there have been numerous occasions when the City has quietly moved with the times. A minor ripple was caused in 1972 when the first Labour Lord Mayor, Lord Mais, was appointed, which occasioned *The Times* to comment, 'a Labour Lord Mayor of the City of London seems as rare as a vegetarian King of the Cannibals.' The first woman to hold the position was Lady Donaldson, in 1983.

Urswick Rush-Bearing

The pretty Lakeland village of Urswick has an annual rush-bearing ceremony that is similar to those of other Cumbrian villages such as Grasmere and Ambleside, but decidedly smaller in scale, local, and quietly religious. In Urswick, the event is organized by the church and the school, and rather than making a carnival day of it, they simply have a cup of tea and a piece of gingerbread after the procession and church service.

The procession starts at 1 p.m. from the school and walks round the village, with a brass band and banners, until it reaches the ancient church of St Mary and St Michael, where the service takes place. Participants carry rushes and flowers, and six children carry a white embroidered rush-sheet, as at Grasmere. There is a Rush Queen, along with her attendants, and on the banners are embroidered the names of all the girls that have served in that capacity.

The custom was revived, or perhaps introduced to Urswick, in 1905 by the Revd Thomas Postelthwaite, and they celebrated their centenary in 2005; however, survival for the next hundred years may not be guaranteed. It is clear that some parts of the ceremony are under threat from changes in the community and society at large, with girls reportedly less interested in being the Rush Queen and parading the village in a white dress. Links to such local community events have also weakened as the local school caters only for primary children, and the older ones have to travel to the nearest town.

See also **Rush-Bearing**, p. 322.

OCTOBER

Quit Rent Ceremonies

In feudal times, a quit rent was a payment or presentation made by tenants to the lord of the manor in order to excuse themselves from having to render customary services. Such payments were often nominal, or could involve customary obligations other than financial. Two of the latter survive in London, concerning two pieces of land, 'the Moors' in Eardington, Shropshire, and the Forge in St Clement Danes, London; they are carried out in October each year. The Comptroller of the City Corporation performs the ceremony at the Law Courts, in the presence of the Queen's Remembrancer. The former land is held by presentation, dating to the year 1211, of two knives, one of which has to be good enough to cut through a hazel stick. Thus, the comptroller brings a hatchet to court, with which he chops a bundle of hazel twigs. For the other land, in a procedure dating to 1295, six horseshoes and sixty-one horseshoe nails are presented and duly counted. There is nowadays much solemn ceremony involved, and the same hatchet, horseshoes, and nails are presented each year.

A Sunday in October

Redcliffe Pipe Walk

In a custom that superficially resembles a 'beating of the bounds', the vicar and churchwardens of St Mary Redcliffe church in Bristol, together with a surveyor, walk the mile-and-a-half course of a medieval water pipe, on a Sunday in October, usually accompanied by two or three dozen interested people. This early water supply for the area runs from the 'Rugewell' (probably meaning 'ridge well'), in Knowle, and was granted in 1190 by Lord Robert de Berkeley, whose tomb can be seen in the church. The pipe's course is marked by a series of stones (marked 'SMP') and manholes, down which the surveyor has to climb, and the walkers have right of way along its course. The water was stopped halfway along the course about fifty years ago, but it still feeds an ornate fountain, and the church authorities still have to make the complete inspection in order to retain certain endowments. A plaque on the outside wall of St Mary Redcliffe church, translated from the Latin, reads:

For the health of the soul of Robert of Berkeley, who gave to God and the church of St. Mary Redcliffe and its ministers the Rugewell and conduit. AD 1190. Erected 1932.

2 October

Braughing Old Man's Day

Matthew Wall was in his coffin, on his way to being buried in St Mary the Virgin's churchyard in the Hertfordshire town of Braughing, when one of the pall-bearers slipped, dropped the coffin, and jolted him awake. Matthew was naturally rather pleased with this outcome, and in his will, dated 1595, he left money to commemorate the event. Among other stipulations, he requested that the church bells be rung on 2 October (the day of his lucky escape), the sexton must look after his grave, and a poor man be paid a shilling to sweep the path up to the church gate.

And so it is that every 2 October, locally called 'Old Man's Day', children of the village gather with brooms and enthusiastically sweep Fleece Lane, while the funeral bell tolls. Brambles are placed on Matthew's grave, to keep the sheep off, and prayers are said at his graveside. Later, the church bells ring a wedding peal, as Matthew lived long enough to re-marry. The present ceremonies date back to a revival in the mid twentieth century, but it is not clear how long it had lapsed before that time.

First Wednesday in October

Nottingham Goose Fair

Various fairs up and down the country were famed for particular wares, reflected in their names, and several were known for the numbers of geese sold, usually because they were held around Michaelmas, the traditional time for goose-eating in England. Many goose fairs have faded from memory, but two that are still going strong, as pleasure fairs, are held in Nottingham and in Tavistock, Devon; both can claim considerable antiquity. A St Matthew Fair at Nottingham was still extant when the town was awarded a second fair in 1284, so it might well be Anglo-Saxon in origin. It was called a 'goose fair' at least as early as 1541, and in its heyday tens of thousands of geese were sold there each year. The change of calendar in 1752 forced the fair to move to 2 October, and continuing popularity brought much congestion to the city centre, where it took place each year. By 1927 it was becoming intolerably cramped, and new municipal building around the Market Square made a move desirable, although there were loud protests against this. It is now held at the Forest Recreation Ground about a mile away, and is one of the biggest pleasure fairs in the country. The actual days on which the Goose Fair is held can vary from year to year. For some time it was regularized as the first Thursday in October, and the following Friday and Saturday, but of late the fair has started on the Wednesday and run for four days.

See also **29 September: Michaelmas/Feast of St Michael and All Angels; Second Wednesday in October: Tavistock Goosie Fair; Fairs, Feasts, Wakes, and Revels, p. 341.**

Goose-Riding

Goose-riding was a 'sport', extant in Derbyshire and probably elsewhere in the 1790s, in which a live goose, its neck well greased to increase the difficulty, was suspended by its legs from a rope strung between two trees or posts. Participants rode at speed under the rope and attempted to pull the head off the goose as they passed; whoever succeeded won the goose.

Second Sunday in October

Harvest of the Sea

The proximity of St Mary-at-Hill church in London's Lovat Lane to the ancient Billingsgate fish market has ensured that it has always had strong links with the fish industry, and the set piece of this historical connection is the Thanksgiving Service for the Harvest of the Sea, which takes place every October, usually on the second Sunday of the month. The church is decorated for the occasion with nets and other seagoing paraphernalia, and houses an intricate design made from a variety of fresh fish and seafood, still supplied by the Billingsgate traders. It is not clear how long this custom has been in operation at St Mary's, but *The Times* of 3 October 1922 described a very similar event at the church of St Magnus the Martyr, at London Bridge, where it had apparently taken place for the previous fifteen years.

Second Wednesday in October

Tavistock Goosie Fair

Various fairs have come and gone in the history of Tavistock, in Devon. The earliest was granted to the Abbey of St Mary and St Rumon by charter of Henry I in the year 1116. But the famous Goosie Fair, held at Michaelmas, is of later foundation (probably the sixteenth century).

The change of calendar in 1752 moved it from 29 September to 10 October, and this was later transferred to the second Wednesday in that month, where it still stands. The ubiquitous presence of roast goose on everybody's dinner table around Michaelmas is detailed under 29 September, and any livestock fair that took place at that time was likely to be termed a 'goose fair', even if other animals were sold in larger quantities. The move to October, the gradual decline in goose-eating, and the inexorable rise of the pleasure side of fairs at the expense of the commercial, all contributed to changes in the event, and by the twentieth century the occasional presence of real geese at the fair always prompted articles in the local and even national press. However, the fair retains its name and importance to the local community, and attracts numerous visitors. As it still takes place in the centre of town, Tavistock is closed to traffic on the day.

The fair also boasts its own song, 'Tavistock Goozey Vair', written by C. John Trythall in 1912, which commences:

> 'Tis just a month come Friday next, Bill Champerdown and me
> Us traipsed across old Darty moor, the Goosey Fair to see
> Us made ourselves quite fitting, us greased and oiled our hair
> Then off we goes in our Sunday clothes, behind old Bill's grey mare.

As with all such 'dialect' pieces, the song sounds fine when sung by locals, but can come across as excruciating stage-yokel in cold print or when sung by anyone else.

See also **29 September: Michaelmas/Feast of St Michael and All Angels; First Wednesday in October: Nottingham Goose Fair; Fairs, Feasts, Wakes, and Revels**, p. 341.

10 October

Old Michaelmas Day

Dog-Whipping Day, a calendar custom apparently confined to Yorkshire, was variously given as occurring on either 10 October or 18 October (St Luke's Day). As folklore writer John Nicholson commented in 1890:

So common was the practice at one time, that every little street arab considered it his bounden duty to prepare a whip for any unlucky dog that might be seen wandering in the streets on that day.

The custom was said to have originated when a dog swallowed the consecrated wafer during service in York Minster. It was suppressed, in Hull at least, by the police in 1853.

Stray dogs were a regular nuisance in past times, and a relatively humble, but no less useful, parish official was the dog-whipper (or dog-rapper) whose job it was to keep stray dogs out of church. The earliest reference known to us is in the Ludlow churchwardens' accounts for 1543, in Shropshire, when Thomas Payver was paid 8d for carrying out the task. Nine years later, Archbishop Holgate of York issued an injunction that the vergers should expel 'beggars, other light persons, and dogs' from the church during divine service. Payments to dog-whippers continue throughout the sixteenth to eighteenth centuries, but they fade out in the first two decades of the nineteenth.

This day was also one of several designated as the last day in the year to eat blackberries (*see* **29 September: Blackberries**).

Pack Monday Fair

Every year, starting on the Monday following 10 October (Old Michaelmas Day), the streets of Sherborne, in Dorset, are given over to Pack Monday Fair – previously an agricultural fair, but now devoted to stalls, sideshows, and a funfair. The second volume of William Hone's *Every-Day Book* contains a lively description of the fair, written by a local man in 1826. It is worth quoting extensively, as an excellent example of the hustle and bustle of a nineteenth-century fair, its activities, and its attractions. The piece demonstrates the way the whole town is taken over by the event, the intermixing of business and pleasure, and of the classes and ages – farmers and farmworkers, tradesmen and customers, adults and children, from town and country:

The fair is annually held on the first Monday after the 10th of October, and is a mart for the sale of horses, cows, fat and lean oxen, sheep, lambs, and pigs; cloth, earthenware, onions, wall and hazel nuts, apples, fruit, trees, and the usual nick nacks for children, toys, gingerbread, sweetmeats, sugar plums, etc., with drapery, hats, bonnets, caps, ribands, etc. for the country belles, of whom, when the weather is favourable, a great number is drawn together from the neighbouring villages . . . To the present time Pack Monday fair is annually announced three or four weeks previous by all the little urchins who can procure and blow a cow's horn, parading the streets in the evenings, and sending forth the different tones of their horny bugles, sometimes beating an old saucepan for a drum, to render the sweet sound more delicious . . .

At four o'clock the great bell is rung for a quarter of an hour. From this time, the bustle commences by the preparations for the coming scene: stalls erecting, windows cleaning and decorating, shepherds and drovers going forth for their flocks and herds, which are depastured for the night in the neighbouring fields, and every individual seems on the alert. The business in the sheep and cattle fairs (which are held in different fields, nearly in the centre of the town, and well attended by the gentlemen farmers of Dorset, Somerset and Devon) takes precedence, and is generally concluded by twelve o'clock, when what is called the in-fair begins to wear the appearance of business-like activity, and from this time till three or four o'clock more business is transacted in the Ship counting house, parlour, hall, and kitchen, than at any other time of day, it being the custom of the tradespeople to have their yearly accounts settled about this time, and scarcely a draper, grocer, hatter, ironmonger, bookseller, or other respectable tradesman, but is provided with an ample store of beef and home-brewed October [ale], for the welcome of their numerous customers . . . Now (according to an old saying) is the town alive. John takes Joan to see the shows – there he finds the giant – here the learned pig – the giantess and dwarf – the menagerie of wild beasts – the conjuror – and Mr. Merry Andrew cracking his jokes with his quondam master. Here it is – 'Walk up, walk up, ladies and gentlemen, we are now going to begin, be in time, the price is only twopence.' Here is Mr. Warr's merry round-about, with 'a horse or a coach for a halfpenny' – Here is Rebecca Swain with her black and red cock, and lucky-bag, who bawls out, 'Come my little lucky rogues, and try your fortune for a halfpenny, all prizes and no blanks, a faint heart never wins a fair lady.' – Here is pricking in the garter – Raffling for gingerbread, with the cry of 'One in, who makes two, the more the merrier.' – Here is the Sheffield hardwareman, sporting a worn-out wig and huge pair of spectacles, offering, in lots, a box of razors, knives, scissors, etc., each lot of which he modestly says, is worth seven shillings, but he'll not be too hard on the gaping crowd, he'll not take seven, nor six, nor five, nor four, nor three, nor two, but one shilling for the lot – going at one shilling – sold again and the money paid. – Here are two earthenware-men bawling their shilling's worth one against the other, and quaffing beer to each other's luck from that necessary and convenient chamber utensil that has modestly usurped the name of the great river Po. Here

continued on page 426 ☞

Wife-Selling

Readers of Thomas Hardy's *Mayor of Casterbridge* (1886) will be familiar with the dramatic scene early in the book when Michael Henchard, in a morose drunken state, decides to sell his wife at a fair:

'For my part I don't see why men who have got wives and don't want 'em, shouldn't get rid of 'em as those gipsy fellows do their old horses,' said the man in the tent. 'Why shouldn't they put 'em up and sell 'em by auction to men who are in need of such articles? Hey? Why, begad, I'd sell mine this minute if anybody would buy her!'

Henchard's decision sets in motion much of the tragic action of the story, but the scene is not simply a novelist's clever trick: it is a fictionalized description of an occurrence that many people of the time would have regarded as nothing particularly unusual. Wife sales, if not exactly an everyday event, were certainly not unknown, and were often advertised in local newspapers, such as the *Windsor & Eton Express* of September 1815:

On Friday last the common bellman gave notice in Staines market that the wife of —— Issey was then at the King's Head Inn, to be sold, with the consent of her husband, to any person inclined to buy her. There was a very numerous attendance to witness this singular sale, notwithstanding which only three shillings and fourpence were offered for the lot, no one choosing to contend with the bidder for the fair object, whose merits could only be appreciated by those who best knew them. This the purchaser could boast from a long and intimate acquaintance.

Hundreds of cases have been recorded over the past 500 years, and Sam Menefee, in the only full-length study of the custom, lists 387 known examples. The earliest definite case is recorded in the diary of London merchant tailor Henry Machyn: 'The 24th day of November [1553] did ride in a cart Cheken, parson of St. Nicholas Cold Abbey, about London, for he sold his wife to a butcher'; and there were several other instances in the sixteenth century, which indicate that this was not an isolated occurrence. Cases were still being reported into the 1920s.

There is no doubt that a wide section of the population genuinely believed that wife sales were not only permissible under law but also legally binding, providing, of course, that the sale was carried out properly. If the decision to sell was made on the spur of the moment, as in Thomas Hardy's novel, the sale will probably not have been recorded for posterity, but the majority of known cases were carefully given a semblance of regularity and legality. The sale often took place in a market or fair, where livestock was normally bought and sold, and the wife was presented with a halter round her neck and displayed to potential buyers. The seller was careful to pay all regular tolls and to get a receipt. Most important of all, the sale was carried out in front of witnesses. The sums involved varied considerably, from fourpence and a pint of beer, to £50.

Occasionally, the sale was a way of sorting out a genuine marital problem, such as when the wife of a sailor had married again, believing him to have been drowned. The embarrassment caused by the man's unexpected return could be resolved by the new husband formally buying his wife from her first husband. Nor is all this necessarily an example of callous male brutality and enforced female submissiveness. There is plenty of evidence that in most cases the wife was pleased to be rid of her unwanted mate, the potential purchaser was known to her, and the whole thing agreed between them beforehand. The business of halters and bidding may have been degrading, but the women believed that this made the transaction legal, and no doubt many thought it was worth it. An example printed in *Notes & Queries* in 1951 makes this point clear:

Brooks, auctioneer, Plymouth, put his wife up for sale [in 1822]. **The police interfered, but Mrs. B. told the magistrates she was anxious to be sold, had made arrangements with a gentleman that he should buy her, an innkeeper being instructed on his behalf to bid to £20. If the reserve was exceeded she was content to go to the highest bidder.**

Nevertheless, nobody seems to have thought that a wife could sell her husband.

Three hundred and eighty-seven cases in 500 years is not indicative of an epidemic of wife-selling, but it was enough to convince some that the English were at it all the time, as reported in Robert Chambers' *Book of Days* (1864):

Rather unfortunately, the occasional instances of wife-sale, while remarked by ourselves with little beyond a passing smile, have made a deep impression on our continental neighbours, who

seriously believe that it is a habit of all classes of our people, and constantly cite it as an evidence of our low civilisation.

Over forty years later, Sabine Baring-Gould agreed:

It is – so far as my experience goes – quite useless to assure a Frenchman that such transfer of wives is not a matter of everyday occurrence and is not legal: he replies with an expression of incredulity, that of course English people endeavour to make light of, or deny, a fact that is 'notorious'.

It might go a little way to salvage our national pride to learn of a French case that took place at Maratz, near Lille, in 1865, and followed the same form as the English custom. The price was 126 francs, and, as reported in *Notes & Queries* in 1874, 'It appeared that neither buyer nor seller had any doubt of the legality of the transaction.'

☞ *continued from page 423*
    is poor Will, with a basket of gingerbread, crying 'toss or buy'. There is a smirking little lad pinning two girls together by their gowns, whilst his companion cracks a Waterloo bang-up [a cracker or firework] *in their faces. Here stands John with his mouth wide open and Joan with her sloe-black ogles stretched to their extremity at a fine painted shawl, which Cheap John is offering for next to nothing; and here is a hundred other contrivances to draw the browns from the pockets of the unwary, and tickle the fancies of the curious; and sometimes the rogue of a pickpocket extracting Farmer Anybody's watch or money from his pockets.*

It is often claimed nowadays that the word 'pack' is here derived from the 'pacts' made between farmer and worker at the fair, but this is unlikely; 'pack' meaning 'pact' is included in some dialect dictionaries, but only from Scotland. On the dialect evidence from elsewhere in England, the word 'pack', which is very common, has two closely related meanings. The first, as in variations on 'Pack Rag Day', refers to the day on which the family packed up their belongings to move house at the end of the annual term of employment (*see* **14 May**). Indeed, 'Pack and Penny Day' was often found in Yorkshire and neighbouring counties as a term for the day after Old Michaelmas or Old Martinmas Day, and as these were two of the most common days for the annual move, and the former is exactly when Sherborne Fair occurs, this seems to be the most likely explanation. Nevertheless, 'pack' is also used all over the country to refer to itinerant sellers and their wares, as in 'pack-man' (pedlar), 'pack-horse', and so on, which is equally apposite for an old-time fair.

An interesting custom that takes place the night before the fair is the perambulation of the town by Teddy Roe's (or Rowe's) Band, made up of the youth of the town, who make a great deal of noise with tin cans, horns, and whistles, in a similar way to **rough music** (p. 95) customs everywhere. The traditional story said to explain both this rough music and the fair's name relates that Teddy Roe was the foreman of some masons who were working on the great fan vault of Sherborne Abbey in 1490. They were given a day off to visit the fair, 'packed up' their tools, and marched in joyful noisy procession to the fairground.

This story is without foundation, however, and Teddy Roe's Band is not at all unusual, as many other fairs up and down the country were heralded by young people going in procession and making noise with toy trumpets and tin cans. The figure of Teddy Roe himself remains a mystery, although one account (*John Bull*, 8 October 1955) states that he was simply the leader of the band in the early nineteenth century. The custom has been associated with vandalism and violence on a number of occasions in the past, and the band has regularly been suppressed by the police, but it always seems to re-emerge.

See also **Fairs, Feasts, Wakes, and Revels,** p. 341.

Weyhill Fair

Weyhill was one of the big agricultural fairs that seemed to survive from habit and custom rather than from a solid legal basis. It had certainly been in existence a long time, as shown by the line in William Langland's *Piers Plowman*, of about 1377 – 'To Wy and to Wynchestre I wente to the feyre' (Passus V, line 201) – but no charter has ever been found. The position of the fair site, on a hillside a few miles from Andover, in Hampshire, is usually explained as the meeting point of several key ancient roads, but more pertinent is the fact that it straddled the boundaries of three parishes and three estates. This geographical ambiguity, coupled with the lack of a charter, made it particularly vulnerable to both legal challenge and more direct methods of takeover, by moving it on to neighbouring land. In the 1550s, for example, a long-running dispute broke out between the traditional owners of the fair and the citizens of the town of Andover, who claimed the fair, and its fees and tolls, for themselves. A similar dispute flared up in the

1670s. The town's claim was bolstered by a royal charter of 1559 that did indeed grant them the right to hold a fair at Weyhill, but the fair owners maintained that this did not apply to *their* fair, which had already been in existence long before.

Weyhill Fair survived these challenges and by the eighteenth century was one of the biggest in England, dominating the livestock trade in the South-West. It was particularly known for its sheep and horses, but hops and cheese were also traded in huge quantities, and a thriving pleasure fair also took place, with its sideshows, rides, freak shows, and boxing booths, along with a hiring fair. However, the nineteenth century saw a long slow decline in many of the country's big fairs. William Cobbett visited Weyhill on 11 October 1822, on one of the journeys that he later described in *Rural Rides*. He had first been to the fair about forty years previously and had fond memories of the trip, so he was shocked to find trade so depressed in the 1820s:

The 11th of October is the sheep-fair. About £300,000 used, some few years ago, to be carried home by the sheep-sellers. Today, less, perhaps, than £70,000, and yet the rents of these sheep-sellers are, perhaps, as high, on an average, as they were then. The countenances of the farmers were descriptive of their ruinous state. I never, in all my life, beheld a more mournful scene. There is a horse fair upon another part of the Down; and there I saw horses keeping pace in depression with the sheep.

Cobbett was not a totally impartial observer – he had political reasons for painting a bad picture, as well as a generalized notion that things had been so much better in his youth – however, his rides took place at a time of real agricultural depression, in the difficult period between the revolution of enclosure and the drastic reorganization of agricultural practice and increased rural prosperity of later in the century. But even without the general agricultural depression, he would have noticed a marked change at Weyhill in the forty years since his first visit. Large-scale fairs all over the country were suffering from changes in economic structure and business practice that were gradually making them redundant as wholesale markets (*see* **14 September: Sturbridge Fair**).

Nevertheless, pleasure-seekers continued to attend Weyhill Fair, and, as with many other places, it was long famous for its burlesque initiation ceremony for newcomers (*see also* **Hocktide: Hungerford**

Described in the Women's Institute book *It Happened in Hampshire*, the ceremony at Weyhill was called 'horning the colt':

The newcomer was seated in a chair, and a hat adorned with a pair of horns and a cup was placed on his head, and the following verses being sung:

> *So swift runs the fox, so cunning runs the fox*
> *Why shouldn't this heifer grow up to be an ox?*
> *And get his living among the briars and thorns*
> *And drink like his daddy with a large pair of horns.*
>> *Horns, boys, horns, boys, horns*
>> *And drink like his daddy with a large pair of horns.*

The cup on his head had to be filled with ale. The newly initiated drank this, and paid for half a gallon, which was consumed by the company.

The ceremony took place at several pubs in the area, and details varied from place to place, other versions of the song including 'So swift runs the hare' in the first line, and 'And die like his daddy' in the fourth. Weyhill also made an appearance in literature, as the model for the fair at which Michael Henchard sold his wife at the start of Thomas Hardy's novel *The Mayor of Casterbridge* (1886); *see* **Wife-Selling,** p. 424.

The dates on which Weyhill Fair was held changed over time. In the earliest records it was a Michaelmas fair, lasting for three days between 28 and 30 September, but it later moved to 8 October, running for six days, and then to 10 October. There were also other smaller fairs, for sheep, in April and July. Weyhill struggled on into the twentieth century, a mere shadow of its former self, and finally ceased in the 1950s.

See also **Fairs, Feasts, Wakes, and Revels,** p. 341; **Hiring Fairs,** p. 470.

11 October

Blackberries

In 1909, the journal *Folk-Lore* reported that in Worcestershire:

All children who either gather or eat blackberries on or after the 11th of October will fall into great trouble. It is said that 'the Devil puts his paw on them' on that day.

See 29 **September: Blackberries** for further details.

16 October

Lion Sermon

This annual sermon takes place at the church of St Katharine Cree, Leadenhall Street, London, on or near 16 October. It commemorates an incident in the life of Sir John Gayer, founder of the Levant Company and later Lord Mayor of London, who died in 1649. While abroad on a trading expedition he became separated from his companions in the desert and met a fierce lion. Praying for assistance, Gayer fell asleep and on being found in the morning he was surrounded by lion prints but had come to no harm. Back in London as a prosperous merchant, he made various charitable gifts, including a bequest for the poor of St Katharine's parish, and he is still commemorated with a special service at which the story is retold and a sermon is preached.

18 October

St Luke's Day

Luke the evangelist, by tradition a Greek physician, was a disciple of St Paul and a key figure in the early development of the Christian Church. He became the patron saint of doctors, surgeons, and artists – the latter because of a tradition that he himself was one. In religious pictures he is sometimes shown painting, but the symbol that accompanies him in most images is an ox with horns, although it is not clear why. The good saint would have been horrified if he knew what connotations those very horns would have in later years, and what they would do to his feast day.

At Charlton, in Kent, where the parish church is dedicated to St Luke, a very famous fair took place each year, starting on 18 October. It was formerly held upon a green opposite the church but later moved to the other end of the village, and at some point became widely known as 'Charlton Horn Fair'; until suppressed in 1872, it was one of the most notorious fairs in the London region.

Horns were the theme of the fair and were ubiquitous on the day. Many of the people who frequented the fair wore or carried horns, the stalls specialized in items made of horn, and even the gingerbread men sported little horns on their heads. However, this was not simply a harmless gimmick; people found the wearing of horns immensely amusing because of their sexual connotations. From at least the mid fifteenth century onwards the phrase 'to wear the horns' referred to a cuckold (i.e. a man whose wife has been unfaithful to him), and anything to do with horns was replete with opportunities for ribald humour. If one held a hand to the forehead, with index and little finger extended, it would be taken as a gross personal insult, and numerous sexual slang phrases that included the word 'horn' traded on the same principle.

The popular story that explained the origin of the fair also traded on this sexual theme. It was said that one St Luke's Day, King John needed a rest while out hunting, and stepped into a nearby mill. The miller's attractive wife was home alone, so the King decided to make advances, and was just in the act of kissing her when the miller returned, drew his dagger, and threatened to kill them both. The King, however, granted him lordship over all the land between Charlton and the bend in the river beyond Rotherhithe, together with the right to hold a fair each year on that same day. The bend in the river bore the popular name of 'Cuckold's Point', and the German traveller Paul Hentzner, who was well aware of the connection between horns and cuckoldry, noted in his *Travels to England* (1598) that a long pole was sited there, with ram's horns affixed.

Although the custom probably began when someone carried a pair of St Luke's horns to open the fair, it soon degenerated into burlesque, with a procession of characters dressed as the King, the miller, and his wife, and hundreds of others wearing horns on their heads. The crowds who flocked to the fair in their thousands were also famous for their habit of cross-dressing (men as women, and vice versa), and as this annual gathering flaunted its ribaldry so openly, it hardly endeared itself to the authorities of Church and State. The idea of horned beings also added a 'devilish' tinge to the fair's reputation.

From the eighteenth century onwards, writers queued up to condemn the goings-on at Charlton. Kent county historian Edward Hasted commented in 1779 that it was 'infamous for rudeness and indecency', and Daniel Defoe described Charlton in the 1720s as:

> ... a village famous, or rather infamous, for the yearly collected rabble of mad-people, at Horn Fair, the rudeness of which I cannot but think, is such as ought to be suppressed ... The mob indeed at that time take all kinds of liberties, and the women are especially impudent for that day; as if it was a day that justified the giving themselves a loose to all manner of indecency and immodesty, without any reproach, or without suffering the censure which such behaviour would deserve.

This bad reputation continued into the nineteenth century, and it is remarkable that the fair lasted as long as it did. However, the Fairs Act of 1871 gave the local authorities the opportunity to get rid of it, which they promptly did.

There are some indications that St Luke's Day was also regarded as a day for love divination. A full description of a ceremony for the day appears in a chapbook printed in 1685 called *Mother Bunch's Closet Newly Broke Open*, in which Mother Bunch instructs young girls how to predict and control their matrimonial prospects. She tells them to take marigold flowers, marjoram, thyme, and wormwood, and then to mix, dry, and pound them to a powder, and simmer them with honey and vinegar over a slow fire. With this concoction, the girl should 'anoint [her] stomach, breast and lips lying down, and repeat these words thrice':

> St. Luke, St. Luke, be kind to me
> In dreams let me my true love see.

She should then go to sleep as fast as she can. This ceremony is so similar to those on other nights (*see*, for example, **20 January: St Agnes' Eve**) that it has been regarded as perhaps a literary fancy on the part of the chapbook author rather than evidence of a genuine popular

of George Chapman's play *Monsieur D'Olive* (1606), in which occurs
the line 'St. Valentine's Day is fortunate to choose lovers, St. Luke's to
choose husbands.'

Somewhat incongruously, St Luke's Day was also 'Dog-Whipping
Day' in nineteenth-century York, when everybody carried whips
with which to assault any dogs found running loose in the town (*see*
10 October: Old Michaelmas Day). And on another note, according
to folklorist Sidney Oldall Addy, writing in 1895, 'A fine autumn is
known as a "St Luke's Summer".'

20 October

Colchester Oyster Feast

The annual Oyster Feast, held on or about 20 October, is a well-
publicized feature in Colchester's municipal calendar. Originally,
it was probably a simple civic luncheon, as found in some form or
other in most corporations up and down the country, and took place
in October because the local fair was on St Denys' Day (9 October,
but moved to 20 October on the change of calendar in 1752). The fact
that Colchester had a thriving local seafood industry added a unique
touch, as reported by the *Essex Standard* of 21 October 1847:

*On Thursday, the Mayor, Aldermen, Assistants, and Common Council
of this borough went in procession to proclaim the Fair of St. Denys.
Proclamation was made according to the ancient custom at the door of the
Town Hall, and repeated at the exchange. A liberal supply of oysters was
furnished by the Colne Fishery Company, which, with wine and cake,
the members of the corporate body partook of at the freeman's club in the
evening.*

The luncheon turned into a more grand affair by stages during the
nineteenth century, as it was opened up to a wider clientele. One particularly extrovert mayor, who served at various times between 1845
and 1862, regularly invited 200 or 300 guests, at his own expense, and
by the turn of the twentieth century, a special train from London had
to be organized each year to bring all the important people who had
been invited and were more than willing to come. Civic pride was well

served by this lavish dinner, which helped to keep Colchester in the public eye.

However, owing to a combination of economics, occasional extreme weather, and pollution, the oyster fishery declined markedly in the twentieth century, and the industry no longer made a significant contribution to the town's economy. The feast, too, seemed increasingly anachronistic and fell on hard times, and between 1939 and 1950 it was not even held. When it was finally revived it became more of a gala evening, as befits the modern view of such affairs. No longer do trainloads of important people arrive from London, but it is still a large event, with celebrities from the world of entertainment, sport, and politics (especially those with local connections), and a number of tickets are available to local people by ballot. Not everyone in attendance eats oysters, which are still always included in the fare; however, the oyster fishery has also undergone a revival, and the sense of pride in a unique aspect of the town's heritage grows stronger every year.

See also **Early September: Colchester Oyster Fishery** for the annual ceremony that starts the oyster dredging season, and **25 July: Whitstable Oyster Festival**.

21 October

Apple Day

This day was designated 'Apple Day' in 1990 by the environment and community charity Common Ground, who are based in Shaftesbury, Dorset. The day is designed as 'an annual celebration of apples, orchards, and local distinctiveness', and apple-related events take place up and down the country.

See also **First Weekend in December: Tree-Dressing Day** for another Common Ground initiative.

Trafalgar Day

A handful of military victories remain in public memory as symbols of national pride, while most are consigned to the history books. The one that appears to have the most resonance in this context is the Battle of Trafalgar of 1805, when the British fleet under Admiral Nelson destroyed the combined French and Spanish fleets in the decisive naval encounter of the Napoleonic Wars. A range of local Trafalgar Day celebrations take place each year on 21 October, particularly in places with strong naval ties, such as Gosport, Portsmouth, Plymouth, and Greenwich.

One of the best known is the annual service aboard the HMS *Victory* at Portsmouth Naval Base, but a more low-key ceremony takes place in Newcastle every October when the Lord Mayor lays a wreath at the foot of the statue of Admiral Lord Collingwood, who took command at Trafalgar when Nelson was killed.

The patriotic potential of Trafalgar Day makes it popular with those who wish to encourage English people to celebrate St George's Day (*see* **23 April**), and it is also the day that is favoured by many who dislike the connotations of May Day and wish to replace it with a different bank holiday later in the year (*see* **Bank Holidays**, p. 373). The year 2005 was the 200th anniversary of the battle, and numerous commemorative events were held around the country, along with the publication of many books and articles, which brought the day to the notice of an even wider audience.

25 October

St Crispin's Day

If they existed at all, the brothers St Crispin and St Crispinian were Roman martyrs who died about the year AD 285, but their cult came to Britain much later via France, where they were reputed to have been buried. By tradition they were shoemakers who even lived for a time at Faversham, in Kent, and they were thus adopted as patron saints of cobblers and leather-workers in general. In some areas these workers held celebratory meetings and processions, as other trades did on their patron saints' days, and there are also traces of other customs that lasted into the mid nineteenth century, as recorded in *Notes & Queries* in 1852:

In the parishes of Cuckfield and Hurst–a–point in Sussex, it is still the cus-tom to observe St. Crispin's Day, and it is kept with much rejoicing. The boys go round asking for money in the name of St. Crispin, bonfires are lighted, and it passes off very much in the same way as the fifth of November does.

However, the real lasting resonance for the day is patriotic rather than occupational, as it was the day that the Battle of Agincourt was fought in 1415, for ever encapsulated in the lines from Act IV, scene 3 of Shakespeare's *Henry V*:

> *This day is called the feast of Crispian.*
> *He that outlives this day, and come safe home,*
> *Will stand a tip-toe when this day is named,*
> *And rouse him at the name of Crispian.*
> *He that shall live this day, and see old age,*
> *Will yearly on the vigil feast his neighbours,*
> *And say, 'Tomorrow is Saint Crispian.'*
> *Then will he strip his sleeve and show his scars,*
> *And say 'These wounds I had on Crispin's day.'*

Last Thursday in October

Bampton Fair

Six miles from Tiverton, on the edge of Exmoor National Park, lies the picturesque Devon village of Bampton, which for centuries was widely known in the region for its annual fair. It is not completely clear when Bampton Fair started. The first documentary record of the fair dates from 1212, but a sheep fair had probably existed there before then, and charters of 1258 and 1267 confirm the right to hold two annual fairs in the village. For most of its history, Bampton was primarily a sheep fair, held on St Luke's Day (18 October). It was one of the biggest in the West Country, and before its decline in the mid nineteenth century over 12,000 animals could be sold each year. There had also been a certain amount of trading in cattle and horses, but as the sheep trade declined, the horse trade increased, and the fair became famous for its Exmoor ponies.

As with nearly all horse fairs, the sale of animals dwindled to nothing in the late twentieth century, and the event seemed destined to survive, if at all, simply as a pleasure fair. However, in 2003 locals completely reorganized the event, and it now offers a street market, an arts and crafts fair, craft workshops, auctions, exhibitions, and a range of other activities, in addition to the funfair, and the event has taken on a heightened profile in the life of the community and as a popular tourist attraction. Pony sales and other related activities have also been re-introduced, and the future for the fair looks promising.

See also **Fairs, Feasts, Wakes, and Revels**, p. 341.

Late October

Punkie Night

> *It's Punky Night tonight*
> *It's Punky Night tonight*
> *Give us a candle, give us a light*
> *It's Punky Night tonight.*

This is one verse of the song chanted by children in certain Somerset villages, as they carry their 'punkies' around the village. A punkie is made from a mangold-wurzel, or a large turnip, on similar lines to the now-standard Hallowe'en pumpkin. The top is sliced off, the insides are scooped out, and designs are cut into the outer skin, leaving a thin membrane intact; a lighted candle is then placed inside to shine through the cuts. These designs vary considerably, and although scary faces are popular, much more imaginative scenes can also be found.

Although Punkie Nights have been reported from several Somerset villages, Hinton St George and Lopen both claim to be the originators of the custom. Various nights in late October have served, including the 28th or 29th, but Hinton St George eventually settled on the last Thursday in the month. It seems to have previously been a simple house-visiting custom, but was reorganized by members of the local Women's Institute in the mid twentieth century and is now celebrated with a procession of children carrying their punkies, and a party where prizes for the best designs are given, a Punkie King and Queen crowned, and money is raised for charity.

The local story usually told to explain the origin of the custom is given in *Notes & Queries* (1931), and is quite simple:

A party of men from Hinton and Lopen visited Chiselborough Fair – a noted cloth fair in years gone by – and did not return to their homes so early

Seed Cakes

It was the custom in certain areas, at the conclusion of the wheat-sowing season, to celebrate by making and distributing a special cake called a 'seed cake'. The 'seed' of the title thus refers to the occasion rather than the ingredients. Anne Baker, in her *Glossary of Northamptonshire Words and Phrases* (1854), referred to them as 'Siblet cakes' and wrote that the ploughmen received them, whereas William Hone, reporting a Bedfordshire example in 1831, called them 'Siblett cakes' and said they were made by farmers' wives and distributed to their friends and relations. In his *Five Hundred Points of Good Husbandry* (1580), Thomas Tusser does not make it clear who gets the cake, but confirms the custom's antiquity:

> **Wife, sometime this week, if ye weather hold clear,**
> **An end of wheat sowing we make for the year;**
> **Remember you therefore, though I do it not,**
> **The seed cake, the pasties, and furmety pot.**

Wheat-sowing in England often ended around All Souls' Day and the custom is therefore confused with, or related to, soul-cakes (*see* 2 **November**).

as promised. Their wives went in search of them, and the attractions of the fair apparently were so great that by the time they commenced their journey home their lamps were innocent of oil, and improvised lanterns, made from mangold-wurzels from the wayside fields, were utilised.

In other versions the emphasis was slightly different, and it was said that the drunkenness of the men, and their inability to find their own way, meant that their wives had to improvise the lanterns so that they could go and bring the men home.

Nobody seems to have made any serious attempt to pin down the history and development of Punkie Night. Many simply assume that it is a localized version of the ubiquitous Hallowe'en (*see below*), or that it is in fact the original of the latter custom, which was exported to America and then re-imported to Britain. The key determining factor is therefore the age of Punkie Night, but despite the usual assumptions of ancient origins, none of the authorities consulted provide any evidence of its existence before the twentieth century.

31 October

Hallowe'en

Hallowe'en is probably the most widely misunderstood and misrepresented day in the festival year, but so many now believe that it was originally a pagan festival of the dead that this belief is virtually impossible to shake. The facts, however, are very different, and are far more elusive and complex.

'Hallowe'en' means the Eve of Hallowtide (1 and 2 November), which was indeed designated as a time to commemorate the dead, but it was a Christian festival inaugurated in the medieval period. There is no evidence that this time of year was celebrated in England before the Christian feast was created. In Ireland, 1 November was 'Samhain', the beginning of winter and of the year, and as such it was an important day of gathering and feasting, but not, it seems, of much religious or supernatural significance. Nor is there any evidence of the supernatural at Hallowe'en in early Welsh or Scottish material, except where Irish influence was strong. Most of the supernatural aura that supposedly surrounded the day in earlier times is an invention from the modern period that has now become entrenched in a way that is depressingly familiar throughout popular writing on folklore.

The modern Hallowe'en developed from the two closely linked Christian festivals of All Saints (1 **November**) and All Souls (2 **November**), which were both concerned in their way with the dead. The festival of All Saints, known in English as All-Hallows or Hallowmas ('hallow' from the Old English word for 'holy man' or 'saint'), was instituted to commemorate all the Christian saints and martyrs, known and unknown, who had been instrumental in forming and perpetuating the faith. It was originally celebrated in May, but was fixed at 1 November in the eighth century, and with this new date soon spread across the Christian west, including England.

The feast of All Souls, on 2 November, was added somewhat later, about the year 1000, and was created to commemorate the faithful departed who had gone before. For centuries there had been debate within the Church about whether Christian souls went straight to Heaven or were detained somewhere to undergo painful purgation to prepare them for eternal bliss; a particular problem was what happened to those who died suddenly without final rites, or who had no time to make proper preparation. It was clear that a halfway house on the way to Heaven was needed, but there was little agreement over the details of what it was, or how it worked. The existence of Purgatory was officially recognized in the Western Church at the Second General Council of Lyons, in 1274, along with the crucial notion that souls could be helped towards Heaven, and their sufferings relieved, by the actions of the living. All Souls thus took shape as an important feast at which special requiem masses were held, with candles and torches, and pious acts were encouraged, such as the giving of alms and offering prayers. For the laity, one of the most tangible methods of assisting souls was the ringing of church bells, and this was done so enthusiastically that the ringing went on for hour after hour at All Souls, and was one of the 'superstitious practices' vigorously attacked by the Protestant reformers of the sixteenth century. At the Reformation the whole idea of Purgatory, and the possibility of intercession on behalf of the dead, were rejected, and All Souls was excluded from the English religious calendar. The bells fell silent in 1559.

In Catholic countries, the festival continued to develop its connection with the supernatural, but in England it seems to have left little more than a vague notion that Hallowe'en was a time when the spirit world was particularly close to the everyday one. In Lincolnshire, as reported in 1908:

On the Eve of All Saints Day, at 12 pm, twelve lights rise from the mound in All Hallows churchyard where the ancient church of Horsington stood (they are blue and rise slowly and do not jump about like jenny wisps), and then slowly proceed in threes toward the following villages – three to Horsington, three to Stixwould, three to Bucknall, and three to Wadingworth.

Even then it was not seen as necessarily the most potently supernatural day in the calendar, but one of several. Activities such as porch-watching, for example – staying up all night in the church porch to see the wraiths of all the local parishioners parade by, in order to determine who would die in the coming year – were far more likely to take place on St Mark's Eve (*see* **24 April**).

Two customs that may have been direct survivals of medieval practices were the house-visiting custom called souling (*see* **2 November: All Souls' Day**), reported in the nineteenth century, and the lighting of fires on Hallowe'en. One of the doctrinal notions about Purgatory was that the purgation of the souls was by holy fire, and the bonfires that were common throughout Hallowtide may be a memory of this connection, although bonfires in northern climes in late autumn or early winter are hardly remarkable, and the influence of the Guy Fawkes bonfires of 5 November cannot be ruled out.

Except for the areas in which souling customs took place, as the twentieth century approached, Hallowe'en had almost died out completely in most of England. The main folklore books of the closing quarter of the nineteenth century, and the early years of the twentieth, hardly mention Hallowe'en at all, except to quote Scottish examples, and the same is true of the mass of autobiographies that provide such telling details of life in England before the Second World War. It is hard to escape the conclusion that for most of the people of England, Hallowe'en passed without notice. When it *is* noticed, it is usually to describe the games and love divinations played on the day, as in John Brockett's *Glossary of North Country Words* (1825):

The vigil of All Saints' Day, on which it is customary with young people in the North of England to dive for apples, or catch at them upon one end of a kind of hanging beam, at the other extremity of which is fixed a lighted candle, and that with their mouths only, their hands being tied behind their backs.

The games mentioned in these accounts have been remarkably stable over the years, utilizing nuts, or apples in buckets of water or hanging from strings, and the prevalence of these edibles does not seem to have any symbolic significance but simply reflects their availability at the time of year.

Hallowe'en was certainly one of the key nights of the year when young people (usually, but not always, girls) could discover who, when, and how they were going to marry, if at all, by following one of many traditional procedures. The *Transactions of the Devonshire Association* recorded:

Mrs. Hook, of Chulmleigh [Devon], aged 70, told me in May 1938, that in her young days it was the custom on All Hallowe'en to pare apples, then whirl the peel three times round the head and then throw it over the left shoulder to the floor. The letter formed on the floor by the apple peel would be the initial of the future husband or wife. Mrs. Hook assured me that her apple peel always formed the letter J., and she eventually married Jack Hook.

As with the games, apples and nuts featured strongly in these divinations. Two nuts, for example, would be chosen to represent two potential lovers and placed side by side on the fire-shovel over the flames of a fire. The future romantic potential for the couple could be gauged by whether the heated nuts jumped apart or drew together. Alternatively, anyone brave enough could brush their hair in front of a mirror at midnight and it was said that they would see the face of their future spouse peering over their shoulder. A much less scary form of fortune-telling was recorded by folklorist Sidney Oldall Addy in the mid 1890s:

In Derbyshire farmers carry a candle down the garden on All Hallow's Een, to see which way the wind blew. As the wind blew that night such would be the prevailing wind for the next three months.

In the mid twentieth century, however, the germs of the modern Hallowe'en were already visible. Iona and Peter Opie discovered that children in 1950s England celebrated either Hallowe'en or Guy Fawkes Night, depending on where they lived:

When darkness closes in on the vigil of All Saints Day, Britain has the appearance of a land inhabited by two nations with completely different cultural backgrounds. While the young of one nation are employed upon their homework, the children of the other are wildly celebrating one of their major festivals.

The demarcation line between these two 'nations' ran from the mouth of the Humber on the east coast across to Knighton, near Stafford, and then southwards along the border with Wales down to the Bristol channel. It was the children to the north and west of this line that enthusiastically celebrated Hallowe'en, by house-visiting in costume and carrying hollowed-out turnips. In some parts, Hallowe'en is also **Mischief Night** (*see below*), and misbehaviour on the day is sanctioned by tradition.

Then there was the explosion of interest in Hallowe'en in the 1970s and 1980s. Children all over England suddenly started dressing up as witches and ghosts, knocking on doors and expecting largesse, and using the words 'trick or treat'; and it is clear that this was largely imported directly from American films and television series, which regularly showed such scenes. The immensely popular film *ET* (1982), for example, provided a model for how to dress and what to do on the

The newspapers were soon full of complaints about children demanding money with menaces, and reports of elderly people being confused and intimidated by this new custom. There is some evidence that the meteoric rise of Hallowe'en in the late twentieth century was deliberately encouraged by teachers trying to shift the attention from Guy Fawkes Night because of widespread criticism of the customs of that night, primarily because of fears over safety. But the teachers quickly found themselves in a different fire, as a howl of protest from fundamentalist Christians broke over their heads about the moral dangers of encouraging children to take an interest in supposed pagan matters and the occult. Dressing up as witches, and reading Harry Potter novels, is no mere game, we are told, but a sure way of endangering our immortal souls.

Hallowe'en parties, with guests dressed as witches and fiends, have been growing in popularity since the 1980s and although they too appear at first glance to have been influenced by American popular culture, they have, in fact, been around for a bit longer than that. In Nella Last's wartime diary, for example, she reflected on pre-war family occasions, and recorded for posterity the details of a family Hallowe'en party, presumably in the 1920s or early 1930s:

Tuesday 31 October 1939 – The wind howled and I could have howled like a banshee with it. Hallowe'en, and the house so straight and quiet, my towels all in a drawer and not in wet heaps in the garage where everybody would have been ducking for apples, no smell of baking potatoes, no decorations – only memories. One year the boys received their guests in a novel way. Cliff painted a placard and put it on the door. It read 'Abandon hope all ye who enter here'. It was in old English lettering and had bats and owls drawn on the border . . . In the pitch-black the boys stood to welcome the guests. Arthur had a black bag over his head and Cliff's fiendishly grinning face, lit by a ghastly green electric bulb, was under his arm. A rubber glove filled with cold water was held out to the hand of each guest – it was a huge success!

Hallowe'en continues to grow in popularity, and the most recent development is the rise of fancy dress at parties for young adults; the day is undoubtedly the busiest time of the year for costume hire and joke shops.

See also **Late October: Punkie Night**.

> *Now ladies and gentlemen, light a fire and strike a light*
> *For in this house there's going to be a dreadful fight*
> *Between King George and the Black Prince*
> *And I hope King George will win*
> *Whether he wins, loses, fights or falls*
> *We'll do our best to please you all*

These are the first words (after the introductory song) of the soul-cakers, who perform in the pubs around Antrobus, in Cheshire, and neighbouring villages from Hallowe'en into the first weeks of November. Their souling play is one form of the ubiquitous mumming play (*see* **Christmas: Mummers**), and thus involves a sword-fight between King George and the Black Prince. The latter is killed, but revived by the Doctor. Other characters include Mary, Beelzebub, Derry Doubt, and the Letter-In, who speaks the introductory lines. Apart from the time of year it is performed, the key characteristic that distinguishes a souling play from other mumming plays is the presence of a man dressed up as the Wild Horse, and his Driver, who come in at the end of the play:

> *In comes Dick and all his men*
> *He's come to see you once again*
> *He was once alive, but now he's dead*
> *He's nothing but a poor old horse's head*
> *Stand around Dick, and show yourself!*

As with other hobby horses across the country, Dick misbehaves, chases people, and causes havoc.

The Antrobus men dress, roughly, in costume depicting their character, and performances nowadays take place primarily in pubs, although in the past they would mainly perform in the local 'big houses' and other homes. It is perhaps because of the modern pub setting that performances nowadays include more ad-libbing and audience involvement than was previously the case.

In the late nineteenth and early twentieth century, there were many such souling teams in Cheshire, but at Antrobus regular performances ceased at the First World War, when some of the team were killed. Local enthusiast Major A. W. Boyd persuaded the local team to re-form, and as they have performed ever since, they are the only local team with a direct connection to the old tradition.

See also **2 November: All Souls' Day; Hobby Horses**, p. 226.

Mischief Night

For many young people in England, a highlight of the traditional year was Mischief Night, when they thought it their right to carry out a range of tricks on their elders and their property. In 1882, Lancashire folklorists John Harland and T. T. Wilkinson reported:

The evening before May Day is termed 'Mischief Night', by the young people of Burnley and the surrounding district. All kinds of mischief are then perpetrated. Formerly shopkeepers' sign-boards were exchanged; 'John Smith, grocer', finding his name and vocation changed, by the sign over his door, to 'Thomas Jones, tailor', and vice versa; but the police have put an end to these practical jokes.

Earlier accounts of the mischief carried out are very similar to each other, and there was clearly a strong tradition of what could and could not be done. Gates and signs were the main targets, as they were easily removed, hidden, or swapped around. Front doors were also the focus of innumerable tricks based on knocking and running away, and tying neighbouring doors together, while tapping on windows and blocking up chimneys, were also popular. Anything not screwed down was fair game, and some tricksters were more inventive, as remembered by members of a local Women's Institute in the collection *Lancashire Lore* (1971):

Mischief Night in Blacko [Lancashire] *was Hallowe'en . . . On one occasion the mischief makers went to Lower Admergill Farm armed with a gun and a tin of blood collected from the slaughterhouse. When the farmer opened the door a shot was fired into the air, and simultaneously the blood was thrown over him. He staggered back, waving his arms and shouting, 'I've been shot.' Needless to say, no-one stayed to find out how long it took him to recover . . .* [Another] *trick was sometimes played on patrons of the Moorcock Inn who left their 'transport' tied up outside. On leaving the inn, they would discover that their horse had been led into a nearby field, the gate closed, the cart still on the roadside, but hitched to the horse through the closed gate.*

The history of Mischief Night continues to puzzle folklorists, from several points of view, but most notably because there are three contenders for the correct day of the year. Most nineteenth-century reports name 30 April as Mischief Night (*see* **30 April: May Day Eve**), but by the 1950s this had changed to 4 November (Guy Fawkes Eve). Iona and Peter Opie, writing in the late 1950s, believed that the change from April to November had only taken place in the previous two decades. In some places in England, however, and throughout Scotland, Ireland, and the United States, Mischief Night has always fallen on Hallowe'en.

The geographical spread of the custom is more easily identified. From the nineteenth century to the 1950s, Mischief Night was regularly recorded in a broad swathe across the country, concentrated in Lancashire and Yorkshire but also found in northern parts of Cheshire, Derbyshire, Nottinghamshire, and Lincolnshire. Since that time, however, it seems to have gradually shrunk to remain in Yorkshire alone, where the tradition is tenaciously vigorous and called 'Miggy Night'. Every year the police in some towns are kept busy dealing with the mayhem caused by children and youths, and the local media bemoan the fact that Mischief Night has changed from relatively harmless fun to mindless vandalism. One has to wonder, however, to what degree the custom is kept alive by the extensive press coverage.

It is certainly true that adults in areas where mischief traditions had been around since their own childhood were until recently relatively tolerant about the tricks played, as long as the children did not 'go too far'. Police, too, seem to have been philosophical about them. Without falling into the trap of believing that the past was a golden age, it is clear from the reminiscences of those involved, as well as press coverage, that today's Mischief Nighters see no difference between vandalism and tricks, and cause much more real damage to public property than previous generations dared – although it has always been widely reported that children who took part in mischievous activities firmly believed that the usual laws of the land did not apply on that night:

When I was a kid I actually thought it was legal – 'coppers can't arrest you on Miggy Night.'

This idea is traditional in itself, and is shared with several other customs (*see* **Lawless Hours and Days**, p. 412).

Although Mischief Night itself was found in a restricted area of the country, children elsewhere enjoyed similar customs. In the West Country, for example, similar tricks were played on neighbours at Shrovetide, under such local names as Nickanan Night and Lansherd Night (*see* **Shrove Tuesday: Shroving and Lent-Crocking**, p. 82).

Some writers have assumed an ancient pagan origin for the custom, but there is no evidence that this is the case. Mischief Night itself only enters the documentary record in the 1830s, although some of the analogous 'tricking' customs may be older.

NOVEMBER

First Sunday in November

London to Brighton Veteran Car Run

The London to Brighton Veteran Car Run, organized by the RAC (Royal Automobile Club) and affectionately known to many as 'the Old Crocks' Race', claims to be the world's longest running motoring event. Participants start at Hyde Park in central London, and then drive sixty miles down the A23 to Brighton. The event is open to vehicles manufactured before 1905, and attracts entrants from around the world. Around 300 entrants usually participate, although the 1996 centenary run attracted a record 680 cars.

The claim to be the longest running motoring event implies a continuous series of runs, but this is not quite the case. In November 1896, when the Act of Parliament was passed that raised the speed limit from 4 mph to 14 mph and abolished the regulation that vehicles must be preceded by a man with a red flag, thirty motorists took part in a semi-spontaneous run to Brighton (only fourteen actually got there). This run was re-enacted in 1927, and the event has taken place every year since, except during the Second World War and in 1947 when severe petrol rationing was in force.

1 November

All Saints' Day

The festival of All Saints, known previously as All-Hallows or Hallowmas ('hallow' from the Old English word for 'holy man' or 'saint'), was originally celebrated in May but moved to 1 November in the eighth century, reaching England soon afterwards. It is the day on which the faithful remember the lives and sacrifices of all saints and martyrs for the Church. In the more secular traditional calendar, however, little distinction seems to have been made between All Saints' Day and All Souls' Day (2 November), as both were concerned with commemorating the dead in one way or another, and similar customs were found on both days.

One of these customs was to make special soul-cakes. The antiquarian John Aubrey noted in 1686 that in Shropshire:

There is set on the board a high heap of soul-cakes, lying one upon another like the picture of sew-bread in the old Bibles. They are about the bigness of 2d. cakes, and nearly all the visitants that day take one; and there is an old rhythm or saying,

> *A soul-cake, a soul-cake*
> *Have mercy on all Christian souls for a soul-cake.*

This custom of giving cakes seems to have been a useful double-sided coin: the act of charity helped the giver's soul, and at the same time, by commemorating the dead, consumption of the cake helped other people's souls to get out of Purgatory and into Heaven. Whenever charities such as this were on offer, house-visiting customs seem to have grown up around them, and in this case it was called 'souling': participants expected to be given cakes, apples, drink, or money at each house at which they called, in response to their singing a souling rhyme similar to that quoted by Aubrey (*see* **2 November: All Souls' Day**). By the nineteenth century, when this custom was adequately recorded, it was predominately carried out by children, but it had previously been a more serious affair, and was commonplace enough for Shakespeare to use the phrase 'to speak puling, like a beggar at Hallowmas' in Act II, scene 1 of *Two Gentlemen of Verona*.

2 November

All Souls' Day

The doctrine of Purgatory was slow to develop in the Christian Church, but was properly codified by the thirteenth century and seemed to answer the problem of what happened to the mass of people who were not good enough to go straight to Heaven, nor sufficiently bad to be consigned straight to Hell. Such souls, it was argued, stayed in Purgatory until they were purified by holy fire and went on to eternal bliss, and they could be helped on their journey by the prayers and other pious actions of the living. Thus, on All Souls' Day, it was the duty of all Christians to concentrate on assisting those souls, by attending special masses, offering special prayers, and making acts of charity. The parish church bells were also rung vigorously on the day, as this holy sound was believed to help.

The whole notion of the living being able to help the dead was rejected at the Reformation, when the 'superstitious' prayers and ringing of bells were condemned, but the basic connections between the time of year, charity, and the dead, lingered on in people's minds and were reflected in several secular customs. As indicated under 1 **November**, most people seem in practice to have made little distinction between All Saints' Day and All Souls' Day, and these customs could occur at any time between Hallowe'en and the night of All Souls.

The most frequently documented example of the charity aspect of the season in the seventeenth century took the form of bread or 'soul-cakes' that were distributed either to the poor or to the whole congregation or community (see 1 **November**). Bonfires were also popular, as in many other autumn and winter customs, but in this case they were directly relevant, echoing the purifying fires of Purgatory.

In later times, however, the main traditional activity for the season was a house-visiting custom in which groups of children knocked on doors, sang a song, and hoped for reward. A version from the Staffordshire/Cheshire border was included in *Note & Queries* (1868):

Bands of children go from house to house, on the evening of All Souls' Day, begging for biscuits, nuts, apples, and the like – all of which they call 'soul-cakes' or 'sou'cakes' (pronounced 'sowl-cake' or 'sow'cake') in doggerel ballads such as these:

I hope you will prove kind with your apples and strong beer
And we'll come no more a-souling until this time next year.
One for Peter, one for Paul
One for Him as made us all
Up with your kettles, and down with your pans
Give us a sou'cake and we will be gone.

Souling was found elsewhere, but the available evidence shows that it was heavily concentrated in the midland counties of Cheshire, Staffordshire, and Lancashire, and it shared this area with two other almost identical visiting customs: clementing (*see* **23 November: St Clement's Day**) and catterning (*see* **25 November: St Catherine's Day**). It is only documented from the early nineteenth century onwards, but it lingered in some places until the 1950s.

A very different custom at this season also went by the name of 'souling' or 'soul-caking', in roughly the same geographical area. This was a local variation of the mummers' play, elsewhere played more commonly at Christmas; *see* **31 October: Antrobus Soul-Cakers** for further details.

First Friday in November

Bridgwater Carnival

Bridgwater, in Somerset, bills itself as 'the home of carnival' and holds what is claimed to be the largest illuminated carnival in the world; it is certainly the biggest and brightest in the region. Crowds of 150,000 pack the town, around 150 entries take part in the procession of floats, and upwards of £24,000 is collected for charity along the way. Since 1909, the carnival had been held on the first Thursday in November, but in 2000 it was moved, after much local debate, to the first Friday, where it is at present.

The most noticeable features of the modern procession are the sheer size of the floats, decorated with thousands of light bulbs that provide stunning illuminated spectacles, the music, and the elaborately costumed 'living statues', which populate the tableaux. The themes vary widely, and an immense amount of thought and effort goes into their planning throughout the year by the carnival clubs (made up of volunteers from particular pubs or organizations), and there is keen competition between them for the numerous sponsored prizes that are awarded in a range of classes. Many of the clubs take their floats to other illuminated carnivals in the region, and in recent years an official tie-up with Notting Hill Carnival (*see* **August Bank Holiday**) has resulted in some reciprocal visits. The procession itself is the climax of weeks of linked events, including a firework display on the evening before, and a series of concerts in late October, at which the clubs present their themes, in costume, on stage.

The organized carnival itself dates back to 1881, and developed directly from the more chaotic traditional 5 November celebrations, following a similar pattern to Lewes (*see* **5 November: Lewes Bonfire Night**), and other towns. At Bridgwater, two features of the modern carnival mark its origins in the old 'Fifth' celebrations. One is the relatively modest float that always leads the procession, which depicts the discovery of Guy Fawkes with his barrels of gunpowder, and the other is the display of synchronized 'squibbing' in the town centre. Over one hundred squibbers stand in lines, holding six-foot poles horizontally at arms' length above their heads. Fireworks fixed to each end of the pole are lit at a signal from the leader, and the result is a very impressive shower of sparks with ghostly figures in the middle. Nowadays, the squibbers wear hard hats and protective clothing, but in the nineteenth century they would run through the crowds, scattering sparks over everybody – just one example of the uncontrolled use of fireworks, blazing tar barrels, and street bonfires that gave the old celebrations such a bad name.

This cavalier attitude to crowd safety is demonstrated in a newspaper report of 1860, which also shows that the tendency for participants to use the event to comment on current affairs, both local and national, was already marked in the mid nineteenth century:

Men, boys and urchins paraded the streets decked out in their colourful costumes during the 1860 Guy Fawkes celebrations. Amongst the usual mix of characters was one young man who had the impudence to mimic 'to an alarming extent' the latest ladies' fashion – crinoline. But the young ladies of the day were able to get their own back by throwing lighted firecrackers at this display from the safety of their upstairs windows.

In other years, the newspapers reported a fashion for aiming roman candles and rockets at open windows.

The year 1880 was the turning point in Bridgwater. 'The Fifth' had long been under threat of suppression from the local authorities, but in that year the celebrations turned nasty and a full-scale riot ensued, focused on the hapless members of the local fire brigade, who had been ordered to put out the bonfires. As a result, the old Fifth lost any remaining respectable support, and the participants faced the choice of complete suppression or the introduction of a relatively tame but properly organized and controlled event, which soon became the central feature of the town's calendar.

4 November

Ringing Night

In some nineteenth-century Cornish parishes, the ringers anticipated the celebratory peals of 5 November, by holding their own 'Ringing Night' on the evening of the 4th. Jonathan Couch described the custom in Polperro, Cornwall, in 1871:

'Ringing-Night' is on the fourth of November, the eve of gunpowder plot. The usual belfry rules, imposing fines on those who in a drunken or 'choleric' mood, should overturn a bell or 'by unskilful handling' mar a peal are, for the time, not rigidly enforced, and I fear that many cracked bells can date their ruin from this night.

Also in the West Country, an apparently unique custom, which also involved bell-ringers, was reported for this night, at East Budleigh, Devon, in 1885:

A very curious custom prevails here on the night of Nov. 4. The children are allowed to 'holloa for biscuits', as they call it. Seventeen shillings and sixpence is allowed by the parish for bell-ringing. Two and sixpence of this is spent in biscuits (i.e. farthing cakes). One shilling's worth of these are retained by the ringers; the remaining ones are given to the children, who formerly came into the churchyard and shouted, the biscuits being distributed from the porch. A few years since the people awoke to the fact that a churchyard was hardly a suitable place for holloaing, and the biscuits were distributed from the church gate. For the last two years the biscuits have been given away at some distance from the sacred edifice. No one appears to know the origin of this custom.

In the northern half of the country, youngsters have had the pleasure of their own 'Mischief Night' for decades, when they believed that tricks could be played with impunity on the adult population. The night chosen for this mayhem varied, and although it was most commonly held on 30 April, Hallowe'en and 4 November were also cited as traditional Mischief Nights in some communities (see **31 October: Mischief Night** for further details.)

See also **5 November: Guy Fawkes Night** for other bell-ringing customs.

5 November

Devil's Stone

On the green just outside the church at Shebbear, between Great Torrington and Holsworthy, in Devon, lies a large boulder, about 6 foot by 4 foot in size, and reputed to weigh a ton. In geological terms it is an 'erratic', a large rock brought from elsewhere by glacial action. The locals call it the 'Shebbear Stone', but because of various stories it has also acquired the name 'Devil's Stone', and the village pub bears this name too. It is the self-inflicted task of the village bell-ringers to turn this boulder over every year on 5 November, or serious misfortune is said to follow. The bell-ringers gather in the church to ring the bells in the usual way, but just before 8 p.m. they give a short discordant jangling peal and then troop outside with torches and crowbars. The vicar says a short prayer, and the stone is duly turned. The actual ceremony is as perfunctory as a dozen men heaving on crowbars can be.

There are several legends that seek to explain the presence of the stone, although all of them are also told of other stones across the country: some say it was dropped by the Devil on his way to Hell, or thrown by him for some reason; while others, that it was chosen as the foundation stone for nearby Henscott church, but for several nights running it was mysteriously moved to Shebbear, so the locals decided it was best to leave it there. It is interesting that these stories explain the stone's presence, but not the custom of turning it over. The usual invented ancient pagan origins are also cited in some quarters, and one website claims it to be the 'oldest folk custom in Europe', but there is no evidence that the custom is older than the twentieth century.

There is nothing unusual about bell-ringing on Guy Fawkes Night; indeed, it was formerly so common that 4 and 5 November were called 'Ringing Night' in various parts of the country, and the most likely explanation of the custom is that it began as a prank by the bell-ringers, or even that it was the result of a drunken conversation in the pub.

Guy Fawkes Night

Remember, remember, the fifth of November
Gunpowder, treason, and plot.

Guy Fawkes Night, Bonfire Night, Squib-Night, Plot Night, or simply 'the Fifth' are just some of the names that have been used to describe one of the most popular events of the traditional year for the last 400 years. People who nowadays flock to the safe and well-organized firework displays mounted by local councils and other respectable bodies will have little idea of the various stages that Guy Fawkes Night has been through since that unfortunate man and his associates tried to blow up the King and Parliament in November 1605. Those old enough will remember the cosy middle-class back-garden family firework parties of the mid twentieth century, which have not quite died out, or the more working-class annual ritual of children exhibiting a guy in the street from late October onwards, begging passers-by for 'a penny for the guy', which is close to extinction. But before these recent manifestations, 5 November had been such a rough and dangerous day that many respectable persons would not venture from their houses, and police fought an annual battle against bonfires and blazing tar barrels in the streets, torch-lit parades and processions, the indiscriminate throwing of fireworks, and the general notion that normal laws do not apply on this special night.

The enormity and astounding audacity of the plot to assassinate the sovereign and all the ruling elite of the country in one fell swoop was bound to mark the day as significant in the history of the nation. The fact that the plotters were Catholics gave the deed an added dimension, in an era when politics and religion were already inextricably mixed, and Parliament immediately decreed public celebrations to mark the miraculous deliverance. These took the normal form for that time – bell-ringing, bonfires, and special prayers and sermons – and a marked feature from the beginning was the notion that the events of that night must never be forgotten. The celebrations rapidly developed most of the features recognizable by later generations. The visiting Dutchman William Schellinks commented, for example, in 1662:

On the 5th ... in the evening the gunpowder plot, or the anniversary of the gunpowder treason of the year in the reign of King James, is celebrated in London: many bonfires are lit all over the town in celebration, and a great lot of fireworks are let off and thrown amongst the people.

However, the anti-Catholic nature of the celebrations was never far beneath the surface. As John Evelyn recorded in his diary on 5 November 1673, 'This night the youths of the city burnt the Pope in effigy after they had made procession with it in great triumph, displeased at the Duke for altering his religion, and now marrying an Italian lady', referring to the marriage of the Duke of York, Charles II's brother and soon to become James II, to the Catholic princess Mary D'Este of Modena.

Over the next 300 years, Guy Fawkes Night continued to develop as a mass working-class event, with the streets of most towns thronged every year with crowds, bonfires everywhere, fireworks thrown, and guns fired indiscriminately, along with spectacular practices such as the rolling of blazing tar barrels. But by the mid nineteenth century, these street celebrations were increasingly seen as dangerous drunken riots that should not be tolerated, and many towns across England, but particularly in the South, saw growing confrontations between the 'bonfire boys', who were determined to keep up their old traditions come what may, and town authorities, who were equally determined to put them down. Pitched battles and 'Guy riots' took place in many towns, including Guildford, Croydon, Exeter, and Worthing, between the police and the bonfire supporters, and it took many years for the authorities to finally gain control of the streets every November.

In the later Victorian period, celebrations then took two main directions. In some places, the bonfire enthusiasts compromised by organizing relatively tame processions, which culminated in a controlled bonfire and firework display on nearby open land, often sponsored by the council or local worthies. But the more respectable people largely withdrew from the public celebrations and started holding family parties in their own gardens. At this point, the next phase of 5 November came into play, and increasingly Guy Fawkes Night was seen either as a private family affair or as an organized community event. Nevertheless, the rough side of the celebration was never far away, and

On 28 November 1931, the *Hampshire Advertiser* reported an incident
in Botley:

*On the night of 5th November, a bonfire of wood, old motor tyres, and other
kinds of rubbish was lighted, and two motor cars were pushed on to the fire
and burnt in the presence of about a thousand people. Twenty-two young
men were subsequently fined at Eastleigh Police Court for lighting a bonfire
within fifty feet of the centre of the highway, and six of them were charged
with stealing a motor car valued at £18 and destroying it by fire. In the
course of the defence it was stated that 'for something like a hundred years
Botley had been loyal to Guy Fawkes'; that the Square, the traditional site
of the bonfire, 'was not treated as part of the highway' and that the owner
of the £18 car 'stood in the crowd laughing while the car was being burned'.
There was no case arising out of the burning of the second car.*

Indeed, newspapers until as late as the 1950s and 1960s regularly reported riots in Oxford and Cambridge, and the centre of London on
Guy Fawkes Night. Something of the old days can still be experienced
at Lewes, in Sussex, and Ottery St Mary, in Devon (*see separate entries,
below*). The later twentieth century saw a sharp decline in the back-
garden style of celebration, primarily because of heightened fears
about safety, and large organized events became more and more the
norm, which still remains the case today.

Within this broad historical framework, there were numerous variations from place to place, and certain aspects of the Fifth are worth
exploring in more detail, in part because they have interesting connections with other customs. As indicated, right from the beginning
the official theme of remembrance was a defining feature of the Fifth.
Church congregations were urged never to forget the enormity of Guy
Fawkes' crime, and this continued to be a theme in the celebrations, as
shown by the rhymes that were chanted as a kind of rallying cry of the
'bonfire boys' and by urchins in the streets to beg pennies. It must be
noted, however, that the longevity of this theme was greatly assisted by
the happy circumstance that 'remember' rhymes with 'November'. In
1903, the journal *Folk-Lore* recorded the following rhyme from 1890s
Hastings, in Sussex:

> *Remember, remember, the fifth of November,*
> *Gunpowder treason and plot;*
> *I see no reason why Gunpowder Treason*

Should ever be forgot.
A stick and a stake
For King George's sake,
Holla, boys! holla, boys! make the town ring!
Holla, boys! holla, boys! God save the King!
Hip, hip, hooray!

Another recurrent theme is the idea of licensed 'lawlessness'. As with many other public customs of long standing, there was a strong feeling in many communities that behaviour that would be prohibited at any other time of year was socially acceptable on this particular night, as in this memory of mid nineteenth-century Yorkshire:

In the days when there were no county police, if not wise enough to securely lock up your yard broom, of a certainty it would be stolen; and if ever you did see it again it would be in the evening of the fifth, soaked with tar, in the hands of some fellow rushing like a mad thing along the street with your property blazing in front of him. I have known scores of brooms which were stolen – aye, and stolen them myself – but I do not recollect an instance of the thief being prosecuted. No, if you did not secure your broom, it went, and that was very much the end of it. There was more fun running with a stolen broom than a bought one.

Indeed, many people seriously believed that normal laws, especially game laws, did not apply on the Fifth. In the *York Herald*, on 15 November 1806, comes the following report:

On Monday last, George Walkitt, farmer of Weaverthorpe, was convicted . . . in the penalty of £5 for destroying hares on that day. We insert this as a caution, as some people ignorantly conceive this to be a day free from all law.

(*See also* **26 December: Hunting and Shooting; Lawless Hours and Days**, p. 412.)

The making and parading of effigies is another widespread theme in English customs, and here, too, normal social rules were felt not to apply. It has a long history, stretching back at least a century before the Gunpowder Plot; as shown, for example, by the celebrations to commemorate the Accession of Elizabeth I (*see* **17 November**). Over the years, countless effigies of political and religious enemies (particularly of the Pope) have been mercilessly parodied and mistreated; social transgressors have found themselves treated in the same way as part of a **rough music** ceremony (p. 95); and other customs, from **Jack-a-Lent** (*see* p. 86) to the Burning of Bartle (*see* **24 August: West Witton Burning of Bartle**) have involved figures made specifically to be ridiculed and mistreated. Strangely, Guy Fawkes himself does not seem to have been singled out for this honour until the turn of the nineteenth century. Whereas nowadays, the word 'guy' is almost synonymous with effigy, the earliest reference to this meaning of the word in the *Oxford English Dictionary* only dates from 1806. Nineteenth-century illustrations usually show a life-size guy, seated upon a chair carried on poles, and paraded around the streets by children who are soliciting money from passers-by. By the early twentieth century, this had been replaced by the more static and individual 'penny for the guy' custom.

Apart from the Pope and Guy Fawkes, the tradition of burning effigies of real people has continued into the present-day, and public enemies such as the Prime Minister of the day, or a current bête noire of popular opinion, such as Saddam Hussein or Osama Bin Laden, are often chosen for this purpose (*see* **Lewes Bonfire Night**, *below*). It could be argued that these are fair game for a traditional form of popular protest, but things look very different when local vendettas or vigilante feelings are played out in this way, as in this example reported in the *Western Morning News* on 8 November 1960:

The Devon village of Chulmleigh, for instance, was no place in which to court unpopularity in the old days. The inhabitants had the tradition of making effigies of people they did not like and then burning them. To make their disfavour as marked as possible they dressed their 'guys' in clothes similar to those worn by their victims, and then set them up for burning right outside the unpopular person's house. One record mentions 'evil doers' and 'evil livers' as people likely to be singled out for the unwelcome 'celebrity'.

Some members of the Bonfire Society of the Sussex village of Firle decided in 2003 to burn an effigy of a Gypsy caravan in protest against local travellers, but no doubt regretted their decision when their actions hit the national headlines and they were arrested under race relations legislation.

Running parallel to the mass community celebrations, there was also the persistent thread of child-centred activity, which was already in place at the turn of the nineteenth century. As the night approached, children all over the country could be seen ferreting about for materials for a bonfire, and trying to raise money for fireworks, and their own traditions naturally evolved. The penny-for-the-guy custom and the making of the guy for the garden bonfire are two widespread homely traditions that have largely disappeared, and numerous others have come and gone. Some families had special food for the evening – jacket potatoes cooked on the edge of the bonfire, or pieces of **parkin** (*see* p. 462) munched as the rockets were set off. Derek Sheffield, describing his childhood in Kent in the early twentieth century, reported a family tradition of home-made fireworks that would make most modern parents go white at the very thought:

There was a massive iron hook embedded in the giant oak beam that straddled the living room, and on which the whole house was supported. The hook had originally been used for hanging slaughtered pigs whilst burning the hairs off with tapers, but in my time it had another purpose; that was in the manufacture of fireworks, and Grandad was firework maker par excellence. About a month before firework night, Grandad would be banging away in the shed producing lath frames on which to support various kinds of fireworks, and sawing five foot long sticks for his rockets. He also produced wooden blocks which were bored out to form a base for his bangers. The old house would become a hive of industry as we worked, under Grandad's guidance, on firework making. The main materials were wood, paper and string, and, of course, gunpowder, which was dried in the family oven. Grandad made all his own gunpowder, which would burn at different rates and in all sorts of magnificent colours depending on the mixtures and formulae that he used.

One further aspect of the Fifth that is largely missing from modern celebrations is the sound of bells. Ringing the church bells was part of the very first Guy Fawkes Night celebrations, and it was a standard part of national and patriotic celebrations for centuries. The Fifth (or its eve) was sometimes called 'Ringing Night' because of the enthusiasm with which ringers carried it out, as bell enthusiast John Camp wrote in 1988:

In some areas the custom of 'firing' the bells (the old method of alarm) is still used on Guy Fawkes Day and is known as 'shooting old Guy'. This also happens at Harlington, Bedfordshire, where the ringers are rewarded with pork pies and beer.

See also **4 November: Ringing Night**.

One of the most spectacular traditional events in the autumn calendar is Bonfire Night at Lewes in East Sussex. It is a direct descendant of the mass Guy Fawkes celebrations of the nineteenth century, and although it may now be safe enough for modern regulations, it still keeps its aura of spectacle and danger. Unlike the celebrations in Bridgwater in Somerset, where the Fifth has been transformed by the glare of thousands of electric light bulbs (*see* **First Friday in November**), at Lewes the light is supplied in the more elemental form of real flames carried on poles through the narrow streets.

Since at least the early nineteenth century, celebrations on the 5th in Lewes have been organized by particular groups, based on geographical territory, and these became the Bonfire Societies, the backbone of the event. Societies have come and gone over the years, but in 2004 there were five: Cliffe, Borough, Commercial Square, South Street, and Waterloo. Each society has a broadly similar way of doing things. They gather at their base in the late afternoon and hold processions around their territory, along with fancy-dress competitions for the children, the racing of tar barrels along the street, and visits to the war memorial. They join the Grand United Parade in the evening, and then return to their own sites for bonfires, firework displays, and effigy burning. Many of the small towns and villages in the Lewes area also have bonfire societies.

The Grand United Parade is the high spot for the visitor to the town, as most of the societies combine to provide a huge torch-lit, costumed, banner-carrying, band-playing procession. Some costumes are simple – such as the characteristic striped jerseys worn by many participants – but there is a strong tradition for the 'pioneers' (the group that leads each contingent in the procession) to be dressed more fantastically, and Zulu, Viking, and Red Indian costumes are a popular and traditional feature.

It is often asked why Lewes, of all the places that had mass Guy Fawkes celebrations in the nineteenth century, should be the one that has retained the spirit of the old Fifth in recognizable form. Taking their cue from the strong anti-Catholic elements of the celebrations, writers often assume a religious basis for this survival, and make reference to the so-called Lewes Martyrs – seventeen local Protestants who were burnt in the High Street in the 1550s during the Catholic backlash of Queen Mary's reign – or to the fact that Lewes always had

Parkin

In the northern counties of England, an oatmeal confection called 'parkin' has long been associated with Guy Fawkes Night. Charlotte Burne recorded her grandmother's recipe in the 1820s:

Another local dainty was 'parkin', or oatmeal gingerbread, which was made for the Fifth of November, and which my grandmother continued to have made within my own memory, long after she had moved away from Lancashire. This is the recipe she used: 3 lbs of sifted meal, 1 lb of butter, 1¾ lb of treacle, ¾ lb of brown sugar, 1 oz of ginger, a few caraway seeds, and a little candied lemon. Bake in a shallow tin, and, when cold, cut into narrow oblong pieces.

Dorothy Wordsworth, the poet's sister, recorded baking parkins in her Lakeland diary on 6 November 1800. Florence White gives several recipes in her classic cookery guide *Good Things in England* (1932).

strong Nonconformist traditions. But these explanations are too facile, and wide of the mark. The Nonconformists were not supporters of the celebrations, and were usually in the forefront of opposition to the event, primarily because of the drunkenness and disorder that took place. In addition, the Lewes Martyrs were hardly mentioned until the end of the nineteenth century, and the erection of the Martyr's Memorial in May 1901 was the result of the long-running bonfire traditions, rather than the cause of them.

The real reason should be sought in the political rather than the religious sphere. When we look at what happened in other towns across southern England, we find the same broad pattern repeated. During the nineteenth century, mass street celebrations came under increasing fire from sections of the local establishment. Mayors, aldermen, councillors, magistrates, clergymen, police chiefs, schoolteachers, businessmen, and tradesmen all had their opinions, and condemned in turn the drunkenness, violence, and danger to property inherent in such events, along with their adverse effect on trade and prosperity. However, while the celebrations had supporters as well as enemies within these groups, they were relatively safe. Put crudely, in Lewes, as elsewhere, the supporters of traditions were on the Conservative wing of local politics, while the opponents were Liberals, but in other places a combination of changing notions of propriety, increasing civic pride, temperance campaigns, and a variety of other social changes gradually eroded that support. In Lewes, however, the particular balance of political power allowed the celebrations to survive long enough to become amenable to change rather than outright suppression.

Survival has also been the result of strategic compromises and retreats at key points on the part of the 'bonfire boys and girls' of the societies. When street fires in the centre of town were banned, the societies found their own fire sites; when 'Lewes Rousers' (large home-made squibs that shot across the ground) were banned, they adopted safer fireworks, and later agreed to abide by a rule of no fireworks in the crowded streets. As Jim Etherington, historian of the Fifth commented:

The bonfire societies transformed a night of riot into an organised and fairly disciplined street celebration. The most significant feature of this change was the introduction of the torchlit processions of costume-clad members carrying banners and accompanied by bands.

Even in recent years there has had to be further compromise as the standards for crowd control and safety have changed, and Lewes has continued to attract controversy over some of the elements of the celebrations that have survived relatively unchanged, in particular the overt anti-Catholic basis of the celebrations and the marked propensity for using the event to comment on political and social issues of the day, in the form of effigies of unpopular figures. The real hardliners in the struggle to uphold tradition, against much criticism, are the Cliffe Bonfire Society, 150 years old in 2004, whose members regularly have to defend themselves against those who call for a toning down of the anti-Catholic elements in their activities. Cliffe still carry their traditional 'No Popery' banner along with seventeen fiery crosses to represent the Lewes Martyrs, and they are still addressed by mock bishops, and burn effigies of the Pope. However, this determination to perpetuate tradition has resulted in their being excluded from the Grand United Parade and, to a certain extent, their ostracism from the other societies, who have moved with the times to avoid trouble.

Ottery St Mary

Bonfire night at Ottery St. Mary, an otherwise sleepy little town twelve miles east of Exeter, is one of the most alarming experiences life has to offer, short of all-out war.

So wrote veteran customs photographer Brian Shuel in 1985. In the traditional calendar, Ottery St Mary in Devon is famous for its barrel-rolling custom, although this is far too pale a phrase to describe what really goes on. The wooden barrels are open-ended, with insides coated in tar, and they are then soaked in paraffin and set alight. They are carried through the crowded streets, one at a time, on the shoulders of the carriers, who wear crude protective gloves made of sacking but no other protection. The barrels are sponsored by the pubs of the town, and there are usually about seventeen barrels of various sizes. In the early part of the evening, there are children's barrels, and also some for women.

Each barrel is fired outside the sponsoring pub and then hoisted on to the shoulders of the first man, who runs off down the road with it. It is passed from one to another, and the carriers take it in turns until the barrel starts to disintegrate, when it is thrown down and left to burn out on the ground. As the evening wears on, the barrels and flames get bigger, and the crowds thicker, and the last one appears in the square about midnight. There is little crowd control, and the barrels pass close enough to the packed spectators to cause real alarm, screams, and rapid retreats, which is all part of the fun – although, as Brian Shuel comments, 'The sight of a large bearded weightlifter, bearing a huge flaming barrel, yelling at the top of his voice, coming at you like a runaway train, is not for the faint-hearted.'

Blazing tar barrels are mentioned as a feature in many descriptions of Guy Fawkes celebrations in the past, and, indeed, a few places still have them. They can be seen at Lewes in Sussex and Hatherleigh in Devon, where they are dragged through the streets, and at Allendale in Northumberland, where they are carried on people's heads, but nowhere else do the flames get so dangerously close to the onlookers. Nineteenth-century celebrations, where burning barrels were rolled and kicked about the streets, seem positively tame by comparison.

As ever, theories of pagan sun worship and fire sacrifice are frequently put forward to explain the origins of the custom, but none has the slightest evidence to support them. The earliest known references date from the 1850s, and there is no reason to think the custom in its present form is any older, although it could have developed from the more usual 5 November tar barrelling at any time over the last 300 years.

The barrel rolling is the most overtly spectacular part of Ottery's annual celebrations, but many other events also take place: a carnival is held a few days before, and on the Fifth itself there is a huge bonfire with guy on the banks of the River Otter, and a funfair going full tilt; there is also the firing of the 'rock cannons'. Before the Second World War, these were ancient muzzle-loading pistols, but the custom lapsed and when it was revived by local resident Nelson Owen in 1956 it was with newly designed and manufactured cannons, on the old principle. The modern rock cannon is made from a 1¼-inch steel bar, 16 inches long, bent in the middle to about 35 degrees, with a half-inch hole bored in one end to a depth of 3 inches, which is filled with well-rammed gunpowder. A cross-hole is drilled to take the percussion cap, which, when struck with a special hammer, sets off the powder with an almighty bang. There are ten or twelve of them, and they are fired three times every 5 November, at 5.30 a.m., 1 p.m., and 4 p.m., usually in rapid sequence, but sometimes all at once. The powder is usually that used for quarry blasting, called 'rock powder'; hence the name of the cannons. They are not quite unique: the Fenny Poppers at Fenny Stratford are quite similar in effect, if not in appearance (*see* 11 November: Fenny Poppers).

Compare 5 November: Lewes Bonfire Night; Second Saturday in November: Hatherleigh Carnival; 31 December: Allendale Guisers.

9 November

Pully Lug Day

See Friday following Ash Wednesday: Pully Lug Day, p. 88.

Second Friday in November

Silent Change

The new Lord Mayor of London, having been in waiting since his or her election on Michaelmas Day, is finally sworn in and takes office on the second Friday in November. At the Guildhall, the symbols of his office are passed to him – the sword, mace, crystal sceptre, seal, and

City purse – and the old and new Lord Mayors exchange seats. Apart from a short declaration by the new incumbent, no words are spoken during the ceremony (hence its title), although nobody seems to know why.

See also 29 **September: Election of the Lord Mayor of London**

Second Saturday in November

Hatherleigh Carnival

The West Country is particularly proud of its carnivals, and the one that takes place at Hatherleigh in Devon is certainly as impressive as any. It started life as a fund-raising event for the local hospital, but later combined with the town's Guy Fawkes celebrations to form an impressive torch-lit procession, usually on the second Saturday in November. Other activities that take place over carnival weekend include decorated shop windows, a children's parade, a funfair, a grand disco, a bonfire, and the crowning of a carnival queen, prince, and princess.

In addition to these interesting, but controlled, events, there is the more spectacular pastime of running blazing tar barrels through the streets early on the Saturday morning, and again in the evening after the main carnival. Three large open-ended tar-soaked barrels are placed on a sledge, set alight, and then dragged as fast as the men can run, round the town centre. Photographer Brian Shuel described the event in 1985:

They came down the hill as the flames took hold. By the time they reached the George Hotel, from a bedroom window of which I was intrepidly recording events, the barrels were a raging inferno. With shouts of joy the men set off up High Street at full speed.

Compare 5 **November: Ottery St Mary.**

Lord Mayor's Show

What is now called the Lord Mayor's Show is actually the procession that accompanies the new Lord Mayor of the City of London on a formal visit to the Law Courts to make a declaration of his or her fealty to the Crown. The new Lord Mayor is elected at or around Michaelmas (29 September) and the procession is his first official duty on taking office, as laid down by a charter granted to the City by King John in 1215. The Mayoralty itself dates to the 1190s, and in many City affairs the Lord Mayor is second only to the sovereign, thus holding a great deal of ceremonial power. The show has long been one of the major pieces of London pageantry, with the Lord Mayor travelling in a gilded horse-drawn coach, built in 1757, which can be seen in the Museum of London when not in use, and accompanied by a bodyguard of pikemen and musketeers, in period costume, and a panoply of military bands and decorated floats sponsored by organizations and companies connected with London. Although the Lord Mayor's visit to the Courts dates from the thirteenth century, the accompanying procession did not take on a high profile until the sixteenth century, when it replaced the older Midsummer Watch procession, which had lost official favour in a time of potential social and political unrest. Initially full of religious themes, after the Reformation the Lord Mayor's Show took on a more patriotic tone, and some elements of entertainment, such as acrobats, were introduced.

The day also includes a banquet, which Samuel Pepys recorded attending on 29 October 1663; however, he was not impressed by the affair, or the women there, and called the pageants 'very silly'. Nowadays, the procession is three miles long and can include 8,000 people. It attracts half a million spectators, plus many more who watch it live on television.

See also **29 September: Election of the Lord Mayor of London**.

10 November

St Martin's Eve

Martinmas (*see* **11 November: St Martin's Day**) was seen as a time of feasting and merrymaking, based on the habit of slaughtering animals at this time for salting down to last through the winter. But Northamptonshire poet John Clare singled out St Martin's Eve, in his poem of that name, which was written about 1830, as a time of indoor gatherings, where tales were told and games played, in defiance of the darkening nights and deteriorating weather of the autumn season:

> *Now that the year grows wearisome with age*
> *And days grow short and nights excessive long*
> *No outdoor sports the village hinds engage*
> *Still is the meadow romp and harvest song.*

See also 10 July for a custom carried out by hill shepherds.

Wroth Silver

Whatever the weather, at daybreak on the eve of Martinmas, a number of people gather on Knightlow Hill near Rugby, in order to pay negligible sums of money to the Duke of Buccleuch's agent, for what rights or privileges nobody quite knows. With everybody gathered, and as soon as it is light enough to see, the agent commences:

Wroth silver due to his Grace the Duke of Buccleuch and payable at Knightlow Cross on Martinmas Eve, 11th November . . . before sun-rising. Non-payment thereof forfeiture of 100 pence for every penny, or a white bull with red ears and red nose.

A list of twenty-five parishes is then read out – 'Arley, Astley, Birdingbury, Bourton and Draycote, Bramcote', and so on – with the amount due from each. As each parish representative places the money into a hole in a large square stone, which is all that is left of Knightlow Cross, he or she says, 'Wroth silver!' After the ceremony, everybody retires to a nearby pub – the Dun Cow at Dunchurch was for many years the favoured location – for a breakfast and the traditional glass of hot rum and milk. This breakfast was formerly open to anyone who wanted to go, but is now by ticket only.

The name 'Wroth silver' has puzzled commentators for some time. The *Oxford English Dictionary* reveals that *wroth* was simply an alternative spelling for 'wrath', and this has led some to assume that the payments are in recompense for some former transgression that angered a lord of the manor. An alternative derivation, however, is suggested by R. T. Simpson, who wrote a description of the custom in 1927. He commented that a seemingly similar payment, in the New

Forest, Hampshire, was termed 'wrather' or 'rother' money, and this brings in the possibility that 'wroth' is derived from *rother*, which is an Old English word for 'ox' or 'cattle' that survived into the current era in some regional dialects. Wroth silver, therefore, may have been simply 'cattle money', given in payment for grazing rights or something similar.

11 November

St Martin's Day

Martin of Tours (*c*.316–97) was a soldier in the Roman army when he decided to convert to Christianity, and was imprisoned for his refusal to fight. He later became a monk, founded the first monastery in Gaul, and then became Bishop of Tours in 372, in which position he served till his death. His reputation for miracles, before and after his death, made him an extremely popular saint in France and neighbouring countries, including Britain, throughout the Middle Ages, and numerous churches were dedicated to him.

The main aspect of this day in the traditional year, however, had little connection with the saint and his life, but everything to do with its position in the farming calendar. Martinmas (or sometimes Martlemas) was traditionally the time when animals were slaughtered to prepare for the coming winter months. It is because of this widespread activity that November was called 'blood-month' in the Anglo-Saxon calendar, and a vague superstition persisted until recent times, in Ireland at least, that something should be killed on this day 'for luck'. The slaughtered meat was salted or dried, and 'Martinmas beef' became a common term for meat preserved in this way. For much of the population, Martinmas itself was therefore one of the last opportunities in the year to eat fresh meat, and was known for food that was a by-product of the slaughter, such as black puddings and offal. The day therefore had something of a reputation for merrymaking.

St Martin's Day also took the place of Michaelmas (*see* 29 **September**) as a 'settling day' in some parts of the country, particularly Cumbria and other parts of the North, although it was never one of the official English quarter days. In these areas it was the day when rents were due, annual terms of employment or occupancy started and finished,

continued on page 475 ☞

Hiring Fairs

Until the turn of the twentieth century, and even later in some parts of the country, most agricultural workers and rural domestic workers were hired by the year. As the end of their term approached, they would enter into negotiation with their employers to decide whether they would be staying for another year or moving on. Those who wished to find a new place travelled to the nearest market town on a set day to attend a hiring fair, where they gathered at a particular spot sanctioned by long custom and waited for the farmer or his agent to come along and, they hoped, offer them a job. Employers would question likely workers about their experience, capabilities, and, most importantly, where they had previously worked, so that a 'character' or reference could be sought. On their side, the labourer or servant had the opportunity to ask about conditions – not only wages but also accommodation, food, and what sort of farm it was. The majority of unmarried year-term agricultural workers lived in, the women in the farmhouse and the men in dormitories in outhouses or above the stable. Living conditions for the latter could be extremely primitive even by contemporary standards, and working conditions harsh, but the advantages were job security and the knowledge that although they had little money in their pocket through the year, they had food and shelter for the foreseeable future, and they could look forward to a lump sum at the end of the year.

If a deal was made, the farmer handed over a small sum of money to seal the bargain. The amount varied from place to place, but was usually between a shilling and half a crown, and went by various local names, such as earnest money, arles, God's penny, fastening penny, and fes. The contract was then legally binding, although there was a strong tradition that the worker could change his or her mind if the money was returned within a specified period. Many places held a second fair a few weeks later, called a 'runaway mop' or something similar, at which those who had not found a place, or whose first choice had been disastrous, had another chance. For those still out of a position, the insecurity of day-labouring was the chief option, although they could travel to another town that held a later fair if they wished. They rarely travelled too far, however, as employers were often suspicious of strangers.

Hiring fairs could be held at any time of year, according to local custom, but were usually conducted at slack times on the farm, for obvious reasons. Candlemas, 12 May, Michaelmas, Martinmas, or their Old Style equivalents, were particularly popular. The fairs also went under various local names, such as Statute, Statty, Mop fair, the Sittings, and the Hirings.

Throughout the eighteenth and nineteenth centuries, hiring fairs were an essential part of the rural scene, and there were numerous published accounts of what went on there. Thomas Hardy's description of a hiring fair in *Far from the Madding Crowd* (1874) is perhaps the best known, in which each farmworker wore a token of their specialism:

Carters and waggoners were distinguished by having a piece of whip-cord twisted round their hats; thatchers wore a fragment of woven straw; shepherds held their sheep-crooks in their hand; and thus the situation required was known to the hirers at a glance.

However, this does not seem to have been the norm, as most eyewitness accounts of hirings describe a much simpler system, whereby those still for hire signified their availability in the same way – a straw in the mouth, a piece of whip-cord in the hatband, twisted straw in a buttonhole, and so on – which was removed as soon as they had found a place.

Once a new place was secured, and the earnest money given over, there were some chores to do before the fun began. Most had accounts to settle – for the year's washing, for the new pair of boots that had been necessary during the year, for next year's working clothes, and so on – and there were presents for parents and sweethearts to purchase. But wherever people gather in holiday mood, tradesmen, entertainers, and food and drink retailers are never far away, and many hiring fairs became large-scale festival events, attended by crowds who were not there to be hired. There were rides, sideshows, gingerbread stalls, and mountebanks, as well as the regular shops and pubs of the town, but there were also pickpockets, prostitutes, card-sharps, and recruiting parties to trap the inexperienced and unwary. It was considered essential to look one's best for the fair, and everyone tried to be as smart as possible, as there was also the rare chance of fraternizing with the opposite sex, and many workers eagerly seized the opportunity. It was a poor fair indeed that could not boast a few musicians and plenty of dancing. After the fair, workers would usually spend a few days with family or friends before starting at their new place.

However, not everybody was in favour of hiring fairs. For a number of vociferous Victorian reformers they were annual affairs of appalling debasement and debauchery, and vigorous campaigns were waged against them from the 1850s onwards. Some commentators were genuinely concerned to improve the bad conditions in which agricultural labourers had to live and work, and they set the need for the reform of annual contracts and hiring fairs in the context of general social improvement. Many argued that standing in the street waiting to be hired, like slaves or beasts, was degrading, especially for young women. There were numerous local attempts to provide indoor venues (away from the young men) where female servants could meet prospective employers in more decorous surroundings. In the long run, these proved popular with the women themselves, especially in bad weather, and became a fixture at many later nineteenth-century fairs. But mostly the reformers were exercised by what went on after the business of hiring had been carried out. To their mind, hordes of unsupervised young people, with money in their pockets, led to widespread drunkenness, fighting, and misbehaviour of all kinds. In November 1858, *The Times* commented:

Drunkenness is the curse to the labouring men of the present day, and love of dress to the young women of the same class. I cannot pretend that the 'mops' are the fountain-head from which these curses flow, but I am sure, from my own observation, that they give great facility to the former and great encouragement to the latter. Instead of young men and women enjoying their holyday in a way that would really make them happy, they simply offer themselves up as victims to the tender mercies of the publican and the beerkeeper.

In particular, young men and women mixing freely, without the usual necessary constraints of their betters, was anathema to them. These are the same familiar strictures that were levied against all working-class leisure pursuits in mid Victorian times by the evangelical middle classes. The young rural workers themselves were determined to enjoy their scarce leisure time as they liked, and it is hardly surprising that their pleasures consisted largely of heavy drinking, eating, and flirting, which were denied them the rest of the year. But eyewitness accounts also show that fighting was endemic to the culture, and the level of violence played into the reformers' hands. By modern standards, the behaviour of many fair-goers was indeed pretty barbaric. 'Binge drinking' and 'yob culture' may be modern concepts, but they are not far off the mark for the way in which some groups regularly behaved. Beyond the practical measures of supplying separate indoor places to stand, however, it is unlikely that the reformers made much difference to the fairs. Their decline in the later nineteenth century was the result of changes in the economic basis of farming that removed their usefulness rather than any new moral climate among farmworkers.

Historians, too, are as divided as their Victorian ancestors on the question of the relative merits of the hiring-fair system. David Kerr Cameron, author of *The English Fair* (1998), writes:

They were days that changed destinies; days of heartbreak and misery for the vast numbers of young girls in domestic service and the men and boys who made up the labour force of the country's farms. Though they might change the milieu, the yearly statute fair offered them little but the opportunity to continue the same drudgery that had dogged their days since leaving school. Few would remember the old 'statty' fairs with affection; for most they were the bitterest of memories.

But Stephen Caunce, writing of East Yorkshire fairs, is much more positive:

The key to the success of the farm servant system was the ease with which lads changed jobs, and that was made possible by the hiring fairs . . . In an age without advertisements, they brought together all the farmers and servants of a district and thereby encouraged the most efficient matching of the requirements of each and the maximum possible choice for both.

The ultimate origins of the hiring-fair system lay in the problems brought about by the acute shortage of labour in the wake of the Black Death. The Ordinance of Labourers (1349) and the Statute of Labourers (1351), passed respectively by Edward III and by Parliament, attempted to regulate the labour market by fixing wages and controlling conditions of employment on a national scale. Among other draconian stipulations, wages were pegged to pre-plague levels, labourers had to be employed by the year or other long term rather than by the day, and those seeking employment had to meet and deal with employers 'in a common place and not privy'. The desperate shortage of manpower, however, meant that these laws were widely ignored, and it was not until the reign of Elizabeth I that further attempts were made to regulate labour. The Statute of Artificers of 1562/3 went much further than previous statutes, and had a more permanent effect on labour relations. Wages were now to be assessed by local Justices of the Peace; all men between twelve and sixty were obliged to work unless they had other means to support themselves, and if they had no other trade or occupation they were forced to do agricultural work; while unmarried women were likewise instructed to undertake domestic service. Workers had to be engaged for a year at a time, and apprentices for seven years, and the working day was set at twelve hours in summer and daylight hours in winter. No one could leave their place without permission. A complex system of enforcement was brought into being, administered by constables, who were required to keep comprehensive lists of local workers and employers and present any who broke the rules to the Justices.

The Elizabethan statute remained the basis of all agricultural labour relations for centuries, but was showing increasing signs of breaking down at the turn of the eighteenth century, and was finally repealed in 1813. By that time, wages had begun to follow market forces, and it was increasingly left to individual workers and farmers to reach a satisfactory bargain. But even without legislative backing, the hiring fair was too essential an institution to be easily dispensed with, and it continued to be a major feature of the agricultural year for many years to come. Huge changes in agriculture and society at large finally made the fairs obsolete, and by the end of the Victorian era they were increasingly seen as anachronistic. Change occurred most rapidly in the south of the country, and new methods of finding work were in place well before the outbreak of the First World War, as recorded by Alfred Williams in Wiltshire in 1912:

There is very little hiring done nowadays in this locality; the farmers generally advertise in the newspapers, or meet with the men on market-days, and make the necessary arrangements; and as for the fair, that is very nearly at an end.

However, the old system persisted in other parts, where local conditions were favourable, and hiring fairs, albeit mere shadows of their former selves, were still being held at some places in northern England between the wars, and a few even into the 1950s. Some hiring fairs continued as pleasure fairs, and it is now only the word 'mop' in their title that betrays their origins.

See also: Fairs, Feasts, Wakes, and Revels, p. 341.

and house-moving took place. Across the whole country, one aspect that made it seem a pale reflection of Michaelmas was the popularity of roast goose for the dinner table.

A useful piece of advice was included by Richard Inwards in his collection of *Weather Lore*, first published in 1869: 'If the wind is in the south-west at Martinmas, it keeps there till after Candlemas [2 February].'

See also **Hiring Fairs**, p. 470.

Fenny Poppers

Fenny Stratford parish church, St Martin's, in Buckinghamshire, was built by Browne Willis, the learned but eccentric local squire, in 1724, in memory of his grandfather Dr Thomas Willis who had lived in St Martin's Lane, London, and had died on St Martin's Day in 1675. Willis himself died in 1760, and left money for an annual sermon in his name. It is also assumed, but cannot be proved, that the 'Fenny Poppers' that are still fired today every St Martin's Day are part of his bequest.

The Poppers are six small cast-iron cannons, which are loaded with gunpowder and fired with the aid of a long iron rod with a red-hot tip. The result is six deafening bangs in quick succession, at 12 noon, 2 p.m., and 4 p.m. They used to be fired in the churchyard, but concern for the church's fabric prompted a move to nearby Leon recreation ground. The present Poppers were cast in 1859 because the originals were becoming dangerous, and they are sometimes fired on other special occasions, such as the death of Queen Victoria and the beginning of the new millennium. Odd as it may seem, the custom is not quite unique, as the rock cannons of Ottery St Mary in Devon are very similar (*see* 5 **November: Ottery St Mary**).

Remembrance Sunday

> *They shall grow not old, as we that are left grow old:*
> *Age shall not weary them, nor the years condemn.*
> *At the going down of the sun and in the morning*
> *We will remember them.*

The poignant third verse of Lawrence Binyon's poem 'For the Fallen' (first published September 1914), engraved on war memorials and recited at countless ceremonies since 1919, neatly encapsulates the widespread postwar feeling that there was a national obligation to remember the fallen and their sacrifice. Other evocative quotations, such as Rudyard Kipling's 'Lest we forget', and 'Their name liveth for evermore', a line taken from Ecclesiasticus, were similarly incorporated into remembrance ceremonies and helped shape the way in which the First World War would be commemorated in Britain and throughout the Empire.

The unprecedented scale of the slaughter, and the fact that so many were volunteers and conscripts rather than regular soldiers, separated this conflict from all the wars that had gone before, and a new level of national response was clearly needed. Even while the fighting continued, there was much public debate about the form that commemoration should take, and a prevailing consensus quickly took hold that the tone must be one of sacrifice and redemption rather than exultation over victory; this has strongly influenced our view of the matter ever since. The Government, and other interested bodies, offered a stream of advice on the design of local memorials and appropriate wording for ceremonies, but many communities went their own way. There were those who wished to see money spent on practical memorials, such as hospital wings and village halls, rather than cenotaphs and churchyard crosses, and there was wide variation in the way different communities chose to honour their dead. However, Armistice Day, the day set aside for national commemoration, symbolically placed on 11 November, the anniversary of the day the armistice was signed, was devised as the official focus, and it rapidly became a major event in the national calendar. It soon acquired rituals and traditions of its own, which in turn have influenced the shape of later responses to other national crises and tragedies.

A temporary cenotaph, designed by Sir Edward Lutyens, was in place in Whitehall for the 1919 ceremony, and the real one in time for November 1920. The Tomb of the Unknown Warrior in Westminster Abbey was unveiled in 1920, and the sale of red poppies by the British Legion started in 1921. On the day, the central core of national commemoration takes place when the sovereign, accompanied by the nation's political and religious leaders, Commonwealth representatives, veterans, and serving military personnel, lay wreaths at the Cenotaph, followed by a two-minute silence at 11 a.m. There are numerous smaller ceremonies on similar lines at war memorials all over the country.

Once the rawness of both individual and national grief began to fade, and other societal problems such as mass unemployment took hold, Armistice Day began to lose some of its support, and drew particular criticism from the burgeoning peace movement. After 1945, the term 'Armistice Day' was thought too specific to the previous conflict, and 'Remembrance Day' became the official title, commemorating the sacrifices of both world wars, and all subsequent conflicts, on the nearest Sunday to 11 November.

Again, the commemoration gradually lost some of its immediacy over the years after the Second World War, and there were even calls for it to be phased out, but there were palpable increases in support for the ceremony when major anniversaries occurred, most notably the fiftieth and sixtieth anniversaries of the Second World War, in 1995 and 2005 respectively. The element that has perhaps attracted the most controversy is the two-minute silence, although largely for reasons far removed from the remembrance of the war dead.

There has been much debate about who first suggested the mass commemorative silence. Although Lord Milner suggested the idea to the government of the day, it is not known for certain who first suggested it to him, and South African Sir Percy Fitzpatrick and Australian journalist Edward George Honey are the main contenders for the honour. Either way, it was already in place in 1919, and has continued ever since, except during the years of the Second World War. Between the wars, the silence was literally imposed at 11 a.m. on 11 November. Police stopped traffic, public transport paused, and people in offices and schools were expected to conform, as the King's proclamation that announced the day decreed that 'All locomotion should cease, so that, in perfect stillness, the thoughts of everyone may be concentrated on reverent remembrance of the glorious dead.'

Moving the ceremony to a Sunday certainly blunted this effect, and there were many who complained that this downgraded the ceremony in national life. However, the real problem in recent years has been that 'silences' have become the standard response to tragedies, large and small, including terrorist attacks such as the New York 9/11 atrocity and the Bali, Madrid, and London bombings, the death of popular famous figures like Princess Diana and the Queen Mother, natural disasters such as the Asian Tsunami, local tragedies, and murders. Social commentator Patrick West has written on the subject: 'They are getting longer and we are having more of them, because we want to be seen to care – and increasingly are compelled to do so.'

West and other critics refer to 'silence inflation' and condemn mass silences as 'conspicuous compassion', which do nothing but make the participants feel superior. Others claim that these other 'silences' devalue the meaning of the original. It is the sacrifice of the fallen on our behalf that should be commemorated in this way, not the unfortunate but unknowing victims of tragedies both natural and man-made.

Nevertheless, these criticisms are strongly countered by those who claim that this method of focusing attention on tragedies or atrocities is one in which ordinary people can participate and demonstrate that they care, that the people involved are not alone, that the terrorists will not win, or whatever else is appropriate to the situation: not only do *I* care, but *we* care. There is no denying the emotional impact of a mass of people – a football crowd or a busy railway station – suddenly and impressively falling silent, in 'perfect stillness'.

As if to demonstrate how the customary calendar is in constant flux, as the above was being written, the Chancellor of the Exchequer and Prime Minister in waiting, Gordon Brown, suggested publicly that Remembrance Day could be developed into a 'British Day', on the lines of the American 4th of July. It remains to be seen whether this idea takes root.

13 November

St Brice's Day

Brice was Bishop of Tours, who died in AD 444 after a long and stormy period in office. He was soon accredited with saintly virtues, and his cult was popular in England until the Conquest, but his fame seems to have waned from about that time onwards.

The most well-known custom that took place on St Brice's Day was the annual bull-running at Stamford, Lincolnshire, which, although not quite unique, was famous countrywide and regarded by locals as an essential part of their town's identity. It was fiercely defended when it became the focus of the campaign to ban working-class blood sports, but by 1840 it had succumbed to the new reformers and was relegated to the town's history. To modern eyes, the custom was indeed barbaric, and it would certainly not be tolerated today, but in the context of the times it was no more cruel than many other so-called sports that involved animals.

The custom was believed to have been founded in the time of King John (1167–1216), when William, Earl of Warren, was said to have been standing on the battlements of his castle and saw two bulls fighting in the field below (later called the Bull Meadow). When butchers attempted to part them, the animals escaped into the town and caused uproar in the streets before they were finally recaptured. The Earl found this so entertaining that he decreed that it should be an annual event.

Every year, on 13 November (or the 14th when that day fell on a Sunday), the town was given over to the bull-running. A little before eleven in the morning, the church bells were rung, to warn the people to clear the streets, and at eleven a bull was released. Side streets and doorways were blocked off, to keep the bull in the town centre for a while, and shop windows were boarded up for safety, but upstairs windows, along with every other relatively safe vantage point, were crowded with spectators. By moving certain barriers, and goading the bull with noise, sticks, stones, and whips, the animal was induced to run a set route through the town, with the participants – the 'bull-ards' – and their dogs, running and yelling before and after. The eventual idea was to 'bridge the bull', by getting it to cross the Welland river, and then the crowd closed in and together heaved it over the parapet into the water. The 'running' continued when it swam ashore in the nearby meadows, where it was finally killed, and later eaten. Sometimes a second bull was then started in the town.

The late eighteenth century saw a sharp rise in feeling against traditional sports that involved mass working-class participation, and also a new revulsion against cruelty to animals at all levels. The *Lincoln, Rutland & Stamford Mercury* of 18 November 1785 commented:

Monday last being our annual bull-running, the same was observed here with the usual celebrity – several men heated with liquor got tossed by the bull, and were most terribly hurt, while some others more sober had little better usage. What a pity it is so barbarous a custom is permitted to be continued, that has no one good purpose to recommend it, but is kept as an orgy of drunkenness and idleness to the manifest injury of many poor families, even tho' the men escape bodily hurt.

continued on page 482 ☞

Bull-Baiting

The spectacle of a bull being baited by dogs was a common enough sight in both rural and urban areas of England right up until the 1830s. Bear-baiting and other similar animal 'sports' were mostly staged at professional arenas, for the enjoyment of paying customers, but bull-baiting was usually carried out in the street, tavern yard, or market-place, free to all and sundry, including women and children. It was this very ordinariness and accessibility, as well as its obvious barbarity, that so incensed the emerging animal rights movement of the early nineteenth century, and made members so determined to rid society of such evil pastimes.

During a baiting, the bull was tethered by a rope attached to a stake driven into the ground or to a permanent metal bull-ring set into the road or a convenient wall. The points of the bull's horns were sawn off, presumably because they would otherwise have been too deadly. Dogs were released either singly or in groups, and were encouraged to attack the bull, which had two main means of defence: the use of its weight to trample them, and its horns, to toss them. The crowd particularly loved the latter, and there were many stories of dogs landing in ladies' laps, or on men's heads, and illustrations of the sport usually show dogs tossed high in the air. The dog owners carried long poles, which they cleverly placed at an angle to break the dogs' fall when they fell to earth. On their part, the dogs simply fastened on to the bull's flesh with their teeth, if possible going for a tender part such as face or throat, and hung on until the bull's own frantic movements shook them free, tearing the flesh off as they fell. The owners thus preferred breeds that would not only attack bravely but would hold on, come what may. After a while, the maddened bull was a mass of open bleeding wounds, and some of the dogs were trampled or had broken their necks from their fall. And the crowd loved it.

It is difficult for most of us in modern times to comprehend why so many people enjoyed spectacles in which animals were pitted against each other, but such 'sports' were almost everyday occurrences, and few before the early nineteenth century gave them much thought. It was genuinely believed that the meat of a bull was much more tender if it had been baited before being slaughtered, and some town councils had regulations insisting on the practice. Staging a bull-baiting was also a standard way of currying favour with the local populace. A candidate up for election, a new mayor who wanted to treat the townsfolk, a squire who wanted to celebrate his son's marriage, a publican who wished to draw a crowd to increase liquor sales – all these were likely to 'give a bull' to the people for baiting, in the sure knowledge that their generosity would be appreciated.

In the early nineteenth century, piecemeal opposition to bull-baiting began to grow into an organized movement determined to get all such blood sports banned, to alleviate the cruelty to the animals. But there were plenty of apologists for blood sports to be found, and many were in high places. Some argued that the sport was natural – both dogs and bull were simply being themselves – while many others, who cared little either way on the cruelty question, were determined to stop any legislation that prevented the individual from freely choosing his own leisure pursuits. Many were well aware that if they legislated against the blood sports of the lower classes, they were opening the way to abolition of their own hunting, shooting, and fishing lifestyles.

From 1800, there was a steady stream of anti-cruelty proposals put to Parliament, but until the breakthrough 1822 Act there was equally steady opposition from a group of determined MPs, led by the most vocal of them all, the Right Honourable William Windham (previously Secretary of State for War). Windham was the scourge of those who sought reform, and helped to scupper all attempts until his death in 1810. He spoke eloquently of liberty and freedom, claiming that such affairs were beneath the dignity of Parliament to discuss, and accusing anti-baiters of being a coalition of Methodists and Jacobins. The most successful of the early reformers was the eccentric Richard Martin, MP for Galway, who, though passionately opposed to the beating of horses, was himself an enthusiastic fox-hunter and was known to boast of the duels he had fought. In 1822, Martin finally managed to get an act passed that penalized anyone who had beaten, abused, or ill-treated a range of named species. However, this legislation failed to prevent bull-baiting because of a problem with the wording, and following a ruling that bulls were not included in the term 'other cattle', the baiters were permitted to continue with their old sport.

The Society for the Prevention of Cruelty to Animals was formed in June 1824, with Martin as one of its founder members; in 1840, Queen Victoria gave permission for the Society's 'Royal' accolade. Though small, the new Society provided a new focus for radical reform, and the 1835 Cruelty to Animals Act finally banned 'running, baiting or fighting any bull, bear, badger, dog, or other animal', and for good measure the Highways Act of the same year made it illegal to bait any animal on the public highway. It is a tribute to the determination of the early campaigners that within thirty years the whole climate of educated opinion had swung dramatically in their direction, and whereas the press of 1802 had derided the reformers as sentimental cranks, that of the 1830s were almost entirely on their side. It must be said, however, that many who supported the campaign against baiting cared little about the plight of animals, but were concerned with the potentially demoralizing effect of such blood sports on the working classes, which they believed encouraged drunkenness and the promiscuous mixing of the sexes, or were equally worried that gatherings of working-class revellers could too easily be used to foment political unrest and rioting. The successful campaign against popular blood sports was not simply a victory for animal-lovers but also for those who sought to control the masses by abolition or reform of their leisure pursuits.

See also **Baiting Bears and Other Animals**, p. 400.

☞ continued from page 479 The Stamford Bull-Running became a *cause célèbre* for the reformers, but it proved remarkably resilient, and supporters managed to keep it going for many years, in the face of mounting opposition and pressure at both national and local levels. Although it was first banned in 1788, by order of the town's quarter sessions, the local authorities met so many difficulties attempting to suppress the custom in subsequent years that they eventually gave up trying. But time was against the running, and after a prolonged campaign by the Society for the Prevention of Cruelty to Animals (founded 1824), aided by the turning of respectable local opinion against the sport, the last bull-running took place in 1839. The suppression of the Stamford Bull-Running was the first major success for the new Society. For years afterwards, however, the cry of 'A bull! A bull!' could unite Stamfordians in feelings of local pride like no other could.

A similar sport existed at Tutbury, Staffordshire (*see* **16 August: Tutbury Bull-Running**). Bull-running is often confused with **bull-baiting** (p. 480), but beyond the cruelty to the animal, the two were very different.

17 November

Queen Elizabeth I/St Hugh's Day

Almost immediately after her death in 1603, the reign of Elizabeth I started to take on the aura of a golden age and she herself the mythic proportions of an unofficial patron saint. The day of her accession, 17 November, was widely celebrated well into the eighteenth century with sermons, bonfires, and bell-ringing. Indeed, by the 1630s, the enthusiastic bells on Elizabeth's day even aroused the jealousy of Charles I, who felt that his birthday, and that of his queen Henrietta Maria (on the 19 and 16 November respectively), were grudgingly and weakly marked. Much of the celebration was spontaneous and local rather than being nationally co-ordinated, but Elizabeth's status as icon of the Protestant revolution meant that the day was always available whenever the government wished to make an anti-Catholic point. The Pope and the Devil were regularly burnt in effigy on the day, as on 5 November.

19 November

The Society of King Charles the Martyr holds events on this day to celebrate the birthday of Charles I (*see* **30 January: Execution of Charles I**).

22 November

St Cecilia's Day

According to legend, first written in the fifth century and completely fictitious, Cecilia was a noble Roman Christian who converted Valerian, her new husband, to the faith by revealing that she was regularly visited by an angel. She insisted on remaining a virgin, and after Valerian and his brother were martyred, she too was condemned to death, first by roasting in her bath, which did not work, and then by beheading. Chaucer made her story famous in England by including it in his *Second Nun's Tale* of the *Canterbury Tales*.

As a line in the story referred to music at her wedding, and claimed that she 'sang in her heart to the Lord', she was frequently portrayed as a lover of music and poetry and, somewhat incredibly, as the inventor of the organ. In paintings, she usually appears playing a musical instrument, and she was chosen as patroness of musicians by the Academy of Music in Rome, in 1584. In Britain, as elsewhere in Europe, she became popular with the likes of Henry Purcell, John Dryden, and Alexander Pope in the late seventeenth century, and concerts and odes were composed for her day.

St Cecilia's fame seems to have been largely confined to the poets and musicians of high art, and never to have reached the hearts and minds of the general public. Periodic revivals of interest in her have always had a slightly forced, refined quality. Writing about English festivals in 1947, Laurence Whistler commented:

In 1945 it would have been fanciful to include St. Cecilia's Day among the English festivals. In 1947 it would be unimaginable to leave it out. If this charming day, twice cared for in England and twice almost forgotten, should come into public remembrance for a third time the year recorded in musical history will be 1946.

One major impetus for this postwar revival was the coincidence that 22 November was also the birthday of the influential English composer Benjamin Britten (1913–76), who dutifully revived the practice of composing odes for the day.

23 November

St Clement's Day

Clement is generally accepted as St Peter's third successor as Pope, and was venerated as a martyr in the early Christian Church, although his martyrdom cannot be proved. The legend of his death states that he was tied to an anchor and thrown into the sea; angels were then said to have built an ornate tomb for him on the seabed, which was miraculously uncovered by the sea every year on his day. The regular appearance of an anchor in pictures of the saint was enough to ensure his adoption as patron saint of seafarers, foundry-workers, and, most famously, blacksmiths. In 1883, the journal of the Sussex Archaeological Society recorded:

At Burwash a few years ago it was the custom to dress up a figure with a wig and a beard and pipe in his mouth, and set it up over the door of the inn where the blacksmiths feasted on St. Clement's Day. The figure was called 'Old Clem'.

One of the regular toasts at such gatherings was 'To the memory of Old Clem, and prosperity to all his descendants'. But the evidence for blacksmiths' particular interest in 'Old Clem' is surprisingly late, dating only from the early nineteenth century onwards. Much earlier material shows that St Clement was celebrated in the sixteenth century by fishermen, sailors, bakers, iron-founders, and other trades. This popularity was probably helped in the early modern period by the general belief that devotion to St Clement protected people from danger, specifically from water and fire, as mentioned in the sermon delivered by Bishop Wimbledon on St Clement's Day, 1388:

For this blessed martyr our Lord God showeth many divers miracles, both by water and by land, and in special for peril of water and fire so far forth that who that prayeth devotedly to God and to this holy martyr Saint Clement is oft delivered from such.

Another custom of the day, probably unrelated to the 'Old Clem' activities of the blacksmiths but sometimes confused with it, was clementing. This was a house-visiting custom, primarily carried out by children, in which a rhyme was recited or sung, and money, food, or sweets were expected in return. A Warwickshire version from the 1870s was printed in *The Times* (10 December 1935):

> *Clementing, clementing once a year*
> *Apples and pears are very good cheer*
> *One for Peter, two for Paul*
> *And three for Him who made us all*
> *Up with the hatchet and down with the shoe*
> *If you have no apples, money will do*
> *Money will do, money will do.*

In some villages, exactly the same was done on St Catherine's Day (*see* **25 November**), and called 'catterning'; both in turn were closely related to the custom called 'souling' (*see* **2 November: All Souls' Day**). The earliest mention of clementing is in 1686, in wording which implies a much longer history.

For earlier blacksmith material, *see* **1 December: St Eligius' Day**.

25 November

St Catherine's Day

Stories of St Catherine of Alexandria's life began to circulate in the ninth century, and her cult was extremely popular in Britain, as elsewhere, from the medieval period onwards. She was reputed to have been tortured on a wheel (hence the term 'Catherine wheel'), before being beheaded. She was adopted by a variety of groups, as listed in David Farmer's *Oxford Dictionary of Saints* (1987):

Patron of young girls, students (and hence the clergy), especially philosophers and apologists, nurses (because milk instead of blood flowed from her severed head) and of craftsmen whose work was based on the wheel, such as wheelwrights, spinners, and millers.

A number of trades therefore celebrated her day, and there are various descriptions of processions and meetings of lacemakers, spinners, and ropemakers, which were presumably founded in late medieval times and continued until the mid nineteenth century before fading away. There seems to have been some confusion between St Catherine and Queen Catherine of Aragon: the latter was reputed to have saved lacemakers from acute distress when she learned of a decline in the trade, and encouraged ladies to burn their old lace and replace it with new.

St Catherine was also invoked in matters of matrimony. At a ruined Norman chapel that bore her name at Abbotsbury in Dorset, for example, folklorist J. S. Udal, writing in 1922, recorded that it had been the custom for women to go and say the following prayer:

> *A husband, St. Catherine;*
> *A handsome one, St. Catherine;*
> *A rich one, St. Catherine;*
> *A nice one, St. Catherine;*
> *And soon, St. Catherine!*

Any custom that took place on St Catherine's Day could be called 'catterning', but in the area where Worcestershire and Staffordshire meet, that name usually referred to a house-visiting custom whereby children sang or recited a rhyme and expected food or money to be given to them in return. This form of 'catterning' was first mentioned in 1730, but almost exactly the same activity, called 'clementing', took place on St Clement's Day (*see* **23 November**) in other villages in the area, and another very similar custom was 'souling' (*see* **2 November: All Souls' Day**); both clementing and souling are documented in earlier times.

Fourth Tuesday in November

Ashburton Court Leet

A court leet was a manorial court that dealt with petty offences and nuisances in areas of communal interest such as highways and ditches, as well as the enforcement of regulations regarding the quality of staples such as ale and bread. It had the power to make by-laws, and to elect officers to enforce them. With successive reorganizations of local government, manorial courts were stripped of their powers, and those which remain are purely ceremonial.

Ashburton, on the edge of Dartmoor in Devon, is one place that preserves at least something of the old court. They still hold a meeting in November (on the fourth Tuesday), at St Lawrence's chapel, attended by freeholders of the town. They elect a portreeve (the equivalent of a mayor) to serve for the coming year, along with other officers including ale-tasters, bread-weighers, pig drivers, scavengers, and surveyors of markets and watercourses. The portreeve takes a leading role in community activities and celebrations, and in July the official ale-tasting and bread-weighing ceremonies take place, in which the local pubs and bakers are duly visited and their wares sampled and assessed. This ceremony is nowadays followed by a medieval fair. It is hardly surprising that such a task as ale-tasting is not taken too seriously these days.

Late November

Stir-Up Sunday

This day, the Sunday before Advent and the twenty-fifth Sunday after Trinity, falling anywhere between 20 and 26 November, was widely known as 'Stir-up Sunday' from at least the 1830s into the mid twentieth century. The collect for the day commenced, 'Stir up, we beseech thee O Lord', but many in the congregation had their own version:

Stir up, we beseech thee, the pudding in the pot
Stir up, we beseech thee, and keep it all hot.

This was particularly apt, because it was generally acknowledged that this was the day to start making the Christmas pudding, and for local shops to ensure that they had all the necessary ingredients in stock.

30 November

St Andrew's Day

St Andrew, fisherman, Apostle (brother of Simon Peter), and martyr, became the patron saint of Scotland when his remains were reputed to have been brought to Fife by St Regulus (Rule) in the eighth century. As the Scottish patron, his day was obviously more celebrated north of the border, but in England several seemingly unrelated customs also took place on the day.

In Buckinghamshire and Northamptonshire, for example, he was considered the patron saint of lacemakers, and before machine-made lace devastated the cottage industry, those involved kept the day as a holiday, and met for what they termed their 'tandering feast' (*see also* **11 December: Old St Andrew's Day**). Indeed, customs that relate to the saint often seem to begin with 'T' in English folklore: some villagers in Bedfordshire ate 'tandry cakes' on the day, and there are also isolated reports of a special bell-ringing on the day, called the 'Tandrew' bell.

There was also a somewhat bizarre custom of going into the local woods, en masse, ostensibly to hunt squirrels; but while some accounts describe the serious attempts made to kill squirrels and small animals, others indicate that the main purpose of the jaunt was to make merry with as much noise and commotion as possible. 'Squirrel hunting' was apparently quite widespread in this form. In Kent and Sussex, it took place on St Andrew's Day, but in other parts of the country it was more common on some other day: in Suffolk on Christmas Day, in Hampshire on Boxing Day (*see* **26 December: Hunting and Shooting**), in Essex on Good Friday, and in Derbyshire in early November. There is some indication that this customary invasion may have been originally a way of preserving a right of access to enclosed and/or private woods, but as all the references so far found are from the late eighteenth and nineteenth century, further research would be necessary to test this theory.

St Andrew's Day was also one of the traditional days for school-children to indulge in locking their teachers out of their schools (*see* **Barring Out**, p. 492). And one final tradition, not perhaps widely known, but reported in the *Church Times* on 22 June 1894, holds that wherever lilies of the valley grow wild, the parish church is dedicated to St Andrew.

Eton Wall Game

The famous Wall Game at Eton College in Buckinghamshire is played at various times in the year, but the big match is held on St Andrew's Day, between the Collegers (scholarship boys) and Oppidans (normal fee-payers). There are ten boys in each team: three 'walls', two 'seconds', three 'outsiders', and two 'behinds'. The leather ball is a bit smaller than a football but with two flattened sides – what Brian Shuel calls an 'oblate spheroid'. The wall against which the game is played is about 110 metres long, and has a vertical white line painted near each end; there are two goals: a door and a tree stump.

Each team tries to move the ball towards their opponents' end, and once past the white line a player tries to lift the ball against the wall with his foot. If he can achieve this, a teammate touches the ball with his hand and cries 'got it'. This scores one point, and the right to throw the ball at one of the goals. Goals score nine points, but are very rarely achieved. The game lasts about an hour and, as with most traditional 'football' games, the players spend much time in a scrum, here called the 'bully'. For the other rules (and arcane terminology), see the College website. The first recorded game was in 1766.

DECEMBER

First weekend in December

Tree-Dressing Day

Since 1990, the environment and culture charity Common Ground has encouraged English people to take part in Tree-Dressing Day on the first weekend in December, as a 'celebration of trees in city and country, in the street, village green – anywhere in the public domain. It highlights our responsibility for looking after trees and reminds us of their enormous cultural and environmental importance.'

Common Ground also supports other traditional tree-based customs (*see* **Last Sunday in May: Arbor Day; 29 June: Bawming the Thorn; Christmas: Wassailing**), along with their own Apple Day (**21 October: Apple Day**).

1 December

St Eligius' Day

St Eligius (*c.*588–660), also Loy or Eloi, was a powerful figure in seventh-century France, acting as adviser to kings Clotaire II and Dagobert I, and the Bishop of Noyon and Tournai, as well as founding monasteries and building churches. He was famed for his piety, his miracles, and for being a skilled metalworker, and his most famous exploit occurred while he was shoeing a difficult horse, when he was said to have removed its leg, applied the shoe, and re-attached the leg. He was also reputed to have taken the Devil by the nose with his red-hot blacksmith's tongs (a story also told of St Dunstan; *see* **19 May**). He was quickly taken as patron saint by metalworkers in the Low Countries, and this soon spread to England, lasting until late medieval times at least, as the charter of the London company of Blacksmiths in 1434 makes clear:

Ordinance and articles and constitution ordained and granted by the worshipful masters and wardens in the worship of the brethren of Saint Loye at the feast of Easter with all the whole Company of the craft of the blacksmiths.

Despite being widely popular in medieval England, very few churches were named after him, and his fame waned so completely that by the nineteenth century blacksmiths were claiming St Clement ('Old Clem') as their patron saint (*see* **23 November**).

6 December

St Nicholas' Day

Nicholas was Bishop of Myra, in south-western Turkey, in the fourth century, but little else is known of him. His lasting popularity is based entirely on the miraculous stories told about him, and the reputation he had for secret assistance to the needy; it was said that he possessed such a degree of holiness that he could work wonders at will. He was already immensely popular in the Eastern Church in the sixth century, and by the tenth century was equally widely known in the West, especially after his relics were transferred to Bari in 1087.

Most of the stories told of him, as recorded in the immensely influential book of saints' tales *The Golden Legend* (*c.*1260), relate how he intervened to save people in groups of three: he raised to life three boys who had been murdered, dismembered, and stored in a brine tub by a butcher; he freed three condemned men; saved three sailors and three princes; and delivered three girls from a fate worse than death:

At the time a certain fellow townsman of his, a man of noble origin but very poor, was thinking of prostituting his three virgin daughters in order

Barring Out

Barring out was a widespread custom particularly common in the northern counties of England, and also in Scotland and Ireland, from Tudor times onwards. It involved pupils taking possession of their school by locking out the staff, and keeping them out until certain demands were met, usually those relating to the perennial concerns of schoolchildren through the ages: holidays, playtimes, food, and the relaxation of corporal punishment. Barring out could take place at the end of any of the school terms, or at any other time if the scholars thought they had a major grievance, but was most common at Shrovetide and on St Nicholas' Day (6 December). Shrove Tuesday had a long history as a half-holiday for apprentices and schoolchildren, and schoolboys claimed Nicholas as their patron saint.

The custom survived into the late nineteenth century in a few places, as in this memory of Northumberland, written in 1929:

We did it every year to Mr. Brown in the old school in the village hall on the shortest day of the year after dinner; he would go round and tap at the windows, and then he would go home, and we would go home too.

But it was not always that easy:

There was a lot of big boys then, they went to school in winter, and worked out all the summer; they brought a lot of ropes to school

to make a living out of this vile transaction. When the saint heard of this, abhorring the crime he wrapped a quantity of gold in a cloth and, under cover of darkness, threw it through a window of the other man's house and withdrew unseen. Rising in the morning the man found the gold, gave thanks to God and celebrated the wedding of his eldest daughter.

He then did the same for the other two girls. As his miraculous acts concerned such a wide variety of people, he was chosen as patron saint of numerous groups, including children, sailors, unmarried girls, merchants, pawnbrokers, apothecaries, and perfumiers. He was popular with the latter group because of the beautiful odour that was said to have emanated from his tomb until long after his death.

Despite his widespread popularity, few traditional customs seem to

that day, and there were a lot of forms, and they tied all three doors, and put forms in front. Mr. Brown got one door a little open, and broke a blade of his favourite penknife trying to cut the rope, and that made him very angry, and when he got in he did thrash them. I *was* frightened. I would be in the infants or standard I.

In earlier reports, the whole affair was more formalized and sanctioned by custom, and was even mentioned in some school rules. The pupils' demands were written out and passed ('through the keyhole') to the master outside, and it was sometimes stipulated that these be written in Latin. Many masters connived in planning the 'rebellion', and thereby exerted some degree of control, but in other instances there was serious violence as the master tried to force entry. Firearms could even be used in defence, and at the High School in Edinburgh in 1595 a local magistrate who had been brought in to help was killed by the 'schot of ane pistol on the forehead out of the scholl'. It is therefore hardly surprising that local authorities and teachers all over the country fought a sustained campaign to abolish the custom. Schoolchildren tried to keep it alive, but in most places by the nineteenth century it had become little more than a token gesture to mark the end of term, accompanied by a rhyme, which was a far cry from the glories of demands written in Latin:

> **Pancake Tuesday** [or other suitable day] **is a very nice day**
> **If you don't give us a holiday, we'll all run away.**

have been associated with his day in Britain. His connection with children made his day particularly appropriate for 'barring out' ceremonies, where schoolchildren tried to keep the master out of the school until he agreed to a holiday (*see* **Barring Out**, p. 492), and also for the medieval custom of electing a **Boy Bishop** (*see* p. 494), but otherwise his appearances in the traditional calendar are sporadic. Nevertheless, St Nicholas' real claim to fame in the modern world is his central role in the development of the Santa Claus figure (*see* **Christmas: Father Christmas/Santa Claus**).

Boy Bishop

The Boy Bishop was a widespread ecclesiastical custom in which a boy – usually a chorister – was elected each year to act as bishop for a short period of time, supported by his fellow choirboys, while some of the normal juvenile tasks were carried out by the adult clergy. This role-reversal custom came to Britain from the Continent, and Ronald Hutton states that the roots of the Boy Bishop lie in the German Church, where there was already a tradition of lower clergy taking charge on certain days by the tenth century. It had reached England by the twelfth century, and it was at first centred on Holy Innocents' Day (28 December), a day on which other child-centred customs already existed, but it was soon influenced by the rapidly growing popularity of St Nicholas, the new patron saint of children. The two festivals of St Nicholas' Day and Holy Innocents' Day gave a natural beginning and end to the Boy Bishop's reign, and he was often elected on the former while his main ceremonial duties fell on the latter.

Almost all the cathedrals and other major religious centres in England had some version of the custom, although the details varied considerably. In essence, the boy was elected, either by his peers or by the real bishop's staff, and was invested with all the accoutrements of a real bishop. In this position he led processions, held services, delivered sermons, and performed all the duties of the normal clergy, except the mass itself. However, the 'role reversal' aspect of this tradition was strictly circumscribed, and only went so far. The boys were expected to behave themselves and were certainly not allowed to parody the services, or puncture the dignity of church officers or ritual. The most that was allowed was a little wry humour in the Boy Bishop's sermons, which were written by the adults. Even so, the Church authorities frequently found it necessary to lay down rules of conduct, and there was often trouble when the boys were out of sight of their masters. One of the most popular aspects of the Boy Bishop custom was when he, accompanied by a few other choristers, went round the parish over the Christmas period singing at people's houses, collecting money for the Church or, occasionally, for himself and his companions.

Sporadic attempts to create ceremonies in which girls were allowed to take on similar exalted positions were firmly stamped on by the Church authorities. Boys may have been allowed a little licence, as they would soon be men, but the idea of females stepping out of their assigned lot in life was too abhorrent to the medieval Church to be tolerated even for a short time.

Despite their apparent popularity, Henry VIII summarily banned Boy Bishops in 1541, on the grounds that they dented ecclesiastical dignity. They returned briefly under Queen Mary, only to be banned again by Elizabeth I. They were not to be seen again until the twentieth century, when periods of nostalgia and heritage consciousness led to the revival of various old church practices. Most such revivals come and go, but the strongest modern example is at Hereford Cathedral. Sometimes romanticism outweighs accuracy, and the revival mixes up traditions in interesting ways. In 1949, the journal *Folk-Lore* recorded that:

It was reported in the Daily Graphic (2 May 1949) that a Kentish vicar revived one May Day custom when, in a church packed with young people, the senior choirboy was proclaimed Boy Bishop. Later the Boy Bishop crowned the May Queen who watched a maypole dance outside the church from her floral throne.

11 December

Old St Andrew's Day

Following the change of calendar in 1752 (*see* p. xxix), some of the St Andrew's Day celebrations of 30 November were carried out by the more traditionally minded participants on the Old Style St Andrew's Day, eleven days later. Dialect collector Thomas Sternberg, for example, described the antics of the lacemakers on this day in his native Northamptonshire, which were still going strong in the mid nineteenth century:

'Tander' – Of all the numerous red-letter days which diversified the lives of our ancestors, this is the only one which has survived to our own times in anything like its pristine manner . . . Drinking and feasting prevail to a riotous extent. Towards evening the sober villagers appear to have become suddenly smitten with a violent taste for masquerading. Women may be seen walking about in male attire, while men and boys have donned the female dress, and visit each other's cottages, drinking hot 'eldern wine', the staple beverage of the season.

13 December

Aldermaston Candle Auction

One of the few surviving **candle auctions** (p. 138) takes place at Aldermaston, Berkshire, every three years on 13 December. The auction is for the lease of the land called Church Acre (although it is more than two acres in size), which was granted to the church there when the parish was enclosed in 1815. A nail is inserted into a lighted candle, about an inch from the top, and bidding continues until the nail falls to the table.

Second Thursday before Christmas

Picrous Day

Cornish tin-miners seem to have had a calendar all of their own, as their festivals were often different from those of the rest of the country. On the last Thursday before Christmas, they celebrated Picrous Day, which was reputedly named after the mythical man who discovered tin. Some called it Chewidden (White) Thursday, as tradition states that this was the day when 'white tin' (smelted tin) was first made or sold in Cornwall. Either way, the tinners claimed a holiday from work, and money to spend on drink.

See also 5 **March: St Piran's Day**.

14 December

St Tibba's Day

Tibba, and her cousin Eabba, lived in Rutland in the seventh century and were probably nieces of Penda, the King of Mercia. They were reputed to be fond of hunting, before becoming devout hermits, and were both made saints after their death. Because of her early liking for the chase, St Tibba was adopted as patroness of falconers and wildfowlers, but otherwise she is only remembered around Ryhall, where she lived and died, and where there is a well named after her. There is some disagreement about her feast day. Most sources give it as 14 December, but David Farmer's *Oxford Dictionary of Saints* (1987) gives it as 6 March.

16 December

Boar's Head

The bringing in of the boar's head is a well-known feature of Christmas past, although few people can have seen it for themselves. In the standard description, the boar's head is served on a silver or gold platter, with some considerable ceremony, at a formal banquet in a university or great house. It is carried in by the butler or other servants, is liberally decorated with bay, rosemary, and laurel, and has a lemon, orange, or apple in its open mouth. Its entrance is heralded by music (often a trumpet fanfare), and one of the attendants sings the 'Boar's Head Carol' in Latin, or at least with a Latin refrain, supported by the company on the chorus. The ceremony almost certainly dates from medieval times, although the majority of descriptions emerged much later. William Husk, for example, printed seven versions of the song that accompanies the ceremony, dating from the fourteenth century onwards, but what is generally considered to be the earliest description of the custom must be taken on trust. It appears in Holinshed's *Chronicles* of 1577 (III, 76), and relates that in the year 1170, King Henry II served a boar's head to his son.

Only the very rich could afford such extravagant fare as boars' heads, dressed peacocks, and swans for dinner, and such dishes were designed as much to impress and inspire awe in their guests as cater for physical appetites. Down the years, there have been numerous descriptions of the ceremony at the substantial Christmas feasts of the royal court, the Inner Temple, and Oxford and Cambridge colleges, but all are suspiciously similar and seem to be more self-conscious and theatrical pieces of pageantry influenced by literary references rather than genuine traditions. Indeed, with its silver platters and Latin refrains, it is hard to escape the feeling that this has always been a pseudo-custom, and it was certainly one of the stock features of the Merrie England view of Christmas created in the nineteenth century and subsequently bequeathed to the twentieth as a component of a largely mythical English golden age (*see* **Merrie England**, p. 510). An early example of this tendency can be found in Washington Irving's best-selling *Sketch-Book* (1820), in which he describes Christmas dinner with a squire who was such a 'strenuous advocate for the revival of the old rural games and holiday observances'. It is no surprise that the squire was careful to re-enact the boar's head ceremony in his own 'baronial hall', with all the necessary trappings.

Nevertheless, this may be simply a jaundiced modern view. There are some indications that the ceremony had a more popular presence, and in his *Wonderful Yeare* (1603) Thomas Dekker reveals that at this time the custom was sufficiently well known to be used proverbially, writing about those who were overly cautious of catching the plague:

They went (most bitterly) miching and muffled up and down, with rue and wormwood stuft into their ears and nostrils, looking like so many boar's heads stuck with branches of rosemary, to be served in for brawn at Christmas.

The boar's head ceremony is still carried out every year at Queen's College, Oxford, around 16 December, where, it is claimed, it has been performed continuously since the fourteenth century. A suitably academic story explains that the ceremony was founded to celebrate an exciting event: a university student was wandering about the Forest of Shotover one day, reading his copy of Aristotle, when he was suddenly confronted by a wild boar, which rushed at him. With no weapon to hand, but with great presence of mind, the student rammed his book into the open mouth of the beast and thus choked it to death.

21 December

St Thomas's Day

By far the most widespread activity of 21 December was to go 'Thomasing' or 'gooding', a custom that clearly relied on the hospitality and charity that had been part of a traditional Christmas for centuries. On this day, poor women tramped round their neighbourhood, calling at the houses and farms of their better-off neighbours, expecting to receive doles of money or food in order to 'keep a good Christmas'. Local customary rules determined who was considered eligible and who gave what; some farmers, for example, gave quantities of wheat, which explains why the custom was called 'corning' in some areas. As Thomas Grey recorded in his memoirs of cottage life in Hertfordshire in the 1870s:

The women that I knew always called at the same houses and were evidently expected, for they told me they always got a 'something' at each place of call. One gentleman gave a new sixpence each year to every 'Thomaser' at his home. I asked what they said or did when calling at the houses. Said they: 'All we ses is please we've cum a–Thomasing, remember St. Thomas's Day.'

Most accounts state that the custom was almost entirely confined to women, often with the help of their children, although sometimes old men would take part.

'Gooding' is recorded as meaning 'begging' from as early as 1560, but there is no direct evidence that the custom of visiting neighbours on St Thomas's Day is any older than the late eighteenth century, although several writers indicate that it was already well established at that time. It was extremely widely practised until the late nineteenth century, when it started to decline. It is clear that these gooding or Thomasing customs could only work in a relatively small close-knit community, where everybody knew each other and understood the local informal rules by which the tradition operated. As rural communities began to change dramatically in the second half of the nineteenth century, many local charities fell by the wayside, or changed as the givers strove to keep a degree of control over what was given, and who should receive it. Charlotte Burne, the leading folklore collector for Shropshire, reported in 1883:

It is in fact a custom very likely to be abused and to degenerate into a nuisance; the strongest, who could walk farthest, getting the greatest number of doles; several members of a family going to the same house at different times in the day, and thus getting an unfair share. In the year 1870, the farmers around Clun determined to put a stop to the begging, and instead of giving to all comers, they agreed to send their contributions of corn to the Town Hall, to be distributed under proper supervision to the deserving poor, in proportion to the size of their families . . .

However, in other places the distribution was put into the hands of the church.

See also **Doles**, p. 115.

24 December

Christmas Eve

In many ways, Christmas Eve has never had much of a character of its own and has generally been seen as a prelude to the big day. Most of the customs and traditions that have taken place on Christmas Eve, including all the various visiting customs, could also be carried out at any time over the Christmas season. However, Christmas Eve was a particularly good time for traditional 'performers' to call, as they would be fairly sure to find someone at home, and the household was likely to be filled with that customary glow of Christmas spirit. In the nineteenth and early twentieth century, the old idea of charity and hospitality at Christmas had not yet died out completely, and even if money were not forthcoming, food and drink could be almost guaranteed. In nearly every part of the country at that time, therefore, you might be visited by the mummers or guisers, who would perform their traditional play, or wassailers, who called to wish good luck or to show you their yule baby. Carol singers or waits might serenade you, and in the North-East you might see sword dancers, in Kent the Hooden Horse, or in Cornwall the guise dancers.

On farms, it was traditional to give extra food to the animals in the evening, partly to give them a Christmas treat but also in the hope that they would need less attention on Christmas Day. As indicated below (*see* **Christmas: Decorations**), the modern way of putting up decorations two weeks before Christmas would have been anathema to our great-grandparents. Most people believed it to be unlucky to decorate their home or church before Christmas Eve, and there would have been much to do to trim the tree and decorate the home with greenery. Similarly, in the days before freezers, there would have been an immense rush to get fresh and perishable food bought or delivered, and the shops would stay open very late on Christmas Eve. The yule log, ashen faggot, and Christmas candles needed to be prepared and lit, and then there was church to go to.

It is not surprising, therefore, that there was little time for other activities, but there are some reports of a few, as recorded in the *Gentleman's Magazine* of 1824:

Christmas Eve is, in Yorkshire, celebrated in a peculiar manner. At eight o'clock in the evening, the bells greet 'old Father Christmas' with a merry peal, the children parade the streets with drums, trumpets, bells, or perhaps, in their absence, with the poker and shovel, taken from the humble cottage fire; the Yule candle is lighted.

As the midnight hour grew closer, nearly every church bell would be ringing (*see also* **Ringing the Devil's Knell**, *below*), and many people would open their door to 'welcome Christmas in'. The cattle in their stalls were said to kneel down in honour of the day at this time, and the bees to hum the Old Hundredth Psalm in their hives. In addition to these beliefs, treated separately below, Christmas Eve was also regarded as a good time for love divination, and there were various procedures, some simple, some complex, to help the enquirer find out who they were destined to marry. Sidney Oldall Addy recorded a relatively straightforward method from Derbyshire in the 1890s:

If a girl walk backwards to a pear tree, on Christmas Eve, and walk round the tree three times, she will see an image of her future husband.

Christmas Eve was believed to be one of the safest times for divination, as ghosts and other spirits were said to be powerless on this night.

Ashen Faggot

A popular Christmas custom in Devon, and in neighbouring parts of Dorset and Somerset, was the burning of the ashen faggot, described here in *Bentley's Magazine* (1847):

On Christmas Eve it is the custom in all the farm-houses of this neighbourhood to 'burn the ashen faggot'. All the labourers and servants are invited and a large fire is heaped up on to the wide hearth . . . We all sat round the hearth in a circle; the fire light deepening the shadows of the hard-featured mahogany countenances around, and setting off the peculiarities of each form. The ashen faggot which lay on the hearth consists of a long, immense log of ash, surrounded with smaller branches, which are bound to it with many withies, forming one large bundle; it filled the whole hearth, and as it burned, the roaring in the large chimney was tremendous. As the fire slowly catches, and consumes the withies, the sticks fly off, and kindle into a sudden blaze, and as each one after the other gives way, all present stand up and shout with might and main; the 'loving cup' of cider is handed round, and each drinks his fill. They then resume their seats, sing songs and crack jokes, till the bursting of another band, and the kindling of a fresh blaze demands renewed shouts, and another pull at the cider flagon. The merriment is allowed to go on till nearly midnight, before which hour the worthy giver of the feast likes to have her house clear, that the 'Holy Day' may begin in peace.

All the descriptions of the custom follow a similar pattern, although they differ in some details. Sometimes a central log, with sticks bound round it, was burned, while others describe a true faggot, or bundle of sticks. Some sources specify ash, but others talk of bands of willow, or other wood.

As is often the case, the antiquarian John Brand identified the earliest known reference – 'Christmas, a Poem', written by Romaine Joseph Thorn and published in 1795, which already mentions the essential features of the custom. It is already called the 'ashen faggot', has nine 'bandages', and as each breaks:

> *A mighty jug of sparkling cyder's brought*
> *With brandy mixt, to elevate the guests.*

It is quite possible that the ashen faggot is a localized offshoot of the more widely known and older **yule log** (*see below*), as they share the same principles of festive and ceremonial burning, but at present this cannot be proved either way. Some pubs in Devon still continue the tradition.

Cattle Kneeling

In former times, it was widely believed that at the stroke of midnight, as Christmas Eve becomes Christmas Day, the cattle in their stalls knelt down in honour of the occasion, and many said that they let out a groan as they did so.

An honest countryman, living on the edge of St. Stephen's Down, near Launceston, Cornwall, informed me, October 28th, 1790, that he once, with some others, made trial of the truth of the above, and watching several oxen in their stalls at the above time, at twelve o'clock at night, they observed the two oldest oxen only fall on their knees, and as he expressed it, in the idiom

*of the country, make 'a cruel moan like Christian creatures'. I could not but
with great difficulty keep my countenance: he saw this, and seemed angry
that I gave so little credit to his tale, and walking off in a pettish humour
seemed to 'marvel at my unbelief '.*

This description, from the 1849 edition of John Brand's *Observations
on the Popular Antiquities of Great Britain*, is the first printed mention of this idea, but his wording suggests that it had already been in
circulation for a while, and it was certainly extremely well known all
over England in the nineteenth and early twentieth centuries. Indeed,
it may still be told to children in some families. Brand was also the
first to suggest that many had been influenced by popular prints of the
Nativity, which showed the cattle kneeling, which is certainly plausible. However, this is not the only belief that maintains that the natural
world follows the Christian calendar: the sun dancing for joy as it rises
on Easter Monday (*see* **Easter Monday: Sun Dancing**, p. 176) and the
Holy Thorn blossoming on Christmas morning (*see* **Christmas: Holy
Thorn(s)**) are based on the same idea. The faith of many in the truth
of the Christian religion was therefore borne out in the idea that even
the dumb beasts knew that Christmas was a special time.

People's faith in these date-related beliefs was severely tested, however, when the Gregorian calendar was introduced in 1752. Would nature follow the new rules, or stick to the old? We do not know whether
the cattle-kneeling belief was around in 1752, but as late as 1847 it was
still an issue, as reported in *Bentley's Magazine*:

*It is said, as the morning of the day on which Christ was born, the cattle in
the stalls kneel down; and I have heard it confidently asserted that, when
the new style came in, the younger cattle only knelt on December 25, while
the older bullocks preserved their genuflections for Old Christmas Day,
January 6.*

Hooden Horse

In a number of East Kent villages, up to the early twentieth century,
Christmas Eve was graced with a house-visiting custom called the
Hooden Horse. The horse consisted of a wooden head (or possibly
a real horse's skull), decorated with ribbons, brasses, and rosettes, and
was mounted on a pole about four feet long. A man (the 'hoodener')
bent over forwards to grasp the pole and was completely covered by
a dark cloth. The jaws of the head were hinged, and could be opened

and closed by the hoodener pulling a string. He was usually joined by the horse's groom or driver, who carried a whip and led him on a rope; a jockey; a character called Molly, played by a man, who carried a broom; and at least one musician. The team called at houses throughout the neighbourhood, where they would sing and play, the horse would play up and have to be restrained, and the jockey would try to ride him. They would then collect money, food, or drink, and move on.

Over thirty local versions of the Hooden Horse were recorded around the turn of the twentieth century, but all from a small restricted area of North and East Kent. Most of the teams came from areas along the coast, but a few were found in villages as far as fifteen miles inland. The tradition was fortunately well documented by Percy Maylam in his privately printed book *The Hooden Horse* (1909), but he was only just in time: the horse was then on its last legs, and there is hardly any evidence of its existence after that date.

The name has intrigued commentators on the custom, and there has been much speculation on its derivation. As far as we can tell, the locals called the custom 'oodening', and only educated writers added the initial 'h'. Nevertheless, the most likely derivation is from 'hood', because that best matches the details of the custom, although another possibility is that it is derived from 'wooden'. Two other suggestions can be dismissed out of hand: one theory is that the name is from Robin Hood (on the strength of the presence of Molly, who, it has been suggested, might represent Maid Marian), but least plausible of all is that it is a survival of the worship of the pagan god Woden, as it is quite improbable that a custom openly named after a pagan god could have survived over a thousand years of jealous Christianity.

The earliest known reference is a little ambiguous: Samuel Pegge defines 'Hooding' in his glossary of Kenticisms (1736) as

> ... *a country masquerade at Christmas time, which in Derb*[yshire] *they call guising (I suppose a contraction of dis-guising), and in other places* '*mumming*'... .

This could conceivably be a simple custom involving disguises, but the next documentary sighting, in Ramsgate in 1807, quite clearly describes the horse, and there are several other accounts from the nineteenth century confirming that the custom had changed little in that time. In fact, apart from the name, the Hooden Horse custom is not

mummers' play in Cheshire (*see* **31 October: Antrobus Soul-Cakers**),
the Mari Lwyd in Wales, and the **Old Horse** and **Old Tup** of the
Midlands (*see below*).

The traditional Hooden Horse may have died out *c*.1910, but the
postwar folk revival created many enthusiasts, and since then many
revival teams have existed in Kent, no Christmas passing without the
appearance of at least a few modern horses.

See also **Hobby Horses**, p. 226.

Old Horse

The Old Horse is both the name of a song and a dramatic Christmas
house-visiting custom, similar to the **Old Tup** or Derby Ram (*see below*). In 1903, George Addy recorded the following version of the song
that was sung during the visit:

> *It is a poor old horse*
> *And he's knocking at your door*
> *And if you choose to let him in*
> *He'll please you all I'm sure*
> *Poor old horse, let him in.*

The same writer also describes the scene in a Derbyshire farmhouse
about the turn of the twentieth century:

*What an eerie monster he looks! He opens his jaws and shuts them with a
horrid metallic sort of a rattle. His painted eyeballs stare around with a
kind of rigid deathlike smile. His lumpy hairy carcase moves uneasily on
four legs – with trousers on. He is shod with collier's clogs. The more timid of
the youngsters, on purpose to hearten each other, whisper, 'He's not real, you
know.' Meanwhile the ponderous jaws and teeth of this mechanically arranged skeleton head clash and gibber weirdly, and snap at the leg of young
Steeve, the farmer's boy. A score or so of young men have by this time trooped
into the house and dressed up in rude theatrical attire and are almost
beyond recognition.*

Young men such as these sang the 'Old Horse' song, and they were
usually accompanied by one or two other characters, including a
blacksmith, who tried to shoe the horse, which of course resisted. At
another point in the song, the horse 'died' and then revived. As in

all other visiting customs, the participants accepted food, drink, or money from the householders, and then moved on. The Old Horse custom was found in a very restricted area around Sheffield, where the counties of Derbyshire, Nottinghamshire, and Yorkshire meet, from the 1840s until the mid twentieth century.

See also **Hobby Horses**, p. 226.

Old Tup

The 'Old Tup', or 'Derby Ram', is a widely collected traditional song found in different versions all over the English-speaking world:

> *As I was going to Derby*
> *'Twas on a Derby day*
> *I saw the finest ram, sir*
> *That ever was fed on hay.*

The song concerns a ram of such prodigious size that its horns reached to the moon and each foot covered an acre of land, and it tells how a butcher killed the ram and its parts were made into useful objects.

> *And all the boys in Derby*
> *Came running for his eyes*
> *To make a pair of footballs*
> *For they were football size.*

Around Sheffield, however, the song is the basis of a Christmas visiting custom, usually performed by children. They make the ram either by simply throwing a cloth over one of their number, or by fixing a pair of horns to a pole and covering the person who holds the pole in the cloth, in exactly the same way as many hobby horses are made (*see* **Hobby Horses**, p. 226). The participants sing the song, while the ram dances about, and then they enact the killing. The custom was common in the area from the mid nineteenth to the mid twentieth centuries, and is still not quite extinct.

Ringing the Devil's Knell

Many church towers resound to peals at midnight on Christmas Eve, but at All Saints, Dewsbury, in Yorkshire, the custom is given a unique twist. Here, they engage in 'tolling the Devil's knell', or ringing 't'owd lad's passin' bell'. The bell-ringers gather at around ten o'clock at night, and commence tolling the church's tenor bell – one stroke for every year since the birth of Christ. At the rate of one stroke every two seconds or so, the whole process takes about two hours and is carefully timed to end exactly at midnight. It has been known for one person to do the lot, but more usually a relay of ringers share the task. Someone is also employed to keep track of the number of strokes on specially prepared squared paper, in order to get the number of strokes exactly right.

The popular explanation of this custom is that the tenor bell used for the toll was presented to the church by local landowner Sir Thomas De Soothill, in the fifteenth century, as penance for murdering a servant; the bell is therefore colloquially called 'Black Tom' in his memory. A more theological explanation is that the toll is to remind parishioners that the Devil died when Christ was born and it is therefore appropriate to mark his demise by ringing a passing bell – as was routinely done for the death of more mortal souls in the parish.

It is unlikely that the Soothill story is true, and it is not clear when the tradition started, but it is generally accepted that the custom had fallen into abeyance and was revived in 1828 by the Revd John Buckworth. It is believed to have been carried out every year since, except when the bells were being recast, and during the Second World War, when all church bells were silent. The custom was depicted on a Christmas postage stamp in 1986.

Although Dewsbury is the only place to greet Christmas in this way nowadays, there is evidence that other places once had analogous, if not identical, customs. In 1866, William Henderson, for example, wrote that 'at Horbury, near Wakefield, and at Dewsbury . . . is tolled the 'Devil's Knell'; a hundred strokes, then a pause, then three strokes three, three strokes, and three strokes again.' Another example of a lengthy peal comes from Gloucestershire, and is recorded in A. R. Wright and T. E. Lones's *British Calendar Customs* (1940):

The Rev. Anthony Sterry, Vicar of Lydney, gave, by deed, in 1599, a sum of 5s per annum . . . for ringing a peal on Christmas Eve, about midnight, for two hours, in commemoration of the Nativity.

Vessel Cups

The 'vessel cup' custom was one in which girls or women would go round houses on or just before Christmas Eve, displaying a doll or two in a decorated box and singing a carol or wassail song. 'Vessel' in this sense is certainly a dialect version of 'wassail', and 'cup' may perhaps indicate that this custom originated with the much more widely known wassail bowl. Another local term for the doll's receptacle was 'milly-box', presumably meaning 'my lady' box.

Vessel cups seem to have been restricted to the North-East. Most of the references to the custom are concentrated in Yorkshire, but one or two are from County Durham and as far south as Lincolnshire; however, none is earlier than the nineteenth century. As described in these sources, the custom was restricted to girls or elderly women, and it is likely that during these women's lives it had been an adult female custom, but had since degenerated into a children's activity. In 1898, local writer Richard Blakeborough documented the following version of the custom from Yorkshire:

The 'vessel-cups'...still come round, with their doll in a box, decked out as the Virgin Mary, lying in pink cotton-wool and evergreens. Some of these vessel-cups are in their way quite little works of art. I remember, up to [five years ago] Lavinia Leather travelled every year all the way from the other side of Leeds, to sing the vessel-cup throughout that part of Cleveland... There was no mistaking the advent of Christmas, when, after unceremoniously opening the door, the old lady commenced saying:

> *God bless the master of this hoos*
> *An' t' mis-ter-ess also*
> *An' all yer lahtle bonny bairns*
> *'At round yer table go!*
> *For it is at this tahm*
> *Straangers travel far an' near*
> *Seea Ah wish ya a merry Kessamus*
> *An' a happy New Year.*

The decorations around the doll varied with the skill of the bearer, but usually included standard Christmas items such as holly, mistletoe, and tinsel, along with fruit and sweets. The vessel cup was therefore an almost exact equivalent of the May dolls custom, especially when in the hands of children, and it was the 'showing' of the box that particularly seemed to matter to them. The following was recorded in the journal *Folk-Lore* (1906):

The children carrying a box never knock or ring, but open each house door and begin to sing, 'God rest you merry gentlemen.' If no notice is taken, they sing the piece over again, until someone goes to speak to them. They then ask if anyone would like to see the 'wassail box'. If no one cares to look at it, they go quietly away. They never uncover the box without first asking, 'Would you like to see the wassail box?'

Compare: **1 May: May Dolls; Christmas: Wassailing.**

Yule Log

The idea that a large log should be burning in the fireplace on Christmas Eve was almost universally acknowledged for at least 300 years. It went under various names, such as yule/Christmas log, block, clog, or brand, and could be found over most of the British Isles during that time. Those in towns may have had to make do with a token gesture, but any self-respecting country family would make the effort to obtain the real thing, as here in Herefordshire in 1886:

A respectable middle-aged labourer (say 42 or 43) tells me that in his boyhood his father was always careful to provide a Christmas Yule-Log. On Christmas morning he would put a bit saved from last year's log on the fire, and lay the new log on top of it, so that it might be kindled from the last year's piece. Before the log was quite burnt out he took it off, extinguished it, and put it by to kindle the next log from.

The yule log was already well known in the seventeenth century, as both Robert Herrick, in his *Hesperides* (1648), and John Aubrey, in his *Remaines of Gentilisme and Judaisme* (1686), refer to it in familiar terms, and Herrick also shows that in his time the idea of saving a piece for next year was already in place:

> *Come, bring with a noise,*
> *My merry, merry boys,*
> *The Christmas log to the firing;*
> *While my good dame, she*
> *Bids ye all be free,*
> *And drink to your heart's desiring.*
> *With the last year's brand*
> *Light the new block, and*
> *For good success in his spending*
> *On your psaltries play,*
> *That sweet luck may*
> *Come while the log is a-teending.*

continued on page 512 ☞

Merrie England

> England was merry England, when
> Old Christmas brought his sports again.

So said Walter Scott in his long poem *Marmion* (1808), setting the scene for a romantic view of the past that would have a profound influence on the way popular customs and traditions would be seen throughout the nineteenth and much of the twentieth centuries. Scott's phrase 'Merry England' has been adopted by historians and folklorists to describe the notion that there was a golden age in the English past, when society functioned without conflict, our rulers were just and kindly, our clergy attentive and understanding, everyone was adequately clothed, fed, and happy in their station, and contentment ruled the land. This is overstating the case a little, but it is not far off the mark for those writers who were disenchanted with the ways in which they saw the nineteenth and twentieth centuries progressing. Many hated the forces of urbanization and mechanization – in particular, the growth of factories, railways, and improved roads – which they saw gathering speed around them, and some even looked askance at education and increasing literacy, believing that these would somehow destroy the essential simplicity of the English peasant. When the present was compared to Merrie England, it was often found wanting. Washington Irving was a chief proponent of the Merrie England school:

One of the least pleasing effects of modern refinement is the havoc it has made among the hearty old holiday customs. It has completely taken off the sharp touchings and spirited reliefs of these embellishments of life, and has worn down society into a more smooth and polished, but certainly a less characteristic, surface. Many of the games and ceremonials of Christmas have entirely disappeared . . . They flourished in times full of spirit and lustihood, when men enjoyed life roughly, but heartily and vigorously; times wild and picturesque . . . The world has become more worldly. There is more of dissipation, and less of enjoyment.

Needless to say, this golden age never really existed, as the non-romantic folklorist A. R. Wright commented in 1928:

'Ye Merrie England of ye Olden Time' of stage and story, with its folk chiefly engaged in dancing around the maypole on the village

green or dragging the yule log into the baronial hall, according to the season of the year, is the creation of the romanticists and poets and painters of the nineteenth century.

In real historical terms, 'Merrie England' was somewhat loosely defined by its proponents, and could slide from era to era as the moment demanded. Feudal times were a contender, as they were considered an age when everyone knew their place and worked together for the common good, as part of an organic, interlinked society – although the small detail of the serfs' lack of freedom tarnished the era's image somewhat. At other times, the period of the Restoration was invoked as a golden age: the colourful monarchy had been returned to its rightful place, and Old Father Christmas and maypoles on the village green had replaced the joyless Puritan rule. But it was the reign of Elizabeth I, and the age of Shakespeare, that was generally considered to be the most golden of all golden ages.

Merrie Englandism is at the root of much popular historical writing from the nineteenth century onwards, but was particularly prevalent in the attitudes of those who sought to revive or recreate the customs of the past, and who tried to remodel local communities on supposedly traditional English lines. As the *Examiner* explained in 1817:

Merry Old England died in the country a great while ago; and the sports, the pastimes, the holidays, the Christmas greens and gambols, the archeries, the May-mornings, the May-poles, the country dances, the masks, the harvest-homes, the new-year's gifts, the gallantries, the golden means, the poetries, the pleasures, the leisures, the real treasures – were all buried with her.

May Day and Christmas were the two festivals most susceptible to this style of re-interpretation, although many other traditional activities, including morris dancing, rush-bearing, and well-dressing, received a similar treatment. Working with the raw data provided by the early antiquarians, a range of writers, including Walter Scott, Leigh Hunt, and Charles Dickens, sought to turn public opinion back to the past. The squire that features in Washington Irving's *Sketch-Book* (1819–20) and *Bracebridge Hall* (1822), and Mr Wardle of Dingley Dell, in Dickens's *Pickwick Papers* (1836–7), were classic creations in this mould. While their re-invention of Christmas worked directly on the middle-class families of the nation, their May Day ideas were filtered through countless organizers of local fêtes, pageants, and other gatherings. Choreographers introduced 'ancient morris dances' and maypole scenes to the stage, and artists joined in the movement, with a new genre of rustic paintings and engravings, starting with *May Day in the Reign of Queen Elizabeth* by Charles Leslie, which was exhibited at the Royal Academy in 1821.

A key characteristic of the genre was that the re-inventions were always billed as true English traditions, despite the fact that they had been concocted a short while before. The 'revivers' decided what was traditional and what was not, and it seemed that everyone was willing to be fooled. Although a few critics were not keen on all this rusticity, hardly anyone questioned its authenticity or cared to expose it, and there was no 'campaign for real traditions'. Little children dressed in white, demure May Queens, controlled processions, and tea on the village green were infinitely more acceptable than drunken morris men, or youths parading the streets throwing squibs, or farm labourers and maidservants mixing indiscriminately in unsupervised dancing booths or local pubs. Such activities were purged of their 'unsavoury' aspects, sanitized, and re-presented to a public eager for the rediscovery of its traditional heritage. In countless fêtes and May Day gatherings, and in our underlying notions of a 'real English Christmas', the spirit of the Merrie Englander lives on.

☞ *continued from page 509* The idea behind keeping part of the wood was twofold: it not only ensured that the luck of the house continued from year to year, but was also believed to offer protection against fire and witchcraft. It was also widely maintained that the log had to burn for the whole of the night of Christmas Eve, and some said all of Christmas Day as well, or the luck would disperse.

Many late Victorian and twentieth-century books include illustrations of baronial halls with impossibly large 'yule logs' burning in huge fireplaces as depictions of 'old-time' Christmases, but it is clear that for the vast majority of families rather more modest logs sufficed to fill the domestic hearth. Nevertheless, there is a sense that size mattered, and where possible a larger than life trunk would be used. Folklorist Charlotte Burne recorded:

In 1845 I was at the Vessons Farmhouse [in Shropshire] . . . *The floor was of flags, an unusual thing in this part. Observing a sort of roadway through the kitchen, and the flags much broken, I enquired what caused it and was told it was from the horses' hoofs drawing in the 'Christmas Brand'.*

Along with many of the traditional features of Christmas, the yule log 513
disappeared from most households during the twentieth century, but
it lives on in spirit, and in chocolate form.

Christmas

In 1807, thirty years before Victoria came to the throne, the poet
Robert Southey wrote:

All persons say how differently this season was observed in their fathers'
days, and speak of old ceremonies and old festivities as things which are
obsolete. The cause is obvious. In large towns the population is continually
shifting; a new settler neither continues the customs of his own province in a
place where they would be strange, nor adopts those which he finds, because
they are strange to him, and thus all local differences are wearing out.

This was the beginning of what could be termed the 'new seasonal nostalgia', when everyone agreed that Christmas was not what it was and
that something should be done about it. Over the following decades,
something was indeed done as, in modern terms, the season was rebrand-
ed and relaunched. To talk about our modern perceptions of the 'real
Christmas', or to investigate the historical development of the festival, is
thus to have a dialogue with the Victorians. They remodelled the season
so thoroughly with their inventions, improvements, and importations
that when we look at any Christmas custom our first question is what
they did with it. Crackers and cards? They invented them. Christmas
trees, stockings, Santa Claus? They imported them. Christmas presents,
Christmas dinner, Father Christmas? They remodelled them.

The Christmas of old, to which so many nineteenth-century writers were constantly hearkening, was largely a figment of their romantic
imaginations, however. It was sited in the mythical **Merrie England**
(p. 510) rather than any real historical era, but it served its purpose.
The golden age was evoked primarily to throw the contemporary festival into unflattering contrast, as a call to action, and it had many
willing readers and followers. The real genius of the Victorians was to
couple this nostalgia with a restless passion for progress, along with
straightforward commercial instincts, and so lay the foundations for
the mammoth spending sprees we experience nowadays. All those

innovations had to be manufactured or grown, packaged, shipped, and bought by the householder, who was increasingly a town dweller. Business began to do very well out of Christmas.

Broadly speaking, the Victorian ideal of Christmas spread to all parts of society in the first half of the twentieth century. Since then, crackers may have got better and bigger, paper decorations may have been augmented with plastics, fairy lights may have proliferated, trees got bigger, and growing affluence resulted in growing piles of presents, but the overall trend has been for more of the same rather than any completely new customs. However, something important has indeed been happening. Whereas the Victorians made the family the focus of Christmas, the twentieth century saw this focus shift to the child. As the century progressed, the idea that Christmas was essentially a time for children pervaded our consciousness, until we took it for granted.

It is a truism to say that there have been huge changes in the last fifty years. The increase in the number and size of presents, and the colossal amount of money spent on them, has taken the season to new commercial heights. A poor Christmas for the retail sector has serious economic consequences for the nation. The television has almost wiped out home-made entertainments, and computer games are replacing board games. But small changes are also happening all the time, and these affect the way we celebrate the season, at least outwardly. In the last twenty years or so, charities have almost cornered the Christmas-card market, and now many office-workers circulate lists of those who would prefer to give money directly to charity instead of exchanging cards. Only a few years ago, a handful of people decorated the outside of their houses with lights, and many people thought it the height of bad taste, but each year more and more households have followed the trend, and the displays get bigger and brighter. Large plastic garden figures that glow, flash, and move are now readily available in the shops.

Many of us hold interesting double standards when it comes to Christmas: we love and hate it at the same time, holding the Dickensian ideal in our hearts and minds, but happily embracing changes, large and small, when convenient. Moreover, the child-friendly nature of the modern Christmas contains its own self-reinforcing gene. Because we believe that the season is a time for children, we constantly strive to recreate for our families the Christmases of our own past – not necessarily the physical realities, but the magical atmosphere, the fun, and the warmth and safety of the family; and although many bored teenagers can only be made to tolerate it because their friends are likewise trapped by their families, when they themselves become parents they will most likely start the cycle again.

Before examining the main individual features of the post-Victorian Christmas, two important elements in the history of the festival should be examined. The first is the antique word 'Yule', and how it relates to our idea of Christmas celebrations before the medieval period. The second is the vehement attack on Christmas launched by the Puritans in the seventeenth century, when they almost succeeded in completely eradicating the festival. Both Yule and 'the time they banned Christmas' have taken on heavy symbolic meaning in the popular view of the early history of our most popular festival.

Yule

The word 'Yule' is sometimes used as a semi-synonym for 'Christmas', but in current everyday language it has the slightly false ring of the deliberately antique. The word certainly pre-dates 'Christmas' in English, but its meaning has been so vague in earlier times that it can confuse even the experts. Variations of 'Yule' existed in most Germanic and Scandinavian languages, signifying an apparently loosely defined midwinter period, although there has been no consensus on its ultimate etymology. Bede reported that our Anglo-Saxon ancestors used the word to refer to both of the modern months of December and January, and it is clear that after the conversion to Christianity it was also used as the standard word for the festival of the Nativity. 'Christmas' only entered the language around the turn of the twelfth century.

The word 'Yule' seems to have simply gone out of fashion, as 'winter', 'midwinter', and 'Christmas' took its various meanings, but it lingered longer in the areas of Danish settlement and thus remained the normal alternative dialect word for Christmas in the northern counties, the East Midlands, and Scotland. It also survived in phrases such as 'yule log', 'yule candle', and 'yule baby'.

The perceived falseness of the word probably originated with the nineteenth-century writers who deliberately adopted it to conjure up the Christmas celebrations of an earlier and largely mythical Merrie England golden age. In more recent times, this tendency has led other popular writers to assume that 'Yule' referred to a pre-Christian midwinter festival, or a suitably muscular Anglo-Saxon Christianity, and to use it as a label for their own romantic inventions.

See also **24 December: Yule Log; Christmas: Candles; Christmas: Food.**

Christmas banned

The banning of Christmas by Parliament in the mid seventeenth century is well known, but is not always understood as the culmination of a long and bitter struggle for the soul of the festival, which had been in play since the Reformation. Sixteenth-century moralists had not been averse to taking shots at the way the people celebrated the birth of Christ, and Philip Stubbes's *Anatomie of Abuses* (1583) provides us with an excellent contemporary view of these celebrations, as well as his objections to them:

But especially in Christmas time there is nothing else used but cards, dice, tables, masking, mumming, bowling, and such like fooleries. And the reason is, for that they think they have a commission and prerogative [at] that time, to do what they list, and to follow what vanity they will. But (alas) do they think that they are privileged at that time to do evil? . . . But what will they say? Is it not Christmas? must we not be merry? Truth it is, we ought both then, and at all times besides, to be merry in the Lord, but not otherwise, not to swill and gull in more than will suffice nature, nor to lavish forth more at that time than at other times. But the true celebration of the feast of Christmas is to meditate . . . upon the incarnation and birth of Jesus Christ, God and man.

These same problems have echoed down the ages, with folk being told to celebrate and be merry on one hand, and then being chastised for doing it the wrong way on the other. However, the real difference sixty years later was not simply that the Puritans were finally in charge and could take drastic action against the parts of the Christmas festivities that they disliked, but that they were against the festival of Christmas *per se*. On 8 June 1647, *An Ordinance for Abolishing of Festivals* was passed:

Forasmuch as the Feasts of the Nativity of Christ, Easter, and Whitsuntide, and other Festivals commonly called Holy-Days, have been heretofore superstitiously used and observed. Be it Ordained, by the Lords and Commons in Parliament assembled, that the said Feast of the Nativity of Christ, Easter and Whitsuntide, and all other Festival days, commonly called Holy-days,

Five years later, on 24 December, they had to try again:

*Resolved by the Parliament: That the markets be kept tomorrow, be-
ing the five-and-twentieth day of December . . . That all such persons as
shall open their shops on that day be protected from wrong or violence, and
the offenders punished. That no observation shall be had of the five-and-
twentieth day of December, commonly called Christmas Day.*

The people were granted the second Tuesday in every month for recreation and relaxation, to compensate for the loss of their old holidays. Nevertheless, the reformers scored something of an own goal
in their efforts to abolish the festival. The fate of Christmas became
a rallying point for those opposed to the new reforms, and a symbolic
personification of 'Old Father Christmas' became spokesman for the
opposition. Numerous pamphlets and prints appeared that featured
him and contrasted the miserable and gloomy piety of the Puritan
outlook with the jolliness of the traditional festivities of 'the old days'.
Opposition to the ban took many forms. Some refused to open their
shops, some continued to eat roast meat and 'Christmas pies' on the
day, and others, like the London diarist John Evelyn, went to semi-
secret church services:

[25 December 1657] *I went with my wife, etc. to London to celebrate
Christmas Day. Mr. Gunning preaching in Exeter Chapel . . . as he was
giving us the holy Sacrament, the chapel was surrounded with soldiers: all
the communicants and assembly surprised and kept prisoners by them, some
in the house, others carried away . . . These wretched miscreants held their
muskets against us as we came up to receive the Sacred Elements, as if they
would have shot us at the altar, but yet suffering us to finish the office of
communion, as perhaps not in their instructions.*

All this was swept aside in England at the Restoration, and Old Father
Christmas was triumphant. The Scottish Church, however, continued
to frown on Christmas and the direct result was the sharp divergence
between the ways the two neighbouring countries celebrated the season. Whereas the English celebrated Christmas as their major winter
festival, the Scots opted for the secular New Year, and it is only in the
last few decades that these national differences have finally begun to
break down.

Candles

The pre-Reformation Church made a point of having plenty of candles ablaze for its Christmas services, as is fitting for a celebration in the darkest days of midwinter. In much later years, there was also a strong tradition of having a special Christmas candle in homes. The 'yule candle' was much larger than an average domestic candle, being about 18 inches tall, and was often presented as a gift to regular customers by grocers and other tradesmen. They were sometimes coloured or decorated with evergreens, and were put in a place of honour in the family home and treated with respect. Several of the superstitions that surrounded the yule log were also appropriated to the candle, in particular the idea of keeping a piece until next year, for luck. It was also considered bad luck if the candle would not light easily, or if it was moved while alight, and it was even more important that no one snuffed it out, as folklorist Sidney Oldall Addy reported from the Sheffield area in the 1890s:

A candle or lamp should be left burning all night on Christmas Eve. Unless this is done there will be a death in the house.

The earliest description of a yule candle only dates from 1817, but several others appeared in the following decades, showing that it was well known before Victoria came to the throne. However, all these nineteenth- and twentieth-century descriptions come from Yorkshire, or closely neighbouring areas, and it would appear that the custom was exclusive to that county, but for a single earlier reference from elsewhere. Parson James Woodforde, of Weston Longeville, in Norfolk, casually recorded in his diary on Christmas Day 1790, 'I lighted my large wax-candle being Xmas day during tea-time this afternoon for about an hour', so it seems that the idea of a special candle had some wider and older presence at that time, although as yet it is not clear just how much.

See also 24 **December: Yule Log**.

Cards

The Christmas card is another example of how the new re-modelled Christmas, taking shape in the mid nineteenth century, stole bits and pieces from other festivals and recycled them into new customs (*see* **Christmas**, *above*). There had long been a tradition of sending New

Year verses to friends and family, but by the mid nineteenth century Christmas was already starting to steal the limelight. The first identifiable Christmas card was designed by John Calcott Horsley, at the instigation of Henry Cole, in 1843. It presented three panels, the larger one in the middle depicting a family sitting round a well-stocked table, while the outer sections showed a man and a woman in the act of giving charity to the poor and needy. The centre panel also bore the legend 'A Merry Christmas and a Happy New Year to You'. The idea caught on relatively quickly, and by the 1860s a range of cheap cards was commercially available.

One superstition concerns the pictures that can be found on Christmas cards, and is linked to the formerly widespread belief that a wild bird entering one's house spells death for someone in the family – a belief that was extended by some to include birds depicted on wallpaper, crockery, and even seasonal cards. Whereas most of us are happy to see chirpy robins on the cards we receive, others are therefore horrified. In 1955, the journal *Folk-Lore* recorded that in Gloucestershire:

A young woman told me it was a death sign to receive a Christmas card with a robin on it. This saying dashed me considerably at the time, as I had just had cards with robins printed. However, I sent them out in spite of the warning, and I am happy to say that there was no undue mortality amongst my friends that year.

The superstition was still being reported in the 1990s, so there are presumably still people who worry about such things.

Carol Singers

The mark of the astonishing success of the modern Christmas as a popular festival is that it can be all things to all people, and within its elastic parameters each person has plenty of room for individual choices. Christmas carols are just one seasonal element among many, but even here there are various ways in which we encounter them. We may sing them at school, hear them piped around the supermarket ad nauseam, or performed by a group in period costume at the shopping centre, in aid of charity, or in a splendid ecclesiastical setting. In his book *The English Folk Carol* (1967), Douglas Brice writes, 'One of the most wonderful experiences that can come the way of anyone living in the north-west of England is to be present in the Anglican cathedral in Liverpool for the annual Carol Service at Christmas time.'

However, we all know, in our Dickensian hearts, that carol singers should be heard through a cottage window on a clear cold frosty night in deepest rural England. This may be an unattainable dream for most of us nowadays, but it was indeed the reality only a hundred years ago, as shown by author Alison Uttley's memories of Derbyshire Christmases about 1890:

She hung her stocking at the foot of the bed and fell asleep. But soon singing roused her, and she sat up, bewildered. Yes, it was the carol-singers. Margaret came running upstairs and wrapped her in a blanket. She took her across the landing to her own room, and pulled up the linen blind. Outside under the stars she could see the group of men and women, with lanterns throwing beams across the paths and on to the stable door. One man stood apart beating time, another played a fiddle and another had a flute. The rest sang in four parts the Christmas hymns, 'While shepherds watched', 'Come all ye faithful', and 'Hark the herald angels sing' ... They trooped, chattering and puffing out their cheeks, and clapping their arms round their bodies, to the front door. They were going into the parlour for elderberry wine and their collection money. A bright light flickered across the snow as the door was flung wide open. Then a bang, and Susan went back to bed.

The songs in today's basic carol repertoire are a pleasantly mixed hotchpotch of different periods and styles, although we like to think of them as timeless. A few are indeed traditional, in the sense that they originated before the mid nineteenth century and show signs of transmission over the generations by informal means, and usually their authors are not known; these include 'The Holly and the Ivy', 'God Rest Ye Merry, Gentlemen', 'As I Sat on a Sunny Bank', and 'The Cherry Tree Carol'. But most are the work of nineteenth-century enthusiasts. Some are American: 'We Three Kings of Orient Are' was written *c.*1857 by Dr John Henry Hopkins of Williamsport, and 'Away in a Manger' was first published in the American Lutheran collection *A Little Children's Book for Schools and Families*, in 1885. 'Silent Night' was written by parish priest Joseph Mohr and schoolteacher/organist Franz Gruber, of Hallein, Austria, in 1818, but 'While Shepherds Watched' is older, being written by Irish clergyman Nahum Tate and Nicholas Brady *c.*1700. While modern carols are written all the time, adding to the repertoire of choirs and professional singers, few new pieces have tunes that are sufficiently memorable to really catch on with the public.

Crackers

The Christmas cracker was invented by London confectioner Tom Smith, in 1847. He got the original idea from seeing *bon-bons* – sugared almonds sold in twists of tissue paper – on sale in Paris in 1840, and although he experimented with the idea for a few years, he was inspired to invent the essential 'snapper' after seeing a log crackling in the fire. The new Christmas novelty was an immediate success, and the firm of Tom Smith's was the leading cracker manufacturer in Britain for the next 150 years, with countless variations on the basic design.

Decorations

Until 150 years ago, the term 'Christmas decorations' simply meant evergreens and candles. Churchwardens' accounts throughout the sixteenth and the first half of the seventeenth century often include payments for plants at Christmas, and we know from John Stow's *Survey of London* (1598) that homes and streets were also decorated in the same way. All kinds of plants seem to have been used, including mistletoe, box, laurel, cypress, yew, rosemary, and bay, or, as Stow commented, 'whatsoever the season of the year afforded to be green'. However, holly and ivy were unquestionably the perennial favourites. Robert Herrick's oft-quoted poem 'Ceremonies for Candlemasse Eve' (1648) cautions readers to take decorations down on the day, and includes the usual items:

> *Down with the rosemary and the bays*
> *Down with the mistletoe*
> *In stead of holly, now up-raise*
> *The greener box (for show).*

And in 1827, a correspondent to the *Gentleman's Magazine* referred to decorations in Surrey:

Then may be seen the windows, the mantel-pieces, and the well-arranged kitchen shelves, clothed in the green holly with its scarlet berry, while in the hall of the hospitable mansion, in the farm house, and even in the humble labourer's cottage, the mystic mistletoe has its share of attraction – frequently suspended from the ceiling, in a large cluster of boughs rich in green leaves and white berries – the mirth-exciting challenger of youth, and the test of maiden coyness. Every kiss beneath it is entitled to the forfeiture of a berry fresh plucked from the bough; and it sometimes happens that ere the Christmas holidays are over the branches and the leaves are all that can be seen of the mistletoe.

It seems that there was little change from Herrick's time to the Victorian watershed, apart from during the Interregnum, when Christmas was banned. However, as in so many other spheres, the Victorians could leave nothing 'unimproved'. New tastes, new sensibilities, and new technology were brought to bear on decorations as on every other aspect of English culture. The *Girls Own Paper* of Christmas 1887 recorded the changing mood:

In this progressive nineteenth century Christmas decorations in churches have attained their highest perfection. Many of our readers may still remember the time when they simply consisted in garnishing the square, high-backed pews with small sprays of scarlet-berried holly, while large, clumsy boughs of box and laurels were distributed promiscuously over the sacred building, with no regard to fitness or symmetry.

Many houses held to the traditional ways for some time, but the scale of the operation had grown. J. S. Fletcher recalled his childhood Christmases in Yorkshire in the 1870s:

On Christmas Eve they completed the decorations. Nowadays one never sees the decorations which everybody used to put up at that time. Every parlour and kitchen in the house was liberally ornamented with holly, ivy, laurel, box, and yew. The kitchens were like green bowers, for the men-servants and maid-servants gave all their spare time to decorating them for a week before Christmas. You may be quite certain that sprigs of mistletoe hung in every room and in every doorway. In those days they knew nothing of the new-fangled importation of German ideas about Christmas, from which we suffer nowadays.

However, for the first time choices were available. Hannah Cullwick, working as a servant in London about the same time as J. S. Fletcher was growing up in Yorkshire, recorded some Christmases in her diary, and occasionally mentioned the decorations. In the 1870s, she was working as general maidservant in a London house, along with a German girl called Clara:

[24 December 1871] I wanted them both to come and see Clara's German way o' decorating for Christmas first thing in the morning . . .

[25 December] Clara was up at 5 o'clock, hammering in the kitchen I could hear but we wasn't to come down afore 7 to see it all finish'd and ready. It was certainly very gay-looking and pretty. Colour'd paper cut and done in festoons all round the top o' the kitchen, and holly trimmings around the lower part [and on] one side o' the kitchen hung a picture of Jesus in the manger, Joseph and Mary and the wise men, and the oxen there too in the stall. Then under the picture was a table spread with presents for each of us, and nuts, biscuits and oranges too, and in the middle was the box o' music playing and a dozen colour'd candles burning. All very pleasing and gay to the senses, but with it all I felt afraid it was too much, too much for Missis to hear of, and Miss Margaret to see, for Missis wouldn't allow us 6d worth of holly and have none themselves.

Little of this would have seemed out of place in an English kitchen a few years later.

One aspect of Victorian Christmas decoration that is not so popular nowadays is the making of mottoes. Although many people still buy a banner, large or small, saying 'Merry Christmas', in the Victorian middle-class home, and church, one of the central features was a lovingly hand-crafted motto proclaiming a suitable text such as 'Peace and Goodwill to All'. These were made in a wide variety of ways, including the use of flower petals and leaves to spell out the words, and they were given pride of place in the room, or the church. On 25 December 1862, George James Dew of Lower Heyford, Oxford, recorded in his diary that:

Heyford church is more neatly decorated this Christmas than it has been before in my recollection. As you enter the church over the porch doorway is 'Emmanuel' in large letters made of bay leaves. The front of the gallery has a border of evergreens with 'Unto us a Child is Born' made of variegated ivy; the word 'Child' is on the middle panel and larger than the rest which gives it an appearance of neatness and good style. On the chancel arch is 'Glory to God in the Highest' made in holly leaves ... Taking it as a whole it is very prettily and neatly arranged.

Christmas decorations were being taken more seriously than ever before, and the pressure was on for more tasteful arrangements, brighter colours, and new materials. Developments can be traced through the issues of popular magazines, especially those aimed at women and girls, which started to run regular pieces on what and what not to do, and set the pattern for the countless articles that still appear every year. One of the many problems on which advice was regularly sought was how to manage in towns, where real evergreens were either hard to come by or not up to standard, for example when the holly for sale had no berries. However, the *Girls Own Paper* for 11 December 1880 had the answer:

Ivy berries or dried peas dyed red (a sixpenny bottle of dye will be sufficient for a very large quantity); or, putty rolled into little balls and coloured either in the same way or in a solution of sealing wax mixed with spirits of wine; or red wax, to be bought at an oil shop, and shaped into berries after slightly softening before the fire. There are many different sorts of red berries to be had in the autumn, which, by soaking in strong salt and water, will keep till Christmas time, and may well pass for holly. And, lastly, easiest of all, artificial berries are sold in bunches very cheaply at most toy shops.

A number of superstitions clustered around Christmas decorations until relatively recent times, but the only real remnant is the question of when they should be taken down, and here again there has been a major sea change. As indicated in Herrick's poem, quoted above, in the mid seventeenth century Christmas decorations were expected to stay in place until Candlemas (2 February), and this remained the norm until the nineteenth century. This may seem a long time, but until the late nineteenth century it was usual to put up home and church decorations on Christmas Eve, and although offices and shops might steal a few days' march, nobody would have thought of putting them up before Christmas week. Nowadays, it is quite common to see home decorations in place two weeks before Christmas Day, and some shops even signal the start of the season in the last two weeks of November. During the Victorian era, however, the Christmas season was dramatically shortened, and people began to remove decorations in early January. It is now almost universally agreed that the day for removing the decorations is Twelfth Night, and that it is 'unlucky' to leave them any longer. But now that Twelfth Night has lost all other meaning, many people think that the Christmas decorations begin to look a bit sad after the New Year celebrations, and it is quite likely that the trend will develop towards removing them around 2 January.

There is little else to concern even the most superstitious among us today, but for the Victorians there was plenty to worry about in this sphere. In 1874, *Notes & Queries* recorded:

It is still a prevailing idea, in some places, that if their decorations be not cleared out of the church by Candlemas Day (2 February), there will within the year, be a death in the family occupying the pew in which a berry or leaf is to be found on the later festival. Mr. Glyde, in his Norfolk Garland, quotes an East Anglian authority as follows: 'An old lady whom I knew was so persuaded of the truth of this superstition that she would not be contented to leave the clearing of her pew to the constituted authorities, but used to send her servant to see that her own seat, at any rate, was free from danger.'

Similarly, bringing holly into the house at any time except Christmas was believed to result in a death. It was also widely believed that the two common types of holly, prickly and smooth, were, respectively, male and female, and that whichever type of holly was brought into the house first determined who would be the master in the coming year. Some people were not keen on ivy, as it reminded them of cemeteries, and made sure it did not dominate in the house.

However, the burning question, quite literally, of the late nineteenth century was what to do with the evergreens when they were taken down. Some people held that they should be burnt, as soon and as completely as possible. But another camp recoiled in horror at this idea, and treated their old decorations with ceremony, even reverence. Some fed them to the farm animals to ensure that they shared in the household's luck, while others laid them carefully on the rubbish heap. It is reasonably clear from the documentary evidence that this is another of the changes that occurred in mid Victorian times. Up to the 1860s, it was commonplace to burn the decorations, and it is only from that point on that people started to worry about it.

One thing the Victorians did not invent was kissing under the mistletoe. Indeed, one of the worries expressed by traditionalists when the Christmas tree began to make inroads into British homes was that it would replace the traditional 'kissing bough'. The latter was the centrepiece of decoration in the early nineteenth century, made in various ways but usually with two hoops set at right angles to make a globe, or a horizontal hoop with vertical semi-circles to make a 'crown' . This was then covered in greenery, with holly predominant, and a large bunch of mistletoe hanging in the centre, and the whole thing was suspended from the ceiling. As already shown, mistletoe formed part of the Christmas greenery since at least the sixteenth century, but we cannot find a mention of kissing underneath it before the 1813 edition of John Brand's *Observations on the Popular Antiquities of Great Britain* – although other references soon afterwards show it was already well known by that time. Charles Dickens gives a delightful picture of Christmas in a country farmhouse in his *Pickwick Papers* (1837), in which the branch of mistletoe hanging from the kitchen ceiling causes such a scene of 'struggling and confusion' and hiding in corners, as the men try to capture and kiss the women, and some maids indeed were so confused that they stood under the branch without realizing it.

Most people nowadays say that the kissing is 'for luck', but a number of ancillary beliefs accrued to the custom in the past. It was believed that any girl who was not kissed, for example, would not get married in the coming year, but that a maiden could dream of her future husband by putting some of the mistletoe under her pillow at night. In an echo of the controversy about burning decorations, some clinched the argument by asserting that 'If mistletoe be not burned all couples who have kissed beneath it will be foes before the end of the year.' It was also believed that mistletoe protected the house from being struck by lightning, but that power is also claimed of many other plants.

A word has to be said about the supposed 'pagan origins' of Christmas decorations. It is usually assumed that the pre-Christian inhabitants of what later became England celebrated the winter solstice by decorating their houses and temples with greenery, but there is no evidence that this was the case, and it is yet another example of a later assumption being used to colour in a past of which we know very little. Another groundless but persistent notion is that mistletoe was officially banned from Christian churches because of its pagan connotations. The idea stems from the well-known description by Pliny, *c.* AD 77, that speaks of Druids holding mistletoe sacred and harvesting it with a golden sickle. However, there is plenty of evidence that mistletoe was once used in Christian churches and homes, along with other evergreens, and it is quite clear that the question of the suitability of mistletoe has only been raised since antiquarians and learned clergymen started reading Pliny about 1,600 years after his time. Indeed, on closer inspection, it can be seen that the notion is based in any case on a series of assumptions: firstly, that Pliny was correct in his description; secondly, that what was written about Gaul was also true of England; thirdly, that the mistletoe ceremony lasted for another 500 years until Christianization, despite the huge upheavals of Romans leaving and Anglo-Saxons settling; fourthly, that the early English churches knew about the mistletoe ceremony and were sufficiently worried to ban this, and only this, plant from their churches; and finally that they did so without leaving any trace in any written laws or regulations. Nevertheless, groundless as it is, there are still occasional reports of local vicars trying to ban the plant from their churches on the grounds of its pagan connotations.

Entertainments

The cake and the nut-brown ale, the toast and the rich elder wine, are freely dispensed to every visitor, and the usual distinctions of rank are in a great degree forgotten amid the general hilarity of the season. It is the holiday of every class, and mirth and good-fellowship reign without control.

Gentleman's Magazine (1827)

Aside from food and drink, the most commonly mentioned desirable for a proper Christmas has long been a good helping of 'mirth and good-fellowship', but with a degree of social conscience. Most of the nineteenth-century writers who bemoaned the Christmas festivities at that time harked back to a golden age of previous generations, focusing on universal hospitality and charity. To a certain extent, they were hankering for a romanticized **Merrie England** (p. 510), but it is true that a strong tradition of hospitality had existed since medieval times and still lingered into the Victorian era. Rural landowners often provided a communal feast for their tenants, farmers for their workers, and others entertained the poor. William Holland, parson of Overstowey, Somerset, from 1779 to 1819, entertained various people from the community in his rectory, and he often recorded his Christmas Day activities in his diary:

[25 December 1799] *The kitchen was tolerably well lined with my poor neighbours, workmen, etc. Many of them staid till past ten o'clock and sang very melodiously. Sent half a crown to our church musicians who had serenaded the family this cold morning at five o'clock.*

Games played by the family have long been another feature of the season, and although the Victorians are rightly credited with making the family the focus of Christmas (*see* **Christmas**), there are indications that family games were played in some quarters well before their time, albeit to a lesser degree. Accounts of earlier festivities often mention what could be called 'parlour games', some of which are still recognizable, while others have gone completely out of fashion: *Round About Our Coal Fire* (1740) lists 'Blind Man's Buff and Puss in the Corner, Questions and Commands, Hoop and Hide, cards and dice', while the *Gentleman's Magazine* of 1828 comments that 'Blind Man's Buff, Hunt the Slipper, the Game of Goose, Snap Dragon, Push Pin, and dancing, form the amusements of the younger part of the assemblage; whilst cards occupy the elders'.

Blind Man's Buff, also known under other names, including 'Hoodman Blind', has a particularly long history. It was first mentioned by name in the sixteenth century, but fourteenth-century illustrations in the Bodleian Library, first published by Joseph Strutt in his *Sports and Pastimes of the People of England* (1801), clearly depict the same game, and it has remained popular until the present day. Many writers have referred to it over the years, including Samuel Pepys, Oliver Goldsmith, Emily Tennyson, and Charles Dickens. In earlier times, the game was rougher than it tends to be nowadays; the word 'buff' means a blow, and the blindfolded player could be buffeted by the others, using their hoods or knotted scarves.

Snap Dragon was also mentioned frequently as a Christmas diversion, but it is unlikely that anyone plays it now, and certainly not if children are around. Raisins were placed in a dish of lighted brandy, and players had to snatch the fruit and eat it without getting burnt, which could only be done with quick decisive movements. Another perennial favourite for the season was cards, and even those who did not play cards during the rest of the year were often persuaded to play at Christmas.

Dancing was a key element of the Christmas party for centuries, which is one of the reasons why the Puritans disliked the festival so much. Thomas Hardy, writing in the 1870s of a previous Dorset generation to his own, provided a slightly romanticized but essentially accurate description of a Christmas party that tranter (horse and cart purveyor) Reuben Dewy and his wife Susan threw for their neighbours and friends, in *Under the Greenwood Tree* (1872). The evening is spent eating and drinking and being sociable, and after a while there is singing, too, and everyone performs their party piece. The young people are ready to dance at ten o'clock, but their elders insist that no 'jigging' take place until after the holy day itself has expired. At the stroke of midnight, the band strikes up, men remove their jackets, and for the next few hours country dances like the Triumph, and Step and Fetch Her, are performed with vigour or grace, depending on the skill and character of the individual dancer. They shortly reach a point where the movement, the music, and the heat seem to possess the cottage room:

. . . when the very fiddlers as well as the dancers get red in the face, the dancers having advanced further still towards incandescence, and entered the cadaverous phase; the fiddlers no longer sit down, but kick back their chairs and saw madly at the strings with legs firmly spread and eyes closed, regardless of the visible world.

Hardy was a fiddler himself, so he must have known all this from first-hand experience. Charles Dickens described a similar farmhouse scene in the *Pickwick Papers* (1837), but higher up the social scale dances will have been less vigorous, with waltzes and quadrilles, but no less enjoyable for the participants.

One element of Christmas past that has virtually disappeared is storytelling. From at least the eighteenth century onwards, there was a very strong tradition of the family gathering to tell stories round the fire which, at this season at least, was often a 'roaring' one. A Christmas storytelling session would almost always be dominated by stories of the supernatural – ghosts, witches, fairies, hobgoblins, and the Devil himself. These tales were all the more scary for the youngsters present because they usually referred to people and places in the immediate neighbourhood, so that many a listener dreaded going to bed, or worse, going outside, for the rest of the evening. They may have drawn some comfort from the widespread notion that Christmas Day was the one day of the year when evil was reputed to have been powerless. Storytelling has long been replaced by radio and television programmes, but the feeling that the time is appropriate for ghost stories still lingers in the media schedules, although it has now been eclipsed by Hallowe'en.

Nevertheless, Christmas was not all polite parlour games, dances, and stories. Some families had broader tastes, and although their entertainments were not usually recorded for posterity, we occasionally get a glimpse of them in a memoir, as in the following description by Derek Sheffield of his family gatherings in Kent in the 1930s:

Most of the games were very physical and earthy in the extreme, but that was country humour; it made us laugh. All would be cleared away, the washing-up done, and the best table cloth laid in preparation for the next event of the day: my Uncle Bill's particular forte, an indoor firework display. A tin tray would be put on the table, and on it would be placed a tissue paper taken from one of the crackers with a map printed on it. One would place a lighted cigarette on the spot marked with an X, and it smouldered away and finally exploded with a sharp bang which would make everyone leap out of their skins. Things would get more interesting, with more adventurous and more revolting fireworks in the form of small pyramids which, when ignited, would give off dense clouds of smoke, splutter like a sparkler, and emit a strange worm-like object that grew at an incredible rate and writhed all over the table, causing the ladies to scream with pretended horror and come over all faint. The pièce de résistance was a white statuette of a little boy about six inches high and made from plaster. He was in crouching position with his trousers down around his ankles, his shirt up over his back, and his bottom exposed for all to see. We waited with baited breath for what was to come – Uncle Bill, by this time laughing so much that he could hardly see, would poke a special indoor firework into the statuette's rear end and light it with a match, the result being that it would begin to blow smoke rings. It would then start to spark and splutter, which would make us weep with hysterics, and finally a large worm-like object would emerge and begin to crawl all over the table. The men would make all sorts of ribald remarks, much to the annoyance of the women. 'I reckon he's bin on one of mother's plum pies,' Grandad would say.

Father Christmas/Santa Claus

The Christmas festival had been personified in song, poetry, and drama centuries before the character of the modern Father Christmas emerged in the late Victorian period. There was a Sir Christmas, for example, in a mid fifteenth-century carol, and Lords of Misrule of the period, appointed to organize the season's festivities at the royal court and in other noble families, were sometimes given titles such as Captain or Prince Christmas. In the pamphlet war during the Puritan attack on the festival in the 1650s, Old Father Christmas emerged as the symbol and spokesman of the 'good old days' of feasting and good cheer, in stark contrast to the gloomy piety offered by the reformers, and from the Restoration to the mid nineteenth century this same character continued to be regarded as the presiding spirit of the festival. Nevertheless, he had a fairly low profile, and none of these pre-Victorian Christmas characters had any connection with presents, nocturnal visits to children, or any of the other trappings of the modern Father Christmas. By the early days of Victoria's reign, however, he had begun to take on a much more active role, as Christmas itself was remodelled (*see* **Christmas**). He started to appear regularly in illustrated magazines, in a wide variety of costumes, but was almost always jolly-faced and bearded, and usually wore holly on his head. He was often surrounded with pictures of plentiful food and drink, and with images of people enjoying themselves. Yet this proto-Father Christmas was in for a great shock, as the figure of Santa Claus was about to appear on the scene.

The development of Santa Claus in America is well known, although some of the details still need to be pinned down. His main creator, Clement C. Moore (1779–1863), an Episcopal minister in New York, is not remembered for his life's work, the *Hebrew and English Lexicon*, but for a poem he composed for his children – 'The Visit of St. Nicholas', now universally known by the title based on its first line, 'The Night Before Christmas'. It was published in 1822, but, despite its immense success, Moore was not proud of his poem and refused to acknowledge authorship for over twenty years. Basing his invention on Dutch folklore, Moore gave to the world St Nicholas as a nocturnal Christmas gift-bringer, with sleigh, reindeer, and a sack of toys on his back, who entered the house via its chimney and filled children's stockings with toys and sweets. The verses imply that St Nicholas is small and elf-like, although he has a jolly rounded shape, and the sleigh is 'miniature' and the reindeer 'tiny'. However, Moore neglected to describe St Nicholas' costume, or even mention its colour, which led to great confusion over the following decades.

'St Nicholas' was soon shortened to Santa Claus, and as he featured in stories such as Susan Warner's *Carl Krinken; or the Christmas Stocking*, published in New York and London in 1854, the details of his visits on Christmas Eve became known to most American families. However, his physical appearance had not yet become fixed. Thomas Nast, illustrating an influential edition of Moore's poem in 1881, depicted Santa as white-bearded, fat, and jolly, and wearing a belted jacket similar to the one he is shown wearing today, but other artists of the time dressed him in a variety of costumes, and even in the early twentieth century he could be portrayed as wearing a green or blue outfit. The well-known Coca-Cola advertising campaign of 1931 put the seal of international mass media approval on the red costume.

Santa Claus seems to have reached England in the 1860s, at the time when many other Christmas innovations, such as stockings, crackers and cards, were being introduced, and slowly but surely Father Christmas took on Santa's attributes so that the two are now, to all intents and purposes, indistinguishable. Nevertheless, some English people still prefer their children to say 'Father Christmas' in preference to 'Santa', nearly 150 years after Santa's importation to England.

Attempts to trace Santa Claus back to shamans of Siberia, whose religious ecstasies were reputedly fuelled by magic mushrooms, are far-fetched and unnecessary.

Food

The one enduring feature of Christmas, since records began, has been the desire to eat well at the season. The wealthy would indulge in huge, lavish banquets during the festival, but they could do that at any time of year. For the vast majority of the population, Christmas was the one time when they could hope to have something special on the table, in sufficient quantity, and everyone tried hard to achieve at least some semblance of a feast. However, it should be remembered that before the mid twentieth century many people could not afford what the rest took for granted. For all the talk of turkeys and geese, many nineteenth-century families were delighted to get a couple of rabbits, or any meat at all, for their Christmas dinner. The strong tradition of charity at Christmas therefore played an important role in providing something special for the poor family's table, especially in rural areas. Farmers often gave a bird or joint to their workers as a sort of Christmas bonus, and paternalistic squires provided meals for poor tenants and workhouse residents. Local clergymen also did the same on a smaller scale, but the effectiveness of this type of charity was naturally patchy, and it only functioned properly in a stable hierarchical society. It also came with the price of expected servility and gratitude on the part of the 'deserving poor'.

Asked to name the staple foodstuffs of the modern Christmas season, most people would answer, 'Turkey, Christmas pudding, Christmas cake, and mince pies.' Even if we choose to ignore tradition and eat something completely different, we know that these four items will be on countless tables each year; and even though we, too, can eat them at any other time of year if we wish, many still feel that these four foodstuffs are an intrinsic part of the season. Each of these items has a long history, but numerous other festive foods, now completely forgotten, were just as popular on a national scale, and an even greater number were eaten at a regional or local level but were not known outside their own area. Add to this the class differences within society, and it is very difficult to summarize seasonal food adequately.

The main meat for the Christmas dinner has always had a high profile and has varied considerably over the past 500 years. The three most widely known staples were roast beef, goose, and turkey. Roast beef had long been the symbolic staple of English food, and until the nineteenth century it was by far the most often quoted symbol of good food at Christmas. As a character in the typical Hampshire mummers' play declaims:

> *Roast beef, plum pudding, and mince pie*
> *Who likes that any better than I?*

Although turkey and goose gradually replaced roast beef as the archetypal Christmas fare, many traditionalist families stuck firmly with beef throughout the Victorian period. Turkeys were already being bred and eaten in Britain in the mid sixteenth century and were quickly associated with Christmas in the more wealthy sections of the community. They joined the ranks of swans, peacocks, and other exotic birds that were regularly served at banquets, and they filtered down the social scale only very gradually. However, by the mid nineteenth century, broadly speaking, the middle classes were eating turkey and the poor ate goose, the turkey only achieving full dominance during the first half of the twentieth century. Geese were considerably cheaper than turkeys, but whatever meat was chosen for the Christmas dinner, it was usually out of the range of most working people's pockets, and one very useful Victorian invention for the working family was the 'goose club', in which members would pay a small sum each week to save up for their Christmas bird or joint of meat. Clubs were organized on a very local scale by pubs, provision dealers, or on an ad hoc basis between members, and they varied widely in what they offered in addition to the basic goose, with some managing to throw in a Christmas pudding or bottle of something in addition to the bird. One standard feature, however, was the drawing of lots to decide who got what. The geese, when delivered for distribution to club members, would vary in size and quality, and lots would be drawn by some impartial person, to ensure fairness. The meeting of the goose club was a convivial event in itself, and some reformers criticized the whole business as leading people to drink, but goose clubs served a very useful purpose, and the idea continued throughout the twentieth century in the form of various Christmas clubs offered by local shops and businesses.

The other convention which has now disappeared is the use of a communal oven to cook the dinner. Few ordinary families, in country or town, had ovens big enough to take a whole turkey or goose, and it was quite common for the whole community to take their main meat to the local baker's shop to be cooked. Around dinner time a procession of figures could be seen, often consisting of the older children of the family, carefully carrying the cloth-covered dinner back home; and woe betide anyone who dropped the precious burden on the way.

Mince pies, also called shred pies, were already associated with Christmas in the later sixteenth century, but they have changed dramatically since that time. Until the mid nineteenth century they contained real meat, but this was gradually replaced by the dried fruit and spices that we know today, when 'mince-meat' superseded 'minced meat'. Their shape has also changed. They were formerly oblong, and generally referred to as 'coffins', although it was popularly believed that the shape commemorated the manger in which the newborn Christ was laid.

In its earliest form, from at least the fifteenth century, the forerunner of the Christmas pudding also contained meat. It was generally known as 'plum pottage', and was made from chopped beef or mutton and onions, together with dried fruit, breadcrumbs, wine, herbs, and spices. The 'plum' in the name refers to the dried fruit – prunes, raisins, etc. – and the dish was much runnier than the modern pudding. The meat was gradually replaced by suet, and the classic spheroid shape was attained when the mixture became much thicker and boiling in a cloth became the norm. The nineteenth-century version was extremely dense and had to be boiled for many hours; the trend in modern times has been for lighter mixtures.

Moving on to less familiar items, there was a wide range of delicacies that would surprise the modern Christmas diner. Haggis, for example, hardly sounds like an English Christmas dish, but in one form or another it was regularly eaten in the counties that border on Scotland, as recorded in John Brockett's *Glossary of North Country Words* (1825):

Haggis – A north country dish . . . It was, till lately, a common custom among the peasantry of the North of England, to have this fare to breakfast every Christmas-day; and some part of the family sat up all night to have it ready at an early hour. It is now used at dinner on the same day. Sold, savoury and hot, in the Newcastle market.

It is clear from the numerous accounts that **frumenty** (p. 536) was also regarded as a particular delicacy at Christmas almost everywhere, although it was eaten at other times of the year as well. Another regular Christmas speciality, especially in Victorian northern England, was the 'yule dough' or 'yule baby', described by William Brockie in his collection of Durham superstitions and legends in 1886:

And when the child wakens in the morning, sure as fate, in the stocking is a Christmas pie – a yule dough, which is a bit of rich paste rolled out, cut, and baked in the shape of a little baby.

Like a gingerbread man, the yule baby had currants for eyes and buttons, and sometimes the figure was of a mother holding a baby in her arms.

The Christmas cake as we know it today was simply transferred from Twelfth Night (*see* **6 January: Twelfth Night**), but many other sorts of cake were found in different parts of the country. In Cornwall in the 1870s, according to the *Folk-Lore Journal* (1886):

In some parts of the county it is customary for each household to make a batch of currant cakes on Christmas-eve. These cakes are made in the ordinary manner, coloured with saffron, as is the custom in those parts. On this occasion the peculiarity of the cakes is that a small portion of the dough in the centre of each top is pulled up and made into a form which resembles a very small cake on the top of a large one, and this centre-piece is usually called 'the Christmas'. Each person in a house has his or her especial cake, and every person should taste a small piece of every other person's cake. Similar cakes are also bestowed on the hangers-on of the establishment, such as laundresses, sempstresses, charwomen, etc., and even some people who are in the receipt of weekly charity call, as a matter of course, for their Christmas cakes. The cakes must not be cut until Christmas-day, it being probably 'unlucky to eat them sooner'.

In East Anglia, there were kichels, as described in Edward Moor's dictionary of the Suffolk dialect in 1823:

Frumenty

Frumenty, or frumety, but often pronounced 'furmety', was both a staple and festive dish often mentioned but rarely described in detail, presumably because its very familiarity made it unnecessary. Its name is derived from the Latin *frumentum*, meaning 'corn'. The basic ingredient was wheat boiled in milk, but as it was made both for everyday use and for ceremonial and festival occasions (especially Christmas), it would have had several degrees of richness and tastiness, depending on the context. The following three descriptions indicate something of the range of variation:

The typical method of preparation was to parboil wholegrains of wheat in water, then strain off and boil in milk, sweeten the boiled product with sugar, and flavour with cinnamon and other spices.

A receipt, three hundred years old, runs thus: 'Take clean wheat and bray it in a mortar till the hulls be all gone off, and seethe it till it burst, and take it up and let it cool; and take clean, fresh broth and sweet milk of almonds, or sweet milk of kine, and temper it all, and take yolks of eggs. Boil it a little and wet it down and mess it forth with fat venison or fresh mutton'.

Somerset–Wiltshire: About forty years ago country women in shawls and sun bonnets used to come to the market at Weston-super-Mare in little carts carrying basins of new wheat boiled to a jelly, which was put into a large pot with milk, eggs and sultanas, and was lightly cooked; the resulting mixture was poured into pie-dishes and served on Mid-Lent Sunday and during the ensuing week. Frumenty is still prepared at Devizes for Mothering Sunday.

It was frumenty (admittedly spiced with rum) that got Michael Henchard into such trouble in Thomas Hardy's novel *The Mayor of Casterbridge* (1886). Numerous references (and almost as many spellings) are given in Joseph Wright's *English Dialect Dictionary* (1900); and references in the *Oxford English Dictionary* commence in the fourteenth century. Folk cookery writer Florence White, who gives detailed instructions on its preparation in her *Good Things in England* (1932), commented, 'It does not seem as if there is any exaggerating in claiming frumenty as our oldest national dish.'

A flat Christmas cake, of a triangular shape, with sugar and a few currants strowd over the top – differing only in shape, I believe, from a bun.

Many accounts of Christmas food in the past make special mention of meat pies, although there is some confusion here because what we now refer to as a 'mince pie' was, in its previous meat-filled incarnation, called a 'Christmas Pie'. Goose pies were particularly popular in the early nineteenth century, often made specifically from the giblets; John Brockett writes, 'At Christmas hardly any person, however poor, is without a giblet pie.' But sometimes it was the grand mixture of meats that made it so special. John Nicholson described the custom in his *Folk Lore of East Yorkshire* (1890):

In keeping with the hospitality of this season, hotels and inns provide a huge game pie for their customers, and none of the good things provided for this festive time are better than these pies, 'standing pies' they are called, being nearly a foot high, and filled with the choicest morsels of hare, rabbit, pheasant, etc.

One of the most obvious fundamental changes that have taken place in the past hundred years is the relative ease and convenience of modern cooking. In the past, the preparation of each item of the family's diet was not only a chore but also a ritual in itself. A Surrey member of the Women's Institute recalled her childhood Christmases in the book *Surrey Within Living Memory* (1992):

Grandmama was less than five feet tall but she ruled her twelve children and 16 grandchildren with a rod of iron. It was she who organised the family preparations for Christmas and as we children became old enough to 'help', the weeks before 25th December became filled with excitement. Pudding making was an activity which involved every member of the family. Raisins, sultanas, prunes, cherries, and lumps of sticky dates had to be washed and laid out on large meat dishes to dry. They took days to reach the stage at which they could be handled. Armed with a sharp knife and a basin of hot water, Grandmama sat in her wing chair before a roaring fire and expertly removed the pips from every single fruit. We children were allowed to grate the suet which came from the butcher in huge lumps. Horrid stuff, suet – so much skin on it, but not on our fingers by the time we had finished. The more responsible of us were given the task of beating the dozens of fresh farm eggs into a foaming yellow mass. Eventually the day dawned for the mixing of all the ingredients. This was done in an earthenware crock normally used for the preserving of eggs. A whole bottle of brandy was added and all the family came together at a set time to stir the mixture and make a wish. If you could get the wooden spoon to stand up in the middle of the glorious-smelling mess then your wish was supposed to come true. I never did get the pony I wished for every time for years. Fourteen greased pudding basins, fourteen cloths, and a ball of string were used to make neat little parcels which were then placed in a scullery copper filled with hot water and kept boiling by means of a roaring fire underneath. The puddings were simmered for three days and nights, filling the house with a mouthwatering aroma and clouds of steam which floated about like a fog. I use my Grandmama's recipe today but my fruit and suet come from packets and I only use a small bottle of brandy. Somehow, my puddings do not taste like Grandmama's.

Geese Dancers

Geese-dancing was a well-known activity in Cornwall at Christmas time. The terms 'geese-dancing' or 'goose-dancing' have almost certainly been derived from a local pronunciation of the word 'guise', which in various local forms such as 'guiser' and 'guising' was found all over the country, signifying a custom in which people dressed up, or disguised themselves (*see* **Guisers**, *below*). Even in Cornwall there were wide variations in the custom, and its exact nature is difficult to pin down. Some geese-dancers performed a local variant of the mummers' play (*see* **Christmas: Mummers**), while others simply entered people's houses and engaged in licensed misbehaviour. Jonathan Couch wrote in his *History of Polperro* (1871):

In town, the family, flocking round the mock [yule log], are interrupted by the cheerfully tolerated intrusion of the goosey-dancers. The boys and girls rifle their parents' wardrobe of old gowns and coats, and disguise themselves, their mien, and speech, so cleverly that it is impossible to identify them. They are allowed, and are not slow to take, the large amount of licence which the season warrants; for it is considered a mark of a churlish disposition to take offence at anything they do or say. Accordingly they enter without ceremony; dance, sing and carry on an extemporaneous dialogue well spiced with native wit. After tasting, unmasked perhaps, whatever may be on the table, they beg some money to make merry with. The children are much amused, and the mummers leave with a benediction.

Folk-Lore Journal of 1886:

From Christmas to twelfth-tide parties of mummers known as Goose or
Geese-dancers, paraded the streets in all sorts of disguises, with masks on.
They often behaved in such an unruly manner that women and children
were afraid to venture out. If the houses were not locked they entered unin-
vited and stayed, playing all kinds of antics, until money was given to them
to go away . . . These goose-dancers became such a terror to the respectable
inhabitants of Penzance that the Corporation put them down about ten
years since, and every Christmas Eve a notice is posted in conspicuous places
forbidding their appearance in the streets, but they still perambulate the
streets of St. Ives . . .

Guisers

One of the highlights of the Christmas season for many families in the
nineteenth and earlier twentieth centuries was a visit from the 'guisers', although the exact nature of this visit varied considerably from
place to place. The word has a long pedigree, and was used all over
the country to describe any custom that featured people dressed up or
disguised in some way. In Yorkshire, Northumberland, and lowland
Scotland, for example, it was one of the regular names for the **mum-**
mers (*see below*), while in Cornwall it was the root of the term **geese**
dancers (*see above*). In many of these customs, the dressing-up simply
took the form of wearing a costume, as in a play, but in some it was the
disguise that played an integral part of the activity, as remembered by
Alison Uttley from her Derbyshire childhood in the 1890s:

[After singing a song outside] *they pushed open the door and half*
entered.

> *God bless the master of this house,*
> *And bless the mistress, too,*
> *And call the little children*
> *That round the table go.*
> *And all your kin and kinsfolk,*
> *That dwell both far and near,*
> *I wish you a merry Christmas,*
> *And a happy New Year.*

'Come in, come in,' shouted Tom, with his broad face wreathed in smiles.

Half a dozen young men and a woman stamped their feet and entered, bringing clots of snow and gusts of sweet icy air. Their faces were masked and they disguised their voices, speaking in gruff tones or high falsettos, which caused much gay laughter. They stood in a row in front of the dresser, and asked riddles of one another: 'How many sticks go to the building of a crow's nest?' – 'None, for they are all carried'; 'When is a man thinner than a lath?' – 'When he's a-shaving' . . . 'I know that voice,' returned Joshua, ''tis Jim Hodges from Over Wood way.' 'You're right, Mester Taberner,' said Jim, as he removed his mask and disclosed his red cheeks. So the guessing went on, until all the mummers were unmasked, Dick, Jolly, Tom Snow, Bob Bird, Sam Roper, and Miriam Webster.

A very similar custom, called 'mummering', was common in Newfoundland, where it had presumably been taken by British settlers.

Holy Thorn(s)

In legendary terms, Glastonbury, in Somerset, is probably the most mystical place in England, with several long-standing stories to its credit. This extraordinary longevity must largely be attributed to the fact that the legends themselves have developed with the times, and have managed to satisfy the needs of successive groups, so as always to be in vogue somewhere. As each group has moved on or faded away, others have taken its place. Over the centuries, Glastonbury devotees have included medieval monks and pilgrims, eighteenth-century anti-Gregorians, 1960s hippies, New Age travellers, modern pagans, King Arthur fans throughout the ages, and nowadays the very fashionable Holy Grail hunters.

The legends themselves have been augmented by new details over the years, but in their basic form they tell of how Joseph of Arimathea came to Britain in AD 63 and founded the first Christian church in the country at Glastonbury, and that King Arthur was buried there. It is difficult to think of a more potent mix in the legend stakes (it only lacks a Robin Hood connection to make it perfect). Joseph appears in the Gospels as the man who rescued Christ's body and placed it in the tomb, and later additions showed him journeying to France, and on to England, with a group of disciples. Some even claimed that he was the Virgin Mary's uncle. However, this Glastonbury connection was a blatant invention by the monks of Glastonbury Abbey, as a clever gambit in the incessant power struggles within the medieval church. They 541

Christmas

were well aware that such stories gave the abbey a distinct edge over rival religious houses, especially its claim to be the first Christian church in the land, and they also encouraged the lucrative pilgrimage trade.

By the time the abbey was suppressed in 1539, the stories had already taken on a life of their own, and had long outlived their original purpose. Their fame has ebbed and flowed over the subsequent centuries, but they have enjoyed a marked renaissance in recent decades. The ability of romantic legend to replace prosaic history has been given a huge boost by the invention of the Internet, and Glastonbury Abbey's official website blithely claims it as the first Christian sanctuary in the country, as do countless others.

The one element of this legend that concerns us from a calendrical point of view is the Holy Thorn, which is said to have sprung from Joseph's staff when he thrust it into the ground on arrival at Glastonbury. This Thorn is internationally famous for blossoming on Christmas Day, and for 500 years has served the faithful as irrefutable proof of the truth of the Christian religion. Innumerable people who have never been near Glastonbury have taken its existence on trust, and have been comforted and inspired by it. Local thorn trees are first mentioned in the poem 'Lyfe of Joseph of Arimathea' (1502), but the Christmas blossom is not recorded until 1535, when it was apparently already well known.

The alleged flowering on Christmas Day became a major *cause célèbre* in the public disquiet after the introduction of the Gregorian calendar in 1752. The idea that there were extensive riots under the rallying cry of 'Give us back our eleven days' has now been exploded, but there was definitely a great deal of concern around the country for what seemed to be the wanton disregard on the part of the Government for the real 'natural' days of the year. Many who had never taken much notice of the custom before suddenly realized that a plant which knew when it was Christmas Day could be used as an 'objective' test of the new calendar, as recorded in the *London Daily Advertiser* of 5 Jan 1753:

We hear from Quainton in Buckinghamshire, that upwards of two thousand people came on the 24th of December at night, with lanthorns and candles, to view a black thorn, which grows in that neighbourhood, and which was remembered (this year only) to be a slip from the famous Glastonbury Thorn, that it always budded on the 24th at night, was full blown the next day, and went off at night. But the people finding no buds, nor the appearance of any, it was agreed by all, that the 25th of December N.S. could not possibly be the right Christmas Day, and accordingly refused going to church.

Other holy thorns suddenly appeared elsewhere in the country and, in public hearsay at least, produced the same result. The oft-repeated tale was used to legitimate the anti-Gregorian sentiments of many sections of the population for years to come, and allowed the celebration of Old Christmas Day to continue as a deep-rooted tradition. Nevertheless, according to one published report, in the *Gloucester Journal* of 2 January 1753, the real Glastonbury Thorn was apparently on the Government's side:

To all tender consciences that are afraid of keeping Christmas Day according to the New Style. This is to certify that the Glastonbury Thorn is in full blossom this day, the 25th of December, New Style, as it was ever known to be on 25th of December Old Style.

A century later, anti-Gregorians had another widespread notion to support their dislike of the New Style Christmas, as by that time cattle were known to kneel down in their stalls on the stroke of midnight on Christmas Eve (*see* **24 December: Cattle Kneeling**).

As indicated, there were many other trees with similar attributes, and indeed, there is a marked tendency to claim any remarkable tree as a descendant of the Glastonbury thorn, as they have done at Appleton, in Cheshire (*see* **29 June: Bawming the Thorn**). In addition to the tree at Quainton, mentioned above, there were several in Herefordshire, one or two in Worcestershire, several in Somerset, and one at Kew Gardens, plus many more. The only partial truth in all this is that it is quite possible for a thorn to flower at Christmas. As Roy Vickery points out in his *Dictionary of Plant-Lore* (1995), *Crataegus monogyna* 'is a variety of common hawthorn which produces flowers in winter as well as at the usual time in early summer'; there is nothing supernatural about it.

Mummers

In comes I, Old Father Christmas
Am I welcome or am I not
I hope Old Father Christmas
Will never be forgot.

Probably the most widespread of calendar customs during the nineteenth century, and into the first decades of the twentieth, was the Christmas mummers, who performed their traditional play over and over again as they visited houses in the neighbourhood. They performed especially at the big houses, where they could be sure of a good fee, but sometimes also at the pub or other local venue. After the play, they entertained the company with a few songs, were given money and other Christmas fare, and then moved on, often walking over thirty miles in a day to visit as many places as possible. Their bizarre costumes and even more bizarre 'play' brought a touch of excitement, colour, and mystery to Christmas at many a country house, and the men could each earn as much as two weeks' normal wages over a couple of days.

Hundreds of villages had their set of mummers, in almost every part of the country; only Norfolk and Suffolk have no traces of the custom. Some teams lasted only a few years, while others continued in unbroken tradition for decades, and as is to be expected from a performance passed down through the generations, each team's version was a little different from the rest. But there were definite regional patterns in both text and characterization, and the similarities between versions across the country far outweigh the differences.

'Mummers' is the generic name used by folklorists and other writers, but most areas had a local dialect name for the custom, including tipteerers in Sussex and Surrey, Johnny Jacks in Hampshire, soul-cakers in Cheshire, pace-eggers in Lancashire, and guisers in Yorkshire. Christmas was the usual time for performance for many of the teams, but some performed at other times of year, most notably at Easter, Hallowe'en, and on Plough Monday.

Scholars have identified three main types of mummers' play: the hero-combat or St George play, the wooing play, and the sword-dance play. The most widely known is the basic hero-combat play, found in all areas and even sometimes embedded in some of the other types. The basic plot is simple, and highly stylized. A presenter introduces the play and says that the mummers are about to perform. A 'knight' appears, who strides about boasting of his martial prowess and challenges anyone who disagrees to a sword-fight. Another character appears, with similar boasts, and accepts the challenge. They fight, and one is wounded or killed. In some plays another knight enters and meets the same fate, and occasionally a third. A character, usually the Presenter, laments the death and calls for a doctor. The Doctor appears, boasts of his medical skill (usually in comic hyperbole or non-sense), bargains with the Presenter, and cures the fallen knight, usually with a drop from his bottle. A string of supernumeraries comes in, one by one, each with a short speech, and at least one of them asks the audience for money, food, and drink.

The pace-egg play, reported mainly from Lancashire and performed at Easter, is similar to the St George type but with different characters, and with a strong tradition of performance by children's teams. The wooing plays of the East Midlands, usually performed around Plough Monday, are longer and more involved and include sung dialogue sections of wooing between male and female characters. Sword-dance plays accompanied some of the traditional sword dances of the North-East. These other forms are described under Easter and Plough Monday, and the following is concerned with the St George hero-combat play only.

It is customary to use the language of theatrical plays to describe the mummers, but in many ways this is misleading. In a mummers' performance there was no stage, no wings, no real entering and exiting, few props, and little or no characterization. Most importantly, you did not go to see the mummers, they came to you. The performance space would vary from place to place, but it was usual for the men to stand in a shallow semicircle and to step forward into the centre to say their piece, then step back into line when finished.

The usual text is mock-heroic, in rhyming couplets, and characters often introduce themselves in formulaic manner:

> *In comes I, King George*
> *That man of courage bold*
> *If his blood be hot*
> *I'll quickly fetch it cold . . .*

And finish by introducing the next player:

> *If you don't believe the words I say*
> *Step in Bold Slasher and clear the way.*

Texts also often include bits and pieces from other sources. The standard doctor's speech, for example, formerly appeared in its own right in eighteenth-century broadsides, in skits parodying the quack doctors of the time, and some mumming plays include occasional fragments from plays performed in theatres.

The names of the characters vary considerably from version to version, and comparative discussion would be difficult if it was not for the fact that this variety masks a very limited number of roles within the play itself: Presenter, Combatants, Doctor, Doctor's Assistant, and Supernumeraries. The sections of the play are even more limited: Introduction, combat(s), cure, quête.

The 'Presenter' is often Father Christmas, although he sometimes has a functional name such as 'Roomer' (as his first words are 'Room, room, I pray'). The main 'hero' is usually the King or Saint George, and his adversary can vary – he is often a Turkish knight, but sometimes a bold soldier, or 'Bold Slasher'. The Doctor is sometimes called 'Doctor Brown' or 'Doctor Dodd', although this seems more to do with fitting the rhyme than anything else:

> *In comes I Doctor Brown*
> *The best old doctor in this town.*

In some regions, there is a 'female' character (always played by a man), called Molly, Betsy, or something similar. Of all the characters, the supernumeraries at the end vary most from region to region – Little Devil Doubt, Johnny Jack, and Billy Sweep, for example – although Beelzebub is sufficiently widespread to make us believe he might have been in the 'original' version:

> *In comes I Beelzebub*
> *Over my shoulder I carry me club*
> *In me hand a dripping pan*
> *Don't you think I'm a fine old man?*

Contrary to popular impression, a dragon rarely appears as a character in the mummers' play, and where it does it can usually be taken as evidence of literary intervention.

Modern descriptions, and revivals, of mumming plays routinely misunderstand and misrepresent what the mummers did and how they did it, mostly by using inappropriate models such as amateur dramatics, pantomime, and melodrama. A traditional mummers' performance was not played for laughs (except for certain well-defined sections); they were not hammed up; the audiences were not expected to join in to cheer the hero or boo the villain; the plays were not ad-libbed; and the presence of St George was not used to engender overt patriotism or nationalism. What evidence there is about performance style all points the same way: little 'acting' was involved, and no attempt was made to portray character. The players' stance was woodenly upright, gestures were stylized, and speech was monotonously declamatory, especially in the boast and challenge sequences. The two characters involved in these sequences counter-marched across the stage, clashing their swords once each time they met and passed, declaiming their lines as they walked. When it was time for the 'fight', they simply met, clashed swords twice, and one fell, or even simply dropped to one knee. The section with the Doctor is the only part that was regularly played for comic effect, but even here it used verbal humour, using topsy-turvy language, for example, rather than physical:

> *I can cure the ips, the pips, the palsy and the gout*
> *The pains within and the pains without*
> *If a man has nineteen devils in his body*
> *I can fetch twenty out.*

However, this is not to argue that a visit from the mummers was in any way dull. Kenneth Grahame, author of the children's classic *The Wind in the Willows* (1908), remembered the mummers of his Berkshire childhood in the 1860s in the following way:

Twelfth Night had come and gone, and life next morning seemed a trifle flat and purposeless. But yester-eve, and the mummers were here! They had come striding into the old kitchen, powdering the red brick floor with snow from their barbaric bedizenments, and stamping, and crossing, and declaiming, till all was whirl and riot and shout. Harold was frankly afraid; unabashed, he buried himself in the cook's ample bosom. Edward feigned a manly superiority to illusion, and greeted these awful apparitions familiarly, as Dick and Harry and Joe. As for me, I was too big to run, too rapt to resist the magic and surprise. Whence came these outlanders, breaking in on us with song and ordered masque and a terrible clashing of wooden swords?

Costumes also varied from place to place. Many of the teams in the South, for example, wore a decidedly weird costume of long strips of wallpaper or rag sewn on to their clothes, which completely obscured their bodies, along with tall cardboard hats decorated with rosettes and tinsel, from which long streamers hung all round, even over their faces. In other areas, patches of material, rosettes, streamers, ribbons, and tassels were in evidence, and many teams blacked their faces. By the time the twentieth century dawned, some performers, and occasionally the whole team, were starting to dress in character – the Doctor in a frock coat and top hat, Father Christmas in red robes and white beard, and the 'knights' in vaguely military costume. It is noticeable that those characters who had easily identifiable costumes were the first to succumb to this modernizing tendency.

For the last fifty years or so, almost every writer on the mummers' play has assumed that it is a direct survival of a pre-Christian fertility ritual. The strange garb, the 'ritual' style of performance, and the elemental themes of death and resurrection are all taken as obvious indications of great age and ritual origin. Unfortunately, there is not the slightest evidence to support these notions, and the whole fabrication rests on the assumption that the plays are very, very old. The fact that they cannot be shown to have existed before the mid eighteenth century is the most telling indictment of a set of theories based entirely on romantic wishful thinking.

There are indeed some mysteries still to be solved, but they are more prosaic historical ones. It seems clear that the play stems from an original, presumably 'literary', form in the early eighteenth century. That form has not yet been identified, but the most likely candidate is some kind of mock-heroic puppet play, although it remains to be seen how that play could have spread so widely and how it was adapted into a village tradition. In some areas, such as Lancashire, chapbooks containing play texts were available in local shops, and we know they were used by performers; another possibility is that it was spread by travelling players or puppets. However, if the original 'play' was popular enough to have taken root across almost the whole country, why has it left so little direct evidence of its existence?

For many years, it was not surprising that these questions remained unanswered. The real problem with the 'pagan origins' theory is that it precludes any other serious enquiry. For generations, nobody thought to look anywhere but pre-history, and eighteenth-century puppet plays were ignored. But we now have a whole new generation of scholars who are desperately keen to find the missing link, as yet to no avail.

Up to the First World War, there were hundreds of local mummers' teams up and down the country, but in the interwar years the majority of them faded away, leaving perhaps a dozen to continue after the Second World War. In the 1960s, however, enthusiasts of the folk revival, and particularly members of morris dance teams, started taking an interest in the custom, and numerous sides started to perform the plays again. The relationship between these new teams and the old ones is still controversial, but any claim to be continuing the pre-war tradition is highly tenuous; one extreme view is that the only thing that connects the modern mummer with that of the pre-war period is a few pieces of text. Nevertheless, some argue, with considerable justification, that many postwar 'revival' teams have now existed for a long enough time to qualify for 'traditional' status, and that the differences between themselves and their predecessors proves that they are part of a living tradition. It is clear that, with each passing year, fewer and fewer people will remember the old style of mumming, and that the 'modern' way will gradually become the norm.

See also **Plough Monday: Plough Plays**, p. 22; **Easter Day: Pace-Egg Plays**, p. 162; **31 October: Antrobus Soul-Cakers**; **2 November: All Souls' Day**; **Christmas: Geese Dancers**; **Christmas: Guisers**; **Christmas: Sword Dance**; **26 December: Marshfield Paper Boys**.

Stockings

The Christmas stocking is one of several elements of the modern Christmas that still puzzles the historian, as it is not at all clear exactly when or how it came into vogue in Britain. Indeed, we are in the difficult position of doubting the word of two contemporary witnesses, including one who provides us with the earliest concrete reference, on the grounds that they assume the stocking had ancient roots. William Henderson, the best folklore collector of his generation, wrote in 1866:

The old custom of hanging up a stocking to receive Christmas presents, a custom which the pilgrim fathers carried to America and bequeathed, curiously enough, to their descendants, has not yet died out in the North of England . . . among my own personal friends [is] *a family in which, without the excuse of a child to be surprised and pleased, each member duly and deliberately hangs out her stocking on Christmas Eve to receive the kindly gifts of mothers and sister.*

In fact, as there is no evidence that Old Father Christmas had a gift-giving function, or any of the trappings of nocturnal visits (*see* **Christmas: Father Christmas/Santa Claus**), it is fairly unlikely that the Christmas stocking pre-dates the introduction of Santa Claus from America, around 1865–70 – although Yorkshire resident J. S. Fletcher, born 1863, who wrote of Christmases of his youth in his *Recollections of a Yorkshire Village* (1910), casts doubt on this interpretation:

Children knew nothing about Santa Claus or about Christmas trees – those are German innovations which should have been left to Germans. We believed that Old Father Christmas brought our Christmas presents and put them in our stockings, which we hung at the foot of our beds, and instead of the German Christmas tree we had the old-fashioned English mistletoe-bough.

This puts the stocking in place before Santa Claus, but Fletcher was writing forty years after the event and his memory might have been confused. Even if the stocking were already making an appearance, it cannot have been widely known. In January 1879, for example, Edwin Lees, from Worcester, heard of a custom in Herefordshire and Worcestershire that clearly puzzled him, and he wrote to *Notes & Queries* to ask if anyone else knew of it:

On Christmas Eve, when the inmates of a house in the country retire to bed, all those desirous of a present place a stocking outside the door of their bedroom, with the expectation that some mythical being called Santiclaus will fill the stocking or place something within it before the morning. This is of course well known, and the master of the house does in reality place a Christmas gift secretly in each stocking; but the giggling girls in the morning, when bringing down their presents, affect to say that Santiclaus visited and filled the stockings in the night. From what region of the earth or air this benevolent Santiclaus takes flight I have not been able to ascertain . . . An Exeter resident tells me this custom prevails also in Devonshire.

Sadly, no one answered his request for further information. Seven years later, another writer confirms the presence of stockings in County Durham, but was also having trouble with the new Christmas gift-giver's name:

On Christmas Eve, each child hangs up one of its stockings in a place where it can be easily reached, in order that Santa Cruz, the Holy Cross, may come into the bedroom during the night, and deposit some little present in it. And when the child wakens in the morning, sure as fate, in the stocking is a Christmas pie – a yule dough, which is a bit of rich paste rolled out, cut, and baked in the shape of a little baby, with currants for eyes – a packet of figs, raisins, bullets – an orange, a ball, a top, or some other article, brought by the mysterious nocturnal visitor, who has come with light and gentle step, when the children were fast asleep.

By 1898, there is no question about its commonplace existence, as Richard Blakeborough could write of Yorkshire Christmases:

By and by the younger ones are packed off to bed, and with us, as the world over, their stockings are hung at the bed-foot to await the mysterious visit of Santa Claus.

Although it seems likely that the Christmas stocking became widespread when the idea of Santa Claus was introduced from America, it is possible that the stocking custom had taken root in some families at an earlier date, and it may even have become a regional feature before going national. Certainly, many British people will have been familiar with the idea, at least, from books. In Clement C. Moore's poem 'The Visit of St. Nicholas' (usually known as 'The Night Before Christmas'), for example, which was written in 1821 and published the following year, the saint comes down the chimney and leaves presents in the stockings left hanging by the children. Similarly, in *Carl Krinken; or the Christmas Stocking*, the novel by the popular American children's author Susan Warner, published in New York and London in 1854, the author's comments have a surprisingly modern ring. After coming down the chimney, Santa Claus examines the family's stockings, which are already full to the brim, as 'they had to hold candy enough to make the child sick, and toys enough to make him unhappy because he did not know which to play with first.'

Superstitions

All the major festivals attracted superstitions, but Christmas seems to have had more than its fair share. Many focused on particular elements, such as **decorations** and **food**, and are discussed under those headings, but others applied more generally to the season. Many people had little rituals to welcome Christmas, as others did the New Year. In 1878, the journal *Folk-Lore Record* reported that in West Sussex:

It is lucky to be the first to open the house-door [at] *Christmas . . . Saying 'Welcome, Old Father Christmas'.*

One of the key underlying motifs of Christmas/New Year superstitions was the fear of the luck of the house and family being lost, as this was believed to seriously affect the well-being of its inhabitants throughout the coming year. Many households up and down the country would not allow anything to leave the house at this period, while others restricted the ban to the symbolic staples of life – money, food, and fire. The prohibition against fire leaving the house was particularly widespread, and although this does not sound a particularly harsh rule by modern standards, before the invention of commercial 'lucifer' matches in the 1830s, it was extremely common for householders to borrow a light from a neighbour, and very inconvenient if one could not. The Shropshire folklore collector Charlotte Burne recorded that around 1805:

We were very good neighbours, willing to help each other in time of need; but there was one time of need when neither neighbour dared insult the other. Asking to borrow a bit of fire, or even to ask for a light to a candle, on Christmas Day or any day until after Old Twelfth Day, was the greatest insult we could offer to a neighbour, as nothing was so certain to cause bad luck to a family for the ensuing year, as to fetch fire from their house during Christmas-time. Consequently, it was no trifling undertaking on Christmas Eve to arrange the tinder box with all its implements in the art of striking a light; first to obtain a piece of old linen rag, and well burn it into a cinder; and then the flint and steel to be looked up and cleaned, or new ones bought in Shrewsbury market; next, the match-making – generally bits of small brown paper cut to sharp points at one end, then the brimstone melted in an old iron spoon, into which the bits of paper were dipped, and all carefully laid by in a dry place until Christmas morning. If each family attended to these precautions carefully, then we should be sure to be good neighbours all the year round.

It was generally agreed that of all days in the year, Christmas Day was the luckiest to be born on, and it was also said that you would not be able to see ghosts or other spirits if you were born on that day. In addition, in Sussex, according to the *Folk-Lore Record* (1878), 'If you were born on Christmas Day you will neither be drowned nor hanged.' There was also a strong aversion to doing any work on the day, or, as in another example from Charlotte Burne's *Shropshire Folk-Lore* (1883), at any time during the season:

The horses might not go to plough during the whole twelve days; nor might any spinning be done; and the distaff, set aside, was not uncommonly dressed with flowers.

See also **New Year Customs and Superstitions**.

Sword Dance

The term 'sword dancers' will mean different things to different people. It might, for example, conjure up a picture of a Scotsman dancing over crossed swords laid on the floor, or the frantic whirling and clashing of real metal swords characteristic of visiting Cossack troupes. But the sword dance found in the counties of Yorkshire, Northumberland, and Durham, traditionally performed around the local neighbourhood over the Christmas/New Year period, is a very different matter. The 'swords' used in this custom are not real swords at all, but are either lathes of wood or metal about three feet long (in the 'longsword' tradition), or shorter ones made of pliable metal with swivelling wooden handles at each end (in the 'rapper' tradition). Mrs Keith, from Cambo in Northumberland, contributed this description to the book of local memories put together by the Women's Institute in 1929:

Almost the first thing I can remember was when we lived at the Dovecot, and sword dancers came at the New Year, in the dark, and danced the sword dance in the back yard by the light of lanterns, all dressed up – there was old Betty, and Nelson, and a doctor, and after they'd finished the dance one held up all the swords. They came from about Boghall. Yes, miners and the lads about. They used to come from Blaydon too. They were given ginger wine, and cake.

The dancers hold one end of a sword in each hand and are thus all linked in a circle, their movements circumscribed by what can be achieved in variations of this formation. The only time they let go of their swords is at the end of the dance when they interlace them to form a 'knot' or 'rose', which can be held aloft in triumph by one dancer. The two types of sword – longsword and rapper – give the dances a very different character, as dances using the rapper are much faster and more spectacular, but the linked circle remains the basic defining feature of the genre. Similar dances are found across most of Europe from the Middle Ages onwards, and while there are a few ambiguous references to such customs in Britain in the seventeenth century, the real bulk of evidence in this country comes from the second half of the eighteenth century onwards.

Sword dance performances often feature a calling-on song to introduce the dancers, and some versions have supernumerary characters, such as a Fool and a Bessie or Betty (always played by a man). These characters do not normally take part in the dance, and may be the remnant of a play which was formerly an integral part of the custom and which scholars have identified as one of the three basic forms of English mumming play (*see* **Christmas: Mummers**). A marked feature of the sword play, which survives in some dances, is when the swords are linked around a character's neck, who is then 'killed' as the swords are smartly withdrawn. The term 'sword dance' is open to some confusion here, because in other customary performances, such as the plough play (*see* p. 22), the participants were locally called 'sword dancers'.

The sword dance is no longer a local house-visiting custom, but many teams still perform, including Handsworth and Grenoside, near Sheffield, Goathland, near Whitby, and Earsdon in Northumberland.

Tree

It is well known that the Christmas tree was directly imported from Germany in the 1840s by Queen Victoria's consort Prince Albert, but this is only partly true. Because of the close connections between the British and German royal families, decorated trees had in fact been a regular feature of court Christmases since at least the days of George III, who married Princess Charlotte of Mecklenburg-Strelitz in 1761. Christmas trees were also seen in other homes with German connections, and were already familiar to many English people. In 1829, for example, when Charles Greville, grandson of a duke, and secretary to the Privy Council, was staying at Pansanger, the Hertfordshire home of Earl Cowper, Greville recorded in his diary that on Christmas Day the Princess Lieven, wife of the Russian Ambassador, had:

. . . *got up a little fête such as is customary all over Germany. Three large trees in large pots were put upon a long table covered with pink linen; each tree was illuminated with three circular tiers of coloured wax candles – blue, green, red and white. Before each tree was displayed a quantity of toys, gloves, pocket handkerchiefs, workboxes, books, and various articles – presents made to the owner of the tree. Here it was only for the children, in Germany the custom extends to persons of all ages.*

However, it was certainly Victoria and Albert's homely Christmas tree in 1848 that caught the public's imagination and started the fashion in Britain. The famous engraving of the royal couple, with their five children admiring the bauble- and present-hung tree, appeared in the Christmas supplement of the *Illustrated London News*, and although it was there described as 'somewhat more of a German than an English custom', it struck a responsive chord with the British middle classes. By 1851, the same journal was running adverts for Christmas trees, and they were increasingly appearing as normal features in illustrations and articles. Not everybody was happy with the development, however. Remembering the Yorkshire of his childhood in the 1870s, J. S. Fletcher wrote:

Children knew nothing about Santa Claus or about Christmas trees – those are German innovations which should have been left to Germans . . . Instead of the German Christmas tree we had the old-fashioned English mistletoe-bough.

But there was no stopping the new fashion, and it gradually filtered down through the layers of society to become one of the essential features of the twentieth-century Christmas. It still retains its important role both in practice and as a recognizable symbol of the season, and most families still have a tree of some sort, whether it is a token one on the sideboard, or as tall as the room will allow, one of the latest non-drop versions, or a synthetic one that plays a tune or changes colour.

Waits

Personal accounts of domestic life in the nineteenth and early twentieth centuries often mention that an essential part of the run-up to Christmas was the evening visits by musicians, called 'the waits'; however, these were just the tail-end of a very long musical tradition that originally was not confined to the festive season.

The word 'wait' is recorded from around 1300 with a variety of linked meanings, and comes from the same root as the word 'watch'. In its earliest sense it probably meant a military sentinel or watchman, who was furnished with a horn or trumpet for signalling, but not long after it was being used to mean a royal or municipal watchman, maintained at public charge, with musical instruments. A number of medieval towns maintained bodies of waits, York, Leicester, and Norwich among them, and those at Norwich were sufficiently famous to be commanded to accompany Edward IV to France in 1475, and Sir Francis Drake on his Lisbon campaign in 1588/9. At home, their duties included providing music at public events, such as dinners and civic gatherings, but their highest public profile came from their role as nightwatchmen – patrolling the streets at night, playing softly, and announcing the time, to reassure the populace that all was well.

The waits were paid for their services, as well as being supplied with instruments, badges of office, and suitable outdoor clothes, and no doubt it was a popular steady position for local musicians, but town records often document quite stormy relationships between employers and employed. In some towns, the waits survived until the early nineteenth century but were swept away by the Municipal Reform Act of 1836. The privatized band continued to function, however, and became particularly associated with Christmas. The word 'wait' therefore came to mean simply a band of musicians who came round at that season, just like the carol singers. In 1827, the *Gentleman's Magazine* recorded that:

About a week before Christmas Day it is the annual custom of the native minstrels in Holmsdale [Surrey] *to serenade the inhabitants every morning at an early hour; then many a delusive dream is broken by 'the concord of sweet sounds'. The instrumental harmonists are welcomed from house to house, and hailed as the harbingers of joyous hours to come . . . I peeped through the chamber window and . . . there stood the venerable figure of Richard Dove, an established musician of the neighbourhood, fiddling with all his might, his head and foot beating time, while every string exulted aloud in 'The Downfall of Paris', and every note tingled in the ear, crying shame to the drowsy sleeper.*

However, not everybody approved of the waits, or their choice of tune; a couple of years earlier, the same magazine reported:

Certain strolling minstrels still occasionally disturb our nocturnal slumbers for a few weeks previous to Christmas, calling themselves 'waites'; but alas! alack the day! instead of playing and singing the good old carol, our ears are saluted with 'Roy's Wife', 'St. Patrick's Day', or the latest quadrille tune.

Wassailing

Of all the traditional customs that are believed to be remnants of ancient luck-bringing rituals, wassailing is the only one with any reasonable claim to this description, as it is overtly concerned with wishing prosperity on those visited; however, even here there is no evidence for the prevailing notion that wassailing customs are pre-Christian, or even that they date back to before the late Middle Ages. The word itself is derived from the Old English *waes haell*, meaning 'be healthy', or, as we would perhaps say nowadays, 'Good health!', and was recorded as a general salutation and also as a drinking toast; the traditional reply was *drinc haell!* But before dreaming of marauding Anglo-Saxons carousing after sacking a British village or two, it is best to consider the linguistic evidence presented in the detailed entry in the *Oxford English Dictionary*. It is there revealed that *wassail* as a general salutation existed in Old Norse as well as in Old English, but that the use of the word as a drinking toast is not found in any of the Teutonic languages, and appears to be a peculiarly 'English' formation from the eleventh or twelfth century: 'It seems probable that this use arose among the Danish-speaking inhabitants of England . . . in the twelfth century it was regarded by Normans as markedly characteristic of Englishmen.' Later uses of the word, in the thirteenth to fifteenth centuries, show that it had undergone a considerable extension of meaning, with a 'wassail' meaning a party, or the drink that was enjoyed there, or the words said when drinking, or even the songs that were sung. Like the word 'Yule', 'wassail' has long been used anachronistically by writers as a shorthand way to conjure up a popular romantic view of England in the Dark Ages (*see* **Merrie England**, p. 510). Indeed, the very first written evidence of the 'wassail-drinkhail' combination appears in Geoffrey of Monmouth's *History of the Kings of Britain* (VI:12), one of our first historical novels, written *c.*1140 but set in the fifth century.

In the sphere of more recent annual customs, there were two related but different forms of wassailing. The first was a domestic house-visiting custom, which could be done by men or women but was traditionally regarded as a predominately female custom, while the second was an agricultural custom carried out primarily in the orchard, in which one wassailed the trees, wishing a good crop and a prosperous coming year.

The key feature of the house-visiting custom was the good-luck drink offered to the householder, with an appropriate song, as in this example from Northamptonshire in 1853:

This friendly and neighbour-loving custom was observed by the young women of the village, who accustomed themselves to go about from door to door on new year's eve, neatly dressed for the occasion, and bearing a bowl richly decorated with evergreens and ribbands, and filled with a compound of ale, roasted apples, and toast, and seasoned with nutmeg and sugar. The

> Good master at your door
> Our wassail we begin
> We all are maidens poor
> So we pray you let us in
> And drink our wassail
> All hail wassail!
> Wassail, wassail!
> And drink our wassail!

Traditions of seasonal goodwill notwithstanding, not everyone was pleased to see them, including John Selden, who wrote the following in his *Table-Talk* (1689):

The Pope in sending rellicks to princes, does as wenches do by their wassals at New-years-tide, they present you with a cup, and you must drink of a slabby stuff; but the meaning is you must give them moneys, ten times more than it is worth.

The whole custom was often referred to as 'the wassail bowl', or 'vessel cup', and the ingredients of the drink varied, but was typically mulled ale spiced with nutmeg, with the pulp from roasted apples – called in some areas **Lamb's Wool** (*see* p. 13). Domestic wassailing was also sometimes combined with the related custom of carrying of 'Christmas dolls' from house to house (*see* **24 December: Vessel Cups**). The earliest reference to a visiting wassail custom appears to be in the records of St Mary of Pré Priory at St Albans, Hertfordshire, between 1461 and 1493, which include payments to wassailers, harpers, and players, and so on, as described in volume 4 of the *Victoria County History* for Hertfordshire. The orchard-visiting custom, which was more spectacular and survived well into the twentieth century, is nowadays probably better known than the house-visiting custom. Often thought to be a West Country custom, it was actually common in some form or other across the southern and western counties, and elsewhere. The exact day varied from place to place, and the custom could take place on Christmas Eve or Day, New Year, Twelfth Night, Plough Monday, or their Old Style equivalents, and in apple-growing areas a team of wassailers could be out on several nights.

Typically, the wassailing party would visit the farmhouse, and then go to the orchard and sing songs under the trees, beat them with sticks, and pour cider over their roots. A marked feature was noise – guns were fired, horns were blown, and there was much loud cheering. It is clear from the wassailers' songs that the purpose of the proceedings was to bring luck and encourage a good crop, and this must have been the case for some time, as in 1648 Robert Herrick included the following in his *Hesperides* collection:

> *Wassaile the trees, that they may beare*
> *You many a plum, and many a peare:*
> *For more or lesse fruits they will bring*
> *As you doe give them wassailing.*

The earliest clear reference to tree wassailing is surprisingly late, in Kent in 1585, as identified by Ronald Hutton in his seminal *Stations of the Sun* (1996).

Numerous versions of the wassailers' song were noted by nineteenth- and early twentieth-century folklorists, and although the songs bear a marked generic similarity, they vary considerably in detail. The first three verses of a version noted in Halse, Somerset, in 1894 are characteristic:

> *Wassail, wassail, all round the town*
> *The cider-cup is white, and the cider is brown*
> *Our cider is made from good apple trees*
> *And now, my fine fellows, we'll drink, if you please*
> *We'll drink your health with all our heart*
> *We'll drink to 'e all before we part.*
> *Here's one, and here's two*
> *And here's three before we go*
> *We're three jolly boys all in a row*
> *All in a row, boys, all in a row*
> *And we're three jolly boys all in a row.*
> *This is our wassail, our jolly wassail*
> *And joy go with our jolly wassail*
> *Hatfuls, capfuls, dree basket, basketfuls*
> *And a littler heap under the stairs.*

Wassailing was also well-reported in Sussex, where it was commonly called 'apple-howling', as recorded in the diary of the Revd Giles Moore, of Horsted Keynes, for 26 December 1670: 'I gave the howling

clared that the 'howling' referred to the style of singing, which was not
always music to the ears of the educated.

Tree wassailing has long been popular with revivalists, and the
sight of morris dancers among the apple trees is common at New
Year. As with other revivals, the temptation to 'improve' the proceedings by dressing up is sometimes too great to resist, as reported in the
Transactions of the Devonshire Association (1954):

*Apple wassailing . . . has been revived at Dunkeswell, Twelfth Night, 1954,
after a lapse of twenty years . . . The only unusual feature was the presence
of two evil spirits, dressed as witches, with tall hats and broomsticks, who
squatted in the branches of an apple tree. When the guns were fired through
the orchard, the spirits fell out of the tree and were chased away by the
delighted crowd.*

See also **6 January: Twelfth Night Fires**

26 December

St Stephen's Day/Boxing Day

Stephen was probably a Hellenistic Jew, appointed by the Apostles
as Deacon in the emerging Christian Church. He was stoned to
death by unbelievers *c.* AD 35, and as one of the first martyrs was giv-
en the day following Christ's birth as his feast. For most people in
this country, however, 26 December is known as Boxing Day, a usage that was already widespread in the 1830s, but not recorded before
that decade. There is little doubt that the name comes from the long-
standing custom of giving and receiving 'Christmas boxes' on the day.

When first mentioned, in the 1620s, Christmas boxes were indeed
the receptacles in which apprentices and servants collected their annual 'tips'. They were made of earthenware, with a slot for coins, and
had to be broken to get the money out. The term 'Christmas box' later
came to cover a variety of payments and presents, but the fundamental
point is that these were not simply gifts, but gratuities for services rendered, and were therefore not transactions between social equals but
between master or client and servant. Who got money from whom
was a complex, and potentially expensive, affair. Anyone who served,

looked after, or delivered goods to the public could expect a gratuity from each of their customers or clients. Parson James Woodforde in his Norfolk parish, for example, recorded the amount of money he gave each year on Boxing Day. In 1782 it was two shillings and six-pence to the bell-ringers, and a shilling each to the butcher's boy, the blacksmith's boy, and the maltster's man. The money went not to the tradesmen themselves, but to their workers, and the good parson never indicates any reluctance or complaint in his writing. But in towns there was a much wider range of potential recipients and the burden was much greater.

Eighty years after Woodforde, Hannah Cullwick, general maid-servant in a London house, noted in her diary for 26 December 1863 how her mistress:

> . . . gave me the money for the Christmas boxes to the men and boys same as last year and I give 'em as they came. I got a lot too – near £2 in all. They was sent to me . . . I put mine in the bank wi' my wages – Mary says hern shall buy a new bonnet.

Hannah's money would have come from regular visitors to the house, and from tradespeople who supplied the family and who wished to keep their custom. Clearly, workers like Hannah were loath to part with a system that was, in effect, a Christmas bonus. But even by the eighteenth century there had been complaints about the number of people who expected a Christmas box, and the abuse and subtle blackmail inherent in the system. Periodicals of the earlier nineteenth century regularly printed letters and articles condemning the practice, and the satirical magazine *Punch* ran a piece on the topic at Christmas almost every year in the 1840s; the following example is from 1849:

> Our postman . . . who has all the year scarcely condescended to greet us with an odd nod, has . . . been making a series of low bows, which for some time we thought were ironically meant, until we remembered the compliments of the season . . . Our newspaper boy, instead of pitching our daily print into our area, as he has done since last Boxing-day, without even troubling himself to ring the bell, has begun to stand at our door, vociferating, in a so-norous tone of voice, the word 'Pa-per' . . . The beadle, whom we have never seen since last Christmas and whom, during the year, we are accustomed to regard as a myth, has come across us, like a phantom, in his gold-laced coat, with crimson cape . . . The milkman has begun for a while to put a little less of the pallida mors, or deadly whitewash, into his milkpails; and even the

butcher boy is on his best behaviour, for he has only broken our bell-wire 561
once a week for the last month, instead of every other day.

26 December

The reformers finally got their way, and by the early twentieth century the Christmas box was a mere shadow of its former self. Nevertheless, remnants of the custom still lingered in post-Second-World-War Britain, by which time the number of recipients had shrunk to a handful: postman, paperboy, milkman, and dustman. Indeed, some families still carry out the custom.

Bleeding Horses

The medical procedure of phlebotomy – blood-letting, or bleeding – is one of the oldest surgical practices known to man, and was a standard method in the treatment of both humans and animals in England until the modern era. For some reason, it was widely believed that the best day to bleed horses and cattle was St Stephen's Day, and most farms and other trades that used horses made sure that this was duly done. The practice was already in place in the late sixteenth century, when Suffolk writer Thomas Tusser compiled his book of agricultural advice, *Five Hundred Points of Good Husbandrie*:

> *Ere Christmas be passed let horse be let blood,*
> *for many a purpose it doth them much good.*
> *The day of St. Stephen old fathers did use:*
> *if that do mislike thee some other day choose.*

Tusser is uncharacteristically blasé about the choice of day, but few others would risk flouting what they regarded as age-old wisdom.

Hunting and Shooting

In various parts of the country, it was traditional for parties of men and boys to invade the local woods on a certain day of the year, to hunt and kill animals – sometimes specifically squirrels or birds, but any small game was apparently at their mercy. The proper day for this custom varied considerably from place to place.

In Suffolk, Hampshire and Essex, it took place on Christmas Day or Boxing Day, but elsewhere it was Good Friday, 5 November, or St Andrew's Day (*see* **30 November**). In all cases, the participants firmly believed that on that particular day the normal game and trespass laws were suspended, and their actions were therefore quite legal (*see* **Lawless Hours and Days**, p. 412). Another striking common element is the noise and general commotion in which they indulged, which were hardly conducive to a genuine desire to find game.

Robert Forby described one version of the custom in his *Vocabulary of East Anglia* (1830):

In many parts of the country, particularly where there is much wood, the custom still prevails of hunting squirrels on this day . . . On Christmas morning half the idle fellows and boys in a parish assemble in any wood, or plantation, where squirrels are known to harbour; and having started their game, pursue it with sticks and stones from tree to tree, hallooing and shouting with all their might, till the squirrel is killed . . . From the general discouragement shown to this sport, probably comes the common saying, 'Hunt squirrels and make no noise'.

The journal *Folk-Lore* (1903) included a Lincolnshire variant from about 1840:

Mr. H., who is more than seventy, told me that when he was a lad, all the young men of Kirton-in-Lindsey, claimed the right of shooting over the whole parish on 5th November. 'When the sport was over,' he added, 'they met together in the market place to fire off their guns.' The belief that the people of a parish may legally shoot 'all over the lordship' on this day is not uncommon in North Lincolnshire.

It is possible that the custom preserves some right of common access to private woodland, but more research would be necessary before such a theory could be tested.

See also **Hunting the Wren** (*below*) for another possible line of enquiry.

Hunting the Wren

Hunting the Wren was a widespread custom in Ireland, Wales, and the Isle of Man, and took place at any time over the Christmas season, but mostly on 26 December. Parties of men and boys killed one or more wrens (or pretended to do so), which they placed in a garland-like 'bush' or special box, and perambulated the village singing, dancing, playing instruments, and collecting money. In many cases, the wren itself was almost forgotten. Some of the wrenboy teams could number up to twenty, and some performed a mummers' play (*see* **Christmas: Mummers**). The traditional song that accompanied the custom usually begins:

The idea that the tiny wren is the king of the birds is known all across Europe, and can be explained by the following folk tale, which portrays the wren as a trickster figure. In the competition to see who should be king of the birds, the eagle flew higher and faster than all the others. But just as he was proclaiming his victory, the wren, who had hidden in the eagle's feathers, popped out and flew a few inches higher, to claim the title. The eagle could do nothing to challenge this, but threw the wren to the ground in a temper – which explains the wren's short tail.

A different story explains why wrens should be hunted down. It seems that at some crucial point in the past, our people were about to ambush and annihilate the enemy, when a wren flew down and alerted them by pecking on a drum. The identity of the enemy changes in each version – for the Irish it can be 'the English', or King William's or Cromwell's army, but for others it is 'the Danes', who served as the archetypal enemy in many tales and traditions across Britain.

The custom was certainly known in England, but it was clearly not very widely known. The few definite references are scattered, and might well be sightings of groups of Irish or Welsh people perpetuating their own customs while living away from home. Edward Armstrong, whose *Folklore of Birds* (1958) is unfortunately influential in the subject, states boldly that 'Contrary to general belief the Hunting of the Wren was an English custom', and lists fifteen English counties in which traces of it have been found. His habit of paraphrasing unnamed sources makes the trail a little difficult to follow, but he appears to have reached this impressive total by uncritically conflating a series of references to two other wren-related traditions that may or may not be relevant.

The first is the simple song often called 'The Cutty Wren', which was widely collected across the British Isles and North America, and takes as its theme the exaggerated size and importance of the wren. A version noted from the singing of Bill Whiting of Longcot, Berkshire, by John Baldwin in 1967, is a good example:

> *I'm goin' to the woods, said Richard to Robin*
> *I'm goin' to the woods, said Robin to Bobbin*
> *I'm goin' to the woods, said John alone*
> *I'm goin' to the woods, boys, ev'ryone.*

Lines in successive verses include: 'What shall us do there?'; 'We'll shoot a wren'; 'How shall us get 'im up?'; 'We must fetch a cart'; 'How shall us get 'im cooked?'; 'Put 'im i' th' oven'; 'We've 'ad a feast'; 'Let's 'ave some ale'. The tunes of different versions are usually simple, often described as more chant than song. The earliest version so far located is in a collection of nursery rhymes dating from around 1744, and although many writers assume that the song originated in some ancient ritual, it is more likely that it started life as a children's song. It can also be assigned to a sub-genre of nonsense songs that could be termed 'hyperbolic animal songs' and includes 'The Derby Ram' and 'The Wonderful Crocodile'.

The second tradition conflated by Armstrong does not always involve wrens. In various parts of the country there was a tradition that on a certain day of the year villagers were allowed to enter local woods to hunt 'game'. The quarry was often specifically named as squirrels, and although wrens were sometimes singled out, this is possibly because it is one of the smallest animals likely to be found. The day varied from place to place, including Good Friday, 5 November, and St Andrew's Day (*see* **30 November**), but Christmas Day or Boxing Day are marginally the most commonly cited (*see* **26 December: Hunting and Shooting** for further examples). The marked characteristic of the event in many reports was that it was hardly a serious hunt at all, and was accompanied by much shouting, hallooing, and crashing about, as if this noise was more important than actually bagging any game. Exactly the same commotion was reported of the Irish wrenboys trying to catch their birds, as in this example from County Cork in the 1840s, printed by Irish folklorist Kevin Danaher:

In the hunt the utmost excitement prevails; shouting, screeching and rushing; all sorts of missiles are flung at the puny mark; and not unfrequently they light upon the head of some less innocent being. From bush to bush, from hedge to hedge is the wren pursued until bagged with as much pride and pleasure, as the cock of the woods by the more ambitious sportsman. The stranger is utterly at a loss to conceive the cause of this hubbub.

This was nothing new, as English antiquarian John Aubrey said of the Irish in 1686, 'You will see sometimes on holidays, a whole parish running like mad men from hedge to hedge a wren-hunting.' This tradition of wren-hunting is particularly strange, in England at least, because at other times 'Jenny Wren' enjoyed considerable protection

from being considered the robin's wife, and to kill a robin was one of
the unluckiest things one could do:

> The robin red-breast and the wren
> Are God Almighty's cock and hen.

This belief was particularly widespread in England, but also known in other parts of the British Isles, from at least 1709 onwards.

To return, therefore, to Armstrong's fifteen English counties, once the song and the general Boxing Day hunting customs are removed from the account, there is little left to show that the Irish-style wren hunt was known in England, although William Henderson included a definite reference in his *Notes on the Folk Lore of the Northern Counties of England and the Border* (1866):

At Christmas-tide, boys are accustomed in Essex to kill wrens and carry them about in furze-bushes, from house to house, asking a present in these words:

> The wren, the wren, the king of the birds
> St. Stephen's Day was killed in the furze
> Although he be little, his honour is great
> And so, good people, pray give us a treat.

In addition, a Boxing Day custom that existed in Devonport until the Second World War was reported in the *Transactions of the Devonshire Association* in 1972, in which participants with blackened faces and improvised costumes visited pubs, carrying a small tree or bush, and chanting a song which started with 'The ram, the ram, the king of the Jews', which, although it does not mention wrens, is clearly a garbled version of the usual wren song.

These references, and one or two others, are all that can be mustered, and the provisional conclusion must be that although wrens were hunted and killed in a customary manner, the perambulation of the village with a dead wren was probably not an English custom after all.

Marshfield Paper Boys

O yes! O yes! O yes! I have much pleasure in introducing the celebrated Marshfield Mummers, the old time Paper Boys. God save the Queen!

In the Cotswold village of Marshfield, Gloucestershire, twelve miles from Bristol, a team of men still performs the old mummers' play every Christmas, in the old-fashioned way. They call themselves the 'old-time Paper Boys' after their outlandish costume, which consists entirely of newspaper cut into strips and sewn on to their clothes and hats. The characters are: Father Christmas, King William, Little Man John, Doctor Phoenix, Saucy Jack, Tenpenny Nit, and Father Beelzebub. They are preceded by a top-hatted Town Crier, with hand-bell, who declaims the lines of introduction quoted above.

As with all 'hero-combat' mumming plays (*see* **Christmas: Mummers**), one character (King William) kills another (Little Man John) in a sword-fight, and the Doctor is summoned to revive him:

I can cure the itch, the stitch, the palsy and the gout, all pains within and none without. Bring me an old woman seven years dead, seven years laid in her grave, take a pill from me, and this gallant boy will rise again.
What's thy fee doctor?
Ten pounds is my fee, but fifteen I'll take of thee, to set this man free.

Apart from a few private performances, the play is acted outdoors, at set points around the village, every Boxing Day, and draws a large crowd from far and wide.

Like many other village customs across the country, the Marshfield play had lapsed in the 1880s, but it was revived in 1932 at the insti-gation of folklorist Violet Alford, whose brother was the local vicar. One of the new team had been in the play as a boy, and he provided the know-how to achieve a relatively faithful replication of the style in which the play was performed fifty years earlier. It is this direct connection with the previous tradition that makes the Marshfield 're-vival' qualitatively different from other revivals that are created from scratch. The Marshfield Paper Boys are also most unusual in that they have resisted the temptation to dress in costume appropriate to each part, or to modernize the style of performance. They do not model themselves on pantomime or melodrama, but still conduct themselves with the serious demeanour of the old teams.

Ludlow Rope-Pulling
See **Shrove Tuesday: Ludlow Rope-Pulling**, p. 76.

A custom that has come under considerable fire recently is the 'Darkie Day' perambulations of Padstow, in Cornwall. Participants don top hats decorated with flowers, fancy waistcoats, chimney-sweep outfits, and other sorts of fancy dress, and go round local pubs and streets singing songs by Stephen Foster and others from the nineteenth-century minstrel days. But what gives 'Darkie Day' its name is that the singers and musicians black their faces.

Darkie Day is thus one of the last vestiges of the blackface minstrel craze of the nineteenth century. 'Nigger minstrels', as they were called then, were introduced to London in 1836, and became an immediate smash sensation, sweeping the country like wildfire. The simple catchy tunes, purporting to be real Negro folk songs but mostly written by white songwriters, were highly suitable for amateur musicians; every village had its minstrel troupe, and every local concert had somebody strumming a banjo and singing minstrel pieces. In London and the big provincial towns, there were semi-permanent minstrel troupes who put on lavish spectacular shows. These lasted into the twentieth century, but declined in the face of competition from new musical crazes. However, the form still had life in it, and survived on BBC television into the 1970s with the 'Black and White Minstrel Show'.

A photograph from *c.*1900 shows the Padstow Darkie Day troupe very smartly dressed in highly patterned suits and black top hats – very much as the big minstrel troupes of the day were dressed. But at the time of writing, the future of the custom is unclear. There are growing calls for its abolition, on the grounds that the blacked-up faces are racist, and police have taken a watching brief – quite literally, as they filmed it in 2005; although according to the *Observer* of 22 January 2006, the local MP has claimed that the blackened faces originated as a form of disguise rather than on the minstrel stage. In the meantime, the participants have renamed the event 'Mummers' Day'.

Pantomimes

The ultimate origins of that strange dramatic beast, the English pantomime, lie in the traditional Italian *commedia dell'arte*, which flourished from the sixteenth to the early eighteenth centuries. This highly stylized dramatic form, with stereotyped characters and plot outlines, but with largely improvised dialogue and action, also included music, dance, and clowning, and, unusually for the period, featured both male and female actors. The basic plot concerned two young lovers whose courtship was frustrated by the girl's aged father and his friend, but who were supported and assisted by comic servants, including the leading girl's maid. The most important stock character was Harlequin, and the plot always included a chase scene, with the lovers fleeing the old man's wrath. *Commedia*-type scenes were already familiar to British audiences by the turn of the eighteenth century, as Harlequin sequences had been included in a few home-grown comedies, but it was the impetus of French *commedia* troupes performing in this country that prompted the growth of the pantomime as a distinct form of entertainment.

The first real pantomime was *The Magician, or Harlequin a Director*, produced in 1721, with actor-manager John Rich as the first English Harlequin; he set the parameters of that character, which lasted for several generations. The 'director' of the title referred to the financial scandal known as the South Sea Bubble, which had burst a few months previously, and this started the trend for topical allusions in the pantomime that lasts to this day. For a while, pantomimes were staged as afterpieces to more conventional fare, but they proved so popular that they were soon extended to fill the whole evening. Indeed, the theatre-going public loved them so much that even those managers that had a distaste for such low-brow material were forced to stage them every year. Even at this time, they were an odd mixture of the romantic, serious, and comic, with song, dance, slapstick, and stunning special effects, and, as now, they were presented in the immediate post-Christmas period. It was quipped that theatres should dispense with their old repertoire of real plays and simply stage pantomimes all year.

The Harlequin created by John Rich was mute, relying on mime and special effects, and his dominance of the genre lasted for decades, but by the early nineteenth century the central role was taken by another comic character, the Clown. The success of this character was almost entirely due to Joseph Grimaldi (1778–1837), the most famous clown of all time, still annually commemorated in London (*see* **First Sunday in February: Clowns' Service**). Pantomime continued to develop, mainly by accretion, and was an integral part of the remodelled Christmas of the mid nineteenth century. Nevertheless, it seems that people have always either loved or hated the pantomime, with no position possible between these extremes. Charles Dickens was firmly in favour, stating in a piece in *Bentley's Miscellany* (1837):

Let us at once confess to a fondness for pantomimes – to a gentle sympathy with clowns and pantaloons – to an unqualified admiration of Harlequins and Columbines – to a chaste delight in every action of their brief existence, varied and many-coloured as those actions are, and inconsistent though they occasionally be with those rigid and formal rules of propriety which regulate the proceedings of meaner and less comprehensive minds. We revel in pantomimes.

By later Victorian times, so much had been added to the performances that chaos reigned. Writing of the later nineteenth century, the *Oxford Companion to the Theatre* justly comments:

With the importation of specialty acts from the music-halls, which held up the action but delighted the audiences, the show became such a hotchpotch of incongruous elements – slapstick, romance, topical songs, male and female impersonation, acrobatics, splendid settings and costumes, precision and ballet dancing, trick scenery and transformation scenes – that for a time the phrase 'a proper pantomime' was used outside the theatre in colloquial English to signify 'a state of confusion'.

Despite these strictures, and the constant lament of reviewers that 'pantomime is not what it used to be', the annual extravaganza still continues, and for many provincial theatres is the only sure-fire money-making venture of the year. Gerald Frow's history of the pantomime (1985) sums it all up:

It all adds up to something refreshingly honest and utterly disarming. We all know the man's a woman; we all know the woman's a man; and anyone can see that the cow has got people in it. But isn't that the whole point?

28 December

Holy Innocents' Day

Holy Innocents' Day, or Childermas, commemorates the day on which King Herod, in his desperate attempt to find the infant Jesus, ordered all children under the age of two in Bethlehem to be killed (Matthew 2:16). It therefore had two slightly conflicting traditional characteristics: the sadness and repentance of a tragic day, coupled with a particular regard for children. In church it was a day of fasting and penance, and the bells were rung in muffled tones. Children were not chastised on the day, and were allowed a certain degree of unaccustomed licence, as recorded by C. J. Billson, one of the editors of the Victorian *County Folklore Printed Extracts* series:

When living in the parish Exton, Rutland, some 15 years ago [i.e. about 1880], *I was told by an old lady that in her girlhood, in the very early years of this century, it was the custom for children to be allowed to play in church on 'Innocents' Day'.*

From the twelfth to the sixteenth centuries, Holy Innocents' Day was also the day on which the Boy Bishop reigned in many cathedrals and other religious institutions, although he was also often elected on the other holy day that was connected with children, St Nicholas' Day (*see* **6 December: Boy Bishop**).

The religious background to the day directly affected the way in which it was seen by the people. All over the country, at least until the early twentieth century, the day was regarded as particularly unlucky. This unluckiness was manifest in various ways – from the general idea that anything started on the day would not be finished, or be doomed to failure, to specific prohibitions against certain activities, such as doing the family washing ('you will wash one of the family away'). Workers in particularly dangerous occupations refused to work at all on the day, first recorded by Richard Carew in Cornwall in 1602:

That proves as ominous to the fisherman as beginning a voyage on the day when Childermas day fell doth to the mariner.

It was still being said of lead-miners in Northumberland over 250 years later.

However, the unluckiness could affect more than the day itself, as reported by Charlotte Burne in 1883:

Innocents' Day, sometimes called 'Cross day', is a day of ill omen. The ancient people of Pulverbatch [Shropshire] *applied this name not only to Innocents' Day but throughout the year to the day of the week on which it had last fallen, such day of the week being believed to be an unlucky day for commencing any work or undertaking. A popular saying about any unfortunate enterprise was: 'It must have been begun on Cross day'.*

On the same principle, Fridays throughout the year were widely regarded as unlucky, simply because the crucifixion took place on that day. There could therefore be two unlucky or 'cross' days every week.

also known as Dyzeman's Day, Dyzemas, or Dizimus Sunday (or
variations thereon); the etymology of these names is unknown.

31 December

New Year's Eve

Until quite recently, it was broadly the case that while people in
Scotland heartily celebrated the New Year and ignored Christmas,
in England people did the reverse. This situation held true for nigh
on 300 years, but it would be a mistake to regard it as evidence of
deep psychological differences between the two peoples. It was simply a result of different paths taken during the religious and political turmoil of seventeenth-century Britain. Christmas was banned in
both countries by Puritan order, but was reinstated in England at the
Restoration of the monarchy in 1660, when the people were positively
encouraged to welcome 'Old Father Christmas' back into their lives.
The Scottish Church, however, continued to frown on the festival,
and their people thus put their festive energies into the secular New
Year instead. It is only in recent years that these national differences
have begun to break down.

In early Victorian England, New Year had a few traditions of its
own which had been around for a long while, such as giving gifts and
sending greetings messages (see **New Year Customs and Superstitions:
Gifts**), but these were eventually usurped by the new-style Christmas
being forged at the time. In 1864, William Chambers could write in
his famous *Book of Days*:

*As a general statement, it may be asserted that neither the last evening of
the old year nor the first day of the new one is much observed in England as
an occasion of festivity. In some parts of the country, indeed, and more especially in the northern counties, various social merry-makings take place; but
for the most part, the great annual holiday-time is now past.*

New Year began to occupy an ambiguous position in the festive calendar. It fell awkwardly between Christmas Eve and Twelfth Night,
which marked the beginning and end of the festive season, and New
Year had no obvious role to play. Nor did New Year's Eve have many

traditional customs of its own, and those that did occur at the season, such as wassailing and mumming, were not fixed to a particular night but could take place at any time over Christmas.

In recent years, however, New Year has quietly undergone a process of major change, which started when New Year's Day became a bank holiday in England in 1974. Increasingly it is seen as the end, not just of Christmas week, but effectively of the whole Christmas season. In this context it has completely eclipsed the old Twelfth Night and has become the new counterbalance to Christmas Day: many workers now get given the whole of Christmas week as holiday, and return to work after the New Year; couples might agree to see one set of parents at Christmas and the other at New Year; and young people who are required to spend Christmas in their parents' houses are often free to see their own friends at New Year.

Nevertheless, despite its lack of overt festivity, New Year has probably always had a quieter, deeper side, brought about by the symbolism inherent in the passing of one year into the next. It seems quite natural that it should be seen as a time of personal stocktaking, engendering those mixed feelings of nostalgia and hope, when even the least romantic of us feels compelled to think back on the past twelve months and make plans for the coming year. Many people who do not celebrate the night in any other way still feel they should stay up till midnight to 'see the New Year in'.

Allendale Guisers

Late in the evening of 31 December, the Northumbrian village of Allendale is quite literally lit up by the spectacular sight of forty fancy-dressed guisers, who parade the streets carrying blazing wooden barrels on their heads. The guisers are aided by a brass band and supported by most of the local population, and the climax is reached at midnight when they light the waiting bonfire in Market Place. In previous times they would dramatically throw their barrels on to the fire, but suitable barrels are not so easy to find these days, so they have to be more circumspect.

The barrels are the ends of ordinary wooden barrels cut down to about twelve inches deep and filled with rags and shavings, soaked in paraffin, although real tar was used in previous times. They can weigh up to 30 lbs, and take some carrying, even when not alight. The guisers take their responsibilities very seriously, and it is rare for a barrel to be especially in the northern counties, and signifies a character dressed up or 'disguised' (*see* **Christmas: Guisers**).

The wishful thinking that automatically assigns ancient origins to traditional customs, repeated all over the country, has operated in Allendale, and the tar barrels have been confidently attributed to acts of ancient fire worship carried out by pagan Celts, Vikings, and Druids; however, the overwhelming evidence points to a far more prosaic explanation. It seems that the tar barrels were introduced in the second half of the nineteenth century as a form of illumination for the members of the local band, who always perambulated the village on New Year's Eve to play the old year out.

Nevertheless, a custom does not need to be ancient to be important to the local inhabitants, and in Allendale it has been preserved, and indeed extended, because it serves a community purpose – and fierce local pride will keep it going for a long time yet. Local determination is often only obvious to the outsider when a tradition is under threat, as many customs were during the Second World War. Venetia Newall's seminal article on the custom, published in 1974, recorded one of these moments:

When war broke out and many of the guysers were called up for military service, blackout regulations enforced the cancellation of the bonfire. To maintain the continuity of the custom, Lancelot Bell, the local carpenter, designed a type of small tar barrel which he carried each New Year's Eve, unlit, along the usual route through the village to the Market Place. On the customary site of the bonfire, he placed it inside a tin trunk, set fire to it, and closed the lid. All the local people then danced around the trunk.

Blazing tar barrels have a long history, and feature in a number of other winter customs, usually on Guy Fawkes Night; *see*, for example **5 November: Ottery St Mary** and **Second Saturday in November: Hatherleigh Carnival**.

Bell-Ringing

The loud ringing of the church bells to honour special occasions has a very long history. On a national scale, military victories and royal events have been regularly marked in this way, and certain nights of the year, such as 5 November and Christmas Eve, have also acquired bell-ringing customs. The ringing of the old year out and the new year in on the night of New Year's Eve is still heard in many places, but in the past it was almost universal, and before the days of radio and television the New Year bell-ringing was for many not only the most evocative sound of the season but the eagerly awaited signal that the midnight hour had officially arrived. The moment inspired numerous poets, including Alfred Lord Tennyson, whose *In Memoriam* (1850) includes the famous verses:

> *Ring out, wild bells, to the wild sky,*
> *The flying cloud, the frosty light;*
> *The year is dying in the night,*
> *Ring out, wild bells, and let him die.*
> *Ring out the old, ring in the new,*
> *Ring happy bells across the snow;*
> *The year is going, let him go,*
> *Ring out the false, ring in the true.*

Many churches had their own ways of welcoming in the New Year, most commonly carried out with a combination of solemnity and joy, as in Nottinghamshire in 1853:

On this night, in many parts of the county as well as in Derbyshire, a muffled peal is rung on the church bells until twelve o'clock, when the bandages are removed from the bells whilst the clock is striking, and a merry peal is instantly struck up; this is called 'ringing the old year out and the new year in'.

See also 4 **November: Ringing Night**; 5 **November: Guy Fawkes Night**; and 24 **December: Ringing the Devil's Knell** for other bell-ringing customs.

Gatherings

The impetus to gather in some key public place on New Year's Eve seems to be fairly widespread, and most cities have a spot where this happens every year. In London, the earliest documented gathering occurred in 1878 when, according to the *Illustrated London News* for 2 January 1897, significant numbers collected outside St Paul's Cathedral to hear the newly installed bells ring in the New Year. The ringing was repeated for a few years, but the crowd became too large and 'uproarious', so the Cathedral authorities put a stop to it. Unfortunately, this did not stop the crowds gathering, and an illustration on the front

of a huge festive crowd. Questions of public order and morality were
regularly voiced, but the crowds continued to grow.

A letter to *The Times* in November 1935 summed up the feeling in
many quarters that while there was nothing inherently bad about New
Year gatherings, trouble might be avoided if they were better organized, and in particular that organized singing would be a good thing:

*In England we seldom sing en masse, except at football matches. In this
respect our shortcomings on New Year's Eve have been particularly deplor-
able. Alike in London and the provincial cities great crowds, obeying a good
and natural emotion, forgather to greet the New Year. Their emotion finds
no orderly outlet. Because they are leaderless they make no united musical
effort. Instead, individuals and small groups sing. The strains of a dozen
banal and tuneless ditties intermingle depressingly. Often the New Year
breaks upon a scene of horseplay and alcoholic excess.*

The Cathedral authorities did indeed provide community singing that
year, along with a broadcast of the service to the crowds outside, which
The Times declared a great success, but it was not repeated the following year. After the Second World War, the focus gradually shifted to
Trafalgar Square, where it has stayed ever since.

Hogmanay

'Hogmanay', the standard Scottish word for New Year's Eve, was also
used in Northumberland, Cumberland, Westmorland, and Yorkshire.
In 1909, Northumbrian writer Hastings M. Neville recorded that:

*Until about five-and-twenty years ago the custom of Hogmanay existed in
our village. This took the form of a round of visits made by the children on
Old New Year's Day. They would assemble at the front door, and, by way
of greeting, sing with great gusto certain quaint catches, always including
the following:*

> Get up, guid wife and shake your feathers
> And dinna think that we are beggars
> We're little children come to play
> Please to give us our Hogmanay
> May God bless all friends dear
> A merry Christmas and happy New Year

. . . Each child went away pleased with a coin, an orange, and a kind word.

The term Hogmanay is not only applied to this custom, but to any gift received at the New Year or at Christmas, and is practically what is called in the South a Christmas Box.

The word has puzzled scholars for many years, and even its spelling was once in dispute. A discussion in the *Gentleman's Magazine* in 1790, for example, gave it as 'hagman heigh' and 'Hagmenai', while others plumped for 'Hagmena' and 'Hogmena'; however, the *Oxford English Dictionary* gives the standard modern spelling and declares that it is from an Old French word:

Hogmanay . . . corresponds exactly in sense and use to Old French aguillanneuf, 'the last day of the year, new year's gift, the festival at which new year's gifts were asked with the shout of aguillanneuf.'

It is not at all clear how the word travelled from France to Scotland (or the north of England) and became attached to a home-grown custom, unless, of course, the custom accompanied the word. The earliest citation given in the *Oxford English Dictionary* for the word 'Hogmanay' in English or Scots is *c.*1680.

Daily Customs

Bainbridge Horn-Blower

Bainbridge in North Yorkshire is proud to possess a horn-blowing tradition, although it is not so well known as the horn-blowing at Ripon (*see* **Ripon Horn-Blower**, *below*). The current instrument is a buffalo horn, dating from 1864, and it is blown daily, at 9 p.m. but only between 28 September and Shrove Tuesday. The honour of being the horn-blower has been in the Metcalfe family for generations.

No one knows when it started, although there are various theories. One belief is that it is a survival from the Roman legions in the area; another is that it was originally used to guide benighted travellers through the surrounding Wensleydale Forest to safety. However, it is more plausible that it functioned as a curfew or a signal, as at Ripon, that the 'watch' was taking over for the night. All this is speculation, as the earliest definite reference to the custom only dates from the 1820s. In a relatively recent extension to the tradition, locals sometimes ask the horn-blower to attend weddings and other functions, 'for luck'.

Chime Hours

Several linked superstitions connect the time of day an individual is born to his/her ability to see ghosts or be otherwise supernaturally gifted. The best-known of these beliefs states that certain times are particularly potent. In 1916, *Notes & Queries* recorded:

A recent experiment in clairvoyance that chanced to be successful evoked the comment from an observer in a Norfolk village that the experimentalist must have been 'born in chime hours'.

However, there is no general agreement on what exactly constituted the 'chime hours'. Nowadays, most people assume they are the quarters on which most chiming clocks strike, i.e. three, six, nine, and twelve, but some take it to mean eight in the evening, midnight, and four in the morning, which were the old monastic hours of prayer, marked by some churches with a bell. It is also unclear how close to the exact hour the birth has to be. But, as reported in *Notes & Queries* of 1862, all are agreed that the most potent hour of all is midnight:

An old Kentish lady, while discussing hobgoblins last Christmas, said that she had never seen a ghost; though she had placed herself in spots visited by the departed, and had been present while others had seen an apparition. She then stated it as a fact, that people born at twelve o'clock at night, and only such, were gifted with this visionary power. An instance in point was, of course, adduced.

And the potency of midnight is said to be further increased if a child is born at that time on certain key dates such as Christmas Eve (good luck) or Hallowe'en (not so good).

Versions of these beliefs have been recorded in most parts of England and in Scotland. They sound like ancient beliefs, but they cannot be shown to have existed before the mid nineteenth century. The earliest known reference is in Charles Dickens's novel *David Copperfield* (1849), in which the hero introduces himself:

I record that I was born (I have been informed and believe) on a Friday, at twelve o'clock at night . . . It was remarked that the clock began to strike, and I began to cry simultaneously. In consideration of the day and hour of my birth, it was declared by the nurse, and by some sage women in the neighbourhood . . . first, that I was destined to be unlucky in life, and, secondly, that I was privileged to see ghosts and spirits.

David Copperfield was probably believed to be destined for unluckiness because he was born on a Friday, but his supposed supernatural ability will have been the result of the midnight hour.

Lady Lee Monument, Aylesbury

In the church of St Mary the Virgin, Aylesbury, in Buckinghamshire, stands an alabaster monument of 1584, brought from the ruined and deserted church at Quarendon. It commemorates Lady Lee, wife of Sir Henry Lee, Queen's Champion to Elizabeth I. Lady Lee kneels

on a tasselled cushion, wearing a full skirt and buttoned bodice, and a
pleated ruff round her neck. Behind her kneels her daughter, Mary, and
two baby boys, John and Henry, in swaddling clothes to show that they
died in infancy. Part of the inscription, which is in pseudo-medieval
verse and is reminiscent of Spenser's *Faerie Queene* (1590), runs:

> *Good frende, stick not to strew with crimson floures*
> *This marble tombe wherin* [sic] *her cinders rest,*
> *For sure her ghost lyes with the heavenly powers,*
> *And guerdon* [reward] *hathe of virtuous life possest.*

Because of this inscription it became the custom to place red flowers
on the tomb, and this is still done. It is not known how long this has
been going on, but a guide to the church published in 1908, and books
on Buckinghamshire by Arthur Mee and Alison Uttley, published in
1940 and 1950 respectively, all mention it.

Ripon Horn-Blower

Ripon, in North Yorkshire, boasts what must be the only traditional
public custom that takes place every day of the year, and has done
so for centuries, although probably not for millennia as is sometimes
claimed by the over-hopeful local council. Every night, the city's horn-
blower dresses himself in his three-cornered hat and antiquated coat
and proceeds to the market-place, where he blows three blasts of his
horn at each of the four sides of the obelisk there.

This ceremony was originally designed to signify that the town was
in the care of the Wakeman and his staff, who would patrol the streets
until morning, keeping the inhabitants safe. The last Wakeman was
Hugh Ripley in 1604, who also became the first mayor when James I
granted the town a charter, but the setting of the watch with the horn
has, apparently, continued ever since. The horn used at present is a
very impressive African ox horn, provided for the purpose in 1865, but
the civic regalia also includes two previous horns – one dating from
1690, and one that is claimed to be the original charter horn given by
King Alfred in the year 886. The latter claim is most unlikely, but it
could be as old as the twelfth century. Plans for carbon-dating work
on the old horn are underway.

Bainbridge, also in Yorkshire, has a similar horn-blowing custom
every night in the winter months (*see* **Bainbridge Horn-Blower**,
above).

Tower of London: Ceremony of the Keys

Every night, at precisely seven minutes to ten, the Chief Yeoman Warder of the Tower of London starts his rounds of the Tower's gates and ceremoniously locks them up until the morning. He is dressed in the formal and colourful Tudor garb so popular with tourists, and is accompanied by an escort of guards. Sentries at each gate 'salute the Queen's Keys' as they pass, and at the Bloody Tower the Warder is challenged and the traditional words are exchanged:

> 'Halt! Who goes there?'
> 'The Keys.'
> 'Whose keys?'
> 'Queen Elizabeth's Keys.'
> 'Pass, Queen Elizabeth's Keys, all's well.'

It is claimed that the ceremony has been carried out for 700 years. Tickets can be purchased to witness the ceremony.

Wayfarers' Dole

Most charitable doles are distributed annually to specific groups of people, but the Wayfarers' Dole at St Cross Hospital, Winchester, is given on any day to anyone who asks for it. The hospital's full name is the Hospital of St Cross and Almshouse of Noble Poverty, and as it was founded in the 1130s, it is probably the oldest continuing charitable institution in Britain. The impressive medieval buildings are home to a number of elderly 'brethren', who wear a traditional black gown and cap. Any passing stranger may ask at the porter's lodge for the Wayfarers' Dole, which consists of some beer (about a fifth of a pint nowadays) and a piece of bread.

See also **Doles**, p. 115.

Weekly Customs

Farthing Bundles

The Fern Street School Settlement in Bow, east London, was founded by Clara Grant in 1907 as one of the many philanthropic schemes of Victorian and Edwardian times designed to alleviate the endemic poverty and deprivation that characterized life in areas of England's cities; in this case the East End of London. One of the innovative ways in which the Settlement sought to reach the children of the area was the provision of 'farthing bundles' every Saturday. These bundles contained a variety of little things that would delight children who had little in the way of real toys or possessions, and included broken toys, bits of dolls, pieces of ribbon or coloured material, pencils, silver paper, cut-out pictures, beads, shells, and whistles. A farthing was charged (the smallest coin of the realm, worth only one quarter of an old penny), and when the bundles became too popular for the Settlement to cope, access was restricted to younger children by making them walk under a purpose-built portable wooden arch, which bore the words:

Enter now ye children small
None can come who are too tall

Only those who could walk under the arch without stooping were eligible, although the height of the arch had to be raised more than once, as growing prosperity resulted in taller children. Distribution of the bundles continued until well after the Second World War, now costing a penny, but changes in society, particularly in the East End, made them increasingly irrelevant, and the last regular distribution was in 1984. The custom is still occasionally revived on special occasions, such

as the eightieth anniversary in 1987, and the Settlement still continues
its good work in other spheres.

John Sayer Charity

This weekly dole is based on the will of John Sayer, who died in 1638.
He left fifteen acres of land, the rent of which was to provide twopenny loaves every Sunday for the poor of Woodbridge in Suffolk. The
charity has continued, but the land was sold in 1958 and the proceeds
invested. A special wooden cage in the porch of St Mary's church,
inscribed with John Sayer's name and the details of his will, holds nine
small loaves every Saturday, to which certain locals help themselves.

See also **Doles**, p. 115.

St Monday

Countless people are familiar with that Monday-morning feeling of
not wanting to go back to work, and one can therefore spare a thought
for workers in the past, before the weekend was invented, who only
had Sunday off each week. Nevertheless, many workers did manage
to achieve their own unofficial weekend, by the simple expedient of
declaring every Monday a day off, which they dedicated to an imaginary saint called 'St Monday'. Clearly, this could only happen in trades
where the workers were largely self-employed and could survive on the
proceeds of the work carried out on other days, and it was the shoemakers who were particularly prone to this self-indulgence. Monday
was often called 'the shoemakers' holiday' in consequence, although
some other workers managed to do something similar.

A spurious explanation for the origin of St Monday was printed in
the *Folk-Lore Record* of 1878, from an undated newspaper cutting. It
explained that when Cromwell's army was encamped outside Perth,
one of his followers, named Monday, hanged himself. Cromwell
offered a reward to the person who could compile the best verse on the
subject, and was so pleased with one shoemaker's contribution that
he declared that no one of that trade needed to work on Monday ever
again. However, the tradition of St Monday was in place long before
Cromwell's time: Thomas Dekker's earliest surviving play, for example, entitled *The Shoemaker's Holiday*, was published in the year 1600,
and his play *If it be not good, the Divel is in it* (1612) contains the line,
'They say Monday's shoemaker's holiday, I'll fall to that trade.'

St Monday survived into the nineteenth century, but the whole idea was anathema to the type of Victorian social reformer who believed that workers should be either at work or at prayer. Those who claimed the St Monday privilege had a reputation for getting drunk and unruly, and were believed to set a bad example to other workers. When better working conditions, stricter time-keeping, and the half-day holiday on Saturday became the norm, St Monday faded away.

St Monday was also popular in Ireland and Scotland, and exactly the same tradition existed in France and Belgium, back to at least the sixteenth century, where the cobblers liked to *faire St Lundi*. Similar customs also existed in Spain, Germany, and elsewhere in Europe.

Occasional Customs

Abingdon Bun-Throwing

At Abingdon, in Oxfordshire, they have a long-standing custom of throwing buns to the waiting crowd on national and royal occasions. The earliest documented instance took place in 1809, to celebrate George III's recovery from illness, but records before 1838 simply refer to the buns being 'distributed'. In 1838, however, a thousand buns were recorded as being thrown to celebrate Victoria's coronation. In more recent times, buns were thrown at the end of the Second World War, in the year 2000 to mark the Millennium, and in 2002, to celebrate the anniversary of Queen Elizabeth's accession in 1952. June 2006 saw 4,000 buns thrown from the roof of the Market House (or county hall) by councillors and freemen to the crowds waiting in the market-square below, to celebrate the 450th anniversary of the granting of the borough charter to Abingdon.

Although it is unusual to find buns being thrown simply for special occasions, buns and other food such as bread and cheese were often thrown to people in other customs around the country, either as part of a charity dole or in mayor-making ceremonies, as at Harwich in Essex (*see* **Third Thursday in May: Harwich Kichel-Throwing**). Jackie Smith, Honorary Archivist for Abingdon Town Council, admitted in 2006 that bun-throwings have certainly become more frequent in Abingdon since the 1980s, and it is not clear whether this is due to an increase in notable occasions. A collection of the buns can be seen in Abingdon Museum.

See also **Scrambling Customs**, p. 172.

Bradshaw Memorial Dusting

Parish churches up and down the country contain thousands of grand memorials to local worthies who were thought important or good enough to be remembered for ever more. Many of the same individuals bequeathed money to the poor or other charitable causes, and sometimes also left instructions for activities that later became regular, and often seemingly eccentric, customs. The memorial to the successful London lawyer Anthonie Bradshaw, of Duffield in Derbyshire, is an interesting example of how a man could contrive to do good for the poor and ensure that his name was remembered after his death.

About 1600, fourteen years before his death, Bradshaw had a huge sandstone and alabaster memorial set against the wall of St Alkmund's church, commemorating himself, his two wives, and their twenty children (although he had three more before he died). He also founded an almshouse for four elderly women. One of the stipulations of Bradshaw's bequest was that the residents of the almshouse should regularly dust the memorial and keep it clean. The almshouse and the dusting disappeared in the 1880s and the monument fell into disrepair. However, it has now been carefully restored and is looked after by a charitable trust, the Friends of the Bradshaw Memorial.

See also **Doles**, p. 115.

Chedzoy Candle Auction

One of two surviving candle auctions in Somerset, the auction at Chedzoy is held once every twenty-one years to lease out Church Acre, which, as its name suggests, is a field that belongs to the parish church, St Mary the Virgin. All proceeds go towards the upkeep of the church. As usual with these affairs, the auction is 'by inch of candle', and the last bid made before the candle goes out is the winner. The auction is usually held at the Manor House Inn, and the next should take place in 2009.

See also **Candle Auctions**, p. 138.

Denby Dale Pie

The West Yorkshire town of Denby Dale is world-renowned for its giant pies. Once every thirty or forty years, the people of the town get the urge to make a huge pie, usually even bigger than the one before.

The reasons behind these urges are various: in 1788, it was to celebrate the return to health of George III; in 1815, a 'Victory Pie' was made to mark the end of the Napoleonic threat; in 1846, the pie celebrated the repeal of the Corn Laws; in 1887, Queen Victoria's Golden Jubilee; in 1896, the jubilee of the repeal of the Corn Laws; in 1928, an 'Infirmary Pie' was made to support the local hospital; in 1964, a pie was made to raise money for a village hall; and in 1988, to celebrate 200 years of pie-making at Denby Dale.

The day the pie is unveiled and shared out has always been a major gala occasion, with speeches, processions, sideshows, funfairs and entertainments, but pie-making and eating has not always gone quite to plan. The 1846 event, to celebrate the repeal of the hated Corn Laws, was marred by a riot, which was probably organized by political opponents, and the pie was trampled underfoot. And in 1887, the pie was found to be rotten and the crowd got dangerously out of control, although the replacement 'Resurrection Pie', which was made a month later, was celebrated without any major hitch. Plans to make a pie to celebrate the end of the Second World War, and the coronation of Elizabeth II in 1953, were scuppered by rationing and food regulation.

The build-up to the 1964 effort was marked with tragi-comedy, and later real tragedy. In June, the specially made steel pie-dish, 18 feet long and 6 feet wide, was launched on to the Calder Navigation Canal at Mirfield, near Huddersfield, where it was to be floated to Denby. Unfortunately, however, it sank. The national press reported that teenagers were holding an impromptu party in the dish at the time of the accident – although it is not clear whether it was their fault – and the dish was duly salvaged by a local garage's rescue truck. The organizing committee revealed that the canal trip had been insured with Lloyd's, so the insurance would foot the bill. In August, however, four members of the organizing committee were killed in a road accident returning from a television interview.

Twentieth-century organizers had clearly got a better handle on crowd control than their Victorian predecessors, and all the events since 1896 have been major successes, attracting ever-increasing numbers of visitors, and with nearly everyone in the town making some contribution. The 1988 pie, organized by the Denby Dale Pie Trust, resulted in a pie that was 20 feet long, 7 feet wide, and 1 foot 6 inches deep, weighing nearly half a ton, but even this was surpassed in both size and technological achievement by the Millennium Pie in the year

This one was baked in a dish that comprised twenty-four compartments, each with its own heating element, specially designed by the School of Engineering at the University of Huddersfield. The pie was 40 feet by 8 feet and nearly 4 foot deep, and contained 5,000 kg of beef, 2,000 kg of potatoes, and 1,000 kg of onions. It was brought in procession to the Pie Field on a lorry, and was blessed by the Bishop of Wakefield before being cut and distributed to the 30,000-strong crowd.

Denby Dale is not quite unique in the big-food stakes, as the village of Aughton, in Lancashire, had a giant-pudding custom. The Aughton feast was a plum pudding 20 feet long and 6 feet thick, weighing 1,000 lb, and was made every twenty-one years. The last one was made in 1886, but in the 1970s the field where the festivities had taken place was still known as 'the Pudding Field'.

Dunmow Flitch

Little Dunmow and Great Dunmow are Essex villages about twelve miles from Chelmsford, and are world famous for their ceremony of awarding a 'flitch of bacon' to couples who have been married for more than a year and a day and who have had neither a cross word nor a single thought regretting their married state during that time. In the modern version of the custom, claimants are brought up before a 'court', presided over by a judge, and complete with claimants' counsel, opposing counsel, a jury of twelve unmarried people (six men and six women), a clerk of the court, and an usher. It is not a competition between couples, as each claim is considered on its merits, and it is possible for them all to win. However, the opposing counsel always tries to demolish each case and persuade the jury to decide 'for the flitch' and against the claimants; and witnesses for and against can be called. Successful couples are carried in the Flitch Chair, shoulder high, to the market-place, and are obliged to take an oath:

> You do swear by custom of confession,
> That you ne'er made nuptial transgression
> Nor since you were married man and wife
> By household brawls or contentious strife
> Or otherwise in bed or at board
> Offended each other in deed or in word
> Or in a twelve months and a day

Repented not in thought in any way
Or since the church clerk said amen
Wish't yourselves unmarried again
But continue true and desire
As when you joined hands in holy quire.

Nowadays, the event is held in a marquee every leap year, and is organized by a committee of volunteers. Judges and counsel often include well-known figures.

Unlike many customs, the Dunmow flitch is genuinely old, and was already well known over 600 years ago. It is mentioned in terms of general familiarity by both William Langland in his *Piers Plowman* (*c*.1377) and Chaucer in the *Wife of Bath's Tale* (*c*.1390), and not long after this, the earliest known awards of the bacon were recorded in the *Cartuleries* of Dunmow Priory, in 1445, 1467, and 1510. The first of these was to one Richard Wright, of Burburgh, near Norwich, which shows that even at this early date the flitch could be claimed by outsiders, and not simply by locals. In this period, the custom was in the province of the Priory of Little Dunmow, but at the Dissolution of the Monasteries in 1539, responsibility was given to the new lord of the manor. Successive lords kept it going until 1751, after which time they started to refuse all requests from prospective recipients, and it lapsed.

There was a tremendous revival of interest, however, after the publication of Harrison Ainsworth's *The Flitch of Bacon, or the Custom of Dunmow* in 1854. Ainsworth was an immensely popular historical novelist of the period, and he took the part of the judge in a well-publicized revival of the custom the following year. As with all such revivals, certain characteristics of the earlier form were maintained, others were dropped, and many were introduced for the first time. In this case, the custom was completely transformed by making it a public event. Whereas previously claimants would come forward of their own volition and would be vetted by the prior, the lord of the manor, or his steward, in private, in the revival version, a 'trial' would be announced and applications invited. After an initial vetting, the actual selection was made in a public mock 'court', with judge, jury, and barristers, and this brought scope for humour and burlesque. So the modern custom was born.

Despite the unusually rich documentary record, the origin of the ceremony is still not known. It is possible that the custom was created as a condition of a bequest to the priory by a benefactor; or perhaps it was some kind of manorial obligation by which land was held, or services rendered. Certainly, whimsical bequests are not unknown, and seemingly bizarre manorial customs were also common, but it is unclear why the prior or a mid sixteenth-century lord would keep up what must have been a potentially expensive custom unless they felt obliged to do so, and it is also unclear why there is no hint of a reason in the surviving priory or manor records.

The exact form of the earliest ceremonies is not known, but by the time of the records found in the *Cartuleries*, a fundamental element was the oath, taken by the applicants, testifying to the truth of everything they had stated. They took this oath while kneeling on uncomfortable (sometimes described as 'sharp') stones, and once the award had been given, the successful couple would be chaired around the vicinity. As far as we can tell, the award was taken seriously in the prior's time, and probably for most of the lord of the manor's jurisdiction as well, but it was not always taken very seriously by outsiders. The custom was regularly featured in novels, poems, ballad operas, and plays, and was also depicted in popular prints and engravings, and in many the flitch ceremony was treated either with broad humour or sentimental romance; a standard motif was the winning of the award by a couple who then argued noisily about how to take it home.

Surprisingly, the Dunmow flitch ceremony was not unique. In October 1714, a writer in the *Spectator* reported:

I find but two couples in this first century that were successful. The first was a sea captain and his wife, who since the day of their marriage had not seen each other till the day of the claim. The second was an honest pair in the neighbourhood. The husband was a man of plain good sense, and a peaceable temper. The woman was dumb.

This writer was in fact satirizing a very similar custom at Wychnor, in Staffordshire, which is reputed to have been first stipulated in the deed by which the Earl of Lancaster granted the manor to Sir Philip de Somerville, in the reign of Edward III, *c.*1336. Francis Steer, who wrote the standard history of the Dunmow custom in 1951, also identified other public flitches in Vienna and Brittany that were closely related to conjugal contentment.

Highgate Horns

Highgate is now a suburb of north London, but in earlier times it was a village in Middlesex, high on a hill, straddling the main road north. Before the railways came, it was an important transport centre, and there were numerous inns catering for the coaching trade and the stream of horse-drawn traffic that passed through every day. An interesting custom grew up at Highgate, in which those who passed through the village for the first time were required to undergo a sort of initiation ceremony, which involved swearing an oath on a pair of horns. By the time the horns custom is first documented, it was carried out by the publicans of the neighbourhood with an eye to what we would now call the tourist trade, and each of the inns kept a pair of horns, mounted on a pole, ready for the purpose. The species from which the horns were taken seemed to matter little, as stag, ram, and bullock horns are mentioned. The burlesque ceremony usually involved the landlord dressing as a judge and administering an oath that included instructions on the lines of 'Never eat the brown bread if white is available, never kiss the maid if you can kiss the mistress, and if you see three pigs asleep in the gutter you may kick out the middle one and take its place.' The applicant had to kiss the horns and then buy drinks for the company or pay the landlord a fee.

The custom was clearly already well known in the mid eighteenth century. The earliest known mention is in the *Weekly Oracle* of 1737, and in 1742 the pantomime *Harlequin Teague* featured a song that already included the traditional jokes of brown bread and kisses. Francis Grose's *Classical Dictionary of the Vulgar Tongue* (1785) confirms the custom's widespread fame:

The proverb 'he has been sworn at Highgate' is more widely circulated than understood. In its ordinary signification it is applied to a 'knowing' fellow who is well acquainted with the 'good things', and always helps himself to the best; and it has its origin in an old usage still kept up at Highgate, in Middlesex.

As the custom is already fully-formed when it enters the documentary record, there is no indication that it was ever anything but burlesque, although some modern writers assume it had previously been a serious ceremony with an ancient lineage. Other customs involving horns existed, but none is quite the same. At Charlton Horn Fair, the horns almost certainly derive from the connection with St Luke (*see* 18 October: St Luke's Day), but the closest analogy to the Highgate Horns was the custom of 'horning the colt' at Weyhill Fair, which was ostensibly an initiation ceremony probably started by cattle dealers (*see* 10 October: Weyhill Fair). One sensible theory is therefore that the swearing was an in-joke of the cattle drovers who regularly passed through Highgate on their way to the northern markets, and this remains a possibility.

The custom finally lapsed in the late nineteenth century, but is revived, from time to time, at local pubs, including The Wrestlers, on North Road, and The Flask, on Highgate West Hill.

Oakham Horseshoes

Every peer of the realm who visits Oakham in Leicestershire (formerly in Rutland) for the first time is obliged by custom to present a horseshoe to the lord of the manor, or to pay a fine. Even royalty is not exempt and Queen Elizabeth II presented a shoe from one of her own racehorses in 1967, although the story that Elizabeth I did so is probably apocryphal. The shoes are exhibited on the walls of the great hall of Oakham Castle, and many of them are not real horseshoes but large, specially made presentation pieces, with the names and crests of the donors. Some have disappeared over the years – the official charged with putting them up often took down older ones to make room – but nearly 250 have survived and are still on show, including one from Edward IV (r. 1461–83). The shoes are all mounted with the prongs facing downwards, regarded as unlucky nowadays, but the general consensus over the orientation of a horseshoe is a relatively recent phenomenon and in the past either way would do.

The origin of the custom remains a mystery, but the first known written reference dates from 1521, and that document mentions the shoe presented by Edward IV, so it was clearly extant in his time. One plausible theory links the shoes to the family of Ferrers, who held the manor direct from the Crown from at least 1166 to 1252. The Ferrers were descended from the Norman Ferrières family, and as the name is clearly connected with iron-working, blacksmiths, and farriers, and the family arms comprise six black horseshoes on a silver background, there seems to be an obvious connection. The fact that the Great Hall was also built in the twelfth century adds circumstantial evidence, but there is no evidence that the arms pre-date the custom, or that either go back to before the fifteenth century.

Virgins' Crowns or Maidens' Garlands

A custom that was carried on for centuries in many parishes up and down the country, and still survives in one, involved the construction of a garland or crown to honour a deceased unmarried parishioner of unblemished character. The garland was carried before the coffin at the funeral and, if unchallenged within a certain period, hung high up in the church for all to see, where it remained until it fell to pieces with age. The construction of these garlands varied considerably, but one common basic form is made in the shape of a crown, with pliable twigs forming a horizontal hoop, and two vertical semicircles arching over it, at right angles to each other. The wood is then covered with cloth or coloured paper, and rosettes and artificial flowers are placed on it at intervals. Some had items hanging down inside, often gloves made of stiff paper, and many had verses from the Scriptures attached. Most had the name of the deceased and the date marked somewhere on the garland or on a small shield fixed to the wall nearby.

William Howitt, born 1792, is one of many writers who were impressed by the garlands in their youth:

Though I never saw a funeral in which so beautiful and appropriate a practice was retained, I well recollect seeing these gloves and garlands hanging in the church of my native village [Heanor] *in Derbyshire, and I have heard my mother say, that in her younger days she has helped to cut and prepare them for the funeral of the young women of the place. The garlands were originally of actual flowers – lilies and roses – and the gloves of white kid. For these had been substituted simple white paper.*

As the garlands were hung in the church, the custom was remembered by the congregation, even if new examples were only rarely made. In many cases, the poignant stories of the deceased recipients also lived on.

The custom was clearly known to Shakespeare, as the references to Ophelia's garlands and 'virgin crants' (crowns) in Act V, scene 1 of *Hamlet* demonstrate, and there are numerous descriptions throughout the eighteenth century. However, it is not clear whether the custom of mounting garlands was ever universal, although it was obviously widespread. A map provided by Gareth Spriggs in his comprehensive survey of garlands published in 1982 includes all known references to the custom, and shows that it was certainly found over most of the country, but was much more common in the Midlands and the North, particularly in Derbyshire and eastern Yorkshire. A fair number of southern examples are included, but there are none west of Hampshire. We will never know how many were swept away by nineteenth-century vicars, church improvers and restorers, but a few can still be seen around the country, and the one place that still keeps the custom alive is St Mary's church, Abbotts Ann, in Hampshire.

Dates for Easter Sunday 2007–20

2007	8 April	2014	20 April
2008	23 March	2015	5 April
2009	12 April	2016	27 March
2010	4 April	2017	16 April
2011	24 April	2018	1 April
2012	8 April	2019	21 April
2013	31 March	2020	12 April

Sources

Brand I (1849) 10–20; Wright & Lones II (1938) 24–32.

Mad Maldon Mud Race
Kent (2005) 47–8; www.maldonlions. co.uk/events/mudrace.

Pop (Pope) Ladies
I happened to sleep: Gent. Mag. 90 (1820) 15. *N&Q* 4S:11 (1873) 412; Wright & Lones I (1938) 29–30.

6 January

Epiphany
Brand I (1849) 21–34; Wright & Lones II (1938) 50–93; Metford (1991) 17–20, 40–42.

Old Christmas Day
My grandfather always kept: Leather (1912) 95.

Twelfth Night
I did bring out my cake: Samuel Pepys, *Diary*, 6 January 1669.
I went to a friend's house: Brand (1810) 228, quoting *Universal Magazine* (1774).
In London: Hone, *The Every-Day Book* I (1827) 24–5.
Hone, *The Every-Day Book* I (1827) 24–31; Brand I (1849) 21–34; Wright & Lones II (1938) 50–91; Hutton (1996) 15–18, 110–11.

Baddeley Cake
Brentnall (1975) 188; Shuel (1985) 127–8.

Brough Holly Night
Formerly the 'Holly-tree': Hone, *The Table Book* (1827) 13–14.
Wright & Lones II (1938) 68; Findler (1968) 47–9.

Haxey Hood
Newall (1980); Cooper (1993).

Moseley's Dole
Edwards (1842) 55–6; Wright & Lones II (1938) 68–74.

Twelfth Night Fires
At the approach of evening: Gent. Mag. (1791) 116.

Plough Sunday

The Times, 11 Jan. 1954, 8.

Plough Monday

Plough Monday, next after: Tusser (1580/1984) 177.
Leading the plough: Dives and Pauper (c.1405–10/1976/1980) 157.
Plough Monday was a great institution: Bird (1911) 39.
Plough Monday – All the boys: Folk-Lore 37 (1926) 76.
Gutch & Peacock (1908) 171–87; Wright & Lones II (1938) 93–103; Porter (1969) 96–103; Palmer (1985) 86–90; Howkins & Merricks (1991); Hutton (1996) 124–33.

Plough Plays
Baskervill (1924); Helm (1980); Howkins & Merricks (1991); Millington (1995); Cass & Roud (2002).

Ploughboys and Maids
When the ploughman returned: Baker II (1854) 123.
It was customary: Bloom (1930) 80.
If ploughman get hatchet: Tusser (1580/1984) 177.

Plough Monday/Plough Tuesday

Straw Bears
When I was at Whittlesey: Folk-Lore 20 (1909) 202–3.
Marshall (1967) 199–201; Tebbutt (1984) 55–6; Frampton (1989).

7 January

St Distaff's Day
Partly work and partly play: Herrick (1648).
Chambers I (1864) 68–9; Wright & Lones III (1940) 91–2.

14 January

Hunting the Mallard
Hone, *The Year-Book* (1832) 44–6; Chambers I (1864) 113–14; Wright & Lones II (1938) 104–5; Hole (1976) 161–3.

17 January

Old Twelfth Night
Patten (1974) 6–8.

21 January

St Agnes' Day
The girl who wished: *Long Ago* 2 (1874) 80.
Wright & Lones II (1938) 106–110; Roud
(2003) 386.

22 January

St Vincent's Day
Remember on St. Vincent's: Balfour (1904) 174.
Wright & Lones II (1938) 111.

24 January

Eve of Conversion of St Paul
St. Paul's Eve: *Folk-Lore Journal* 4 (1886) 127.
On entering a house: *Western Antiquary* 3
(1884) 67.

25 January

St Paul's Day
If Paul's Fair: *Western Antiquary* 3 (1884) 193.
Brand I (1849) 39–42; Chambers I (1864)
157–8; Wright & Lones II (1938) 112–15.

30 January

Execution of Charles I
Chambers I (1864) 189–92; Brentnall (1975)
174–6; Society of King Charles the
Martyr website, www.skcm.org.

January/February

Chinese New Year
Buddha, on the turn of the year: www.china
townchinese.com/rooster.htm.

Games and Sports
but all play and no work: Samuel Smiles, *Self
Help* (1859), quoted in Flavell (1993) 144.
In the records: Govett (1890) 73.
The favourite pastimes: Hole (1949) 1.
Strutt (1801); Govett (1890); Hole (1949);
Malcolmson (1973); Opie (1997a).

Camping
Of the sport itself: Forby (1830) 51.
camping is not football: *N&Q* 5S:2 (1892) 137.
At times a large football: Moor (1823) 65.
Moor (1823) 63–6; Forby (1830) 50–54; Porter
(1969) 230–31.

Pell-Mell
Chambers I (1864) 465-6; Hazlitt (1905)
470–71.

Shuttlecock
The play at shuttlecocke: Manningham (1868),
quoted in Hazlitt (1905) 33.
On the day itself: *N&Q* 3S:3 (1863) 87.
Gomme II (1894–8) 192-6; Wright & Lones
I (1936) 28; Strutt (1801/1876) 400–401.

Stoolball
Stoolball: this game: *N&Q* 3S:11 (1867) 457–8.
a certain number: Strutt (1801/1876) 165.
Strutt (1801/1876) 165–6; Grantham (1931);
Arlott (1975) 996–9; Lowerson (1995);
Sussex Arch. Colls. 133 (1995) 263-74; *Sussex
Arch. Colls.* 136 (1998) 204–5; National
Stoolball Association website, www.
stoolball.co.uk.

Tipcat
Strutt (1801/1876) 86; Hole (1949) 48; Opie
(1997a) 316–21.

Trapball / Knurr and Spell
Strutt (1801/1876) 176-9; Hone, *The Every-
Day Book* I (1827) 215; Hole (1949) 48–9;
Atkinson (1963); Opie (1997a) 322–8.

FEBRUARY

Trial of the Pyx
Brentnall (1975) 42–7; www.thegoldsmiths.
co.uk/company/trial.htm.

First Sunday in February

Clowns' Service
Shuel (1985) 79.

2 February

**Candlemas (Purification of the Blessed
Virgin Mary)**
If Candlemas day be dry: Hewett (1900) 107.
Candlemas day was also known: Tebbutt
(1984) 56–7.
Brand I (1849) 43–51; Wright & Lones II
(1938) 118–29; Opie & Tatem (1989) 54–5;
Metford (1991) 74–6; Duffy (1992) 15–22;
Roud (2003) 56–9.

Forty Shilling Day
Kightly (1986) 117; information from the
Revd Pam Robson of Holmbury St Mary
church, Surrey, August 2005.

3 February

St Blaise's Day
This day, Munday: Gurdon (1893) 110.
Chambers I (1864) 219–20.

St Ives Hurling
Rabey (1972); Kightly (1986) 144–5; Williams (1987) 16–19.

Hurling
The game called the Hurlers: Defoe (1724–6) Letter IV: Cornwall.
Carew (1602/1969) 147–50; Rabey (1972); Williams (1987) 16–19, 20–21.

10 February

St Scholastica's Day
Dyer (1876) 97–8.

14 February

St Valentine's Day
I'll tell you something: Hart (1968) 167, citing Dorothy Osborne.
Valentining: Children going: Baker II (1854) 373–4.
Young girls grow eager: John Clare, *The Midsummer Cushion* (1832/1990)
On Valentine's day: Halliwell (1849) 219–20.

20 February

John Cass Commemoration
Brentnall (1975) 167–8.

Shrovetide and Lent

At the beginning of Lent: Fisher (1865) 463.
Brand I (1849) 62–102; Chambers I (1864) 236–41; Wright & Lones I (1936) 1–42; Hutton (1996) 151–68.

Shrove Tuesday

the children expect: Nicholson (1890) 12
It was the day: Pasquils Palinodia (1619/1886) 29.
The custom of apprentices: The Times, 3 March 1954.

Alnwick Football
Before the Alnwick Improvement Act: Folk-Lore Journal 2 (1884) 123–4.
Independent, 11 Feb. 1989, 47.

Ashbourne Football
Porter (1992); Porter (1995); www.derby shireuk.net/dcustom4.html.

Football
Moreover, each year: Fitz Stephen (*c.*1180/1990) 56–7.
And because of the great: N&Q 7S:2 (1886) 26–7.
The Kinge forbiddes: Sc. Act Jas. I c. 18.
Foote balle wherin is nothinge: The Boke named the Governour I (1531) xxvii.
In the town of Derby: Glover I (1829) 310.
The old custom: The Times, 10 Feb. 1932, 9.
Any exercise, which withdraweth us: Stubbes (1595/2002) 251–3.
Nicholson (1890) 34–9; Magoun (1938); Elias & Dunning (1971); Alexander (1986); Reid (1988).

Cock Throwing and Threshing
Their entertainment then: Schellinks (1993) 73.
Hone, *The Every-Day Book* II (1827) 123–9; Wright & Lones I (1936) 22–4; Malcolmson (1973) 48–9, 118–22.

Cockfighting
Each year upon the day: Fitz Stephen (*c.*1180/1990) 56.
In the afternoon we went: Schellinks (1993) 93.
Wright & Lones I (1936) 24–6; Malcolmson (1973) 49–50.

Cookeels (or Coquilles)
Forby (1830) 76; N&Q 1S:1 (1850) 293, 412–3.

Dough-Nut Day
Hone, *The Year-Book* (1832) 796.

Egg Shackling
In the 19th century: Dacombe (1935) 90.

Ludlow Rope-Pulling
Hone, *The Every-Day Book* II (1827) 128–9; Brand I (1849) 92; Wright & Lones I (1936) 29; Palmer (2004) 291–2.

Pancakes
It was the day: Pasquils Palinodia (1619/1866) 29.
The excitement of pancake day: Harris (1969) 149–51.
The 'pancake bell' is still rung: Folk-Lore 61 (1950) 167.
Shrove Tuesday: Ill-luck: Forby (1830) 242.

Pancake Races
Folk-Lore 60 (1949) 301–2; Lenton (2003).

Westminster Pancakes
Then, suddenly, the frying pan: Brentnall
    (1975) 158.
Brentnall (1975) 157–61; Shuel (1985) 151–2.

Purbeck Marblers and Stonecutters
www.uk-genealogy.org.uk/genuki/DOR/
    CorfeCastle/articles.html; Shuel (1985)
    120; Kightly (1986) 156–7.

St Columb Hurling
Many a young hurler: Rabey (1972) 15.
Williams (1987) 20–21; Kightly (1986) 144–5.

Sedgefield Ball Game
The ball was put through: *Folk-Lore Journal* 2
    (1884) 124.

Shroving and Lent-Crocking
Pit-a-pat! the pan's hot: *Folk-Lore* 14 (1903)
    167–8.
On the day termed 'Hall Monday': Couch
    (1871) 151.
Wright & Lones I (1936) 16–20; Hutton
    (1996) 163–7; Robson (1996).

Skipping
brought back memories: *Dalesman*, Apr. 1994,
    74–5.
Smith (1989) 3–8; *Dalesman*, Feb. 1994, 23–4.

Whipping Toms
Palmer (1985) 223–4.

Ash Wednesday

On Ash Wednesday the good people: Fisher
    (1865) 463.
On Ash Wednesday, many folks: *Folk-Lore* 40
    (1929) 283.

Jack-a-Lent
An old custom: Couch (1871) 152.
How like a Jack a Lent: Quarles (1646) 88.
Brand I (1849) 94–102; Wright & Lones I
    (1936) 39–42.

Scambling Days
Dyer (1876) 95; *OED*; *EDD*.

Friday Following Ash Wednesday

Pully Lug Day
I have a recollection: *N&Q* 5S:10 (1878) 249.
N&Q 7S:2 (1886) 294. Wright, *EDD* IV
    (1898–1905) 644.

29 February

Leap Year Day
In Leap Year they have power: Lean I
    (1902–4) 468.
Some priests assert: Hampson II (1841) 31–2.
N&Q 4S:8 (1871) 505, citing *Courtship, Love
    and Matrimony* (1606).

MARCH

Dame Elizabeth Marvyn Charity
Sykes (1977) 37.

1 March

St David's Day
being St. David's Day: Schellinks (1993) 75.
A house-maid advised: Hewett (1892) 52.
The Devil shakes a bag: *Bye-Gones* (1899–
    1900) 344.
Lean I (1905) 357; for March coming in like a
    lion, *see* Inwards (1893) 19–20.

2 March

St Chad's Day
Chambers I (1864) 320–21.

3 March

St Winwaloe's Day
Wright & Lones II (1938) 159–62.

Rough Music
There is a man: *Surrey Gazette*, 9 Jan. 1869.
A thrice married man: *Croydon Advertiser*, 1
    Oct. 1881, 5.
A few months ago: *Folk-Lore Journal* 2 (1884)
    187–8.
'Rough music' was heard: Horn (1986) 52–3.
Ingram (1984); Thompson (1991).

5 March

St Piran's Day
Wright & Lones II (1938) 162; Doble IV
    (1998) 3–30.

9 March

St Constantine's Day
Wright & Lones II (1938) 163–4; Doble II
    (1997) 15–24.

10 March

If it does not freeze: Hewett (1900) 109
Mists or hoar frosts: Thomas Passenger, *The Shepherd's Kalendar* (London, c.1680), quoted in *N&Q* 1S:8 (1853) 50.

11 March

Penny Loaf Day
Newark Advertiser, 14 Mar. 1997, 36; J. Potter Briscoe, *Nottinghamshire Facts and Fictions* (1876), quoted in Wright & Lones II (1938) 164.

12 March

St Gregory's Day
Wright & Lones II (1938) 164–5.

17 March

St Patrick's Day
The Irish folks: Swift, *Journal to Stella* (1710–13) letter lxi.
My grandmother would send: Sutton (1997) 39.
St. Patrick's Day today: Bruley (2001) 173.
The early English calendars: Chambers I (1864) 385.

Pudding-Pies
Woe betide the farmer: *N&Q* 4S:4 (1869) 506–7.
Throughout Lent: *Folk-Lore* 23 (1912) 353.

Wiggs
N&Q 5S:1 (1874) 474; 5S:2 (1874) 138, 178–9; *EDD* VI (1905) 489.

Braggot Sunday

Hir mouth was swete: Geoffrey Chaucer, *The Canterbury Tales: The Miller's Tale*, line 3261.

Mothering Sunday

Every mid-Lent Sunday: Symonds (1644/1909) 27.
I'll to thee a simnell bring: Herrick (1648) 'A Ceremonie in Gloster'.
I happened to reside: *Gent. Mag.* (1784) 343.
The pretty custom: Leather (1912) 97.
They are very rich plum-cakes: Burne (1883) 325
To 3lbs of flour: *Folk-Lore* 20 (1909) 203–4.
Long ago: Chambers II (1864) 337.
Chambers I (1864) 335–7; Wright & Lones I (1936) 42–51.

19 March

St Joseph's Day
Sutton (1997) 35.

21 March

St Benedict's Day
Where the wind is: Devonshire Assoc. 105 (1973) 214.
Saint Benedick: Ray (1670/1818) 30.
Wright & Lones II (1938) 165–6.

Weekday in late March

Oranges and Lemons Service
Brentnall (1975) 171; Opie (1997b) 398–401.

25 March

Annunciation/Lady Day
Although servants are hired: Devonshire Assoc. 57 (1926) 127.
Wright & Lones II (1938) 166–8.

Tichborne Dole
Baigent (1855); Shuel (1985) 127–9; James (1987); Westwood and Simpson (2005) 312.

Doles
to lay out six nobles: Edwards (1842) 112.
As for legacies: Chambers II (1864) 702–4.
In the course of 30 years' ministry: *The Times*, 12 Jan. 1898, 6.
Edwards (1842); Shuel (1985) 125–35; Kightly (1986) 58–9, 127–8.

Care or Carling Sunday

The rustics go: Brand I (1810) 361–2.
Wright & Lones I (1936) 53.

March/April

Borrowed Days
Give me (says March): *N&Q* 1S:5 (1852) 342.
The three last days: *N&Q* 1S:5 (1852) 278–9.
March borrowed of April: Brockett (1846) 47.
March said to April: Chambers I (1864) 448.
They who are very superstitious: Hampson I (1841) 211.
The first three days in March: Whitcombe (1874) 7.
Brand II (1849) 41–4; Hampson I (1841) 210–11; Chambers I (1864) 448; *N&Q* 9S:12 (1903) 23; Wright & Lones II (1938) 168–170.

Great Barmote Court

Porteous (1976) 12–13; www.duchyoflancas
ter.org.uk; www.en.wikipedia.org/wiki/
Derbyshire_lead_mining_history.

1 April

All Fools' Day

Fooles Holy Day: Aubrey (1686/1880) 10.
Thursday 1 April: Bruley (2001) 124.
in March 1860: Chambers I (1864) 462.
Hone, *The Every-Day Book* I (1827) 205–7;
Brand I (1849) 131–41; Wright & Lones II
(1938) 171–6; Opie (1959) 243–7; Hutton
(1996) 177–8; Sutton (1997) 82–3.

Palm Sunday

We always went out: Sutton (1997) 62.
several hundreds of the workers: *Time's
Telescope* (1826) 66–7.
Popularly, Palm Sunday: Burne (1883) 330.
Brand I (1849) 118–31; Chambers I (1864)
395–8; Dyer (1876) 126–35; Wright &
Lones I (1936) 54–61; Opie & Tatem
(1989) 297; Metford (1991) 56–8.

Caistor Gad-Whip Ceremony

The whip is taken: Dyer (1876) 129, quoting a
sale document of 1845.
Dyer (1876) 128–32; Gomme (1883) 195–7;
Andrews (1891) 91–104; *N&Q* 9S:7 (1901)
286; Sutton (1997) 63–5.

Figs

This day is called: *Folk-Lore Journal* 3 (1885)
283.
Palm Sunday is called: *Folk-Lore* 40 (1929)
82–3.

Martinsell Hill

In the eighteenth and nineteenth: Bradley
(1913) 222.
Wilts. Arch. & Nat. Hist. Mag. 17 (1878)
289–90; Wright & Lones I (1936) 55;
Whitlock (1976) 52.

Pax Cakes

Leather (1912) 97–8; Shuel (1985) 83–4;
Palmer (2002) 64–5.

Water

On Palm Sunday: *Folk-Lore* 40 (1929) 381.

Fig Sunday

The fig-pies are made: *N&Q* 2S:1 (1856) 227.

½ lb breadcrumbs: White (1932) 335–6.
Hone, *The Year-Book* (1832) 797; Brand I
(1849) 124; *EDD* II (1900) 352; Wright &
Lones I (1936) 58–9.

Holy Week Monday

Bourne Running Auction

Sutton (1997) 80.

Maundy Thursday

On the 5th April: Ratcliffe & Wright (1960)
13–14, citing Edward Walford's *Old and
New London* III (1890) 368.
Stone (1906) 52–4; Ratcliffe & Wright,
(1960); Robinson (1992).

Henry Travice Charity

Sykes (1977) 39; Shuel (1985) 132; Kightly
(1986) 127.

Peter's Pence

At Exeter Cathedral: Cossins (1878) 36.

5 April

John Stow Commemoration

on three market-days: Stow (1603/1994)
Shuel (1985) 73; Kightly (1986) 82.

6 April

Flitting Day

We always had to move: Sutton (1997) 83.

Tatworth Candle Auction

Independent, 14 Apr. 1994, 4; Kightly (1986)
65.

Candle Auctions

Learmount (1985); Kightly (1986) 65–6; *New
Law Journal*, 23 Apr. 1993, 598.

Easter

Easter Day is the first Sunday: *Whitaker's
Almanack* (1996 edn) 82.
Eosturmonath has a name: Wallis (1999) 54.
In the village of Berkley: *N&Q* 1:1 (1850) 294.
Brand I (1849) 157–84; Chambers I (1864)
423–31; Wright & Lones I (1936) 85–122;
Duffy (1992); Hutton (1996) 198–213.

Good Friday

Brand I (1849) 150–57; Metford (1991) 62–7;
Roud (2003) 218–22.

Sources

Bread and Eggs
Last Christmas: N&Q 12S:9 (1921) 489.
Roud (2003) 219–20.

Burning Judas
A custom that is peculiar: Folk-Lore 65 (1954)
47.
Opie (1959) 248–9.

Butterworth Charity
Brentnall (1975) 184–5; Kightly (1986) 127.

Hartfield Dole
Sussex County Magazine 13 (1939) 282; 24
(1950) 138; 30 (1956) 197.

Hot Cross Buns
Good Friday comes this month: Poor Robin's
Almanack (1733), quoted in Brand I (1849)
154.
I am a butcher: Gutch (1901) 243–4, cit-
ing *The Testimony, Trial, Conviction,
Condemnation, Confession, and Execution
of William Smith* (1753).
Brand I (1949) 155.

Skipping
In Brighton on this day: N&Q 3S:3 (1863) 444.
The custom continues: Sussex Arch. Colls. 33
(1883) 241–2.
Until early in the evening: Porter (1969) 107.
Wales (1990) 50–51; Porter (1969) 107–8; for
skipping as a children's activity, *see* Opie
(1997a) 160–306.

Tinsley Green Marbles
First player knuckles down: Opie (1997) 32–3.
Some of the original: Wales (1979) 30.
Wales (1990) 52–3; Opie (1997a); www.
marblemuseum.org.

Washing Molly Grime
Edwards (1842) 100–101; Rudkin (1936) 44–5.

Widow's Son
In the houses of some: Hone, *The Every-Day
Book* I (1827) 203.
Brentnall (1975) 192–3; *London Lore* 1:2 (Sept.
1978) 15–16; Shuel (1985) 16.

Workington Football
Cumbria, Mar. 1970, 647–8; Shuel (1985)
160–61; Murfin (1990) 110–14.

Easter Saturday

Bacup Coco-Nut Dancers
Buckland (1986).

Easter Day

Eggs
Newall (1971).

Greenwich Fair
What immediately perplexed me: Hawthorne
(1863) 198.
Then you must go: Douglas Jerrold, 'Mrs.
Caudle's Curtain Lectures', *Punch* (1845).
Half the private houses: Charles Dickens,
Sketches by Boz (1836) chap. 12.
Grant (1838) chap. 9; Addison (1953)
100–105; Cameron (1998).

New Clothes
Whether from respect: Neville (1909) 8.
After leaving the Sunday School: Cumbrian
Federation of Women's Institutes (1994)
234.
The farmer that was contented: Lodge (1596)
14.
Roud (2003) 100.

Old Ball
He runs first at one: Harland & Wilkinson
(1867) 234–5.
Cawte (1978) 140–42.

Pace-Egging
Fasting days, years of grace: Beehive of the
Romishe Churche (1579), quoted in Brand
I (1849) 173.
The children have dyed: Hutchinson II (1778)
Supp. p. 10.
Here's two or three jolly boys: Journal of Folk
Song Society 5 (1915) 214.
Young men in groups: Harland & Wilkinson
(1882) 229–30.
Around Easter: Lancashire Federation of
Women's Institutes (1997) 205–6.
The children all assemble: Neville (1909) 8.
On Easter Monday: N&Q 6S:1 (1880) 337.
Holding his egg in his hand: Brand I (1849)
169.
In the North of England: Brand I (1849) 168.
Year by year: Chambers's Journal, 10 Mar.
1894, 159.
Brand I (1849) 168–76; Wright, *EDD* IV
(1903) 399–400; Wright & Lones I (1936)
87–8; Opie (1959) 250–55; Newall (1971);
Hutton (1996) 198–203.

Pace-Egg Plays
In steps I: Helm (1980) 67.
Cass (2001); Cass & Roud (2002).

Riding the Lord
The morning's interlude: Cheshire Sheaf, NS 1
(1895) 63–4.

Easter Monday

Biddenden Maids Charity
There is a vulgar tradition: Hasted III (1790)
66.
Bread and cheese lands: Edwards (1842) 19–20.

Black Knight of Ashton
It was easy to see: Axon (1870) 20–25.
Hone, *The Every-Day Book* II (1827) 234–5;
Axon (1870); Hole (1978) 248-9; Williams
& Williams (1998).

Epping Stag Hunt
Brand III (1849) 395; Wright & Lones I
(1936) 106–7.

Gawthorpe Coal-Carrying
Smith (1989) 27–8; www.gawthorpe.ndo.
co.uk/coal.htm.

Hallaton Hare Pie and Bottle-Kicking
[t]*he scramble was a token*: Shuel (1985) 165.
The scrum writhes: Morison & Daisley
(2000) 12.
Morison & Daisley (2000).

Scrambling Customs
It was truly reviving: The Times, 7 Nov.
1956, 11.
There was an ancient custom: Daniel Lysons,
Environs of London (1792), quoted in
Hone, *The Every-Day Book* II (1827) 225.

Harness Horse Parade
Shuel (1985) 60–61.

Legging Day
At Easter, boys and girls: Nicholson (1890) 12

Leicester Hare Hunt
Folk-Lore 3 (1892) 441–66; Billson (1895)
76–7.

Sun Dancing
I was awoke: Devonshire Assoc. 8 (1876) 57-8.
There is a tradition: Parish (1875) 57.
Roud (2003) 160–61.

Water
Elecampane on East Monday: N&Q 4S:5
(1870) 595.
Wright & Lones I (1936) 100–101, 112; Hole
(1978) 285–6.

Easter Monday and Tuesday

Lifting
The men lift the women: Gent. Mag. (1784:
i) 96.
a case heard before: Folk-Lore Journal 1 (1883)
269–70.
It was a very pretty: Burne (1883) 336.
At Kidderminster: N&Q for Worcestershire
(1856) 212.
On Easter Sunday: Fisher (1865) 463–4.
Wright & Lones I (1936) 107–10; Hutton
(1996) 208–13; Palmer (2004) 296–8.

Easter Tuesday

Holly Bussing
N&Q 2S:3 (1857) 344.

Tuppenny Starvers
Shuel (1985) 84.

Low Sunday

Upon little Easter Sunday: Carew
(1602/2000) 164.

Hocktide

Chambers I (1864) 498–9; Wright & Lones
I (1936) 124–9; Hutton (1996) 207–14;
MacLean (1996).

Hungerford Hocktide Court
Basically all we do: Independent, 23 Apr.
1993, 20.
*Report of Charity Commissioners: Parish of
Hungerford* (Mar 1906); Summers (1926);
Pihlens (1983).

Two weeks after Easter

Spital Sermon
Brentnall (1975) 185

19 April

Primrose Day
Vickery (1995) 295; Sutton (1997) 84–5.

21 April

Queen Elizabeth II's Birthday
www.royal.gov.uk.

23 April

St George's Day
my mam used to say: Sutton (1997) 91–2.

Wright & Lones II (1938) 178–83; *History Today* 30 (Apr. 1980) 17–22; Fox (1983); Palmer (1994) 290; Hutton (1996) 214–17.

24 April

St Mark's Eve
A youth or girl: Andrews (1891) 90.
I never watched myself: Blakeborough (1898) 80–81.
Wright & Lones II (1938) 183–92; Menefee (1989) 80–99; Roud (2003) 366–7.

25 April

St Mark's Day
After meeting in the market place: *History of Berwickshire Naturalists' Club* 14 (1892–3) 135.
Horn (1986) 39; *FLS News* 48 (2006) 13–14.

29 April

Chambers I (1864) 385.

30 April

May Day Eve
At Oldham: Ditchfield (1896) 104–5.
On the Eve of May Day: Leather (1912) 44.
Wright & Lones II (1938) 195–9.

MAY

Corby Pole Fair
Two thousand people: *The Times*, 12 June 1962, 6.
www.polefair.com.

Maids' Money
Surrey Magazine 4 (1902) 119–20.

Weighing the Mayor
Shuel (1985) 104; Wycombe District Council website, www.wycombe.gov.uk.

1 May

We, with our coal fires: Burne (1883) 354.
In the month of May: Stow (1603/1994) 123.
A woman from the extreme north: *Folk-Lore* 9 (1898) 365.
When . . . I lived at Kington: *Transactions of the Woolhope Naturalists' Field Club* (1877–80) 26.
When she was young: *Folk-Lore* 12 (1901) 426.

It hath been a custom: Billson (1895) 102.
It was formerly a custom: Harland & Wilkinson (1882) 238–40.

Bank Holiday
On May Day the entire: Mitford (1960) 145.

Bears
One went to the grocer's shop: *Burnley Express*, 11 Feb. 1983, 9.
Opie (1959) 261; *Burnley Express*, 1 Feb. 1983, 11 Feb. 1983.

Casting Clouts
Till April is dead: Devonshire Assoc. (1932).
Don't change a clout: *N&Q* 4S:6 (1870) 131.

Charlton-on-Otmoor Garland
During the upheavals: Hole (1976) 113.
Bloxham (2002) 81–9.

Children's Garlands
In Huntingdonshire: *N&Q* 1S:10 (1854) 91–2.
I was at Wilton: *Folk-Lore* 11 (1900) 210.
The garlands of this year: Mantell (1940).
Wright & Lones II (1938) 213–17; Thompson (1939) chap.13; *JEFDSS* 9 (1961) 81–90; *Transactions of the Leicestershire Archaeological & Historical Society* 40 (1964/5) 69-84; Tebbutt (1984) 59–66; Judge (1987); Judge (1993); Hutton (1996) 237–41; Bloxham (2002) 63–136; *see* Bloxham in particular for excellent photographs of garlands.

Ducking or Dipping Day
On May morning the children: Couch (1871) 153–4.
In 1894 the practice: Devonshire Assoc. 27 (1895) 72–3.

Fighting
Annually, on the first of May: Rudder (1779) 533.
Every hamlet used: Jefferies (1880) 65-6.

Horse Decorations
They took places: Gent. Mag (1754) 354.
There was on May-day: *Pall Mall Gazette* (1880), quoted in *N&Q* 6S:1 (1929) 434–5.
Everything that went on wheels: *Stockport Advertiser*, 2 May 1890, 8, quoted in Judge (1987) 132.

International Labour Day
The idea of a May-day festival: *Oxford Chronicle*, 4 May 1906, 2.
Judge (1987).

Jack-in-the-Green
A lusty sweep: Bennett (1924) 69–70.
Walking along Jamaica Road: Judge (2000)
126.
A reasonable conclusion: Judge (2000) 24.
Judge (2000).

Magdalen College Singing
more like a Baccanalian: Judge (1987) 425.
Hone (1832) 797; Porter (1969) 115; *Folklore*
97:1 (1986) 15–40; Judge (1987) 422–58;
Bloxham (2002) 70–78;

May Dew
I overheard this conversation: *Folk-Lore* 23
(1912) 451.

May Dolls
At a very early hour: *Devonshire Assoc.* 8
(1876) 50.
Porter (1969) 111–15.

May Goslings
A May gosling: *Gent Mag.* (Apr. 1791) 327.
Opie (1959) 255–7; Wright & Lones II (1938)
242.

May Queens
At Albrighton: Burne (1883) 361.
Wright & Lones II (1938) 223–8; Cole (1981);
Judge (1993); Sutton (1997) 99–101.

Maypoles
Feast week was in Maytime: Rudkin (1936) 46.
On May 1, 1952: Opie (1959) 258.
The manner of May games: Stubbes
(1583/2002).
Judge (1983); Judge (1987).

Milkmaids' Garland
Judge (2000); Phythian-Adams (1983).

Minehead Hobby Horse
obeisance to onlookers: Kille (1931) 67.
Kille (1931); Cawte (1978).

Hobby Horses
Maylam (1909); Alford (1978); Cawte (1978).

Padstow Hobby Horse
Well we had all sorts: Rowe (1982) 7.
man drest up: R. Polwhele, *History of
Cornwall* (1803), quoted in Cawte (1978).
canvas being extended: F. Hitchins and
Samuel Drew, *History of Cornwall*,
quoted in Cawte (1978).
Arise up Mrs.——: Rawe (1982) 6.
Cawte (1978) 157–67; Rawe (1982); Rowe
(1982).

Randwick Cheese-Rolling
Three large cheeses: Hone, *The Table Book*
(1827) 277.

3 May

**The Day of the Invention of the Holy
Cross**
The first of May: *Devonshire Assoc.* 12 (1880)
105–8.

First Saturday in May

Gawthorpe Celebrations
Smith (1989) 33–6; www.gawthorpe.ndo.
co.uk/home.

Knutsford Royal May Day Festival
Strand Magazine, May 1892, 484–8; Shuel
(1985) 34–9; www.virtual-knutsford.co.uk.

First Sunday in May

Tyburn Walk
London Tourist Board, *Traditional London*
(1987) 56.

8 May

Helston Flora Day
At Helstone: *Gent. Mag.* 60:1 (1790) 520.
Toy (1936) 368–79; Kennedy (1964) 71–5;
Newton (1978); Jones (1997).

12 May

The May
Our May Day is not: Neville (1909) 27–33.
children wore a May gollen: *Lancashire Lore*
(1971) 74.

Second Saturday in May

Randwick Wap
One of the parish is: *Gent. Mag.* (1784) 334–5.
Briggs (1974) 183–6; Palmer (1994) 295–7.

13 May (Old May Day)

Abbotsbury Garland Day
Robson (1993).

Cowslips
When spring had really come: Harris (1969)
138–9.

Miners' Holiday
On the 13th of May: Glover I (1829) 261.

Rook Sunday
White (1932) 202; Sutton (1997) 108–9.

14 May

Pack Rag Day
Bank holidays pass almost: Gutch & Peacock
(1908) 205.

Mid to late May

Scorton Silver Arrow
Hird (1972); Smith (1989) 65–72; www.
scortonarrow.com.

Rogationtide

Beating the Bounds
Boundary roll from Tudor Cheshire: Head
(1887) 119–23.
On the 16th [May]: Schellinks (1993) 85.
At Beverley: Nicholson (1890) 31–2.
Mr. Checkley, a farmer: *The Graphic*, 28 Nov.
1874, 527.
If, by chance: Cossins (1878) 11.
One vicar said: Smith (1989) 89–90.
Brand I (1849) 197–212; Wright & Lones I
(1936) 129–38; Winchester (1990); Hutton
(1996) 277–87; Bloxham (2002) 50–62.

Rogation Monday

Wishford Auction
Whitlock (1976) 54–5.

Ascension Eve

Whitby Penny Hedge
Charlton (1779); Young (1817); Atkinson
(1894); Turton (1909); Jeffrey (1923) 38–45;
Smith (1989) 29–32.

Ascension Day

At daybreak on Ascension: *Folk-Lore Record* 5
(1882) 160.
To hang an egg: Scot (1584/1972) Bk 12, chap.
18.
If you hang clothes: *Folk-Lore* 20 (1909) 345.
Hailing the Lamb: *Devonshire Assoc.* 68 (1936)
246, quoting *Gent. Mag.* 57 (1787) 718.
The parochial bounds: Cossins (1878) 34.
Wright & Lones I (1936) 129–48; Roud
(2003) 10–12.

Tower of London Beating the Bounds
Brentnall (1975) 77, 79; Shuel (1985) 106.

18 May

Newbiggin Freeholders
Sykes (1977) 72–3; Shuel (1985) 114.

19 May

St Dunstan's Day
St. Dunstan bought: *N&Q* 2S:12 (1861) 303.
No luck will follow: Blakeborough (1898) 131.
N&Q 2S:12 (1861) 303; Westwood (1985) 95–7.

23 May

Rye Mayor-Making
Hogg (1971) 84–5; Simpson (1973) 119.

24 May

Empire Day
The morning shall be: *The Times*, 20 Mar.
1899, 8.
When I was at school: East Kent Federation of
Women's Institutes (1993) 246.
For Wesley Day, *see* Sutton (1997) 116.

Whitsun

On Whit Monday: Whitsun poster cited by
Wright & Lones I (1936) 161.
Whit week, however: Philpott (1961/2) 173–4.
It is customary: Harland & Wilkinson (1882)
247.

Eton School Montem
Aubrey (1686/1880) 132; Wright & Lones I
(1936) 167–9; Hazlitt (1905); *N&Q* 3S:12
(1867) 377–8; Chambers II (1864) 665–6.

Food
The village policeman: Porter (1969) 118.
Goosnargh cakes: Wilson (1991) 137.

Morris Dance
Then every one: Stubbes (1583/2002) 206–7.
The bibliography of the morris dance is
voluminous. The following is a selection
of the best recent treatments: *Folklore* 96:1
(1985) 29–37; Heaney (1985); *Traditional
Dance* 5/6 (1988) 191–215; *Folk Music
Journal* 6:2 (1991) 169–86; 7:3 (1997) 311–51;
8:4 (2004) 513–15; Chandler (1993a);
Forrest (1999).

Superstitions
It was traditional: East Yorkshire Federation
of Women's Institutes (1998) 203–4.

Whit Walks

At Manchester: *The Times*, 7 June 1949, 4.

It was 1958: www.haveyoursay.freeserve.
co.uk/hys11/then1.htm *Have Your Say
Magazine* (used by permission of Lillian
Barlow).

This annual event: West Yorkshire Federation
of Women's Institutes (1996) 29.

Whit Sunday

St Briavels Bread and Cheese Dole

They have a custom: Rudder (1779) 307.

So after Evensong: Crawford (1938) 160–61.
Edwards (1842) 17–22; Bushaway (1982)
16–18; Palmer (1994) 298–9.

Church Ales

entertaining of Christian love: Carew
(1602/2000) 141–2.

Hazlitt (1905) 631–2; Wright & Lones I
(1936) 151–7; Chandler (1993a) 59–79;
Hutton (1994); Hutton (1996) 244–61.

St Mary Redcliffe Rush Sunday

www.bristol-city.gov.uk/aboutbris/civic_
services; www.stmaryredcliffe.co.uk

Whit Tuesday

Dicing for Bibles

N&Q 5S:12 (1879) 238; Hole (1975) 148;
Kightly (1986) 101.

Whit Wednesday

Mother Shipton's Day

Porter (1969) 118–19; for Hindley's confession, *see N&Q* 4S:11 (1873) 355.

Whit Friday

Brass Bands

The Black Dyke Mills band: Greenhalgh
(1992) 18.

They [the churches] *take this day*: Stalybridge
Reporter (1926), quoted in Greenhalgh
(1992) 36.

Greenhalgh (1992).

Late May

Blessing of the Sea

Brixham: Information supplied by Bridget
Cusack, churchwarden and archivist of
All Saints' Church, Lower Brixham.
Hastings: Shuel (1985) 82. For a list of
some other coastal blessings extant in the
mid 1980s, *see* Kightly (1986) 55.

Last Sunday in May

Arbor Day

Shuel (1985) 39–40; Palmer (2004) 304; www.
members.aol.com/arbortreefest.

29 May

Royal Oak Day

going round to the houses: *Listener*, 23 May
1957.

These pinches are: Durand (1913) 10.

I was travelling from Crewe: *Bye-Gones*
(1889–90) 169.

Wright & Lones II (1938) 254–70; Opie
(1959) 263–6; Cressy (1989).

Castleton Garland Day

Addy (1901); Boyes (1993); Membury example: *Devonshire Assoc*. 102 (1970) 269.

Grovely Ceremonies

Bushaway (1982); Frampton (1992).

Neville's Cross Commemoration

Hole (1975) 132–3; Kightly (1986) 174.

Royal Hospital Chelsea Founder's Day

Brentnall (1975) 125–8; www.chelsea-
pensioners.co.uk.

Spring Bank Holiday

Bampton Morris

Another season of festivity: Giles (1847) lxv.

Sharp and MacIlwaine (1924) 38–72;
Chandler (1983); *Musical Traditions* 10
(1992) 18–24; Chandler (1993a).

Barwick Maypole

Smith (1989) 36–40; *Dalesman*, Jan. 1986,
849–50; www.hjsmith.clara.co.uk.

Cooper's Hill Cheese-Rolling

The master of the ceremonies: *Folk-Lore* 23
(1912) 351.

Folk-Lore 23 (1912) 351; Palmer (1994) 193–6;
Daily Telegraph, 26 May 1998, 3.

Hunting the Earl of Rone

Devonshire Assoc. 49 (1917) 71–5; Brown
(1997).

Kingsteignton Ram-Roasting

A lamb is drawn: *N&Q* 6S:7 (1883) 345.

My husband started: Crawford (1938) 131–2.

Wright & Lones I (1936) 169–70.

Robert Dover's Olimpick Games
Burns (2000); Haddon (2004).

JUNE

Trinity Sunday

Burne (1883) 352; Sutton (1997) 127–8.

Thursday after Trinity Sunday

Corpus Christi
On the day before: Wright & Lones I (1936)
176–7.

8 June

If on the 8th of June: Inwards (1869) 30.

11 June

St Barnabas' Day
Brand I (1849) 293–4; Wright & Lones III
(1940) 1–3.

20 June

Mayor of Ock Street
Chandler (1993b).

21 June

Brecknell Bequest
A bachelor named: Noake (1868) 218.

Mock Mayors and Courts
The Mayors were nominated: Cossins (1878)
9–10.
And that you may: Cossins (1878) 46–8.
The youthlier sort of Bodmin: Carew
(1602/2000) 197–8.
[t]he police interfered: *Antiquary* 4 (1881) 80.
Chambers I (1864) 659–64; Gutch (1901)
325–31; *N&Q* 12S:12 (1923) 194; Wright &
Lones II (1938) 254; III (1940) 29–30, 94,
158–9; Shaw (1980).

24 June

Midsummer's Day/St John the Baptist's Day
In [John] Aubrey's: Piggott (1968) 133.
In the months: Stow (1603/1994) 126–7.
But whatever reason: Bourne (1725) 214–15.
Before St John's Day: Hewett (1900) 112.

Stow (1603/1994) 125–9; Brand I (1849)
298–338; Wright & Lones III (1940) 6–23;
Shortt (1988).

Dumb Cake
Opie & Tatem (1989) 127–8; Roud (2003)
156–7.

Divination
I remember, the maids: Aubrey (1686/1880)
25–6.
It is said here: Bray (1838) 287.
Wright & Lones III (1940) 12–19; Opie &
Tatem (1989) 295, 332; Roud (2003) 247–8,
307–8, 383.

Election of Sheriffs
Brentnall (1975); www.cityoflondon.gov.uk.

Knollys Red Rose
Brentnall (1975) 47–9.

Magdalen Outdoor Sermon
Hole (1975) 81–2; Shuel (1985) 81–2.

Midsummer Cushions
The young lads and lasses: Denham II (1895)
1–2.

29 June

St Peter's Day/St Paul's Day
Unless the apples: *Folk-Lore Journal* 4 (1886)
167.

Bawming the Thorn
Up with fresh garlands: Appleton Parish
Council (1997) 11.
At Appleton it was the custom: Wilbraham
(1826) 16.
Kightly (1986) 47; diary information sup-
plied by Warrington Local Studies
Library.

Jankyn Smith's Charity
Kightly (1986) 145; St Mary's Church
Magazine (*View from Honey Hill*), June
1999.

Warcop Rush-Bearing
The girls of the village: *Cumbrian*, June 1995,
37–8.
The Globe, 30 June 1913; www.edenonline.
net/pages/warcoprush.

June/July

Yarnton Lot Meadow
Kightly (1986) 153–4; Bloxham (2002)
208–13.

Well-Dressing
In the village of Tissington: Gent. Mag. 64
(1794) 114–15.
newly-gathered flowers: Rhodes (1818).
Porteous (1949); Christian (1983); Rattue
(1995); Naylor & Porter (2002).

JULY

Early July

Fairlop Fair
According to ancient custom: Illustrated
London News, 15 July 1843, 44.
Muncey (c.1935) 68–73; www.hainaultforest.
co.uk/3Fairlop%20Fair.

4 July

Stagshawbank Fair
Besides horses, sheep, cattle: Forster (1881) 65–6.
Forster (1881) 63–70; Muncey (c.1935) 147–52.

Whalton Baal Fire
Wright & Lones III (1940) 11; Shuel (1985)
183.

5 July

Old Midsummer's Day
In the parishes: Collinson III (1791) 586.

6 July

Duck-Racing
Duck racing isn't as easy: John Bull, 9 July
1955, 41.
Reading Mercury, 5 Aug. 1961; Bloxham
(2002) 214–15.

Kilburn Feast
Johnny Kirk, whose family: Smith (1989) 85–7.

First Friday in July

Warrington Walking Day
www.shef.ac.uk/nfa/history/worlds_fair/
articles/warrington.

First Saturday in July

Ambleside Rush-Bearing
The 'burthens' were devices: Rawnsley (1953)
26–8.
N&Q 5S:2 (1892) 141–2; Rawnsley (1953)
26–8.

Medway Admiralty Court
There is in the River Medway: Defoe (1724–6)
Letter II: Kent.
Goodsall (1965); www.medway.gov.uk.

Rush-Bearing
I remember going: Folk-Lore 20 (1909) 204.
About the latter: Clarke (1789) 134.
every part of the church: Diary of Benjamin
Newton, quoted by Rawnsley (1953) 10.
In their wisdom: Country Home, June 1909, 80.
Chambers I (1864) 505–7; Burton (1891);
Buckland (1982); Rawnsley (1953); Helm
(1970); Kightly (1986) 199–201; Brears
(1989) 178–203; Fletcher (1997/8).

Sunday in Early July

Oxenhope Straw Race
Smith (1989) 92–5; www.strawrace.co.uk.

7 July

Bodmin Riding
On Monday, a grand procession: Munn (1975) 26.
the two Mondays right: Munn (1975) 20.
Munn (1975); Wright & Lones III (1940)
31–2.

Rose Queens
A vicar in Bury: Independent Magazine, 1
Apr. 1989, 9.
The crowning of a Rose Queen: Lancashire
Lore (1971) 59.

10 July
Twice a year: Neville (1909) 72–3.

Second Wednesday in July

Pretty Maid's Charity
Sykes (1977) 108; Shuel (1985) 129–30;
Kightly (1986) 190–91.

Second/Third Saturday in July

Durham Miners' Gala
Richardson (2001).

15 July

St Swithun's Day
St. Swithin's Day: N&Q 11:4 (1911) 45.
You won't have the jam: Wright & Lones III
(1940) 35.
Opie & Tatem (1989) 337–8.

16 July

Anne Askew Day
Sutton (1997) 146.

19 July

Little Edith's Treat
Information supplied by Valerie Mellor, historian of Piddinghoe.

25 July

St Christopher's Day
There was a colossal figure: Rudder (1779) 286.

Ebernoe Horn Fair
Sussex County Magazine 2 (1928) 331, 338; 29 (1955) 320–23, 403, 501.
Song text: verse 4, line 3, and verse 5, lines 3 and 4, added from Vaughan Williams' manuscripts, as collected from Frederick Teal at Kingsfold, Surrey, 23 December 1904.

25 July

John Knill Charity
Hone, *The Every-Day Book* II (1827) 505–6; Shuel (1985) 129; Kightly (1986) 146–7.

Whitstable Oyster Festival
www.whitstableoysterfestival.co.uk.

Fairs, Feasts, Wakes, and Revels
They love a crowd: Neville (1909) 85–6.
A farmer's wife: Folk-Lore 23 (1912) 352.
For the children: Kightly (1986) 184–5.
Our village church: West Yorkshire Federation of Women's Institutes (1996) 211.
Heyford Feast: Horn (1986) 31.
Because you couldn't go: Kightly (1986) 182–3.
Walford (1883); Muncey (*c*.1935); Wright & Lones (1936–1940); Addison (1953); Cameron (1998).

26 July

Mace Monday
In the course of the day: Hone, *The Every-Day Book* II (1827) 523.
Ditchfield (1896) 246–7.

28 July

Old St Kenelm's Day
The custom of crabbing: John Noake, *N&Q for Worcestershire* (1856) 206.
Wright & Lones III (1940) 38–9, 59–60, 99.

Doggett's Coat and Badge Race
Doggett was stranded on the wrong side: Guardian, 19 July 1974.
Chambers II (1864) 157–8; Brentnall (1975) 94–9; Paget (1989) 56.

Swan-Upping
Stone (1906) 13–15; Hole (1975) 111–12; Kightly (1986) 213–14.

July/August

St Wilfrid Feast Procession
Shortcrust pastry base: Smith (1989) 107–8.

AUGUST

Early August

Grottoes
When was Grotto Day?: The Times, 21 Nov. 1957, 12.
Please remember the grotto: Gamble (1979) 107.
Opie (1959) 266–7; Folklore 88:2 (1977) 183–90.

First Wednesday in August

Knighthood of the Old Green
Shuel (1985) 142–4; Southampton Old Bowling Green website, www.sobg.co.uk/index.

The King's Book of Sports 1618 and 1633
Govett (1890).

First week in August

Woodmen of Arden
Shuel (1985) 141–2.

1 August

Lammas/St Peter ad Vincula
On that day: Brand I (1849) 348.
Certain lands were used: Wright & Lones III (1940) 43.
was a pleasure fair: Cossins (1878) 20–21.
Brand I (1849) 347–9; Wright & Lones III (1940) 43–6; Hutton (1996) 327–31.

Late July

4 August

Kit-Dressing
At Baslow the rural: Glover I (1829) 261.

5 August

Grasmere Rush-Bearing
I chanced to be in Grasmere: N&Q 5S:4 (1875)
    162–3.
Rawnsley (1953); Shuel (1985) 85–7; www.
    visitcumbria.com.

James I
Cressy (1989) 57–9.

10 August

St Lawrence's Day
For more on 'The History of Lawrence
    Lazy', see *Folklore* 107 (1996).

12 August

Congleton Bells
On the Wake Sunday: *Monthly Packet* 24
    (1862) 660.
Head (1887) 203–4; Andrews (1895) 137–43;
    Congleton museum website,
    www.comcarenet.com/museum/default.

Gibson Tomb
FLS News 10 (1990) 11–12.

16 August

St Roch's Day
Brand I (1849) 350.

Tutbury Bull-Running
Raven (1978) 110-14; Bushaway (1993).

17 August

Lee Gap Fair
www.travellersinleeds.
    co.uk/_travellers/LeeGapFair.

23 August

St Bartholomew's Eve
I myself, in my youth: Stow (1603/1994)
    100–101.

24 August

St Bartholomew's Day
In the morning a number of maidens: Hone,
    The Year-Book (1832) 492.
At St. Bartholomew: Inwards (1869) 32.

Wright & Lones III (1940) 49–52.

Bartholomew Fair
Ward (1703/1927) 176–206; Hone, *The
    Every-Day Book* I (1827) 583–626; Morley
    (1859).

Sandwich Bun Race
The Times, 24 Aug. 1953, 8; Kightly (1986)
    202.

West Witton Burning of Bartle
Smith (1989) 119–22; *John Bull*, 27 Aug. 1955,
    43.

Sparrow Mumbling
'Twill be most ridiculous: George Chapman,
    Andromeda Liberata (1614), cited in N&Q
    4S:10 (1872) 184.
All the Year Round, 3 June 1865.

29 August

Preston Guild
Crosby (1991).

August Bank Holiday

Marldon Apple Pie Fair
The Marldon Apple Pie: *Devonshire Assoc.* 67
    (1935) 377–8.

Notting Hill Carnival
www.london.gov.uk/mayor/carnival/index.
    jsp.

Bank Holidays
www.dti.gov.uk/er/bankhis; Michael Jacobs,
    'More Bank Holidays!', www.fabian-
    society.org.uk.

SEPTEMBER

Harvest Customs
The in-gathering: Williams (1912) 116–17.
A practical joke: Neville (1909) 50–51.
A farm-worker from: Folk-Lore 14 (1903)
    92–4.
Now, when all the corn: Folk-Lore 1 (1890) 280.
On certain Ramsey manors: Bennett (1948)
    111–12.
On the last night of harvest: Folk-Lore 13
    (1902) 180.
At Kingsbridge, the following: Folk-Lore 1
    (1890) 280.
The top of the last load: N&Q 4S:10 (1872) 359.

No further back: Gutch & Peacock (1908)
209, quoting Heanley (1902) 11–12.

[An] *explanation was given to me*: The Times,
2 Oct. 1934, 10.

Hone, *Every-Day Book* II (1827) 577–91;
Jenkin (1934); Wright & Lones I (1936)
82–90; Evans (1969); Bushaway (1982)
107–66; Hutton (1996) 332–47; Main
(1998–9).

Gleaning

The gleaning season: Grey (1934) 118–24.

Harvest Suppers

Tomorrow the men: N&Q 4S:10 (1872) 411.
Here's a health: Dacombe (1935) 93.
Later in the evening: Gutch (1901) 266.
In the first quarter: N&Q 8S:9 (1896) 128.
There could be no better: Horn (1986) 22, 86.

Harvest Festivals

Harvest festival is upon us again: Daily
Telegraph, 23 Sept 2000, Weekend section, 5.

Hop-Picking

Plenty of hands: Arthur Young, *Farmer's
Kalendar* (1771) quoted in Filmer (1982) 17.
These were all people and *In the shop*: Warren
(1938) 18–35.
Our farm was a small and *The smell of the
hops*: East Kent Federation of Women's
Institutes (1993) 138.
Leather (1912) 105–6; Warren (1938) chap.
2; Filmer (1982); East Kent Federation
of Women's Institutes (1993) 137–42;
Heffernan (1996); Doel (2003) 59–66.

Early September

Colchester Oyster Fishery

The company were about: The Times, 22 Sept.
1928, 15.
Victoria County History: Essex II (1907)
425–39.

1 September

St Giles's Day

Probably the greatest: Muncey (c.1935) 100.
Victoria County History: Hampshire V (1912)
36–41; Muncey (c.1935) 79–85, 92–102;
Wright & Lones III (1940) 59–60;
Victoria County History: Oxfordshire IV
(1979) 310–12.

3 September

Cromwell Day

www.olivercromwell.org.

Merchant Navy Day

www.mna.org.uk.

4 September

Abbots Bromley Horn Dance

There was no audience: English Dance & Song
3:2 (Nov. 1938) 27–8.
Sharp I (1911–13) 105–12; Cawte (1978) 65–79;
Buckland (1980); Heaney (1987).

Barnet Horse Fair

My first impression: Greenwood (1867) 198.
Barnet Fair is still: Addison (1953) 147.
In a 20-acre field: The Times, 6 Sept. 1954, 2.
Daily Telegraph, 2 Sept. 1995, Weekend
section, 10; www.barnet4u.
co.uk/Barnet%20History/barnetfair.

14 September

Holy Rood or Holy Cross Day

On Holy Rood day: Clare (1993) 140.
Brand I (1849) 353; Cross (1957) 480; Metford
(1991) 85; Vickery (1995) 276–7; Roud
(2003) 343–4; Westwood & Simpson
(2005) 750–51.

Shaftesbury Byzant

a trophy or mace: Frampton (1990) 155.

Sturbridge Fair

It is kept in a large corn-field: Defoe I (1724–6)
80.
The fair was proclaimed: Victoria County
History: Cambridge III (1959) 95.
Walford (1883); Muncey (c.1935) 20–36;
Victoria County History: Cambridge III
(1959) 91–5.

Baiting Bears and Other Animals

In winter on almost every feast day: Fitz
Stephen (c.1180/1990) 58.
Concerning a case: Home (1915) 224–6.
Chambers II (1864) 57–9; Porter (1969)
227–8; Malcolmson (1973); Richardson
(2000).

Third Thursday in September

Chalk-Back Day

It is customary: N&Q 1S:4 (1851) 501–2.
At Bridlington: Nicholson (1890) 29.

Pursehouse (1966) 130–32; for Chalk Sunday
in Ireland, *see* Danaher (1972) 47–8.

Egremont Crab-Apple Fair
We haven't been able: John Bull, 17 Sept. 1955.
Shuel (1985) 14–16; Kightly (1986) 98–9;
www.egremontcrabfair.org.uk.

Warden Pies
Wardens were not soft: Candlin (1987) 73.

18 September

Samuel Johnson Commemoration
www.lichfieldrambler.co.uk.

Southwark Fair
noted chiefly for shows: John Strype, *Survey
of the Cities of London and Westminster*,
quoted in Rosenfeld (1960) 71.
only to the destruction: Rosenfeld (1960) 74.
Rosenfeld (1960) 71–107; Muncey (*c.*1935)
54–8.

19 September

Painswick Church-Clipping
gave time to re-organizing: *N&Q* 181 (1941) 36
'When I was a girl': John Bull, 24 Sept. 1955, 47.
Folk-Lore 23 (1912) 196–203.

21 September

St Matthew's Day
Inwards (1869) 32–3.

29 September

**Michaelmas/Feast of St Michael and All
Angels**
If you don't baste: Forby (1830) 414.
I dined upon goose: Jane Austen, quoted in Le
Faye (1995) 235.
The election of Mayors: Cossins (1878) 9.
Brand I (1849) 367–71; Wright & Lones III
(1940) 80–90.

Lawless Hours and Days
According to the Staffordshire Advertiser: *Folk-
Lore* 42 (1931) 466.
At Kidderminster is a singular: *Gent. Mag.*
(1790), quoted in Burne (1883) 221–2.

Blackberries
The belief that it is unlucky: *Western
Antiquary* 2 (1882) 137.
Opie & Tatem (1989) 29; Roud (2003) 39.

Crack-Nut Sunday
the cracking noise was: Edward Wedlake
Brayley, *A Topographical History of Surrey*
III (1850) 41–2.
They kept up the Christmas: Goldsmith (1766)
chap. 4.

Election of the Lord Mayor of London
a Labour Lord Mayor: The Times, 30
September 1972.
Brentnall (1975) 19–53; Paget (1989) 15–18.

Urswick Rush-Bearing
Cumbrian Federation of Women's Institutes
(1994) 240–42; information (May 2005)
from Miss Joan Wood, Urswick resident
of eighty-three years standing.

OCTOBER

Quit Rent Ceremonies
Brentnall (1975) 153–6.

A Sunday in October

Redcliffe Pipe Walk
Shuel (1985) 106–7; www.members.lycos.
co.uk/brisray/bristol/bstmary1.

2 October

Braughing Old Man's Day
Jones-Baker (1977) 164; www.braughing.
org.uk.

First Wednesday in October

Nottingham Goose Fair
Wilkes (1989); www.nottinghamgoosefair.
co.uk.

Goose-Riding
Hazlitt (1905) 284.

Second Sunday in October

Harvest of the Sea
Brentnall (1975) 183–4.

Second Wednesday in
October

Tavistock Goosie Fair
Gunnell (1978); Gerrish (2004).

10 October

Old Michaelmas Day
So common was the practice: Nicholson (1890)
22.
Hone, *The Table Book* (1827) 838; *Wilts.
Arch. & Nat. Hist. Mag.* 1 (1854) 89–91;
Andrews (1900) 175–85; Hazlitt (1905)
377; Wright & Lones III (1940) 94, 100.

Pack Monday Fair
The fair is annually held: Hone, *The Every-
Day Book* II (1827) 654–5.
Wright & Lones III (1940) 95–6; Hole
(1976) 291–2.

Weyhill Fair
The 11th of October: Cobbett (1830) 'Through
Hampshire . . .'
The newcomer was seated: Beddington &
Christy (1936) 18.
Hampshire Field Club 3 (1894–7) 127–42; *Folk-
Lore* 22 (1911) 300–302; *Victoria County
History: Hampshire* IV (1911) 394–99;
Beddington & Christy (1936) 17–19.

Wife-Selling
For my part I don't see: Hardy (1886) chap. 1.
On Friday last: Windsor & Eton Express,
10–17 Sept. 1815, quoted in *N&Q* 196
(1951) 82.
Brooks, auctioneer: N&Q 196 (1951) 460.
Rather unfortunately: Chambers I (1864) 487.
It is – so far as my experience: Baring-Gould
(1908) 58.
Menefee (1981); Thompson (1991).

11 October

Blackberries
All children who either gather: Folk-Lore 20
(1909) 343.

16 October

Lion Sermon
N&Q 6S:1 (1880) 236, 303, 344; Brentnall
(1975) 181–2.

18 October

St Luke's Day
a village famous: Defoe (1724–6) Letter II:
Kent.
A fine autumn is known: Addy (1895) 117.

20 October

Colchester Oyster Feast
On Thursday, the Mayor: Essex Standard, 21
Oct. 1847, quoted in *Past & Present* 94
(1982) 112.
Cannadine (1982); Kightly (1986) 82.

21 October

Apple Day
www.commonground.org.uk.

Trafalgar Day
Brentnall (1975) 114–16.

25 October

St Crispin's Day
In the parishes: N&Q 1S:5 (1852) 30.
Wright & Lones III (1940) 102–4.

Last Thursday in October

Bampton Fair
Gerrish (2004); www.bampton.org.
uk/bampton_fair.

Seed Cakes
Wife, sometime this week: Tusser (1580/1984).
Hone, *The Year-Book* (1832) 798; Baker II
(1854) 211.

Late October

Punkie Night
A party of men: N&Q 161 (1931) 372.
Opie (1959) 267–8; *Folklore* 83 (1972) 240–44;
Palmer (1976) 105–7.

31 October

Hallowe'en
On the Eve of All Saints Day: Gutch &
Peacock (1908) 212.
The vigil of All Saints' Day: Brockett (1825)
145.
Mrs. Hook, of Chulmleigh: Devonshire Assoc.
70 (1938) 116.
In Derbyshire farmers: Addy (1895) 118.
When darkness closes in: Opie (1959) 268–75.
Tuesday 31 October: Last (1981) 21.

Antrobus Soul-Cakers
Helm (1968); *Lore & Language* 3 (1970) 9–11;
5 (1971) 11–15.

Mischief Night
The evening before May Day: Harland &
Wilkinson (1882) 239.
Mischief Night in Blacko: *Lancashire Lore*
(1971) 11.
When I was a kid: www.bbc.co.uk/
northyorkshire/iloveny/2004/halloween/
mischief_night.
Opie (1959) 255, 276–80.

NOVEMBER

First Sunday in November
London to Brighton Veteran Car Run
www.lvcr.com.

1 November
All Saints' Day
There is set on the board: Aubrey (1686/1880)
23.

2 November
All Souls' Day
Bands of children: *N&Q* 4S:2 (1868) 553.
Burne (1914); Wright & Lones III (1940)
121–45.

First Friday in November
Bridgwater Carnival
Men, boys and urchins: Hocking (2004) 9.

4 November
Ringing Night
'Ringing-Night' is on the fourth: Couch (1871)
161.
A very curious custom: Gibbons (1885) 14.

5 November
Devil's Stone
Shuel (1985) 19.

Guy Fawkes Night
On the 5th: Schellinks (1993) 172.
On the night of 5th November: *Hampshire
Advertiser*, 28 Nov. 1931, quoted in *Folk-
Lore* 42 (1931).
Remember, remember the fifth of November:
Folk-Lore 14 (1903) 91.
In the days when there was no: Blakeborough
(1898) 87.

On Monday last: *York Herald*, 15 Nov. 1806,
quoted in Morsley (1979).
The Devon village of Chulmleigh: *Western
Morning News*, 8 Nov. 1960, quoted in
Devonshire Assoc. 102 (1970) 270.
There was a massive: Sheffield (1993) 274–7.
In some areas: Camp (1988) 69.
Wright & Lones III (1940) 145–56;
History Today, Nov. 1981, 5–9; *Surrey
Archaeological Collections* 76 (1985) 61–8;
Folklore 95:2 (1984) 191–203; Cressy (1989);
Buchanan *et al.* (2005); Sharpe (2005).

Parkin
Another local dainty: *Folk-Lore* 20 (1909) 204.

Lewes Bonfire Night
The bonfire societies: Etherington (1993) 23.
Shuel (1985) 186–7; Etherington (1993).

Ottery St Mary
Bonfire night at Ottery and *The sight of a
large*: Shuel (1985) 187.
Owen (1984/5).

Second Friday in November
Silent Change
Brentnall (1975) 21–4; Paget (1989) 15–16.

Second Saturday in November
Hatherleigh Carnival
They came down the hill: Shuel (1985) 189.
Shuel (1985) 188–9; www.hatherleigh.org.
uk/carnival.

Lord Mayor's Show
Guildhall Miscellany 10 (1959) 3–18; Shuel
(1985) 54–6; www.lordmayorsshow.org.

10 November
St Martin's Eve
Now that the year: Clare (1990) 112–17.

Wroth Silver
Chambers (1864) 571–2; Shuel (1985) 123–4;
Waddilove & Eadon (1994).

11 November
St Martin's Day
If the wind: Inwards (1869) 33.
Brand I (1849) 399–404; Wright & Lones III
(1940) 159–66.

Hiring Fairs

Carters and waggoners: Thomas Hardy, *Far from the Madding Crowd* (1874), chap. 6.
Drunkenness is the curse: *The Times*, 17 Nov. 1858, 8.
They were days: Cameron (1998) 120.
The key to the success: Caunce (1991) 54.
There is very little hiring: Williams (1912) 238–9.
Trotter (1919) 130–62; Catt (1986); Kightly (1986) 23–32; Roberts (1988); Caunce (1991) 54–73; Cameron (1998).

Remembrance Sunday

They are getting longer: West (2004) 19.
Bushaway (1992); West (2004) 19–22. For the contenders for the origin of the two-minute silence, see *The Times*, 14 Nov. 1930, 14 and *N&Q* 162 (1932) 412. For 'British Day', see the *Guardian*, 14 Jan. 2006.

13 November

St Brice's Day

Monday last being our annual: Lincoln, Rutland & Stamford Mercury, 18 Nov. 1785, quoted in Morsley (1979) 112.
Chambers II (1864) 574–6; Malcolmson (1973) 126–55.

Bull-Baiting

Turner (1964); Malcolmson (1973), *passim*.

17 November

Queen Elizabeth I/St Hugh's Day

Brand I (1849) 404–8; Cressy (1989), *passim*.

22 November

St Cecilia's Day

In 1945 it would have been: Whistler (1947) 213–18.

23 November

St Clement's Day

At Burwash a few years ago: Sussex Arch. Colls. 33 (1883) 252.
For this blessed martyr: *N&Q* 195 (1950) 531–2.
Clementing, clementing: *The Times*, 10 Dec. 1935, 17.
Folk-Lore Journal 2 (1884) 321–9; *Folk-Lore* 25 (1914) 285–99; Wright & Lones III (1940) 167–76; *N&Q* 195 (1950) 443–4, 530–32, 535–6.

25 November

St Catherine's Day

Patron of young girls: Farmer (1987) 77–8.
A husband, St. Catherine: Udal (1922) 102.
Folk-Lore 25 (1914) 285–99; Wright & Lones III (1940) 177–86.

Fourth Tuesday in November

Ashburton Court Leet

Kightly (1986) 97; www.ashburton.org.

30 November

St Andrew's Day

Church Times, 22 June 1894, 689; Wright & Lones III (1940) 136–7, 186–91, 261, 277.

Eton Wall Game

Shuel (1985) 167–8; www.etoncollege.com.

DECEMBER

First weekend in December

Tree-Dressing Day

www.commonground.org.uk.

1 December

St Eligius' Day

Ordinance and articles: *N&Q* 195 (1950) 532.

6 December

St Nicholas

At the time a certain fellow: De Voragine (*c.*1260/1993) I, 21–7.

Barring Out

We did it every year and *There was a lot of big boys*: Bosanquet (1929/1989) 21.
schot of ane pistol: Quoted in Cathcart (1988) 51.
Pancake Tuesday: *Folk-Lore* 36 (1925) 256.
Hone, *The Year-Book* (1832) 653–4; Brand I (1849) 441–54; Chambers I (1864) 238–9; *N&Q* 187 (1944) 37, 83–4, 218–19; Thomas (1976); Cathcart (1988); *History Today*, Dec. 1988, 49–50.

Boy Bishop

It was reported: *Folk-Lore* 60 (1949) 302.
History Today 37 (1987) 10–16; Hutton (1996) 100–104.

11 December

Old St Andrew's Day
Tander – Of all the numerous: Sternberg (1851) 183–5.

14 December

St Tibba's Day
Hampson I (1841) 81–2; Palmer (1985) 31–2.

16 December

Boar's Head
They went (most bitterly): Thomas Dekker, *Wonderful Yeare* (1603).
Brand I (1849) 484–6; Husk (1868) 115–27; Wright & Lones III (1940) 252, 267, 279.

21 December

St Thomas' Day
The women that I knew: Grey (1934) 195.
It is in fact a custom: Burne (1883) 393.

24 December

Christmas Eve
Christmas Eve is: Gent. Mag. (1824:ii) 587–90.
If a girl walk: Addy (1895) 84.
Wright & Lones III (1940) 209–29.

Ashen Faggot
On Christmas Eve: Bentley's Magazine 21 (1847) 310.
Brand I (1849) 470; Wright & Lones III (1940) 213–14.

Cattle Kneeling
An honest countryman: Brand I (1849) 473–4.
It is said, as the morning: Devonshire Assoc. 70 (1938) 346, quoting Bentley's Magazine 21 (1847) 306.
Roud (2003) 7–8.

Hooden Horse
a country masquerade: Pegge (1736/1876), under *Hooding*.
Maylam (1909); Cawte (1978) 85–93.

Old Horse
What an eerie monster: Addy (1903) 3–6.
Cawte (1978) 117–24.

Ringing the Devil's Knell
at Horbury, near Wakefield: Henderson (1866) 40.
The Rev. Anthony Sterry: Wright & Lones III (1940) 219.
Colbeck (1983) 198–9; Smith (1989) 163–4.

Vessel Cups
The 'vessel-cups': Blakeborough (1898) 67–8.
The children carrying a box: Folk-Lore 17 (1906) 349–51 (includes a photograph of a 'wassail box' from Yorkshire).
Gent. Mag. (1832) 491–4; Brand I (1849) 454–5; Henderson (1879) 64–6; Wright & Lones II (1938) 32–3; III (1940) 239–41.

Yule Log
A respectable middle-aged: Folk-Lore Journal 4 (1886) 167.
Come, bring with a noise: Herrick (1648), 'Ceremonies for Christmasse'.
In 1845 I was at: Burne (1883) 399.
Brand I (1849) 467–74; Wright & Lones III (1940) 210–13; Hutton (1996) 38–40.

Merrie England

England was merry England then: Walter Scott, *Marmion* (1808) canto VI.
One of the least pleasing effects: Irving (1819–20) 'Christmas' chapter.
Ye Merrie England of ye Olden Time: Wright (1928) 37.
Merry old England died: Examiner, 21 Dec. 1817, 801.

Christmas

All persons say: Robert Southey, *Letters from England*, ed. Jack Simmons (London: Cresset Press, 1951) 362.
But especially in Christmas: Stubbes (1595/2002) 238–9.
Durston (1985); Golby & Purdue (1986); Weightman & Humphries (1987); Davis (1990); Miller (1993); Dickens (1976), *passim*.

Candles
A candle or lamp: Addy (1895) 105.
Wright & Lones III (1940) 215; Opie & Tatem (1989) 75.

Cards
A young woman told me: Folk-Lore 66 (1955) 324.
Buday (1964); Higgs (1999).

Carol Singers
One of the most wonderful: Brice (1967) 1.
She hung her stocking: Uttley (1931) 119.
Poston (1965); Brice (1967); Poston (1970).

Crackers

A History of the Cracker, booklet issued by Tom Smith Group Ltd. (*c*.1997).

Kimpton (2004).

Decorations

Down with the rosemary: Herrick (1648).

Then may be seen: Gent. Mag. (1827:ii) 483–6.

In this progressive nineteenth century: Girls Own Paper, Christmas 1887, 32.

On Christmas Eve: Fletcher (1910) 152–3.

I wanted them both: Cullwick (1984) 184–5

Heyford Church is more neatly: Horn (1986) 6.

Ivy berries or dried peas: Girls Own Paper, 11 Dec. 1880, 170.

It is still a prevailing idea: N&Q 5S:2 (1874) 509.

If mistletoe be not burned: Igglesden (1932) 69–70.

Entertainments

The cake and the nut-brown ale: Gent. Mag. (1827:ii) 484–6.

The kitchen was tolerably: Ayres (1984) 23.

Blind Man's Buff: Gent. Mag. (1828) 506.

when the very fiddlers: Thomas Hardy, *Under the Greenwood Tree* (1872) chaps. 7–8.

Most of the games: Sheffield (1993) 269–70.

Food

Haggis – A north country: Brockett (1825) 144.

And when the child wakens: Brockie (1886/1974) 93, 99–100.

In some parts of the county: Folk-Lore Journal 4 (1886) 115.

A flat Christmas cake: Moor (1823) 192.

At Christmas hardly any: Brockett (1825) 132.

In keeping with the hospitality: Nicholson (1890) 19.

Grandmama was less: Surrey Federation of Women's Institutes (1992) 267–8.

Hone, *The Every-Day Book* I (1827) 819–20; Brand I (1849) 526–32; Davidson (2002) 221–2; 607.

Frumenty

The typical method: Wright and Lones I (1936) 50.

A receipt, three hundred years old: Esther Singleton, 'Ceremonial Dishes of England', *Cosmopolitan* 19 (1895) 51.

Somerset–Wiltshire: White (1932) 348.

It does not seem: White (1932) 363.

White (1932) 26–7, 341, 348, 361–5; Brears (1987) 172–4.

Geese Dancers

In town, the family: Couch (1871) 161-2.

From Christmas to twelfth-tide: Folk-Lore Journal 4 (1886) 118–19.

Guisers

they pushed open the door: Uttley (1931) 111–14.

Holy Thorn(s)

We hear from Quainton: London Daily Advertiser, 5 Jan. 1753, quoted in Mullan & Reid (2000) 214.

To all tender consciences: Gloucester Journal, 2 Jan. 1753.

Wright & Lones II (1938) 76–8 (for trees in Somerset); *The Times*, Jan. 1949 (for trees in Herefordshire); Vickery (1995) 184–8; Mullan & Reid (2000) 208-219; Westwood & Simpson (2005) 642–3.

Mummers

Twelfth Night had come: Grahame (1898) 121–2.

Cawte, Helm & Peacock (1967); Helm (1980); Cass (2001); Cass & Roud (2002).

Stockings

The old custom: Henderson (1866/1973) 50.

Children knew nothing: Fletcher (1910) 152–3.

On Christmas Eve, when the inmates: N&Q 5S:11 (1879) 66.

On Christmas Eve, each child: Brockie (1886/1974) 93.

By and by the younger ones: Blakeborough (1898) 67–9.

they had to hold candy: Warner (1854) 10.

Superstitions

It is lucky to be the first: Folk-Lore Record 1 (1878) 9.

We were very good neighbours: Burne (1883) 400.

If you were born: Folk-Lore Record 1 (1878) 9.

The horses might not go: Burne (1883) 403.

Sword Dance

Almost the first thing: Bosanquet (1929/1989) 23.

Sharp (1911–13); Helm (1980) 19–27; Shuel (1985) 47–9; Corrsin (1993); Corrsin (1997).

Tree

got up a little fête: Greville (2005) 27 December 1829.

Children knew nothing: Fletcher (1910) 152–3.

Waits
About a week before: Gent. Mag. (1827:ii)
483–6.
Certain strolling minstrels: Gent. Mag. (1824:
ii) 587–90.
Stephen (1933); Wilshere (1970).

Wassailing
This friendly and neighbour–loving: Jewitt
(1853) 230.
The Pope in sending: John Selden, *Table–Talk*
(1689/1934) 86.
Wassaile the trees: Herrick (1648), 'Another
[Christmasse Eve Ceremonie]'.
Wassail, wassail, all round the town: Antiquary
29 (1894) 122–4.
Apple wassailing: Devonshire Assoc. 86 (1954)
299.
Brand I (1849) 2–8; Wright & Lones III
(1940) 223–4; Hutton (1996) 46; Sutton
(1997) 13–14, 45–63.

26 December

St Stephen's Day/Boxing Day
gave me the money: Cullwick (1984) 145, 261.
Our postman: Punch (1849) 237.
Brand I (1849) 532–4; Wright & Lones III
(1940) 273; Hutton (1996) 23–4.

Bleeding Horses
Ere Christmas be past: Tusser (1580/1984) 57:2.
Brand I (1849) 532–4; Wright & Lones III
(1940) 275.

Hunting and Shooting
In many parts of the country: Forby (1830)
420.
Mr. H., who is more: Folk-Lore 14 (1903) 89.

Hunting the Wren
I'm goin' to the woods: Folk Music Journal 1:5
(1969) 346.
In the hunt the utmost: Danaher (1972) 243.
You will see sometimes: Aubrey (1686/1880)
47–8.
The robin red-breast: Forby (1830) 409–10.
At Christmas-tide: Henderson (1866) 93.
Armstrong (1958) 141–66; Opie (1997b)
437–40; Roud (2003) 381–2, 529–30;
For Irish traditions, *see* Danaher (1972)
243–50; for Welsh traditions, *see* Owen
(1987) 63–9; for traditions from the Isle of
Man, *see* Moore (1891) 133–40.

Marshfield Paper Boys
Folklore 93 (1982) 105–11.

Pantomimes
Let us at once confess: Charles Dickens,
Bentley's Miscellany (1837).
With the importation: Hartnoll (1983) 625.
It all adds up: Frow (1985) 186.
Wilson (1974); Frow (1985).

28 December

Holy Innocents' Day
When living in the parish: Billson (1895) 96.
That proves as ominous: Carew (1602/2000)
32.
Innocents' Day, sometimes called: Burne (1883)
408–9.
Wright & Lones III (1940) 280–3; for lead-
miners' refusal to work on the day, *see*
N&Q 1:12 (1855) 201.

31 December

New Year's Eve
As a general statement: Chambers II (1864)
787.
Brand I (1849) 1–10; Wright & Lones III
(1940) 284–93.

Allendale Guisers
When war broke out: Newall (1974) 95.
Newall (1974); Shuel (1985) 190–91.

Bell-Ringing
On this night: Jewitt (1853) 230.
Wright & Lones II (1938) 18–21.

Gatherings
In England we seldom: The Times, 18 Nov.
1935, 15.
Wright & Lones II (1938) 16–18.

Hogmanay
Until about five-and-twenty: Neville (1909) 2.

Daily Customs

Bainbridge Horn-Blower
Kightly (1986) 141; Smith (1989) 142–5.

Chime Hours
A recent experiment: N&Q 12S:1 (1916) 329.
An old Kentish lady: N&Q 3S:1 (1862) 223.
I record that I was born: Charles Dickens,
David Copperfield (1849) chap. 1.
Opie & Tatem (1989) 71; Roud (2003) 36–7.

Lady Lee Monument, Aylesbury
Information from Jennifer Westwood
(2006).

Tower of London: Ceremony of the Keys
Brentnall (1975) 77–9; Paget (1989) 22–3.

Wayfarers' Dole
Shuel (1985) 127; James (1987).

Weekly Customs

Farthing Bundles
Beer & Pickard (1987).

John Sayer Charity
Sykes (1977) 165.

St Monday
N&Q 8S:1 (1892) 88, 232–3, 252, 441, 523;
Merceron (2002) 337–44.

Occasional Customs

Abingdon Bun-Throwing
Bloxham (2005) 124.

Bradshaw Memorial Dusting
Porteous (1976) 9; www.duffieldparish
church.co.uk/bradshaw.

Chedzoy Candle Auction
Somerset & Avon Life, Apr. 1986, 85.

Denby Dale Pie
Bostwick (1987–8); Smith (1989) 125–9; for
the Aughton plum pudding *see N&Q*
7S:2 (1886) 26.

Dunmow Flitch
I find but two couples: *Spectator*, 18 Oct. 1714.
Hackwood (1924) 67–9; Steer (1951); www.
dunmowflitchtrials.co.uk.

Highgate Horns
The proverb 'he has been sworn at Highgate':
Grose (1785).
Hone, *The Every-Day Book* II (1827) 40–44,
189; Bell (1866) 188–91; Thorne (1876)
346–7.

Oakham Horseshoes
Clough (1987).

Virgins' Crowns or Maidens' Garlands
Though I never saw: *Reliquary* 1 (1860–61)
8–9.
Chambers I (1864) 271–4; Brears (1982/3);
Spriggs (1982/3).

Bibliography

Addison, William, *English Fairs and Markets* (London: Batsford, 1953).

Addy, George H., *Some Old Customs of Derbyshire* (London: London Society of Derbyshiremen, 1903).

Addy, Sidney Oldall, 'Garland Day at Castleton', *Folk-Lore* 12 (1901) 394–430.

——, *Folk Tales and Superstitions* (Wakefield: EP, 1973); previously published as *Household Tales with Other Traditional Remains* (1895).

Alexander, Matthew, 'Shrove Tuesday Football in Surrey', *Surrey Archaeological Collections* 77 (1986) 197–205.

Alford, Violet, *The Hobby Horse and other Animal Masks* (London: Merlin, 1978).

Andrews, William, *Bygone Lincolnshire* (Hull: A. Brown, 1891).

——, *Bygone Cheshire* (London: Simpkin Marshall, 1895).

——, *Old Church Life* (Hull: W. Andrews, 1900).

Appleton Parish Council, *A History of Appleton* (Appleton: Appleton Parish Council, 1997).

Arlott, John, *The Oxford Companion to Sports and Games* (Oxford: Oxford University Press, 1975).

Armstrong, Edward M., *The Folklore of Birds* (London: Collins, 1958).

Atkinson, Frank, 'Knur and Spell and Allied Games', *Folk Life* 1 (1963) 43–65; plus note by Ralph Merrifield in *Folk Life* 2 (1964) 116–17.

Atkinson, J. C., *Memorials of Old Whitby* (London: Macmillan, 1894).

Aubrey, John, *Remaines of Gentilisme and Judaisme* (1686); ed. James Britten (London: The Folklore Society, 1880).

Axon, William, *The Black Knights of Ashton* (Manchester: John Heywood, 1870).

Ayres, Jack (ed.), *Paupers and Pig Killers: The Diary of William Holland, a Somerset Parson, 1799–1818* (Gloucester: Alan Sutton, 1984).

Baigent, Francis Joseph, 'On the Family of de Lymerston', *Journal of the British Archaeological Association* 11 (1855) 277–302.

Baker, Anne Elizabeth, *Glossary of Northamptonshire Words and Phrases*, 2 vols. (London: Russell Smith, 1854).

Balfour, M. C., *County Folklore: Northumberland* (London: David Nutt, 1904).

Baring-Gould, S., *Devonshire Characters and Strange Events* (London: John Lane, 1908).

Baskervill, Charles Read, 'Mummers' Wooing Plays in England', *Modern Philology* 21 (1924) 225–72.

Beddington, Winifred G., and Christy, Elsa B., *It Happened in Hampshire* (Winchester: Hampshire Federation of Women's Institutes, 1936).

Bede, Venerable, *De Temporum Ratione*, in Wallis (1999).

Beer, R., and Pickard, C. A., *Eighty Years on Bow Common* (London: Fern Street Settlement, 1987).

Bell, Robert, *Ballads and Songs of the Peasantry of England* (London: Charles Griffin, 1866).

Bennett, A. R., *London and Londoners in the Eighteen-Fifties and Sixties* (London: Fisher Unwin, 1924).

Bennett, H. S., *Life on the English Manor: A Study of Peasant Conditions 1150–1400* (Cambridge: Cambridge University Press, 1948).

Billson, C. J., *County Folklore Printed Extracts 3: Leicestershire and Rutland* (London: The Folklore Society, 1895).

Bird, F. W., *Memorials of Godmanchester: Reminiscences of F. W. Bird* (Peterborough: Peterborough Advertiser, 1911).

Blakeborough, Richard, *Wit, Character, Folklore and Customs of the North Riding of Yorkshire* (London: Frowde, 1898).

Bloom, J. Harvey, *Folk Lore, Old Customs and Superstitions in Shakespeare Land* (London: Mitchell Hughes & Clarke, c.1930).

Bloxham, Christine, *May Day to Mummers: Folklore and Traditional Customs in Oxfordshire* (Charlbury: Wychwood Press, 2002).

——, *Folklore of Oxfordshire* (Stroud: Tempus, 2005).

Bosanquet, Rosalie E., *In the Troublesome Times* (Northumberland Press, 1929; reprinted Stocksfield: Spredden Press, 1989).

Bostwick, David, 'The Denby Dale Pies: An Illustrated Narrative History', *Folk Life* 26 (1987–8) 12–42.

Bourne, Henry, *Antiquitates Vulgares, or the Antiquities of the Common People* (Newcastle: privately printed, 1725).

Boyes, Georgina, 'Dressing the Part: The Role of Costume as an Indicator of Social Dynamics in the Castleton Garland Ceremony', in Buckland & Wood (1993) 105–18.

Bradley, A. G., *Round About Wiltshire* (1907; 3rd edn, London: Methuen, 1913).

Brand John, *Observations on Popular Antiquities* (London: Vernon, Bood & Sharpe, 1810).

Brand, John, *Observations on the Popular Antiquities of Great Britain*, new edn, ed. Henry Ellis, 3 vols. (London: Bohn, 1849).

Bray, Mrs A. E., *Traditions, Legends, Superstitions, and Sketches of Devonshire* (London: Murray, 1838).

Brears, Peter, *Traditional Food in Yorkshire* (Edinburgh: John Donald, 1987).

——, *North Country Folk Art* (Edinburgh: John Donald, 1989).

Brears, Peter C. D., 'Construction of a Maiden's Garland', *Folk Life* 21 (1982/83) 34–5.

Brentnall, Margaret, *Old Customs and Ceremonies of London* (London: Batsford, 1975).

Brice, Douglas, *The English Folk Carol* (London: Herbert Jenkins, 1967).

Briggs, Katharine M., *The Folklore of the Cotswolds* (London: Batsford, 1974).

British Film Institute, *Electric Edwardians: The Films of Mitchell and Kenyon*, DVD (London: BFI, 2005).

Brockett, John Trotter, *A Glossary of North Country Words* (Newcastle: Emerson Charnley, 1825; 3rd edn, 1846).

Brockie, William, *Legends and Superstitions of the County of Durham* (Sunderland, 1886; reprinted Wakefield: EP, 1974).

Brown, Tom, *The Hunting of the Earl of Rone*, revised edn (Combe Martin: Earl of Rone Council, 1997).

Bruley, Sue (ed.), *Working for Victory: A Diary of Life in a Second World War Factory* (Stroud: Sutton, 2001).

Buchanan, Brenda, *et al.*, *Gunpowder Plots* (London: Allen Lane, 2005).

Buckland, Theresa, 'The Reindeer Antlers of the Abbots Bromley Horn Dance: A Re-examination', *Lore and Language* 3:7 (1980) 1–8 (*see also* correspondence in vols. 3:7 (1982) 87; 4:1 (1985) 86–7; 5:2 (1986) 101).

——, 'Wakes and Rushbearing c. 1780–c. 1830: A Functional Analysis', *Lore & Language* 3:6 (1982) 29–44.

——, 'The Tunstead Mill Nutters of Rossendale, Lancashire', *Folk Music Journal* 5:2 (1986) 132–49.

Buckland, Theresa, and Wood, Juliette, *Aspects of British Calendar Customs* (Sheffield: Sheffield Academic Press, 1993).

Buday, George, *The History of the Christmas Card* (London: Spring Books, 1964).

Burne, Charlotte, *Shropshire Folk-Lore: A Sheaf of Gleanings* (London: Trübner, 1883).

——, 'Souling, Clementing, and Catterning: Three November Customs of the Western Midlands', *Folk-Lore* 25 (1914) 285–99.

Burns, Francis, *Heigh for Cotswold! A History of Robert Dover's Olimpick Games*, new edn (Chipping Campden: Robert Dover's Games Society, 2000).

Burton, Alfred, *Rush-Bearing* (Manchester: Brook & Chrystal, 1891).

Bushaway, Bob, *By Rite: Custom, Ceremony and Continuity in England 1700–1880* (London: Junction Books, 1982).

——, 'Name Upon Name:The Great War and Remembrance', in Porter (1992) 136–67.

——, 'Bulls, Ballads, Minstrels and Manors: Some Observations on the Defence of Custom in Eighteenth-Century England', in Buckland & Wood (1993) 75–93.

Bushaway, R. W., 'Grovely, Grovely, Grovely, and all Grovely: Custom, Crime and Conflict in the English Woodland', *History Today* 31 (March 1981) 37–43.

Byng, John, *The Torrington Diaries*, 4 vols. (London: Eyre & Spottiswoode, 1934–8).

Cameron, David Kerr, *The English Fair* (Stroud: Sutton, 1998).

Camp, John, *In Praise of Bells: The Folklore and Traditions of British Bells* (London: Robert Hale, 1988).

Candlin, Lilian, *Memories of Old Sussex* (Newbury: Countryside Books, 1987).

Cannadine, David, 'The Transformation of Civic Ritual in Modern Britain: The Colchester Oyster Feast', *Past & Present* 94 (1982) 107–30.

Capp, Bernard, *Astrology and the Popular Press: English Almanacs 1500–1800* (London: Faber, 1979).

Carew, Richard, *The Survey of Cornwall* (London: John Jaggard, 1602; reprinted Redruth: Tamar Books, 2000).

Cass, Eddie, *The Lancashire Pace-Egg Play: A Social History* (London: FLS Books, 2001).

Cass, Eddie, and Roud, Steve, *Room, Room, Ladies and Gentlemen: An Introduction to the English Mummers' Play* (London: English Folk Dance & Song Society, 2002).

Cathcart, Rex, 'Festive Capers? Barring-Out the Schoolmaster', *History Today* (Oct 1988) 49–53.

Catt, Jon, *Northern Hiring Fairs* (Chorley: Countryside Publications, 1986).

Caunce, Stephen, *Amongst Farm Horses: The Horselads of East Yorkshire* (Stroud: Alan Sutton, 1991).

Cawte, E. C., *Ritual Animal Disguise* (Cambridge: Brewer, 1978).

Cawte, E. C., Helm, Alex, and Peacock, Norman, *English Ritual Drama* (London: The Folklore Society, 1967).

Chambers, Robert, *The Book of Days: A Miscellany of Popular Antiquities*, 2 vols. (London: Chambers, 1864).

Chandler, Keith, *Morris Dancing at Bampton Until 1914* (Minster Lovell: privately printed, 1983).

——, *Ribbons, Bells and Squeaking Fiddles: The Social History of Morris Dancing in the English South Midlands, 1660–1900* (Enfield Lock: Hisarlik, 1993) [cited as 1993a].

——, 'The Abingdon Morris and the Election of the Mayor of Ock Street', in Buckland & Wood (1993) 119–36 [cited as 1993b].

Charlton, Lionel, *The History of Whitby and of Whitby Abbey* (York: A. Ward, 1779).

Christian, Roy, *Well-Dressing in Derbyshire* (Derby: Derbyshire Countryside, 1983).

Clare, John, *The Midsummer Cushion* (Manchester: Carcanet, 1990).

——, *Cottage Tales* (Manchester: Carcanet, 1993).

——, *The Midsummer Cushion*, in Eric Robinson, David Powell, and P. M. S. Dawson (eds.), *John Clare: Poems of the Middle Period* III (Oxford: Clarendon Press, 1998).

Clarke, James, *Survey of the Lakes of Cumberland, Westmorland, and Lancashire*, 2nd edn (London: privately printed, 1789).

Clough, T. H. McK., *The Horseshoes of Oakham Castle*, 2nd edn (Leicester: Leicestershire Museums, 1987).

Cobbett, William, *Rural Rides* (London: William Cobbett, 1830).

Colbeck, Maurice, *The Calendar Year: A Celebration of Events in the Yorkshire Television Region* (East Ardsley: EP, 1983).

Cole, Malcolm, *Whitelands College May Queen Festival 1881–1981* (London: Whitelands College, 1981).

Collinson, John, *The History and Antiquities of the County of Somerset*, 3 vols. (Bath: R. Cruttwell, 1791).

Cooper, Jeremy J., *A Fool's Game: The Ancient Tradition of Haxey Hood* (Haxey: Lord & Boggins of the Haxey Hood, 1993).

Corrsin, Stephen D., *Sword Dancing in Britain: An Annotated Bibliography* (London: English Folk Dance & Song Society, 1993).

——, *Sword Dancing in Europe: A History* (Enfield Lock: Hisarlik, 1997).

Cossins, James, *Reminiscences of Exeter Fifty Years Since* (Exeter: privately printed, 1878).

Couch, Jonathan, *The History of Polperro* (Truro: W. Lake, 1871).

Crawford, Phyllis, *In England Still* (London: Arrowsmith, 1938).

Cressy, David, *Bonfires and Bells: National Memory and the Protestant Calendar in Elizabethan and Stuart England* (London: Weidenfeld & Nicolson, 1989).

Crosby, Alan, *The History of the Preston Guild* (Preston: Lancashire County Books, 1991).

Cross, F. L., *The Oxford Dictionary of the Christian Church* (London: Oxford University Press, 1957).

Cullwick, Hannah, *The Diaries of Hannah Cullwick, Victorian Maidservant*, ed. Liz Stanley (London: Virago, 1984).

Cumbrian Federation of Women's Institutes, *Cumbria Within Living Memory* (Newbury: Countryside Books, 1994).

Dacombe, Marianne R. (ed.), *Dorset Up Along and Down Along* (Dorchester: Dorset Federation of Women's Institutes, 1935).

Danaher, Kevin, *The Year in Ireland: Irish Calendar Customs* (Cork: Mercier, 1972).

Davidson, Alan, *The Penguin Companion to Food* (London: Penguin, 2002).

Davis, Paul, *The Life and Times of Ebenezer Scrooge* (New Haven: Yale University Press, 1990).

De Carle, Donald, *British Time* (London: Crosby Lockwood, 1947).

De Voragine, Jacobus, *The Golden Legend: Readings on the Saints* (c.1260), trans. William Granger Ryan (Princeton: Princeton University Press, 1993).

Deane, Tony, and Shaw, Tony, *The Folklore of Cornwall* (London: Batsford, 1975).

Defoe, Daniel, *A Tour through the Whole Island of Great Britain* (1724–6; London: Dent, 1962).

Denham Tracts: A Collection of Folklore by Michael Aislabie Denham, ed. James Hardy, 2 vols. (London: The Folklore Society, 1892–5).

Dickens, Charles, *The Annotated Christmas Carol*, ed. Michael Patrick Hearn (New York: Clarkson N. Potter, 1976).

Ditchfield, P. H., *Old English Customs* (London: Methuen, 1896).

Dives and Pauper (c.1405–10; London: Early English Text Society, 1976/1980).

Doble, Gilbert H., *The Saints of Cornwall: Part 2, Saints of the Lizard District* (Felinfach: Llanerch, 1998).

Doel, Fran, and Doel, Geoff, *Folklore of Kent* (Stroud: Tempus, 2003).

Donoghue, Paul, and Capstick, Tony, *Appleby Horse Fair: A Collection of Stories, Poems, and Photographs* (Northallerton: Appleby Fair, 2002).

Dowden, John, *The Church Year and Kalendar* (Cambridge: Cambridge University Press, 1910).

Duffy, Eamon, *The Stripping of the Altars* (London: Yale University Press, 1992).

Duncan, David Ewing, *The Calendar* (London: Fourth Estate, 1998).

Duncomb, John, *Words Used in Herefordshire* (1804), in Walter W. Skeat, *Reprinted Glossaries, Series B* (London: English Dialect Society, 1874).

Durand, Mortimer, *The Life of the Rt. Hon. Sir Alfred Comyn Lyall* (London: Blackwood, 1913).

Durston, Chris, 'Lords of Misrule: The Puritan War on Christmas 1642–60', *History Today* (Dec. 1985) 7–14.

Dyck, Ian, *William Cobbett and Rural Popular Culture* (Cambridge: Cambridge University Press, 1992).

Dyer, T. F. Thiselton, *British Popular Customs, Past and Present* (London: George Bell, 1876).

East Kent Federation of Women's Institutes, *East Kent Within Living Memory* (Newbury: Countryside Books, 1993).

East Yorkshire Federation of Women's Institutes, *East Yorkshire Within Living Memory* (Newbury: Countryside Books, 1998).

Edwards, E., *A Collection of Old English Customs* (London: John Bower Nichols, 1842).

Elias, N., and Dunning, E., 'Folk Football in Medieval and Early Modern Britain', in E. Dunning, *The Sociology of Sport* (London: F. Cass, 1971).

Etherington, Jim, *Lewes Bonfire Night: A Short History of the Guy Fawkes Celebrations* (Seaford: S.B. Publications, 1993).

Evans, George Ewart, *The Farm and the Village* (London: Faber, 1969).

——, *Where Beards Wag All: The Relevance of the Oral Tradition* (London: Faber, 1972).

Evelyn, John, *The Diary of John Evelyn*, 3 vols. (London: Routledge/Thoemmes, 1996).

Farmer, David, *Oxford Dictionary of Saints*, 2nd edn (Oxford: Oxford University Press, 1987).

Filmer, Richard, *Hops and Hop Picking* (Princes Risborough: Shire, 1982).

Findler, Gerald, *Folk Lore of the Lake Counties* (Clapham: Dalesman, 1968).

Fisher, John, *The History and Antiquities of Masham and Mashamshire* (London: Simpkin Marshall, 1865).

Fitz Stephen, William, *Description of London* (*c.*1180; reprinted as *Norman London*, New York: Italica, 1990).

Flavell, Linda and Roger, *Dictionary of Proverbs and their Origins* (London: Kyle Cathie, 1993).

Fletcher, J. S., *Recollections of a Yorkshire Village* (London: Digby Long, 1910).

Fletcher, Linda, 'Strewings', *Folk Life* 36 (1997/8) 66–71.

Forby, Robert, *The Vocabulary of East Anglia* (London: Nichols, 1830).

Forrest, John, *The History of Morris Dancing 1458–1750* (Cambridge: James Clarke, 1999).

Forster, Robert, *History of Corbridge* (Newcastle: J. Beall, 1881).

Fox, David Scott, *Saint George: The Saint with Three Faces* (Windsor: Kensal Press, 1983).

Frampton, George, *Whittlesey Straw Bear* (Peterborough: Cambridgeshire Libraries, 1989).

——, 'The Shaftesbury Byzant: A South of England Morris?', *Folklore* 101:2 (1990) 152–61.

——, *Grovely! Grovely! Grovely! and All Grovely! The History of Oak Apple Day in Great Wishford* (York: Quacks Books, 1992).

Frow, Gerald, *Oh Yes It Is! A History of Pantomime* (London: BBC, 1985).

Fry, Lewis G., *Oxted, Limpsfield and Neighbourhood* (Oxted: privately printed, 1932).

Gamble, Rose, *Chelsea Child* (London: BBC, 1979).

Gardner, Keith, 'Apples in the Landscape: The Puxton Dolmoors', *Bristol and Avon Archaeology* 4 (1985) 13–20.

Gerould, Gordon Hall, *Saints' Legends* (Boston: Houghton Mifflin, 1916).

Gerrish, Tricia, *The Glove is Up! Devon's Historic Fairs* (unpublished typescript, West Country Studies Library, 2004) [unpaginated].

Gibbons, M. S., *We Donkeys in Devon* (Exeter: Eland, 1885).

Gibson, A. Craig, 'Ancient Customs and Superstitions in Cumberland', *Transactions of the Historical Society of Lancashire & Cheshire* 10 (1858) 96–110.

Giles, John A., *History of the Parish and Town of Bampton* (Oxford: J. H. Parker, 1847).

Glover, Stephen, *The History of the County of Derby*, 2 vols. (Derby: Henry Mozley, 1829).

Golby, J. M. and Purdue, A. W., *The Making of the Modern Christmas* (London: Batsford, 1986).

Golden Legend, see De Voragine.

Goldsmith, Oliver, *The Vicar of Wakefield* (London: F. Newbery, 1766).

Gomme, Alice Bertha, *The Traditional Games of England, Scotland and Ireland*, 2 vols. (London, David Nutt, 1894–8).

Gomme, G. L. (ed.), *The Gentleman's Magazine Library: Manners and Customs* (London: Eliot Stock, 1883).

Goodsall, Robert H., 'Oyster Fisheries on the North Kent Coast', *Archaeologia Cantiana* 80 (1965) 118–51.

Govett, L. A., *The King's Book of Sports* (London: Eliot Stock, 1890).

Grahame, Kenneth, *The Golden Age* (London: John Lane, 1898).

Grant, James, *Sketches in London* (London: W. S. Orr, 1838).

Grantham, W. W., *Stoolball and How to Play It*, 2nd edn (London: W. B. Tattershall, 1931).

Greenhalgh, Alec, *Hail Smiling Morn: Whit Friday Brass Band Contests, 1884–1991* (Oldham: Oldham Library, 1992).

Greenwood, James, *Unsentimental Journeys* (London: Lock & Tyler, 1867).

Greville, Charles, *The Diaries of Charles Greville*, ed. Edward Pearce (London: Pimlico, 2005).

Grey, Edwin, *Cottage Life in a Hertfordshire Village* (St Albans: Fisher, Knight & Co., 1934).

Grose, Francis, *Classical Dictionary of the Vulgar Tongue* (London: S. Hooper, 1785).

Gunnell, Clive, *To Tavistock Goosie Fair* (Bodmin: Bossiney, 1978).

Gunnell, Terry, *The Origins of Drama in Scandinavia* (Cambridge: Brewer, 1995).

Gurdon, E. C., *County Folk-Lore: Suffolk* (London: The Folklore Society, 1893).

Gutch, Mrs, *County Folk-Lore: North Riding of Yorkshire and the Ainsty* (London: David Nutt, 1901).

Gutch, Mrs and Peacock, Mabel, *County Folk-Lore Vol. 5: Lincolnshire* (London: David Nutt, 1908).

Hackwood, Frederick William, *Staffordshire Customs, Superstitions and Folklore* (Lichfield: Mercury Press, 1924).

Haddon, Celia, *The First Ever English Olimpick Games* (London: Hodder & Stoughton, 2004).

Halliwell, James Orchard, *The Popular Rhymes and Nursery Tales of England* (London: John Russell Smith, 1849).

Hampson, R. T., *Medii Aevi Kalendarium*, 2 vols. (London: Causton, 1841).

Hardy, Thomas, *The Mayor of Casterbridge* (London: Macmillan, 1886).

Harland, John, and Wilkinson, T. T., *Lancashire Legends, Traditions, Pageants and Sports* (London: Routledge, 1867).

——, *Lancashire Folk-Lore* (Manchester: Heywood, 1882).

Harris, Mollie, *A Kind of Magic: An Oxfordshire Childhood in the 1920s* (London: Chatto & Windus, 1969).

Harrison, Kenneth, *The Framework of Anglo-Saxon History to AD 900* (Cambridge: Cambridge University Press, 1967).

Hart, Kingsley, *The Letters of Dorothy Osborne to Sir William Temple 1652–54* (London: Folio Society, 1968).

Hartnoll, Phyllis, *The Oxford Companion to the Theatre*, 4th edn (Oxford: Oxford University Press, 1983).

Hasted, Edward, *History and Topographical Survey of the County of Kent*, 4 vols. (Canterbury: Simmons & Kirby, 1778–99).

Hawthorne, Nathaniel, *Our Old Home* (London: Smith Elder, 1863).

Hazlitt, W. C., *A Dictionary of Faiths and Folk-Lore* (London: Reeves & Turner, 1905).

Head, Robert, *Congleton Past and Present* (Congleton: privately printed, 1887).

Heaney, Michael, *An Introductory Bibliography on Morris Dancing* (London: English Folk Dance and Song Society, 1985).

——, 'New Evidence for the Abbots Bromley Hobby-Horse', *Folk Music Journal* 5:3 (1987) 359–60.

Heanley, R. M., 'The Vikings: Traces of their Folklore in Marshland', *Saga-Book* 3 (1902).

Heffernan, Hilary, *The Annual Hop London to Kent* (Stroud: Tempus, 1996).

Helm, Alex, *Cheshire Folk Drama* (Ibstock: Guizer Press, 1968).

——, 'Rushcarts of the North-West of England', *Folk Life* 8 (1970) 20–31.

——, *The English Mummers' Play* (Woodbridge: D.S. Brewer, 1980).

Henderson, William, *Notes on the Folk Lore of the Northern Counties of England and the Border* (London: Longmans Green, 1866; reprinted Wakefield: EP, 1973; 2nd edn, London: The Folklore Society, 1879).

Herrick, Robert, *Hesperides* (1648), in *The Poems of Robert Herrick* (London: Oxford University Press, 1965).

Hewett, Sarah, *The Peasant Speech of Devon*, 2nd edn (London: Elliot Stock, 1892).

——, *Nummits and Crummits: Devonshire Customs, Characteristics, and Folk-Lore* (London: Thomas Burleigh, 1900).

Higgs, Michelle, *Christmas Cards from the 1840s to the 1940s* (Princes Risborough: Shire, 1999).

Hird, Ben, *The Antient Scorton Silver Arrow* (London: Society of Archer-Antiquaries, 1972).

Hocking, Chris, *Remember, Remember: The Story of Bridgwater Guy Fawkes Carnival* (Bridgwater: privately printed, 2004).

Hogg, Garry, *Customs and Traditions of England* (Newton Abbot: David & Charles, 1971).

Hole, Christina, *English Sports and Pastimes* (London: Batsford, 1949).

——, *English Traditional Customs* (London: Batsford, 1975).

——, *Dictionary of British Folk Customs* (London: Hutchinson, 1976).

——, *A Dictionary of British Folk Customs* (London: Paladin, 1978).

Home, Gordon, *The Evolution of an English Town* (London: Dent, 1915).

Hone, William, *The Every-Day Book*, 2 vols. (London: Thomas Tegg, 1827).

——, *The Table Book* (London: Thomas Tegg, 1827).

——, *The Year-Book* (London: Thomas Tegg, 1832).

Horn, Pamela (ed.), *Oxfordshire Country Life in the 1860s: The Early Diaries of George James Dew (1846–1928) of Lower Heyford* (Sutton Courtenay: Beacon Publications, 1986).

Howkins, Alun, and Merricks, Linda, 'The Ploughboy and the Plough Play', *Folk Music Journal* 6:2 (1991) 187–208.

Hughes, Thomas, *The Scouring of the White Horse* (Cambridge, Macmillan, 1859).

Husk, William Henry, *Songs of the Nativity* (London: Hotten, 1868).

Hutchinson, W., *A View of Northumberland*, 2 vols. (Newcastle: T. Saint, 1778).

Hutton, Ronald, *The Rise and Fall of Merry England: The Ritual Year 1400–1700* (Oxford: Oxford University Press, 1994).

——, *Stations of the Sun: A History of the Ritual Year in Britain* (Oxford: Oxford University Press, 1996).

Hyett, F. A., *Glimpses of the History of Painswick* (Gloucester: British Publishing, 1957).

Igglesden, Charles, *Those Superstitions* (London: Jarrolds, 1932).

Ingram, Martin, 'Ridings, Rough Music and the Reform of Popular Culture in Early Modern England', *Past & Present* 105 (1984) 79–113.

Inwards, R., *Weather Lore* (London: W. Tweedie, 1869; new edn, London: Elliot Stock, 1893).

Irving, Washington, *The Sketch-Book of Geoffrey Crayon, Gent.* (1819–20; rev. edn, New York: Putnam, 1848).

——, *Bracebridge Hall* (London: John Murray, 1822).

James, Nicholas, 'The Survival of the Traditional Dole in Hampshire Today', *Lore Language* 6:1 (1987) 59–64.

Jefferies, Richard, *Round About a Great Estate* (London: Smith Elder, 1880).

Jeffrey, Percy Shaw, *Whitby Lore and Legend*, 2nd edn (Whitby: Horne, 1923).

Jenkin, A. K. Hamilton, *Cornish Homes and Customs* (London: Dent, 1934).

Jewitt, Llewellyn, 'On Ancient Customs and Sports of the County of Nottingham', *Journal of the British Archaeological Association* 8 (1853) 229–40.

Jones, Kelvin I., *The Furry Dance: An Ancient Tradition* (Penzance: Oakmagic, 1997).

Jones-Baker, Doris, *The Folklore of Hertfordshire* (London: Batsford, 1977).

Judge, Roy, 'Tradition and the Plaited Maypole Dance', *Traditional Dance* 2 (1983) 1–22.

——, *Changing Attitudes to May Day 1844–1914* (unpublished Ph.D. thesis, University of Leeds, 1987).

——, 'Fact and Fancy in Tennyson's May Queen and Flora Thompson's May Day', in Buckland & Wood (1993) 167–83.

——, *The Jack-in-the-Green*, 2nd edn (London: FLS Books, 2000).

Kennedy, Douglas, *English Folk Dancing Today and Yesterday* (London: Bell, 1964).

Kent, Sylvia, *Folklore of Essex* (Stroud: Tempus, 2005).

Kightly, Charles, *The Customs and Ceremonies of Britain: An Encyclopaedia of Living Traditions* (London: Thames & Hudson, 1986).

Kille, Herbert W., 'West Country Hobby-Horses and Cognate Customs', *Proceedings of the Somerset Archaeological & Natural History Society*, 4th series, 17 (1931) 63–77.

Kilvert, Francis, *Kilvert's Diary*, ed. William Plomer, 4 vols. (London: Jonathan Cape, 1938–9).

Kimpton, Peter, *Tom Smith's Christmas Crackers: An Illustrated History* (Stroud: Tempus, 2004).

Kitchen, Fred, *Brother to the Ox: The Autobiography of a Farmer's Boy* (London: Dent, 1940).

Lancashire Federation of Women's Institutes, *Lancashire Within Living Memory* (Newbury: Countryside Books, 1997).

Lancashire Lore (Preston: Lancashire Federation of Women's Institutes, 1971).

Last, Nella, *Nella Last's War: A Mother's Diary*, ed. Richard Broad and Suzie Fleming (London: Falling Wall, 1981).

Le Faye, Deirdre, *Jane Austen's Letters*, new edn (Oxford: Oxford University Press, 1995).

Lean, Vincent Stuckey, *Lean's Collectanea*, 5 vols. (Bristol: Arrowsmith, 1902–4).

Learmount, Brian, *A History of the Auction* (Iver: Barnard & Larmount, 1985).

Leather, Ella Mary, *The Folk-Lore of Herefordshire* (London: Sidgwick and Jackson, 1912).

Leeds Mercury (4 Oct. 1879), 'Notes & Queries No. XL: Yorkshire Folk Lore' (contributed by Samuel Smith).

Lenton, Graham, *The Story of the Olney Pancake Race* (Whitney: gml art, 2003).

Lodge, Thomas, *Wit's Miserie* (London: Adam Islip, 1596).

Lowerson, John, 'Stoolball: Conflicting Values in the Revivals of a Traditional Sussex Game', *Sussex Archaeological Collections* 133 (1995) 263–74.

Machyn, Henry, *The Diary of Henry Machyn*, ed. John Gough Nichols (London: Camden Society, 1848).

MacLean, Sally-Beth, 'Hocktide: A Reassessment of a Popular Pre-Reformation Festival', in Twycross (1996) 233–41.

Magoun, F. P., *History of Football from the Beginnings to 1871* (Bochum-Langendreer: H. Poppinghaus, 1938).

Main, Veronica, 'Corn Dollies: Searching for the Seed of Truth', *Folk Life* 37 (1998–9) 44–63.

Malcolmson, Robert W., *Popular Recreations in English Society 1700–1850* (Cambridge: Cambridge University Press, 1973).

Manningham, John, *The Diary of John Manningham of the Middle Temple 1602–1603* (London: Camden Society, 1868).

Mantell, Gideon, *Journal of Gideon Mantell (Surgeon and Geologist)* (London: Curwen, 1940).

Marshall, Sybil, *Fenland Chronicle* (Cambridge: Cambridge University Press, 1967).

Maylam, Percy, *The Hooden Horse: An East Kent Christmas Custom* (Canterbury: privately printed, 1909).

Menefee, Samuel Pyeatt, *Wives for Sale* (Oxford: Blackwell, 1981).

——, 'Dead Reckoning: the Church Porch Watch in British Society', in Hilda Ellis Davidson (ed.), *The Seer in Celtic and Other Traditions* (Edinburgh: John Donald, 1989).

Merceron, Jacques E., *Dictionnaire des Saints Imaginaires et Facétieux* (Paris: Editions du Seuil, 2002).

Metford, J. C. J., *The Christian Year* (London: Thames & Hudson, 1991).

Miller, Dan (ed.), *Unwrapping Christmas* (Oxford: Clarendon Press, 1993).

Millington, Peter, 'The Ploughboy and the Plough Play', *Folk Music Journal* 7:1 (1995) 71–3.

Mitford, Jessica, *Hons and Rebels* (London: Gollancz, 1960).

Moor, Edward, *Suffolk Words and Phrases* (Woodbridge: Loder, 1823).

Moore, A. W., *The Folk-Lore of the Isle of Man* (London: D. Nutt, 1891).

Morison, John, and Daisley, Peter, *Hare Pie Scrambling & Bottle Kicking: Hallaton's Strange and Ancient Custom* (Hallaton: Hallaton Museum Press, 2000).

Morley, Henry, *Memoirs of Bartholomew Fair* (London: Chapman & Hall, 1859).

Morris, M. C. F., *Yorkshire Folk-Talk*, 2nd edn (London: A. Brown, 1911).

Morsley, Clifford, *News from the English Countryside 1750–1850* (London: Harrap, 1979).

Mullan, John, and Reid, Christopher, *Eighteenth-Century Popular Culture: A Selection* (Oxford: Oxford University Press, 2000).

Muncey, R. W., *Our Old English Fairs* (London: Sheldon Press [*c.*1935]).

Munn, Pat, *Bodmin Riding and Other Similar Celtic Customs* (Bodmin: Bodmin Books, 1975).

Murfin, Lyn, *Popular Leisure in the Lake Countries* (Manchester: Manchester University Press, 1990).

Naylor, Peter, and Porter, Lindsey, *Well Dressing* (Ashbourne: Landmark, 2002).

Neasham, George, *North-Country Sketches* (Durham: privately printed, 1893).

Neville, Hastings M., *A Corner in the North: Yesterday and Today with Border Folk* (Newcastle: Andrew Reid, 1909).

Newall, Venetia, *An Egg at Easter* (London: Routledge & Kegan Paul, 1971).

——, 'The Allendale Fire Festival in Relation to its Contemporary Social Setting', *Folklore* 85 (1974) 93–103.

——, 'Throwing the Hood at Haxey: A Lincolnshire Twelfth Night Custom', *Folk Life* 18 (1980) 7–23.

Newton, Jill, *Helston Flora Day* (Bodmin: Bossiney, 1978).

Nicholson, John, *Folk Lore of East Yorkshire* (London: Simpkin Marshall, 1890).

Noake, John, *Guide to Worcestershire* (London: Longman, 1868).

Opie, Iona and Peter, *The Lore and Language of Schoolchildren* (Oxford: Oxford University Press, 1959).

——, *Children's Games with Things* (Oxford: Oxford Univ. Press, 1997) [cited as 1997a].

——, *Oxford Dictionary of Nursery Rhymes* (2nd edn., Oxford: Oxford University Press, 1997) [cited as 1997b].

Opie, Iona, and Tatem, Moira, *A Dictionary of Superstitions* (Oxford: Oxford University Press, 1989).

Oruch, Jack, 'St. Valentine, Chaucer, and Spring in February', *Speculum* 56:3 (1981) 534–65.

Osborne, Dorothy, Letters of, in Hart (1968).

Owen, Nelson, 'Old Custom Goes with a Bang', *The Countryman* (Winter 1984/5) 70–74.

Owen, Trefor M., *Welsh Folk Customs*, new edn (Llandysul: Gomer, 1987).

Paget, Julian, *Discovering London Ceremonial and Traditions* (Princes Risborough: Shire, 1989).

Palmer, Kingsley, *The Folklore of Somerset* (London: Batsford, 1976).

Palmer, Roy, *The Folklore of Leicestershire and Rutland* (Wymondham: Sycamore Press, 1985).

——, *The Folklore of Gloucestershire* (Tiverton: Westcountry Books, 1994).

——, *Herefordshire Folklore* (Woonton Almeley: Logaston, 2002).

——, *The Folklore of Shropshire* (Almeley: Logaston Press, 2004).

Parish, W. D., *A Dictionary of the Sussex Dialect*, 2nd edn (Lewes: Farncombe, 1875).

Pasquils Palinodia and His Progress to the Taverne (London: Thomas Snodham, 1619); reprinted in J. Payne Collier, *Illustrations of Old English Literature* I (London: privately printed, 1866).

Patten, R. W., *Exmoor Custom and Song* (Dulverton: Exmoor Press, 1974).

Pegge, Samuel, *Glossary of Kenticisms* (1736); reprinted in English Dialect Society, *Original Glossaries* III (London: Trubner, 1876).

Philpott, Olive M., 'Whitsuntide in Our Village', *Dorset Year Book* (1961/2) 173–7.

Phythian-Adams, Charles, 'Milk and Soot: The Changing Vocabulary of a Popular Ritual in Stuart and Hanoverian London', in D. Fraser and A. Sutcliffe, *The Pursuit of Urban History* (London: Edward Arnold, 1983) 83–104.

Piggott, Stuart, *The Druids* (London: Thames & Hudson, 1968).

Pihlens, Hugh, *The Story of Hungerford* (Newbury: Local Heritage Books, 1983).

Pollard, A. F., 'New Year's Day and Leap Year in English History', *English Historical Review* 55 (1940) 177–93.

Poole, Robert, *Time's Alteration: Calendar Reform in Early Modern England* (London: UCL Press, 1998).

Porteous, Chrichton, *The Beauty and Mystery of Well-Dressing* (Derby: Pilgrim Press, 1949).

——, *The Ancient Customs of Derbyshire* (Derby: Derbyshire Countryside, 1976).

Porter, Enid, *Cambridgeshire Customs and Folklore* (London: Routledge & Kegan Paul, 1969).

Porter, Lindsey, *Ashbourne Royal Shrovetide Football: the Official History* (Ashbourne: Ashbourne Editions, 1992).

——, *Ashbourne Shrovetide Football: 100 Years in Photographs* (Ashbourne: Ashbourne Editions, 1995).

Poston, Elizabeth, *The Penguin Book of Christmas Carols* (Harmondsworth: Penguin, 1965).

——, *The Second Penguin Book of Christmas Carols* (Harmondsworth: Penguin, 1970).

Pursehouse, Eric, *Waveney Valley Studies: Gleanings from Local History* (Diss: Diss Publishing, 1966).

Quarles, Francis, *The Shepheards' Oracles* (London: printed for John & Richard Marriott, 1646).

Rabey, A. Ivan, *Hurling at St. Columb: and in Cornwall* (Padstow: Lodenek Press, 1972).

Ratcliffe, E. E., and Wright, Peter A., *The Royal Maundy: a Brief Outline of its History and Ceremonial*, 7th edn (London: Royal Almonry, 1960).

Rattue, James, *The Living Stream: Holy Wells in Historical Context* (Woodbridge: Boydell, 1995).

Raven, Jon, *The Folklore of Staffordshire* (London: Batsford, 1978).

Rawe, Donald R., *Padstow's Obby Oss*, enlarged edn (Padstow: Lodenek, 1982).

Rawnsley, E. F., *The Rushbearing in Grasmere and Ambleside* (booklet, no publisher, 1953).

Ray, John, *A Complete Collection of English Proverbs* (1670; London: Allman, 1818).

Reid, Douglas A., 'Folk-Football, the Aristocracy and Cultural Change', *International Journal of the History of Sport* 5 (1988) 224–38.

Rhodes, Ebenezer, *Peak Scenery* (London: privately printed, 1818).

Richardson, John, *The Annals of London* (London: Cassell, 2000).

Richardson, Michael, *The Durham Miners' Gala 1935–1960* (Derby: Breedon, 2001).

Roberts, Michael, 'Waiting Upon Chance: English Hiring Fairs and their Meanings from the 14th to the 20th Century', *Journal of Historical Sociology* 1:2 (1988) 119–60.

Robertson, John, *Uppies & Doonies: The Story of the Kirkwall Ba' Game* (Aberdeen: Aberdeen University Press, 1967).

Robinson, Brian, *Silver Pennies and Linen Towels: The Story of the Royal Maundy* (London: Spink, 1992).

Robson, Peter, 'Dorset Garland Days on the Chesil Coast', in Buckland & Wood (1993) 155–66.

——, 'Shrove-tide House-Visiting Customs in Dorset', *Lore & Language* 14:1 (1996) 31–47.

Rosenfeld, Sybil, *The Theatre of the London Fairs in the Eighteenth Century* (Cambridge: Cambridge University Press, 1960).

Roud, Steve, *The Penguin Guide to the Superstitions of Britain and Ireland* (London: Penguin, 2003).

Round About Our Coal Fire; or, Christmas Entertainments (London: J. Roberts, 1740; reprinted Whitstable: Pryor Publications, 1991).

Rowe, Doc, *We'll Call Once More Unto Your House* (Padstow: Padstow Echo, 1982).

Rudder, Samuel, *A New History of Gloucestershire* (Cirencester: privately printed, 1779).

Rudkin, E. M., *Lincolnshire Folklore* (Gainsborough, 1936).

Schellinks, William, *The Journal of William Schellinks' Travels in England 1661–1663* (London: Royal Historical Society, 1993).

Scot, Reginald, *The Discoverie of Witchcraft* (1584; reprinted New York: Dover, 1972).

Selden, John, *Table-Talk* (London: E. Smith, 1689); reprinted in James Thornton, *Table Talk from Ben Jonson to Leigh Hunt* (London: Dent, 1934).

Sharp, Cecil J., *The Sword Dances of Northern England*, 3 vols. (London: Novello, 1911–13).

Sharp, Cecil, and MacIlwaine, Herbert C., *The Morris Book*, Part III, 2nd edn (London: Novello, 1924).

Sharpe, James, *Remember Remember the Fifth of November: Guy Fawkes and the Gunpowder Plot* (London: Profile, 2005).

Shaw, Anthony, *The Mayor of Garratt* (Wandsworth: Wandsworth Borough Council, 1980).

Sheffield, Derek, *This Forgotten Place: a Kentish Chronicle* (Gillingham: Meresborough, 1993).

Shortt, Hugh, *The Giant and Hob-nob* (booklet, Salisbury and South Wiltshire Museum, 1988).

Shuel, Brian, *The National Trust Guide to the Traditional Customs of Britain* (Exeter: Webb & Bower, 1985).

Simpson, Jacqueline, *The Folklore of Sussex* (London: Batsford, 1973).

Smith, Julia, *Fairs, Feasts and Frolics: Customs and Traditions in Yorkshire* (Otley: Smith Settle, 1989).

Spriggs, Gareth, 'Maiden's Garlands', *Folk Life* 21 (1982/83) 12–32.

Steer, Francis W., *The History of the Dunmow Flitch Ceremony* (Chelmsford: Essex Record Office, 1951).

Stephen, George A., *The Waits of the City of Norwich* (Norwich: Goose, 1933).

Sternberg, Thomas, *The Dialect and Folk-Lore of Northamptonshire* (London: Russell Smith, 1851; reprinted East Ardsley: S. R. Publishers, 1971).

Stone, Benjamin, *Sir Benjamin Stone's Pictures* (London: Cassell, 1906).

Stow, John, *A Survey of London* (1598; 2nd edn, 1603; reprinted Stroud: Alan Sutton, 1994).

Strickland, Agnes, *Old Friends and New Acquaintances*, 2nd series (London, Simpkin Marshall, 1861).

Strutt, Joseph, *Glig-Gamena Angel-Deod, or The Sports and Pastimes of the People of England* (1801); later edition published as *The Sports and Pastimes of the People of England*, ed. William Hone (London: Chatto & Windus, 1876).

Stubbes, Philip, *The Anatomie of Abuses* (1583; 4th edn 1595), ed. Margaret Jane Kidnie (Tempe: Arizona Center for Medieval and Renaissance Studies, 2002).

Summers, W. H., *The Story of Hungerford in Berkshire* (London: Trustees of the Borough of Hungerford, 1926).

Surrey Federation of Women's Institutes, *Surrey Within Living Memory* (Newbury: Countryside Books, 1992).

Sutton, Maureen, *A Lincolnshire Calendar* (Stamford: Paul Watkins, 1997).

Swainson, C., *A Handbook of Weather Folk-Lore* (Edinburgh: Blackwood, 1873).

Swift, Jonathan, *Journal to Stella* (1710–13; Gloucester: Alan Sutton, 1984).

Sykes, Homer, *Once a Year: Some Traditional British Customs* (London: Gordon Fraser, 1977).

Symonds, Richard, *Diary of the Marches of the Royal Army during the Great Civil War* (1644; London: Camden Society, 1909).

Tebbutt, C. F., *Huntingdonshire Folklore* (St. Neots: Tomson & Lendrum, 1952).

——, *Huntingdonshire Folklore* (St Ives: Friends of Norris Museum, 1984).

Thomas, Keith, *Religion and the Decline of Magic* (London: Weidenfeld and Nicolson, 1971).

——, *Rule and Misrule in the Schools of Early Modern England* (Reading: University of Reading, 1976).

Thompson, E. P., *Customs in Common* (London: Merlin, 1991).

Thompson, Flora, *Lark Rise* (Oxford: Oxford University Press, 1939).

Thorne, James, *Handbook to the Environs of London* (London: J. Murray, 1876).

Toy, H. Spencer, *The History of Helston* (London: Oxford University Press, 1936).

Trotter, Eleanor, *Seventeenth-Century Life in the Country Parish* (Cambridge: Cambridge University Press, 1919).

Turner, E. S., *All Heaven in a Rage* (London: Michael Joseph, 1964).

Turton, Robert B., 'The Service of Horngarth', *Yorkshire Archaeological Journal* 20 (1909) 51–67.

Tusser, Thomas, *Five Hundred Points of Good Husbandry* (1580; Oxford: Oxford University Press, 1984).

Twycross, Meg (ed.), *Festive Drama* (Cambridge: Brewer, 1996).

Udal, J. S., *Dorsetshire Folk-Lore* (Hertford: Stephen Austin & Sons, 1922).

Uttley, Alison, *The Country Child* (London: Faber, 1931).

Vickery, Roy, *A Dictionary of Plant Lore* (Oxford: Oxford University Press, 1995).

Victoria County History: Cambridge III (London: Oxford University Press, 1959).

Victoria County History: Essex II, ed. William Page and J. Horace Round (London: Constable, 1907).

Victoria County History: Hampshire IV, ed. William Page (London: Constable, 1911).

Victoria County History: Hampshire V, ed. William Page (London: Constable, 1912).

Victoria County History: Hertfordshire IV, ed. William Page (London: Constable, 1914).

Victoria County History: Oxford IV, ed. Alan Crossley (London: Oxford University Press, 1979).

Waddilove, William, and Eadon, David, *Wroth Silver Today: An Ancient Warwickshire Custom* (Rugby: privately printed, 1994).

Wales, Tony, *A Sussex Garland* (Newbury: Countryside Books, 1979).

——, *Sussex Customs, Curiosities and Country Lore* (Southampton: Ensign, 1990).

Walford, Cornelius, *Fairs Past and Present: A Chapter in the History of Commerce* (London: Elliot Stock, 1883).

Wallis, Faith, *Bede: The Reckoning of Time* [English translation of Bede's *De Temporum Ratione*] (Liverpool: Liverpool University Press, 1999).

Ward, Ned, *The London Spy* (1703; London: Cassell, 1927).

Warner, Susan, *Carl Krinken; or the Christmas Stocking* (London: Routledge, 1854).

Warren, C. Henry, *A Boy in Kent* (London: G. Bles, 1938).

Weightman, Gavin, and Humphries, Steve, *Christmas Past* (London: Sidgwick & Jackson, 1987).

West, Patrick, *Conspicuous Compassion: Why Sometimes it Really is Cruel to be Kind* (London: Civitas, 2004).

West Yorkshire Federation of Women's Institutes, *West Yorkshire: Within Living Memory* (Newbury: Countryside Books, 1996).

Westwood, Jennifer, *Albion: A Guide to Legendary Britain* (London: Grafton, 1985).

Westwood, Jennifer, and Simpson, Jacqueline, *The Lore of the Land: A Guide to England's Legends* (London: Penguin, 2005).

Whistler, Laurence, *The English Festivals* (London: Heinemann, 1947).

Whitcombe, H. P., *Bygone Days* (London: R. Bentley, 1874).

White, Florence, *Good Things in England* (London: Jonathan Cape, 1932; reprinted London: Persephone, 1999).

Whitlock, Ralph, *The Folklore of Wiltshire* (London: Batsford, 1976).

Wilbraham, Roger, *An Attempt at a Glossary of Some Words used in Cheshire* (1817; London: T. Rodd, 1826).

Wilkes, Peter, *The Great Nottingham Goose Fair* (Burton-on-Trent: Trent Valley Publications, 1989).

Williams, Alfred, *A Wiltshire Village* (London: Duckworth, 1912).

Williams, Douglas, *Festivals of Cornwall* (Bodmin: Bossiney, 1987).

Williams, Philip Martin, and Williams, David L., *The Knight Rides Out* (Ashton-under-Lyne: History on Your Doorstep, 1998).

Wilshere, Jonathan E. O., *Leicester Towne Waytes* (Leicester: Leicester Research Services, 1970).

Wilson, A. E., *The Story of Pantomime* (1949; Wakefield: EP, 1974).

Wilson, C. Anne (ed.), *Traditional Food East and West of the Pennines* (Edinburgh: Edinburgh University Press, 1991).

Winchester, Angus, *Discovering Parish Boundaries* (Princes Risborough: Shire, 1990).

Woodforde, James, *The Diary of a Country Parson*, ed. John Beresford, 4 vols. (London: Oxford Univesity Press, 1924–9).

Woodman, William, 'Reminiscences and Desultory Notes of Morpeth Social Customs Now Obsolete', *History of the Berwickshire Naturalists' Club* 14 (1892–3) 125–38.

Wright, A. R., *English Folklore* (London: Benn, 1928).

Wright, A. R., and Lones, T. E., *British Calendar Customs: England*, 3 vols. (London: The Folklore Society, 1936–40).

Young, George, *A History of Whitby and Streoneshalh Abbey*, 2 vols. (Whitby: Clark & Medd, 1817).

Index